Dictionary of Abbreviations

Dictionary of Abbreviations

DAVID PICKERING

CASSELL

First published 1996
by Cassell
Wellington House
125 Strand
London WC2R 0BB

Distributed in the United States
by Sterling Publishing Co., Inc.
387 Park Avenue South, New York, NY 10016–8810

Distributed in Australia
by Capricorn Link (Australia) Pty Ltd
2/13 Carrington Road, Castle Hill, NSW 2154

British Library Cataloguing in Publication Data
A catalogue record for this book is available from the British Library

ISBN 0–304–34612–8 (hardback)

Typeset by Gem Graphics, Trenance, Cornwall

Printed and bound by Mackays of Chatham

Contents

Preface

In an age when virtually every organization, invention or cultural, technological and social concept is immediately and irreversibly reduced in technical and common parlance to its initialized form, a good dictionary of abbreviations is an essential aid. The bewildering proliferation of abbreviations in recent decades has meant that conventional language dictionaries and brief lists of such truncated names in yearbooks and so forth are now rarely adequate for readers' requirements, be they watching the television news, puzzling over a detailed newspaper report of some scientific breakthrough, wrestling with the small print on a car insurance document, or curious to know why a lover has scrawled SWALK or HOLLAND on the back of an envelope.

The aim of this book is to provide a comprehensive, internationally-ranging reference guide, offering simple explanations of the more commonly encountered abbreviations, as well as many more specialized ones and those of purely historical interest. Comprising some 40,000 abbreviations collected under 20,000 headword entries, the text includes all manner of shortened forms, initializations, acronyms and slangy colloquialisms.

The text has been carefully arranged to enable the reader to get to the desired item with the least delay. Thus, field labels and glosses shedding light on the more obscure abbreviations have been deliberately kept to a minimum and, unlike most other similar guides, placed at the end of the entry, so that the reader is not obliged to wade through reams of italicized information before finding out what an abbreviation actually stands for. With the same aim in mind, the abbreviations themselves are given in the form in which they are most usually seen (though many may be rendered in different ways by different users) and the use of fullstops has been restricted for the sake of clarity, in line with modern convention. One exception to this rule is where an abbreviation comprises the truncated form of a longer word (for instance, Eras. for Erasmus, Kash. for Kashmir or lexicog. for lexicographer), in which cases fullstops are always used.

If an abbreviation is equally common in a variety of forms, the simplest of these is usually the one given, with variations noted by parentheses within the headword (although any parenthesis that has been set in bold is part of the abbreviation and not a variation). Similarly, many abbreviations will be seen both with and without spaces between the letters: here, once more, they are rendered in their simplest form, with all letters closed up. (It should be noted that the fact that a particular abbreviation is given here in upper case roman with no fullstops is no guarantee that it will not be seen elsewhere in lower case italic with fullstops between each letter.)

Foreign-language abbreviations are italicized in their full form, with a translation into English following in parentheses. Coverage is ambitiously international, and abbreviations commonly used around the world, both now and in the past, may be found alongside those specific to the UK, USA and the EC countries (with appropriate geographic labels).

At the end of the book, the reader will find several pages of appendices offering further information about the various symbols that are commonly used in alphabets and in scientific data. Such symbols (for instance, Greek and Russian letters and the signs of the zodiac) often have a strong graphical quality and are thus better listed separately from the main text.

My thanks go, as ever, to the editors and production staff at Cassell for their assistance and to Jan, Edward and Charles for the TLC.

David Pickering

Dictionary

A

a *année* (French: year); *annus* (Latin: year); answer; are (measure of land); atto-
a acceleration (physics); amplitude (physics)
a. about; *accepté* (French: accepted); accepted; acre; acreage; acting; actual; address; adjective; advance(d); afternoon; age; *akzeptiert* (German: accepted); alto; amateur; *anno* (Latin: in the year); anonymous; answer; *ante* (Latin: before); *aqua* (Latin: water); arrive; arriving; assist (sport)
A Aberdeen (UK fishing port registration); absolute (physics); Academician; ace (cards); adult (cinema certification); advanced (education); ammeter; ampere; anode; arterial road; assault; Associate; atom; atomic; Austria (international vehicle registration); mass number (physics); nucleon number (physics); top grade; top mark; top rank
A absorbance (physics); area (mathematics); Helmholtz function (chemistry); magnetic vector potential (physics)
Å angstrom unit (physics)
A. Academician; academy; acre; acreage; adjutant; admiral; air; *Altesse* (French: Highness); alto; America; American; Amos (Bible); annual (horticulture); answer; anterior; April; armoured; article; art; artillery; assistant; associate; athletic; August; Australia(n)
A1 ships maintained in first-class condition (Lloyd's Register)
A2 Botswana (international civil aircraft marking)
A3 Tonga (international civil aircraft marking)
A5 Bhutan (international civil aircraft marking)
A6 United Arab Emirates (international civil aircraft marking)
A7 Qatar (international civil aircraft marking)
A9C Bahrain (international civil aircraft marking)
A40 Oman (international civil aircraft marking)
aa absolute alcohol; acting appointment; after arrival; always afloat (shipping); *ana* (Greek: of each; medicine); approximate absolute; area

administrator; arithmetic average; attendance allowance; author's alteration
AA accompanied by an adult (cinema certification); administrative assistant; advertising agency; Advertising Association; age allowance (taxation); air attaché; Alcoholics Anonymous; Alloa (UK fishing port registration); American Airlines (airline flight code); American Aviation (aircraft); amino acid (biochemistry); Anglers' Association; anti-aircraft (military); Architectural Association; Army Act; ascorbic acid (biochemistry); Associate in Accounting; Associate in Agriculture; Associate in Arts; Associate of Arts; Association of Agriculture; atomic absorption; atomic adsorption; Augustinians of the Assumption; author's alteration; Automobile Association; Bournemouth (UK vehicle registration)
AAA Agricultural Adjustment Act (US); Agricultural Adjustment Administration (US); Allied Artists of America; Amateur Athletic Association; American Accounting Association; American Automobile Association; anti-aircraft artillery; Army Audit Agency (US); Association of Average Adjusters; Australian Association of Accountants; Australian Automobile Association; Automobile Association of America
AAAA Amateur Athletic Association of America; American Association of Advertising Agencies; Associated Actors and Artistes of America; Australian Association of Advertising Agencies
AAAI American Association for Artificial Intelligence; Associate of the Institute of Administrative Accountants
AAAL American Academy of Arts and Letters
AAAM American Association of Aircraft Manufacturers
AA&QMG Assistant Adjutant and Quartermaster-General
AAAS American Academy of Arts and Sciences; American Academy of Asian Studies; American Association for the Advancement of Science; Associate of the American Antiquarian Society

AAB Aircraft Accident Board; Association of Applied Biologists
AABC American Amateur Baseball Congress
AABL Associated Australian Banks in London
AABM Australian Association of British Manufacturers
AABT American Association of Behavior Therapists
AABW Antarctic Bottom Water
AAC Alaskan Air Command (US Air Force); Aeronautical Advisory Council; Agricultural Advisory Council; Amateur Athletic Club; *anno ante Christum* (Latin: in the year before Christ); Army Air Corps
AACB Aeronautics and Astronautics Coordinating Board (US); Association of African Central Banks
AACC American Association of Clinical Chemists; area-approach control centre (aeronautics)
AACE American Association of Cost Engineers; Association for Adult and Continuing Education
AACP American Association for Child Psychiatry; Anglo-American Council on Productivity
AACS Aberdeen-Angus Cattle Society; Airways and Air Communications Service (US)
AADC air aide-de-camp; Army-Air Defense Command (US)
AADS Army-Air Defense System (US)
AAE American Association of Engineers
AAEC Australian Atomic Energy Commission
AAeE Associate in Aeronautical Engineering
AAEE Aircraft and Armament Experimental Establishment; American Association of Electrical Engineers
AAES Association of Agricultural Education Staffs; Australian Army Education Service
AAEW Atlantic airborne early warning
AAF Allied Air Forces; Army Air Force (US)
AAFC anti-aircraft fire control
AAFCE Allied Air Forces in Central Europe
AAFIS Army and Air Force Intelligence Staff
AAFNE Allied Air Forces in Northern Europe

AAFSE Allied Air Forces in Southern Europe
AAG Air Adjutant-General; Assistant Adjutant-General; Association of American Geographers
AAgr Associate in Agriculture
AAGS Association of African Geological Surveys
AAHPER American Association for Health, Physical Education and Recreation
AAIA Associate of the Association of International Accountants; Associate of the Australian Institute of Advertising; Association of American Indian Affairs
AAIB Associate of the Australian Institute of Bankers
AAII Associate of the Australian Insurance Institute
AAIL American Academy and Institute of Art and Letters
AAL above aerodrome level (meteorology); Academy of Art and Literature; Association of Assistant Librarians
AALA American Association for Laboratory Accreditation
AALD Australian Army Legal Department
AALL American Association of Law Libraries
AAM air-to-air missile; American Association of Microbiology; American Association of Museums; Anti-Apartheid Movement; Association of Assistant Mistresses in Secondary Schools; Australian Air Mission
AAMD American Association on Mental Deficiency
AAMI age-associated memory impairment
AAMW Association of Advertising Men and Women (US)
AAMWS Australian Army Medical Women's Service
AANA Australian Association of National Advertisers
A&A additions and amendments
A&AEE Aeroplane and Armament Experimental Establishment
A&C addenda and corrigenda
A&E accident and emergency
a&h accident and health (insurance)
a&i accident and indemnity (insurance)
A&I Agricultural and Industrial (college; US)
A&M Agricultural and Mechanical

(college; US); Ancient and Modern (hymn book)

A&N Army and Navy Club; Army and Navy Stores

A&NI Andaman and Nicobar Islands

A&P advertising and promotion

A&R artists and recording; artists and repertoire; artists and repertory

a&s accident and sickness (insurance)

A&SH Argyll and Sutherland Highlanders

AANS Australian Army Nursing Service

AAO American Association of Orthodontists

AAOC Australian Army Ordnance Corps

AAOM American Academy of Occupational Medicine

AAOO American Academy of Ophthalmology and Otolaryngology

AAP Association of American Publishers; Australian Associated Press (news agency)

AAPA Advertising Agency Production Association; American Association of Port Authorities

AAPB American Association of Pathologists and Bacteriologists

AAPC All African People's Conference

AAPE American Academy of Physical Education

AAPG American Association of Petroleum Geologists

AAPHI Associate of the Association of Public Health Inspectors

AAPM American Association of Physicists in Medicine

AAPS American Association for the Promotion of Science

AAPSO Afro-Asian People's Solidarity Organization

AAPSS American Academy of Political and Social Science

AAPSW Associate of the Association of Psychiatric Social Workers

AAPT American Association of Physics Teachers; Associate of the Association of Photographic Technicians

aar after action report; against all risks (insurance); aircraft accident record; aircraft accident report; average annual rainfall

AAR Association of American Railroads

AARP American Association of Retired Persons

AAS *Academiae Americanae Socius* (Latin: Fellow of the American Academy of Arts and Sciences); *Acta Apostolicae Sedis*

(Latin: Acts of the Apostolic See); American Academy of Sciences; American Antiquarian Society; American Astronautical Society; American Astronomical Society; Army Air Service; Associate in Applied Science; Association of Architects and Surveyors; Association of Asian Studies; atomic absorption spectrometry; atomic absorption spectrophotometry; atomic absorption spectroscope; Australian Academy of Science; Auxiliary Ambulance Service

AASA *Agence Arabe Syrienne d'Information* (news agency); Associate of the Australian Society of Accountants

AASB American Association of Small Businesses

AASC Allied Air Support Command; Australian Army Service Corps

AASF Advanced Air Striking Force

AASG Association of American State Geologists

AASM Associated African States and Madagascar (treaty)

AASR Airport and Airways Surveillance Radar

AASS *Americanae Antiquarianae Societatis Socius* (Latin: Associate of the American Antiquarian Society)

AAT achievement anxiety test (psychology); Australian Antarctic Territory

AATA Anglo-American Tourist Association

AATNU *Administration de l'assistance technique des Nations Unies* (French: United Nations Technical Assistance Administration)

AATT American Association of Textile Technology

AATTA Arab Association of Tourism and Travel Agents

AAU Amateur Athletic Union (US); Association of American Universities

AAUN American Association for United Nations; Australian Association for United Nations

AAUP American Association of University Presses; American Association of University Professors

AAUW American Association of University Women

AAV assault amphibious vehicle

AAVC Australian Army Veterinary Corps

AAVS American Anti-Vivisection Society

AAWC Australian Advisory War Council

AAZPA American Association of Zoological Parks and Aquariums
ab anchor bolt; at bat (baseball)
ab. about; abridgement
a/b airborne
aB *auf Bestellung* (German: on order)
AB Aberdeen (UK postcode); Aberystwyth (UK fishing port registration); able-bodied seaman; advisory board; air board; airborne; Airman Basic (US Air Force); Alberta (Canada); antiballistic; *Artium Baccalaureus* (Latin: Bachelor of Arts; US); asthmatic bronchitis; at bat (baseball); automated bibliography; Worcester (UK vehicle registration)
A/B *Aktiebolaget* (Swedish: joint-stock company)
ABA Amateur Boxing Association; American Badminton Association; American Bankers' Association; American Bar Association; American Basketball Association; American Book Award; American Booksellers' Association; American Broadcasting Association; Antiquarian Booksellers' Association; Associate in Business Administration; Association of British Archaeologists; Australian Bankers' Association
ABAA Antiquarian Booksellers' Association of America
ABAC Association of British Aero Clubs and Centres
abb. abbey; *abbuono* (Italian: allowance or discount)
Abb. abbess; abbey; abbot
ABBA Amateur Basketball Association; American Board of Bio-Analysis
abbr(ev). abbreviate; abbreviated; abbreviation
ABC advance booking charter (airline tickets); advanced biomedical capsule; airbridge to Canada; airway, breathing, circulation (first aid); America-Britain-Canada; American Broadcasting Company; analysis of benefits and costs; animal birth control; Argentina-Brazil-Chile; Aruba-Bonaire-Curaçao (island group); Associated British Cinemas; atomic, biological and chemical (warfare or weapons); Audit Bureau of Circulation; Australian Broadcasting Commission; automatic brake control
ABCA American Business Communication Association; Army Bureau of Current Affairs

ABCC Association of British Chambers of Commerce; Association of British Correspondence Colleges
ABCD American, British, Chinese, Dutch (World War II alliance); atomic, biological and chemical protection and damage control
ABCFM American Board of Commissioners for Foreign Missions
ABCM Associate of Bandsmen's College of Music
abd. abdicate; abdicated; abdomen; abdominal
ABD advanced base depot (US Navy); average body dose (radiation)
ABDA American, British, Dutch, Australian (World War II)
abdom. abdomen; abdominal
ABDP Association of British Directory Publishers
ABEd Bachelor of Arts in Education (US)
Aber. Aberdeen; Aberdonian
ABERCOR Associated Banks of Europe Corporation
abf absolute bloody final (drink)
Abf. *Abfahrt* (German: departure)
ABF Actors' Benevolent Fund; Associated British Foods
ABFD Association of British Factors and Discounters
ABFM American Board of Foreign Missions
ABGB *Allgemienes Bürgerliches Gesetzbuch* (German: Austrian Civil Code)
abgk. *abgekürzt* (German: abbreviated)
ABGWIU Aluminum Brick and Glass Workers International Union (US)
Abh. *Abhandlungen* (German: transactions or treatises)
ABI Associate of the Institute of Book-keepers; Association of British Insurers
ABIA Association of British Introduction Agencies
ab. init. *ab initio* (Latin: from the beginning)
ABINZ Associate of the Bankers' Institute of New Zealand
abl(at). ablative
Abl. *abril* (Spanish: April)
ABL atmospheric boundary layer
ABLA American Business Law Association
ABLJ adjustable buoyancy lifejacket
ABLS Association of British Library Schools; Bachelor of Arts in Library Science (US)
ABM antiballistic missile; Associate in

Business Management; Australian Board of Missions
ABMA Army Ballistic Missile Agency
ABMAC Association of British Manufacturers of Agricultural Chemicals
ABMEWS antiballistic missile early warning system
ABMPM Association of British Manufacturers of Printers' Machinery
ABMT allogeneic bone-marrow transplantation (medicine)
abn airborne
Abn Aberdeen
ABNE Association for the Benefit of Non-contract Employees
ABO American Board of Ophthalmology; American Board of Orthodontics; American Board of Otolaryngology
ABOF Association of British Organic Fertilizers
ABOG American Board of Obstetrics and Gynecology
A-bomb atomic bomb
ABOS American Board of Oral Surgery; American Board of Orthopedic Surgery
Abp archbishop
ABP American Board of Pathology; American Board of Pediatrics; American Board of Peridontology; American Board of Prosthodontics; arterial blood pressure (medicine); Associated Book Publishers; Associated British Ports
ABPA Australian Book Publishers' Association
ABPC American Book Publishers' Council; Associated British Picture Corporation
ABPI Association of the British Pharmaceutical Industry
ABPN American Board of Psychiatry and Neurology; Association of British Paediatric Nurses
ABPO Advanced Base Personnel Officer
ABPS American Board of Plastic Surgery
ABPVM Association of British Plywood and Veneer Manufacturers
abr. abridge; abridged; abridgment
ABRACADABRA Abbreviations and Related Acronyms Associated with Defense, Astronautics, Business and Radio-electronics (US publication)
ABRC Advisory Board for the Research Councils
ABRES advanced ballistic re-entry system
ABRO Animal Breeding Research

Organization; Army in Burma Reserve of Officers
ABRS Association of British Riding Schools
ABRSM Associated Board of the Royal Schools of Music
ABRV advanced ballistic re-entry vehicle
abs *aux bons soins* (French: care of)
abs. absence; absent; absolute; absolutely; absorbent; abstract
ABS acrylonitrile-butadiene-styrene (plastic); alkyl benzene sulphonate (chemistry); American Bible Society; American Board of Surgery; American Bureau of Shipping; *Antiblockiersystem* (German: antilocking system; brakes); Architects' Benevolent Society; Australian Bureau of Statistics
ABSA Association of Business Sponsorship of the Arts
abse. re. *absente reo* (Latin: the defendant being absent; law)
abs. fed. *absente febre* (Latin: when there is no fever; medicine)
ABSIE American Broadcasting Station in Europe (World War II)
ABSM Associate of the Birmingham School of Music
ABSM(TTD) Associate of the Birmingham School of Music (Teacher's Training Diploma)
absol. absolute; absolutely
abs. re. *absente reo* (Latin: the defendant being absent; law)
abstr. abstract; abstracted
abs. visc. absolute viscosity
ABSW Association of British Science Writers
abt about
Abt. *Abteilung* (German: division or part)
ABT Association of Building Technicians
ABTA Allied Brewery Traders' Association; Association of British Travel Agents; Australian British Trade Association
ABU Asian Broadcasting Union; Assembly of the Baptist Union
A-BU Anglo-Belgian Union
abv. above
ABWR advanced boiling water reactor (nuclear physics)
ac *a capo* (Italian: new line); *à compte* (French: on account); advisory committee; alternating current; *année courante* (French: this year); *anno corrente* (Latin: this year); *ante cibum* (Latin: before meals; medicine); *assegno circolare*

(Italian: banker's draft or cashier's check); author's correction

ac. acre; activity

a/c account; account current; *ao cuidado de* (Portuguese: care of)

aC *antes de Cristo* (Portuguese: before Christ); *avanti Cristo* (Italian: before Christ)

Ac acetyl (chemistry); actinium (element); altocumulus (meteorology)

AC Air Canada (airline flight code); activated carbon (chemistry); activated charcoal (chemistry); aero club; Air Command; air commodore; air conditioning; air control; Air Corps; Air Council; aircraftman; Alcohol Concern; Alpine Club; alternating current; altocumulus (meteorology); Ambulance Corps; analogue computer; analytical chemist; annual conference; *ante Christum* (Latin: before Christ); appeal case; appeal court; *appellation contrôlée* (French wine classification); Army Corps; Army Council; artillery college; Arts Council; assistant commissioner; athletic club; Atlantic Charter; *Auditor Camerae* (Latin: Auditor of the Papal Treasury); *Azione Cattolica* (Italian: Catholic Action); Companion of the Order of Australia; Coventry (UK vehicle registration)

A/C account; account current; air conditioning; aircraft; aircraftman

ACA advanced combat aircraft; Agricultural Cooperative Association; American Camping Association; American Canoe Association; Anglers' Cooperative Association; Arts Council of America; Associate of the Institute of Chartered Accountants; Association of Consulting Actuaries; Australian Consumers' Association; Australian Council for Aeronautics

ACAA Agricultural Conservation and Adjustment Administration; American Coal Ash Association; Associate of the Australasian Institute of Cost Accountants

ACAB Army Contract Adjustment Board (US)

acad. academic; academical; academy

Acad. academy

Acad. fran. *Académie française* (French: French Academy)

ACADI *Association des cadres dirigeants de l'industrie* (French: Association of Industrial Executives)

Acad. med. academy of medicine

Acad. mus. academy of music

Acad. sci. academy of science

ACAE Advisory Council for Adult and Continuing Education

AC&U Association of Colleges and Universities (US)

ACAO Assistant County Advisory Officer

Acap. Acapulco

ACAS Advisory, Conciliation and Arbitration Service; Assistant Chief of Air Staff

ACB *Association Canadienne des Bibliothèques* (French: Canadian Library Association); Australian Cricket Board

ACBI Associate of the Institute of Book-keepers

ACBS Accrediting Commission for Business Schools

ACBSI Associate of the Chartered Building Societies Institute

ACBWS automatic chemical-biological warning system

acc. accelerate; acceleration; accent; acceptance (commerce); accepted (commerce); accompanied (music); accompaniment (music); according (to); account (book-keeping); accountant; accusative (grammar)

ACC Accident Compensation Corporation (New Zealand); accumulator (computing); acute cardiovascular collapse (medicine); Administrative Coordination Committee; advanced communications course; Agricultural Credit Corporation Limited; Anglican Consultative Council; annual capital charge; army cadet college; Army Catering Corps; Assistant County Commissioner (Scouts); Associated Chemical Companies; Association of County Councils

ACCA Aeronautical Chamber of Commerce of America; Agricultural Central Cooperative Association; Associate of the Chartered Association of Certified Accountants; Association of Certified and Corporate Accountants

ACCC Association of Canadian Community Colleges

ACCD American Coalition of Citizens with Disabilities

acce. acceptance (commerce)

accel. *accelerando* (Italian: getting faster; music)

access. accessory

ACCHAN Allied Command Channel (NATO)

ACCM Advisory Council for the Church's Ministry

ACCO Association of Child Care Officers

accom. accommodation

accomp. accompanied; accompaniment; accompany

ACCP American College of Chest Physicians

accred. accredited; accreditation

ACCS Associate of the Corporation of Secretaries

acct. account(ing); accountant

ACCT Association of Cinematograph, Television and Allied Technicians

acctd accented

accum. accumulative

accus. accusative (grammar)

accy accountancy; accuracy

acd accord

ACDA Advisory Committee on Distinction Awards; Arms Control and Disarmament Agency; Aviation Combat Development Agency

ACDAS automatic control and data acquisition system

AC/DC alternating current/direct current (physics); bisexual

ACDCM Archbishop of Canterbury's Diploma in Church Music

ACdre Air Commodore

ACDS Assistant Chief of Defence Staff

acdt accident

ACE advanced cooled engine (engineering); Advisory Centre for Education; alcohol-chloroform-ether (anaesthetic); Allied Command Europe; American Council on Education; Association for the Conservation of Energy; Association of Conference Executives; Association of Consulting Engineers; Association of Cultural Exchange; Australian College of Education; Automatic Computing Engine (computing)

ACEA Action Committee for European Aerospace

ACEd. Associate in Commercial Education

ACEEE American Council for an Energy-Efficient Economy

ACEF Australian Council for Employers' Federations

ACER Australian Council for Educational Research

ACERT Advisory Council for Education of Romanies and other Travellers

acet. acetate; acetone

ACET Advisory Committee on Electronics and Telecommunications; Aids care, education and treatment

ACEWEX Allied Command Europe Weather Exchange

ACF *Académie Canadienne Française* (French: French Canadian Academy); Army Cadet Force; *Automobile Club de France* (French: French Automobile Club)

ACFA Army Cadet Force Association

ACFAS *Association Canadienne-Française pour l'avancement des sciences* (French: French-Canadian Association for the Advancement of Science)

ACFHE Association of Colleges of Further and Higher Education

ACFI Associate of the Clothing and Footwear Institute

acft aircraft

ACG *An Comunn Gaidhealach* (Gaelic: The Gaelic Society; Highland Association); Assistant Chaplain-General; automatic control gear

ACGB Arts Council of Great Britain

ACGBI Automobile Club of Great Britain and Ireland

ACGI Associate of the City and Guilds Institute

ACGS Assistant Chief of the General Staff

ACH automated clearing house (banking)

ACHR American Society of Human Rights

AChS Associate of the Society of Chiropodists

ACI *Alliance coopérative internationale* (French: International Cooperative Alliance); Alloy Castings Institute; American Concrete Institute; army council instruction; Associate of the Institute of Commerce; Automobile Club d'Italia

ACIA Associate of the Corporation of Insurance Agents

ACIAA Australian Commercial and Industrial Artists' Association

ACIArb Associate of the Chartered Institute of Arbitrators

ACIB Associate of the Chartered Institute of Bankers; Associate of the Corporation of Insurance Brokers

ACIC Aeronautical Charting and Information Center (US)

ACIGS Assistant Chief of the Imperial General Staff

ACII Associate of the Chartered Insurance Institute

ACINF Advisory Committee on Irradiated and Novel Foods (US)

ACIOPJF *Association catholique internationale des oeuvres de protection de la jeune fille* (French: International Catholic Girls' Society)

ACIS American Committee for Irish Studies; Associate of the Institute of Chartered Secretaries and Administrators

ACIT Associate of the Chartered Institute of Transport

ACJP airways corporations joint pensions

ack. acknowledge; acknowledgment

ACK acknowledgment (computing, telecommunications)

ack-ack anti-aircraft

ack(g)t acknowledgment

ACL access control list (computing); action-centred leadership

ACLA Anti-Communist League of America

ACLANT Allied Command Atlantic

ACLC Air Cadet League of Canada

ACLP Association of Contact Lens Practitioners

ACLS American Council of Learned Societies; automatic carrier landing system

ACLU American Civil Liberties Union; American College of Life Under-writers

ACM Air Chief Marshal; air combat manoeuvring; American Campaign Medal; asbestos-containing material; Assistant Chief of Mission (US); Association for Computing Machinery (US); authorized controlled material

ACMA Agricultural Cooperative Managers' Association; Associate of the Institute of Cost and Management Accountants

ACMC Association of Canadian Medical Colleges

ACME advanced computer for medical research; Advisory Council on Medical Education (US); Association of Consulting Management Engineers (US)

ACMET Advisory Council on Middle East Trade

ACMF Air Corps Medical Forces (US); Allied Central Mediterranean Forces; Australian Commonwealth Military Forces

ACMM Associate of the Conservatorium of Music, Melbourne

acmp. accompany

ACMP Advisory Committee on Marine Pollution; Assistant Commissioner of the Metropolitan Police

ACMRR Advisory Committee on Marine Resources Research (FAO)

ACMT American College of Medical Technologists

acn all concerned notified

ACN alkane carbon number (chemistry); American College of Neuropsychiatrists; *ante Christum natum* (Latin: before the birth of Christ)

ACNA Advisory Council on Naval Affairs (US); Arctic Institute of North America

ACNS Assistant Chief of Naval Staff; Associated Correspondents News Service

ACNY Advertising Club of New York

ACO Association of Children's Officers

AC of S Assistant Chief of Staff

acog aircraft on ground

ACom(m) Associate in Commerce

Acops Advisory Commission on Pollution of the Sea

ACOR American Center for Oriental Research

ACORD Advisory Council on Research and Development

ACORN A Classification of Residential Neighbourhoods; associative content retrieval network (computing); automatic checkout and recording network (computing)

ACOS Advisory Committee on Safety; American College of Osteopathic Surgeons; Assistant Chief of Staff

ACOST Advisory Council on Science and Technology

ACP advanced computer program; advanced computer project; African, Caribbean and Pacific; American College of Pharmacists; American College of Physicians; Associate of the College of Preceptors; Association of Circus Proprietors of Great Britain; Association of Clinical Pathologists; *Automóvel Clube de Portugal* (Portuguese: Automobile Club of Portugal)

ACPA Associate of the Institute of Certified Public Accountants (US)
ACPM American Congress of Physical Medicine and Rehabilitation
ACPO Association of Chief Police Officers
acpt. acceptance (commerce)
acq. acquire; acquittal
ACR Admiral Commanding Reserves; advanced capabilities radar; aircraft control room; American College in Rome; approach control radar (aeronautics); Association of College Registrars; audio cassette recorder
acrd accrued
ACRE Action with Rural Communities in England; automatic climatological recording equipment
ACRF Advanced Computing Research Facility
acrg. acreage
ACRI Air-Conditioning and Refrigeration Institute (US)
ACRL Association of College and Research Libraries (US)
acron. acronym
ACRR American Council on Race Relations
ACRS accelerated cost recovery system (taxation); Advisory Committee on Reactor Safeguards
a/cs aircraft security vessel
ACS active control system (aeronautics); Admiral Commanding Submarines; advanced communications system; airport catering services; air-conditioning system; altitude control system (aeronautics); American Cancer Society; American Ceramic Society; American Chemical Society; American College of Surgeons; assembly control system; Associate in Commercial Science; automated confirmation service (finance); automated control system (computing)
ACSA Allied Communciations Security Agency
ACSE Association of Consulting Structural Engineers (Australia)
ACSEA Allied Command South East Asia
ACSET Advisory Committee on the Supply and Training of Teachers
ACSL advanced continuous simulation language (computing); assistant cub-scout leader

ACSM American Congress on Surveying and Mapping
ACSN Association of Collegiate Schools of Nursing
ACSOS Acoustical Society of America
ACSPA Australian Council of Salaried and Professional Associations
a/cs pay. accounts payable
a/cs rec. accounts receivable
ACSS automated colour separation system (printing)
act. acting; active; activities; actor; actual; actuary
ACT advance corporation tax; advanced coal technology; Advisory Council on Technology; Air Council for Training; American College Test; Associated Container Transportation; Associate of the College of Technology; Association of Corporate Treasurers; Australian Capital Territory; Australian College of Theology
a cta. *a cuenta* (Spanish: on account)
ACTC Art Class Teacher's Certificate
actg acting
ACTH adrenocorticotrophic hormone (biochemistry)
ACTO Advisory Council on the Treatment of Offenders
ACTP American College Testing Program
ACTS Acoustic Control and Telemetry System (US); Associate of the Society of Certified Teachers of Shorthand
ACTT Association of Cinematograph, Television and Allied Technicians
ACTU Australian Council of Trade Unions
ACTWU Amalgamated Clothing and Textile Workers Union (US)
ACU Actors' Church Union; American Congregational Union; Asian Clearing Union; Association of Commonwealth Universities; Auto-Cycle Union
ACUA Association of Cambridge University Assistants
ACUE American Committee of United Europe
ACUS Atlantic Council of the United States
ACV actual cash value; air-cushion vehicle (hovercraft); Associated Commercial Vehicles; Associate of the College of Violinists
ACW agricultural crop waste; Air Command and Warning; Air Control and Warning; aircraftwoman;

alternating continuous wave (physics); automatic car wash

ACWS aircraft control and warning system

ACWW Associated Country Women of the World

ACY average crop yield

ad after date; *ante diem* (Latin: before the day); autograph document

ad. adapt; adaptation; adapter; *addantur/adde* (Latin: let there be added or add; medicine); advantage (tennis); adverb; advertisement

aD *ausser Dienst* (German: retired, on half pay)

AD accidental damage (insurance); accumulated dose (radiation); active duty (military); administrative department; aggregate demand; air defence (military); air dried; Algerian dinar (monetary unit); Alzheimer's disease; *anno Domini* (Latin: in the year of the Lord); Ardrossan (UK fishing port registration); armament depot; Art Director; assembly district; Assistant Director; Australian Democrat/s; autograph document; average deviation; Dame of the Order of Australia; Gloucester (UK vehicle registration)

A-D Albrecht Dürer (German artist)

A/D aerodrome; after date; analog-to-digital (computing)

ADA Agricultural Development Association; Air Defense Agency (US); Aluminium Development Association; American Dental Association; American Diabetes Association; Americans for Democratic Action; Association of Drainage Authorities; Atomic Development Authority; Australian Dental Association

ADAA Art Dealers Association of America

ADAD automatic telephone dialing-announcing device (US)

adag. adagio (music)

adap. adapted

ADAPSO Association of Data Processing Organizations (US)

Adapt Access for Disabled People to Arts Today

ADAPTS Air-Deliverable Antipollution Transfer System (US Coast Guard)

ADAWS action data automation and weapons systems (military); Assistant Director of Army Welfare Services

A-day assault day

ADB accidental death benefit; African Development Bank; Asian Development Bank; Bachelor of Domestic Arts (US)

ADC advanced developing country/ countries; advice of duration and charge (telecommunications); aerodrome control; aide-de-camp; Aids dementia complex; Aid to Dependent Children; Air Defense Command (US); amateur dramatic club; analog-to-digital converter (computing); Art Directors' Club; Assistant District Commissioner (Scouts); Association of District Councils; automated distribution control (computing); automatic digital calculator

ADCC Air Defense Control Center (US)

ADCCP advanced data communication control procedure (computing)

ADCI American Die Casting Institute

ADCM Archbishop of Canterbury's Diploma in Church Music

ADCONSEN advice and consent of the Senate (US)

ADC(P) personal aide-de-camp to the Queen

add. *addantur/adde* (Latin: let there be added or add; medicine); addenda; addendum; addition; additional; address; addressed

ADD airstream direction detector (aeronautics)

ADDC Air Defense Direction Center (US)

add(n)l additional

addn addition

ADDS Association of Directors of Social Services

addsd addressed

ad effect. *ad effectum* (Latin: until effective; medicine)

ADEME Assistant Director, Electrical and Mechanical Engineering

ad eund. *ad eundem gradum* (Latin: to the same degree)

adf after deducting freight

ADF approved deposit fund (finance; Australia); Asian Development Fund; Australian Defence Force; automatic direction finder (navigation)

ad fin. *ad finem* (Latin: at or near the end)

ADFManc Art and Design Fellow, Manchester

ADFW Assistant Director of Fortifications and Works

ADG Assistant Director-General

ADGB Air Defence of Great Britain

ADGMS Assistant Director-General of
Medical Services
ADH antidiuretic hormone
(biochemistry); Assistant Director of
Hygiene; Association of Dental
Hospitals
ADHD attention deficit and hyperactivity
disorder (medicine)
ad h.l. *ad hunc locum* (Latin: at this place)
ADI acceptable daily intake (medicine);
approved driving instructor
ad inf. *ad infinitum* (Latin: to infinity)
ad init. *ad initium* (Latin: at the
beginning)
ad int. *ad interim* (Latin: in the meantime)
ADIZ air defense identification zone (US)
adj. adjacent; adjective; adjoining;
adjourned; adjudged; adjunct;
adjustment; adjutant
Adj. adjutant
Adj.A Adjunct in Arts (US)
ADJAG Assistant Deputy Judge
Advocate-General
Adjt adjutant
Adjt-Gen adjutant-general
ADL assistant director of labour
ad lib. *ad libitum* (Latin: at pleasure or
freely)
ad loc. *ad locum* (Latin: at the place)
ADLP Australian Democratic Labour
Party
adm. administration; administrative;
administrator; admission; admitted
Adm. admiral; Admiralty; admission
ADM Advanced Diploma in Midwifery;
annual delegate meeting; Association of
Domestic Management; atomic
demolition munitions; average daily
membership
ADMA American Drug Manufacturers'
Association; Aviation Distributors' and
Manufacturers' Association
Ad. Man. Advertisement Manager
admin. administration; administrator
Admin. Apost. Administrator Apostolic
Adml admiral
admov. *admoveatur* (Latin: let it be
applied; medicine)
Adm. Rev. *Admodum Reverendus* (Latin:
Very Reverend)
ADMS Assistant Director of Medical
Services
ADMT Association of Dental
Manufacturers and Traders of the
United Kingdom
admx administratrix
ADN *Allgemeiner Deutscher*

Nachrichtendienst (news agency,
Germany); Yemen PDR (international
vehicle registration)
ADNA Assistant Director of Naval
Accounts
ADNC Assistant Director of Naval
Construction
ad neut. *ad neutralizandum* (Latin: until
neutral; medicine)
ADNI Assistant Director of Naval
Intelligence
ADNOC Abu Dhabi National Oil
Company
ADNS Assistant Director of Nursing
Services
ADO advanced development objective
(US); air defence officer; assistant district
officer; Association of Dispensing
Opticians; automotive diesel oil
ADP adenosine diphosphate
(biochemistry); air defence position;
Association of Dental Prosthesis;
automatic data processing
ADPA Associate Diploma of Public
Administration
ADPLAN advanced planning
ADPR Assistant Director of Public
Relations
ADPSO Association of Data Processing
Service Organizations
ADR accident data recorder; alternative
dispute resolution (law); American
Depository Receipt (stock exchange)
ADRA Animal Diseases Research
Association (Edinburgh)
ads autograph document, signed
ad s. *ad sectam* (Latin: at the suit of; law)
AdS *Académie des Sciences* (French:
Academy of Sciences)
ADS accurately defined systems
(computing); advanced dressing station;
air defense sector (US); American Dialect
Society; articulated drill string
(engineering); automatic depressur-
ization system (engineering)
ad saec. *ad saeculum* (Latin: to the
century)
ADS&T Assistant Director of Supplies
and Transport
ad sat. *ad saturandum* (Latin: to
saturation; medicine)
ADSOC Administrative Support
Operations Center (US)
ADSS Australian Defence Scientific
Service
ADST approved deferred share trust
(finance)

adst. feb. *adstante febre* (Latin: when fever is present; medicine)
ADT American District Telegraph; Assistant Director of Transport; average daily traffic
ADTECH advanced decoy technology
ADTS Automated Data and Telecommunications Service
ad us. *ad usum* (Latin: according to custom)
ad us. ext. *ad usum externum* (Latin: for external use; medicine)
adv. advance; adverb; adverbial; *adversus* (Latin: against); advertisement; advertising; advice; advise; adviser; advisory; advocate
Adv. Advent; Advocate
ad val. *ad valorem* (Latin: according to value)
advb adverb
adven. adventure
adv. pmt advance payment
ADVS Advanced Diploma in Voice Studies; Assistant Director of Veterinary Services
advt advertisement
advv. adverbs
ADW air defence warning; Assistant Director of Works
ADWE&M Assistant Director of Works, Electrical and Mechanical
ADX automatic data exchange (computing); automatic digital exchange (telecommunications)
ae. *aeneus* (Latin: made of copper; numismatics); *aetatis* (Latin: at the age of)
AE account executive; acoustic emission (physics); adult education; aeronautical engineer; aeronautical engineering; age exemption (taxation); *Agence Europe* (news agency); agricultural engineer; agricultural engineering; Air Efficiency Award; *Aktiebolaget Atomenergi* (Swedish: Atomic Energy Corporation); All England; American English; army education; Associate in Education; Associate in Engineering; atomic energy; Bristol (UK vehicle registration); George Russell (Irish poet; pseudonym); third-class ships (Lloyd's Register)
AEA Actors' Equity Association (US); American Economic Association; Atomic Energy Act (US); Atomic Energy Authority (UK)
AEAF Allied Expeditionary Air Force

AE&MP Ambassador Extraordinary and Minister Plenipotentiary
AE&P Ambassador Extraordinary and Plenipotentiary
AEAUSA Adult Education Association of the United States of America
AEB Area Electricity Board; Associated Examining Board
AEBP atmospheric equivalent boiling point
AEC additional extended coverage (insurance); Agricultural Executive Council; American Express Company; Army Electronics Command; Associated Equipment Company; Association of Education Committees; Atomic Energy Commission (US); Atomic Energy Corporation (South Africa); Atomic Energy Council (US)
AECB Atomic Energy Control Board (US)
AECCG African Elephant Conservation Coordinating Group
AECI African Explosives and Chemical Industries; Associate of the Institute of Employment Consultants
AECL Atomic Energy of Canada Limited
AEd Associate in Education
AED advanced electronics design; *Artium Elegantium Doctor* (Latin: Doctor of Fine Arts); Association of Engineering Distributors; automated engineering design
AEDE *Association européenne des enseignants* (French: European Teachers' Association)
AEDOT Advanced Energy Design and Operation Technologies
AEDP Alternative Energy Development Program (US)
AEDS Association for Educational Data Systems (US); Atomic Energy Detection Systems
AEDU Admiralty Experimental Diving Unit
AeE Aeronautical Engineer
AEE airborne evaluation equipment; Atomic Energy Establishment
AEEC Airlines Electronic Engineering Committee (US); Army Equipment Engineering Establishment (Canada)
AEEN *Agence européenne pour l'energie nucléaire* (French: European Agency for Atomic Energy)
AEEU Amalgamated Engineering and Electrical Union
AEF Allied Expeditionary Force;

American Expeditionary Force; Australian Expeditionary Force

A-effect alienation effect (theatre)

AEFM *Association européenne des festivals de musique* (French: European Association of Music Festivals)

aeg *ad eundem gradum* (Latin: to the same degree); all edges gilt (bookbinding)

AEG *Allgemeine Elektrizitäts-Gesellschaft* (German: General Electric Company)

AEGIS Aid for the Elderly in Government Institutions

AEGM Anglican Evangelical Group Movement

AEI Alternative Energy Institute (US); American Express International; Associated Electrical Industries; *Association des écoles internationales* (French: International Schools Association)

AEIOU *Austriae Est Imperare Orbi Universi* (Latin: it is given to Austria to rule the whole world); *Austria Erit In Orbe Ultima* (Latin: Austria will be the world's last survivor)

AEJ Association for Education in Journalism

AEL aeronautical engine laboratory; aircraft engine laboratory; Associated Engineering Limited; automation engineering laboratory

AELE *Association européenne de libre-échange* (French: European Free Trade Association)

AELTC All England Lawn Tennis Club

AEM Air Efficiency Medal; analytical electron microscopy

AEMT Association of Electrical Machinery Trades

AEMU advanced extra-vehicular mobility unit (astronautics)

aen. *aeneus* (Latin: made of copper; numismatics)

AEn Associate in English

AENA All England Netball Association

AEng Associate in Engineering

AEO Assistant Education Officer; Assistant Experimental Officer; Association of Exhibition Organisers

AEP *Agence européenne de productivité* (French: European Production Agency); American Electric Power

AEPI American Educational Publishers Institute

aeq. *aequalis* (Latin: equal)

aer. aeronautics; aeroplane

AER Army Emergency Reserve

aera. aeration

AERA American Educational Research Association; Associate Engraver, Royal Academy; Associate of the British Electrical and Allied Industries Research Association

AerE Aeronautical Engineer

AERE Atomic Energy Research Establishment (Harwell)

AERI Agricultural Economics Research Institute (Oxford)

AERNO aeronautical equipment reference number

aero. aeronautic(al)

AERO Air Education and Recreation Organization

aeron. aeronautical; aeronautics

aerosp. aerospace

AES advanced energy system; Aerospace Electrical Society (US); Airways Engineering Society (US); atomic emission spectrum (physics); Audio Engineering Society

AESE Association of Earth Science Editors (US)

AESL Aerospace Energy Systems Laboratory (US)

aesth. aesthetics

aet(at). *aetatis* (Latin: at the age of)

AET Associate in Electrical Engineering; Associate in Electronic Engineering

AETR advanced engineering test reactor

AEU Amalgamated Engineering Union; American Ethical Union

AEU(TASS) Amalgamated Engineering Union (Technical, Administrative and Supervisory Section)

AEV air evacuation

AEW Admiralty Experimental Works; airborne early warning (aircraft)

AEWHA All England Women's Hockey Association

AEWLA All England Women's Lacrosse Association

AEWS advanced earth satellite weapons system; aircraft early warning system

af advanced freight; *a favor* (Spanish: in favour); *anno futuro* (Latin: next year); as found (auctions); audio-frequency

Af afgháni (monetary unit of Afghanistan)

Af. Africa(n); Afrikaans; Aruban florin (monetary unit of Aruba)

AF *Académie française* (French: French Academy); Admiral of the Fleet; air force; Air Foundation (US); Air France (airline flight code); Anglo-French; *Armée française* (French: French Army); Associated Fisheries; associate fellow; audio-frequency; autofocus (photography); automatic filter (smoke filter); Truro (UK vehicle registration)

A/F antiflooding; as found (auctions)

AFA advanced fuel assembly (nuclear engineering); African Football Association; Air Force Act; Air Force Association (US); Amateur Fencing Association; Amateur Football Alliance; American Foundrymen's Association; Associate in Fine Arts; Associate of the Faculty of Actuaries (Scotland)

AFAC American Fisheries Advisory Committee

AFAEP Association of Fashion Advertising and Editorial Photographers

AFAIAA Associate Fellow of the American Institute of Aeronautics and Astronautics

AFAIM Associate Fellow of the Australian Institute of Management

AFAITC Armed Forces Air Intelligence Training Center (US)

AFAL Air Force Astronautical Laboratory (US)

AFAM Ancient Free and Accepted Masons

AFAS *Association française pour l'avancement des sciences* (French: French Association for the Advancement of the Sciences)

AFASIC Assocation for All Speech-impaired Children

AFB Air Force Base (US); American Federation for the Blind

AFBD Association of Futures Brokers and Dealers

AFBF American Farm Bureau Federation

AFBMD Air Force Ballistic Missile Division (US)

AFBPsS Associate Fellow of the British Psychological Society

AFBS American and Foreign Bible Society

AFC Air Force Cross; amateur football club; American Football Conference; Association Football Club; Australian Flying Corps; automatic flight control; automatic frequency control; average fixed costs

AFCAI Associate Fellow of the Canadian Aeronautical Institute

AFCE Associate in Fuel Technology and Chemical Engineering; automatic flight control equipment

AFCEA Armed Forces Communications and Electronics Association (US)

AFCENT Allied Forces in Central Europe (NATO)

afco automatic fuel cut-off (engineering)

AFCO Admiralty Fleet Confidential Order

AFCS Air Force Communications Service; automatic flight control system

AFCU American and Foreign Christian Union

AFCW Association of Family Case Workers

AFD accelerated freeze dried; accelerated freeze drying; air force depot; Doctor of Fine Arts (US)

AFDC Aid to Families with Dependent Children (US)

AFDCS Association of First Division Civil Servants

AFDS Air Fighting Development Squadron

AFEA American Farm Economics Association; American Film Export Association

AFEE Airborne Forces Experimental Establishment

AFEIS Advanced Further Education Information Service

AFERO Asia and the Far East Regional Office (FAO)

AFES Admiralty Fuel Experimental Station

AFESC Air Force Engineering and Services Center (US)

AFESD Arab Fund for Economic and Social Development

AFEX Air Forces Europe Exchange (US); Armed Forces Exchange (US)

aff. affairs; affectionate; affiliate; affiliated; affirmative; affix

Aff.IP Affiliate of the Institute of Plumbing

AFFL Agricultural Finance Federation Limited

afft affidavit

AFFTC Air Force Flight Test Center (US)

Afg. Afghan; Afghanistan

AFG Afghanistan (international vehicle registration)

AFGE American Federation of Government Employees

Afgh(an). Afghan(istan)

AFGM American Federation of Grain Millers

AFH American Foundation for Homeopathy

AFHC Air Force Headquarters Command

AFHQ Allied Forces Headquarters; Armed Forces Headquarters

AFI American Film Institute

AFIA American Foreign Insurance Association; Apparel and Fashion Industry Association; Associate of the Federal Institute of Accountants (Australia)

AFIAP *Artiste de la Fédération internationale de l'art photographique* (French: Artist of the International Federation of Photographic Art)

AFICD Associate Fellow of the Institute of Civil Defence

AFII American Federation of International Institutes

AFIIM Associate Fellow of the Institution of Industrial Managers

AFIMA Associate Fellow of the Institute of Mathematics and its Applications

AFIPS American Federation of Information Processing Services Incorporated

AFL Air Force List; American Federation of Labor; American Football League

AFLA Amateur Fencers' League of America; Asian Federation of Library Associations

AFLC Air Force Logistics Command (US)

AFL-CIO American Federation of Labor and Congress of Industrial Organizations

aflt afloat

AFM Air Force Medal; American Federation of Musicians of the United States and Canada; assistant field manager; Associated Feed Manufacturers; atomic force microscope; atomic force microscopy; audio-frequency modulation (telecommunications)

AFMA Armed Forces Management Association; Artificial Flower Manufacturers' Association of Great Britain

AFMDC Air Force Missile Development Center (US)

AFMEC African Methodist Episcopal Church

AFMED Allied Forces Mediterranean

afmo. *afectísimo* (Spanish: very affectionately)

AFMTC Air Force Missile Test Center (US)

AFN American Forces Network; Armed Forces Network; Association of Free Newspapers

AFNE Allied Forces Northern Europe

AFNOR *Association française de normalisation* (French: French Standardisation Association)

AFNORTH Allied Forces Northern Europe

AFO Admiralty Fleet Order; army forwarding officer

AFOAR Air Force Office of Aerospace Research (US)

AFOAS Air Force Office of Aerospace Sciences (US)

AF of M American Federation of Musicians of the United States and Canada

AFOM Associate of the Faculty of Occupational Medicine

AFOSR Air Force Office of Scientific Research (US)

AFP *Agence France Presse* (news agency)

AFPRB Armed Forces Pay Review Board

Afr. Africa; African; Afrikaan/s

AFr. Anglo-French

AFR accident frequency rate; air-fuel ratio; automatic fingerprint recognition

AFRA American Farm Research Association

AFRASEC Afro-Asian Organization for Economic Cooperation

AFRC Agricultural and Food Research Council

Afrik. Afrikaans

AFRO Africa Regional Office (FAO)

AFRTS Armed Forces Radio and Television Service (US)

AFS Advanced Flying School; air force station; Alaska Ferry Service; American Field Service; Army Fire Service; Atlantic Ferry Service; auxiliary fire service

AFSA American Foreign Service Association; Armed Forces Security Agency (US)

AFSBO American Federation of Small Business Organizations

AFSC Air Force Systems Command; American Friends Service Committee; Armed Forces Staff College

AFSCME American Federation of State, Country and Municipal Employees

afsd aforesaid

AFSIL Accommodation for Students in London

AFSLAET Associate Fellow of the Society of Licensed Aircraft Engineers and Technologists

AFSOUTH Allied Forces in Southern Europe

aft. after; afternoon

AFT American Federation of Teachers

AFTE American Federation of Technical Engineers

AFTM American Foundation of Tropical Medicine

aftn afternoon

AFTN Aeronautical Fixed Telecommunications Network

AFTR American Federal Tax Reports

AFTRA American Federation of Television and Radio Artists

AFU advanced flying unit

AFULE Australian Federated Union of Locomotive Engineers

AFV armoured fighting vehicle; armoured force vehicle

AFVG Anglo-French variable geometry (aeronautics)

AFVPA Advertising Film and Videotape Producers' Association

AFW army field workshop

ag anti-gas

ag. agent; agreement; agricultural; agriculture

Ag silver (element)

Ag. August

AG accountant-general; adjutant-general; agent-general; *Aktiengesellschaft* (German: public limited company); *Alberghi per la Gioventù* (Italian: youth hostels); art gallery; attorney-general; Hull (UK vehicle registration)

Aga Aktiebolaget Gasackumulator (Swedish oven)

AGA air-to-ground-to-air (military); Amateur Gymnastics Association; American Gas Association; American Genetic Association; appropriate for gestational age (obstetrics); Australian Garrison Artillery

AGAC American Guild of Authors and Composers

AGACS automatic ground-to-air communications system

AGARD Advisory Group for Aerospace Research and Development (NATO)

agb a good brand; any good brand

AGB Audits of Great Britain

AGBI Artists' General Benevolent Institution

AGC advanced graduate certificate (US); American Grassland Council; automatic gain control

AGCA automatic ground-controlled approach (aeronautics)

AGCAS Association of Graduate Careers Advisory Service

AGCC Arab Gulf Cooperation Council

AGCL automatic ground-controlled landing (aeronautics)

agcy agency

agd agreed

AGDL Attorney-General of the Duchy of Lancaster

AgE Agricultural Engineer

AGE Admiralty Gunnery Establishment; aerospace ground equipment; Associate in General Education; automatic guidance electronics

AGES Association of Agricultural Education Staffs

AGF Adjutant-General to the Forces; army ground forces

Agfa *Aktiengesellschaft fur Anilinfabrikation* (German: Limited Company for Dye Manufacturing)

ag. feb. *aggrediente febre* (Latin: when the fever increases; medicine)

agg(r). aggregate

AGH Australian General Hospital

AGI adjusted gross income (US); American Geographical Institute; American Geological Institute; annual general inspection; *Artistes graphiques internationaux* (French: International Graphic Artists); Associate of the Institute of Certificated Grocers

AGIP *Agenzia Generale Italiana Petroli* (Italian national oil company)

agit. *agitatum* (Latin: shaken)

agit. ante sum. *agita ante sumendum* (Latin: shake before taking; medicine)

agitprop agitation and propaganda

AGL above ground level

aglm. agglomerate

AGM advisory group meeting; air-to-ground missile; annual general meeting

AGMA American Guild of Musical Artists

agn again; agnomen

agnos. agnostic

ago. *agosto* (Italian: August)

AGOR Auxiliary-General Oceanographic Research

AGP Academy of General Practice; aviation general policy

AGPA American Group Psychotherapy Association

agr. agreement; agricultural; agriculture; agriculturalist
AGR advanced gas-cooled reactor (nuclear physics); Association of Graduate Recruiters
AGRA Army Group Royal Artillery; Association of Genealogists and Record Agents
AGREE Advisory Group on Reliability of Electronic Equipment
AGRF American Geriatric Research Foundation
agric. agricultural; agriculture; agriculturist
AGRM Adjutant-General, Royal Marines
agron. agronomy
AGS abort guidance system (astronautics); aircraft general standard; Air Gunnery School; Alpine Garden Society; American Geographical Society; Associate in General Studies
AGSM Associate of the Guildhall School of Music and Drama; Australian Graduate of the School of Management
AGSRO Association of Government Supervisors and Radio Officers
AGSS American Geographical and Statistical Society
agst against
agt agent; agreement
AGT advanced gas turbine; Association of Geology Teachers (US)
AGU American Geophysical Union
AGV automatic guided vehicle
AGVA American Guild of Variety Artists
agw actual gross weight
AGWI Atlantic, Gulf, West Indies (insurance)
agy agency
ah aft hatch (shipping); after hatch (shipping); ampere-hour; armed helicopter
AH Air Algerie (airline flight code, Algeria); *anno Hebraico* (Latin: in the Jewish year); *anno Hegirae* (Latin: in the year of the Hegira); Antwerp-Hamburg coastal ports (insurance); Arbroath (UK fishing port registration); aromatic hydrocarbon (chemistry); Norwich (UK vehicle registration)
AHA American Heart Association; American Historical Association; American Hospitals Association; Australian Hotels Association
AHAM Association of Home Appliance Manufacturers (US)

AH&FITB Agricultural, Horticultural and Forestry Industry Training Board
AHAUS Amateur Hockey Association of the United States
AHC Accepting Houses Committee; American Horticultural Council; Army Hospital Corps
ahd ahead
AHE Associate in Home Economics (US)
AHEM Association of Hydraulic Equipment Manufacturers
AHF antihaemophilic factor (medicine)
AHI American Health Institute; American Hospital Institute
AHIL Association of Hospital and Institutional Libraries (US)
ahl *ad hunc locum* (Latin: on this passage)
AHL American Hockey League
AHMC Association of Hospital Management Committees
AHMPS Association of Headmistresses of Preparatory Schools
AHMS American Home Mission Society
AHNCV Area of High Nature Conservation Value
AHP absorption heat pump (engineering); air horsepower; assistant house physician
AHPR Association of Health and Pleasure Resorts
AHQ Air Headquarters; Allied Headquarters; Army Headquarters
ahr acceptable hazard rate
AHRC Australian Humanities Research Council
AHRHS Associate of Honour of the Royal Horticultural Society
AHS adult health study; American Helicopter Society; *anno humanae salutis* (Latin: in the year of human salvation); annual housing survey; assistant house surgeon
AHSA American Horse Shows Association
AHSB Authority, Health and Safety Branch (Atomic Energy Authority)
AHSM Associate of the Institute of Health Services Management
AHT acoustic homing torpedo; Animal Health Trust; Association of Highway Technicians
ahv *ad hanc vocem* (Latin: at this word)
AHWA Association of Hospital and Welfare Administrators
ai *ad interim* (Latin: for the meantime)
AI Admiralty Instruction; Admiralty Islands; Air India (airline flight code); air

interdiction; *Altesse Impériale* (French:
Imperial Highness); American Institute;
Amnesty International; *anno inventionis*
(Latin: in the year of the discovery);
Anthropological Institute; Army
Intelligence; artificial insemination;
artificial intelligence; Meath (Irish
vehicle registration)
AIA Aerospace Industries Association
(US); American Institute of Aeronautics;
American Institute of Architects;
American Insurance Association;
Anglo-Indian Association;
Archaeological Institute of America;
Associate of the Institute of Actuaries;
Association of International
Accountants; Association of
International Artists
AIAA Aircraft Industries Association of
America; American Institute of
Aeronautics and Astronautics;
Association of International Advertising
Agencies
AIAB Associate of the International
Association of Book-keepers
AIAC Air Industries Association of
Canada; *Association internationale
d'archéologie classique* (French:
International Association for Classical
Archaeology)
AIAE Associate of the Institution of
Automobile Engineers
AIAgrE Associate of the Institution of
Agricultural Engineers
AIAL Associate Member of the
International Institute of Arts and
Letters
AIAS Associate Surveyor Member of the
Incorporated Association of Architects
and Surveyors; Australian Institute of
Agriculture and Science
AIB accidents investigation branch;
American Institute of Banking;
Association of Independent Businesses
AIBA *Association internationale de boxe
amateur* (French: International Amateur
Boxing Association)
AIBC Architectural Institute of British
Columbia
AIBD Associate of the Institute of British
Decorators; Association of International
Bond Dealers
AIBE Associate of the Institute of
Building Estimators
AIBM Associate of the Institute of Baths
Management; *Association internationale
des bibliothèques musicales* (French:

International Association of Music
Libraries)
AIBP Associate of the Institute of British
Photographers
AIBS American Institute of Biological
Sciences
AIBScot Associate of the Institute of
Bankers in Scotland
AIC Agricultural Improvement Council;
Agricultural Institute of Canada;
American Institute of Chemists; artificial
insemination centre; Art Institute of
Chicago
AICA Associate Member of the
Commonwealth Institute of
Accountants; *Association internationale
des critiques d'art* (French: International
Association of Art Critics)
AICB *Association internationale contre le
bruit* (French: International Association
Against Noise)
AICBM anti-intercontinental ballistic
missile
AICC All India Congress Committee
AICE American Institute of Chemical
Engineers; American Institute of
Consulting Engineers; Associate of the
Institution of Civil Engineers
AICeram Associate of the Institute of
Ceramics
AIChE American Institute of Chemical
Engineers
AICMA *Association internationale des
constructeurs de matériel aérospatial*
(French: International Association of
Aerospace Equipment Manufacturers)
AICPA American Institute of Certified
Public Accountants
AICS Associate of the Institute of
Chartered Shipbrokers; *Association
internationale du cinéma scientifique*
(French: International Scientific Film
Association)
AICV armoured infantry combat vehicle
AID acute infectious disease; Aeronautical
Inspection Directorate; Agency for
International Development; agricultural
industrial development; Aircraft
Intelligence Department; American
Institute of Decorators; American
Institute of Interior Designers; Army
Intelligence Department; artificial
insemination by donor (medicine);
*Association internationale pour le
développement* (French: International
Development Association)
AIDA *Association internationale de droit*

Africain (French: International African Law Association); *Association internationale de la distribution des produits alimentaires* (French: International Association of Food Distribution); attention, interest, desire, action (advertising)

AIDAS Agricultural Industry Development Advisory Service

AIDB Association of International Bond Dealers

AIDD American Institute for Design and Drafting

AIDF African Industrial Development Fund

AIDIA Associate of the Industrial Design Institute of Australia

AIDP Associate of the Institute of Data Processing; *Association internationale de droit pénal* (French: International Association of Penal Law)

Aids acquired immune deficiency syndrome

AIDS accident information display system; acquired immune deficiency syndrome; aircraft integrated data system; air force intelligence data-handling system

AIE Associate of the Institute of Education

AIEA *Agence internationale de l'énergie atomique* (French: International Atomic Energy Agency)

AIED *Association internationale des étudiantes dentaires* (French: International Association of Dental Students)

AIEE Associate of the Institution of Electrical Engineers; *Association des instituts d'études européennes* (French: Association of Institutes for European Studies)

AIEP Association of Independent Electricity Producers (US)

AIF *Alliance internationale des femmes* (French: International Alliance of Women); Atomic Industrial Forum (US); Australian Imperial Forces

AIFA Associate of the International Faculty of Arts

AIFireÉ Associate of the Institution of Fire Engineers

AIFM Associate of the Institute of Factory Managers; *Association internationale des femmes médecins* (French: International Association of Women Doctors)

AIG Adjutant Inspector-General;

Assistant Inspector-General; Assistant Instructor of Gunnery

AIGA American Institute of Graphic Arts

AIGCM Associate of the Incorporated Guild of Church Musicians

AIH all in hand; artificial insemination by husband (medicine); *Association internationale de l'hôtellerie* (French: International Hotel Association)

AIHA American Industrial Hygiene Association

AIHsg Associate of the Institute of Housing

AIIA Associate of the Indian Institute of Architects; Associate of the Insurance Institute of America; Australian Institute of International Affairs

AIIAL Associate of the International Institute of Arts and Letters

AIIE American Institute of Industrial Engineers

AIInfSc Associate of the Institute of Information Scientists

AIITech Associate Member of the Institute of Industrial Technicians

AIJD *Association internationale des juristes démocrates* (French: International Association of Democratic Lawyers)

AIJPF *Association internationale des journalistes de la presse féminine et familiale* (French: International Association of Women's Press Journalists)

AIL air intelligence liaison; Associate of the Institute of Linguists

AILAS automatic instrument landing approach system (aeronautics)

AILO air intelligence liaison officer

AILocoE Associate of the Institution of Locomotive Engineers

AIM Africa Inland Mission; American Indian Movement; American Institute of Management; Association of Industrial Machinery Merchants; Australian Institute of Management

aima as interest may appear

AIMarE Associate of the Institute of Marine Engineers

AIMCO Association of Internal Management Consultants (US)

AIME American Institute of Mechanical Engineers; American Institute of Mining Engineers

AIMEchE Associate of the Institution of Mechanical Engineers

AIMI Associate of the Institute of the Motor Industry

AIMinE Associate of the Institution of Mining Engineers

AIMM Australasian Institute of Mining and Metallurgy

AIMO Association of Industrial Medical Officers

AIMS Association for Improvement in Maternity Services

AIMSW Association of the Institute of Medical Social Workers

AIMU American Institute of Marine Underwriters

AIN American Institute of Nutrition

AInstBCA Associate of the Institute of Burial and Cremation Administration

AInstCE Associate of the Institution of Civil Engineers

AInstExE Associate of the Institute of Executive Engineers and Officers

AInstFF Associate of the Institute of Freight Forwarders Limited

AInstMO Associate of the Institute of Market Officers

AInstP Associate of the Institute of Physics

AInstPI Associate of the Institute of Patentees and Inventors

AINucE Associate of the Institution of Nuclear Engineers

AIO *Agencia Informativa Orbe de Chile* (news agency)

AIP *Agence Ivoirienne de Presse* (news agency); American Institute of Physics; Associate of the Institute of Plumbing; Association of Independent Producers

AIPA Associate Member of the Institute of Practitioners in Advertising; *Association internationale de psychologie appliquée* (French: International Association of Applied Psychology)

AIPO American Institute of Public Opinion

AIPR Associate of the Institute of Public Relations

AIProdE Associate of the Institution of Production Engineers

AIPS *Association internationale de la presse sportive* (French: International Sports Press Association)

AIQS Associate Member of the Institute of Quantity Surveyors

AIR All India Radio; American Institute of Refrigeration

AIRA air attaché (US)

AIRC Association of Independent Radio Companies

AIRCENT Allied Air Forces, Central Europe

AIRCOM airways communications system

AIRH *Association internationale de recherches hydrauliques* (French: International Association of Hydraulic Research)

airmiss aircraft miss

AIRPASS aircraft interception radar and pilots attack sight system

AIRTE Associate of the Institute of Road Transport Engineers

AIRTO Association of Independent Research and Technology Organizations

AIS agreed industry standard (commerce); Anglo-Italian Society; *Association internationale de sociologie* (French: International Sociological Association)

AISA Associate of the Incorporated Secretaries Association

AISE *Association internationale des sciences économiques* (French: International Economics Association)

AISI American Iron and Steel Institute; Associate of the Iron and Steel Institute

AISJ *Association internationale des sciences juridiques* (French: International Association of Legal Science)

AISS *Association internationale de la sécurité sociale* (French: International Social Security Organization)

AIST Agency of Industrial Science and Technology (US); Associate of Science and Technology

AIStructE Associate of the Institution of Structural Engineers

AIT *Alliance internationale de tourisme* (French: International Tourist Alliance); Asian Institute of Technology; Association of HM Inspectors of Taxes; Association of Investment Trusts

AITA *Association internationale du théâtre d'amateurs* (French: International Amateur Theatre Association)

AITC *Association internationale des traducteurs de conférence* (French: International Association of Conference Translators); Association of Investment Trust Companies

AITI Associate of the Institute of Translators and Interpreters

AITO Association of Independent Tour Operators

AIU *Association internationale des*

universités (French: International Association of Universities)

AIV *Association internationale de volcanologie* (French: International Association of Volcanology)

AIW Allied Industrial Workers of America; Atlantic-Intercoastal Waterway (US)

AIWC All-India Women's Conference

AIWEM Associate of the Institution of Water and Environmental Management

AIWM American Institute of Weights and Measures

AJ anti-jam (telecommunications); Associate in Journalism; Middlesbrough (UK vehicle registration)

AJA American of Japanese ancestry; Anglo-Jewish Association; Australian Journalists' Association

AJAG Assistant Judge Advocate-General

AJC Australian Jockey Club

AJCC American Joint Committee on Cancer

AJEX Association of Jewish Ex-Service Men and Women

AJPM *ad Jesum per Mariam* (Latin: to Jesus through Mary)

AJR Association of Jewish Refugees

AJY Association for Jewish Youth

AK Alaska (zip code); automatic Kalashnikov (rifle); Knight of the Order of Australia; Sheffield (UK vehicle registration)

aka also known as

Akad. *Akademie* (German: academy)

AKC American Kennel Club; Associate of King's College (London)

Aktb *Aktiebolaget* (Swedish: joint-stock company)

al allotment letter (finance); *après livraison* (French: after delivery); autograph letter

al. alcohol(ic); *alia* (Latin: other things)

Al aluminium (element)

AL activity of living (medicine); Admiralty letter; Alabama (zip code); Albania (international vehicle registration); *América Latina* (Spanish: Latin America); American League (baseball); American Legion; Anglo-Latin; *anno lucis* (Latin: in the year of light); army list; Nottingham (UK vehicle registration); St Albans (UK postcode)

Ala. Alabama

ALA Air Licensing Authority; all letters answered; American Library Association; Associate in Liberal Arts;

Associate of the Library Association; Association of London Authorities; Authors' League of America

ALAA Associate of Library Association of Australia; Associate of the London Association of Certified Accountants

ALAC Artificial Limb and Appliance Centre

ALACP American League to Abolish Capital Punishment

ALADI *Asociación Latino-Americana de Integración* (Spanish: Latin-American Integration Association)

ALAI *Association littéraire et artistique internationale* (French: International Literary and Artistic Association)

ALA-ISAD American Library Association-Information Science and Automation Division

ALAM Associate of the London Academy of Music and Dramatic Art

Alap as low as practicable (radiation)

Alara as low as reasonably achievable (radiation)

Alas. Alaska

alb. albumin (medicine)

Alb. Albania(n); Alberta; Albion

Alban. *Albanensis* (Latin: (Bishop) of St Albans)

ALBM air-launched ballistic missile

Albq. Albuquerque

ALBSU Adult Literacy and Basic Skills Unit

alc à la carte

alc. alcohol

ALC Agricultural Land Commission

ALCAN Aluminium Company of Canada

ALCD Associate of the London College of Divinity

alch. alchemy

ALCM air-launched cruise missile; Associate of London College of Music

ALCS Authors' Lending and Copyright Society

Ald. Alderman

ALD *Agencia Los Diarios* (news agency, Argentina)

ALDEV African Land Development

Aldm. Alderman

ALE additional living expense (insurance); Association for Liberal Education

A level advanced level (education)

ALF Animal Liberation Front; Arab Liberation Front (Iraq); automatic letter facer (letter-sorting)

ALFSEA Allied Land Forces South-East Asia
alg advanced landing ground
alg. algebra(ic)
Alg. Algeria(n); Algiers
ALGES Association of Local Government Engineers and Surveyors
ALGFO Association of Local Government Financial Officers
Algol algorithmic language (computing)
ALH Australian Light Horse
ALI *Agencia Lusa de Informacao* (news agency, Portugal); American Library Institute; Argyll Light Infantry; Associate of the Landscape Institute
ALICE Autistic and Language-Impaired Children's Education
align. alignment
ALJ Administration Law Judge
alk. alkali
ALL acute lymphatic/lymphoblastic/lymphocytic/lymphoid leukaemia
ALLC Association for Literary and Linguistic Computing
alleg. allegory
All H. All Hallows
all'ingr. *all'ingrosso* (Italian: wholesale)
allo. allegro (music)
all'ott *all'ottava* (Italian: an octave higher; music)
All S. All Souls
All SS All Saints
ALM *Artium Liberalium Magister* (Latin: Master of the Liberal Arts)
ALO air liaison officer; allied liaison officer
ALOE A Lady of England (pseudonym of British novelist Charlotte M. Tucker)
alp. alpine
ALP American Labor Party; Australian Labor Party; automated learning process; automated library program (US)
ALPA Airline Pilots' Association
alph. alphabetical
ALPO Association of Land and Property Owners; Association of Lunar and Planetary Observers
ALPSP Association of Learned and Professional Society Publishers
ALPURCOMS all-purpose communications system
alr *aliter* (Latin: otherwise)
ALR American Law Reports
ALRC Anti-Locust Research Centre

ALRI airborne long-range input
als autograph letter, signed
ALS accident localization system; Agricultural Land Service; approach lighting systems (aeronautics); Associate of the Linnean Society; automated library system
Alsat. Alsatian
al seg. *al segno* (Italian: to or at the sign; music)
alt. alteration; alternate; alternative; alternator; altimeter; altitude; alto
Alt. *Altesse* (French: Highness)
ALT Agricultural Land Tribunal
Alta. Alberta
alt. dieb. *alternis diebus* (Latin: every other day; medicine)
alter. alteration
alt. hor. *alternis horis* (Latin: every other hour)
alt. noct. *alternis noctibus* (Latin: every other night)
ALTPR Association of London Theatre Press Representatives
ALTU Association of Liberal Trade Unionists
ALU arithmetic and logic unit (computing)
alum. aluminium; alumna; alumnae; alumni; alumnus
ALWR advanced light-water reactor (nuclear physics)
am amplitude modulation (radio); *ante meridiem* (Latin: before noon); attometre (physics)
am. ammeter; ammunition
a/m above mentioned
aM *am Main* (German: on the River Main)
Am americium (element)
Am. America(n); Amos (Bible)
AM Academy of Management; administrative memorandum; Aeromexico (airline flight code); *Agencia Meridional* (news agency, Brasil); airlock module (astronautics); air mail; Air Marshal; Air Ministry; Albert Medal; Alpes-Maritime (French department); amplitude modulation (radio); angular momentum (physics); *anno mundi* (Latin: in the year of the world); *annus mirabilis* (Latin: year of wonders); *ante meridiem* (Latin: before noon); area manager; army manual; *Artium Magister* (Latin: Master of Arts); assistant manager; Associate Member; *assurance mutuelle* (French: mutual assurance); *Ave Maria* (Latin: Hail Mary); Member of the Order

of Australia; Swindon (UK vehicle registration)

AMA against medical advice; American Management Association; American Marketing Association; American Medical Association; American Missionary Association; American Motorcycle Association; Assistant Masters Association; Associate of the Museums Association; Association of Metropolitan Authorities; Australian Medical Association

AMAB Army Medical Advisory Board

AMAE American Museum of Atomic Energy

amal. amalgamated

AMAmIEE Associate Member of the American Institute of Electrical Engineers

AMARC Associated Marine and Related Charities

AMASCE Associate Member of the American Society of Civil Engineers

amat. amateur

AMAusIMM Associate Member of the Australasian Institute of Mining and Metallurgy

Amb. Ambassador; ambulance

AMB Air Ministry bulletin; Airways Modernization Board (US)

AMBAC Associate Member of the British Association of Chemists

Ambas. Ambassador

ambig. ambiguous

AMC Aerospace Manufacturers' Council (US); Agricultural Mortgage Corporation Limited; American Motors Corporation; Army Missile Command (US); Army Mobile Command (US); Army Munitions Command (US); Art Master's Certificate; Association of Management Consultants; Association of Municipal Corporations

AMCA Architectural Metal Craftsmen's Association

AMCIB Associate Member of the Corporation of Insurance Brokers

AMCIOB Associate Member of the Chartered Institute of Building

AMCL Association of Metropolitan Chief Librarians

AMCS airborne missile control system

AMCT Associate of the Manchester College of Technology

am. cur. *amicus curiae* (Latin: a friend of the court)

amd amend

AMD Admiralty machinery depot; aerospace medical division; air movement data; Army Medical Department

AMDB Agricultural Machinery Development Board

AMDEA Association of Manufacturers of Domestic Electrical Appliances

AMDEC Agricultural Marketing Development Executive Committee

AMDG *ad majorem Dei gloriam* (Latin: to the greater glory of God; Jesuit motto)

amdt amendment

AME Advanced Master of Education (US); African Methodist Episcopal; Association of Municipal Engineers

AMEC Australian Minerals and Energy Council

AMEDS Army Medical Service

AMEE Admiralty Marine Engineering Establishment; Association of Managerial Electrical Executives

AMEIC Associate Member of the Engineering Institute of Canada

AMEM African Methodist Episcopal Mission

Am. Emb. American Embassy

AMEME Association of Mining Electrical and Mechanical Engineers

amend(t). amendment

Amer. Ind. American Indian

Amer. Std. American Standard

AMES Air Ministry Experimental Station; Association of Marine Engineering Schools

AMet Associate of Metallurgy

AMEWA Associated Manufacturers of Electric Wiring Accessories

Amex American Express; American Stock Exchange

AMEZC African Methodist Episcopal Zion Church

AMF Australian Marine Force; Australian Military Forces

amg among; automatic magnetic guidance (aeronautics)

AMG Allied Military Government

AMGO Assistant Master-General of Ordnance

AMGOT Allied Military Government of Occupied Territory (World War II)

ami advanced manned interceptor (military); air mileage indicator (aeronautics)

AMI acute myocardial infarction (medicine); American Meat Institute; American Military Institute; Ancient

Monuments Inspectorate; *Association Montessori internationale* (Italian: International Montessori Association)

AMIAE Associate Member of the Institution of Automobile Engineers

AMIAP Associate Member of the Institution of Analysts and Programmers

AMIBF Associate Member of the Institute of British Foundrymen

AMICEI Associate Member of the Institution of Civil Engineers of Ireland

AMIChemE Associate Member of the Institution of Chemical Engineers

AMICW Associate Member of the Institute of Clerks of Works of Great Britain

AMIE Associate Member of the Institute of Engineers and Technicians

AMIE(Aust) Associate Member of the Institution of Engineers (Australia)

AMIED Associate Member of the Institute of Engineering Designers

AMIE(Ind) Associate Member of the Institution of Engineers (India)

AMIElecIE Associate Member of the Institution of Electrical and Electronic Incorporated Engineers

AMIERE Associate Member of the Institute of Electronic and Radio Engineers

AMIEx Associate Member of the Institute of Export

AMIFireE Associate Member of the Institution of Fire Engineers

AMIGasE Associate Member of the Institution of Gas Engineers

AMIH Associate Member of the Institute of Housing

AMIHT Associate Member of the Institution of Highways and Transportation

AMII Association of Musical Instrument Industries

AMIIM Associate Member of the Institution of Industrial Managers

AMILocoE Associate Member of the Institution of Locomotive Engineers

AMIMarE Associate Member of the Institute of Marine Engineers

AMIMGTechE Associate Member of the Institution of Mechanical and General Technician Engineers

AMIMI Associate Member of the Motor Industry

AMIMinE Associate Member of the Institution of Mining Engineers

AMIMM Associate Member of the Institution of Mining and Metallurgy

Am. Ind. American Indian

AMinIsTech Associate in Minerals Technology

AMInstBE Associate Member of the Institution of British Engineers

AMInstEE American Institute of Electrical Engineers

AMInstR Associate Member of the Institute of Refrigeration

AMInstTA Associate Member of the Institute of Traffic Administration

AMINucE Associate Member of the Institution of Nuclear Engineering

AMIOP Associate Member of the Institute of Printing

AMIPA Associate Member of the Institute of Practitioners in Advertising

AMIPE Associate Member of the Institute of Production Engineers

AMIPM Associate Member of the Institute of Personnel Management

AMIPRE Associate Member of the Incorporated Practitioners in Radio and Electronics

AMIProdE Associate Member of the Institution of Production Engineers

AMIQA Associate Member of the Institute of Quality Assurance

AMIRA Australian Mineral Industries Association

AMIRSE Associate Member of the Institute of Railway Signalling Engineers

AMIStructE Associate Member of the Institution of Structural Engineers

AMITA Associate Member of the Industrial Transport Association

AMITE Associate Member of the Institute of Traffic Engineers (US)

AMIWEM Associate Member of the Institution of Water and Environmental Management

AMIWM Associate Member of the Institution of Works Managers

AMJ *Assemblée mondiale de la jeunesse* (French: World Assembly of Youth)

AML abandoned mine land; acute myelocytic/myeloid/myelogenous leukaemia; Admiralty materials laboratory

AMLS Master of Arts in Library Science (US)

amm. ammunition

AMM antimissile missile; assistant marketing manager; *Association médicale*

mondiale (French: World Medical Association)
AMMA Assistant Masters' and Mistresses' Association
AMMI American Merchant Marine Institute
amn ammunition
AMNECInst Associate Member of the North East Coast Institution of Engineers and Shipbuilders
AMNILP Associate Member of the National Institute of Licensing Practitioners
AMNZIE Associate Member of the New Zealand Institute of Licensing Practitioners
AMO Air Ministry order; area medical officer; assistant medical officer
AMOB automatic meteorological oceanographic buoy
AMORC Ancient Mystical Order Rosae Crucis (Rosicrucians)
amort. amortization
AMOS automatic meteorological observing station
amp. amperage; ampere; amplified; amplifier; amplitude
AMP Air Member for Personnel (RAF); Associated Master Plumbers and Domestic Engineers; Australian Mutual Provident Society
AMPAS Academy of Motion Picture Arts and Sciences (US)
AMPC automatic message processing center (US); auxiliary military pioneer corps
amph. amphibian; amphibious
AMPHIBEX amphibious exercise
ampl. amplifier
AMPS automatic message processing system
AMPSS advanced manned precision strike system
AMQ American medical qualification
AMR Atlantic missile range; automated meter reading; automatic message routing
Amraam advanced medium-range air-to-air missile
AMRINA Associate Member of the Royal Institution of Naval Architects
Amrit. Amritsar
AMRO Association of Medical Record Officers
AMRS Air Ministry radio station
AMS accelerator mass spectrometer; accelerator mass spectrometry; accident-

monitoring system; Agricultural Marketing Service (US); American Mathematical Society; American Meteorological Society; American Microscopal Society; American Musicological Society; Ancient Monuments Society; army map service; army medical services; army medical staff; assistant military secretary; Australian medical services; automatic music search
AMSA advanced manned strategic aircraft
AMSAIEE Associate Member of the South African Institution of Electrical Engineering
Am. Sam. American Samoa
AMSAM anti-missile surface-to-air missile
AMSE Associate Member of the Society of Engineers
AMSEF antiminesweeping explosive float
AMSERT Associate Member of the Society of Electronic and Radio Technicians
AMSGA Association of Manufacturers and Suppliers for the Graphic Arts
AMSL above mean sea level
AMSO Air Member for Supply and Organization (RAF); Association of Market Survey Organizations
AMSST Associate of the Society of Surveying Technicians
Amst. Amsterdam
AMSTRAD Alan Michael Sugar Trading (computer manufacturers)
AMSW Master of Arts in Social Work (US)
amt amount
AMT airmail transfer; Air Member for Training (RAF); alternative minimum tax; area management team; Associate in Mechanical Technology; Associate in Medical Technology; Association of Marine Traders; Master of Arts in Teaching (US)
AMTA Association of Multiple Travel Agents
AMTC Academic Member of the Trinity College of Music; Art Master's Teaching Certificate
AMTDA Agricultural Machinery Tractor Dealers' Association
AMTE Admiralty Marine Technology Establishment
AMTI airborne moving target indicator
AMTRI Advanced Manufacturing Technology Research Institute

AMTS Associate Member of the Television Society

amu atomic mass unit

AMU Associated Midwestern Universities (US); Association of Master Upholsterers

AMUA Associate of Music, University of Adelaide (Australia)

AMus Associate in Music

AMusD Doctor in Musical Arts

AMusLCM Associate in Music, London College of Music

AMusTCL Associate in Music, Trinity College of Music, London

AMV *Association mondiale vétérinaire* (French: World Veterinary Association)

AMVAP Associated Manufacturers of Veterinary and Agricultural Products

AMVETS American Veterans

AMW average molecular weight

an above named

an. *anno* (Latin: in the year); anonymous; answer

An actinon (chemistry)

An. Annam

AN acid number (chemistry); *Agencia Nacional* (news agency, Brasil); ammonium nitrate (chemistry); Anglo-Norman; Ansett Australia (airline flight code); ante-natal; Associate in Nursing; audible noise (physics); Reading (UK vehicle registration)

A/N advice note

ANA All Nippon Airways; American Nature Association; American Neurological Association; American Newspaper Association; American Numismatic Association; American Nurses' Association; Associate National Academician (US); Association of Nurse Administrators; *Athenagence* (news agency, Greece); Australian Natives' Association

anac(r). anacreon

anaes. anaesthesia; anaesthetic

anag. anagram

anal. analogous; analogy; analyse; analysis; analytic

ANAPO *Alianza Nacional Popular* (Spanish: National Popular Alliance)

ANARE Australian National Antarctic Research Expedition

anat. anatomical; anatomy

anc. ancient

ANC African National Congress; Army Nurse Corps; Australian Newspapers Council

anch. anchored

ANCOM Andean Common Market

anct ancient

ANCUN Australian National Committee for the United Nations

and. *andante* (Italian: at a moderate speed; music)

AND Andorra (international vehicle registration)

ANDB Air Navigation Development Board (US)

ANEC American Nuclear Energy Council

ANECInst Associate of the North-East Coast Institution of Engineers and Shipbuilders

ANERI Advanced Nuclear Equipment Research Institute (US)

anes. anesthetic (US)

ANF Advanced Nuclear Fuels (US); antinuclear factor; Atlantic Nuclear Force; Australian National Flag Association

ang. angle; angular

Ang. Anglesey

ANG Air National Guard (US); Australian Newspaper Guild

ANGB Air National Guard Base (US)

Angl. *Angleterre* (French: England); Anglican; Anglicized

Anglo-Fr. Anglo-French

Anglo-Ind. Anglo-Indian

Anglo-Ir. Anglo-Irish

Anglo-L. Anglo-Latin

Anglo-Sax. Anglo-Saxon

ANGUS Air National Guard of the United States

Anh. *Anhang* (German: appendix)

anhyd(r). anhydrous (chemistry)

ANI American Nuclear Insurers

anim. *animato* (Italian: in a spirited manner; music)

Ank. *Ankunft* (German: arrival)

ANL automatic noise limiting (engineering); National Library of Australia

Anm. *Anmerkung* (German: note)

ANM Admiralty Notices to Mariners

ann. annals; *anni* (Latin: years); *anno* (Latin: in the year); annual; annuity

ANNA Army-Navy-NASA-Air Force satellite (US)

anniv. anniversary

annot. annotate; annotation; annotator

annuit. annuitant

annul. annulment

Annunc. Annunciation

ANO Association of Nuclear Operators (US)

anon. anonymous; anonymously
ANP advanced nursing practice; aircraft nuclear propulsion; *Algemeen Nederlands Persbureau* (news agency); ammonium nitrate-phosphate (fertilizer); Australian National Party
ANPA American Newspaper Publishers' Association; Australian National Publicity Association
anr another
anrac aids navigation radio control
ANRC American National Red Cross; Australian National Research Council
ANRE advanced nuclear rocket engine
ANRPC Association of Natural Rubber Producing Countries
ans autograph note, signed
ans. answer
ANS American Nuclear Society; Army News Service; Army Nursing Service; autonomic nervous system
ANSA *Agenzia Nazionale Stampa Associate* (news agency, Italy)
ANSI American National Standards Institute
ANSL Australian National Standards Laboratory
ANSP Academy of Natural Sciences of Philadelphia; Australian National Socialist Party
ANSR advanced neutron source reactor (nuclear physics)
ANSTI African Network of Scientific and Technological Institutions
ANSTO Australian Nuclear Science and Technology Organization
ant. antenna; anterior; antilog; antiquarian; antique; antiquity; antonym
Ant. Antarctica; Antigua; Antrim
ANTA American National Theatre and Academy; Australian National Travel Association
ANTARA Indonesian National News Agency
Antarc. Antarctic
anthol. anthology
anthrop(ol). anthropological; anthropology
Antig. Antigua
antilog antilogarithm
antiq. antiquarian; antiquity
Ant. Lat. antique Latin
ant. ld antique laid (paper)
anton. antonym
ANTOR Association of National Tourist Office Representatives
Antr. Antrim

ant. wo. antique wove (paper)
ANU Australian National University
ANWR Arctic National Wildlife Refuge
anx annex
ANZ Australia and New Zealand Banking Group
ANZAAS Australian and New Zealand Association for the Advancement of Science
Anzac Australian and New Zealand Army Corps (World War I)
ANZAM Australia, New Zealand and Malaysia (defence force)
ANZCAN Australia, New Zealand and Canada
ANZIA Associate of the New Zealand Institute of Architects
ANZIC Associate of the New Zealand Institute of Chemistry
ANZLA Associate of the New Zealand Library Association
ANZUK Australian, New Zealand and United Kingdom (defence force)
ANZUS Australia, New Zealand and US Defence Pact
aO *an der Oder* (German: on the River Oder)
AO accountant officer; air officer; air ordnance; *anno ordinis* (Latin: in the year of the order); anthracene oil (chemistry); area office; army order; Australian Opera; Carlisle (UK vehicle registration); Officer of the Order of Australia
A/O account of; and others
AOA Administration on Ageing; Aerodrome Owners Association; Air Officer in charge of Administration; American Ordnance Association; American Orthopedic Association; American Orthopsychiatric Association; American Osteopathic Association; American Overseas Association
aob any other business; at or below
AOB advanced operational base; Antediluvian Order of Buffaloes; any other business
AOC Air Officer Commanding; *anno orbis Conditi* (Latin: in the year of the Creation); *appellation (d'origine) contrôlée* (French: controlled place of origin; wine classification); Army Ordnance Corps
AOCB any other competent business
AOC-in-C Air Officer Commanding-in-Chief
AOCM aircraft out of commission for maintenance (US Air Force)
AOD advanced ordnance depot; Ancient

Order of Druids; Army Ordnance Department
AOER Army Officers' Emergency Reserve
AOF *Afrique Occidentale Française* (French: French West Africa); Ancient Order of Foresters; Australian Olympic Federation
A of F Admiral of the Fleet
A of S Academy of Science
AOG aircraft on ground
AOH Ancient Order of Hibernians
AoI aims of industry
aoiv automatically operated inlet valve (engineering)
A-OK all OK
AOL absent over leave (US)
AOM amorphous organic matter
AONB area of outstanding natural beauty
AOP Association of Optical Practitioners
AOPU Asian Oceanic Postal Union
AOQ average outgoing quality
AOQL average outgoing quality limit
aor. aorist
a/or and/or
AOR adult-oriented rock (music); advice or rights (law; US); album-oriented radio; album-oriented rock (music)
AOS American Opera Society; American Ophthalmological Society; Ancient Order of Shepherds; automated office system
AOSO advanced orbiting solar observatory
AOSS *Americanae Orientalis Societatis Socius* (Latin: Fellow of the American Oriental Society)
AOSW Association of Official Shorthand Writers
AOT allowed outage time (engineering); allowed out-of-service time (engineering)
AOTA American Occupational Therapy Association
AOU American Ornithologists' Union
ap above proof; additional premium; advanced post; *ante prandium* (Latin: before a meal; medicine); arithmetical progression; author's proof
ap. apothecary; apparent; *apud* (Latin: in the works of, according to)
Ap. apostle; April
AP additional premium; adjective phrase; aerosol particle; airplane (US); Air Police (US); air pollution; *Alianza Popular* (Spanish: Popular Alliance); Andhra Pradesh; angina pectoris (medicine); anteroposterior (medicine);

antipersonnel; armour-piercing; array processor (computing); arterial pressure (medicine); Associated Presbyterian; Associated Press (news agency); atomic power; authority to pay; authority to purchase; automotive products; average payable (insurance); Brighton (UK vehicle registration); Pakistan (international civil aircraft marking)
APA additional personal allowance (taxation); Alaska Power Authority; All Parties Administration (Australia); American Philological Association; American Physicists Association; American Pilots Association; American Press Association; American Protestant Association; American Psychiatric Association; American Psychoanalytic Association; American Psychological Association; Associate in Public Administration; Association for the Prevention of Addiction; Association of Public Analysts; Australian Physiotherapy Association; *Austria Presse Agentur* (news agency)
APACL Asian People's Anti-Communist League
APACS Association for Payment Clearing Services
APAE Association of Public Address Engineers
APANZ Associate of the Public Accountants of New Zealand
apart. apartment
APB all-points bulletin (US police alert)
APBA American Power Boat Association
APBF Accredited Poultry Breeders' Federation
apc average propensity to consume
APC advanced process control (engineering); air-pollution control; American Philatelic Congress; Appalachian Power Company; armoured personnel carrier; Assistant Principal Chaplain; Associated Portland Cement; automatic phase control; automatic power control (electronics); automatic public convenience
APCA Air Pollution Control Association (US); Anglo-Polish Catholic Association
APCK Association for Promoting Christian Knowledge (Church of Ireland)
APCN *anno post Christum natum* (Latin: in the year after the birth of Christ)
APCO Association of Pleasure Craft Operators

APCOL All-Pakistan Confederation of
Labour
apd approved
APD Administrative Planning Division;
Air Pollution Division (US); Army Pay
Department
APDC Apple and Pear Development
Council
Ap. Deleg. Apostolic Delegate
APE Amalgamated Power Engineering;
automatic photomapping equipment;
available potential energy (physics)
APEC Asia-Pacific Economic
Cooperation Conference
APEX advance-purchase excursion (UK
railway fare scheme); Association of
Professional, Executive, Clerical and
Computer Staff
APF Association for the Propagation of
the Faith
APFC Asia-Pacific Forestry Commission
APG air proving ground (US Air Force)
APGA American Public Gas Association
aph. aphorism
APH antepartum haemorrhage
(obstetrics); anterior pituitary hormone
aphet. aphetic
APHI American Public Health
Association; Association of Public
Health Inspectors
APHIS Animal and Plant Health
Inspection Service (US)
API air-pollution index; air-position
indicator; American Petroleum Institute;
application programmer interface
(computing); *Association phonétique
internationale* (French: International
Phonetic Association)
APIS Army Photographic Intelligence
Service
ap. J-C *après Jésus-Christ* (French: after
Jesus Christ)
Apl April
APL A Programming Language
(computing)
APLE Association of Public Lighting
Engineers
APM Academy of Physical Medicine
(US); airborne particulate matter;
Assistant Paymaster; Assistant Provost-
Marshal
APMC Allied Political and Military
Commission
APMG Assistant Postmaster-General
APMI Associate of the Pensions
Management Institute
apmt appointment

apo. apogee
APO acting pilot officer; African People's
Organization; Armed Forces Post Office;
Army Post Office; Asian Productivity
Organization
Apoc. Apocalypse; Apocryphal
apog. apogee
apos. apostrophe
APOTA automatic positioning
telemetering antenna
apoth. apothecary
app. apparatus; apparent; apparently;
appeal; appended; appendix; applied;
appointed; apprentice; approved;
approximate; approximately
App. Apostles
APP African People's Party (Kenya);
Agence Parisienne de Presse (news agency,
France); Associated Press of Pakistan
APPA African Petroleum Producers
Association
appar. apparatus; apparent; apparently
appd approved
APPES American Institute of Chemical
Engineers Physical Properties
Estimation System
APPITA Australian Pulp and Paper
Industries Technical Association
appl appeal
appl. appellant; applicable; applied
appos. appositive
appr. apprentice
appro. approbation; approval
approx. approximate; approximately
apps appendices
appt appoint; appointment
apptd appointed
APPU Australian Primary Producers
Union
appurts appurtenances
appx appendix
Apr. April
APR Accredited Public Relations
Practitioner; annual percentage rate;
annual progress report; annual purchase
rate
APRA *Alianza Popular Revolutionaria
Americana* (Spanish: American Popular
Revolutionary Alliance); *anno post
Romam conditam* (Latin: in the year after
the foundation of Rome)
APRI Associate of the Plastics and Rubber
Institute
A/Prin. Assistant Principal
apr. J-C *après Jésus-Christ* (French: after
Jesus Christ)
APRS acoustic position reference system

(navigation); Association for the Protection of Rural Scotland; Association of Professional Recording Studios

aps autograph poem, signed; average propensity to save

APS Aborigines' Protection Society; *Agence de Presse Senegalaise* (news agency, Senegal); *Algeria Press Service* (news agency); American Peace Society; American Philatelic Society; American Philosophical Society; American Physics Society; American Physiological Society; American Protestant Society; Arizona Public Service Company; army postal service; Assistant Private Secretary; Associate of the Philosophical Society

APSA American Political Science Association; Associate of the Photographic Society of America; Australian Political Studies Association

APSL Acting Paymaster Sublieutenant

APsSI Associate of the Psychological Society of Ireland

APST Association of Professional Scientists and Technologists

APSW Association of Psychiatric Social Workers

apt apartment

APT advanced passenger train; advanced process technology; Association of Printing Technologists; Association of Private Traders; automatic picture transmission

APTC Army Physical Training Corps

APTI Association of Principals of Technical Institutions

APTIS all purpose ticket issuing system

APTS Automatic Picture Transmission Subsystem (NASA)

APTU African Postal and Telecommunications Union

APU acute psychiatric unit; Arab Postal Union; Assessment of Performance Unit (education); auxiliary power unit (aeronautics)

APUC Association for Promoting Unity of Christendom

apv adjusted present value

APWA American Public Welfare Association; American Public Works Association

APWR advanced pressurized water reactor (nuclear physics)

APWU American Postal Workers Union

aq. *aqua* (Latin: water); aqueous

Aq. aquatic (horticulture)

AQ accomplishment quotient

(psychology); achievement quotient (psychology); Administration and Quartering (military); Aloha Airlines (airline flight code, Hawaii)

aq. bull. *aqua bulliens* (Latin: boiling water; medicine)

AQC Associate of Queen's College (London)

aq. cal. *aqua calida* (Latin: warm water; medicine)

aq. com. *aqua communis* (Latin: tap water; medicine)

aq. dest. *aqua destillata* (Latin: distilled water; medicine)

aq. ferv. *aqua fervens* (Latin: hot water; medicine)

aq. frig. *aqua frigida* (Latin: cold water; medicine)

AQI air-quality index

AQL acceptable quality level

AQMG Assistant Quartermaster-General

aq. m. pip. *aqua menthae piperitae* (Latin: peppermint water; medicine)

aq. pur. *aqua pura* (Latin: pure water; medicine)

aq. tep. *aqua tepida* (Latin: tepid water; medicine)

aque. aqueduct

ar all risks (insurance); *anno regni* (Latin: in the year of the reign)

ar. arrival; arrive/s; arrived

Ar argon (element)

Ar. Arabia; Arabian; Arabic; Aramaic

AR accomplishment ratio (psychology); achievement ratio (psychology); account receivable; acid resisting; acrylic rubber; acute rejection (medicine); advice of receipt; Aerolineas Agentinas (airline flight code); airman recruit (US Air Force); *Altesse Royale* (French: Royal Highness); *Anna Regina* (Latin: Queen Anne); annual register; annual report; annual return (taxation); *argentum* (Latin: silver; numismatics); Arkansas (zip code); Army Regulations; aspect ratio (image technology); Assistant Resident; Associated Rediffusion; Autonomous Region; Ayr (UK fishing port registration); Chelmsford (UK vehicle registration)

ARA Aircraft Research Association; American Railway Association; Army Rifle Association; Associate of the Royal Academy

Arab. Arabia; Arabian; Arabic

ARAC Associate of the Royal Agricultural College

arach. arachnology

ARACI Associate of the Royal Australian Chemical Institute

ARAD Associate of the Royal Academy of Dancing

ARAeS Associate of the Royal Aeronautical Society

ARAIA Associate of the Royal Australian Institute of Architects

Aram. Aramaic

ARAM Associate of the Royal Academy of Music

ARAMCO Arabian-American Oil Company

ARAS Associate of the Royal Astronomical Society

arb. arbiter; arbitrageur; arbitrary; arbitration; arbitrator

ARB Air Registration Board (aviation); Air Research Bureau

ARBA Associate of the Royal Society of British Artists

ARBE *Académie Royale des Beaux-Arts, École Supérieure des Arts Décoratifs et École Supérieure d'Architecture de Bruxelles* (French: Brussels Royal Academy of Fine Arts)

arbor. arboriculture

ARBS Associate of the Royal Society of British Sculptors

arc. *arcato/coll'arco* (Italian: with the bow; music)

ARC Aeronautical Research Council; Agricultural Research Council; Aids-related complex (medicine); American Red Cross; Archaeological Resource Centre (York); Architects' Registration Council; Arthritis and Rheumatism Council; Atlantic Research Corporation

ARCA Associate of the Royal Cambrian Academy; Associate of the Royal Canadian Academy (of Arts); Associate of the Royal College of Art

arch. archaic; archaism; archery; archipelago; architect; architectural; architecture

Arch. archbishop; archdeacon; archduke

archaeol. archaeology

Archb. archbishop

Archd. archdeacon; archduke

archit. architecture

archt. architect

ARCIC Anglican-Roman Catholic International Commission

ARCM Associate of the Royal College of Music

ARCO Associate of the Royal College of Organists

ARCO(CHM) Associate of the Royal College of Organists with Diploma in Choir Training

ARCOS Anglo-Russian Cooperative Society

ARCPsych Associate of the Royal College of Psychiatrists

ARCS Associate of the Royal College of Science; Associate of the Royal College of Surgeons; Australian Red Cross

ARCST Associate of the Royal College of Science and Technology (Glasgow)

ARCUK Architects' Registration Council of the United Kingdom

ARCVS Associate of the Royal College of Veterinary Surgeons

ARD acute radiation disease

ARDC Air Research and Development Command (US)

ARDEC Army Research Development and Engineering Center (US)

ARDMS automated route design and management system

ARDS adult respiratory distress syndrome (medicine)

ARE Admiralty Research Establishment; Arab Republic of Egypt; Associate of the Royal Society of Painter-Etchers and Engravers

AREI Associate of the Real Estate and Stock Institute of Australia

ARELS Association of Recognized English Language Schools

ARF acute renal failure (medicine); acute respiratory failure (medicine); Advertising Research Foundation

Arg. argent (heraldry); Argentina; Argentine; Argentinian; Argyll; Argyllshire

a. Rh. *am Rhein* (German: on the River Rhine)

ARHA Associate of the Royal Hibernian Academy of Painting, Sculpture and Architecture

ARHS Associate of the Royal Horticultural Society

ARI acute respiratory infection

ARIAS Associate of the Royal Incorporation of Architects in Scotland

ARIBA Associate of the Royal Institute of British Architects

ARICS Professional Associate of the Royal Institution of Chartered Surveyors

ARIEL Automated Real-time Investments

Exchange Limited (share-dealing system)

ARINA Associate of the Royal Institution of Naval Architects

ARIS advanced range instrumentation ship

Arist. Aristotle (Greek philosopher)

Aristoph. Aristophanes (Greek playwright)

arith. arithmetic; arithmetical; arithmetician

Ariz. Arizona

Ark. Arkansas

ARL Association of Research Libraries; Australian Rugby League

Arm. Armagh; Armenia; Armenian; Armorica; Armorican

ArM *Architecturae Magister* (Latin: Master of Architecture)

ARM adjustable-rate mortgage; *Alliance réformée mondiale* (French: Worldwide Presbyterian Alliance); antiradar missile; antiradiation missile; atomic resolution microscope; Australian Republican Movement

ARMCM Associate of the Royal Manchester College of Music

armd armoured

ARMIT Associate of the Royal Melbourne Institute of Technology

ARMS Action for Research into Multiple Sclerosis; Associate of the Royal Society of Miniature Painters

ARNA Arab Revolution News Agency

ARO army routine order; Asian Regional Organization; Associate Member of the Register of Osteopaths

AROD airborne remote operated device

AROS African Regional Organization for Standardization

arp. arpeggio (music)

ARP adjustable rate preferred (stock; US); air-raid precautions; Associated Reformed Presbyterian

ARPA Advanced Research Projects Agency

ARPANET Advanced Research Projects Agency Network (computing)

ARPO Association of Resort Publicity Officers

ARPS Associate of the Royal Photographic Society; Association of Railway Preservation Societies

arr. arranged (music); arrangement (music); arrival; arrive/s; arrived

ARR accounting rate of return; *anno regni Reginae/Regis* (Latin: in the year of the

Queen's or King's reign); Association of Radiation Research

ARRC Associate of the Royal Red Cross

arron. *arrondissement* (French: administrative district)

ARS acute radiation syndrome (medicine); Agricultural Research Service (US); American Records Society; American Recreation Society; American Rocket Society; *anno reparatae salutis* (Latin: in the year of our redemption); Army Radio School

ARSA Associate of the Royal Scottish Academy; Associate of the Royal Society of Arts

ARSCM Associate of the Royal School of Church Music

ARSH Associate of the Royal Society for the Promotion of Health

ARSL Associate of the Royal Society of Literature

ARSM Associate of the Royal School of Mines

ARSR air route surveillance radar

ARSW Associate of the Royal Scottish Society of Painting in Watercolours

art. article; artificer; artificial; artillery; artist

ARTC air route traffic control

artic articulated vehicle

artif. artificer

art. pf. artist's proof

arty artillery

ARU American Railway Union; audio response unit (computing)

ARV American Revised Version (Bible)

ARVIA Associate of the Royal Victoria Institute of Artists

ARWA Associate of the Royal West of England Academy

ARWS Associate of the Royal Society of Painters in Water-Colours

as account sales; aggregate supply

As arsenic (element)

As. Asia; Asian; Asiatic

AS Academy of Science; Admiral Superintendent; advanced supplementary (education); air speed; air staff; Alaska Airlines (airline flight code); all sections (insurance); *al segno* (Italian: to or at the sign; music); American Samoa; Anglo-Saxon; *anno salutis* (Latin: in the year of salvation); *anno Salvatoris* (Latin: in the year of the Saviour); antisubmarine; Assistant Secretary; assistant surgeon; Associate in Science; Inverness (UK vehicle registration); personal allowance (taxation)

A/S account sales; Advanced Supplementary (education); after sight (banking); *Aktieselskab* (Danish: joint-stock company); *Aktjeselskap* (Norwegian: limited company); alongside

ASA Acoustic Society of America; Addiction Services Agency (US); Advertising Standards Authority; Amateur Swimming Association; American Sociological Association; American Standards Association; American Statistical Association; Army Sailing Association; Associate Member of the Society of Actuaries; Associate of the Society of Actuaries; Australian Society of Accountants

ASAA Associate of the Society of Incorporated Accountants and Auditors

ASAB Association for the Study of Animal Behaviour

ASAI Associate of the Society of Architectural Illustrators

ASAM Associate of the Society of Art Masters

AS&TS of SA Associated Scientific and Technical Societies of South Africa

asap as soon as possible

ASAP automated shipboard aerological programme

ASAT anti-satellite (interceptor) (military)

asb aircraft safety beacon

asb. asbestos

ASB Alternative Service Book; American Society of Bacteriologists

ASBAH Association for Spina Bifida and Hydrocephalus

ASBM air-to-surface ballistic missile

ASBSBSW Amalgamated Society of Boilermakers, Shipwrights, Blacksmiths and Structural Workers

asc. ascend; ascent

ASc Associate in Science

ASC Administrative Staff College (Henley); Air Service Command (US); altered state of consciousness; American Society of Cinematographers; Asian Socialist Conference

ASCA Associate of the Society of Company and Commercial Accountants

ASCAB Armed Services Consultant Approval Board

ASCAP American Society of Composers, Authors and Publishers

ASCC Association of Scottish Climbing Clubs; automatic sequence controlled calculator (computing)

ASCE American Society of Civil Engineers

ASCII American Standards Code for Information Interchange (computing)

ASCM Australian Student Christian Movement

ASCU Association of State Colleges and Universities (US)

ASD Admiralty Salvage Department; Armament Supply Department

ASDAR aircraft-to-satellite data relay

ASDC Associate of the Society of Dyers and Colourists

a/s de *aux soins de* (French: care of)

ASDE airport surface detection equipment

Asdic Admiralty Submarine Detection Investigation Committee; Armed Services Documents Intelligence Center (US)

ASE Admiralty Signal Department; American Stock Exchange; amplified spontaneous emission (physics); Army School of Education; Associate of the Society of Engineers; Association for Science Education

ASEA Association of South East Asia

ASEAN Association of South East Asian Nations

ASEC Applied Solar Energy Corporation (US)

ASEE American Society for Engineering Education; Association of Supervisory and Executive Engineers

ASF Associate of the Institute of Shipping and Forwarding Agents

ASG acting secretary-general; assistant secretary-general

ASGB Aeronautical Society of Great Britain; Anthroposophical Society of Great Britain

ASGBI Anatomical Society of Great Britain and Ireland

asgd assigned

asgmt assignment

ASH Action on Smoking and Health

ashp airship

ASHRAE American Society of Heating, Refrigeration and Air-Conditioning Engineers

ASI airspeed indicator; *Association soroptimiste internationale* (French: Soroptimist International Association)

ASIA Airlines Staff International Association

ASIAD Associate of the Society of Industrial Artists and Designers

ASIA(Ed) Associate of the Society of Industrial Artists (Education)

ASIF Amateur Swimming International Federation

ASIO Australian Security Intelligence Organization

ASIS American Society for Information Science

asl above sea level

ASL Acting Sublieutenant; Advanced Student in Law; American Sign Language; American Soccer League; assistant scout leader

ASLA American Society of Landscape Architects

ASLB Atomic Safety and Licensing Board (US)

ASLE American Society of Lubrication Engineers

Aslef Associated Society of Locomotive Engineers and Firemen

A/S level advanced supplementary level (education)

ASLIB Association for Information Management/Association of Special Libraries and Information Bureaux

ASLO American Society of Limnology and Oceanography; Australian Scientific Liaison Office

ASLP Amalgamated Society of Lithographic Printers

ASLW Amalgamated Society of Leather Workers

ASM Acting Sergeant-Major; air-to-surface missile; American Society for Metals; assistant sales manager; assistant scoutmaster; assistant sergeant-major; assistant stage manager; assistant station master; Association of Senior Members

ASME American Society of Mechanical Engineers; Association for the Study of Medical Education

As. Mem. Associate Member

ASMO Arab Organization for Standardization and Metrology

ASMP American Society of Magazine Photographers

ASN army service number; average sample number

ASNE American Society of Newspaper Editors

ASO Air Staff Officer; American Symphony Orchestra; area supplies officer

ASOS automatic storm observation service

ASP *accepté sous protêt* (French: accepted under protest); aerospace plane (US Air Force); African Special Project (IUCN); American selling price; Anglo-Saxon Protestant; Astronomical Society of the Pacific

ASPA Australian Sugar Producers' Association

ASPAC Asian and Pacific Council

ASPC *accepté sous protêt, pour compte* (French: accepted under protest for account); Association of Swimming Pool Contractors

ASPCA American Society for the Prevention of Cruelty to Animals

ASPEP Association of Scientists and Professional Engineering Personnel

ASPF Association of Superannuation and Pension Funds

ASR airport surveillance radar; air-to-sea rescue

ASRE Admiralty Signal and Radar Establishment

A/SRS air-sea rescue service

ass. assembly; assistant; association; assurance

ASS automatic space station

ASSC Accounting Standards Steering Committee

Ass-Com-Gen Assistant-Commisary-General

ASSET Association of Supervisory Staffs, Executives and Technicians

ASSGB Association of Ski Schools in Great Britain

AssIE Associate of the Institute of Engineers and Technicians

assigt assignment

assim. assimilate

assmt assessment

assn association

assoc. associate(d); association

AssocEng Associate of Engineering

AssocIMinE Associate of the Institution of Mining Engineers

AssocISI Associate of the Iron and Steel Institute

AssocMCT Associateship of Manchester College of Technology

AssocMIAeE Associate Member of the Institution of Aeronautical Engineers

assocn association

AssocSc Associate in Science

ASSR Autonomous Soviet Socialist Republic
asst assistant
asstd assorted
ASSU American Sunday School Union
assy assembly
Assyr. Assyrian
AST above-ground storage tank; air service training; assured shorthold tenancy; Atlantic Standard Time; automated screen trading
ASTA American Society of Travel Agents
ASTC Administrative Service Training Course; Associate of the Sydney Technical College
ASTIA Armed Services Technical Information Agency (US)
ASTM American Society for Testing Materials
ASTMS Association of Scientific, Technical and Managerial Staffs
ASTOR antisubmarine torpedo ordnance rocket
astr. astronomer; astronomical; astronomy
astro. astronautics; astronomer; astronomy
ASTRO Air Space Travel Research Organization (US)
astrol. astrologer; astrological; astrology
astron. astronomer; astronomical; astronomy
astrophys. astrophysical
Ast. T. astronomical time
ASU American Students Union; Arab Socialist Union
ASUA Amateur Swimming Union of the Americas
ASV aircraft-to-surface vessel; American Standard Version (Bible)
ASVA Associate of the Incorporated Society of Valuers and Auctioneers
ASVU Army Security Vetting Unit
ASW Amalgamated Society of Wood Workers; antisubmarine warfare; antisubmarine work; Association of Scientific Workers; Association of Social Workers
ASWDU Air Sea Warfare Development Unit
ASWE Admiralty Surface Weapons Establishment
at. atmosphere; atomic; attitude (navigation); attorney
At ampere-turn; astatine (element); Auxiliary Territorial Service
AT alternative technology; antitank;

apparent time; arrival time; Atlantic Time; attainment target (education); Hull (UK vehicle registration); Royal Air Maroc (airline flight code, Morocco)
A/T American terms
ATA advanced test accelerator (nuclear physics); Air Transport Association; Air Transport Auxiliary; Albanian Telegraphic Agency (newsagency); American Translators' Association; Amusement Trades Association; Animal Technicians' Association; Associate Technical Aide; Atlantic Treaty Association
ATAC Air Transport Advisory Council
ATAE Association of Tutors in Adult Education
ATAF Allied Tactical Air Force
ATAM Association for Teaching Aids in Mathematics
AT&T American Telephone and Telegraph Company
ATAS Air Transport Auxiliary Service
ATB advanced technology bomber; at the time of the bomb; at the time of bombing
ATBM antitactical ballistic missile
atc average total costs
ATC air traffic control; Air Training Command; Air Training Corps; Air Transport Command; Annotated Tax Cases (law); Art Teacher's Certificate; authorization to copy (computing); automatic temperature control; automatic train control
ATCC air traffic control centre
atchd attached
ATCL Associate of Trinity College of Music, London
ATCO Air Traffic Control Officer
ATCRBS Air Traffic Control Radar Beacon System
ATCSP Association of Teachers of the Chartered Society of Physiotherapists
ATD actual time of departure; advanced technology development; Art Teacher's Diploma
ATDS Association of Teachers of Domestic Science
ATE Amusement Trades Exhibition; Automatic Telephone and Electric Company; automatic test equipment (electronics)
ATEC Air Transport Electronics Council
a tem. *a tempo* (Italian: in time; music)
ATF accelerator test facility (nuclear physics)
ATFS Association of Track and Field Statisticians

ath. athlete; athletic
ATHE Association of Teachers in Higher Education
Athen. Athenian
athl. athlete; athletic
ATI Associate of the Textile Insistute; Association of Technical Institutions
ATII Associate Member of the Institute of Taxation; Associate of the Taxation Institute Incorporated
Atl. Atlantic
ATL actual total loss (insurance)
ATLAS airborne tunable laser absorption spectrometer (astronomy)
ATLB Air Transport Licensing Board
ATLV adult T-cell leukaemia virus
atm atmosphere (unit of pressure)
atm. atmospheric
ATM air training memorandum; antitank missile; Association of Teachers of Management; Association of Teachers of Mathematics; automated teller machine (banking)
ATMS assumption-based truth maintenance system
ATNA Australasian Trained Nurses' Association
at. no. atomic number
ATO Ammunition Technical Officer (bomb disposal); assisted take-off (aeronautics)
A to A air-to-air
ATOL Air Travel Organisers' Licence
ATP adenosine triphosphate (biochemistry); Association of Tennis Professionals; automatic train protection (railways)
ATPAS Association of Teachers of Printing and Allied Subjects
ATPG automatic test-pattern generation
ATPL(A) Airline Transport Pilot's Licence (Aeroplanes)
ATPL(H) Airline Transport Pilot's Licence (Helicopters)
ATR advanced test reactor (nuclear physics); advanced thermal reactor (nuclear physics); air turbo-ram jet engine (aeronautics); Association of Teachers of Russian; automatic target recognition (military)
ATRAN automatic terrain recognition and navigation
atrima as their respective interests may appear (law)
ats at the suit of (law)
ATS Amalgamated Television Services (Australia); American Temperance

Society; American Tract Society; American Transport Service; anti-tetanus serum (medicine); Army Transport Service (US); Associate of Theological Study; automated trade system; Auxiliary Territorial Service (World War II)
ATSC Associate of the Tonic Sol-Fa College
ATSDR Agency for Toxic Substances and Disease Registry (US)
ATSIS automated technical-specification information system (computing)
ATSS Association for the Teaching of Social Sciences
att. attached; attention; attorney
ATT antitetanus toxoid
Att-Gen. Attorney-General
attn attention; for the attention of
attrib. attribute; attributed; attribution; attributive; attributively
atty. attorney
Atty-Gen. Attorney-General
ATU Amalgamated Transit Union (US)
ATUC African Trade Union Confederation
ATV all-terrain vehicle; Associated Television
at. wt atomic weight
Au gold (element)
AU Actors' Union (US); all up (printing); angstrom unit; arithmetic unit; astronomical unit; Nottingham (UK vehicle registration)
AUA agricultural unit of account (EC); American Unitarian Association; American Urological Association
AUBC Association of Universities of the British Commonwealth
AUBTW Amalgamated Union of Building Trade Workers
AUC *ab urbe condita* (Latin: in the year of the foundation of Rome); *anno urbis conditae* (Latin: in the year of the founding of the city); Association of Underwater Contractors; Australian Universities Commission
AUCAS Association of University Clinical Academic Staff
aud. audit; auditor
Aud-Gen. auditor-general
AUEW Amalgamated Union of Engineering Workers
Aufl. *Auflage* (German: edition)
AUFW Amalgamated Union of Foundry Workers

aug. augmentative (grammar);
augmented
Aug. August
augm. augmentative (grammar)
AULLA Australasian Universities
Language and Literature Association
AUM air-to-underwater missile
AUMLA Australian Universities Modern
Language Association
aun *absque ulla nota* (Latin: with no
identifying mark)
AUO African Unity Organization
AUP Aberdeen University Press;
Australian United Press (news agency)
Aus. Australia; Australian; Austria;
Austrian
AUS Army of the United States; Assistant
Undersecretary; Australia (international
vehicle registration)
AUSA Association of the United States
Army
Ausg. *Ausgabe* (German: edition)
Austral. Australasia; Australasian;
Australia; Australian
aut. autograph; autumn
Aut. *Autriche* (French: Austria)
AUT Association of University Teachers
AUTEC Atlantic Underwater Test
Evaluation Center (US Navy)
auth. authentic; author; authoress;
authority; authorized
Auth. Ver. Authorized Version (Bible)
auto. automatic; automobile; automotive
autobiog. autobiographical;
autobiography
autog. autograph
AUT(S) Association of University
Teachers (Scotland)
auw all-up-weight
AUWE Admiralty Underwater Weapons
Establishment
aux. auxiliary
AUX auxiliary verb (linguistics)
av *ad valorem* (Latin: according to value;
finance); *annos vixit* (Latin: he/she lived
(so many) years); asset value (finance)
av. avenue; average; avoirdupois; *avril*
(French: April)
Av. Avenue; *Avocat* (French: lawyer)
AV acid value (chemistry); *ad valorem*
(Latin: according to value; finance);
Artillery Volunteers; audiovisual; *aurum*
(Latin: gold; numismatics); Authorized
Version (Bible); average value; Avianca
(airline flight code, Colombia); Peter-
borough (UK vehicle registration)
AVA Amateur Volleyball Association of

Great Britain; audiovisual aids;
Audiovisual Association; Australian
Veterinary Association
avc automatic volume control
(electronics); average variable costs
av. C. *avanti Cristo* (Italian: before
Christ)
AVC additional voluntary contribution
(pensions); American Veterans'
Committee; automatic volume control
(electronics)
Av. Cert. Aviator's Certificate
AVCM Associate of Victoria College of
Music
AVD Army Veterinary Department
avdp. avoirdupois
ave. avenue; average
AVF all-volunteer force (US military)
avg. average
AVGAS aviation gasoline
avge average (cricket)
AVI Association of Veterinary Inspectors
avia. aviation
av. J-C *avant Jésus-Christ* (French: before
Jesus Christ)
AVL automatic vehicle location
AVLA Audio Visual Language
Association
AVM Air Vice-Marshal
AVMA Action for the Victims of Medical
Accidents; Automatic Vending Machine
Association
avn aviation
AVO Administrative Veterinary Officer;
average vehicle occupancy
avoir. avoirdupois
AVR Army Volunteer Reserve
AVRI Animal Virus Research Institute
AVRO A.V. Roe & Company (aircraft
manufacturers)
AVRP audiovisual recording and
presentation
AVS Anti-Vivisection Society
AVSL assistant venture scout leader
AVTRW Association of Veterinary
Teachers and Research Workers
aw actual weight; all water (shipping);
atomic weight
AW added water (foodstuffs); Armstrong
Whitworth (aircraft manufacturers);
Articles of War; atomic warfare;
Shrewsbury (UK vehicle registration)
A/W actual weight; airworthy; artwork
AWA Amalgamated Wireless (Australia)
Limited
AWACS airborne warning and control
system

AWAM Association of West African Merchants

AWAS Australian Women's Army Service

AWASM Associate of the Western Australia School of Mines

AWB Agricultural Wages Board; air waybill (US); Australian Wool Board

AWBA American World's Boxing Association

AWC Allied Works Council; Army War College (US); Australian Wool Corporation

AWE Atomic Weapons Establishment

AWEA American Wind Energy Association

AWeldI Associate of the Welding Institute

AWG American Wire Gauge; Art Workers' Guild

AWHA Australian Women's Home Army

AWJ abrasive water jet (building, engineering)

AWL absent without leave

AWMC Association of Workers for Maladjusted Children

AWNL Australian Women's National League

AWO American Waterways Operators Incorporated; Association of Water Officers

AWOL absent without (official) leave

AWP amusements with prizes; annual wood production

AWPR Association of Women in Public Relations

AWR Association for the Study of the World Refugee Problem

AWRA Australian Wool Realization Agency

AWRE Atomic Weapons Research Establishment

aws Graduate of Air Warfare Course

AWS Agricultural Wholesale Society; American Welding Society; automatic warning system

AWSA American Water Ski Association

AWU Australian Workers' Union

ax. axiom

AX Cardiff (UK vehicle registration)

AY Finnair (airline flight code, Finland); Leicester (UK vehicle registration)

AYH American Youth Hostels

Ayr. Ayrshire

az. azimuth; azure

AZ Alitalia (airline flight code, Italy); Arizona (zip code); Belfast (UK vehicle registration)

az. ld azure laid (paper)

Azo. Azores

AZT azidothymidine (Aids drug)

az. wo. azure wove (paper)

B

b barn (physics); blue sky (meteorology)

b. back to engine (railways); bag; bale; ball; base; bass (music); bath; batsman; bay; beam; bedroom; before; billion; *bis* (Latin: twice); bitch; bloody; book; born; bound; bowels (medicine); bowled (cricket); breadth; brother; bugger; bust; by; bye (cricket)

B baht (Thai monetary unit); balboa (Panamanian monetary unit); baryon number (physics); Baumé (temperature scale); Belfast (UK fishing port registration); Belgium (international vehicle registration); best (wrought iron); Birmingham (UK postcode); black (pencils); bolívar (Venezuelan monetary unit); bomber (US); boron (element); breathalyser; B-setting (photography); bone marrow/bursa of Fabricius

(immunology); Taiwan (international civil aircraft marking); human blood group; of the second rank; secondary road

B magnetic flux density (physics)

B. bachelor; Baptist; baron; bass (music); battle; bay (cartography); *Beatus* (Latin: Blessed); benediction; Bey; Bible; billion; bishop; Blessed; blue; board; boatswain; book; breadth; British; brotherhood; building

ba balancing allowance (taxation); blind approach

Ba barium (element)

BA able-bodied seaman; Bachelor of Arts; Ballantrae (UK fishing port registration); bank acceptance (finance); banker's acceptance (finance); Bath (UK postcode); Biological Abstracts (US);

Board of Agriculture; Booksellers' Association; boric acid; British Academy; British Airways (airline flight code); British America; British Association; bronchial asthma; Buenos Aires; bus automaton (computing); Manchester (UK vehicle registration)
BAA Bachelor of Applied Arts; Booking Agents' Association; British Airports Authority; British Archaeological Association; British Astronomical Association
BAA&A British Association of Accountants and Auditors
BAAB British Amateur Athletics Board
BA(Admin) Bachelor of Arts in Administration
BAAF British Agencies for Adoption and Fostering
BAAL British Association for Applied Linguistics
BA(Art) Bachelor of Arts in Art
BAAS British Association for the Advancement of Science
Bab. Babylonia; Babylonian
BABIE British Association for Betterment of Infertility and Education
BABS beam approach beacon system (aeronautics); blind approach beacon system (aeronautics)
Bac. baccalauréat (France); *Baccalaureus* (Latin: Bachelor)
BAc Bachelor of Acupuncture
BAC blood-alcohol concentration; blood-alcohol content; British Aircraft Corporation; British Association of Chemists; Business Archives Council
BACAH British Association of Consultants in Agriculture and Horticulture
BACAT barge aboard catamaran; barge canal traffic
BAcc Bachelor of Accountancy
bach. bachelor
BACIE British Association for Commercial and Industrial Education
BACM British Association of Colliery Management
BACO British Aluminium Company Ltd
BACS Bankers' Automated Clearing Service
bact. bacteria; bacterial; bacteriology
bacteriol. bacteriological; bacteriology
BAD base air depot; British Association of Dermatology
BADA British Antique Dealers' Association

BADGE base air defence ground environment
BAdmin Bachelor of Administration
BAe British Aerospace
BAE Bachelor of Aeronautical Engineering; Bachelor of Arts in Education; Badminton Association of England; Belfast Association of Engineers; Bureau of Agricultural Economics (US)
BAEA British Actors' Equity Association
BAEC Bangladesh Atomic Energy Commission; British Agricultural Export Council
BA(Econ) Bachelor of Arts in Economics
BA(Ed) Bachelor of Arts in Education
BAED Bachelor of Arts in Environmental Design
BAEF Belgian-American Educational Foundation
BAF biological aerated filter; British Air Force; British Athletics Federation
BAFM British Association of Forensic Medicine
BAFMA British and Foreign Maritime Agencies
BAFO British Air Forces of Occupation; British Army Forces Overseas
BAFSC British Association of Field and Sports Contractors
BAFSV British Armed Forces Special Vouchers
Bafta British Academy of Film and Television Arts
BAGA British Amateur Gymnastics Association
BAgEc Bachelor or Agricultural Economics
BAgr Bachelor of Agriculture
BAgrSc Bachelor of Agricultural Science
Bah. Bahamas
BAHA British Association of Hotel Accountants
BAHOH British Association for the Hard of Hearing
BAHS British Agricultural History Society
BAI *Baccalaureus Artis Ingeniariae* (Latin: Bachelor of Engineering); battlefield air interdiction (military); Book Association of Ireland
BAIE British Association of Industrial Editors
BA(J) Bachelor of Arts in Journalism
bal. balance (book-keeping)
Bal. Ballarat

BAL blood-alcohol level; British anti-lewisite (dimercaprol)

BALH British Association for Local History

ball. ballast; ballistics

Ball. Balliol College (Oxford)

BALPA British Airline Pilots' Association

bals. balsam

Balt. Baltic; Baltimore

balun balanced unbalanced (telecommunications)

BAM Bachelor of Applied Mathematics; Bachelor of Arts in Music

BAMA British Aerosol Manufacturers' Association; British Amsterdam Maritime Agencies; British Army Motoring Association

BAMBI ballistic missile boost intercept

BAMTM British Association of Machine Tool Merchants

BA(Mus) Bachelor of Arts in Music

BAMW British Association of Meat Wholesalers

Ban. Bangor; Bantu

BAN British Association of Neurologists

Banc. Sup. *Bancus Superior* (Latin: higher bench; Queen's or King's Bench)

B&B bed and breakfast

B&C building and contents (insurance)

B&D bondage and discipline; bondage and domination

b&e beginning and ending

B&FBS British and Foreign Bible Society

B&S brandy and soda; Brown and Sharpe (wire gauge)

B&W black and white

B&WE Bristol and West of England

BANS British Association of Numismatic Societies

BANZARE British, Australian, New Zealand Antarctic Research Expedition

BAO Bachelor of Arts in Obstetrics; Bankruptcy Annulment Order; British American Oil

BAOD British Airways Overseas Division

BA of E Badminton Association of England

BAOMS British Association of Oral and Maxillo-Facial Surgeons

BAOR British Army of the Rhine

b. à p. *billets à payer* (French: bills payable)

bap. baptize; baptized

Bap. Baptist

BAPA British Amateur Press Association; British Airline Pilots' Association

BAPC British Aircraft Preservation Council

BAPCO Bahrain Petroleum Company

BA(PE) Bachelor of Arts in Physical Education

BAPLA British Association of Picture Libraries and Agencies

BAPM British Association of Physical Medicine

BAppArts Bachelor of Applied Arts

BAppSc Bachelor of Applied Science

BAppSc(MT) Bachelor of Applied Science (Medical Technology)

BAPS beacon automated processing system (lighthouses); British Association of Paediatric Surgeons; British Association of Plastic Surgeons

bapt. baptism; baptized

Bapt. Baptist

BAPT British Association for Physical Training

b. à r. *billets à recevoir* (French: bills receivable)

bar. barleycorn (measurement of length); barometer; barometric; barrel; barrister

Bar. baritone; Barrister; Baruch (Bible)

BAR base address register (computing); book auction records; Browning Automatic Rifle

Barb. Barbados

BARB British Association of Rose Breeders; British Audience Research Bureau; Broadcasters' Audience Research Board

BARC British Automobile Racing Club

BArch Bachelor of Architecture

BArchE Bachelor of Architectural Engineering

barg. bargain

barit. baritone

BARP British Association of Retired Persons

Barr. Barrister

BARR British Association of Rheumatology and Rehabilitation

BARS behaviourally anchored rating scales; British Association of Residential Settlements

Bart. baronet

Bart's St Bartholomew's Hospital (London)

BAS Bachelor in Agricultural Science; Bachelor of Applied Science; British Antarctic Survey

BASA British Architectural Students' Association; British Australian Studies Association

BASAF British and South Africa Forum
BASc Bachelor of Agricultural Science; Bachelor of Applied Science
BASC British Association for Shooting and Conservation
BASCA British Academy of Songwriters, Composers and Authors
BASF Badische Anilin und Soda-Fabrik (German chemical and electronics company)
BASI British Association of Ski Instructors
Basic beginners' all-purpose symbolic instruction code (computing); British-American scientific international commercial (simplified language)
BASMA Boot and Shoe Manufacturers' Association and Leather Trades Protection Society
bass. con. *basso continuo* (Italian: continuous bass; music)
BASW British Association of Social Workers
bat. battalion; battery; battle
Bat. Batavia
BAT best available technology; British Aerial Transport (aircraft); British-American Tobacco Company
BATF Bureau of Alcohol, Tobacco and Firearms (US)
bath. bathroom
BA(Theol) Bachelor of Arts in Theology
BATO balloon-assisted take-off
BA(TP) Bachelor of Arts in Town and Country Planning
BATS biosphere-atmosphere transfer scheme (ecology)
batt. battalion; battery (military)
battn. battalion
BAU British Association Unit; business as usual
BAUA Business Aircraft Users' Association
BAUS British Association of Urological Surgeons
b. à v. *bon à vue* (French: good at sight)
Bav. Bavaria(n)
BAWA British Amateur Wrestling Association
BAWLA British Amateur Weightlifters' Association
BAYS British Association of Young Scientists
bb ball bearing; bearer bonds; below bridges (nautical); books
Bb. Bishops
BB bail bond; balloon barrage; bank

book; bed and breakfast; best best (wrought iron); Blackburn (UK postcode); Blue Book (HMSO); B'nai B'rith (Jewish society); Boys' Brigade; Brigitte Bardot (French actress); double black (pencils); Newcastle upon Tyne (UK vehicle registration); papers in order (nautical certificate); Sansa (airline flight code, Costa Rica); standard size of lead shot (0.18in. diameter)
BBA Bachelor of Business Administration; Big Brother of America; born before arrival (obstetrics); British Bankers' Association; British Beekeepers' Association; British Bloodstock Association; British Board of Agreement; British Bobsleigh Association
BBAC British Balloon and Airship Club
BBB bed, breakfast and bath; Better Business Bureau (US); blood-brain barrier (physiology); treble black (pencils)
BBBC British Boxing Board of Control
BBC baseball club; British Broadcasting Corporation
BBCM Bandmaster of the Bandsmen's College of Music
BBCMA British Baby Carriage Manufacturers' Association
BBEM bed, breakfast and evening meal
BBFC British Board of Film Censors
BBI British Bottlers' Institute
BBIP British Books in Print
BBIRA British Baking Industries' Research Association
B. Bisc. Bay of Biscay
bbl barrel
BBldg(Sc) Bachelor of Building Science
bbls/d barrels per day
BBMA British Brush Manufacturers' Association; British Button Manufacturers' Association
BBQ barbecue
BBS Bachelor of Business Science; Bachelor of Business Studies; bulletin board system (computing)
BBSR Bermuda Biological Station for Research
BBT basal body temperature (medicine)
BBV Banco Bilbao Vizcaya (Spanish bank)
bc *basso continuo* (Italian: continuous bass; music); blind copy; sky partly clouded (meteorology)
BC *Baccalaureus Chirurgiae* (Latin: Bachelor of Surgery); Bachelor of Chemistry; Bachelor of Commerce; bad

character (military); badminton club; balancing charge (taxation); bank clearing; bankruptcy court; basketball club; *basso continuo* (Italian: continuous bass; music); Battery Commander; battle cruiser; bayonet cap (light bulbs); before Christ; bicycle club; billiards club; bills for collection; bishop and confessor; blood consumption (medicine); board of control; boat club; boating club; body composition (biochemistry); Bomber Command; borough council; bowling club; bowls club; boxing club; boys' club; Bristol Channel; British Coal; British Columbia; British Commonwealth; British Council; bronchial carcinoma (medicine); Brymon Airways (airline flight code, UK); budgeted cost; Burnham Committee (education); Leicester (UK vehicle registration)

B/C bills for collection

BCA Bachelor of Commerce and Administration (New Zealand); Boys' Club of America; British-Caribbean Association; British Casting Association (angling); British Chiropractic Association

BCAB Birth Control Advisory Bureau

BCAC British Conference on Automation and Computation

BCal British Caledonian (airline)

BC&T Bakery, Confectionery and Tobacco Workers International Union

BCAP British Code of Advertising Practice

BCAR British Civil Airworthiness Requirements; British Council for Aid to Refugees

BCAS British Compressed Air Society

BCBC British Cattle Breeders' Club

bcc blind carbon copy

BCC British Coal Corporation; British Colour Council; British Copyright Council; British Council of Churches; British Crown Colony

BCCA British Cyclo-Cross Association

BCCG British Cooperative Clinical Group

BCCI Bank of Credit and Commerce International

BCD bad conduct discharge (US); binary coded decimal (computing); blue compact dwarf (astronomy)

BCDTA British Chemical and Dyestuffs Traders' Association

BCE Bachelor of Chemical Engineering; Bachelor of Civil Engineering; before common era; before Christian era; Board of Customs and Excise

BCEAO *Banque centrale des états de l'Afrique de l'Ouest* (French: Central Bank of West African States)

BCECC British and Central European Chamber of Commerce

BCF battle cruiser force; billion cubic feet; British Chess Federation; British Cycling Federation; bromochlorodi-fluoromethane (chemical used in fire-fighting); bulked continuous filament (textiles); Bureau of Commercial Fisheries (US)

BCFA British-China Friendship Association

BCG bacille Calmette-Guérin (tuberculosis vaccine); blue compact galaxy (astronomy)

BCGA British Commercial Gas Association; British Cotton Growing Association

bch branch; bunch

BCh(ir) *Baccalaureus Chirurgiae* (Latin: Bachelor of Surgery)

BCh(D) *Baccalaureus Chirurgiae Dentalis* (Latin: Bachelor of Dental Surgery)

BChE Bachelor of Chemical Engineering

BChemEng Bachelor of Chemical Engineering

BCINA British Commonwealth International Newsfilm Agency

BCIRA British Cast-Iron Research Association

BCIS Building Cost Information Service; *Bureau central international de séismologie* (French: International Central Bureau of Seismology)

BCK Buckie (UK fishing port regis-tration)

BCL Bachelor of Canon Law; Bachelor of Civil Law

BCM Boston Conservatory of Music (US); British Commercial Monomark; British Consular Mail

BCMA British Colour Makers' Asso-ciation; British Columbia Medical Association

BCMD biological and chemical munitions disposal

BCMF British Ceramic Manufacturers' Federation

BCMG Birmingham Contemporary Music Group

BCMS Bible Churchmen's Missionary Society

bcn beacon

BCN British Commonwealth of Nations
BCNZ Broadcasting Corporation of New Zealand
BCoIP British Columbia Pine
BCom(m) Bachelor of Commerce
BComSc Bachelor of Commercial Science
BCP Book of Common Prayer; Bulgarian Communist Party
BCPC British Crop Protection Council
BCPIT British Council for the Promotion of International Trade
BCPL Basic Computer Programming Language
BCPMA British Chemical Plant Manufacturers' Association
BCR battlefield casualty replacement
BCRA British Carbonization Research Association; British Ceramic Research Association
BCRC British Columbia Research Council
BCRD British Council for the Rehabilitation of the Disabled
BCS Bachelor of Chemical Science; Bachelor of Commercial Science; Bardeen-Cooper-Schrieffer (theory of superconductivity); battle cruiser squadron; Bengal Civil Service; British Calibration Service; British Cardiac Society; British Ceramic Society; British Computer Society; Bureau of Criminal Statistics (US)
BCSA British Constructional Steelwork Association
bcst broadcast
BCT Belfast Chamber of Trade; body computer tomograph (medicine)
BCTA British Canadian Trade Association; British Children's Theatre Association
BCTGA British Christmas Tree Growers Association
BCTV beet curly top virus (microbiology)
BCU big close-up (cinema); British Canoe Union; British Commonwealth Union
BCURA British Coal Utilization Research Association
BCVA British Columbia Veterinary Association
BCWMA British Clock and Watch Manufacturers' Association
BCYC British Corinthian Yacht Club
bd *bid die* (Latin: twice a day; medicine); bill discounted (commerce); board; bold; bond (insurance, finance); bound (books); broad; bundle

b/d barrels per day; brought down (book-keeping)
Bd *Band* (German: volume); baud (computing); board; boulevard
BD Bachelor of Divinity; Bahrain dinar (monetary unit); Bangladesh (international vehicle registration); battle dress; beam deflection (physics); Bideford (UK fishing port registration); bile duct (medicine); bill discounted (commerce); bomb disposal; bone density (medicine); boom defence; Bradford (UK postcode); British Midland (airline flight code, UK); *Bundesrepublik Deutschland* (German: Federal Republic of Germany); Northampton (UK vehicle registration)
B/D bank draft; bill discounted (commerce); brought down (book-keeping)
BDA Bachelor of Domestic Arts; Bachelor of Dramatic Art; bomb-damage assessment; British Deaf Association; British Dental Association; British Diabetic Association
bdc bottom dead centre (engineering)
BDC Book Development Council
BDCC British Defence Coordinating Committee
BDDA British Deaf and Dumb Association
Bde *Bände* (German: volumes); brigade
BDentSc Bachelor in Dental Science
BDes Bachelor of Design
BDF backward differentiation formulae (computing)
BDFA British Dairy Farmers' Association
bd ft board foot (timber)
BDG binding (books)
BDG/ND binding, no date can be given (books)
BDH British Drug Houses
bdi bearing deviation indicator; both dates included; both days included
BDI *Bundesverband der Deutschen Industrie* (German: Federal Association of German Industry)
bdl(e). bundle
BDL British Drama League
BDM births, deaths, marriages; bomber defence missile; branch delegates' meeting
BDMA British Direct Marketing Association; British Disinfectant Manufacturers' Association
BDMAA British Direct Mail Advertising Association

Bdmr Bandmaster
BDO Boom Defence Officer
BDP breakdown pressure
Bdr Bombardier; Brigadier
bdrm bedroom
bds *bis in die sumendus* (Latin: to be taken twice a day; medicine); boards (bookbinding); bundles
BDS Bachelor of Dental Surgery; Barbados (international vehicle registration); bomb disposal squad; British Diving Society
BDSA Business and Defense Services Administration (US)
BDSc Bachelor of Dental Science
BDST British Double Summer Time
BDU bomb disposal unit
Bdx Bordeaux
be bill of exchange; binding edge
be. *bezüglich* (German: regarding or with reference to)
Be beryllium (element)
Bé Baumé (temperature scale)
BE Bachelor of Economics; Bachelor of Education; Bachelor of Engineering; Bank of England; Barnstaple (UK fishing port registration); best estimate; bill of exchange; binary encounter (computing); Board of Education (US); borough engineer; Bose-Einstein (physics); British Element; British Embassy; British Empire; Lincoln (UK vehicle registration)
B/E bill of entry; bill of exchange
BEA British East Africa; British Epilepsy Association; British Esperanto Association; British European Airways
BEAB British Electrical Approvals Board
BEAC *Banque des états de l'Afrique centrale* (French: Bank of Central African States)
BEAIRE British Electrical and Allied Industries' Research Association
BEAM brain electrical activity mapping (medicine)
BEAMA (Federation of) British Electricotechnical and Allied Manufacturers' Associations
bearb. *bearbeitet* (German: compiled or edited)
BEAS British Educational Administration Society
bec. because
BEc Bachelor of Economics
BEC Building Employers' Confederation; *Bureau européen du café* (French: European Coffee Bureau); Bureau of Employees' Compensation (US)

BECA British Exhibition Contractors' Association
Bech. Bechuanaland
BE(Chem) Bachelor of Chemical Engineering
BECO booster-engine cut-off
BEcon Bachelor of Economics
BEcon(IA) Bachelor of Economics in Industrial Administration
BEcon(PA) Bachelor of Economics in Public Administration
BECTU Broadcasting, Entertainment and Cinematograph Technicians Union
BEd Bachelor of Education
BEDA British Electrical Development Association; Bureau of European Designers' Associations
BEd(Com) Bachelor of Education in Commerce
BEd(HEc) Bachelor of Education in Home Economics
BEd(N) Bachelor of Education in Nursing
BEd(PE) Bachelor of Education in Physical Education
beds. bedrooms
Beds Bedfordshire
BEd(Sc) Bachelor of Education in Science; Bachelor of Educational Science
BEE Bachelor of Electrical Engineering
bef blunt end first
bef. before
BEF British Equestrian Federation; British Expeditionary Force (military)
BEFA British Emigrant Families Association
beg. beginning
BEG Bureau of Economic Geology
BEHA British Export Houses Association
BEI Bachelor of Engineering (Dublin); *Banque européenne d'investissement* (French: European Investments Bank)
Beibl. *Beiblatt* (German: supplement)
beigeb. *beigebunden* (German: bound, in with something else)
beil. *beiliegend* (German: enclosed)
Bel. Belgian; Belgium
BEL British Electrotechnical Committee
bel ex. *bel exemplaire* (French: fine copy)
Belf. Belfast
Belg. Belgian; Belgic; Belgium
BELGA *Agence Belga* (news agency, Belgium)
BEM British Empire Medal; bug-eyed monster
BEMA British Essence Manufacturers' Association; Business Equipment Manufacturers' Association

BEMAC British Exports Marketing Advisory Committee
BEMAS British Education Management and Administration Society
BEMB British Egg Marketing Board
BEME Brigade Electrical and Mechanical Engineer
BEMSA British Eastern Merchant Shippers' Association
ben. *benedictio* (Latin: blessing)
BEN broadband electrostatic noise (electronics)
Bend. Bendigo (Australia)
BenDr *Bachelor en droit* (French: Bachelor of Law)
benef. benefice
Benelux Belgium, Netherlands and Luxembourg (customs union)
Beng. Bengal(i)
BEng Bachelor of Engineering
BEngr Bachelor of Engraving
BenH *Bachelier en humanités* (French: Bachelor of Humanities)
BEO Base Engineer Officer
BEpA British Epilepsy Association
BEPC British Electrical Power Convention
beq. bequeath
beqt bequest
Ber(l). Berlin
BERCO British Electric Resistance Company
Berks Berkshire
Berm. Bermuda
BERNAMA Malaysia National News Agency
Berw. Berwickshire
bes. *besonders* (German: especially)
BES Bachelor of Engineering Science; Bachelor of Environmental Studies; Biological Engineering Society; British Ecological Society; Business Expansion Scheme
BèsA *Bachelier ès arts* (French: Bachelor of Arts)
BESA British Esperanto Scientific Association
BESI bus electronic scanning indicator
BèsL *Bachelier ès lettres* (French: Bachelor of Letters)
BESO British Executive Service Overseas
BèsS(c) *Bachelier ès sciences* (French: Bachelor of Science)
BESS Bank of England Statistical Summary; bottom environmental sensing system (oceanography)

Best. *Bestellung* (German: order; commerce)
BEST British Expertise in Science and Technology (database)
bet. between
BET British Electric Traction Company; buildings energy technology
BETA Broadcasting and Entertainment Trades Alliance; Business Equipment Trades' Association
BETAA British Export Trade Advertising Association
BETRO British Export Trade Research Organization
betw. between
BEU batch extraction unit (engineering); Benelux Economic Union
BEUC *Bureau européen des unions de consommateurs* (French: European Bureau of Consumers' Unions)
bev. bevel
BeV billion electronvolts (US)
BEV Black English Vernacular
BEVA British Exhibition Venues' Association
BEXA British Exporters Association
bez. *bezahlt* (German: paid); *bezüglich* (German: regarding or with reference to)
bezw. *beziehungsweise* (German: respectively)
bf bankruptcy fee; base frequency; beer firkin; bloody fool; bold face (printing); bona fide; brief
b/f bring forward; brought forward (book-keeping)
BF Bachelor of Forestry; Banff (UK fishing port registration); *Banque de France* (French: Bank of France); Belgian franc; black face (sheep); blast furnace; bloody fool; body fat; breathing frequency; British Funds; Stoke-on-Trent (UK vehicle registration)
B/F bring forward; brought forward (book-keeping)
BFA Bachelor of Fine Arts; British Film Academy
BFAP British Forces Arabian Peninsula
BFASS BWR fuel assembly sealing system (nuclear physics)
BFBPW British Federation of Business and Professional Women
BFBS British and Foreign Bible Society; British Forces Broadcasting Service (World War II)
BFCA British Federation of Commodity Associations
BFCS British Friesian Cattle Society

BFEBS British Far Eastern Broadcasting Service

BFFA British Film Fund Agency

BFFC British Federation of Folk Clubs

BFI British Film Institute

BFIA British Flower Industry Association

BFMA British Farm Mechanization Association

BFMF British Federation of Music Festivals; British Footwear Manufacturers' Association

BFMIRA British Food Manufacturing Industries' Research Association

BFMP British Federation of Master Printers

Bfn Bloemfontein

BFN British Forces Network

bfo beat-frequency oscillator (electronics)

BFor Bachelor of Forestry

BForSc Bachelor of Forestry Science

BFP Bureau of Freelance Photographers

BFPA British Film Producers' Association

BFPC British Farm Produce Council

BFPO British Forces Post Office

BFr Belgian franc

BFS blast-furnace slag (mining); British Fuchsia Society

BFSA British Fire Services' Association

BFSS British and Foreign Sailors' Society; British Field Sports Society

BFTA British Fur Trade Alliance

BFUW British Federation of University Women

BFV Bradley fighting vehicle (military)

bg bag (commerce); bay gelding (horse racing)

b/g bonded goods

BG Biman Bangladesh Airlines (airline flight code); Birmingham Gauge (wire gauge); blood group; brigadier general; British Guiana; Bulgaria (international vehicle registration); Liverpool (UK vehicle registration)

BGA Better Government Association (US); British Gliding Association; British Graduates Association

BGB Booksellers' Association of Great Britain and Ireland; *Bürgerliches Gesetzbuch* (German: code of civil law)

BGC bank giro credit; British Gas Corporation

BGCS Botanic Gardens Conservation Secretariat

BGEA Billy Graham Evangelistic Association

BGenEd Bachelor of General Education

BGF Banana Growers' Federation (Australia)

BGIRA British Glass Industry Research Association

bgl below ground level

BGL Bachelor of General Laws

bglr bugler

BGM Bethnal Green Museum

BGMA British Gear Manufacturers' Association

BGS Brigadier General Staff; British Geological Survey; British Geriatrics Society; British Goat Society; Brothers of the Good Shepherd

bgt bought

BGV below-ground vault

bh barrels per hour; bloody hell; *bougie-heure* (French: candle-hour)

BH Augusta Airways (airline flight code, Australia); base hospital; Belize (international vehicle registration); black hole (astronomy); Blyth (UK fishing port registration); Bournemouth (UK postcode); Brinell hardness (metallurgy); British Honduras; British Hovercraft; Burlington House (London); Luton (UK vehicle registration)

B/H bill of health

BHA bottom-hole assembly (mining); British Homeopathic Association; British Humanist Association

B'ham Birmingham

BHB British Hockey Board

BHC benzene hexachloride (insecticide); British High Commissioner

bhd beachhead; billhead; bulkhead

BHDF British Hospital Doctors' Federation

BHE Bachelor of Home Economics

B'Head Birkenhead

Bhf *Bahnhof* (German: railway station)

BHF British Heart Foundation

BHGA British Hang Gliding Association

BHI British Horological Institute; *Bureau hydrographique international* (French: International Hydrographic Bureau)

Bhm Birmingham

BHMRA British Hydromechanics' Research Association

Bhn Brinell hardness number (metallurgy)

BHort Bachelor of Horticulture

BHortSc Bachelor of Horticultural Science

bhp brake horsepower

BHP Broken Hill Proprietary Company (Australia)

bhpric bishopric
BHQ Brigade Headquarters
BHRA British Hydromechanics' Reasearch Association
BHRCA British Hotels, Restaurants and Caterers' Association
BHS boys' high school; British Home Stores; British Horse Society
BHTA British Herring Trade Association
Bhu. Bhutan
BHy Bachelor of Hygiene
Bi bismuth (element)
BI background information; Bahama Islands; Balearic Islands; base ignition; Bermuda Islands; bone injury (medicine); bulk issue; Monaghan (Irish vehicle registration); Royal Brunei Airlines (airline flight code)
BIA British Institute of Acupuncture; British Insurance Association; British Ironfounders' Association; Bureau of Indian Affairs (US)
BIAA British Industrial Advertising Association
BIAC Business and Industry Advisory Committee
BIAE British Institute of Adult Education
BIAS Bristol Industrial Archaeological Society
BIATA British Independent Air Transport Association
bib. *bibe* (Latin: drink; medicine); *bibliothèque* (French: library)
Bib. Bible; Biblical
BIB baby incendiary bomb (military)
BIBA British Insurance Brokers' Association
BIBC British Isles Bowling Council
BIBF British and Irish Basketball Federation
bibl(iog). bibliographer; bibliographical; bibliography
BIBRA British Industrial Biological Research Association
BIC Bahá'í International Community; *Bureau international du cinéma* (French: International Cinema Bureau); Butter Information Council
bicarb. bicarbonate of soda
BICC Berne International Copyright Convention
BICE *Bureau international catholique de l'enfance* (French: International Catholic Child Bureau)
BICEMA British Internal Combustion Engine Manufacturers' Association

BICEP British Industrial Collaborative Exponential Programme
BICERI British Internal Combustion Engine Research Institute
bid *bis in die* (Latin: twice a day; medicine)
BID Bachelor of Industrial Design; Bachelor of Interior Design; brought in dead (medicine)
BIDS British Institute of Dealers in Securities
BIE Bachelor of Industrial Engineering; *Bureau international d'éducation* (French: International Bureau of Education); *Bureau international des expositions* (French: International Exhibition Bureau)
BIEE British Institute of Energy Economics
bien. biennial
BIET British Institute of Engineering Technology
BIF banded iron formation (geology); British Industries Fair
BIFFEX Baltic International Freight Futures Market
BIFU Banking, Insurance and Finance Union
BIH *Bureau international de l'heure* (French: International Time Bureau)
BIHA British Ice Hockey Association
BIIBA British Insurance and Investment Brokers Association
bim. *bimestrale* (Italian: twice monthly); *bimestre* (Italian: two-month period)
BIM Bachelor of Indian Medicine; British Institute of Management; British Insulin Manufacturers
BIMCAM British Industrial Measuring and Control Apparatus Manufacturers' Association
bin. binary (mathematics)
BIN Bulletin of International News
BINC Building Industries' National Council
bind. binding
BIO Bedford Institute of Oceanography (Canada)
biochem. biochemistry
biog. biographer; biographic; biographical; biography
biogeog. biogeography
biol. biological; biologist; biology
BIOS basic input-output system (computing); Biological Investigation of Space; biological satellite (astronautics);

British Intelligence Objectives Subcommittee

BIOT British Indian Ocean Territory

BIP British Industrial Plastics; British Institute in Paris

BIPCA *Bureau international permanent de chimie analytique pour les matières destinées à l'alimentation de l'homme et des animaux* (French: Permanent International Bureau of Analytical Chemistry of Human and Animal Food)

BIPL Burmah Industrial Products Limited

BIPM *Bureau international des poids et mesures* (French: International Bureau of Weights and Measures)

BIPP bismuth, iodoform, paraffin paste (medicine); British Institute of Practical Psychology

BIR Board of Inland Revenue; British Institute of Radiology

BIRD *Banque internationale pour la reconstruction et le développement* (French: International Bank for Reconstruction and Development; IBRD)

BIRE British Institution of Radio Engineers

BIRF Brewing Industry Research Foundation

Birm. Birmingham

BIRMO British Infra-Red Manufacturers' Organization

BIRS British Institute of Recorded Sound

bis. bissextile

BIS Bank for International Settlements; British Information Services; British Interplanetary Society; *Bureau international du scoutisme* (French: Boy Scouts International Bureau)

BISA British International Studies Association

Bisc. Biscayan

BISF British Iron and Steel Federation

BISFA British Industrial and Scientific Film Association

bish. bishop

bis in 7d. *bis in septem diebus* (Latin: twice a week; medicine)

BISPA British Independent Steel Producers' Association

BISRA British Iron and Steel Research Association

BISYNC binary synchronous communications (computing)

bit binary digit (computing, mathematics)

BIT *Bureau international du travail* (French: International Labour Office)

BITA British Industrial Truck Association

bitm. bituminous

BITNET Because It's Time Network (computing)

BITO British Institution of Training Officers

BITOA British Incoming Tour Operators' Association

bitum. bituminous

BIU Bermuda Industrial Union; *Bureau international des universités* (French: International University Bureau)

biv. bivouac

BIWF British-Israel World Federation

BIWS Bureau of International Whaling Statistics

BIZ *Bank für Internationalen Zahlungsausgleich* (German: Bank for International Settlements)

BJ Bachelor of Journalism; Ipswich (UK vehicle registration)

BJA British Judo Association

BJCEB British Joint Communications Electronics Board

BJOS British Journal of Occupational Safety

BJP Bharatiya Janata Party (India)

BJSM British Joint Services Mission

BJT bipolar junction transistor (electronics)

BJTRA British Jute Trade Research Association

Bjur(is) Bachelor of Jurisprudence

bk backwardation; bank; bark; barrack; black; block; book; break

Bk berkelium (element)

BK Berwick-on-Tweed (UK fishing port registration); Portsmouth (UK vehicle registration)

BKA *Bundeskriminalamt* (German: criminal investigations office)

bkble bookable

bkcy bankruptcy

bkd blackboard; booked

BKD bacterial kidney disease

bkg banking; booking; book-keeping

bkgd background

bkkg book-keeping

bklr black letter (printing)

bklt booklet

Bklyn Brooklyn (US)

bkm buckram

BKN broken cloud (meteorology)

bk(r)pt bankrupt

bks barracks; books

BKSTS British Kinematograph, Sound and Television Society

bkt basket; bracket; bucket
bl barrel; bill of lading; breech-loading
bl. bale; black; blue
Bl. *Blat* (German: newspaper); Blessed
BL Bachelor of Law; Bachelor of Letters; Bachelor of Literature; Barrister-at-Law; base line; bill lodged; bill of lading; black letter (printing); boatswain lieutenant; Bodleian Library (Oxford); Bolton (UK postcode); Bristol (UK fishing port registration); British Leyland; British Library; Reading (UK vehicle registration)
B/L bill of lading
BLA Bachelor of Landscape Architecture; Bachelor of Liberal Arts; British Legal Association; British Liberation Army (post World War II)
BLACC British and Latin American Chamber of Commerce
BLAISE British Library Automated Information Service
BLB bacterial leaf blight (horticulture); Boothby, Lovelace and Bulbulian (oxygen mask)
BLC British Lighting Council
bld bold (printing)
bldg building
BLE Brotherhood of Locomotive Engineers (trade union)
BLESMA British Limbless Ex-Servicemen's Association
BLEU Belgo-Luxembourg Economic Union; Blind Landing Experimental Unit (aeronautics)
BLG Burke's Landed Gentry
BLH British Legion Headquarters
BLI British Lighting Industries
BLib(Sc) Bachelor of Library Science
BLIC *Bureau de liaison des industries du caoutchouc de la CE* (French: Rubber Industries Liaison Bureau of the EC)
BLIS Bibliographic Literature Information Service (US)
Bliss baby life support system; bend, low silhouette, irregular shape, small, secluded (military)
BLit Bachelor of Literature
BLitt *Baccalaureus Litterarum* (Latin: Bachelor of Letters)
blk black; blank; block; bulk
BLL Bachelor of Laws
BLM Bachelor of Land Management; blind landing machine; Bureau of Land Management (US)
BLMA British Lead Manufacturers' Association

BLMAS Bible Lands Missions' Aid Society
BLMRA British Leather Manufacturers' Research Association
BLO below clouds (meteorology)
BLOF British Lace Operatives' Federation
BLOX block order exposure system (finance)
BLP Barbados Labour Party
blr breech-loading rifle
BLRA British Launderers' Research Association
BLS Bachelor of Library Science; basic life support; *benevolenti lectori salutem* (Latin: greeting to the well-wishing reader); Branch Line Society; Bureau of Labor Statistics (US)
BLSN blowing snow (meteorology)
blt built
BLT bacon, lettuce and tomato (sandwich)
BLV bovine leukaemia virus (microbiology); British Legion Village
Blvd Boulevard (France)
BLWA British Laboratory Ware Association
BLWN band-limited white noise (electronics)
bm *bene merenti* (Latin: to the well-deserving); black mare (horse racing); board measure (timber); bowel movement (medicine); breech mechanism (firearms)
BM Bachelor of Medicine; Bachelor of Music; bandmaster; base metal; *beatae memoriae* (Latin: of blessed memory); *Beata Maria* (Latin: the Blessed Virgin); benchmark (surveying); Bishop and Martyr; *bonae memoriae* (Latin: of happy memory); bone marrow (medicine); brigade major; British Monomark; British Museum; Brixham (UK fishing port registration); bronze medallist; Bureau of Mines (US); Luton (UK vehicle registration)
BMA Bahrain Monetary Agency; British Manufacturers' Association; British Medical Association
BMath Bachelor of Mathematics
BMC bone marrow cell (medicine); Book Marketing Council; British Match Corporation; British Medical Council; British Metal Corporation; British Motor Corporation; British Mountaineering Council; British Museum Catalogue
BMCIS Building Maintenance Cost Information Service

BMD ballistic missile defence; births, marriages and deaths
BMDM British Museum Department of Manuscripts
Bmdr Bombardier
BME Bachelor of Mechanical Engineering; Bachelor of Mining Engineering; Bachelor of Music Education
BMEC British Marine Equipment Council
BMed Bachelor of Medicine
BMedSci Bachelor of Medical Science
BMEF British Mechanical Engineering Federation
BMEG Building Materials Export Group
BMEO British Middle East Office
BMEP brake mean effective pressure (engineering)
BMet Bachelor of Metallurgy
BMetE Bachelor of Metallurgical Engineering
BMEWS ballistic missile early-warning system
BMFA Boston Museum of Fine Arts
BMH British Military Hospital
BMI ballistic missile interceptor; Birmingham and Midland Institute; body-mass index; Broadcast Music Incorporated
BMJ British Medical Journal
BML Bachelor of Modern Languages; British Museum Library
BMM British Military Mission
BMMA Bacon and Meat Marketing Association
bmo business machine operator
B'mouth Bournemouth
bmp brake mean power
BMP biochemical methane potential; biochemical methane production
BMPA British Metalworking Plantmakers' Association
BMPS British Musicians' Pension Society
BMR basal metabolic rate (physiology)
BMRA Brigade Major Royal Artillery
BMRB British Market Research Bureau
BMRMC British Motor Racing Marshals' Club
BMS Bachelor of Marine Science; Baptist Missionary Society; British Mycological Society; building management system; business modelling system
BMSE Baltic Mercantile and Shipping Exchange
BMT basic motion-time study; bone-marrow transplant; British Mean Time
BMTA British Motor Trade Association

BMus Bachelor of Music
BMusEd Bachelor of Music Education
BMV Blessed Mary the Virgin
BMW *Bayerische Motorenwerke* (German: Bavarian Motor Works)
BMWE Brotherhood of Maintenance of Way Employees (US trade union)
BMWS ballistic missile weapon system
BMX bicycle motocross
bn bassoon; battalion; beacon; been; billion; born
Bn Baron; Battalion
BN Bachelor of Nursing; bank note; Boston (UK fishing port registration); Brighton (UK postcode); Britten-Norman (aircraft); Manchester (UK vehicle registration)
BNA British Naturalists' Association; British North America; British North Atlantic (insurance); British Nursing Association
BNAF British North Africa Force
BNB British National Bibliography
BNBC British National Book Centre
BNC Brasenose College (Oxford); British National Corpus (linguistics)
BNCC British National Committee for Chemistry
BNCI *Banque nationale pour le commerce et l'industrie* (French: National Bank for Commerce and Industry; Madagascar)
BNCM *Bibliothèque nationale du conservatoire de musique* (French: National Library of Music)
BNCS British National Carnation Society
BNCSAA British National Committee on Surface-Active Agents
BNCSR British National Committee on Space Research
BND *Bundesnachrichtendienst* (German: national intelligence service)
B/ND binding, no date given (books)
BNDD Bureau of Narcotics and Dangerous Drugs (US)
Bndr Bandmaster
BNEC British National Export Council; British Nuclear Energy Conference
BNES British Nuclear Energy Society
BNF Backus-Naur form (computing); Backus normal form (computing); British National Formulary (pharmacology); British Nuclear Fuels (Limited); British Nutrition Foundation
BNFC British National Film Catalogue
BNFL British Nuclear Fuels Limited
BNFMF British Non-Ferrous Metals Federation

BNGA British Nursery Goods Association
BNGM British Naval Gunnery Mission
BNHQ battalion headquarters
bnkg banking
BNL *Banca Nazionale del Lavoro* (Italian: National Bank of Lavoro)
BNM *Bureau national de meteorologie* (French: National Bureau of Meteorology)
BNMAU Mongolia (international civil aircraft marking)
BNOC British National Oil Corporation; British National Opera Company
BNP *Banque national de Paris* (French: National Bank of Paris); Barbados National Party; British National Party
BNS Bachelor of Natural Science; Bathymetric Navigation System; British Numismatic Society; buyer no seller
BNSc Bachelor of Nursing Science
BNSC British National Space Centre
BNTA British Numismatic Trade Association
BNurs Bachelor of Nursing
BNX British Nuclear Export Executive
bnzn benzoin
bo back order; blackout; body odour; bowels opened (medicine); box office; branch office; broker's order; buyer's option
b/o brought over (book-keeping)
BO Bachelor of Oratory; biological oceanography; body odour; Borrowstowness (UK fishing port registration); Bouraq Indonesia Airlines (airline flight code); box office; bowels opened (medicine); Cardiff (UK vehicle registration)
B/O brought over (book-keeping); buyer's option
BOA British Olympic Association; British Optical Association; British Orthopaedic Association; broad ocean area
BOAC British Overseas Airways Corporation
BOAD *Banque ouest-africaine de développement* (French: West African Development Bank)
BOA(Disp) British Optical Association, Dispensing Certificate
BOBA British Overseas Banks' Association
BOBMA British Oil Burner Manufacturers' Association
BOC beginning of cycle (computing); bimodal optical computer; British

Oxygen Corporation; Burmah Oil Company
BOCE Board of Customs and Excise
Bod. Bodleian Library (Oxford)
BOD biochemical oxygen demand (sewage treatment)
BOE Board of Education; brick on edge (building)
BOF beginning of file (computing); British Orienteering Federation; British Overseas Fairs
B of E Bank of England
B of H Band of Hope Union
BOGMC Bangladesh Oil, Gas and Minerals Corporation
Boh. Bohemia; Bohemian
BoJ Bank of Japan
bol. *bolus* (Latin: large pill; medicine)
Bol. Bolívar; Bolivia; Bolivian
BOL beginning of life
Boltop better on lips than on paper
bom bill of materials
Bom. Bombay
BOM Bureau of Mines (US)
Bomb. Bombardier; Bombay
BomCS Bombay Civil Service
BomSC Bombay Staff Corps
bon *bataillon* (French: battalion)
BONUS Borrower's Option for Notes and Underwritten Standby (finance)
BOP basic oxygen process (chemistry); Boy's Own Paper
BOPA Botswana Press Agency (news agency)
BOptom Bachelor of Optometry
BOQ bachelor officers' quarters (US); base officers' quarters (US)
bor. borough
BOr Bachelor of Orientation
BORAD British Oxygen Research and Development Association
boro. borough
bos'n boatswain
Bos Pops Boston Pops Orchestra (US)
BOSS Bioastronautic Orbiting Space Station; Bureau of State Security (South Africa)
Boswash Boston-Washington D.C.
bot. botanic; botanical; botanist; botany; bottle; bottom; bought
BOT beginning of tape (computing); Board of Trade
BOTB British Overseas Trade Board
BOU British Ornithologists' Union
boul. boulevard
BOV brown oil of vitriol (commercial sulphuric acid)

BOWO Brigade Ordnance Warrant
Officer
bp below proof (alcohol); bills payable;
boiling point (chemistry); *bonum
publicum* (Latin: the public good)
bp. baptized; birthplace
b/p blueprint; bills payable
Bp Bishop
BP Air Botswana (airline flight code);
Bachelor of Pharmacy; Bachelor of
Philosophy; back projection; (Robert)
Baden-Powell (founder of the scout
movement); barometric pressure; basis
point (finance); beach party (military);
Be Prepared (Scout motto); before
present; between perpendiculars
(shipping); blood pressure; boiling point
(chemistry); British Patent; British
Petroleum; British Pharmacopoeia;
British Public; Portsmouth (UK vehicle
registration)
B/P bills payable
BPA Bachelor of Professional Arts;
Bahnpostamt (German: railway post
office); Biological Photographic
Association (US); Bookmakers' Protec-
tion Association; British Paediatric Asso-
ciation; British Parachute Association;
British Philatelic Association; Business
Publications Audit of Circulation (US)
BPAA British Poster Advertising
Association
BPAGB Bicycle Polo Association of Great
Britain
BPAS British Pregnancy Advisory
Service
bpb bank post bills
BPBF British Paper Box Federation
BPBIRA British Paper and Board
Industry Research Association
BPBMA British Paper and Board Makers'
Association
BPC Book Prices Current; British
Pharmaceutical Codex; British
Pharmacopoeia Commission; British
Printing Corporation; British
Productivity Council; Business and
Professional Code (US)
bpcd barrels per calendar day
BPCF British Precast Concrete
Federation
BPCR Brakes on Pedal Cycle Regu-
lations
BPCRA British Professional Cycle Racing
Association
bpd barrels per day
BPd Bachelor of Pedagogy

BPDB Bangladesh Power Development
Board
BPDMS basic point defence missile
system (military)
BPE Bachelor of Physical Education
bpf *bon pour francs* (French: value in
francs)
BPF British Plastics Federation; British
Polio Fellowship
BPG Broadcasting Press Guild
BPh Bachelor of Philosophy
BPH Bachelor of Public Health
BPharm Bachelor of Pharmacy
BPhil Bachelor of Philosophy
bpi bits per inch (computing)
BPI Booksellers' Provident Institution;
British Pacific Islands
BPICA *Bureau permanent international des
constructeurs d'automobiles* (French:
International Permanent Bureau of
Motor Manufacturers)
BPIF British Printing Industries'
Federation
bpl. birthplace
Bpl. Barnstaple
bpm barrels per minute; beats per minute
(music)
BPMA British Premium Merchandise
Association; British Pump
Manufacturers' Association
BPMF British Postgraduate Medical
Federation; British Pottery
Manufacturers' Federation
BPO base post office; Berlin Philharmonic
Orchestra
BPOE Benevolent and Protective Order
of Elks (US)
BPP Botswana People's Party
BPPMA British Power-Press
Manufacturers' Association
BPRA Book Publishers' Representatives'
Association
BPRO Blind Persons Resettlement Officer
bps bits per second (computing)
BPs Bachelor of Psychology
BPS border patrol sector; border patrol
station; British Pharmacological Society;
Bureau of Professional Standards (US)
BPsS British Psychological Society
Bp Suff. Bishop Suffragan
BPsych Bachelor of Psychology
bpt bits per track (computing)
b. pt boiling point
BPT Bachelor of Physiotherapy; battle
practice target; British Petroleum Tanker
BPV bovine papilloma virus
(microbiology)

bq(ue). barque
Bq becquerel (physics)
BQ *bene quiescat* (Latin: may he/she rest well)
BQA British Quality Association
BQMS battery quartermaster-sergeant
br bank rate; bills receivable; breeder reactor
br. bearing; branch; bridge; brief; brig; bronze; brother; brown
Br birr (Ethiopian monetary unit); Bombardier; bromine (element); Brother (Roman Catholic Church); bugler
Br. Branch; Brazil; Breton; Britain; British
BR *Bancus Reginae/Regis* (Latin: Queen's or King's Bench; law); block release (education); book of reference; Brazil (international vehicle registration); Bridgwater (UK fishing port registration); British Rail; Bromley (UK postcode); (poly)butadiene rubber; buyl rubber; Newcastle upon Tyne (UK vehicle registration)
B/R bills receivable; Bordeaux or Rouen (grain); builders' risks (insurance)
bra brassière
BRA Bee Research Association; Brigadier Royal Artillery; British Records Association; British Rheumatism and Arthritis Association
Brad. Bradford
Br. Am. British America
Bras. *Brasil* (Portuguese: Brazil)
BRAS ballistic rocket air suppression
Braz. Brazil(ian)
Brazza. Brazzaville
Br. C. British Columbia
BRC base residence course (US); Biological Records Centre, Nature Conservancy Council; British Rabbits Council; British Radio Corporation
brch branch
BRCS British Red Cross Society
BRD Broadford (UK fishing port registration); Building Research Division, National Bureau of Standards (US)
BRDC British Racing Drivers' Club
brdcst broadcast
BRE Bachelor of Religious Education; Building Research Establishment
b. rec. bills receivable
Brec. Brecon
BREL British Rail Engineering Limited
BREMA British Radio Equipment Manufacturers' Association
Br'er Brother

Bret. Breton
brev. brevet; *breveté* (French: patent); *brevetto* (Italian: patent)
brew. brewer; brewery; brewing
brf brief (law)
BRF Bible Reading Fellowship; British Road Federation
BRFC British Record Fish Committee (angling)
brg bearing
br. g. brown gelding (horse racing)
Br. I. British India; British Isles
BRI *Banque des règlements internationaux* (French: Bank for International Settlements); Biological Research Institute (US); Brain Research Institute (US)
Brig brigade; brigadier
Brig. Gen. brigadier general
brill. *brillante* (Italian: brilliant; music)
BRIMEC British Mechanical Engineering Confederation
BRINCO British Newfoundland Corporation Limited
Brisb. Brisbane
Brist. Bristol
Brit. Britain; Britannia; British; Briton
Brit. Mus. British Museum
Brit. Pat. British Patent
Britt. *Britanniarum* (Latin: of Great Britain; numismatics)
brk brick
brkt bracket
brkwtr breakwater
brl barrel
BRL Ballistic Research Laboratory; Bible Research Library
BRM binary-rate multiplier (computing); British Racing Motors
BRMA Board of Registration of Medical Auxiliaries; British Rubber Manu-facturers' Association
BRMCA British Ready-Mixed Concrete Association
BRMF British Rainwear Manufacturers' Federation
brn brown
BRN Bahrain (international vehicle registration)
BRNC Britannia Royal Naval College
brng bearing (navigation); burning
bro brother
Bro. Brotherhood
BRO brigade routine order
brom. bromide
bros. brothers
BRP biological reclamation process

BRS British Record Society; British Road Services; Building Research Station
BRSA British Rail Staff Association
BRSCC British Racing and Sports Car Club
brt bright
BRT *Belgische Radio en Televisie* (Belgian broadcasting company); *Brutto-Register-tonnen* (German: gross register tons; shipping)
BRTA British Racing Toboggan Association; British Regional Television Association; British Road Tar Association
BRU Brunei (international vehicle registration)
Brum. Birmingham
Brunsw. Brunswick
BRurSc Bachelor of Rural Science
Brux. *Bruxelles* (French: Brussels)
BRW British Relay Wireless
bry(ol). bryology
brz. bronze
bs backstage; bags; balance sheet; bales; bill of sale
Bs bolívars (Venezuelan monetary unit); bolivianos (Bolivian monetary unit)
BS Bachelor of Science (US); Bachelor of Surgery; Bahamas (international vehicle registration); battleship; battle squadron; Beaumaris (UK fishing port registration); below specification; Bibliographical Society; bill of sale; binary state (computing); Biochemical Society; Blessed Sacrament; Boy Scouts; breaking strain (angling); Bristol (UK postcode); Bristol Siddeley (aircraft); British Standard; British Steel; Budgerigar Society; building society; bullshit; bus switch (computing); Inverness (UK vehicle registration)
B/S bill of sale; bill of store (commerce)
BSA Bachelor of Science in Agriculture; Bachelor of Scientific Agriculture; Bibliographical Society of America; Birmingham Small Arms Company; body surface area (medicine); bovine serum albumin (medicine); Boy Scouts' Association; Boy Scouts of America; British School at Athens; British Speleological Association; Building Societies' Association
BSAA Bachelor of Science in Applied Arts; British School of Archaeology at Athens
BSAC British Sub-Aqua Club

BSAdv Bachelor of Science in Advertising
BSAE Bachelor of Science in Aeronautical Engineering; Bachelor of Science in Agricultural Engineering
BSAeEng Bachelor of Science in Aeronautical Engineering
BSAgE Bachelor of Science in Agricultural Engineering
BSAgr Bachelor of Science in Agriculture
BS&W basic sediment and water; bottom sediment and water
BSAP British Society of Animal Production
BSArch Bachelor of Science in Architecture
BSAS British Ship Adoption Society
BSAVA British Small Animals Veterinary Association
Bsb. Brisbane
BSB British Satellite Broadcasting; British Standard brass (screw thread)
BSBA Bachelor of Science in Business Administration
BSBC British Social Biology Council
BSBI Botanical Society of the British Isles
BSBus Bachelor of Science in Business
bsc basic
BSc Bachelor of Science
BSC Bachelor of Science in Commerce; Bengal Staff Corps; Bibliographical Society of Canada; binary synchronous communications (computing); Biomedical Sciences Corporation; British Safety Council; British Shoe Corporation; British Society of Cinematographers; British Standard Channel; British Stationery Council; British Steel Corporation; British Sugar Corporation; British Supply Council; Broadcasting Standards Council
BSCA British Swimming Coaches' Association; Bureau of Security and Consular Affairs (US)
BScA Bachelor of Science in Agriculture
BSc(Acc) Bachelor of Science in Accounting
BSc(Ag) Bachelor of Science in Agriculture
BScApp Bachelor of Science in Applied Science
BScArch Bachelor of Science in Architecture
BSCC British Society of Clinical Cytology; British Synchronous Clock Conference

BScD Bachelor of Dental Science
BSc(Dent) Bachelor of Science in Dentistry
BSCE Bachelor of Science in Civil Engineering
BSc(Econ) Bachelor of Science in Economics
BSc(Ed) Bachelor of Science in Education
BSChE Bachelor of Science in Chemical Engineering
BSc(Hort) Bachelor of Science in Horticulture
BScMed Bachelor of Medical Science
BSc(Nutr) Bachelor of Science in Nutrition
BSCP British Standard Code of Practice
BSCRA British Steel Castings Research Association
BScSoc Bachelor of Social Sciences
BSD Bachelor of Science in Design; ballistic system division; British Society of Dowsers; British Space Development
bsdl boresight datum line
bse base support equipment
BSE Bachelor of Science in Education; Bachelor of Science in Engineering; bovine spongiform encephalopathy; breast self-examination (medicine)
BSEc Bachelor of Science in Economics
BSEd Bachelor of Science in Education
BSEE Bachelor of Science in Electrical Engineering; Bachelor of Science in Elementary Education
BSEEng Bachelor of Science in Electrical Engineering
BSEIE Bachelor of Science in Electronic Engineering
BSEM Bachelor of Science in Engineering of Mines
BSEng Bachelor of Science in Engineering
BSES Bachelor of Science in Engineering Sciences; British Schools Exploring Society
BSF Bachelor of Science in Forestry; British Slag Federation; British Standard fine (screw thread); British Stone Federation
BSFA British Science Fiction Association; British Steel Founders' Association
bsfc brake specific fuel consumption
BSF(L) British Shipping Federation (Limited)
BSFM Bachelor of Science in Forestry Management
BSFor Bachelor of Science in Forestry

BSFS Bachelor of Science in Foreign Service
BSFT Bachelor of Science in Fuel Technology
BSG British Standard Gauge
bsgdg *breveté sans garantie du gouvernment* (French: patented without government guarantee)
BSGE Bachelor of Science in General Engineering
bsh. bushel
BSH British Society of Hypnotherapists; British Standard Hardness
BSHA Bachelor of Science in Hospital Administration
BSHE(c) Bachelor of Science in Home Economics
BSHS British Society for the History of Science
BSHyg Bachelor of Science in Hygiene
BSI British Sailors' Institute; British Standards Institution; Building Societies' Institute
BSIA British Security Industry Association
BSIB Boy Scouts International Bureau
BSIC British Ski Instruction Council
BSIE Bachelor of Science in Industrial Engineering
BSIP British Solomon Islands Protectorate
BSIRA British Scientific Instrument Research Association
BSIS Business Sponsorship Incentive Scheme
BSIU British Society for International Understanding
BSJ Bachelor of Science in Journalism
BSJA British Show Jumping Association
bsk(t). basket
BSkyB British Sky Broadcasting
Bs/L bills of lading
BSL Bachelor of Sacred Literature; Bachelor of Science in Linguistics; boatswain sublieutenant; British Sign Language
BSLS Bachelor of Science in Library Science
BSM Bachelor of Sacred Music; Bachelor of Science in Medicine; battery sergeant-major; branch sales manager; British School of Motoring; bronze star medal (US)
BSMA British Skate Makers' Association
BSME Bachelor of Science in Mechanical Engineering; Bachelor of Science in Mining Engineering

BSMedTech Bachelor of Science in
Medical Technology
BSMet Bachelor of Science in Metallurgy
BSMetE Bachelor of Science in
Metallurgical Engineering
BSMGP British Society of Master Glass-
Painters
bsmt basement
BSMT Bachelor of Science in Medical
Technology
bsn bassoon
BSN Bachelor of Science in Nursing
BSNE Bachelor of Science in Nuclear
Engineering
BSNS Bachelor of Naval Science
BSO base supply officer; Boston
Symphony Orchestra; Bournemouth
Symphony Orchestra; Business Statistics
Office
BSocSc Bachelor of Social Science
BSOT Bachelor of Science in
Occupational Therapy
BSP Bachelor of Science in Pharmacy;
Bering Sea Patrol; Birmingham School of
Printing; British Standard pipe (screw
thread); Bulgarian Socialist Party;
business systems planning
BSPA Bachelor of Science in Public
Administration
BSPE Bachelor of Science in Physical
Education
BSPH Bachelor of Science in Public
Health
BSPhar(m) Bachelor of Science in
Pharmacy
BSP(h)T(h) Bachelor of Science in
Physical Therapy
BSR Birmingham Sound Reproducers;
blood sedimentation rate (medicine);
British School at Rome
BSRA British Ship Research Association;
British Society for Research on Ageing;
British Sound Recording Association
BSRAE British Society for Research in
Agricultural Engineering
BSRC Biological Serial Record Center
(US)
BSRT Bachelor of Science in Radiological
Technology
BSS Bachelor of Secretarial Science;
Bachelor of Social Science; basic safety
standards; Bibliothèque Saint-Sulpice
(Montreal); British Sailors' Society;
British Standard size; British Standards
Specification
BSSA Bachelor of Science in Secretarial
Administration

BSSc Bachelor of Social Science
BSSE Bachelor of Science in Secondary
Education
BSSG Biomedical Sciences Support Grant
(US)
BSSO British Society for the Study of
Orthodontics
BSSS Bachelor of Science in Secretarial
Studies; Bachelor of Science in Social
Science; British Society of Soil Science
BST Bachelor of Sacred Theology; British
Standard Time; British Summer Time;
bulk supply tariff
B/St bill of sight
BSTA British Surgical Trades' Association
BSTC British Student Travel Centre
bstd bastard
bstr booster
bstr rkt booster rocket
BSU bench scale unit (engineering)
BSurv Bachelor of Surveying
bsw barrels of salt water
BSW Bachelor of Social Work; British
Standard Whitworth (screw thread)
BSWB Boy Scouts World Bureau
BSWE British Scouts in Western Europe
BSWIA British Steel Wire Industries'
Association
bt beat; benefit; bent; bought
Bt baronet; brevet (military)
BT Bachelor of Teaching; Bachelor of
Theology; basic trainer; basic training;
behaviour therapy (psychology);
Belfast (UK postcode); benign
tumour (medicine); bishop's
transcript; Board of Trade (UK);
British Telecom(munications);
Leeds (UK vehicle registration)
BTA Billiards Trade Association; Blood
Transfusion Association (US); British
Theatre Association; British Tourist
Authority; British Tuberculosis
Association; *Bulgarska Telegrafitscheka
Agentzia* (news agency, Bulgaria)
BTAC binary tree algebraic computation
(computing)
BTASA Book Trade Association of South
Africa
Btb. bass tuba (music)
BTBA British Ten Pin Bowling
Association
BTBS Book Trade Benevolent Society
BTC Bankers' Trust Company; basic
training center (US); British Textile
Confederation; British Transport
Commission
btca *biblioteca* (Spanish: library)

BTCC Board of Transportation Commissioners of Canada
BTCh Bachelor of Textile Chemistry
BTCP Bachelor of Town and Country Planning
BTCV British Trust for Conservation Volunteers
btd bomb testing device
BTDB Bermuda Trade Development Board
BTDC before top dead centre (engineering)
bté *breveté* (French: patent)
BTE Bachelor of Textile Engineering
BTEC Business and Technician Education Council
BTech Bachelor of Technology
BTechEd Bachelor of Technical Education
BTechFood Bachelor of Food Technology
BTEF Book Trade Employers' Federation
BTEMA British Tanning Extract Manufacturers' Association
BTEX benzene, toluene, ethyl-benzene and xylene (solvents)
btf barrels of total fuel; bomb tail fuse
BTF British Tarpaviors' Federation; British Trawlers Federation; British Turkey Federation
BTG British Technology Group
bth bath; bathroom; berth
BTh Bachelor of Theology
BTHMA British Toy and Hobby Manufacturers' Association
BThU British thermal unit
BTI British Technology Index
BTIA British Tar Industries' Association
btk buttock
btl. bottle
BTL between layers (meteorology)
btm bottom
BTM bromotrifluoromethane (used in firefighting)
BTMA British Typewriter Manufacturers' Association
btn baton; button
BTN Brussels Tariff Nomenclature
BTO big time operator; British Trust for Ornithology
BTP Bachelor of Town Planning
BTR British Tax Review; British Telecommunications Research
BTRA Bombay Textile Industry's Research Association
BTRP Bachelor of Town and Regional Planning

btry battery (military)
BTS Blood Transfusion Service; British Telecommunications Systems
Btss Baroneness
BTTA British Thoracic and Tuberculosis Association
Btu British thermal unit
BTU Board of Trade unit; British thermal unit (US)
BTUC Bahamas Trade Union Congress
BTW by the way
btwn between
BTX benzene, toluene and xylene (solvents); *Bildschirmtext* (German videotext system)
bty battery (military)
B-type Basedow type (psychology)
bu base unit; break-up (finance)
bu. bureau; bushel
Bu butyl group (chemistry)
BU Baptist Union of Great Britain and Ireland; Braathens SAFE (airline flight code, Norway); Brown University, Rhode Island; Burntisland (UK fishing port registration); Manchester (UK vehicle registration)
BuAer Bureau of Aeronautics (US)
BUAF British United Air Ferries
BUA of E Badminton Umpires' Association of England
BUAV British Union for the Abolition of Vivisection
BUC Bangor University College
buck. buckram
Bucks Buckinghamshire
BUCOP British Union Catalogue of Periodicals
bud. budget
Bud(d). Buddhism; Buddhist
BuDocks Bureau of Yards and Docks (US Navy)
Budpst Budapest
bue built-up edges
BUF British Union of Fascists
BUIC back-up interceptor control
BUJ *Baccalaureus utriusque juris* (Latin: Bachelor of Canon and Civil Law)
bul. bulletin
Bulg. Bulgaria; Bulgarian
bull. bulla (papal seal); bulletin; *bulliat* (Latin: let it boil; medicine)
buloga business logistics game
BULVA Belfast and Ulster Licensed Vintners' Association
BuMed Bureau of Medicine and Surgery (US Navy)

BUNA butadiene and natrium (synthetic rubber)

BUNAC British Universities North America Club

BUNCH Burroughs, Univac, NCR, Control Data, Honeywell (computer companies)

BuOrd Bureau of Ordnance (US Navy)

BUP British United Press

BUPA British United Provident Association

BuPers Bureau of Naval Personnel (US Navy)

Bu. Pub. Aff. Bureau of Public Affairs (US)

bur. bureau; buried

Bur. Burma; Burmese

BUR Burma (international vehicle registration)

BuRec Bureau of Reclamation (US)

burg. burgess; burgomaster

burl. burlesque

Burm. Burma; Burmese

Burma be undressed ready, my angel

Burs. Bursar

bus. bushel; business

BuSandA Bureau of Supply and Accounts (US Navy)

BUSF British Universities' Sports Federation

bush. bushel

BuShips Bureau of Ships (US Navy)

bus. mgr business manager

but. butter; button

buy. buyer; buying

bv balanced voltage; book value (accounting)

BV *Beata Virgo* (Latin: Blessed Virgin); *Beatitudo Vestra* (Latin: Your Holiness); *bene vale* (Latin: farewell); *Besloten Vennootschap* (Dutch: private limited company); Bible Version (Psalms); Blessed Virgin; blood volume (medicine); Preston (UK vehicle registration)

BVA British Veterinary Association

BVDs one-piece underwear for men, originally made by the Bradley, Voorhees & Day firm (US)

BVetMed Bachelor of Veterinary Medicine

BVetSc Bachelor of Veterinary Science

BVI British Virgin Islands

BVJ British Veterinary Journal

BVK *Bundesverdienstkreuz* (German: Federal Cross of Merit)

BVM Bachelor of Veterinary Medicine;

Beata Virgo Maria (Latin: Blessed Virgin Mary)

BVMA British Valve Manufacturers' Association

BVMS Bachelor of Veterinary Medicine and Surgery

BVO *Bundesverdienstorden* (German: Federal Order of Merit)

BVP British Visitors' Passport; British Volunteer Programme

BVS Bachelor of Veterinary Surgery

BVSc Bachelor of Veterinary Science

BVSc&AH Bachelor of Veterinary Science and Animal Husbandry

bvt brevet

bw *bitte wenden* (German: please turn over); bridleway

b/w black and white

BW bacteriological warfare; Barrow (UK fishing port registration); Bath and Wells; biological warfare; black and white; Black Watch; Board of Works; body weight (medicine); bonded warehouse; British Waterways; business week; BWIA International Trinidad and Tobago Airways (airline flight code); Oxford (UK vehicle registration)

B/W black and white; black to white

BWA backward wave amplifier; Baptist World Alliance; British Waterworks Association; British West Africa

B-way Broadway (US)

BWB British Waterways Board

BWC Board of War Communications; British War Cabinet

BWCC British Weed Control Conference

bwd backward

BWD bacillary white diarrhoea (veterinary science)

BWF British Whiting Federation; British Wool Federation

BWG Birmingham Wire Gauge (engineering)

BWI British West Indies

BWIA British West Indian Airways

BWIR British West India Regiment

BWISA British West Indies Sugar Association

bwk brickwork; bulwark

BWM British War Medal

BWMA British Woodwork Manufacturers' Association

BWMB British Wool Marketing Board

BWO backward wave oscillator

BWP basic war plan

BWPA backward wave power amplifier;

British Waste Paper Association; British Word Preserving Association
bwpd barrels of water per day
bwph barrels of water per hour
BWPUC British Wastepaper Utilization Council
BWR boiling-water reactor (nuclear physics)
BWS battered wife syndrome; battered woman syndrome; British Watercolour Society
BWSF British Water Ski Federation
BWTA British Women's Temperance Association
BWU Barbados Workers' Union
bwv back water valve
BWV *Bach Werke-Verzeichnis* (German: Catalogue of Bach's Works)
BWVA British War Veterans of America
BWWA British Waterworks Association
bx box
BX Base Exchange (US Air Force); British Xylonite; Haverfordwest (UK vehicle registration)
by billion years
By barony
BY Britannia Airways (airline flight code, UK); northwest London (UK vehicle registration)
Bye. Byelorussia; Byelorussian
Byo Bulawayo
BYO bring your own
BYOB bring your own beer/booze/bottle
BYOG bring your own girl/grog
byr billion years
BYT bright young things
BYU Brigham Young University (US)
Byz. Byzantine; Byzantium
Bz benzene
BZ B'nai Zion; Brazil; British Zone; Down (UK vehicle registration)
bzw. *beziehungsweise* (German: respectively)

C

c centi-; concentration (chemistry); constant (mathematics); cubic
c specific heat capacity (physics); speed of light in a vacuum (physics)
c. canine (tooth); capacity; cape; *caput* (Latin: chapter); carat; carbon (paper); carton; case; catcher (baseball); cathode; cattle; caught (cricket); cent; centavo (currency); centigram; centime; centimetre; central; centre; century; chairman; chairperson; chairwoman; chapter; charge; chest; child; church; *cibus* (Latin: meal; medicine); *circiter* (Latin: approximately); *circum* (Latin: around); city; class; cloudy; club; cold; collected; colt; compound; conductor; constable; consul; *contra* (Latin: against); contralto; contrast; convection; copy; copyright; corps; coupon; court; cousin; creation; crowned; *cum* (Latin: with; medicine); cup; currency; current (electricity); cycle
c. *circa* (Latin: about)
c/- care of (Australia, New Zealand); case; coupon; currency
C Caesar; Cambrian (geology); carbon (element); Carboniferous (geology); cargo transport (US aircraft); Celsius; centigrade; centre stage (theatre); century; cocaine; cold (water); Command Paper (Parliament); Companion (chivalry); complement (immunology); compliance (physics); *congius* (Latin: gallon; pharmacology); Conservative; copyright; Cork (Irish fishing port registration); corolla (botany); coulomb (physics); crown (paper); Cuba (international vehicle registration); hundred (Roman numerals)
C capacitance (physics); charm quantum number (physics); Euler number (physics); heat capacity (physics); molecular concentration (chemistry)
C. *Caballeros* (Spanish: gentlemen); Caesar; *caldo* (Italian: hot); *caliente* (Spanish: hot); *calle* (Spanish: street); calorie; candle; canon; canto; Cape; Captain; Cardinal; catechism; Catholic; Celtic; Chancellor; Chancery; *chaud* (French: hot); chief; Christ(ian); circuit; *ciudad* (Spanish: town); clubs (cards); Commander; commended; Commodore; Confessor; Congregation(al); Congress; Conservative; contract; Corps; council; Count; counter-tenor; county; coupon;

cross; cruiser; curacy; curate
C2 Nauru (international civil aircraft marking)
C3 Andorra (international civil aircraft marking)
C4 Channel Four (television); crown quarto (paper size)
C5 Gambia (international civil aircraft marking)
C6 Bahamas (international civil aircraft marking)
C8 crown octavo (paper size)
C9 Mozambique (international civil aircraft marking)
ca capital asset (commerce); close annealed (engineering); *coll'arco* (Italian: with the bow; music); *corriente alterna* (Spanish: alternating current; physics); *courant alternatif* (French: alternating current; physics)
ca. carcinoma (medicine); cases (law); centiare
ca. *circa* (Latin: about)
c/a cash account
Ca calcium (element)
Cª *companhia* (Portuguese: company); *compañia* (Spanish: company)
Ca. California; Canada; Canadian
CA Air China (airline flight code); California (zip code); Canadian Army; capital allowances (taxation); Cardigan (UK fishing port registration); Carlisle (UK postcode); Caterers' Association; Catholic Association; cellulose acetate (chemistry); Central America; Certificate of Airworthiness; chargé d'affaires; Chartered Accountant; Chemical Abstracts; Chester (UK vehicle registration); chief accountant; chronological age; Church Army; Church Assembly; citric acid; city architect; civil affairs; civil aviation; Classical Association; clean air; coast artillery; College of Arms; commercial agent; community association; Companies Act; Confederate Army (US); constituent assembly; consular agent; Consumers' Association; controller of accounts; cooperative agreement; *Corps d'Armée* (French: Army Corps); county alderman; county architect; court of appeal; Croquet Association; Crown Agent; Cruising Association; current assets (commerce)
C/A capital account; credit account; current account
CAA Canadian Authors' Association;

Capital Allowances' Act (commerce); Central African Airways Corporation; Civil Aeronautics Administration (US); Civil Aeronautics Administrator (US); Civil Aviation Authority; Clean Air Act; Commonwealth Association of Architects; Community Action Agency (US); Concert Artists' Association; Cost Accountants' Association; county agricultural adviser
CAAA Canadian Association of Advertising Agencies
CAADRP civil aircraft airworthiness data recording program
CAAE Canadian Association of Adult Education
CAAIS computer-assisted action information systems
CAAR compressed-air accumulator rocket
CAARC Commonwealth Advisory Aeronautical Research Council
CAAT College of Applied Arts and Technology (Canada)
CAAtt Civil Air Attaché
CAAV Central Association of Agricultural Valuers
cab. cabalistic; cabin; cabinet; cable
CAB Canadian Association of Broadcasters; cellulose acetate buyrate (chemistry); Citizens' Advice Bureau; Civil Aeronautics Board; Commonwealth Agricultural Bureaux
CABAS City and Borough Architects' Society
CABEI Central American Bank for Economic Integration
CABM Commonwealth of Australia Bureau of Meteorology
CABMA Canadian Association of British Manufacturers and Agencies
CABS coronary artery bypass surgery (medicine)
cabtmkr cabinetmaker
CAC Canadian Armoured Corps; Central Advisory Committee; Central Arbitration Committee; Climate Analysis Center (US); Colonial Advisory Council; *Compagnie des agents de change* (French: stockbrokers' association); Consumer Advisory Council; County Agricultural Committee
CACA Canadian Agricultural Chemicals Association
CAC&W continental aircraft control and warning
CACC Civil Aviation Communications

Centre; Council for the Accreditation of Correspondence Courses
CACD computer-aided defence
CACDS Centre for Advanced Computing and Decision Support
CACE Central Advisory Council for Education
CACGP Commission on Atmospheric Chemistry and Global Pollution
CACM Central Advisory Council for the Ministry; Central American Common Market
CACSD computer-aided control system design
CACUL Canadian Association of College and University Libraries
cad cash against disbursements; cash against documents; contract award date
c-à-d *c'est-à-dire* (French: that is to say)
cad. cadaver (medicine); cadenza (music); cadet; *cadauno* (Italian: each)
Cad. Cádiz
CAD Civil Air Defense (US); *comité d'aide au développement* (French: development assistance committee); computer-aided design; coronary artery disease (medicine); Crown Agent's Department
cadav. cadaver (medicine)
CADC central air-data computer; colour analysis display computer
CADCAM computer-aided design, computer-aided manufacturing
CADD computer-aided drafting and design
CADE computer-assisted data evaluation
CADF Commutated Antenna Direction Finder
CADIN continental air defense integration north (US)
CADIS computer-aided design information system
CADMAT computer-aided design, manufacturing and testing
CADO central air documents office
CADPO communications and data-processing operation
CADS computer-aided design system
CAE Canadian Aviation Electronics; Chartered Automobile Engineer; *cóbrese al entregar* (Spanish: cash on delivery); College of Advanced Education (Australia); computer-aided education; computer-aided engineering
CAEC County Agricultural Executive Committee
CAEM *Conseil d'assistance économique*

mutuelle (Council for Mutual Economic Aid; France)
CAER Conservative Action for Electoral Reform
Caern(s). Caernarvonshire
Caes. Caesar
CAES compressed-air energy storage
caf. cafeteria
CAF cardiac assessment factor (medicine); Central African Federation; charities aid fund; charities aid foundation; clerical, administrative and fiscal; cost and freight (commerce); *coût, assurance, fret* (French: cost, insurance, freight)
CAFE Corporate Average Fuel Economy (cars)
CAFEA-ICC Commission on Asian and Far Eastern Affairs of the International Chamber of Commerce
CAFIC Combined Allied Forces Information Centre
cafm commercial air freight movement
CAFS content-addressable file system
CAFU civil aviation flying unit
CAG Canadian Association of Geographers; carrier air group (US Navy); civil air guard (US); commercial arbitration group; Commercial Artists' Guild; Composers'-Authors' Guild; Concert Artists' Guild
CAGI Compressed Air and Gas Institute (US)
CAGR civil advanced gas-cooled reactor; commercial advanced gas-cooled reactor
CAGS Certificate of Advanced Graduate Study (US)
CAH cyanacetic hydrazide (chemistry)
Cai. Caithness; Caius College (Cambridge)
CAI Canadian Aeronautical Institute; *Club Alpino Italiano* (Italian: Italian Alpine Club); computer-aided instruction; computer-assisted instruction
CAIB Certified Associate of the Institute of Bankers
CAIRC Caribbean Air Command (US)
CAISM Central Association of Irish Schoolmistresses
CAISSE computer-aided information system on solar energy
Caith. Caithness
cal calibre; calorie
cal. *calando* (Italian: calming; music); calendar; calibre
Cal kilocalorie

Cal. Calcutta; Caledonia; Calends; California

CAL computer-aided learning; computer-assisted learning; Continental Airlines; conversational algebraic language (computing); Cornell (University) Aeronautical Laboratory (US)

CALA Civil Aviation (Licensing) Act

CALANS Caribbean and Latin American News Service

calc. calculate; calculated; calculator; calculus

Calc. Calcutta

Calç *Calçada* (Portuguese: street)

cald calculated

CALE Canadian Army Liaison Executive

calg calculating

Calg. Calgary (Canada)

calibr. calibrate; calibration

Calif. California

caln calculation

CALPA Canadian Air Line Pilots' Association

CALS computer-aided (acquisition and) logistics support

Caltech California Institute of Technology

Caltex California Texas Petroleum Corporation

Calv. Calvin; Calvinism

Calz. *Calzada* (Spanish: boulevard)

cam. camber; camouflage

Cam. Cambodia; Cambodian; Cambrian; Cambridge; Cameroon

CAM commercial air movement; communication, advertising and marketing; computer-aided manufacture; computer-assisted manufacture; content-addressable memory (computing)

CAMA Civil Aerospace Medical Association

CAMAL continuous airborne missile-launched and low-level system

Camb. Cambrian; Cambridge

Cambs Cambridgeshire

CAMC Canadian Army Medical Corps

CAMD computer-aided molecular design

CAMDA Car and Motorcycle Drivers' Association

CAMDS chemical agent munitions disposal system (military)

CAMM computer-aided maintenance management; computer-assisted maintenance management

CAMRA Campaign for Real Ale

CAMRIC Campaign for Real Ice Cream

CAMS Certificate of Advanced Musical Study; computer-aided manipulation system (engineering)

CAMW Central Association for Mental Welfare

can. canal; cancel; cannon; canon (music); canto; canton

Can. Canada; Canadian; Canberra; canon (ecclesiastical); canonry (ecclesiastical); *Cantoris* (Latin: place of the cantor)

CAN customs-assigned number

CANA Caribbean News Agency

Canad. Canada; Canadian

canc. cancellation; cancelled

Canc. *Cancellarius* (Latin: Chancellor)

CANCIRCO Cancer International Research Cooperative

cand. candidate

C&A Clemens and Auguste Breeninkmeyer (shopping chain)

c&b caught and bowled (cricket)

c&c carpets and curtains; command and control

c&d collection and delivery

c&e consultation and education

C&E Customs and Excise

c&f cost and freight

C&G City and Guilds

c&i cost and insurance

C&I commerce and industry; commercial and industrial

C&J clean and jerk (weightlifting)

c&m care and maintenance

c&p carriage and packing; collated and perfect (bookbinding)

CANDU Canadian Deuterium Uranium Reactor

C&W country and western (music)

C&W Ck caution and warning (system) check

CANEL Connecticut Advanced Nuclear Engineering Laboratory (US)

Can. Fr. Canadian French

Can. I. Canary Islands

CANO Chief Area Nursing Officer

Can. Pac. Canadian Pacific

CANSG Civil Aviation Navigational Services Group

cant. cantilever

Cant. Canterbury; Canticles (Bible); Cantonese

Cantab. *Cantabrigiensis* (Latin: of Cambridge)

canton. cantonment (military)

CANTRAN cancel in transmission

Cantuar: *Cantuariensis* (Latin: (Archbishop) of Canterbury)

CANUS Canada-United States (military)

canv. canvas

CAO Chief Accountant Officer; Chief Administrative Officer; County Advisory Officer; County Agricultural Officer; Crimean Astrophysical Observatory

CAORB Civil Aviation Operational Research Branch

CAORG Canadian Army Operational Research Group

CAOT Canadian Association of Occupational Therapy

cap *codice di avviamento postale* (Italian: postcode number)

cap. capacity; *capiat* (Latin: let him/her take; medicine); capital; capitalize; capital letter; *capitulum/caput* (Latin: chapter or heading); foolscap

Cap. captain

CAP Canadian Association of Physicists; civil air patrol (US); Code of Advertising Practice; College of American Pathologists; combat air patrol; Common Agricultural Policy (EC); Community Action Program (US); computer-aided planning; computer-aided production

CAPA Canadian Association of Purchasing Agents

CAPAC Composers', Authors' and Publishers' Association of Canada

CAPCOM capsule communicator (NASA)

CAPD continuous ambulant peritoneal dialysis (medicine)

CAPE Clifton Assessment Procedures for the Elderly

Capn Captain

CAPO Canadian Army Post Office; Chief Administrative Pharmaceutical Officer

CAPP computer-aided process planning

Capric. Capricorn

caps. capital letters; capsule

CAPS Center for Analysis of Particle Scattering (US)

capt. caption

Capt. captain

car compounded annual rate (finance)

car. carat

Car. Carlow

CAR Canadian Association of Radiologists; Central African Republic; Civil Air Regulations; cloudtop altitude radiometer (aeronautics); Commonwealth Arbitration Reports (Australia); compound annual rate (finance); compound annual return (finance);

computer-aided retrieval; contents of address register (computing)

CARA combat air rescue aircraft

CARAC Civil Aviation Radio Advisory Committee

carb. carbon; carbonate; carburettor

CARB California Air Resources Board

card. cardinal (mathematics, logic)

Card. Cardinal (Roman Catholic Church)

CARD Campaign Against Racial Discrimination; compact automatic retrieval device; computer-augmented road design

CARDE Canadian Armament Research and Development Establishment

Cards Cardiganshire

CARE Christian Action for Research and Education; communicated authenticity, regard, empathy (psychiatry); computer-aided risk evaluation; continuous aircraft reliability evaluation; Cooperative for American Relief Everywhere; Cottage and Rural Enterprises

CAREC Caribbean Epidemiology Centre

Carib. Caribbean

CARIBANK Caribbean Investment Bank

CARICAD Caribbean Centre for Administration Development

Caricom Caribbean Community and Common Market

Carifta Caribbean Free Trade Area

Carliol: (Bishop) of Carlisle

Carms Carmarthenshire

carn. carnival

Carns Caernarvonshire

carp. carpenter; carpentry

Carp. Carpathian Mountains; Carpentaria (Australia)

carr. carriage

carr. fwd carriage forward (commerce)

CARS Canadian Arthritis and Rheumatism Society

cart. cartage

CART collision avoidance radar trainer

Carth. Carthage

cartog. cartographer; cartography

cas. castle; casual; casualty

CAS Cambridge Antiquarian Society; Centre for Administrative Studies; CERN Accelerator School; Certificate of Advanced Studies (US); Chemical Abstracts Service; Chief of Air Staff; Children's Aid Society; close air support; collision avoidance system (aeronautics); *Connecticutensis Academiae Socius* (Latin: Fellow of the Connecticut Academy of Arts and Sciences); controlled airspace

ca. sa. *capias ad satisfaciendum* (Latin: writ of execution)

CA(SA) Chartered Accountant (South Africa)

CASA Coal Advisory Service Association (US); Contemporary Art Society of Australia

CASAC Clean Air Scientific Advisory Committee (US)

CASE Centre for Advanced Studies in Environment (Architecture Association); Committee on Academic Science and Engineering (US); computer-aided software/system engineering; computer-assisted software/system engineering; Confederation for the Advancement of State Education; Cooperative Awards in Science and Engineering

casevac casualty evacuation (military)

cash. cashier

CASI Canadian Aeronautics and Space Institute

CASIG Careers Advisory Service in Industry for Girls

CASLE Commonwealth Association of Surveying and Land Economy

Caspar Cambridge analog simulator for predicting atomic reactions

Cast. Castile; Castilian

CAST Consolidated African Selection Trust

CASTE Civil Aviation Signals Training Establishment

CASU Cooperative Association of Suez Canal Users

CASW Council for the Advancement of Scientific Writing

cat. catalogue; catamaran; cataplasma (poultice); catapult; catechism (Christianity); category; caterpillar tractor; cattle

Cat. Catalan; Catholic; Catullus (Roman poet)

CAT Centre for Alternative Technology; Children's Apperception Test (psychology); Civil Air Transport; cleanup and treatment; clear-air turbulence (aeronautics); College of Advanced Technology; compressed-air tunnel; computer-aided teaching; computer-assisted teaching; computer-aided testing; computer-assisted testing; computer-aided trading; computer-assisted trading; computer-aided

training; computer-assisted training; computer-aided translation; computer-assisted translation; computer-aided typesetting; computer-assisted typesetting; computer-assisted tomography (medicine); computerized axial tomography (medicine)

Cata Commonwealth Association of Tax Administrators

catachr. catachrestic

Catal. Catalan

CATC Commonwealth Air Transport Commission

CATCC Canadian Association of Textile Colorists and Chemists

cath. cathode

Cath. Cathedral; Catholic; St Catherine's College (Oxford)

CATI computer-assisted telephone interviewing

catk counterattack

CATOR Combined Air Transport Operations Room

CATRA Cutlery and Allied Trades Research Association

CATS credit accumulation transfer scheme (education)

CATscan computerized axial tomography

CATV cable antenna television; community antenna television

caus. causation; causative

cav. cavalier; cavalry; caveat (law)

Cav. *Cavaliere* (Italian: Knight); Cavalry

CAV constant angular velocity (computing); *curia advisari* (Latin: the court wishes to consider it; law)

CAVD Completion, Arithmetic Problems, Vocabulary, following Directions (intelligence test)

CAVI *Centre audio-visuel international* (French: International Audio-Visual Centre)

CAWU Clerical and Administrative Workers' Union

Cay. Cayenne; Cayman Islands

cb cash book; cast brass; centre of buoyancy; circuit breaker; compass bearing; continuous breakdown

c/b caught and bowled (cricket)

Cb columbium; *contre-bass* (French: double bass; music); cumulonimbus (meteorology)

CB Bolivia (international civil aircraft marking); Cambridge (UK postcode); Cape Breton (Canada); carbon black; carte blanche; cavalry brigade; Census

Bureau (US); centre back (theatre); chemical and biological (warfare or weapons); Chief Baron; chloro-bromomethane (used in fire fighting); citizens' band (radio); Coal Board; Common Bench (law); Companion of the Order of the Bath; conduction band (physics); confidential book (Navy); confined to barracks; construction battalion (military); cost benefit; county borough; currency bond; Manchester (UK vehicle registration)

CBA colliding-beam accelerator (physics); Commercial Bank of Australia; Commonwealth Broadcasting Association; Community Broadcasters' Association; cost benefit analysis; Council for British Archaeology

CBAA Canadian Business Aircraft Association

CB&PGNCS circuit breaker and primary guidance navigation control system

CBAT College Board Achievement Test (US)

CBB Campaign for Better Broadcasting

CBC Canadian Broadcasting Corporation; Caribbean Broadcasting Company; Children's Book Council (US); Christian Brothers' College (Australia); combined blood count (medicine); complete blood count (medicine); county borough council

CBCRL Cape Breton Coal Research Laboratory

CBCS Commonwealth Bureau of Census and Statistics (Australia)

cbd cash before delivery

CBD central business district; common bile duct (anatomy)

CBDC Cape Breton Development Corporation

CBE chemical, biological and environmental; Commander of the Order of the British Empire; Council for Basic Education

CBEL Cambridge Bibliography of English Literature

CBEVE Central Bureau for Educational Visits and Exchanges

CBF Central Board of Finance; cerebral blood flow (medicine)

cbi complete background investigation

CBI Cape Breton Island; Central Bureau of Information (US); computer-based information; computer-based

instruction; Confederation of British Industry; Cumulative Book Index (US)

CBIM Companion of the British Institute of Management

CBiol Chartered Biologist

CBIS computer-based information system

CBIV computer-based interactive videodisc

CBJO Coordinating Board of Jewish Organizations

cbk cheque-book

cbl commercial bill of lading

cbl. cable

CBL computer-based learning

CBM Californian Business Machines; confidence building measure; conveyor belt monitor(ing); *kubikmeter* (German: cubic metre)

CBMIS computer-based management information system

CBMM Council of Building Materials Manufacturers

CBMPE Council of British Manufacturers of Petroleum Equipment

CBMS Conference Board of Mathematical Sciences (US)

CBNM Central Bureau for Nuclear Measurements (US)

CBNS Commander British Navy Staff

Cbo Colombo (Sri Lanka)

CBO Conference of Baltic Oceanographers; Congressional Budget Office (US); Counter-Battery Officer

CBOE Chicago Board of Options Exchange

C-bomb cobalt bomb

CBOT Chicago Board of Trade

CBPC Canadian Book Publishers' Council

CBQ civilian bachelor quarters

CBR Center for Brain Research (US); chemical, bacteriological and radiation (warfare or weapons); cloud base recorder (aeronautics); cosmic background radiation (astronomy); crude birth rate

CBRI Central Building Research Institute (India)

CBS Canadian Biochemical Society; *Centraal Bureau voor de Statistiek* (Dutch: Central Statistical Bureau); Church Building Society; close binary system (computing); Columbia Broadcasting System; computerized bone scanning (medicine); Confraternity of the Blessed Sacrament (Roman Catholic Church)

CBSA Clay Bird Shooting Association
CBSI Chartered Building Societies Institute
CBSM conveyor-belt service machine
CBSO City of Birmingham Symphony Orchestra
CBT Chicago Board of Trade; computer-based training
cbu cluster bomb unit; clustered bomb unit; completely built-up (commerce)
CBW chemical and biological warfare
CBX company branch exchange (telecommunications)
CBZ coastal boundary zone
cc carbon copy/copies; cash credit; change course; chronometer correction; close control; colour code; *compte courant* (French: current account); *conto corrente* (Italian: current account); contra credit; *courant continu* (French: direct current); cubic centimetre(s)
cc. centuries; chapters
Cc cirrocumulus (meteorology)
CC Bangor (UK vehicle registration); Caius College (Cambridge); Cape Colony; Caribbean Commission; central committee; chamber of commerce; Charity Commission; chess club; chief clerk; Chile (international civil aircraft marking); circuit court; city council; city councillor; civil commotion; civil court; closed circuit (television); collision course; colour correction (photography); community council; Companion of the Order of Canada; company commander; compensating current (electronics); computer code; concave; confined to camp (military); consular clerk; continuation clause (commerce); *corriente continua* (Spanish: direct current); Countryside Commission; county clerk; county commissioner; county council; county councillor; county court; credit card; cricket club; croquet club; Crown Clerk; cruising club; curate in charge; cycling club
CCA Canadian Construction Association; carrier-controlled approach (US Navy); Chief Clerk of the Admiralty; Circuit Court of Appeals (US); common carotid artery (medicine); Commonwealth Correspondents' Association; Consumers' Cooperative Association (US); continental control area; Council for Colored Affairs (US); County Councils' Association; County Court of Appeals (US); current-cost accounting

CCAB Canadian Circulations Audit Board; Consultative Committee of Accountancy Bodies
CCAFS Cape Canaveral Air Force Station (US)
CCAHC Central Council for Agricultural and Horticultural Cooperation
CCAM Canadian Congress of Applied Mechanics
CCAMLR Commission for the Conservation of Antarctic Marine Living Resources
ccb cubic capacity of bunkers
CCB Civil Cooperation Bureau (South Africa)
CCBI Council of Churches for Great Britain and Ireland
CCBN Central Council for British Naturism
CCBW Committee on Chemical and Biological Warfare
ccc *cwmni cyfyngedig cyhoeddus* (Welsh: public limited company)
CCC Canadian Chamber of Commerce; Central Control Commission; Central Criminal Court (Old Bailey, London); Chemical Control Corporation; Christ's College, Cambridge; Civilian Conservation Corps (US); Club Cricket Conference; Commodity Credit Corporation; *Conseil de coopération culturelle* (French: European Council for Cultural Cooperation); Corpus Christi College (Oxford, Cambridge); Council for the Care of Churches; county cricket club; cross-country club; Customs Cooperation Council
CCCA Cocoa, Chocolate and Confectionery Alliance; Corps Commander, Coast Artillery
CCCC Corpus Christi College, Cambridge
CCCI command, control, communications and intelligence (military)
CCCM Central Committee for Community Medicine
CCCO Committee on Climatic Changes and the Ocean
CCCP *Soyuz Sovietskikh Sotsialisticheskikh Respublik* (Russian: Union of Soviet Socialist Republics)
CCCS Commonwealth and Continental Church Society
CCD Central Council for the Disabled; charged-coupled device (electronics);

Conseil de coopération douanière (French: Customs Cooperation Council)
CCDA Commercial Chemical Development Association
CCE carbon-chloroform extract (chemistry); Chartered Civil Engineer; *Conseil des communes d'Europe* (French: Council of European Municipalities); Council of Construction Employers (US)
ccei composite cost effectiveness index
CCETSW Central Council for Education and Training in Social Work
CCETT *Centre commun d'études de télédiffusion et de télécommunications* (French: National Television and Telecommunications Research Centre)
CCF central computing facility; Combined Cadet Force; Common Cold Foundation; concentrated complete fertilizer; congestive cardiac failure (medicine); Cooperative Commonwealth Federation (Canada)
CCFA Combined Cadet Force Association
CCFM Combined Cadet Forces Medal
CCFP Certificate of the College of Family Physicians
CCG Control Commission for Germany
CCGB Cycling Council of Great Britain
cch commercial clearing house; cubic capacity of holds
CCHE Central Council for Health Education
CChem Chartered Chemist
CCHF Children's Country Holidays Fund
CCHMS Central Committee for Hospital Medical Services
cc hr cubic centimetres per hour
CCI *Chambre de commerce internationale* (French: International Chamber of Commerce); Commission for Climatology
CCIA Commission for the Churches on International Affairs; Consumer Credit Insurance Association (US)
CCIC *Comité consultatif international du coton* (French: International Cotton Advisory Committee)
CCIR Catholic Council for International Relations; *Comité consultatif international des radiocommunications* (French: International Radio Consultative Committee)
CCIS command control information system
CCITT *Comité consultatif international télégraphique et téléphonique* (French:

International Telegraph and Telephone Consultative Committee)
CCJ Circuit Court Judge; Council of Christians and Jews; County Court Judge
CCJO Consultative Council of Jewish Organizations
CCK cholecystokinin-pancreozymin (biochemistry)
CCL Canadian Congress of Labour; commodity control list (US)
C.Cls Court of Claims (US)
ccm cubic centimetre
CCM constant current modulation (physics); controlled carrier modulation (physics)
CCMA Canadian Council of Management Association; Commander, Corps Medium Artillery; Contract Cleaning and Maintenance Association
CCMD Carnegie Committee for Music and Drama (US); continuous-current monitoring device (physics)
CCMS Committee on the Challenge of Modern Society (NATO)
CCN cloud condensation nuclei (meteorology); command control number; contract change notice; contract change notification
CCNDT Canadian Council for Non-Destructive Technology
CCNR Consultative Committee for Nuclear Research (Council of Europe)
CCNSC Cancer Chemotherapy National Service Center
CCNY Carnegie Corporation of New York; City College of the City University of New York
CCO Central Coding Office; current-controlled oscillator (physics)
CCOA County Court Officers' Association
CCOFI California Cooperative Oceanic Fisheries Investigations
ccp credit-card purchase
CCP Chinese Communist Party; Code of Civil Procedure; Committee on Commodity Problems (FAO); Court of Common Pleas; critical compression pressure (nuclear physics)
CCPE Canadian Council of Professional Engineers
CCPF *Comité central de la propriété forestière de la CE* (French: Central Committee on Forest Property for the EC)

CCPIT China Committee for the Promotion of International Trade
CCPL Computer Center Program Library (US)
CCPO *Comité central permanent de l'opium* (French: Permanent Central Opium Board)
CCPR Central Council of Physical Recreation
CCPS Consultative Committee for Postal Studies
CCR camera cassette recorder; Commission of Civil Rights (US); Common Centre of Research
CCRA Commander Corps of Royal Artillery
CCRE Commander Corps of Royal Engineers
CCREME Commander Corps of Royal Electrical and Mechanical Engineers
CCRSigs Commander Corps of Royal Signals
CCRU Common Cold Research Unit
CCS Canadian Cancer Society; Canadian Ceramic Society; casualty clearing station; child-care service; collective call sign; Combined Chiefs of Staff (US); controlled combustion system
CCSA Canadian Committee on Sugar Analysis
CCSATU Coordinating Council of South African Trade Unions
CCSEM computer-controlled scanning electron microscopy
CCSS centrifugally cast stainless steel
CCST Center for Computer Sciences and Technology (US)
CCSU Council of Civil Service Unions
CCT clean coal technology (US); common customs tariff; correct corps time
CCTA Central Computer and Telecommunications Agency; *Commission de coopération technique pour l'Afrique* (French: Commission for Technical Cooperation in Africa); Coordinating Committee of Technical Assistance
CCTS Canaveral Council of Technical Societies (US); Combat Crew Training Squadron
CCTV closed-circuit television
CCU coronary care unit (medicine)
CCUS Chamber of Commerce of the United States
CCV control-configured vehicle (aeronautics)
ccw counterclockwise

CCW Curriculum Council for Wales
cd candela (physics); carried down (book-keeping); cash discount; *ciudad* (Spanish: city); command; cord; could; *cum dividend* (Latin: with dividend; finance)
Cd cadmium (element); Command (military); Command Paper (Parliament); Commissioned (military)
CD Brighton (UK vehicle registration); Canadian Forces Decoration; carrier density (electronics); certificate of deposit; Chancery Division (law); Civil Defence; civil disobedience; closing date; coal dust; College Diploma; Commander of the Order of Distinction (Jamaica); commercial dock; compact disc; Conference on Disarmament (UN); confidential document; Congressional District (US); contagious disease (medicine); core damage (nuclear engineering); *Corps Diplomatique* (French: Diplomatic Corps); countdown; Court of Deliberation (Freemasonry); current density (electronics)
C/D consular declaration; customs declaration
CDA Canadian Dental Association; Christian Democratic Alliance (South Africa); Civil Defence Act; College Diploma in Agriculture; Colonial Dames of America; Conference of Defence Associations (Canada); Copper Development Association
CDAAA Committee to Defend America by Aiding the Allies
Cd Armn Commissioned Airman
CDAS Civil Defence Ambulance Service
CdB Commissioned Boatswain
CDB comprehensive database (computing)
cdbd cardboard
Cd Bndr Commissioned Bandmaster
CDC Canada Development Corporation; Caribbean Defence Command; Center for Disease Control (US); Combat Development Command (US); command and datahandling console (computing); Commissioners of the District of Columbia; Commonwealth Development Corporation; cost determination committee
Cd CO Commissioned Communication Officer
Cd Con Commissioned Constructor
CDD certificate of disability for discharge

(US); charge-density distribution (electronics)

CDE chemical defence ensemble; compact disc erasable

CDEE Chemical Defence Experimental Establishment

C de G Croix de Guerre

CDEM crop disease environment monitor

Cd Eng Commissioned Engineer

CDF central database facility (computing)

CDFC Commonwealth Development Finance Company

cd fwd carried forward (book-keeping)

Cdg. Cardigan(shire)

Cd Gr Commissioned Gunner

CDH College Diploma in Horticulture

CDHS California Department of Health Services

CDI compact disc interactive

CDIC Carbon Dioxide Information Center (US)

Cd In O Commissioned Instructor Officer

CDipAF Certified Diploma in Accounting and Finance

c. div. *cum dividend* (Latin: with dividend; finance)

Cdl Cardinal

CDL Central Dockyard Laboratory (Ministry of Defence); Council of the Duchy of Lancaster; County and Democratic League (Australia)

CDM cold dark matter (astronomy)

Cd MAA Commissioned Master-at-Arms

Cdn Canadian

CDN Canada (international vehicle registration); Chicago Daily News

cDNA complementary DNA (biochemistry)

Cdo Commando

Cd O Commissioned Officer

Cd Obs Commissioned Observer

Cd OE Commissioned Ordnance Engineer

CDOI Colorado Department of Institutions

Cd OO Commissioned Ordnance Officer

CDP Committee of Directors of Polytechnics

CDPE continental daily parcels express

Cdr commander; conductor

CDR Committees for the Defence of the Revolution (Cuba); compact-disc recordable; critical design review; crude death rate

CDRA Committee of Directors of Research Associations

Cd Rad O Commissioned Radio Officer

CDRB Canadian Defence Research Board

CDRC Civil Defence Regional Commissioner

CDRD Carbon Dioxide Research Division (US)

Cdre commodore

CDRF Canadian Dental Research Foundation

CDRH Center for Devices and Radiological Health (US)

CDRI Central Drug Research Institute (India)

CD-ROM compact disc read-only memory (computing)

CDRS Civil Defence Rescue Service

CDS Chief of the Defence Staff; Civil Defence Services

CDSE computer-driver simulation environment

Cd Sh Commissioned Shipwright

Cd SO Commissioned Stores Officer; Commissioned Supply Officer

CDSO Companion of the Distinguished Service Order

Cdt cadet; commandant

CDT Carnegie Dunfermline Trust; Central Daylight Time (US, Canada); craft, design and technology

Cdt Mid cadet midshipman

CDTV Commodore Dynamic Total Vision (computing); compact-disc television

CDU *Christlich-Demokratische Union* (German: Christian Democratic Union)

CDUCE Christian Democratic Union of Central Europe

cdv *carte-de-viste* (French: visiting card)

CDV CD-video; Civil Defence Volunteers; current domestic value

cdw chilled drinking water; cold drinking water

Cd Wdr Commissioned Wardmaster

CDWR California Department of Water Resources

CDWS Civil Defence Wardens' Service

Cdz Cádiz

ce *caveat emptor* (Latin: let the buyer beware); compass error; critical examination

Ce cerium (element)

CE Canada East; carbon equivalent; centre of effort (architecture); Chancellor of the Exchequer; Chemical Engineer; Chief Engineer; Christian Endeavour; Christian Era; Church of England; circular error (computing); Civil Engineer; Coleraine (UK fishing port registration); Common Entrance;

Common Era; *Communauté européenne* (French: European Community); compass error; compression engine; computing efficiency (computing); Corps of Engineers; Council of Europe; counter-espionage; Peterborough (UK vehicle registration)
CEA Canadian Electrical Association; Central Electricity Authority; Cinematograph Exhibitors Association; Combustion Engineering Association; *Comité européen des assurances* (French: European Insurance Committee); commodity exchange authority (commerce); *Confédération européenne de l'agriculture* (French: European Confederation of Agriculture); Conference of Educational Associations; control electronics assembly; Council of Economic Advisers; Council of Educational Advance
CEAA Center for Editions of American Authors (US); Council of European-American Associations
CEAC Citizens Energy Advisory Committee; *Commission européenne de l'aviation civile* (French: European Civil Aviation Commission)
CEB Central Electricity Board
CEBAR chemical, biological, radiological warfare
CEC California Energy Commission; Canadian Electrical Code; Catholic Education Council; Church Education Corporation; Civil Engineering Corps; Clothing Export Council; Commission of the European Communities; Commonwealth Economic Committee; Commonwealth Education Conference; Commonwealth Engineering Conference; Council for Exceptional Children
CECA *Communauté européenne du charbon et de l'acier* (French: European Coal and Steel Community)
CECD *Confédération européenne du commerce de détail* (French: European Confederation of Retail Trades)
CECE Committee for European Construction Equipment
CECG Consumers in the European Community Group
CECLES *Conseil européen pour la construction de lanceurs d'engins spatiaux* (French: European Launching Development Organization)
CECS Church of England Children's

Society; civil engineering computing system; Communications Electronics Coordination Section
CED Committee for Economic Development; computer entry device; Council for Economic Development (US)
CEDA Committee for Economic Development of Australia
CEDI *Centre européen de documentation et d'information* (French: European Documentation and Information Centre)
CEDIC Church Estates Development and Improvement Company
CEDO Centre for Educational Development Overseas
CEDR Centre for Dispute Resolution
CEE Central Engineering Establishment; Certificate of Extended Education; *Commission économique pour l'Europe* (French: Economic Commission for Europe); *Commission internationale de réglementation en vue de l'approbation de l'équipement électrique* (French: International Commission on Rules for the Approval of Electrical Equipment); Common Entrance Examination; *Communauté économique européenne* (French: European Economic Community); Council of Environment Education
CEEA *Communauté européenne de l'énergie atomique* (French: European Atomic Energy Community)
CEEB College Entrance Examination Board (US)
CEEC Council for European Economic Cooperation
CEED Centre for Economic and Environment Development
CEEP *Centre européen d'études de population* (French: European Centre for Population Studies)
CEF Canadian Expeditionary Force; Chinese Expeditionary Force
CEFTRI Central Food Technological Research Institute (India)
CEG *Collège d'enseignement général* (French: College of General Education)
CEGB Central Electricity Generating Board
CEGGS Church of England Girls' Grammar School
CEGS Church of England Grammar School
CEI *Centres d'études industrielles* (French: Centre for Industrial Studies; Switzerland); *Commission électro-*

technique internationale (French: International Electrotechnical Commission); communications-electronics instructions; cost-effectiveness index; Council of Engineering Institutions

CEIF Council of European Industrial Federations

CEIR Corporation for Economic and Industrial Research

cel. celebrate; celebrated; celebration; celery; celesta (music); celibate

Cel(s). Celsius

CEL Constitutional Educational League (US)

CELA Council for Exports to Latin America

CELC Commonwealth Education Liaison Committee

CELEX *Communitatis Europeae Lex* (Latin: European Community Law)

CELJ Conference of Editors of Learned Journals

CELSS controlled ecological life-support system

Celt. Celtic

cem. cement; cemetery

CEM *Companhia Electricidade de Macáu* (Portuguese: Electricity Company of Macau); cost and effectiveness method; crew-escape module (astronautics)

CEMA Canadian Electrical Manufacturers' Association; Catering Equipment Manufacturers' Association; Conveyor Equipment Manufacturers' Association; Council for Economic Mutual Assistance; Council for the Encouragement of Music and the Arts

CEMAC Committee of European Associations of Manufacturers of Active Electronic Components

CEMAP *Commission européenne des méthodes d'analyse des pesticides* (French: Collaborative Pesticides Analytical Committee)

cemf counter-electromotive force (electronics)

CEMLA *Centro de Estudios Monetarios Latino-Americanos* (Spanish: Latin-American Centre for Monetary Studies)

CEMR Council of European Municipalities and Regions

CEMS Church of England Men's Society

cen. central; centre; century

CEN *Comité européen de normalisation* (French: European Standardization Committee)

CEND Civil Engineers for Nuclear Disarmament

CENEL European Electrical Standards Coordinating Committee

CENELEC *Comité européen normalisation électro-technique* (French: European Electrotechnical Standardization Committee)

CEng Chartered Engineer

cens. censor; censored; censorship

cent. centavo (currency); centesimo (currency); centigrade; centime (currency); central; centrifugal; *centum* (Latin: 100); century

CENTAG Central (European) Army Group (NATO)

centig. centigrade

Cento Central Treaty Organization

CEO Chief Education Officer; Chief Executive Officer; Confederation of Employee Organizations

CEOA Central European Operating Agency (NATO)

CEP circular error probability (computing)

CEPCEO *Comité d'études des producteurs de charbon d'Europe occidentale* (French: Western European Coal Producers' Association)

CEPES *Comité européen pour le progrès économique et social* (French: European Committee for Economic and Social Progress)

CEPO Central European Pipeline Office

CEPS Central European Pipeline System; Cornish Engine Preservation Society

CEPT *Conférence européenne des administrations des postes et des télécommunications* (French: European Conference of Postal and Tele-communications Administrations)

CEQ Council on Environmental Quality (US)

CEQA California Environmental Quality Act (US)

cer(am). ceramic

CERC Center for Energy Research Computation (US)

CERCA Commonwealth and Empire Radio for Civil Aviation

CERCLA Comprehensive Environmental Response, Compensation and Liability Act (US)

CERES Coalition for Environmentally Responsible Economies

CERG Conservative European Reform Group

CERI Centre for Educational Research and Innovation (OECD)

CERL Central Electricity Research Laboratories

CERN *Conseil européen pour la recherche nucléaire* (French: European Organization for Nuclear Research/European Laboratory for Particle Physics)

CERP *Centre européen des relations publiques* (French: European Centre of Public Relations)

cert. certain; certainty; certificate; certificated; certification; certified; certify

CERT Charities Effectiveness Review Trust

CertCAM Certificate in Communication, Advertising and Marketing

Cert Ed Certificate in Education

CertHE Certificate in Higher Education

certif. certificate

cert. inv. certified invoice

CertITP Certificate of International Teachers' Program (US)

cerv. cervical (medicine)

CES Center for Energy Studies (US); Christian Evidence Society; *Collège d'enseignement secondaire* (French: College of Secondary Education); community energy system; cost-estimating system

CESAR Center for Engineering Systems Advanced Research (US)

CESE Center for Earth Science and Engineering

CESSAC Church of England Soldiers', Sailors' and Airmen's Clubs

CESSI Church of England Sunday School Institution

CEST Centre for Exploitation of Science and Technology

Cestr: *Cestrensis* (Latin: (Bishop) of Chester)

CET Central European Time; *Collège d'enseignement technique* (French: College of Technical Education); Common External Tariff; Council for Educational Technology

CETA Comprehensive Employment and Training Act (US)

CETEX Committee on Extra-Terrestrial Exploration

CETHV Council for the Education and Training of Health Visitors

CETI communications with extra-terrestrials

CETO Centre for Educational Television Overseas

cet. par. *ceteris paribus* (Latin: other things being equal)

CETS Church of England Temperance Society

CEU Christian Endeavour Union

CEUS Central and Eastern United States

CEUSA Committee for Exports to the United States of America

CEWMS Church of England Working Men's Society

Cey. Ceylon

CEYC Church of England Youth Council

Ceyl. Ceylon

CEZMS Church of England Zenana Missionary Society

cf *cantus firmus* (Latin: fixed song; music); carried forward (book-keeping); center-fielder (baseball); centre-forward (football); *chemin de fer* (French: railway); communication factor; context free; cost and freight; cubic feet

cf. calfskin (bookbinding); *confer* (Latin: compare)

Cf californium (element)

Cf. Confessions (Roman Catholic Church)

CF Canada (international civil aircraft marking); Canadian Forces; Cardiff (UK fishing port registration; postcode); carriage forward (commerce); centre of flotation; Chaplain to the Forces; charcoal-filtered; *Comédie Française* (French theatre); Commonwealth Fund; Comorian franc (monetary unit of Comoros); corresponding fellow; cost and freight; cystic fibrosis (medicine); Faucett Peruvian Airlines (airline flight code); Reading (UK vehicle registration)

CFA Canadian Federation of Agriculture; Canadian Field Artillery; Canadian Forestry Association; Chartered Financial Analyst (US); Commission of Fine Arts; Commonwealth Forestry Association; *Communauté financière africaine* (French: African Financial Community); Consumer Federation of America; Cookery and Food Association; Council for Acupuncture; Council of Foreign Affairs; cross field amplifier

CFAF *Communauté financière africaine franc* (French: African Financial Community franc)

CFAL Current Food Additives Legislation

CFAP Canadian Foundation for the Advancement of Pharmacy
CFAR constant false alarm rate
CFAT Carnegie Foundation for the Advancement of Teaching
CFB Consumer Fraud Bureau (US); Council of Foreign Bondholders
CFBS Canadian Federation of Biological Sciences
CFC carbon-fibre composite; chlorofluorocarbon; Common Fund for Commodities (UN); *Congregatio Fratrum* (Latin: Congregation of Christian Brothers); consolidation freight classification
CFCE *Conseil des fédérations commerciales d'Europe* (French Council of European Commercial Federations)
cfd cubic feet per day
CFD computational fluid dynamics (engineering)
CFDC Canadian Film Development Corporation
CFDT *Confederation française démocratique du travail* (French: French Democratic Federation of Labour)
CFE Central Fighter Establishment; College of Further Education; Conventional Forces in Europe (military)
CFF *Chemins de fer fédéraux Suisses* (French: Swiss National Railway); critical fusion frequency (physics)
CFFLS Consortium for Fossil Fuel Liquefaction Science (US)
cfh cubic feet per hour
CFHT Canada-France-Hawaii Telescope (Hawaii)
cfi cost, freight and insurance
CFI Chief Flying Instructor
CFL Canadian Football League; ceasefire line; Central Film Library
cfm confirm(ation); cubic feet per minute
CFM Cadet Forces Medal; chlorofluoromethane (chemistry); Council of Foreign Ministers
cfo calling for orders; channel for orders; coast for orders (shipping)
CFO Central Forecasting Office (meteorology); Chief Financial Officer; Chief Fire Officer
CFOA Chief Fire Officers' Association
CFOD Catholic Fund for Overseas Development
CFP Common Fisheries Policy (EC); *Communauté financière du Pacifique* (French: Pacific Financial Community);

Compagnie Française des Pétroles (French: French Petroleum Company)
CFPF *Communauté financière du Pacificique franc* (French: Pacific Financial Community franc)
CFPP coal-fired power plant
cfr chauffeur
cfr. *confronta* (Italian: compare)
CFR Code of Federal Regulations (US); Commander of the Order of the Federal Republic of Nigeria; commercial fast reactor (nuclear engineering); Cooperative Fuel Research (Committee) (engineering); Council on Foreign Relations
CFRI Central Fuel Research Institute (US)
CFRP carbon-fibre reinforced plastic
cfs cubic feet per second
CFS Central Flying School; Clergy Friendly Society; common file system (computing)
CFSAN Center for Food Safety and Applied Nutrition (US)
CFSTI Clearinghouse for Federal Scientific and Technical Information (US)
cft craft
CFT *Compagnie française de télévision* (French television company)
CFTB Commonwealth Forestry and Timber Bureau
CFTC Commodity Futures Trading Commission; Commonwealth Fund for Technical Cooperation
cftmn craftsman
CFWI County Federation of Women's Institutes
CFX *Congregatio Fratrum Xaverianorum* (Latin: Congregation of Xaverian Brothers)
cg centigram; centre of gravity
CG Bournemouth (UK vehicle registration); Captain-General; Captain of the Guard; centre of gravity; cloud-to-ground (aeronautics); coastguard; Commanding General (US); Commissary-General; computer graphics; Consul-General; Croix de Guerre
C-G Chaplain-General
CGA cargo's proportion of general average (commerce); Certified General Accountant; Coast Guard Academy (US); Coast Guard Auxiliary (US); colour graphics adapter (computing); Community of the Glorious Ascension; Country Gentlemen's Association

CGBR Central Government Borrowing Requirement
CGC Coast Guard cutter (US); *Confédération générale des cadres* (French: General Confederation of Executive Staff)
CGDK Coalition Government of Democratic Kampuchea
cge carriage; charge
CGE Conservative Group for Europe
cge fwd carriage forward
cge pd carriage paid
CGH Cape of Good Hope
cgi corrugated galvanized iron
CGI Chief Ground Instructor; Chief Gunnery Instructor; City and Guilds Institute; commercial grade item; computer graphics interface
CGIA City and Guilds of London Insignia Award
CGIAR Consultative Group on International Agricultural Research
CGIL *Confederazione Generale Italiana del Lavoro* (Italian: General Italian Confederation of Labour)
CGL corrected geomagnetic latitude
CGLI City and Guilds of London Institute
cgm centigram
CGM computer graphics metafile; Conspicuous Gallantry Medal
CGMW Commission for the Geological Map of the World
cgo cargo; contango (finance)
CGOU Coast Guard Oceanographic Unit (US)
CGP College of General Practitioners
CGPM *Conférence générale des poids et mesures* (French: General Conference of Weights and Measures); *Conseil général des pêches pour la Méditerranée* (French: General Fisheries Council for the Mediterranean)
CGPS Canadian Government Purchasing System
CGRI Central Glass and Ceramic Research Institute (India)
CGRM Commandant-General, Royal Marines
cgs centimetre-gram(me)-second
CGS central gunnery school; Chief of General Staff; Coast and Geodetic Survey; Commissary General of Subsistence (US Army)
CGSB Canadian Government Specifications Board
CGSC Command and General Staff College (US)

CGSS Command and General Staff School (US)
CGSUS Council of Graduate Schools in the United States
CGT capital gains tax; *Compagnie générale transatlantique* (French shipping line); *Confederación general del trabajo* (Spanish: General Federation of Workers); *Confédération générale du travail* (French: General Confederation of Labour)
CGTB Canadian Government Travel Bureau
CGT-FO *Confédération générale du travail-force ouvrière* (French: General Confederation of Labour-Workers' Force)
cgu ceramic glazed units
ch candle hour; central heating; centre-half (sport); clearing house; club house; compass heading; cosh (mathematics); court house; custom(s) house
ch. chain; chaldron (unit of capacity); *chambre* (French: room); chaplain; chapter; charge; chart; chase (horse racing); check (chess); cheese; chemical; chemistry; cheque; chestnut (horse racing); *cheval-vapeur* (French: horsepower); *chevaux* (French: horses); chief; child; children; choir; choke; church
Ch. chairman; chairperson; chairwoman; Chaldean; Chaldee; Chamber; Champion; Chancellor; Chancery; Chapter; Chile(an); China; Chinese; *Chirurgiae* (Latin: of surgery); Christ; Church
CH Captain of the Horse (military); Captain of the Host (Freemasonry); Carnegie Hall; cerebral haemorrhage (medicine); chapter house; Chester (UK fishing port registration; postcode); Christ's Hospital; clearing house; Companion of Honour; *Confédération Helvétique* (international vehicle registration for Switzerland); corporate hospitality; custom(s) house; Nottingham (UK vehicle registration)
C/H central heating
CHA Catholic Hospital Association; Chest and Heart Association; Community Health Association; Country-wide Holidays Association
chacom chain of command
chal. chaldron (unit of capacity); *chaleur* (French: heat); challenge
Chal(d). Chaldaic; Chaldaism; Chaldee; Chaldean
Chamb. Chamberlain; Chambers

chan. chancel; channel
Chan(c). Chancellor; Chancery
CHANCOM Channel Committee (NATO)
chap. chapel; chaplain; chaplaincy; chapter
Chap. chaplain; chapter
Chap-Gen Chaplain-General
CHAPS Clearing House Automatic Payments System
char. character; characteristic; characterize; charity; charter
CHAR Campaign for Homeless People
charact. characterize
charc. charcoal
Chauc. Geoffrey Chaucer
Chb. Cherbourg
ChB *Chirurgiae Baccalaureus* (Latin: Bachelor of Surgery); Chief of the Bureau (US)
CHB Companion of Honour of Barbados
CHC child health clinic; choke coil; Clerk to the House of Commons; Community Health Council; Confederate High Command (US); cyclohexylamine carbonate (chemistry)
ch. cent. *chauffage central* (French: central heating)
Ch. Ch. Christ Church (Oxford)
Ch. Clk Chief Clerk
Ch. Coll. Christ's College (Cambridge)
ChD *Chirurgiae Doctor* (Latin: Doctor of Surgery); Doctor of Chemistry
Ch. D. Chancery Division (law)
CHD congenital heart disease; coronary heart disease
CHDL computer hardware description language
ChE Chemical Engineer; Chief Engineer
CHE Campaign for Homosexual Equality
CHEAR Council on Higher Education in the American Republics
CHEC Commonwealth Human Ecology Council
Cheka *Chrezvychainaya Comissiya* (Russian: Extraordinary Commission; security organization)
CHEL Cambridge History of English Literature
Chelm. Cheltenham
chem. chemical; chemically; chemist; chemistry
ChemE Chemical Engineer
Ches. Cheshire
CHESS Cornell high-energy synchrotron source (US)
chev. chevron
Chev. Chevalier

Chevy Chevrolet (US car make)
chf chief
ChF Chaplain of the Fleet
CHF Carnegie Hero Fund; congestive heart failure (medicine)
ch. fwd charges forward
chg. change; charge (commerce, finance)
chgd charged
chgph choreographer; choreographic; choreography
Ch. hist. Church history
Chi. Chicago; China; Chinese
Chich. Chichester
Chicom Chinese communist
Chin. China; Chinese
CHIPS Clearing House Inter-Bank Payments System
CHIRP Confidential Human Incidence Reporting Programme (civil aviation safety progamme)
Chi. Trib. Chicago Tribune (newspaper)
chiv. chivalry
Ch. J. Chief Justice
chk check
Ch. K. Christ the King
chkd checked
chkr checker
chl. chloride; chloroform
Chl chlorophyll (biochemistry, botany)
Ch. Lbr. Chief Librarian
ChLJ Chaplain of the Order of St Lazarus of Jerusalem
chlo. chloride; chloroform
CHLW commercial high-level waste (nuclear engineering)
chm. chairman; checkmate; choirmaster
ChM *Chirurgiae Magister* (Latin: Master of Surgery)
CHMC Children's Hospital Medical Center (US)
CHMR Center for Hazardous Materials Research (US)
CHNT Community Health Nurse Tutor
cho. choral; chorister; chorus
CHO Crop Husbandry Officer
choc. chocolate
Ch. of S. Chamber of Shipping
Ch. of the F. Chaplain of the Fleet
chor. choral; chorister; chorus
CHP combined heat and power; *Cumhuriyet Halk Partisi* (Turkish: Republican People's Party)
ch. pd charges paid
Ch. ppd charges prepaid
chq. cheque
CHQ Commonwealth Headquarters (Girl Guides); Corps Headquarters (military)

Chr. Christ; Christian; Christianity; Christmas; Chronicles (Bible)
chrm. chairman
chron. chronicle; chronological; chronologically; chronology; chronometry
Chron. Chronicles (Bible)
Chrs Chambers
chs chapters; charges on account (accountancy)
CHS Canadian Hydrographic Service; Church Historical Society
CHSA Chest, Heart and Stroke Association
CHSC Central Health Services Council
ch'ship championship
Ch. Skr Chief Skipper
ChStJ Chaplain of the Order of St John of Jerusalem
cht cylinder-head temperature
chtg charting
chu centigrade heat unit
ch. v. check valve
chw constant hot water
chwdn churchwarden
chyd churchyard
Chy Div. Chancery Division (law)
ci cast iron
Ci cirrus (meteorology); curie (physics)
CI Channel Islands; Chapter of Instruction (Freemasonry); chemical inspectorate; chemical ionization; chief inspector; chief instructor; China Airlines (airline flight code, Taiwan); colour index (astronomy); Commonwealth Institute; Communist International; compression-ignition; configuration interaction; consular invoice; corrosion inhibitor (engineering); Côte d'Ivoire (international vehicle registration); counter-intelligence; (Imperial Order of the) Crown of India; Laois (Irish vehicle registration)
C3I command, control, communications and intelligence (military)
Cia *compagnia* (Italian: company); *companhia* (Portuguese: company); *compañia* (Spanish: company)
CIA cash in advance; Central Intelligence Agency (US); Chemical Industries' Association; Chief Inspector of Armaments; *Conseil international des archives* (French: International Council on Archives); Corporation of Insurance Agents; Culinary Institute of America
CIAA *Centre international d'aviation*

agricole (French: International Agricultural Aviation Centre); Coordinator of Inter-American Affairs
CIAB Coal Industry Advisory Board (US); *Conseil international des agences bénévoles* (French: International Council of Voluntary Agencies)
CIAgrE Companion of the Institution of Agricultural Engineers
CIAI Commerce and Industry Association Institute
CIAL Corresponding Member of the International Institute of Arts and Letters
CIAPG *Confédération internationale des anciens prisonniers de guerre* (French: International Confederation of Former Prisoners of War)
CIArb Chartered Institute of Arbitrators
CIAS Changi International Airport Services; Conference of Independent African States
CIB Central Intelligence Board; Chartered Institute of Bankers; Corporation of Insurance Brokers; Criminal Investigation Branch (New Zealand)
CIBS Chartered Institution of Building Societies
CIBSE Chartered Institution of Building Services Engineers
Cic. Cicero
CIC Capital Issues Committee; Chemical Institute of Canada; Combat Information Center (US); Commander-in-Chief; Command Information Center (US); Commonwealth Information Centre; Counter-Intelligence Corps (US); Critical Issues Council (US)
CICA Canadian Institute of Chartered Accountants
CICADA central instrumentation control and data acquisition
CICAR Cooperative Investigations of the Caribbean and Adjacent Regions
CICB Criminal Injuries Compensation Board
CICC *Conférence internationale des charités catholiques* (French: International Conference of Catholic Charities)
Cicestr: *Cicestrensis* (Latin: (Bishop) of Chichester)
CICG *Centre international du commerce de gros* (French: International Centre for Wholesale Trade)
CICHE Committee for International Cooperation in Higher Education

CICI Confederation of Information Communication Industries

CICP Committee to Investigate Copyright Problems (US)

CICR *Comité international de la Croix-Rouge* (French: International Committee of the Red Cross)

CICRC *Commission internationale contre le régime concentrationnaire* (French: International Commission Against Concentration Camp Practices)

CICRIS Cooperative Industrial and Commercial Reference and Information Service

CICT *Conseil international du cinéma et de la télévision* (French: International Film and Television Council)

CID Committee for Imperial Defence; computer-assisted imaging device; Council of Industrial Design; Criminal Investigation Department

CIDA Canadian International Development Agency; *Comisión interamericano de desarrollo agrícola* (Spanish: Inter-American Committee for Agricultural Development); *Comité intergouvernemental du droit d'auteur* (French: Intergovernmental Copyright Committee)

CIDADEC *Confédération internationale des associations d'experts et de conseils* (French: International Confederation of Associations of Experts and Consultants)

CIDE *Comisión de inversion y desarrollo económico* (Spanish: Commission for Investment and Economic Development; Uruguay)

CIDESA *Centre international de documentation économique et sociale africaine* (French: International Centre for African Social and Economic Documentation)

CIDOC Centre for Intercultural Documentation (Mexico)

Cie *Companie* (French: company)

CIE captain's imperfect entry; *Centre international de l'enfance* (French: International Children's Centre); *Commission internationale de l'éclairage* (French: International Commission on Illumination); Companion of the Order of the Indian Empire; *Confédération internationale des étudiants* (French: International Confederation of Students); *Córas Iompair Éireann* (Irish: Transport Organization of Ireland)

CIEC *Centre international d'études criminologiques* (French: International Centre of Criminological Studies); *Commission internationale de l'état civil* (French: International Commission on Civil Status)

CIEE Companion of the Institution of Electrical Engineers

CIEM *Conseil international pour l'exploration de la mer* (French: International Council for the Exploration of the Sea)

CIEO Catholic International Education Office

CIEPS *Conseil international de l'éducation physique et sportive* (French: International Council of Sport and Physical Education)

cif cost, insurance and freight

CIF Canadian Institute of Forestry; *Clube internacional de futebol* (Portuguese: International Football Club); *Conseil international des femmes* (French: International Council of Women)

cifc cost, insurance, freight and commission (commerce)

cifci cost, insurance, freight, commission and interest (commerce)

cife cost, insurance, freight and exchange (commerce)

CIFE Colleges and Institutes for Further Education; *Conseil des fédérations industrielles d'Europe* (French: Council of European Industrial Federations); *Conseil international du film d'enseignement* (French: International Council for Educational Films)

cifi cost, insurance, freight and interest (commerce)

CIFJ *Centre international du film pour la jeunesse* (French: International Centre of Films for Children)

cifLt cost, insurance and freight, London terms (commerce)

CIG *Comité international de géophysique* (French: International Geophysical Committee)

CIGA *Compagnia Italiana dei Grandi Alberghi* (Italian hotel group)

CIGasE Companion of the Institute of Gas Engineers

CIGR *Commission internationale du génie rural* (French: International Commission of Agricultural Engineering)

CIGS Chief of the Imperial General Staff

CIH Certificate in Industrial Health

CIHA *Comité international d'histoire de l'art* (French: International Committee on the History of Art)

CII Centre for Industrial Innovation; Chartered Insurance Institute; *Conseil international des infirmières* (French: International Council of Nurses)

CIIA Canadian Institute of International Affairs; *Commission internationale des industries agricoles* (French: International Commission for Agricultural Industries)

CIIR Catholic Institute for International Relations

CIJ *Commission internationale de juristes* (French: International Commission of Jurists)

CIL Confederation of Irish Labour

CILB *Commission internationale de lutte biologique contre les ennemis des plantes* (French: International Commission for Biological Control)

CILECT *Central international de liaison des écoles de cinéma et de télévision* (French: International Association of National Film Schools)

CILG Construction Industry Information Liaison Group

CIM Canadian Institute of Mining; China Inland Mission; Commission for Industry and Manpower; computer input on microfilm; computer-integrated manufacturing; *Conférence islamique mondial* (French: World Muslim Conference); *Conseil international de la musique* (French: International Music Council); Cooperative Investment Management

CIMA Chartered Institute of Management Accountants; Construction Industry Manufacturers' Association (US)

CIMarE Companion of the Institute of Marine Engineers

CIMAS continuous iron-making and steel-making

CIME *Comité intergouvernemental pour les migrations européennes* (French: Intergovernmental Committee for European Migration); Council of Industry for Management Education

CIMechE Companion of the Institution of Mechanical Engineers

CIMEMME Companion of the Institution of Mining Electrical and Mining Mechanical Engineers

CIMGTechE Companion of the Institution of Mechanical and General Technician Engineers

CIMM Canadian Institute of Mining and Metallurgy

CIMPM *Comité international de médecine et de pharmacie militaires* (French: International Committee of Military Medicine and Pharmacy)

CIMS chemical information management systems (US)

CIMTP *Congrès international de médecine tropicale et de paludisme* (French: International Congress of Tropical Medicine and Malaria)

CIN *Commission internationale de numismatique* (French: International Numismatic Commission)

C-in-C Commander-in-Chief; curate-in-charge

CINCAFMED Commander-in-Chief Allied Forces Mediterranean

CINCEASTLANT Commander-in-Chief Eastern Atlantic Area

CINCENT Commander-in-Chief Allied Forces Central Europe

CINCEUR Commander-in-Chief Europe

CINCHAN Commander-in-Chief Channel

CINCLANT Commander-in-Chief, Atlantic Fleet (US Navy)

CINCMED Commander-in-Chief British Naval Forces in the Mediterranean

CINCNELM Commander-in-Chief US Naval Forces in Europe, the East Atlantic and the Mediterranean

CINCNORTH Commander-in-Chief Allied Forces Northern Europe

CINCPAC Commander-in-Chief Pacific

CINCPACFLT Commander-in-Chief, Pacific Fleet (US Navy)

CINCSOUTH Commander-in-Chief Allied Forces Southern Europe

CINCWESTLANT Commander-in-Chief Western Atlantic Area

CINFO Chief of Information

Cinn. Cincinnati

CINO Chief Inspector of Naval Ordnance

CINR Central Institute for Nuclear Research (US)

CINS Child in Need of Supervision (US); Children in Need of Supervision (US)

CInstR Companion of the Institute of Refrigeration

CInstRE(Aust) Companion of the Institution of Radio Engineers (Australia)

CIO Church Information Office; *Comité international olympique* (French: International Olympic Committee); *Commission internationale d'optique*

(French: International Commission for Optics); Congress of Industrial Organizations (US)
CIOB Chartered Institute of Building
CIOMS Council for International Organizations of Medical Sciences
CIOS Combined Intelligence Objectives Subcommittee; *Conseil international pour l'organisation scientifique* (French: International Committee of Scientific Management)
CIP Cataloguing-in-Publication; *Centre d'Information de la Presse* (news agency, Belgium); Common Industrial Policy (EC)
CIPA Canadian Industrial Preparedness Association; Chartered Institute of Patent Agents
CIPFA Chartered Institute of Public Finance and Accountancy
CIPL *Comité international permanent de linguistes* (French: Permanent International Committee of Linguists)
CIPM *Commission internationale des poids et mesures* (French: International Committee on Weights and Measures); Companion of the Institute of Personnel Management; Council for International Progress in Management (US)
CIPO *Comité internatonal pour la préservation des oiseaux* (French: International Committee for Bird Preservation)
CIPP *Conseil indo-pacifiques des pêches* (French: Indo-Pacific Fisheries Council)
CIPR *Commission internationale de protection contre les radiations* (French: International Commission on Radiological Protection)
CIPS Central Illinois Public Service (US company); Choice in Personal Safety
CIPSH *Conseil international de la philosophie et des sciences humaines* (French: International Council for Philosophy and the Humanities)
cir. *circa* (Latin: about); circle; circuit; circular; circulation; circumference; circus
CIR Canada India reactor; Commission on Industrial Relations; Council on Industrial Relations; Commissioners of Inland Revenue; cost information report
CIRA Conference of Industrial Research Associations
circ. *circa* (Latin: about); circle; circuit; circular; circulation; circumcision; circumference; circus

CIRCCE *Confédération internationale de la représentation commerciale de la communauté européenne* (French: International Confederation of Commercial Representation in the European Community)
circs. circumstances
circum. circumference
CIRF *Centre international d'information professionelle* (French: International Vocational Training Information and Research Centre); Corn Industries Research Foundation
CIRIA Construction Industry Research and Information Association
CIRIEC *Centre international de recherches et d'information sur l'économie collective* (French: International Centre of Research and Information on Collective Economy)
CIRP *Collège internationale pour recherche et production* (French: International Institution for Production Engineering Research)
CIRRPC Committee on Inter-agency Radiation Research and Policy Coordination (US)
CIRT Community Initiative Research Trust
CIS cataloguing in source; Catholic Information Society (US); Center for International Studies (US); Central Information Service on Occupational Health and Safety (RoSPA); Chartered Institute of Secretaries; Coal Industry Society; Commonwealth of Independent States (Russia and former Soviet republics); Cooperative Insurance Society
CISA Canadian Industrial Safety Association
CISAC Centre for International Security and Arms Control; *Confédération internationale des sociétés d'auteurs et compositeurs* (French: International Confederation of Societies of Authors and Composers)
CISBH *Comité international de standardisation en biologie humaine* (French: International Committee for Standardization in Human Biology)
CISC complex instruction-set computer
CISCO Civil Service Catering Organization
CIS-COBOL compact interactive standard COBOL (computing)
CISF *Confédération internationale des sages-*

femmes (French: International Confederation of Midwives)

CISL *Confédération internationale des syndicats libres* (French: International Confederation of Free Trade Unions); *Confederazione italiana sindacati lavoratori* (Italian: Italian Confederation of Workers' Trade Unions)

CISM *Conseil international du sport militaire* (French: International Military Sports Council)

CISPR *Comité international spécial des perturbations radioélectriques* (French: International Special Committee on Radio Interference)

CISS *Conseil international des sciences sociales* (French: International Social Science Council)

Cist. Cistercian

CISTI Canadian Institute for Scientific and Technological Information

CISV Children's International Summer Village Association

cit compression in transit

cit. citadel; citation; cited; citizen; citrate

CIT California Institute of Technology (US); Carnegie Institute of Technology (US); Central Institute of Technology (New Zealand); Chartered Institute of Transport; *Comité international des transports par chemins de fer* (French: International Railway Transport Committee)

CITB Construction Industry Training Board

CITC Canadian Institute of Timber Construction; Construction Industry Training Centre

CITCE *Comité international de thermodynamique et de cinétique électrochimiques* (French: International Committee of Electrochemical Thermodynamics and Kinetics)

CITEL Committee for Inter-American Telecommunications

CITES Convention on International Trade in Endangered Species

CITI *Confédération internationale des travailleurs intellectuels* (French: International Confederation of Professional and Intellectual Workers)

cito disp. *cito dispensetur* (Latin: let it be dispensed quickly; medicine)

CIU Club and Institute Union

CIUS *Conseil international des unions scientifiques* (French: International Council of Scientific Unions)

CIUSS Catholic International Union for Social Service

civ. civil; civilian; civilization; civilize

CIV City Imperial Volunteers; *Commission internationale du verre* (French: International Glass Commission); *Convention internationale concernant le transport des voyageurs et des bagages par chemin de fer* (French: International Convention Concerning the Carriage of Passengers and Baggage by Rail)

CivE Civil Engineer

CIW Carnegie Institute of Washington (US)

CIWF Compassion in World Farming

CIWO Companion of the Institute of Welfare Officers

cj. conjectural

CJ Chief Justice; Gloucester (UK vehicle registration)

CJA Commonwealth Journalists' Association

CJCC Commonwealth Joint Communications Committee

CJD Creutzfeldt-Jakob disease

CJM *Code de justice militaire* (French: Code of Military Justice); Congregation of Jesus and Mary (Roman Catholic Church); *Congrès juif mondial* (French: World Jewish Congress)

ck cask; check; cook

CK Colchester (UK fishing port registration); Preston (UK vehicle registration)

CKD completely knocked down (commerce)

ckpt cockpit

ckw. clockwise

cl carload; centilitre; centre line; *cum laude* (Latin: with praise); cut lengths

cl. claim; clarinet; class; classical; classics; classification; clause; clearance; clergy(man); clerk; climb; close; closet; closure; cloth (bookbinding); clove; council

c/l cash letter; craft loss

Cl chlorine (element)

CL calendar line; Carlisle (UK fishing port registration); civil law; Civil Lord; Commander of the Order of Leopold (Belgium); common law; Communication Lieutenant; craft loss; critical list; Norwich (UK vehicle registration); Sri Lanka (international vehicle registration)

Cla(ck). Clackmannan

CLA Canadian Library Association;

Canadian Lumbermen's Association;
Copyright Licensing Agency; Country
Landowners' Association

CL(ADO) Contact Lens Diploma of the
Association of Dispensing Opticians

CLAM chemical ramjet low-altitude
missile

CLAPA Cleft Lip and Palate Association

clar. clarendon type (printing); clarinet

Clar. Clarenceaux (King of Arms;
heraldry)

class. classic(al); classification; classified;
classify

CLASS Computer-based Laboratory for
Automated School Systems

clav. clavier (music)

CLB Cape Lookout Bight (North
Carolina); Church Lads' Brigade

CLC Canadian Labour Congress;
Chartered Life Underwriter of Canada;
Commonwealth Liaison Committee

CLCB Committee of London Clearing
Bankers; Committee of London Clearing
Banks

CLCert(BOA) Supplementary Contact
Lens Certificate of the British Optical
Association

CLCert(SMC) Supplementary Contact
Lens Certificate of the Worshipful
Company of Spectacle Makers

CLCr Communication Lieutenant-
Commander

cld called (stock exchange); cancelled;
cleared; coloured; cooled; could

CLD chronic liver disease; Doctor of Civil
Law

CLE Council of Legal Education

CLEA Council of Local Education
Authorities

CLEAPSE Consortium of Local
Education Authorities for the Provision
of Science Equipment

cler. clerical

cl. gt cloth gilt (bookbinding)

CLH *Croix de la Légion d'Honneur* (French:
Cross of the Legion of Honour)

CLIC Cancer and Leukaemia in Children

clim. climate; climatic

CLIMAP Climate: Long-range
Interpretation, Mapping and Prediction

clin. clinic; clinical

CLit(t) Companion of Literature

CLJ Commander of the Order of St
Lazarus of Jerusalem

clk clerk; clock

clkw. clockwise

cl. L. classical Latin

Cllr Councillor

clm column

CLML Current List of Medical Literature

CLNS connectionless network service
(computing)

clo. closet; clothing

CLO chief liaison officer; cod liver oil

CLP concurrent logic programming
(computing); Constituency Labour Party

CLPA Common Law Procedure Acts

clr clear; colour; cooler

CLR Central London Railway; City of
London Rifles; computer-language
recorder; Council on Library Resources
(US)

CLRAE Conference of Local and Regional
Authorities of Europe

clrm classroom

CLRU Cambridge Language Research
Unit

CLS Certificate in Library Science;
Christian Literature Society; Courts of
London Sessions

CLT Canadian Law Times; computer-
language translator

CLTech(ADO) Contact Lens Diploma of
the Association of Dispensing Opticians

CLU Chartered Life Underwriter

CLV constant linear velocity (computing)

clvd clavichord

cm *carat métrique* (French: metric carat);
causa mortis (Latin: by reason of death);
centimetre; common metre (music);
court martial; *cras mane* (Latin:
tomorrow morning; medicine)

Cm curium (element)

CM Canadian Militia; Catholic Mission;
Central Maine (US); central meridian;
centre of mass (physics); certificated
master; certified master; certificate of
merit; Chelmsford (UK postcode);
Chirurgiae Magister (Latin: Master of
Surgery); church mission; church
missionary; circulation manager;
command module (astronautics);
Common Market; common metre
(music); composite material;
configuration management (computing);
Congregation of the Mission (Roman
Catholic Church); COPA (*Compania
Panamena de Aviación*; airline flight code,
Panama); core meltdown (nuclear
physics); corporate membership;
corresponding member; Liverpool (UK
vehicle registration); *Membre de l'Ordre
du Canada* (French: Member of the Order
of Canada)

CMA Cable Makers' Association; Canadian Medical Association; Catering Managers' Association; Certificate of Management Accounting (US); Church Music Association; civil-military affairs; Commonwealth Medical Association; Communication Managers' Association; cost and management accountant (New Zealand); Court of Military Appeals

CMAC Catholic Marriage Advisory Council

CMACP *Conseil mondial pour l'assemblée constituante des peuples* (French: World Council for the People's World Convention)

CMAS Clergy Mutual Assurance Society; *Confédération mondiale des activités subaquatiques* (French: World Underwater Federation)

CMB Central Medical Board; Central Midwives Board; Chase Manhattan Bank; coastal motor boat

CMBHI Craft Member of the British Horological Institute

CMBI Caribbean Marine Biological Institute

cmbt combat

CMC Canadian Marconi Company; Canadian Meteorological Centre; Canadian Music Council; carboxymethyl cellulose (chemistry); Central Manpower Committee; certified management consultant (US); Collective Measures Committee (UN); Commandant of the Marine Corps; Conservation Monitoring Centre

CMChM Master of Surgery

CMCW Calvinistic Methodist Church of Wales

Cmd Command Paper (Parliament)

CMD common metre double (music); conventional munitions disposal (bomb disposal)

cmdg commanding

Cmdr Commander (military)

Cmdre Commodore

Cmdt Commandant

CME Chicago Mercantile Exchange; *Conférence mondiale de l'energie* (French: World Power Conference); cost and manufacturability expert (US)

CMEA Council for Mutual Economic Assistance (Comecon)

CMF Cement Makers' Federation; Central Mediterranean Force; Citizen Military Forces (Australia); coherent memory filter (physics); Commonwealth Military Forces; *Cordis Mariae Filii* (Latin: Missionary Sons of the Immaculate Heart of Mary; Roman Catholic Church)

CMG Commission on Marine Geology; Companion of the Order of St Michael and St George; Computer Management Group

CMH Campaign for the Mentally Handicapped; combined military hospital; Congressional Medal of Honour (US)

CMHA Canadian Mental Health Association

CMHC Central Mortgage and Housing Corporation (Canada)

CMI *Comité maritime international* (French: International Maritime Committee); *Commission mixte internationale pour la protection des lignes de télécommunication et des canalisations* (French: Joint International Committee for the Protection of Telecommunication Lines and Ducts); Commonwealth Mycological Institute; computer-managed instruction

CMIA Coal Mining Institute of America

CMIR Center for Medical Imaging Research (US)

CMJ Church's Ministry among the Jews

cml commercial; current mode logic (computing)

CML Central Music Library

CMLA Chief Martial Law Administrator

CMLJ Commander of Merit of the Order of St Lazarus of Jerusalem

CMM Commander of the Order of Military Merit (Canada)

CMMA Concrete Mixer Manufacturers' Association

CMMC Coal Mining Management College (US)

cmn commission

Cmnd Command Paper (Parliament)

cmnr commissioner

CMO Central Merchandising Office (Zambia); Chief Medical Officer

CMOPE *Confédération mondiale des organisations de la profession enseignante* (French: World Confederation of Organizations of the Teaching Profession)

CMOS complementary metal oxide semiconductor (electronics); complementary metal oxide silicon (electronics)

cmp. compromise

CMP command module pilot

(astronautics); Commissioner of the
Metropolitan Police; cost of maintaining
project
cmpd compound
CMPDI Central Mine Planning and
Design Institute Ltd (US)
cm. pf. cumulative preference shares;
cumulative preferred shares
Cmpn Companion
cmps centimetres per second
CMR Cape Mounted Rifles; central meter
reading; common mode rejection
(electronics)
CMRA Chemical Marketing Research
Association
CMRC Coal Mining Research Company
(US)
CMRO County Milk Regulations
Officer
CMRS Central Mining Research Station
(US)
cms *cras mane sumendus* (Latin: to be
taken tomorrow morning; medicine)
CMS Center for Measurement of Science
(US); central materials supply;
Certificate in Management Studies;
Church Missionary Society
CMSER Commission on Marine Science,
Engineering and Resources (US)
cmsgt chief master sergeant (US)
CM/SM command module service
module (astronautics)
cmt cement
CMZS Corresponding Member of the
Zoological Society
cn *cras nocte* (Latin: tomorrow night;
medicine)
Cn canon (ecclesiastical)
CN Campbeltown (UK fishing port
registration); Canadian National
(Railway); cellulose nitrate (chemistry);
Chinese Nationalists; chloracetophenone
(chemistry); *Code Napoléon* (French:
Napoleonic Code); common network;
Confederate Navy; Morocco
(international civil aircraft marking);
Newcastle upon Tyne (UK vehicle
registration)
C/N circular note; consignment note;
contract note; cover note (insurance);
credit note (commerce)
CNA Canadian Nuclear Association;
Center for Naval Analyses (US Navy);
Central News Agency (Taiwan);
Chemical Notation Association (US);
cosmic noise absorption (astronomy);
Cyprus News Agency

CNAA Council for National Academic
Awards
CNADS Conference of National
Armaments Directors (NATO)
CNAR compound net annual rate
(finance)
CNAS Chief of Naval Air Services
CNC computer numerical control
Cncl Council
Cnclr Councillor
CNCMH Canadian National Committee
for Mental Hygiene
cncr. concurrent
CND Campaign for Nuclear
Disarmament
CNDC China Nuclear Data Centre
CNE *Comisión nacional de energia* (Spanish:
National Energy Commission)
CNEAF coal, nuclear, electric and
alternate fuels
CN(Eng)O Chief Naval Engineering
Officer
CNES *Centre National d'Espace* (French:
National Space Centre)
CNF Challis National Forest;
Commonwealth Nurses' Federation
CNFD Commercial Nuclear Fuel Division
(US)
CNG compressed natural gas;
consolidated natural gas
CNI Chief of Naval Information;
Companion of the Nautical Institute
CNIPA Committee of National Institutes
of Patent Agents
cnl cancel
CNL Canadian National Library;
Commonwealth National Library
(Australia)
CNLA Council of National Library
Associations
CNM Certified Nurse-Midwife (US)
CNN Cable News Network; Certified
Nursery Nurse
CNO Chief Nursing Officer; Chief of
Naval Operations
CNP Chief of Naval Personnel
cnr corner
CNR Canadian National Railway; Civil
Nursing Reserve; *Conseil National de la
Révolution* (French: National
Revolutionary Council; Burkina Faso);
Council of National Representatives
CNRE cooperative networks on rural
energy (US)
CNRS *Centre national de la recherche
scientifique* (French: National Centre for
Scientific Research)

CNS central nervous system (anatomy); Chief of the Naval Staff; China News Service (news agency); Community Nursing Services; Congress of Neurological Surgeons
CNSI Chem-Nuclear Systems, Inc. (US)
CNSLD chronic non-specific lung disease
CNSSO Chief Naval Supply and Secretariat Officer
CNT Canadian National Telegraphs; celestial navigation trainer; Center for Neighborhood Technology (US); *Confederación nacional del trabajo* (Spanish: National Confederation of Labour)
cntn contain
cntr. container; contribute; contribution
cnvt convict
co complains of (medicine)
c/o care of; carried over (book-keeping); cash order; change over
Co cobalt (element); company; county
Co. Coalition; Colorado; Company; County; course (navigation)
CO Air Micronesia (airline flight code, Mariana Islands); Cabinet Office; Caernarvon (UK fishing port registration); Careers Officer; Central Office; Chief Officer; Clerical Officer; Colchester (UK postcode); Colombia (international vehicle registration); Colorado (zip code); combined operations; Commanding Officer; command order; Commissioner of Oaths; Commonwealth Office; *compte ouvert* (French: open account; finance); conscientious objector; Continental Airlines (airline flight code, USA); criminal offence; Crown Office; Exeter (UK vehicle registration)
C/O case oil; cash order; certificate of origin
CO² carbon dioxide gas
COA change of address; College of Aeronautics; condition on admission
coad. coadjudicator
Coal. Coalition
COAS Council of the Organization of American States
cob close of business
COBCCEE *Comité des organisations de la boucherie et charcuterie de la CE* (French: Committee of the Meat Trade Organizations of the EC)
Cobol Common Business Oriented Language (computing)

cobq *cum omnibus bonis quiescat* (Latin: may he/she rest with all good souls)
Cobra Cabinet Office Briefing Room
coc. cocaine
COC Chamber of Commerce; Clerk of the Chapel; combat operations center (US); combined oral contraceptive (medicine); Corps of Commissionaires
COCA consent order and compliance agreement (US)
COCAST Council for Overseas Colleges of Arts, Science and Technology
COCEMA *Comité des constructeurs européens de matériel alimentaire* (French: Committee of European Machinery Manufacturers for the Food Industries)
coch(l). *cochleare* (Latin: spoonful; medicine)
coch. amp. *cochleare amplum* (Latin: heaped spoonful; medicine)
coch. mag. *cochleare magnum* (Latin: tablespoonful; medicine)
coch. med. *cochleare medium* (Latin: dessertspoonful; medicine)
coch. parv. *cochleare parvum* (Latin: teaspoonful; medicine)
COCI Consortium on Chemical Information
COCOM Coordinating Committee for Multinational Export Controls
COCOMO constructive cost model (computing)
cod cargo on deck; cash on delivery; collect on delivery
cod. codicil; codification
Cod. codex
COD cash on delivery; collect on delivery; Chamber of Deputies; chemical oxygen demand; Concise Oxford Dictionary
CODAG combined diesel and gas turbine (engineering)
CODAN carrier-operated device anti-noise (telecommunications)
CODASYL Conference on Data Systems Languages (computing)
CODATA Confederation of Design and Technology Associations
codd. codices
codec coder-decoder (computing)
CODIPHASE coherent digital phased array system (computing)
CODOG combined diesel or gas turbine (engineering)
CODOT Classification of Occupations and Directory of Occupational Titles (Department of Employment)
COE *Conseil oecuménique des églises*

(French: World Council of Churches);
Corps of Engineers (US); cost of
electricity; cost of energy
co-ed co-educational
COED computer operated electronic
display; Concise Oxford English
Dictionary
coeff. coefficient
CoEnCo Committee for Environmental
Conservation
COESA Committee on Extension to the
Standard Atmosphere (US)
COF *Comité olympique française* (French:
French Olympic Committee)
C of A Certificate of Airworthiness;
College of Arms
C of B confirmation of balance
C of C Chamber of Commerce
C of E Church of England; Council of
Europe
C of ECS Church of England Children's
Society
C of F Chaplain of the Fleet; chief of
finance; coefficient of friction
(mechanical engineering)
c of g centre of gravity
C of GH Cape of Good Hope
C of I Church of Ireland
COFI Committee on Fisheries (FAO)
C of L City of London
C of M Certificate of Maintenance
(aeronautics)
C of S Chief of Staff; Church of Scotland;
conditions of service
cog. cognate; cognisant; cognomen
CoG centre of gravity
COG Cleansing Officers' Guild
COGAG combined gas and gas turbine
(engineering)
COGB certified official government
business
COGECA *Comité général de la coopération
agricole des pays de la CE* (French: General
Committee for Agricultural Cooperation
in the EC Countries)
COGLA Canada Oil and Gas Lands
Administration
COGS continuous orbital guidance
system (astronautics)
coh cash on hand
coh. coheir
COHO coherent oscillator (physics)
COHSE Confederation of Health Service
Employees
COI Central Office of Information;
certificate of origin and interest;
Commission océanographique inter-

gouvernementale (French:
Intergovernmental Oceanographic
Commission); cost of illness
COIC Canadian Oceanographic
Identification Centre; Careers and
Occupational Information Centre
CoID Council of Industrial Design
COIN counter-insurgency (US)
COINS Committee on Improvement of
National Statistics (US)
COJO Conference of Jewish
Organizations
col. collect; collected; collection; collector;
college; collegiate; colon; colonial;
colony; colour; coloured; column
Col. Colombia; Colombian; Colonel;
Colorado; Colossians (Bible)
COL computer-oriented language; cost of
living
COLA cost of living adjustment (US
employment contracts)
Col. Comdt colonel commandant
coll. collateral; colleague; collect;
collected; collection; collector; college;
collegiate; colloquial; colloquialism;
collyrium (eyewash)
collab. collaborate; collaboration;
collaborator
collat. collateral; collaterally
collect. collective; collectively
Coll. of FE College of Further Education
colloq. colloquial; colloquially;
colloquialism
coll'ott *coll'ottava* (Italian: in octaves;
music)
collr collector
colly colliery
Colo. Colorado
colog. cologarithm
Coloss. Colossians (Bible)
Col. P. colour page (advertising)
Colprensa (news agency, Colombia)
cols columns
COLS communications for online
systems (computing)
Col-Sgt Colour-Sergeant
com. comedy; comic; comma;
commentary; commerce; commercial;
commission; commissioner; committee;
common; commonly; commoner; commune; communicate; communicated;
communication; community
Com. Commander; Commissary;
Commissioner; Committee;
Commodore; Commonwealth;
Communist
COM computerized operations

management; computer output on microfilm; computer output on microfiche

COMA Committee on Medical Aspects of Food Policy

COMACA Corresponding Member of the Academy of Arts (Russia)

COMAF *Comité des constructeurs de matériel frigorifique de la CE* (French: Committee of Refrigerating Plant Manufacturers of the EC)

COMAIRCHAN Maritime Air Commander Channel

COMAIREASTLANT Air Commander Eastern Atlantic Area

COMAIRLANT Commander Air Force, Atlantic (US)

COMAL common algorithmic language (computing)

COMAR Code of Maryland Air Regulations (US)

COMARE Committee on Medical Aspects of Radiation in the Environment (US)

COMART Commander, Marine Air Reserve Training

comb. combination; combine; combined; combining; combustible; combustion

combine combined harvester

combu. combustion

COMCRULANT Commander Cruisers, Atlantic (US)

comd command; commanding

Comd. commander

COMDEV Commonwealth Development Finance Company

Comdg commanding (military)

Comdr commander (military)

Comdt commandant (military)

COME Chief Ordnance Mechanical Engineer

COMECON Council for Mutual Economic Aid; Council for Mutual Economic Assistance

Comet Committee for Middle East Trade; computer-operated management evaluation technique

COMEX Commodity Exchange (US)

COMEXO Committee for Exploitation of the Oceans

Com-Gen Commissary-General

COMIBOL *Corporación Minera de Bolivia* (Spanish: Bolivian State Mining Company)

Cominform Communist Information Bureau

COMINT communications intelligence

Comintern Communist International

COMISCO Committee of International Socialist Conference

coml commercial

COMLOGNET combat logistics network (US Air Force)

comm. commentary; commerce; commercial; commercially; committee; commonwealth; communication

Comm. commander; commodore

Commd commissioned (military)

commem. commemoration; commemorative

Commiss. commissary

Commissr commissioner

Commn commission

Commnd commissioned (military)

Commr commissioner

commun. communication; community

Commy commissary; communist

COMNAVNORTH Commander Allied Naval Forces Northern Europe

COMO Committee of Marketing Organizations

comp. companion; comparative; compare; comparison; compass; compensation; compete; competition; competitive; competitor; compilation; compiled; compiler; complete; compose; composer; composite; composition; compositor; compound; compounder; comprehensive; compression; comprising

Comp Companion

COMPAC Commonwealth Trans-Pacific Telephone Cable

compar. comparative; comparison

compd compound

Comp-Gen comptroller-general

compl. complement; complete; compliment; complimentary

complt complainant; complaint

compo. composition

compr. compressive

compt compartment

Compt(r). comptroller

Comr commissioner

Com. Rom. Common Romance (language)

comsat communications satellite

ComSec Commonwealth Secretariat

COMSER Commission on Marine Science and Engineering Research (UN)

COMSUBEASTLANT Commander Submarine Force Eastern Atlantic

Com. Teut. Common Teutonic (language)

Com. Ver. Common Version (Bible)

Com W. Ger. Common West Germanic (language)
Comy-Gen Commissary-General
con. concentration; concerning; concerto; conclusion; confidence; conics; *conjunx* (Latin: wife); connection; consolidate; consolidated; consols; continue(d); *contra* (Latin: against); convenience; conversation
Con. Conformist; Conservative; consols (finance); constructor (military); consul; contralto (music)
CONAC Continental Air Command (US Air Force)
CONAD Continental Air Defense Command (US)
CONARC Continental Army Command (US)
conbd contributed
conc. concentrate; concentrated; concentration; concerning; concerto
Con. C constructor captain
concd concentrated
concg concentrating
conch. conchology
concn concentration
concr. concrete
con. cr. contra credit (book-keeping)
Con. Cr constructor commander
cond. condense; condenser; condition; conditional; conduct; conducted; conductivity; conductor
condr conductor
con esp(r). *con espressione* (Italian: with expression; music)
conf. confection (medicine); confectionery; *confer* (Latin: compare); conference; confessor
confab. confabulation
confed. confederated; confederation
Confed. Confederacy; Confederate; Confederation
Conf. Pont. *Confessor Pontifex* (Latin: Confessor and Bishop)
cong. *congius* (Latin: gallon; pharmacology); congregation(ist)
Cong. Congregational(ist); Congress; Congressional
Cong. R(ec). Congressional Records (US)
CONGU Council of National Golf Unions
CONI *Comitato olimpico nazionale italiano* (Italian: Italian National Olympic Committee)
con. inv. consular invoice
conj. conjugation; conjunction; conjunctive
Con. L constructor lieutenant

Con. LCr constructor lieutenant-commander
conn. connect; connected; connection; connotation
Conn. Connecticut
conq. conquer; conqueror
cons. consecrate; consecrated; consecration; consecutive; consequence; conservation; conservative; conserve (medicine); consigned; consignment; consolidated; consonant; constable; constitution; constitutional; construction; consul; consult; consulting
Cons. Conservative; conservatoire; conservatorium; conservatory; constable; constitution; consul
CONS connection-oriented network service (computing)
con. sec. conic section
Conserv. conservatoire; conservatorium; conservatory
cons. et prud. *consilio et prudentia* (Latin: by counsel and prudence)
consgt consignment
consid. consideration
Con. SL constructor-sub-lieutenant
consols consolidated annuities (government securities); consolidated stock (government securities)
const. constable; constant; constituency; constitution; constitutional; construction
constl constitutional
constr. construct; construction; construe
cont. container; containing; contents; continent; continental; continue; continued; continuo (music); continuum; *contra* (Latin: against); contract; contraction; control; controller
contag. contagious
contbd contraband
contbg contributing
cont. bon. mor. *contra bonos mores* (Latin: contrary to good manners)
contd contained; continued
contemp. contemporary
contg containing
contn continuation
contr. contract; contracted; contraction; contralto; contrary; contrast; contrasted; control; controller
contrail condensation trail (aircraft)
contr. bon mor. *contra bonos mores* (Latin: contrary to good manners)
cont. rem. *continuantur remedia* (Latin: let the medicines be continued; medicine)
contrib. contributed; contributing; contribution; contributor

CONUS continental United States
conv. convenient; convent; convention; conventional; conversation; converter; convertible
Conv. Convocation
convce conveyance
COOC contact with oil or other cargo (insurance)
co-op cooperative
Co-Op Cooperative Building Society; Cooperative Building Union
COORS communications outage restoral section
cop. copper; copulative; copyright; copyrighted
Cop. Copernican; Coptic
COP Certificate of Proficiency (New Zealand universities); coefficient of performance (thermodynamics); community-oriented policing (US); custom of port
COPA *Comité des organisations professionelles agricoles de la CE* (French: Committee of Agricultural Organizations in the EC)
COPAL Cocoa Producers' Alliance
Copec Conference on Christian Politics, Economics and Citizenship
COPPSO Conference of Professional and Public Service Organizations
copr. copyright
COPS Council of Polytechnic Secretaries
Copt. Coptic
coptr copartner
COPUS Committee on the Public Understanding of Science
coq. *coque* (Latin: boil)
cor. corner; cornet; coroner; *corpus* (Latin: the body); correct; corrected; correction; correlative; correspondence; correspondent; corresponding; corrupt
Cor. Corinthians (Bible)
Corat Christian Organizations Research and Advisory Trust
cord. corduroy
CORE Congress of Racial Equality (US)
CORES Computer-Assisted Order Routing and Execution System (Japanese commerce)
CORGI Confederation for Registration of Gas Installers
Cor. Mem. Corresponding Member
Corn. Cornish; Cornwall
Cornh. Cornhill Magazine
corol(l). corollary
Corp. Corporal; Corporation; Corpus Christi College (Oxford)

Corpl Corporal
Corpn Corporation
corr. correct; corrected; correction; corrective; correlative; *corrente* (Italian: current); correspond; correspondence; correspondent; corresponding; corrigenda; corrugated; corrupt; corrupted; corruption
CORRA Combined Overseas Rehabilitation Relief Appeal
correl. correlative
corresp. correspondence; corresponding
Corresp. Mem. corresponding member
corrupt. corruption
Cors. Corsica; Corsican
CORS Chief of the Regulating Staff
Cor. Sec. corresponding secretary
CORSO Council of Organizations for Relief Services Overseas
cort. cortex
cos cash on shipment (commerce); cosine (mathematics)
Cos. companies; counties
COS cash on shipment (commerce); Chamber of Shipping; Charity Organization Society; chief of staff
co. sa *come sopra* (Italian: as above)
COSA Colliery Officials and Staffs Association
COSAG combined steam turbine and gas turbine (shipping)
COSAR compression scanning array radar
COSATI Committee on Scientific and Technical Information
COSATU Congress of South African Trade Unions
COSBA Computer Services and Bureaux Association
cosec cosecant (mathematics)
COSEC Coordinating Secretariat of the National Union of Students
cosech hyperbolic cosecant (mathematics)
COSFPS Commons, Open Spaces, Footpaths Preservation Society
cosh hyperbolic cosine (mathematics)
COSHH Control of Substances Hazardous to Health
CoSIRA Council for Small Industries in Rural Areas
COSLA Convention of Scottish Local Authorities
COSMD Combined Operations Signals Maintenance Division
cosmog. cosmogony; cosmographical; cosmography

COSMOS Coast Survey Marine Observation System
co. so. *come sopra* (Italian: as above)
COSPAR Committee on Space Research
Coss. *Consules* (Latin: Consuls)
COSSAC Chief of Staff to Supreme Allied Commander
COST Committee for Overseas Science and Technology (Royal Society)
cot cotangent (mathematics)
CoT college of technology
COT change of temperature (physics)
cotan cotangent (mathematics)
COTC Canadian Officers' Training Corps
COTE Committee for the Accreditation of Teacher Education
coth hyperbolic cotangent (mathematics)
COTR contracting officers' technical representative
COTT Central Organization for Technical Training (South Africa)
couch. couchant (heraldry)
Coun. council; councillor; counsellor
cour. *courant* (French: currently or this month)
cov. covenant
Cov. Coventry
COV coefficient of variation (statistics); concentrated oil of vitriol (chemistry); covariance (statistics); crossover value (genetics)
covers coversed sine (mathematics)
cov. pt cover point (cricket)
COWAR Committee on Water Research
COWPS Council on Wages and Price Stability
Cox. Coxswain
Coy company (military)
coz. cousin
COZI communications zone indicator
cp candlepower; carriage paid; centre of pressure (aeronautics); condensation product; constant pressure
cp. compare
Cp. compline (Roman Catholic Church)
CP Bolivia (international civil aircraft marking); Canadian Airlines International (airline flight code); Canadian Pacific (Railway); Canadian Press (news agency); Cape Province (South Africa); Captain of the Parish (Isle of Man); cardinal point (navigation); *casella postale* (Italian: post office box); central processor (computing); centrifugal pump; cerebral palsy (medicine); change point (surveying); charge-parity (physics);

charter party; chemically pure; chief of police; Chief Patriarch; civil power; civil procedure; Clarendon Press; clerk of the peace; code of procedure; *Codice Penale* (Italian: Penal Code); College of Preceptors; colour printing; command post (military); commercial paper; common pleas; Common Prayer; Communist Party; community physician; community programme; *Companhia dos Caminhos de Ferro Portugueses* (Portuguese railway company); concert party; conference paper; conference proceedings; *Congregatio Passionis* (Latin: Congregation of the Passion); Congress Party (India); convict prison; corporal punishment; Country Party (Australia); court of probate; current paper; Huddersfield (UK vehicle registration)
C/P charter party
CPA Canadian Pacific Airlines; Canadian Pharmaceutical Association; Canadian Psychological Association; central planning area; Certified Public Accountant (US); Chartered Patent Agent; Chick Producers' Association; claims payable abroad (insurance); Clyde Port Authority; Commonwealth Parliamentary Association; Communist Party of Australia; Construction Plant Association; Contractors' Plant Association; contract price adjustment; cost planning and appraisal; Council of Provincial Associations; critical path analysis (computing)
CPAC Collaborative Pesticides Analytical Committee; Consumer Protection Advisory Committee
CPAG Child Poverty Action Group; Collision Prevention Advisory Group (US)
CPAI Canvas Products Association International
C. Pal. Crystal Palace
CPAM Committee of Purchasers of Aircraft Material
CPAS Catholic Prisoners' Aid Society; Church Pastoral Aid Society
CPB casual payments book (bookkeeping); Central Planning Bureau; Communist Party of Britain
CPC City Planning Commission (US); City Police Commissioner; Clerk of the Privy Council; Communist Party of China; Conservative Political Centre

CPCIZ *Comité permanent des congrès internationaux de zoologie* (French: Permanent Committee of International Zoological Congresses)

CPCU Chartered Property and Casualty Underwriter (US)

cpd charterers pay dues (commerce); compound

CPD continuing professional development

CPDL Canadian Patents and Developments Limited

CPDM Centre for Physical Distribution Management

CPE Certificate of Physical Education; Certified Property Exchanger (US); College of Physical Education; *Congrès du peuple européen* (French: Congress of European People); contractor performance evaluation

CPEA Catholic Parents' and Electors' Association; Cooperative Program for Educational Administration (US)

c. pén. *code pénal* (French: penal code)

CPEQ Corporation of Professional Engineers of Quebec

CPF contributory pension fund

CPFF cost plus fixed fee

CPFS Council for the Promotion of Field Studies

CPGB Communist Party of Great Britain

cph cycles per hour

CPH Certificate in Public Health

CPHA Canadian Public Health Association

CPhys Chartered Physicist

cpi characters per inch (printing)

CPI chief pilot instructor; Communist Party of India; consumer price index

CPJI *Cour permanente de justice internationale* (French: Permanent Court of International Justice)

Cpl corporal (military)

CPL central public library; Colonial Products Laboratory; Commercial Pilot's Licence

cpm cycles per minute

CPM Certified Property Manager (US); Colonial Police Medal; common particular metre (music); computer program module; critical path method (computing)

CP/M control program monitor (computing, trademark)

CPMEE&W Council for Postgraduate Medical Education in England and Wales

cpn coupon

Cpn Copenhagen

CPN *Communistische Partij van Nederland* (Dutch: Netherlands Communist Party); Community Psychiatric Nurse

CPNA Council of Photographic News Agencies

Cpnhgn Copenhagen

CPNZ Communist Party of New Zealand

CPO cancel previous order; Chief Petty Officer; command pay office; Commonwealth Producers' Organization; compulsory purchase order; County Planning Officer

cpp controllable pitch propeller

CPP chemical processing plant; Convention People's Party (Ghana); critical path planning (computing); current purchasing power

CPPA Canadian Pulp and Paper Association

CPPCC Chinese People's Political Consultative Conference

CPPS critical path planning and scheduling (computing)

cpr copper

CPR Canadian Pacific Railway; cardio-pulmonary resuscitation (medicine)

CPRC Central Price Regulation Committee

CPRE Council for the Protection of Rural England

CPRS Central Policy Review Staff

CPRW Council for the Protection of Rural Wales

cps characters per second (computing); cycles per second (physics)

CPS Centre for Policy Studies; cents per share; Certified Professional Secretary (US); Church Patronage Society; Clerk of Petty Sessions; Commonwealth Public Service; Congregational Publishing Society; Crown Prosecution Service; *Custos Privati Sigilli* (Latin: Keeper of the Privy Seal)

CPSA Civil and Public Services Association; Clay Pigeon Shooting Association

CPSC Consumer Product Safety Commission (US)

CPSS Certificate in Public Service Studies

CPSU Communist Party of the Soviet Union

CPsychol Chartered Psychologist

cpt cockpit; counterpoint

Cpt. captain

CPT Canadian Pacific Telegraphs; charge-parity-time (physics); cost per thousand; critical path technique (computing)
CPTB Clay Products Technical Bureau
CPU central packaging unit; central processing unit (computing); collective protection unit; Commonwealth Press Union
CPUSA Communist Party of the United States of America
CPVE Certificate of Pre-vocational Education
CPWC Central People's Workers' Council (Burma)
CQ call to quarters (radio code); charge of quarters (military); conditionally qualified
CQM chief quartermaster; company quartermaster
CQMS company quartermaster-sergeant
CQR Church Quarterly Review
CQS Court of Quarter Sessions
CQSW Certificate of Qualification in Social Work
cr *con riserva* (Italian: with reservations); cum rights (finance)
cr. created; creation; credit; creditor; creek; crescendo (music); crew; crimson; crown; cruise; *crux* (Latin: cross)
c/r company's risk
Cr chromium (element); commander; councillor; cruiser
CR *Carolina Regina* (Latin: Queen Caroline); *Carolus Rex* (Latin: King Charles); carriage return; carrier's risk; cash receipts; central railway; central registry; Chief Ranger; *Civis Romanus* (Latin: Roman citizen); Commendation Ribbon (US); Community of the Resurrection (Anglican Church); company's risk; compression ratio (engineering); conditioned reflex (psychology); conditioned response (psychology); conference report; Congo red (dye); consciousness raising; control relay; cosmic rays; Costa Rica; Costa Rica (international vehicle registration); crease-resistant; credit rating; credit report; Croydon (UK postcode); current rate; *Custos Rotulorum* (Latin: Keeper of the Rolls); Portsmouth (UK vehicle registration)
CRA California Redwood Association; Canadian Rheumatism Association; Civil Rights Association (Northern Ireland); Coal Research Association of

New Zealand; Commander of the Royal Artillery; Commercial Rabbit Association; composite research aircraft; corrosion-resistant alloy
CrAA commander-at-arms
CRAC Careers Research and Advisory Centre; Central Religious Advisory Committee; Construction Research Advisory Council
CRAD Committee for Research into Apparatus for the Disabled
CRAeS Companion of the Royal Aeronautical Society
CRAF Civil Reserve Air Fleet (US)
CRAMRA Convention on the Regulation of Antarctic Mineral Resource Activities
cran(iol). craniology
craniom. craniometry
CRASC Commander of the Royal Army Service Corps
CRB central radio bureau
CRC camera-ready copy (printing); Cancer Research Campaign; child-resistant closure; Civil Rights Commission; coal rank code; community relations council; Coordinating Research Council (US); cycle racing club; cyclic redundancy check (computing); cyclic redundancy code (computing)
CRCC Canadian Red Cross Committee
CRCH central register and clearing house
CRCP Certificant of the Royal College of Physicians
CRCS Certificant of the Royal College of Surgeons
CRD chronic respiratory disease; Crop Research Division
CRDEC Chemical Research, Development and Engineering Center (US)
CRDF cathode-ray direction-finding
CRE Coal Research Establishment (US); Commander of the Royal Engineers; Commercial Relations and Exports; Commission for Racial Equality
CREFAL *Centro Regional de Educación Fundamental para la América Latina* (Spanish: Regional Centre of Fundamental Education for Latin America; UNESCO)
cres(c). crescendo (music)
Cres. Crescent
CRF capital recovery factor (finance); chronic renal failure (medicine)
crg. carriage
CRI Caribbean Research Institute; *Croce Rossa Italiana* (Italian: Italian Red Cross)

CRIB Current Research in Britain
CRIC Canons Regular of the Immaculate Conception (Roman Catholic Church)
crim. criminal
crim. con. criminal conversation (law)
criminol. criminology
Crimp. Crimplene (textiles, trademark)
CRIS clinical radiology imaging system (medicine); command retrieval information system (computing); current research information system
crit. criterion; critic; critical; critically; criticism
Crk Cork (Ireland)
CRL Canons Regular of the Lateran (Roman Catholic Church); Certified Record Librarian; Certified Reference Librarian; Chemical Research Laboratory
CRM Central Rocky Mountains; certified reference material; counter-radar missile; count-rate meter; cruise missile
CRMA Cotton and Rayon Merchants' Association
CRMF Cancer Relief Macmillan Fund
CRMP Corps of Royal Military Police
crn crown
crn. crane
CRNA Clinical Research Nurses' Association
CRNCM Companion of the Royal Northern College of Music
CRNSS Chief of the Royal Naval Scientific Service
CRO cathode-ray oscilloscope; cathode-ray oscillograph; chief recruiting officer; Commonwealth Relations Office; community relations officer; compulsory rights order; Criminal Records Office
Croat. Croatia; Croatian
CRP *Calendarium Rotulorum Patentium* (Latin: Calendar of the Patent Rolls); Canons Regular of Prémontré (Roman Catholic Church); Central Reserve Police (India); coordinated research programme
CRPL Central Radio Propagation Laboratory (US)
CRPPH Committee on Radiation Protection and Public Health (US)
CRR Curia Regis Roll
CRS Catholic Record Society; cold-rolled steel; Cooperative Retail Society; cosmic radio source
CRSA Cold Rolled Sections Association; Concrete Reinforcement Steel Association

CRSI Concrete Reinforcing Steel Institute (US)
Crt Court
CRT cathode-ray tube; combat readiness training; composite rate tax
CRTC Canadian Radio-Television Commission
crtkr caretaker
CRTS Commonwealth Reconstruction Training Scheme
CRU civil resettlement unit; control register user (computing)
CRUDESPAC Cruiser-Destroyer Forces, Pacific (US Navy)
CRULANT Cruiser Forces, Atlantic (US Navy)
crypto. cryptographic; cryptography
cryst. crystal; crystalline; crystallography
crystd crystallized
crystn crystallation
CRZZ *Centralna Rada Zwiazkow Zawadowych* (Polish: Central Council of Trade Unions)
cs capital stock; census; *come sopra* (Italian: as above)
cs. case; consul
c/s cases; cycles per second
Cs caesium/cesium (element); cirrostratus (meteorology)
CS calcium silicate (chemistry); capital stock; carbon steel; cast steel; Certificate in Statistics; Chartered Surveyor; Chemical Society; Chief of Staff; Chief Secretary; Christian Science; Christian Scientist; city surveyor; civil servant; Civil Service; Clerk of Session; Clerk to the Signet; close shot; close support; College of Science; colliery screened; Common Sergeant; Confederate States (US); Congregation of Salesians (Roman Catholic Church); coolant system (physics); Cooperative Society; county surveyor; court of session; Cowes (UK fishing port registration); credit sales; cruiser squadron; *Custos Sigilli* (Latin: keeper of the seal); Czech and Slovak Republics (international vehicle registration); Glasgow (UK vehicle registration); Portugal (international civil aircraft marking)
C/S channel shank (buttons); cycles per second
CSA Canadian Standards Association; Casualty Surgeons' Association; Child Support Agency; Common Services Agency; Community Services Administration (US); Computer Science

Association (Canada); Confederate States Army; Confederate States of America

CSAA Child Study Association of America

CSAE Canadian Society of Agricultural Engineering

CSAP Canadian Society of Animal Production

CSAR Communication Satellite Advanced Research

CSB Bachelor of Christian Science; calcium silicate brick (engineering); Central Statistical Board; chemical stimulation of the brain (medicine)

CSBGM Committee of Scottish Bank General Managers

CSBM Confidence- and Security-Building Measures (military)

csc cosecant (mathematics)

CSC Civil Service Commission; Commonwealth Science Council; Comprehensive Schools Committee; *Confédération des syndicats chrétiens* (French: Federation of Christian Trade Unions); Congregation of the Holy Cross; Conspicuous Service Cross

CSCBS Commodore Superintendent, Contract-Built Ships

CSCC Civil Service Commission of Canada; Council of Scottish Chambers of Commerce

CSCE Conference on Security and Cooperation in Europe

CSD Chartered Society of Designers; Civil Service Department; Commonwealth Society for the Deaf; constant speed drive (engineering); Cooperative Secretaries Diploma; Doctor of Christian Science

CSDE Central Servicing Development Establishment (Royal Air Force)

cse course

CSE Central Signals Establishment; Certificate of Secondary Education; cognitive systems engineering (computing); Council of the Stock Exchange

CSEA Civil Service Employees Association (US)

CSED coordinated ship electronics design (US Navy)

CSEU Confederation of Shipbuilding and Engineering Unions

CSF cerebrospinal fluid (medicine); Coil Spring Federation

CSFA Canadian Scientific Film Association

CSFE Canadian Society of Forest Engineers

CSG Catholic Social Guild; Companion of the Order of the Star of Ghana

CSGA Canadian Seed Growers' Association

CS gas Carson Staughton gas (tear gas named after its inventors, Ben Carson and Roger Staughton)

csh cash

CSH calcium silicate hydrate (chemistry)

CSI Chartered Surveyors' Institution; Church of South India; compact source iodide; *Commission sportive internationale* (French: International Sporting Commission); Companion of the Order of the Star of India; Construction Specifications Institute (US)

CSICC Canadian Steel Industries Construction Council

CSIEJB Certificate of the Sanitary Inspectors Examination Joint Board

CSIP Committee for the Scientific Investigation of the Paranormal

CSIR Council for Scientific and Industrial Research

CSIRA Council for Small Industries in Rural Areas

CSIRO Commonwealth Scientific and Industrial Research Organization

CSJ Christian Science Journal

csk cask; countersink

CSL Communication Sub-Lieutenant; computer simulation language; cub scout leader

CSLATP Canadian Society of Landscape Architects and Town Planners

CSLO Canadian Scientific Liaison Office; Combined Services Liaison Officer

CSLT Canadian Society of Laboratory Technologists

CSM cerebrospinal meningitis; Christian Science Monitor; Christian Socialist Movement; command service module (astronautics); Commission for Synoptic Meteorology; Committee on Safety of Medicines; company sergeant-major; corn, soya, milk (food supplement)

CSMA Chemical Specialities Manufacturers' Association; Civil Service Motoring Association

CSMA/CD carrier sense multiple access, collision detection (computing)

CSMMG Chartered Society of Massage and Medical Gymnastics

CSN Confederate States Navy
CSNI Committee on the Safety of Nuclear Installations (US)
CSO Central Selling Organization; Central Statistical Office; chief scientific officer; chief signal officer; chief staff officer; Colonial Secretary's Office; colour separation overlay; command signals officer; Commonwealth Scientific Office; community service order
CSP Chartered Society of Physiotherapists; Chartered Society of Physiotherapy; Civil Service of Pakistan; Congregation of Saint Paul; Council for Scientific Policy
CSPAA *Conférence de solidarité des pays afro-asiatiques* (French: Afro-Asian People's Solidarity Conference)
CSPCA Canadian Society for the Prevention of Cruelty to Animals
CSPR chlorosulphonated polyethylene rubber (chemistry)
CSR Colonial Sugar Refining Company (Australia); combat-stress reaction; Czechoslovak Socialist Republic
CSS Certificate in Social Service; computer systems simulator; Congregation of the Holy Ghost; Council for Science and Society
CSSA Civil Service Supply Association
CSSB Civil Service Selection Board
CSSDA Council for Social Science Data Archives (US)
CSSR *Congregatio Sanctissimi Redemptoris* (Latin: Congregation of the Most Holy Redeemer)
CSSS Canadian Soil Science Society
CST Central Standard Time (US); College of Science and Technology
CSTA Canadian Society of Technical Agriculturists; Canterbury Science Teachers' Association (New Zealand)
CSTI Council of Science and Technology Institutes
CStJ Commander of the Most Venerable Order of the Hospital of St John of Jerusalem
CSU Central Statistical Unit; *Christlich-Soziale Union* (German: Christian Social Union); Civil Service Union; Colorado State University; constant speed unit (engineering)
CSV community service volunteer
CSW continuous seismic wave
CSYS Certificate of Sixth year Studies (Scotland)
ct carat; caught; cent; circuit; *courant*

(French: currently or this month); court; crate; credit; current
ct. *centum* (Latin: 100); certificate
Ct count; court
Ct. canton; Connecticut; countertenor (music)
CT cable transfer; Candidate in Theology; Canterbury (UK postcode); Cape Town; Castletown (UK fishing port registration); Central Time (US); certificated teacher; certified teacher; Civic Trust; code telegrams; college of technology; commercial traveller; *commissario tecnico* (Italian: sports coach); computed tomography (medicine); computerized tomography (medicine); Connecticut (zip code); corporation tax; counter trade; Lincoln (UK vehicle registration)
C/T Californian Terms (grain trade)
cta *cum testamento annexo* (Latin: with the will annexed)
CTA Camping Trade Association; Canadian Tuberculosis Association; Caribbean Technical Assistance; Caribbean Tourist Association; Catering Teachers' Association; Chaplain Territorial Army; Chicago Transit Authority; Commercial Travellers' Association; commodities trading adviser (US)
CTAU Catholic Total Abstinence Union
CTB Commonwealth Telecommunications Board; comprehensive test ban
CTBT comprehensive test ban treaty
CTC Canadian Transport Commission; carbon tetrachloride (chemistry); centralized traffic control; Citizen's Training Corps (US); city technology college; Civil Technical Corps; Commando Training Centre; *Confederación de Trabajadores Cubanos* (Spanish: Confederation of Cuban Workers); *Congrès du travail du Canada* (French: Canadian Labour Congress); corn trade clauses; crushing, tearing and curling (machine); Cyclists' Touring Club
ctd crated
CTD central training depot; charge-transfer device (electronics); classified telephone directory
Cte *comte* (French: count)
CTEB Council of Technical Examining Bodies
Ctesse *comtesse* (French: countess)

CTETOC Council for Technical Education and Training for Overseas Countries
CText Chartered Textile Technologist
ctf. certificate; certify
CTF Chaplain to the Territorial Forces; coal-tar fuel
ctge cartage; cartridge; cottage
CTH Corporation of Trinity House
CTK *Ceskoslovenska Tiskova Kancelar* (news agency, Czech Republic)
ctl central
CTL constant tensile load; constructive total loss (insurance)
ctn carton; cotangent (mathematics)
CTN confectioner, tobacconist and newsagent
CTO cancelled to order (philately); Central Telegraph Office; Central Treaty Organization; Chief Technical Officer; concerto
CTOL conventional take-off and landing
CTP *Confederación de Trabajadores del Peru* (Spanish: Peruvian Confederation of Labour)
ctpt counterpoint (music)
ctptal contrapuntal (music)
ctptst contrapuntist (music)
ctr. centre; contribution; contributor
CTR certified test record; controlled thermonuclear reaction; controlled thermonuclear research
CTRA Coal Tar Research Association
CTRP *Confederación de Trabajadores de la República de Panama* (Spanish: Confederation of Workers of the Republic of Panama)
CTRU Colonial Termite Research Unit
cts centimes; cents; certificates; crates
CTS Catholic Truth Society; computed tomographic scanner (medicine); computerized tomographic scanner (medicine); Consolidated Tin Smelters
CTSA Crucible and Tool Steel Association
CTT capital transfer tax
CTTB Central Trade Test Board (Royal Air Force)
Cttee committee
CTTSC Certificate in the Teaching and Training of Subnormal Children
CTUS Carnegie Trust for the Universities of Scotland
CTV cable television; Canadian Television Network Limited; *Confederación de Trabajadores de Venezuela* (Spanish: Confederation of Venezuelan Workers)

Cty city
CTZ control traffic zone (aircraft)
cu. cubic
Cu copper (element); cumulus (meteorology)
CU Cambridge University; Church Union; close-up (photography); Congregational Union of England and Wales; Cooperative Union; Cornell University (US); Cuba (international civil aircraft marking); *Cubana De Aviation* (airline flight code, Cuba); Customs Union; Newcastle upon Tyne (UK vehicle registration)
CUA Canadian Underwriters' Association; Catholic University of America; Colour Users' Association
CUAC Cambridge University Athletic Club
CUAFC Cambridge University Association Football Club
CUAS Cambridge University Agricultural Society; Cambridge University Air Squadron
cub. cubic
CUBC Cambridge University Boat Club; Cambridge University Boxing Club
CUC Canberra University College; Coal Utilization Council
CUCC Cambridge University Cricket Club
CUDAT Community Urban Development Assistance Team
CUDS Cambridge University Dramatic Society
CUEW Congregational Union of England and Wales
CUF *Catholicarum Universitatum* (Latin: Federation of Catholic Universities); common university fund
CUGC Cambridge University Golf Club
CUHC Cambridge University Hockey Club
cuis. cuisine
CUKT Carnegie United Kingdom Trust
cul. culinary
CUL Cambridge University Library
CULTC Cambridge University Lawn Tennis Club
cum. cumulative (finance)
CUM Cambridge University Mission
Cumb. Cumberland
cum div. cum (with) dividend (finance)
cum. pref. cumulative preference (shares)
CUMS Cambridge University Musical Society

CUNA Credit Union National Association
CUNY City University of New York
CUOG Cambridge University Opera Group
CUP Cambridge University Press; Cuban peso (monetary unit)
cur. currency; current
CURAC Coal Utilization Research Advisory Committee (Australia)
cur. adv. vult *curia advisari vult* (Latin: the court wishes to consider it)
CURE Care, Understanding and Research (organization for drug addicts)
curt current
CURUFC Cambridge University Rugby Union Football Club
CURV cable-controlled undersea recovery vehicle (US Navy)
CUS Catholic University School
CUSO Canadian University Services Overseas
CUSRPG Canada-United States Regional Planning Group (NATO)
custod. custodian
CUTF Commonwealth Unit Trust Fund
CUTS Computer Users' Tape System
cv *cheval-vapeur* (French: horsepower); chief value; *cras vespere* (Latin: tomorrow evening; medicine); curriculum vitae; *cursus vitae* (Latin: course of life)
cv. cultivar (botany)
CV calorific value; *cavallo vapore* (Italian: horsepower); *cavalos vapor* (Portuguese; horsepower); common valve; Common Version (Bible); convertible (finance); Coventry (UK postcode); Cross of Valour (Canada); curriculum vitae; Truro (UK vehicle registration)
CVA cerebrovascular accident (medicine); Columbia Valley Authority (US)
CVCP Committee of Vice-Chancellors and Principals (UK universities)
cvd cash versus documents (commerce)
CVD common valve development
CVE Certificate of Vocational Education; Council for Visual Education
CVEsc Cape Verde escudo (monetary unit of Cape Verde)
CVK centre vertical keel
CVM Company of Veteran Motorists
CVO Commander of the Royal Victorian Order
C.voc. *colla voce* (Italian: with the voice; music)
CVP *Christelijk Volkspartif* (Belgium: (Flemish) Christian Social Party)

CVS chorionic villus sampling (medicine); Council of Voluntary Service
CVSNA Council of Voluntary Service National Association
cvt. convertible (finance)
CVT constant variable transmission (vehicles)
Cvt Gdn Covent Garden (London)
CVWS combat vehicle weapons system
cw carrier wave (physics); continuous weld
cw. clockwise
c/w chainwheel (cycling)
CW Air Marshall Islands (airline flight code); Canada West; cavity wall; chemical warfare; chemical weapons; child welfare; clerk of works; cold-worked (metals); commercial weight; Commissions and Warrants (Admiralty department); complete with; continuous wave; Crewe (UK postcode); Curie–Weiss (physics); Preston (UK vehicle registration)
C/W Country and Western (music)
CWA Catering Wages Act; chemical warfare agent; Civil Works Administration (US); Clean Water Act (US); Country Women's Association (Australia); Crime Writers' Association
CWB Canadian Wheat Board; Central Wages Board
CWBW chemical warfare-bacteriological warfare
CWC Catering Wages Commission; Commonwealth of World Citizens
CWD civilian war dead
CWDE Centre for World Development Education
C'wealth Commonwealth
CWF coal-water fuel
CWGC Commonwealth War Graves Commission
CWINC Central Waterways, Irrigation and Navigation Commission (India)
CWL Catholic Women's League
Cwlth Commonwealth
CWME Commission on World Mission and Evangelism (World Council of Churches)
CWNA Canadian Weekly Newspapers Association
cwo cash with order
CWO Chief Warrant Officer
CWOIH Conference of World Organizations Interested in the Handicapped

CWP Christian Workers' Party (Malta); Communist Workers' Party (US)
CWR continuous welded rail
CW radar continuous-wave radar
CWS Cooperative Wholesale Society; Court Welfare Service
cwt hundredweight
CWT central war time
CWU Chemical Workers' Union
cx cervix (medicine); convex
CX Cathay Pacific Airways (airline flight code, Hong Kong); Huddersfield (UK vehicle registration); Uruguay (international civil aircraft marking)
CXR chest X-ray
CXT Common External Tariff (EC)
cy capacity; currency; cyanide; cycle
CY calendar year; Castlebay (UK fishing port registration); Cyprus (international vehicle registration); Cyprus Airways (airline flight code); Swansea (UK vehicle registration)

cyath. *cyathus* (Latin: glassful; medicine)
cyath. vin. *cyathus vinarius* (Latin: wineglassful)
cyber. cybernetics
cyc. cycle; cycling; cyclopedia; cyclopedic
CYCA Clyde Yacht Clubs Association
cyclo. cyclopedia
CYEE Central Youth Employment Executive
cyl. cylinder; cylindrical
Cym. Cymric
CYMS Catholic Young Men's Society
CYO Catholic Youth Organization (US)
Cyp. Cyprian; Cyprus
Cz Cenozoic (geology)
Cz Czechoslovakia(n)
CZ Belfast (UK vehicle registration); Canal Zone
CZMA Coastal Zone Management Act (US)

D

d day; deci-; deuteron (physics); *denarius* (Latin: penny); drizzle (meteorology); old pence
d diameter; relative density; thickness
d. dam (animal pedigrees); damn; date; daughter; day; deacon; dead; deceased; deciduous (dentistry); decree; degree; delete; deliver(y); delta; density; depart(s); depth; deputy; desert; deserter; *destro* (Italian: right); dextrorotatory; diameter; died; dime; dinar (Tunisian currency unit); discharge; distance; dividend; dollar; dose (medicine); drachma (Greek currency unit); drama; *droite* (French: right); dump; penny/pennies
D absorbed dose (radioactivity); dalasï (Gambian monetary unit); darcy (geology); defence; Democrat (US); Department; Detective; deuterium; Devonian (geology); dimension(al); dinar (Tunisian monetary unit); dioptre (optics); dong (Vietnamese monetary unit); Dublin (Irish fishing port registration); Germany (international vehicle registration); Germany (international civil aircraft marking); 500 (Roman numerals)

D diameter; diffusion coefficient (chemistry); dispersion (physics); drag (aeronautics); electric flux density (physics); electric flux displacement (physics)
D. *Damen* (German: ladies); December; Democrat (US); Democratic (US); demy (paper); destroyer; *Deus* (Latin: God); *Deutschland* (German: Germany); diamonds (cards); director; *Diretto* (Italian: slow train); distinguished; doctor; *dogana* (Italian: customs); Dom (monastic title); *Dominus* (Latin: Lord); Don (Spanish title); *douane* (French: customs); dowager; duchess; duke; Dutch
D2 Angola (international civil aircraft marking)
D4 Cape Verde Islands (international civil aircraft marking)
D6 Comoros Islands (international civil aircraft marking)
da deca-
d/a days after acceptance (commerce); documents against acceptance (commerce)
Da dalton (biochemistry)
Da. Danish

D/a deposit account; discharge afloat
DA Birmingham (UK vehicle registration); Dan-Air Services (airline flight code, UK); Dartford (UK postcode); Daughters of America; deed of arrangement; Defence Act; delayed action (bomb); Department of Agriculture (US); Deputy Advocate; deputy assistant; design automation; destructive analysis; dinar (Algerian monetary unit); Diploma in Anaesthesia; Diploma in Anaesthetics; Diploma in Art; direct action; dissolved acetylene; District Attorney (US); doesn't answer; dopamine (medicine); Drogheda (Irish fishing port registration); duck's arse (hairstyle)
D/A days after acceptance (commerce); delivery on acceptance (commerce); deposit account; digital-to-analog (computing); documents against acceptance (commerce)
D-A digital-to-analog (computing)
DAA *défense anti-aérienne* (French: anti-aircraft defence); diacetone acrylamide (chemistry); diacetone alcohol (chemistry); Diploma of the Advertising Association
DAA&QMG deputy assistant adjutant and quartermaster-general
DAAG deputy assistant adjutant-general
DA&QMG deputy adjutant and quartermaster-general
DAAS data acquisition and analysis system
DAB daily audience barometer; *Deutsches Apothekerbuch* (German: German Pharmacopoeia); Dictionary of American Biography; digital audio broadcasting
dac deductible average clause (insurance); direct air cycle
DAc Doctor of Acupuncture
DAC data analysis and control; Development Assistance Committee (OECD); digital-to-analog converter (computing)
DACC Dangerous Air Cargoes Committee
DACG deputy assistant chaplain-general
dacr. dacron (fabric)
DAD deputy assistant director
DADG deputy assistant director general
DAdmin Doctor of Administration
DAE Department of Atomic Energy (US); Dictionary of American English; differential algebraic equation; Diploma in Advanced Engineering; Director of Army Education
DAEP Division of Atomic Energy Production
DAER Department of Aeronautical and Engineering Research
daf described as follows; *Doorn Automobielfabriek* (Dutch: Dutch gearless car)
DAF Department of the Air Force (US); dry ash free (coal)
DAFS Department of Agriculture and Fisheries for Scotland
dag decagram
DAG deputy adjutant-general; *Deutsche Angestellten-Gewerkschaft* (German trade union); development assistance group
DAGMAR defining advertising goals for measured advertising results (commerce)
DAgr Doctor of Agriculture
DAgrSc Doctor of Agricultural Science
DAH disordered action of the heart (medicine)
dai death from accidental injuries
DAI disease activity index; distributed artificial intelligence
DAJAG deputy assistant judge advocate general
Dak. Dakota
dal decalitre
DAL direct acid leaching
DALR dry adiabatic lapse rate (meteorology)
dal S. *dal segno* (Italian: (repeat) from the sign; music)
dam decametre
DAM Diploma in Ayurvedic Medicine
DAMS defense against missiles system (US); deputy assistant military secretary
Dan. Daniel (Bible); Danish
DAN (People's) Direct Action Network
Dan-Air Davies and Newman Ltd (UK airline)
D&AD Designers and Art Directors Association
D&B discipline and bondage; Dun and Bradstreet (financial reports)
D&C dean and chapter; dilation and curettage (medicine)
D&D deaf and dumb; death and dying; drunk and disorderly
D&HAA Dock and Harbour Authorities' Association
d and p developing and printing
d&s demand and supply

D and V diarrhoea and vomiting (medicine)
DAO district advisory officer
DAOT director of air organization and training
dap do anything possible; documents against payment
DAP director of administrative planning; distributed array processor (computing); draw a person (psychology)
DAP&E Diploma in Applied Parasitology and Entomology
DAPM deputy assistant provost-marshal
DAppSc Doctor of Applied Science
DAPS director of army postal services
DAQMG deputy assistant quartermaster-general
DAR Daughters of the American Revolution; Defense Aid Reports (US); Directorate of Atomic Research (Canada)
DArch Doctor of Architecture
DARD Directorate of Aircraft Research and Development
DARE demand and resource evaluation
DARPA Defense Advanced Research Projects Agency (US)
DArt Doctor of Art
das delivered alongside ship (commerce)
DAS data-acquisition system (computing); development advisory service; director of armament supply; double algebraic sum; Dramatic Authors' Society
DASA Defense Atomic Support Agency (US)
DASc Doctor of Agricultural Science
DASC Direct Air Support Center (US)
DASD direct-access storage device (computing); director of army staff duties
DASH drone antisubmarine helicopter
DASM delayed-action space missile
dat. dative
DAT digital analogue technology; digital audio tape
DATA Draughtsmen's and Allied Technicians' Association
DATEC Art and Design Committee, Technician Education Council
Datel data telex (telecommunications; trademark)
DATV digitally assisted television
dau. daughter
DAV Disabled American Veterans
DAvMed Diploma in Aviation Medicine

DAW dry active waste (nuclear engineering)
DAWS director of army welfare services
DAX *Deutsche Aktien-index* (German: German share price index)
DAyM Doctor of Ayurvedic Medicine
db daybook; double bass (music); double bed; double-breasted; drawbar
dB decibel
Db dobra (monetary unit of São Tomé and Príncipe)
DB dark blue; database; daybook; deals and battens (timber); delayed broadcast; *Deutsche Bundesbahn* (German: German Federal Railway); *Deutsche Bundesbank* (German: German Federal Bank); *Divinitatis Baccalaureus* (Latin: Bachelor of Divinity); dock brief; Domesday Book; double-barrelled; Manchester (UK vehicle registration)
dba doing business as; doing business at
DBA database administrator (computing); Doctor of Business Administration
DBB deals, battens and boards (timber); *Deutscher Beamtenbund* (German: German civil servants' trade union)
DBC Deaf Broadcasting Council
DBE Dame Commander of the Order of the British Empire; design-basis event
DBEATS dispatch payable both ends all time saved
DBELTS dispatch payable both ends on lay time saved
dbh diameter at breast height (forestry)
DBib Douay Bible
DBIU Dominion Board of Insurance Underwriters (Canada)
dbk debark; drawback
dbl(e). double
DBM Diploma in Business Management
DBMS database management system (computing)
Dbn Durban (South Africa)
DBO Diploma of the British Orthoptic Board
dbre *diciembre* (Spanish: December)
DBS direct broadcasting from satellite
DBST double British summer time
dc dead centre; direct current; double column (printing); double crotchet (music); drift correction (navigation)
dC *depois de Cristo* (Portuguese: after Christ); *dopo Cristo* (Italian: after Christ)
DC *da capo* (Italian: from the beginning; music); Daughters of Charity of St Vincent de Paul; death certificate;

decimal currency; *Democrazia Cristiana* (Italian: Christian Democratic Party); Dental Corps (US); depth charge; deputy chief; deputy commissioner; deputy consul; deputy counsel; detective constable; diagnostic centre; diplomatic corps; direct current; Disarmament Conference; Disciples of Christ; district commissioner; district council; district court; District of Columbia; Doctor of Chiropractic; Douglas Commercial (aircraft); down centre (theatre); Middlesbrough (UK vehicle registration)

D/C deviation clause (insurance)

DCA Defense Communications Agency (US); Department of Civil Aviation (Australia)

DCAe Diploma of the College of Aeronautics

DCAO deputy county advisory officer

dcap double foolscap (paper)

DCAS deputy chief of air staff

DCB Dame Commander of the Order of the Bath

DCC deputy chief constable; digital compact cassette; diocesan consistory court; Diploma of Chelsea College

DCD department of community development; Diploma in Chest Diseases

DCE data-communication equipment (computing); design and construction error; Diploma in Chemical Engineering; Doctor of Civil Engineering; domestic credit expansion

DCEP Diploma of Child and Educational Psychology

DCF discounted cash flow (accounting)

dcg dancing; decigramme

DCG deputy chaplain-general

DCGS deputy chief of the general staff

DCh *Doctor Chirurgiae* (Latin: Doctor of Surgery)

DCH Diploma in Child Health

DChD Doctor of Dental Surgery

DChE Doctor of Chemical Engineering

DCI detective chief inspector; double column inch (advertisements); ductile cast iron

DCJ district court judge (US)

dcl. declaration

DCL Distillers' Company Limited; Doctor of Canon Law; Doctor of Civil Law

DCLI Duke of Cornwall's Light Infantry

DCLJ Dame Commander of the Order of St Lazarus of Jerusalem

DClSc Doctor of Clinical Science

DCM Diploma in Community Medicine; Distinguished Conduct Medal (military); district court-martial; Doctor of Comparative Medicine

DCMG Dame Commander of the Order of St Michael and St George

DCMS deputy commissioner medical services

DCnL Doctor of Canon Law

DCNS deputy chief of naval staff

DCO Duke of Cambridge's Own (regiment)

DC of S deputy chief of staff

dcol double column (printing)

DComL Doctor of Commercial Law

DComm Doctor of Commerce

DCompL Doctor of Comparative Law

DCP Diploma in Conservation of Paintings; Diploma in Clinical Pathology; Diploma of Clinical Psychology

DCPA Defense Civil Preparedness Agency (US)

DCPath Diploma of the College of Pathologists

DCR Diploma of the College of Radiographers

DCrim Doctor of Criminality

DCS deputy chief of staff; deputy clerk of sessions; digital camera system; Doctor of Christian Science; Doctor of Commercial Studies

DCSO deputy chief scientific officer

DCST deputy chief of supplies and transport

dct document

DCT Doctor of Christian Theology

DCVO Dame Commander of the Royal Victorian Order

DCW dead carcass weight; domestic cold water

dd dated; days after date; *de dato* (Latin: today's date); dedicated; delayed delivery; delivered; delivered dock (commerce); demand draft; detergent dispersant; *dono dedit* (Latin: given as a gift); drilled; dry dock; due date; due day

Dd *Deo dedit* (Latin: gave to God)

D/d days after date; delivered (commerce)

DD damage done (insurance); demand draft (banking); Department of Defense (US); deputy director; deputy directorate; Diploma in Dermatology; direct debit; *direttissimo* (Italian: fast train); discharged dead; dishonourable discharge; Doctor of Divinity; double

demy (paper); Dundee (UK postcode); Gloucester (UK vehicle registration)
D/D delivered at docks; demand draft; dock dues
DDA Dangerous Drugs Act; Disabled Drivers' Association
D-Day Day Day (World War II: Allied invasion of France, 6 June 1944)
DDC Dewey Decimal Classification (libraries); direct digital control (computing)
DDD *dat, dicat, dedicat* (Latin: gives, devotes and dedicates); deadline delivery date; *dono dedit dedicavit* (Latin: gave and consecrated as a gift)
DDDS deputy director of dental services
DDE direct data entry (computing); Dwight David Eisenhower (US President)
DDG deputy director-general
DDGAMS deputy director-general, army medical services
DDH Diploma in Dental Health
DDI divisional detective inspector
dd in d *de die in diem* (Latin: from day to day; medicine)
DDL data description language (computing); deputy director of labour
DDM Diploma in Dermatological Medicine; Doctor of Dental Medicine
DDME deputy director of mechanical engineering
DDMI deputy director of military intelligence
DDMOI deputy director of military operations and intelligence
DDMS deputy director of medical services
DDMT deputy director of military training
DDNI deputy director of naval intelligence
DDO Diploma in Dental Orthopaedics; district dental officer
DDOS deputy director of ordnance services
DDPH Diploma in Dental Public Health
DDPR deputy director of public relations
DDPS deputy director of personal services; deputy director of postal services
DDR *Deutsche Demokratische Republik* (German: German Democratic Republic); Diploma in Diagnostic Radiology
DDRA deputy director, Royal Artillery

DDRD deputy directorate of research and development
dd/s delivered sound
DDS deep diving system; deputy directorate of science; Dewey Decimal System (libraries); director of dental services; Doctor of Dental Science; Doctor of Dental Surgery
DDSD deputy director of staff duties
DDSM Defense Distinguished Service Medal (US)
DDSR deputy director of scientific research
DDST deputy director of supplies and transport
DDT dichlorodiphenyltrichloroethane (insecticide)
DDVS deputy director of veterinary services
DDWE&M deputy director of works, electrical and mechanical
de deckle edge; diesel-electric; direct elimination (fencing); double entry (book-keeping)
DE Dáil Éireann (Irish parliamentary chamber); deflection error; Delaware (zip code); Department of Employment; Derby (UK postcode); destroyer escort; destruction efficiency; diesel engine; direct electrolysis; Doctor of Engineering; Doctor of Entomology; double elephant (paper); Dundee (UK fishing port registration); Haverfordwest (UK vehicle registration)
Dea. Deacon; Dean
DEA Department of Economic Affairs; Department of External Affairs; Drug Enforcement Administration (US); Drug Enforcement Agency (US)
deb. debenture (finance); debit; debut
deb. stk debenture stock (finance)
dec declination (astronomy)
dec. deceased; *décembre* (French: December); decimal; decimetre; declaration; declare; declared; declension (grammar); decoration; decorative; decrease; *decrescendo* (Italian: decrease loudness; music)
Dec *Decani* (Latin: of the dean); *Decanus* (Latin: Dean); December
DEc Doctor of Economics
DEC dental examination centre; Department of Environmental Conservation (US); Digital Equipment Corporation (US); Dollar Export Council
decd deceased
decid. deciduous

decl. declension (grammar)
decn decontamination
DEcon Doctor of Economics
DEconSc Doctor of Economic
Science
DECR decrease (meteorology)
decresc. *decrescendo* (Italian: decrease
loudness; music)
ded. dedicate; dedicated; dedication;
deduce; deduction
DEd Doctor of Education
de d in d *de die in diem* (Latin: from day to
day; medicine)
DEE Diploma in Electrical Engineering
DEED Department of Energy and
Economic Development (US)
dee jay disc jockey
DEEP Directly Elected European
Parliament
def. defecate; defecation; defect;
defection; defective; defector; defence;
defendant; deferred; deficit; define;
definite; definition; definitive;
deflagrate; deflect(ion); defoliate;
defrost; defunct; *defunctus* (Latin:
deceased)
def. art. definite article (grammar)
DEFCON defence readiness condition
(military)
defl. deflate; deflation; deflect(ion)
deft defendant
deg. degree
DEG degrees (meteorology)
DEI Dutch East Indies
del. delegate; delegation; delete; *delineavit*
(Latin: he/she drew it); deliver(ed)
Del. Delaware; Delhi
deld delivered
deleg. delegate; delegation
deli delicatessen
DEIo Doctor of Elocution
delv. deliver; delivered
dely delivery
dem. demand; demerara; democracy;
demurrage
Dem. Democrat (US); Democratic (US)
DEME Directorate of Electrical and
Mechanical Engineering
demo demonstration
demob. demobilize; demobilization
demon. demonstrate; demonstrative
DEMS defensively equipped merchant
ships
DemU Democratic Unionist (Northern
Ireland)
demur. demurrage
den. *dernier* (French: last); denotation;

denote; denoted; dental; dentist;
dentistry
Den. Denbighshire; Denmark; Denver
(US)
DEn Department of Energy; Doctor of
English
DEN District Enrolled Nurse
dend(rol). dendrology
DenD *Docteur en droit* (French: Doctor of
Laws)
DEng(g) Doctor of Engineering
DEngS Doctor of Engineering Science
DenM(ed) *Docteur en médecine* (French:
Doctor of Medicine)
denom. denomination
DENR Department of Energy and
Natural Resources (US)
dens. density
dent. dental; dentist; dentistry;
denture
DEnt Doctor of Entomology
DEOVR Duke of Edinburgh's Own
Volunteer Rifles
dep. depart; department; departure;
dependant; dependency; dependent;
deponent; depose; deposed; deposit;
deposition; depositor; depot; deputize;
deputized; deputy
dép. *département* (French: department;
administrative division); *député* (French:
deputy)
DEP Department of Employment and
Productivity; Department of
Environmental Protection (US)
dept. department; deponent
deptn. deputation
der. *derecha* (Spanish: right); derivation;
derivative; derive; derived; *dernier*
(French: last)
DER Department of Environmental
Resources (US)
Derby(s). Derbyshire
deriv. derivation; derivative; derive;
derived
DERL derived emergency reference level
(radioactivity)
derm. dermatitis; dermatology
dermat(ol). dermatology
DERR Duke of Edinburgh's Royal
Regiment
derv diesel-engined road vehicle (oil)
des. desert; design; designer; designate;
designated; designation; desire; dessert
Des. deaconess; designer
DES data encryption standard
(computing); Department of Education
and Science; diethylstilboestrol

(medicine); director of educational services

desc. descend; descendant; descent; describe

desid. *desideratum* (Latin: something wanted)

desig. designate

DèsL *Docteur ès lettres* (French: Doctor of Letters)

desp. despatch; despatched

DesRCA Designer of the Royal College of Art

DèsS(c) *Docteur ès sciences* (French: Doctor of Science)

DèsScPol *Docteur ès science politique* (French: Doctor of Political Science)

dest. destroyer

destn destination

det. detach; detached; detachment; detail; determine; *detur* (Latin: let it be given)

Det Detective

DET determiner (linguistics); direct energy transfer

Det Con detective constable

Det Insp detective inspector

detn detention; determination

Det Sgt detective sergeant

Det Supt detective superintendent

Deut. Deuteronomy (Bible)

dev. develop; developed; developer; development; deviate; deviation (navigation)

Dev. Devon

devp develop

devpt development

devs. devotions

DEW directed-energy weapon; distant early-warning

dez. *dezembro* (Portuguese: December)

Dez. *Dezember* (German: December)

df dead freight (commerce); drinking fountain

df. draft

DF dean of faculty; decontamination factor (nuclear engineering); Defender of the Faith; direction finder (telecommunications); direction finding (telecommunications); Djibouti franc (monetary unit); Doctor of Forestry; double foolscap (paper); Gloucester (UK vehicle registration)

DFA Department of Foreign Affairs (US); Diploma in Foreign Affairs; Doctor of Fine Arts

DFC Distinguished Flying Cross

DFD dataflow diagram

DFHom Diploma of the Faculty of Homeopathy

DFLS Day Fighter Leaders' School

DFM Diploma in Forensic Medicine; Distinguished Flying Medal

dfndt defendant

dfr decreasing failure rate

DFS Department for Education; disease-free survival

DFSc Doctor of Financial Science

dft defendant; draft

DFW director of fortifications and works

dg decigram

DG *Dei gratia* (Latin: by the grace of God); *Deo gratias* (Latin: thanks be to God); directional gyro (navigation); director-general; Dragoon Guards; Dumfries (UK postcode); Gloucester (UK vehicle registration)

D-G director-general

DGA director-general, aircraft; Directors' Guild of America

DGAA Distressed Gentlefolks Aid Association

DGAMS director-general, army medical services

DGB *Deutscher Gwerkschaftsbund* (German: German Trade Union Federation)

DGC Diploma in Guidance and Counselling

DGCA director-general of civil aviation

DGCE Directorate-General of Communications Equipment

DGCStJ Dame Grand Cross of the Order of Saint John of Jerusalem

DGD director, gunnery division

DGD&M director-general, dockyards and maintenance

DGE Directorate-General of Equipment

DGEME director-general, electrical and mechanical engineering

DGI director-general of information; director-general of inspection

DGLP(A) director-general, logistic policy (army)

DGM Diploma in General Medicine; director-general of manpower

DGMS director-general of medical services

DGMT director-general of military training

DGMW director-general of military works

Dgn Dragoon

DGNPS director-general of naval personnel services

DGO Diploma in Gynaecology and Obstetrics
DGP director-general of personnel; director-general of production
DGPS director-general of personal services
DGR director of graves registration
DGS Diploma in General Studies; Diploma in General Surgery; Diploma in Graduate Studies; Directorate-General of Signals; director-general, ships
DGSRD Directorate-General of Scientific Research and Development
DGT director-general of training
DGW director-general of weapons; director-general of works
dh *das heisst* (German: that is); dead heat
Dh dirham (monetary unit of the United Arab Emirates)
DH Dartmouth (UK fishing port registration); dead heat (sport); De Havilland (aircraft); Department of Health; designated hitter (baseball); dirham (Moroccan monetary unit); district heating; Doctor of Humanities; Dudley (UK vehicle registration); Durham (UK postcode)
DHA district health authority
Dhc *Doctoris honoris causa* (Latin: honorary doctorate)
DHHS Department of Health and Human Services (US)
DHL Doctor of Hebrew Letters; Doctor of Hebrew Literature; Doctor of Humane Letters
DHMSA Diploma in the History of Medicine (Society of Apothecaries)
DHQ district headquarters; divisional headquarters
DHS Diploma in Horticultural Science; Doctor of Health Services
DHSA Diploma of Health Service Administration
DHSS Department of Health and Social Security
DHumLit Doctor of Humane Letters
DHW domestic hot water
DHyg Doctor of Hygiene
di daily inspection; *das ist* (German: that is); de-ice; diplomatic immunity; document identifier
di. diameter
Di didymium
Di. dinar (currency)
DI Defence Intelligence; *Delta Air Regionalflung* (airline flight code, Germany); Department of the Interior;

detective inspector; direct injection (aeronautics); director of infantry; district inspector; divisional inspector; donor insemination (medicine); double imperial (paper); drill instructor; Roscommon (Irish vehicle registration)
dia. diagnose; diagram; dialect; diameter
DIA Defense Intelligence Agency (US); Design and Industries Association; Diploma in International Affairs; Driving Instructors' Association
diag. diagnose; diagonal; diagram
dial. dialect; dialectal; dialectic; dialectical; dialogue
diam. diameter
diamat dialectical materialism (economics; philosophy)
DIANE Direct Information Access Network for Europe
diap. diapason (music)
diaph. diaphragm
DIAS Dublin Institute of Advanced Sciences
dic. *dicembre* (Italian: December); *diciembre* (Spanish: December)
DIC Diploma of Membership of the Imperial College of Science and Technology (London); drunk in charge
DIChem Diploma in Industrial Chemistry
dict. dictate; dictated; dictation; dictator; dictionary
dicta. dictaphone
DICTA Diploma of Imperial College of Tropical Agriculture
DIE Diploma in Industrial Engineering; Diploma of the Institute of Engineering
dieb. alt. *diebus alternus* (Latin: on alternate days; medicine)
DIEME Directorate of Inspection of Electrical and Mechanical Equipment
diet. dietary; dietetics; dietician
dif. differ; differential
DIF diffuse (meteorology); district inspector of fisheries
diff. differ; difference; different; differential
dig. digest (books); digestion; digestive; digit; digital
DIG deputy inspector-general; disablement income group
DIH Diploma in Industrial Health
Dij. Dijon (France)
dil. dilute; diluted; dilution
diln dilution
dim. *dimanche* (French: Sunday); dimension; *dimidium* (Latin: one-half);

diminish; diminuendo (music);
diminutive
DIM Diploma in Industrial Management
dimin. diminutive
DIMS data and information management
system (computing)
din. dining-car; dining-room; dinner
Din dinar (monetary unit)
Din. *Dinsdag* (Dutch: Tuesday)
DIN *Deutsches Institut für Normung*
(German: German National Standards
Organization); digital imaging network
(computing)
DIng *Doctor Ingeniariae* (Latin: Doctor of
Engineering)
Dinky double income, no kids yet
DInstPA Diploma of the Institute of Park
Administration
dio. diocese
DIO district intelligence officer
dioc. diocesan; diocese
dioc. syn. diocesan synod
dip. Diploma
DipAD Diploma in Art and Design
DipAe Diploma in Aeronautics
DipAgr Diploma in Agriculture
DipALing Diploma in Applied
Linguistics
DipAm Diploma in Applied Mechanics
DipAppSc Diploma of Applied Science
DipArch Diploma in Architecture
DipArts Diploma in Arts
DipASE Diploma in Advanced Study of
Education, College of Preceptors
DipAvMed Diploma of Aviation
Medicine (Royal College of Physicians)
DipBA Diploma in Business
Administration
DipBac Diploma in Bacteriology
DipBMS Diploma in Basic Medical
Sciences
DipBS Diploma in Fine Art, Byam Shaw
School
DipCAM Diploma in Communication,
Advertising and Marketing of the CAM
Foundation
DipCC Diploma of the Central College
DipCD Diploma in Child Development;
Diploma in Civic Design
DipCE Diploma in Civil Engineering
DipChemEng Diploma in Chemical
Engineering
DipCom Diploma in Commerce
DipDHus Diploma in Dairy Husbandry
DipDP Diploma in Drawing and Painting
DipDS Diploma in Dental Surgery
DipEcon Diploma in Economics

DipEd Diploma in Education
DipEl Diploma in Electronics
DipEng Diploma in Engineering
DipESL Diploma in English as a Second
Language
DipEth Diploma in Ethnology
DipFA Diploma in Fine Arts
DipFD Diploma in Funeral Directing
DipFE Diploma in Further
Education
DipFor Diploma in Forestry
DipGSM Diploma in Music, Guildhall
School of Music and Drama
DipGT Diploma in Glass Technology
DipHA Diploma in Hospital
Administration
DipHE Diploma in Higher Education;
Diploma in Highway Engineering
DipHSc Diploma in Home Science
diphth. diphthong
DipHum Diploma in Humanities
DipJ Diploma in Journalism
dipl. diploma; diplomacy; diplomat;
diplomatic
DipL Diploma in Languages
DipLA Diploma in Landscape
Architecture
DipLib Diploma of Librarianship
DipLSc Diploma of Library Science
DipM Diploma in Marketing
DipMechE Diploma of Mechanical
Engineering
DipMet Diploma in Metallurgy
DipMFOS Diploma in Maxial, Facial and
Oral Surgery
DipMusEd Diploma in Musical
Education
DipN Diploma in Nursing
DipNEd Diploma in Nursery School
Education
DipO&G Diploma in Obstetrics and
Gynaecology
DipOL Diploma in Oriental Learning
DipOrth Diploma in Orthodontics
DipPA Diploma in Public Administration
DipP&OT Diploma in Physiotherapy and
Occupational Therapy
DipPharmMed Diploma in
Pharmaceutical Medicine
DipPhysEd Diploma in Physical
Education
DipQS Diploma in Quantity Surveying
DipRADA Diploma of the Royal
Academy of Dramatic Art
DipREM Diploma in Rural Estate
Management
DIPS digital image-processing system

DipS&PA Diploma in Social and Public Administration
DipSMS Diploma in School Management Studies
DipSoc Diploma in Sociology
DipSpEd Diploma in Special Education
DipSS Diploma in Social Studies
DipSW Diploma in Social Work
DipT Diploma in Teaching
DipTA Diploma in Tropical Agriculture
DipT&CP Diploma in Town and Country Planning
Dip Tech Diploma in Technology
DipTEFL Diploma in the Teaching of English as a Foreign Language
DipTh Diploma in Theology
DipTP Diploma in Town Planning
DipTPT Diploma in Theory and Practice of Teaching
dir. direct; directed; direction; director; dirham (Moroccan currency)
DIR developer inhibitor release (photography)
Dir-Genl director-general
dis. discharge; disciple; discipline; disconnect; discontinue; discount; dispense; distance; distant; distribute
DIS Defense Intelligence School (US)
disab(l). disability
disb. disbursement
disc. disciple; discipline; discount; discover; discovered; discoverer; discovery
disch. discharge
dishon. dishonourable; dishonourably
disp. dispensary; dispensation; dispense; disperse; dispersion
displ. displacement
diss. dissenter; dissertation; dissolve
dist. distance; distant; distilled; distinguish; distinguished; district
Dist. Atty District Attorney (US)
distr. distribution; distributor
distrib. distributive
DistTP Distinction in Town Planning
DIT Detroit Institute of Technology; double income tax
div divergence (mathematics)
div. diversion; divide; divided; dividend; divine; division; divisor; divorce; divorced
Div. Divine; Divinity
div. in par. aeq. *dividatur in partes aequales* (Latin: divide into equal parts; pharmacology)
divn division
divnl divisional

DIY do-it-yourself
dJ *der Jüngere* (German: Junior); *dieses Jahres* (German: of this year)
DJ dinner jacket; Diploma in Journalism; disc jockey; district judge; divorce judge; *Doctor Juris* (Latin: Doctor of Law); Dow Jones (finance); dust jacket (books); Liverpool (UK vehicle registration)
DJAG deputy judge advocate-general
DJI Dow Jones Index (finance)
DJIA Dow Jones Industrial Average (finance)
DJS Doctor of Juridical Science
DJT Doctor of Jewish Theology
DJTA Dow Jones Transportation Average (finance)
DJUA Dow Jones Utilities Average (finance)
DJur *Doctor Juris* (Latin: Doctor of Law or Jurisprudence)
dk dark; deck; dock; duck
DK Denmark (international vehicle registration); Dundalk (Irish fishing port registration); Manchester (UK vehicle registration)
DKB distributed knowledge base (computing)
Dkr krone (monetary unit of Denmark and Greenland)
DKS Deputy Keeper of the Signet
dkt docket
dkyd dockyard
dl decilitre
DL Darlington (UK postcode); Deal (UK fishing port registration); Delta Air Lines (airline flight code, USA); Deputy Lieutenant; diesel; *Doctor Legum* (Latin: Doctor of Laws); dog licence; dose level (physics); double ledger (book-keeping); down left (theatre); driving licence; Portsmouth (UK vehicle registration)
D/L data link; demand loan
dlc direct lift control
DLC Diploma of Loughborough College; divisional land commissioner; Doctor of Celtic Literature; down left centre (theatre)
dld deadline date; delivered
DLES Doctor of Letters in Economic Studies
DLett *Docteur en lettres* (French: Doctor of Letters)
DLG David Lloyd George (UK Prime Minister)
DLI Durham Light Infantry
D-Lib Liberal Democrat (US)
DLit Doctor of Literature

DLitt *Doctor Litterarum* (Latin: Doctor of Letters)
DLittS Doctor of Sacred Letters
DLJ Dame of Justice of the Order of St Lazarus of Jerusalem
DLO dead letter office; Diploma in Laryngology and Otology; Diploma in Laryngology and Otorrhinolaryngology; dispatch loading only
DLOY Duke of Lancaster's Own Yeomanry
DLP Democratic Labor Party (Australia); Democratic Labour Party (Barbados, Trinidad and Tobago, etc)
dlr dealer
DLR Docklands Light Railway (London)
DLS debt liquidation schedule; Doctor of Library Science; Dominion Land Surveyor
dlvd delivered
DLW Diploma in Labour Welfare
dly daily
dlyv delivery
dm decimetre
dM *dieses Monats* (German: this month)
DM Chester (UK vehicle registration); Daily Mail; dark matter (astronomy); deputy master; design manual; Deutschmark (German monetary unit); direct mail; Director of Music; dispersion measures; distributed memory (computing); district manager; *Docteur en médecine* (French: Doctor of Medicine); Doctor of Mathematics; Doctor of Medicine; Doctor of Music
DMA Diploma in Municipal Administration; direct memory access (computing)
DM&CW Diploma in Maternity and Child Welfare
D-mark Deutschmark (German monetary unit)
DMath Doctor of Mathematics
DMC direct manufacturing costs; district medical committee
DMD Doctor of Mathematics and Didactics; Doctor of Dental Medicine; Doctor of Medical Dentistry; Duchenne muscular dystrophy (medicine)
DME Diploma in Mechanical Engineering; distance-measuring equipment (aeronautics)
DMed Doctor of Medicine
DMet Doctor of Metallurgy; Doctor of Meteorology
DMFOS Diploma in Maxillofacial and Oral Surgery

dmg. damage
DMGO divisional machine-gun officer
DMHS director of medical and health services
DMI director of military intelligence
DMin Doctor of Ministry
DMJ Diploma in Medical Jurisprudence
DMJ(Path) Diploma in Medical Jurisprudence (Pathology)
DMK *Dravida Munnetra Kazgham* (India: Dravidian Progressive Forum)
dml. demolish
DML data-manipulation language (computing); Defence Medal for Leningrad; Doctor of Modern Languages
DMLJ Dame of Merit of the Order of St Lazarus of Jerusalem
DMLS Doppler Microwave Landing System
DMLT Diploma in Medical Laboratory Technology
DMM Defence Medal for Moscow
dmn dimension; dimensional
DMO Defence Medal for Odessa; director of military operations; district medical officer
DMO&I director, military operations and intelligence
DMP Diploma in Medical Psychology; director of manpower planning
DMPB Diploma in Medical Pathology and Bacteriology
DMR Diploma in Medical Radiology; Directorate of Materials Research
DMRD Diploma in Medical Radiological Diagnosis; Directorate of Materials Research and Development
DMR(&)E Diploma in Medical Radiology and Electrology
DMRT Diploma in Medical Radiotherapy
DMS data management system (computing); Diploma in Management Studies; Directorate of Military Survey; director of medical services; *Dis manibus sacrum* (Latin: consecrated to the souls of the departed); Doctor of Medical Science; Doctor of Medicine and Surgery
DMSO dimethyl sulphoxide (medicine)
DMSSB Direct Mail Services Standard Board
dmst(n) demonstration
dmstr demonstrator
DMSV Defence Medal for Sevastopol
DMT director of military training
DMU decision-making unit (commerce); directly managed unit (NHS)

D Mus Doctor of Music
DMV Department of Motor Vehicles (US); *Docteur en médecine vétérinaire* (French: Doctor of Veterinary Medicine)
DMZ demilitarized zone
dn down; dozen
Dn deacon; dragoon
Dn *Don* (Spanish: Mr)
DN debit note; *de novo* (Latin: from the beginning); Diploma in Nursing; Diploma in Nutrition; *Dominus noster* (Latin: our Lord); Doncaster (UK postcode); Leeds (UK vehicle registration)
Dna *Doña* (Spanish: Mrs)
DNA Defense Nuclear Agency (US); deoxyribonucleic acid (genetics); *Det Norske Arbeiderpartiet* (Norwegian: Norwegian Labour Party); *Deutscher Normenausschuss* (German: German Committee of Standards); did not attend (medicine); director of naval accounts; District Nursing Association
DNAD director of naval air division
DNB Dictionary of National Biography
DNC delayed-neutron counting (nuclear engineering); director of naval construction; distributed numerical control (computing)
DND director of navigation and direction
dne. *douane* (French: customs)
DNE Diploma in Nursing Education; director of naval equipment; director of nurse education
DNES director of naval education service
DNF did not finish (sport)
DNHW Department of National Health and Welfare (US)
DNI director of naval intelligence
DNJC *Dominus noster Jesus Christus* (Latin: Our Lord Jesus Christ)
DNMS director of naval medical services
DNO director of naval ordnance; district naval officer; district nursing officer; divisional nursing officer
D notice defence notice
DNP declared national programme
DNPP *Dominus Noster Papa Pontifex* (Latin: Our Lord the Pope)
DNR Department of Natural Resources (US); director of naval recruiting; do not resuscitate (medicine)
dns downs (cartography)
DNS Department of National Savings
DNSA Diploma in Nursing Service Administration

DNT director of naval training
DNWS director of naval weather service
do. *ditto* (Latin: the same)
d/o delivery order
DO defence order; deferred ordinary (shares); delivery order; Diploma in Ophthalmology; Diploma in Osteopathy; direct object (grammar); direct order (commerce); district office; district officer; divisional office; divisional officer; Doctor of Optometry; Doctor of Oratory; Doctor of Osteopathy; *Dominicana De Aviación* (airline flight code, Dominican Republic); Douglas (UK fishing port registration); drawing office; Lincoln (UK vehicle registration)
DOA date of availability; dead on arrival; Department of the Army (US); dissolved oxygen analyser
DOAE Defence Operational Analysis Establishment (Ministry of Defence)
dob date of birth
DObstRCOG Diploma of the Royal College of Obstetricians and Gynaecologists
doc. document; documents
Doc. doctor
DOC *Denominazione di Origine Controllata* (Italian: name of origin controlled; wines); Department of Commerce (US); direct operating cost; district officer commanding
doca date of current appointment
doce date of current enlistment
DocEng Doctor of Engineering
DOCG *Denominazione di Origine Controllata Garantita* (Italian: name of origin guaranteed controlled; wines)
docu. document; documentary; documentation
dod date of death; died of disease
DOD Department of Defense (US)
doe depends on experience
DoE Department of the Environment; director of education
DOE Department of Energy (US); Department of the Environment; depends on experience; director of education
D. of Corn. LI Duke of Cornwall's Light Infantry
D of H degree of honour
D of L Duchy of Lancaster
D of S director of stores
DoH Department of Health

DOHC double overhead camshaft; dual overhead camshaft
DOI Department of Industry; Department of the Interior (US); died of injuries; director of information
DOJ Department of Justice (US)
dol. *dolce* (Italian: sweetly; music); dollar
DOL Department of Labor (US); Doctor of Oriental Learning
dolciss. *dolcissimo* (Italian: very sweetly; music)
dom. domain; *domenica* (Italian: Sunday); domestic; domicile; dominant; *domingo* (Spanish, Portuguese: Sunday); dominion
Dom. Dominica; Dominical; Dominican (religion); *Dominus* (Latin: Lord)
DOM *Deo Optimo Maximo* (Latin: to God, the best and greatest); dirty old man; Dominican Republic (international vehicle registration); *Dominus omnium magister* (Latin: God the Lord of all)
Dom. Bk. Domesday Book
Dom. Proc. *Domus Procerum* (Latin: House of Lords)
DOMS Diploma in Ophthalmic Medicine and Surgery
Dom. Sc. domestic science
don. *donc* (Latin: until)
Don(eg). Donegal
DON Department of the Navy (US); Diploma in Orthopaedic Nursing
DOpt Diploma in Ophthalmic Optics
Dor. Dorian; Doric
DOr Doctor in Orientation
DOR director of operational requirements
Dora Defence of the Realm Act (World War I)
dorm. dormitory
Dors. Dorset
DOrth Diploma in Orthodontics; Diploma in Orthoptics
DOS day of sale; Department of State (US); Diploma in Orthopaedic Surgery; Directorate of Overseas Surveys; director of ordnance services; disk operating system (computing); Doctor of Ocular Science
DOSV deep ocean survey vehicle
dot. dotation/endowment (law)
DoT Department of Transport
DOT Department of Overseas Trade; Department of Transportation (US); designated order turnaround (finance); Diploma in Occupational Therapy
dott. *dottore* (Italian: doctor)
DOV double oil of vitriol (sulphuric acid)

DOVAP Doppler velocity and position (physics)
dow. dowager
DOW died of wounds
doz. dozen
dp damp-proof; damp-proofed; damp-proofing; deep; deep penetration; departure point; depreciation percentage (finance); *directione propria* (Italian: with proper direction; medicine); direct port; double paper; double play (baseball); dry powder; dual purpose
DP data processing; decimal pitch; degree of polymerization; delivery point; Democratic Party; diametral pitch; Diploma in Psychiatry; direction of the President; disabled person; displaced person; Doctor of Philosophy; domestic prelate; *Domus Procerum* (Latin: House of Lords); durable press; duty paid; dynamic programming (computing); Reading (UK vehicle registration)
D/P delivery on payment; documents against payment (commerce); documents against presentation (commerce)
dpa deferred payment account
DPA *Deutsche Presse-Agentur* (news agency, Germany); Diploma in Public Administration; discharged prisoners' aid; Doctor of Public Administration (US)
DPath Diploma in Pathology
DPB deposit pass book (finance)
DPC Defence Planning Committee (NATO)
DPCP Department of Prices and Consumer Protection
DPD Data Protection Directive; Diploma in Public Dentistry
DPE Diploma in Physical Education
DPEc Doctor of Political Economy
DPed Doctor of Pedagogy
DPh Doctor of Philosophy
DPH Department of Public Health; Diploma in Public Health; director of public health; Doctor of Public Health (US)
DPharm Doctor of Pharmacy
DPHD Diploma in Public Health Dentistry
DPhil Doctor of Philosophy
DPHN Diploma in Public Health Nursing
DPhyMed Diploma in Physical Medicine
dpi dots per inch (computing)
dpl. diploma; diplomat; duplex

DPM data processing manager; deputy prime minister; deputy provost-marshal; Diploma in Psychological Medicine

DPMI DOS/Protected Mode Interface (computing)

DPO distributing post office; district pay office

dpob date and place of birth

DPolSc Doctor of Political Science

DPP deferred payment plan (insurance); Diploma in Plant Pathology; director of public prosecutions

DPR Data Protection Register; director of public relations

DPRK Democratic People's Republic of Korea (North Korea)

DPS director of personal services; director of postal services; dividend per share; Doctor of Public Service

DPSA Diploma in Public and Social Administration

DPsSc Doctor of Psychological Science

DPsy *Docteur en psychologie* (French: Doctor of Psychology)

DPsych Diploma in Psychiatry; Doctor of Psychology

dpt department; deponent; deposit; depot

DPT diphtheria, pertussis, tetanus

dpty deputy

DPW Department of Public Works

dpx duplex

dq direct question

DQ dispersion quotient; disqualify (sport); Fiji (international civil aircraft marking)

DQMG deputy quartermaster-general

DQMS deputy quartermaster-sergeant

dr debtor; deficiency report; design requirements; development report; document report; dram; drizzle and rain (meteorology)

dr. debit; door; drachm; drachma (Greek monetary unit); drama; draw; drawer; drawn; dresser; driver; drum; drummer

Dr director; doctor; drachma (Greek monetary unit); drive

DR Daughters of the Revolution (US); dead reckoning (navigation); decay ratio (physics); defence regulation; *Deutsches Reich* (German: German Empire); dining-room; Diploma in Radiology; discount rate; dispatch rider; district railway; double royal (paper); Dover (UK fishing port registration); down right (theatre); Dutch Reformed; Exeter (UK vehicle registration)

D/R deposit receipt

Dra *Doctora* (Spanish: (female) doctor); *Doutora* (Portuguese: (female) doctor)

DRA de-rating appeals

DRAC Director Royal Armoured Corps

DrAgr Doctor of Agriculture

dram. drama; dramatic; dramatist

DRAM dynamic random-access memory (computing)

drams. pers. *dramatis personae* (Latin: characters in the play)

Drav. Dravidian

DRAW direct read after write (computing)

DrBusAdmin Doctor of Business Administration

DRC Diploma of the Royal College of Science and Technology (Glasgow); down right centre (theatre); Dutch Reformed Church

DrChem Doctor of Chemistry

DRCOG Diploma of the Royal College of Obstetricians and Gynaecologists

DRCPath Diploma of the Royal College of Pathologists

DRD Diploma in Restorative Dentistry

DRDW direct read during write (computing)

DRE Director of Religious Education; Doctor of Religious Education

DrEng Doctor of Engineering

drg drawing

DRG diagnosis-related group (medicine)

Dr hc *Doctor honoris causa* (Latin: honorary doctor)

Dr ing Doctor of Engineering

Dr jur Doctor of Laws

DRK *Deutsches Rotes Kreuz* (German: German Red Cross)

DRLS dispatch-rider letter service

DRM Diploma in Radiation Medicine; Diploma in Resource Management

DrMed Doctor of Medicine

drn drawn

DrNatSci Doctor of Natural Science

DRO daily routine order; disablement resettlement officer; divisional routine order

DrOecPol *Doctor Oeconomiae Politicae* (Latin: Doctor of Political Economics)

DRP dividend reinvestment plan

DrPH Doctor of Public Health

DrPhil Doctor of Philosophy

DrPolSci Doctor of Political Science

Dr rer. nat. Doctor of Natural Science

DRS Diploma in Religious Studies

DRSAMD Diploma of the Royal Scottish Academy of Music and Drama

DRSE drug-related side-effects (medicine)
DRSN drifting snow (meteorology)
DRT diagnostic rhyme test (psychiatry)
DrTheol Doctor of Theology
Dr. und Vrl. *Druck und Verlag* (German: printed and published by)
DRurSc Doctor of Rural Science
drx drachma
ds date of service; daylight saving; days after sight; day's sight; *destro* (Italian: right); document signed
Ds *Deus* (Latin: God); *Dominus* (Latin: Lord)
DS Air Senegal (airline flight code); *dal segno* (Italian: (repeat) from the sign; music); debenture stock (finance); defect score; dental surgeon; Department of State; detective sergeant; directing staff; Doctor of Science; Doctor of Surgery; Down's syndrome; driver seated; Dumfries (UK fishing port registration); Glasgow (UK vehicle registration)
DSA Diploma in Social Administration; *Docteur en sciences agricoles* (French: Doctor of Agriculture)
DSAC Defence Scientific Advisory Council
DSAO Diplomatic Service Administration Office
DSASO deputy senior air staff officer
DSB Drug Supervisory Body (UN)
DSc Doctor of Science
DSC Distinguished Service Cross; Doctor of Surgical Chiropody
DScA *Docteur en sciences agricoles* (French: Doctor of Agricultural Sciences); *Docteur en sciences appliquées* (French: Doctor of Applied Sciences)
DSc(Agr) Doctor of Science in Agriculture
DScEng Doctor of Science in Engineering
DScFor Doctor of Science in Forestry
DSCHE Diploma of the Scottish Council for Health Education
DScMil Doctor of Military Science
DScTech Doctor of Technical Science
DSD director of signals division; director of staff duties
dsDNA double-stranded DNA (genetics)
DSDP deep-sea drilling project
DSE Doctor of Science in Economics
Dsf. Düsseldorf
dsgn design; designer
DSIR Department of Scientific and Industrial Research (New Zealand)

DSL district scout leader; Doctor of Sacred Letters
DSM deputy stage manager; Directorate of Servicing and Maintenance; Distinguished Service Medal; Doctor of Sacred Music
dsmd dismissed
DSN Deep-Space Network (astronautics)
DSO Distinguished Service Order; district staff officer
DSocSc Doctor of Social Science(s)
dsp *decessit sine prole* (Latin: died without issue)
DSP Democratic Socialist Party; digital signal processing (electronics); *Docteur en sciences politiques* (French: Doctor of Political Science; Canada)
dspl *decessit sine prole mascula* (Latin: died without legitimate issue); disposal
dspm *decessit sine prole legitima* (Latin: died without legitimate issue)
dspms *decessit sine prole mascula superstite* (Latin: died without surviving male issue)
dspn disposition
dsps *decessit sine prole superstite* (Latin: died without surviving issue)
dspv *decessit sine prole virile* (Latin: died without male issue)
dsq discharged to sick quarters
DSR debt service ratio (commerce); director of scientific research
DSRD Directorate of Signals Research and Development
Dss deaconess
DSS decision-supporting system (computing); Department of Social Security; director of social services; Doctor of Social Science; *Doctor Sacrae Scripturae* (Latin: Doctor of Holy or Sacred Scripture)
DSSc Diploma in Sanitary Science; Doctor of Social Science
DST daylight-saving time; deep-sleep therapy; director of supplies and transport; Doctor of Sacred Theology; double summer time
DStJ Dame of Justice/Grace of the Order of St John of Jerusalem
dstn destination
D. Surg. dental surgeon
DSW Department of Social Welfare (New Zealand); Doctor of Social Welfare; Doctor of Social Work
dt delirium tremens; double throw
DT Daily Telegraph; damage-tolerant; daylight time; dead from tumour

(medicine); delirium tremens; dental technician; Department of Transportation (US); Department of Treasury (US); destructive testing; detective (US); director of transport; *Doctor Theologiae* (Latin: Doctor of Divinity or Theology); Dorchester (UK postcode); Sheffield (UK vehicle registration); TAAG-Angola Airlines (airline flight code)

DTA Diploma in Tropical Agriculture; Distributive Trades' Alliance

dtba date to be advised (commerce)

DTC Diploma in Textile Chemistry; Docklands Transportation Consortium

DTCD Department of Technical Cooperation for Development (US); Diploma in Tuberculosis and Chest Diseases

dtd dated; *detur talis dosis* (Latin: let such a dose be given; medicine)

DTD Diploma in Tuberculous Diseases; Director of Technical Development

DTE data terminal equipment (computing)

DTech Doctor of Technology

Dtg *Dienstag* (German: Tuesday)

DTh(eol) Doctor of Theology

DTH Diploma in Tropical Hygiene

DThPT Diploma in Theory and Practice of Teaching

DTI Department of Trade and Industry

DTL diode-transistor logic (electronics); down the line (shooting)

Dtm. Dortmund

DTM Diploma in Tropical Medicine

DTM(&)H Diploma in Tropical Medicine and Hygiene

dt° *direito* (Portuguese: right)

DTOD director of trade and operations division

DTp Department of Transport

DTP desk-top publishing

DTPH Diploma in Tropical Public Health

DTR Diploma in Therapeutic Radiology; double taxation relief

DTRP Diploma in Town and Regional Planning

DTRT deteriorate (meteorology); deteriorating (meteorology)

DT's delirium tremens

DTVM Diploma in Tropical Veterinary Medicine

Du. ducal; duchy; duke; Dutch

DU Coventry (UK vehicle registration);

died unmarried; Doctor of the University

dub. dubious; *dubitans* (Latin: doubting)

Dub(l). Dublin

DUC dense upper cloud (meteorology)

Dumf. Dumfries and Galloway Region

Dun. Dundee

Dunelm: *Dunelmensis* (Latin: (Bishop) of Durham)

DUniv Doctor of the University

duo. duodecimo (paper)

dup. duplicate

DUP Democratic Unionist Party (Northern Ireland); *Docteur de l'Université de Paris* (French: Doctor of the University of Paris)

Dur. Durban; Durham

DUS Diploma of the University of Southampton

DUSC deep underground support center (US Air Force)

Dut. Dutch

DUV damaging ultra-violet

DV defective vision; double vision; *Deo volente* (Latin: God willing); Diploma in Venereology; direct vision; distinguished visitor; district valuer; Domestic Violence Division (Scotland Yard); Douay Version (Bible); Exeter (UK vehicle registration)

DVA Diploma of Veterinary Anaesthesia

DV&D Diploma in Venereology and Dermatology

DVH Diploma in Veterinary Hygiene

DVI digital video imaging (computing)

DVLA Driver and Vehicle Licencing Authority

DVLC Driver and Vehicle Licencing Centre (Swansea)

dvm *decessit vita matris* (Latin: died in the lifetime of the mother)

DVM Doctor of Veterinary Medicine

DVMS Doctor of Veterinary Medicine and Surgery

DVO District Veterinary Officer

dvp *decessit vita patris* (Latin: died in the lifetime of the father)

DVPH Diploma in Veterinary Public Health

dvr driver

DVR Diploma in Veterinary Radiology; discrete-variable representation (computing)

DVS Doctor Of Veterinary Surgery

DVSc(i) Doctor of Veterinary Science

DVT deep-vein thrombosis (medicine)

dw dead weight; delivered weight

d/w dust wrapper (books)
DW Cardiff (UK vehicle registration);
dock warrant (commerce)
D/W deadweight; dock warrant
(commerce)
DWA driving without awareness
dwc deadweight capacity
dwel. dwelling
DWEM dead white European male
dwg drawing; dwelling
DWI driving while intoxicated (US);
Dutch West Indies
dwr drawer
DWR Duke of Wellington's Regiment
dwt deadweight tonnage; pennyweight
DWU Distillery, Wine and Allied Workers
International Union (US)
DX Dan-Air (airline flight code,
Denmark); daylight exposure
(photography); Ipswich (UK vehicle
registration); long-distance
(telecommunications)
DXR deep X-ray (medicine)
DXRT deep X-ray therapy

dy delivery; demy (paper)
Dy dysprosium (element)
DY Alyemda-Democratic Yemen Airlines
(airline flight code, Republic of Yemen);
Benin (international vehicle registration); Brighton (UK vehicle
registration); dockyard; Dudley (UK
postcode)
DYB Do Your Best (Boy Scouts)
Dyd dockyard
dyn dyne (physics)
dyn. dynamics; dynamite; dynamo;
dynasty
DYS Duke of York's Royal Military
School
dz. dozen
DZ Algeria (international vehicle
registration); Antrim (UK vehicle
registration); Doctor of Zoology;
drizzle (meteorology); drop zone
(military)
DZool Doctor of Zoology
D-Zug *Durchgangszug* (German: express
train)

E

e base of natural (Napierian) logarithms
(mathematics); east; eastern;
electromotive; electron (physics);
positron (physics); unit coordinate
vectors (mathematics); wet air
(meteorology)
e eccentricity (mathematics);
electron/proton charge (physics);
equatorial conformation (of molecules)
e. edition; educated; elder; eldest;
electric(ity); electromotive;
engineer(ing); Erlang (telephony); error
(baseball); evening; excellence; excellent
E earl; earth (electrics); east London (UK
postcode); Ecstasy (drug); electromeric
effect (chemistry); elimination reaction
(chemistry); elliptical galaxy (astronomy);
emalangeni (monetary unit of Swaziland); English shilling (numismatics);
E-number (food additives); exa-; Exeter
(UK fishing port registration); second-
class merchant ship (Lloyd's Register);
Spain (international vehicle registration);
universal negative categorical
proposition (logic)
E electric field strength (physics);

electrode potential (chemistry);
electromotive force (physics); energy
(physics); illuminance (physics);
irradiance (physics); Young modulus
(physics)
E. earl; earth (planet); east; eastern;
Easter; Edinburgh; efficiency; Egypt;
Egyptian; elocution; eminence; enemy;
engineer; engineering; England; English;
envoy; equator; España (Spain); evening;
evensong
ea. each
EA Dudley (UK vehicle registration);
early antigen; East Anglia; economic
adviser; educational age; effective
action; effective agent; electrical artificer;
Ente Autonomo (Italian: Autonomous
Corporation); Entered Apprentice
(Freemasonry); enterprise allowance;
environmental assessment; Evangelical
Alliance; experimental area; exposure
age
E/A enemy aircraft; experimental aircraft
EAA Edinburgh Architectural
Association; Electrical Appliance
Association; Engineer in Aeronautics

and Astronautics (US); ethylene/ethene
acrylic acid (chemistry)
EAAA European Association of
Advertising Agencies
EAAC European Agricultural Aviation
Centre
EAAFRO East African Agriculture and
Forestry Research Organization (Kenya)
EAAP European Association for Animal
Production
EAC East African Community;
Educational Advisory Committee;
Engineering Advisory Council;
European Atomic Commission
EACA East Africa Court of Appeal
Reports
EACC East Asia Christian Conference
EACSO East African Common Services
Organization
EAEG European Association of
Exploration Geophysicists
EAES European Atomic Energy Society
eaf emergency advisory file
EAF electric-arc furnace
EAFFRO East African Freshwater
Fisheries Research Organization
EAG Economists Advisory Group
EAGGF European Agricultural Guidance
and Guarantee Fund (EC)
EAK Kenya (international vehicle
registration)
EAM *Ethniko Apelentherotiko Metopo*
(Greek: National Liberation Front;
World War II)
EAMF European Association of Music
Festivals
EAMFRO East African Marine Fisheries
Research Organization
EAMTC European Association of
Management Training Centres
EAN effective atomic number (chemistry);
European Academic Network
(computing)
e and e each and every
E and OE errors and omissions expected
(invoices)
eaon except as otherwise noted
EAP East Africa Protectorate; Edgar
Allan Poe; employee-assistance
programme (US); English for academic
purposes
EAPR European Association for Potato
Research
EAR employee advisory resource;
employee attitude research; energy-
absorbing resin (engineering)
EARCCUS East African Regional

Committee for Conservation and
Utilization of Soil
EARM electrically alterable read-only
memory (computing)
EARN European Academic and Research
Network (computing)
EAROM electrically alterable read-only
memory (computing)
EAROPH East Asia Regional
Organization for Planning and Housing
EAS equivalent air speed (aeronautics);
estimated air speed (aeronautics)
EASA Entertainment Arts Socialist
Association
EASEP Early Apollo Scientific
Experiments Package (astronautics)
EASHP European Association of Senior
Hospital Physicians
east. eastern
EASTROPAC Eastern Tropical Pacific
eat earliest arrival time
EAT Employment Appeal Tribunal;
Tanzania (international vehicle
registration)
EATRO East African Trypanosomiasis
Research Organization
EAU Uganda (international vehicle
registration)
EAVRO East African Veterinary Research
Organization
EAW Electrical Association for Women;
equivalent average words
EAX electronic automatic exchange
(telecommunications)
EAZ Tanzania (international vehicle
registration)
EB Electricity Board; electron beam;
Evans blue (dye); Peterborough (UK
vehicle registration)
EB Encyclopedia Britannica
EBA English Bowling Association
EB&RA Engineer Buyers' and
Representatives' Association
ebar edited beyond all recognition
EBC English Benedictine Congregation;
European Billiards Confederation;
European Brewery Convention
EBCDIC extended binary-coded decimal
interchange code (computing)
e-beam electron beam
EBICON electron-bombardment-induced
conductivity (physics)
ebit earnings before interest and taxes
EBL European Bridge League
EBM expressed breast milk
EBMC English Butter Marketing
Company

EbN east by north
EBNF extended Backus normal form (computing)
E-boat Enemy War Motorboat (World War II)
Ebor: *Eboracensis* (Latin: Archbishop of York)
EBR experimental breeder reactor
EBRA Engineer Buyers' and Representatives' Association
EBRD European Bank of Reconstruction and Development
EbS east by south
EBS Emergency Bed Service; emergency broadcast system; engineered barrier system; English Bookplate Society
EBT electron-beam therapy (medicine)
EBU English Bridge Union; European Badminton Union; European Boxing Union; European Broadcasting Union
EBV Epstein-Barr virus (medicine)
EBWR experimental boiling-water reactor (nuclear physics)
ec earth closet; enamel coated; enamel covered; error correction; *exempli causa* (Latin: for example); extended coverage; extension course
Ec. Ecuador
EC East Caribbean; east central London (UK postcode); east coast; Eastern Command; Ecclesiastical Commissioner; Ecuador (international vehicle registration); eddy current (physics); education committee; educational committee; effective concentration (chemistry); electricity council; electrolytic corrosion; electron capture (physics); electron cyclotron (physics); electronic computer; emergency commission; Engineering Corps; Enzyme Commission (biochemistry); Episcopal Church; Established Church; ethene carbonate (chemistry); ethlyene carbonate (chemistry); *Étoile du Courage* (French: Star of Courage; Canada); European Commission; European Community; executive committee; Preston (UK vehicle registration); Spain (international civil aircraft marking)
ECA Early Closing Association; Economic Commission for Africa (UN); Economic Cooperation Administration (US); Educational Centres Association; Electrical Contractors' Association; European Commission on Agriculture; European Congress of Accountants
ECAC Engineering College Admin-

istrative Council; European Civil Aviation Conference
ECAFE Economic Commission for Asia and the Far East
ECAS Electrical Contractors' Association of Scotland
ECB electronic components board
ecc *eccetera* (Italian: etc)
Ecc. *Eccellenze* (Italian: Excellency)
ECC energy-conscious construction; European Cultural Centre
Ecc. Hom. *Ecce Home* (Latin: Behold the Man)
eccl. ecclesiastic; ecclesiastical
eccles. ecclesiastic; ecclesiastical
Eccles. Ecclesiastes (Bible)
Ecclus. Ecclesiasticus (Bible)
ECCM electronic counter-countermeasure (military)
ECCP European Committee on Crime Problems
ECCS emergency core-cooling system (physics)
ECCU English Cross Country Union
ECD early closing day; electron-capture detector (physics); electron-capture detection (physics); electrostatic charge decay (electronics); estimated completion date
ECE Economic Commission for Europe (UN); electron-cyclotron emission (physics)
ECF extended-care facility (US); extracellular fluid
ECFA European Committee for Future Accelerators
ECFMB Educational Council for Foreign Medical Graduates
ECFMS Educational Council for Foreign Medical Students
ECG electrocardiogram (medicine); electrocardiograph (medicine); Export Credit Guarantee
ECGB East Coast of Great Britain
ECGC Empire Cotton Growing Corporation
ECGD Export Credits Guarantee Department
ech. echelon
ECHP Environmental Compliance and Health Protection (US)
ECI East Coast of Ireland; energy-cost indicator
ECIA European Committee of Interior Architects
ECITO European Central Inland Transport Organization

ECLAC Economic Commission for Latin America and the Caribbean (UN)
eclec. eclectic; eclecticism
ecli. eclipse; ecliptic
ECLOF Ecumenical Church Loan Fund
ECLSS environmental control and life-support systems
ECM electric coding machine; electro-chemical machining; electronic countermeasure (military); energy conservation measure; environmental corrosion monitor; European Common Market
ECMA East Coast Magnetic Anomaly (geology); European Computer Manufacturers' Association
ECMF Electric Cable Makers' Federation
ECMRA European Chemical Market Research Association
ECMT European Conference of Ministers of Transport
ECMWF European Centre for Medium-range Weather Forecast
ECN epoxy-cresol-novolak (synthetic resin)
ECNSW Electricity Commission of New South Wales
ECO energy conservation opportunity; English Chamber Orchestra; European Coal Organization
ECODU European Control Data Users
ecol. ecological; ecology
Ecol. Soc. Am. Ecological Society of America
econ. economic(al); economics; economist; economy
Econ. J. Economic Journal
Econ. R. Economic Review
ECOR Engineering Committee on Ocean Resources (US)
ECOSOC Economic and Social Council (UN)
ECOVAST European Council for the Village and Small Town
ECOWAS Economic Community of West African States
ECP Euro-commercial paper (finance); European Committee on Crop Protection; *Evangelii Christi Praedicator* (Latin: Preacher of the Gospel of Christ)
ECPA Electric Consumers Protection Act
ECPD Engineers' Council for Professional Development (US)
ECPS European Centre for Population Studies
ECQAC Electronic Components Quality Assurance Committee

ECR electronic cash register
ECS electron-capture spectroscopy (physics); emergency cooling system (physics); emergency coolant system (physics); environmental control system; European Communications Satellite; European Components Service
ECSC European Coal and Steel Community
ECT electroconvulsive therapy (medicine); emission-computed tomography (medicine); emission-computerized tomography (medicine)
ECTA Electrical Contractors' Trading Association
ECTD Emission Control Technology Division (US)
ECTG European Channel Tunnel Group
ecu European currency unit
ECU English Church Union; environmental control unit; European Chiropractic Union; extra close-up (photography)
ECUA. Ecuador
ECUK East Coast of the United Kingdom
ECV external cephalic version (obstetrics)
ECWA Economic Commission for Western Asia (UN)
ECWEC European Community Wind Energy Conference and Exhibition
ECWS English Civil War Society
ECY European Conservation Year
ECYO European Community Youth Orchestra
ed edge distance; enemy dead; error detecting; excused duty; extra duty
ed. *edile* (Italian: building); edited; edition; editor; educated; education
éd. *édition* (French: edition)
Ed. Edinburgh; editor
ED Department of Education (US); Doctor of Engineering (US); economic dispatch; Education Department; effective dose (pharmacology); Efficiency Decoration; election district; electromagnetic dissociation (physics); electron device (electronics); electron diffraction (chemistry; physics); embryonic day (medicine); Employment Department; endiastole (medicine); endiastolic (medicine); entertainments duty; equilibrium dialysis; equivalent dose (radioactivity); European Democrat; ex dividend (finance); existence doubtful; experimental detector; extensive disease (medicine); extra

dividend (finance); Liverpool (UK vehicle registration)

eda early departure authorized

EDA Economic Development Administration (US); Electrical Development Association; electronic design automation; *Eniea Dimokratiki Aristera* (Greek: Union of the Democratic Left)

ED&S English Dance and Song

EDAS enhanced data-acquisition system (computing)

EdB Bachelor of Education

EDB ethene dibromide (soil fumigant and fuel additive)

EDBS expert database system (computing)

edc error detection and correction; extra dark colour

EDC Economic Development Committee; electron-distribution curve (physics); Engineering Design Centre; European Defence Community; expected date of confinement (obstetrics)

edd. *ediderunt* (Latin: published by); *editiones* (Latin: editions)

EdD Doctor of Education

EDD exactly delayed detonator; expected date of delivery (obstetrics)

EDE effective dose equivalent (radioactivity)

EDF *Électricité de France* (French: French electricity corporation); Environmental Defense Fund (US); European Development Fund

EDG emergency diesel generator; European Democratic Group

EDHA experimental data handling equipment

EDI electronic data interchange (computing)

Edin. Edinburgh

Ed. in Ch. editor in chief

EDIP European Defence Improvement Programme (NATO)

EDIS Engineering Data Information System

edit. edited; edition; editor; editorial; *editore* (Italian: publisher)

edl edition de luxe

EDL economic discard limits

EdM Master of Education

EDM electronic distance measurement (surveying)

EDMA European Direct Marketing Association

Edm. and Ipswich: Bishop of St Edmundsbury and Ipswich

Edmn Edmonton (Canada)

edn edition

Ednbgh Edinburgh

EDNS expected demand not supplied

edoc effective date of change

EDP electron-diffraction pattern (physics); electronic data processing; emergency defence plan; end-diastolic pressure (medicine)

EDPS electronic data-processing system (computing)

EDR electronic decoy rocket; Electronic Dictionary Research (Japan); European Depository Receipts; except during rain (pollen count)

EDRF European Demonstration Reprocessing Plant (nuclear fuel)

EdS Education Specialist

EDS Electronic Data Systems Corporation; English Dialect Society; exchangeable disk store (computing)

EDSAC Electronic Delay Storage Automatic Calculator (computing)

EDSAT Educational Television Satellite

EDSS expert decision-support system

EDT Eastern Daylight Time; energy design technique

EDTA European Dialysis and Transplant Association

EDU European Democratic Union

educ. educated; education(al)

educn education

EDV end-diastolic volume (medicine)

EDVAC Electronic Discrete Variable Automatic Computer

ee errors excepted; eye and ear

EE Early English; Eastern Electricity; edge-to-edge; electrical engineer(ing); electron emission; electronic engineer(ing); employment exchange; environmental education; environmental engineering; Envoy Extraordinary; errors excepted; ewe equivalent (New Zealand); explosive emission; expressed emotion; Lincoln (UK vehicle registration)

EEA Electronic Engineering Association; European Economic Area

EEAIE Electrical, Electronic and Allied Industries, Europe

EE&MP Envoy Extraordinary and Minister Plenipotentiary

EEB European Environmental Bureau

EEC energy-energy correlation; English Electric Company; European Economic Community; explosive-emission cathode (electronics)

EECS electrical-energy conversion system

EED effective equivalent dose (radioactivity); electro-explosive device

EEDC Economic Development Committee for the Electronics Industry

EEF Egyptian Expeditionary Force; Engineering Employers' Federation; equivalent-energy function

EEG electroencephalogram; electroencephalograph; Essence Export Group

EEI Edison Electric Institute (US); Environmental Equipment Institute (US)

EEIBA Electrical and Electronic Industries Benevolent Association

EEMJEB Electrical and Electronic Manufacturers' Joint Education Board

EEMS enhanced expanded memory specification (computing)

EEMUA Engineering Equipment and Materials Users Association

E Eng. Early English

EENT eye, ear, nose and throat (medicine)

EEO equal employment opportunity

EEOC Equal Employment Opportunity Commission (US)

EER energy-efficiency ratio

EERI Earthquake Engineering Research Institute (US)

EEROM electrically erasable read-only memory (computing)

EES electron-energy spectroscopy (physics); electron-energy spectrum (physics); European Exchange System

EET Eastern European Time

EETPU Electrical, Electronic, Telecommunication and Plumbing Union

EETS Early English Text Society

EEZ exclusive economic zone

EF edge-to-face; education(al) foundation; elevation finder; elongation factor (genetics); emergency fleet; enrichment factor (physics); expectant father; expeditionary force; experimental flight; extra fine; Middlesbrough (UK vehicle registration)

EFA engine fault analysis; essential fatty acid (biochemistry); Eton Fives Association; European Fighter Aircraft

EFB energy from biomass

EFC European Federation of Corrosion; European Forestry Commission

EFCE European Federation of Chemical Engineering

EFCT European Federation of Conference Towns

EFD early fault detection (engineering)

EFDSS English Folk Dance and Song Society

EFE *Agencia EFE* (news agency, Spain)

eff. *effetto* (Italian: bill or promisory note); efficiency; effigy

EFF European Furniture Federation

EFG electric-field gradient

EFGF epitaxial ferrite-garnet film (electronics)

EFI electronic fuel injection

EFIS electronic flight-information system (aeronautics)

EFL English as a foreign language; external financial limit

EFM electronic fetal/foetal monitor (medicine); European Federalist Movement

EFNS Educational Foundation for Nuclear Science

EFP Einstein-Fokker-Planck (differential equation); electronic filed production (photography); exchange of futures for physicals (commerce); explosively formed penetrator; explosively formed projectile

EFPD effective full-power day

EFPH effective full-power hour

EFPW European Federation for the Protection of Waters

EFPY effective full-power year

EFR European fast reactor; experimental fast reactor

EFRC Edwards Flight Research Centre (US)

EFSA European Federation of Sea Anglers

EFSC European Federation of Soroptimist Clubs

EFT electronic funds-transfer

EFTA European Free Trade Association

EFTC Electrical Fair Trading Council

EFTPOS electronic funds-transfer at point of sale

EFTS electronic funds-transfer system; elementary flying training school

EFU energetic feed unit; European Football Union

EFVA Educational Foundation for Visual Aids

EFW energy from waste

eg *ejusdem generis* (Latin: of a like kind); *exempli gratia* (Latin: for the sake of example)

Eg. Egypt; Egyptian; Egyptologist; Egyptology

EG Engineers' Guild; ethylene glycol (chemistry); Peterborough (UK vehicle registration)

EGA Elizabeth Garrett Anderson (Hospital); enhanced graphics adapter (computing); European Gold Association

EGARD environmental gamma-ray and radon detector

EGAS Educational Grants Advisory Service

EGCI Export Group for the Construction Industries

EGCS English Guernsey Cattle Society

EGD epithermal gold deposit

EGEAS Electric Generating Expansion Analysis System

EGF epidermal growth factor (medicine)

EGFR epidermal-growth-factor receptor (medicine)

EGIFO Edward Grey Institute of Field Ornithology

EGL Engineers' Guild Limited

EGM Empire Gallantry Medal; European Glass Container Manufacturers' Committee; extraordinary general meeting

EGmbH *Eingetragene Gesellschaft mit beschränkter Haftung* (German: registered limited company)

EGO eccentric (orbit) geophysical observatory

EGR earned growth rate (finance); exhaust gas recirculation

EGSP electronics glossary and symbol panel

egt exhaust gas temperature

EGT Einstein-invariant gauge theory (physics)

EGU English Golf Union; external gelation of uranium (chemistry)

Egypt. Egyptian

EGYPT Eager to grab your pretty tits

Egyptol. Egyptologist; Egyptology

eh. *ehrenhalber* (German: honorary)

EH Edinburgh (UK postcode); English horn (music); essential hypertension (medicine); Stoke-on-Trent (UK vehicle registration)

EHC effective heat capacity (buildings); European Hotel Corporation; external heart compression (medicine)

EHF European Hockey Federation; experimental husbandry farm; extremely high frequency (radio)

EHL effective half-life (physics)

EHO environmental health officer

ehp effective horse power

EHP electric and hybrid propulsion

EHR environmental hazard ranking

EHS Environmental Health Services (US); European hybrid spectrometer; extra-high strength

EHT extra-high tension (electronics)

EHV electric and hybrid vehicle; extra-high voltage

EHWS extreme high water-level spring tides

EI Aer Lingus (airline flight code, Irish Republic); earth interface (atmosphere); East Indian; East Indies; electrical insulation; electromagnetic interaction; electron impact; electron ionization; endorsement irregular (finance); energy intake; environmentally induced illness; exposure index (photography); external irradiation; Irish Republic (international civil aircraft marking); Sligo (Irish vehicle registration)

EIA East Indian Association; economic impact assessment; Electronic Industries Association (US); Engineering Industries Association; environmental impact analysis; environmental impact assessment; Environmental Investigation Agency; exercise-induced asthma (medicine)

EIB European Investment Bank; Export-Import Bank

EIC East India Company; Electrical Industries' Club; Engineering Institute of Canada

EICM employers' inventory of critical manpower

EICS East India Company's Service

EID East India Dock; Electrical Inspection Directorate (military)

EIDCT Educational Institute of Design, Craft and Technology

EIEMA Electrical Installation Equipment Manufacturers' Association

EIF Elderly Invalids Fund

EIFAC European Inland Fisheries Advisory Committee (FAO)

E-in-C Engineer-in-Chief

E Ind. East Indies

einschl. *einschliesslich* (German: including or inclusive)

Einw. *Einwohner* (German: inhabitant)

EIPC European Institute of Printed Circuits

EIR earned income relief (taxation)

EIRMA European Industrial Research Management Association

EIS economic information system; Educational Institute of Scotland; effluent information system; energy information system; environmental impact statement; epidemic intelligence service

EISA extended industry standard architecture (computing)

EITB Engineering Industry Training Board

EIU Economist Intelligence Unit

EIVT European Institute for Vocational Training

ej. *ejemplo* (Spanish: example)

EJ exajoule (physics); Haverfordwest (UK vehicle registration)

EJC Engineers' Joint Council (US)

EJMA English Joinery Manufacturers' Association

ejusd. *ejusdem* (Latin: of the same)

eK *etter Kristi* (Norwegian: after Christ)

EK East Kilbride; Emirates (airline flight code, United Arab Emirates); *Enosis Kentron* (Greek: Centre Union); Liverpool (UK vehicle registration)

EKD *Evangelische Kirche in Deutschland* (German: Protestant Church in Germany)

EKG electrocardiogram; electrocardiograph (US; Germany)

el. elect; elected; electric; electrical; electricity; element; elevated; elevated railway; elevation; elongation

EL easy listening (music); Bournemouth (UK vehicle registration); electrical laboratory; electronics laboratory; Engineer Lieutenant; epitaxial layer; Everyman's Library; explosive limit; Liberia (international civil aircraft marking)

ELA electronic learning aid; Eritrean Liberation Army (Ethiopia)

elas. elasticity

ELAS *Ethnikos Laikos Apeleutherotikos Stratos* (Greek: Hellenic People's Army of Liberation; World War II)

ELB Bachelor of English Literature

ELBS English Language Book Society

ELC Environment Liaison Centre (Nairobi)

eld. elder; eldest

ELD economic load distribution

ELDC economic load dispatching centre

ELDO European Launcher Development Organization

elec. election; elector(al); electric(al); electrically; electrician; electricity; electron(ic); electuary (medicine)

ELEC European League for Economic Cooperation

electr. electrical

Electra Electrical, Electronics and Communications Trades Association

electron. electronics

elem. element(s); elementary

elev. elevation; elevator

elf early lunar flare

ELF Eritrean Liberation Front (Ethiopia); European Landworkers' Federation; extremely low frequency (radio)

ELG emission-line galaxy (astronomy)

ELH egg-laying hormone (biochemistry)

Eli electronic line indicator (sport)

Eli. Elias; Elijah

Elien: *Eliensis* (Latin: Bishop of Ely)

Elint electronic intelligence (military)

elix. elixir

Eliz. Elizabethan

ELLA European Long Lines Agency

ellipt. elliptical

ELM edge-localized mode

ELMA electromechanical aid

Elmint electromagnetic intelligence (military)

elo. elocution; eloquence

ELOISE European Large Orbiting Instrumentation for Solar Experiments

elong. elongate(d); elongation

E. Long. east longitude

ELR environment lapse rate (meteorology); exceptional leave to remain (immigration); export licensing regulations

elsewh. elsewhere

ELSIE electronic speech information equipment

ELT English language teaching; European letter telegram

ELU English Lacrosse Union

ELV expendable launch vehicle; extra-low voltage

ELWS extreme low water-level spring tides

ely easterly

em electromagnetic; electron microscope; emergency maintenance; expanded metal; external memorandum

em. emanation; embargo; eminent

Em. Eminence

EM Earl Marshal; Edward Medal; effective mass (physics); Efficiency Medal; electrical and mechanical;

electromagnetic; electromotive;
electronic mail; electron microscope;
electron microscopy; emission measure;
engineering model; Engineer of Mines;
enhanced mutagenesis (genetics);
enlisted man; environmental modelling;
equipment module; *Equitum Magister*
(Latin: Master of the Horse); European
Movement; evaluation model;
expectation maximization; Liverpool
(UK vehicle registration)
EMA European Marketing Association;
European Monetary Agreement;
Evangelical Missionary Alliance
EMAD engine maintenance and
disassembly
e-mail electronic mail
EMAS Edinburgh multi-access system
(computing); Employment Medical
Advisory Service
emb. embargo
Emb. Embankment (London); Embassy
EMB Energy Mobilization Board
EMBD embedded in cloud (meteorology)
EMBL European Molecular Biology
Laboratory (Heidelberg)
EMBO European Molecular Biology
Organization
embr. embroider; embroidery
embryol. embryology
EMC Einstein Medical Centre (US);
energy management centre; energy
management company; Engineering
Manpower Commission (US);
environmental monitoring and
compliance
EMCB earth-mounded concrete bunker
EMCC European Municipal Credit
Community
EMCCC European Military
Communications Coordinating
Committee
EMCOF European Monetary Cooperation
Fund
EMCS energy monitoring and control
system
EME East Midlands Electricity
emer. emergency
Emer. Emeritus
EMet Engineer of Metallurgy
EMEU East Midlands Educational Union
emf electromotive force (physics)
EMF European Metalworkers' Federation;
European Monetary Fund; European
Motel Federation
EMFI Energy and Minerals Field Institute
(US)

EMG electromyogram (medicine);
electromyograph (medicine)
EMI Earth Mechanics Institute (US);
Electric and Musical Industries Limited;
electromagnetic interference
(computing)
EMIC emergency maternity and infant
care
EMK *elektromotorische Kraft* (German:
electromotive force)
EML Environmental Measurement(s)
Laboratory; Everyman's Library
Emm. Emmanuel College (Cambridge)
E. Mn. E. Early Modern English
EMNRD Energy, Minerals and Natural
Resources Department
emos earth's mean orbital speed
emp. *emplastrum* (Latin: in plaster;
medicine)
Emp. Emperor; Empire; Empress
EMP ecological monitoring programme;
electromagnetic pulse; electronic
materials programme; environmental
management plan/programme;
environmental monitoring
plan/programme
emp. agcy employment agency
empld employed
EMR Eastern Mediterranean Region;
electromagnetic radiation
EMRIC Educational Media Research
Information Centre (US)
EMRS East Malling Research Station
EMS emergency management system;
emergency medical service; energy
management system; European
Monetary System; expanded memory
specification (computing)
EMSA Electron Microscopy Society of
America
EMSC Electrical Manufacturers'
Standards Council (US)
EMT effective-mass theory (physics);
emergency medical technician
EMTA Electro-Medical Trade Association
emu electromagnetic unit; European
monetary unit
EMU economic and monetary union;
electrical multiple unit; extravehicular
activity
EMW energy from municipal waste
en. enemy
En. Engineer; English
EN El Niño (meteorology); *Emissora
Nacional* (Portuguese: national
broadcasting station); Enfield (UK
postcode); Enrolled Nurse; *Estrada*

Nacional (Portuguese: national highway); exceptions noted; extrapolation number; Manchester (UK vehicle registration)
ENA Eastern News Agency (Bangladesh); Eastern North America; *École Nationale d'Administration* (French: graduate college for top civil servants); English Newspaper Association
ENAB Evening Newspaper Advertising Bureau
enam. enamel(led)
ENB English National Ballet; English National Board for Nursing, Midwifery and Health Visiting
enc. enclosed; enclosure
ENCA European Naval Communications Agency
Enc. Brit. Encyclopedia Britannica
encl. enclosed; enclosure
ency. encyclopedia; encyclopedic; encyclopedism; encyclopedist
END European Nuclear Disarmament
ENDO Ethiopian National Democratic Organization
endow. endowment
endp. endpaper
ENDS Euratom Nuclear Documentation System
ENE east-northeast
ENEA European Nuclear Energy Agency
ENF European Nuclear Force
eng. engine; engineer(ing); engraved; engraver; engraving
Eng. England; English
ENG electronic news gathering
EN(G) Enrolled Nurse (General)
EngD Doctor of Engineering
engg engineering
Eng. hn English horn (music)
engin. engineer(ing)
Engl. England; English
engr engineer; engraver
engr. engrave(d); engraving
EngScD Doctor of Engineering Science
ENIAC Electronic Numeral Indicator and Calculator
ENIT *Ente Nazionale Industrie Turistiche* (Italian: state tourist office)
enl. enlarge(d); enlargement; enlisted
EN(M) Enrolled Nurse (Mental)
EN(MH) Enrolled Nurse (Mental Handicap)
eno *enero* (Spanish: January)
ENO English National Opera
ENR Energy and Natural Resources
Ens. ensemble (music); Ensign

ENSA Entertainments National Service Association (World War II)
ENSDF Evaluated Nuclear Structure Data File
ENSO El Niño southern oscillation (meteorology)
ent. entomology; entertainment; entrance
Ent. enter (theatre)
ENT ear, nose and throat (medicine)
entom(ol). entomological; entomology
Ent. Sta. Hall entered at Stationers' Hall (copyright)
env. envelope; environs
Env. Envoy
Env. Ext. Envoy Extraordinary
eo ex officio
Eo Easter offerings
EO Eastern Orthodox (religion); education officer; electro-optic; electro-optical; emergency operation; employers' organization; engineer officer; entertainments officer; equal opportunities; executive officer; executive order; experimental officer; Preston (UK vehicle registration)
EOA Essential Oil Association (US); examination, opinion and advice
EOARDC European Office of the Air Research and Development Command (US)
EOB end of block (computing); Executive Office Building
Eoc Eocene (geology)
EOC electron-optical camera; Emergency Operations Center (US); Emergency Operating Center (US); end of cycle; Equal Opportunities Commission
eod entry on duty; every other day
EOD end of data (computing); explosive ordnance demolition (military); explosive ordnance disposal (military)
EOE enemy-occupied Europe; equal opportunity employer; errors and ommissions excepted (invoices); European Options Exchange
EOF Emergency Operating Facility (US); Emergency Operations Facility (US); end of file (computing)
eohp except otherwise herein provided
EOJ end of job (computing)
Eoka *Ethniki Organosis Kipriakou Agonos* (Greek: National Organization for Cypriot Struggle)
EOL end of life
EOLM electro-optical light modulator

eom end of the month (commerce); every other month

EOM Egyptian Order of Merit; extractable organic material; extractable organic matter

EONR European Organization for Nuclear Research

eooe *erreur ou omission exceptée* (French: errors and omissions excepted; invoices)

EOP emergency operating procedure

EOPH Examined Officer of Public Health

EOQC European Organization for Quality Control

EOQL end of qualified life

EOR earth-orbit rendezvous (astronautics); end of record (computing); enhanced oil recovery

EORI Economic Opportunity Research Institute (US)

EORTC European Organization for Research on Treatment of Cancer

EOS erasable optical storage (computing); European Orthodontic Society

eot enemy-occupied territory

EOT end of tape; end of transmission (computing)

EOTP European Organization for Trade Promotion

ep easy projection; *editio princeps* (Latin: first edition); electrically polarized; endpaper; engineering personnel; en passant (chess); estimated position (navigation); extreme pressure

Ep. *Episcopus* (Latin: Bishop); Epistle (Bible)

EP educational psychologist (US); electrically conducting polymer (electronics); electroplate(d) (metallurgy); end point; environmental protection; estimated position (navigation); European Parliament; expanded polystyrene; extended-play (gramophone records); extraction procedure; Extraordinary and Plenipotentiary; Iran (international civil aircraft marking); Swansea (UK vehicle registration)

EPA educational priority area; Emergency Powers Act; Employment Protection Act; energy-performance assessment; Environmental Protection Agency (US); European Productivity Agency

EPAA Emergency Petroleum Allocation Act (US)

EPACCI Economic Planning and Advisory Council for the Construction Industries

EPAQ electronic parts of assessed quality

EPB equivalent pension benefit

EPC easy-processing channel; Economic and Planning Council; Educational Publishers' Council; evaporative pattern-casting (foundry)

EPCA Energy Policy and Conservation Act (US); energy production and consumption account; European Petro-Chemical Association

EPCOT Experimental Prototype Community of Tomorrow (Disney World, Florida)

EPD earliest practicable date

EPDA Emergency Powers Defence Act

EPDC Electric Power Development Company (US)

EPEA Electrical Power Engineers' Association

EPF emulsified petroleum fuel; European Packaging Federation

EPFM elastic-plastic fracture mechanics

EPG Electronic Proving Ground (US); Emergency Procedure Guidelines; Eminent Persons Group

EPGS electric power generating system

Eph(es). Ephesians (Bible)

EPI echo planar imaging; electronic position indicator

EPIC Engineering and Production Information Control; European Prospective Investigation into Cancer

Epict. Epictetus (Greek philosopher)

epid. epidemic

epil. epilogue

Epiph. Epiphany (Bible)

EPIRB emergency position indicator radio beacon (navigation)

Epis(c). Episcopal(ian)

Epist. Epistle (Bible)

epit. epitaph; epitome

EPLD erasable programmable logic device (computing)

EPLF Eritrean People's Liberation Front

EPNS electroplated nickel silver; English Place-Name Society

EPOC Eastern Pacific Oceanic Conference

EPOCH End Physical Punishment of Children

EPOS electronic point of sale

EPP European People's Party; executive pension plan

EPPO European and Mediterranean Plant Protection Organization

EPPT European printer performance test (computing)

EPR Einstein-Podolsky-Rosen (paradox); electron paramagnetic resonance; ethylene-propylene rubber

EPRI Electric Power Research Institute (US)

EPROM electronically programmable read-only memory (computing)

eps earnings per share

EPS electric(al) power system; Environmental Protection Service (US)

EPSS electrical power supervision system

EPT early pregnancy test (medicine); excess profits tax

EPTA Expanded Programme of Technical Assistance (UN)

Ep. tm. Epiphany term (law)

EPU European Payments Union

Epus. *Episcopus* (Latin: bishop)

EPW earth-penetrator weapon; enemy prisoner of war

eq. equal; equate; equation; equator(ial); equipment; equitable; equity; equivalent

Eq. Equerry

EQ educational quotient; equipment qualification; equivalence (electronics)

EQC external quality control

EQD Electrical Quality Assurance Directorate

EQDB equipment qualification data bank

EQI exhaust quality index

eqn equation

eqpt equipment

equil. equilibrium

equip. equipment

EQUIP equipment usage information programme

equiv. equivalent

er echo ranging; effectiveness report; elder; electronic reconnaissance; emergency request; emergency rescue; established reliability; external resistance

Er erbium (element)

ER Eastern Region (UK Rail); East Riding (Yorkshire); *Eduardus Rex* (Latin: King Edward); efficiency report; *Elizabeth Regina* (Latin: Queen Elizabeth); emergency room (medicine); engine room; entity relationship (computing); Peterborough (UK vehicle registration)

ERA earned run average (baseball); Economic Regulatory Administration (US); Education Reform Act; Electrical Research Association; electronic reading automation; Electronic Rentals

Association; Emergency Relief Administration (US); engine-room artificer; Equal Rights Amendment (US); European Ramblers' Association; Evangelical Radio Alliance

ERAB Energy Research Advisory Board

ERAMS Environmental Radiation Ambients Monitoring System

Eras. Erasmus

ERBM extended range ballistic missile

ERBS Earth Radiation Budget Satellite

ERC Economic Research Council; Electronics Research Council; Employment Rehabilitation Centre; Energy Research Corporation (US)

ERC&I Economic Reform Club and Institute

ERCB Energy Resources Conservation Board (US)

ERCS emergency response computer system

ERD elastic recoil detection; Emergency Reserve Decoration; emergency return device; environmental radiation data; equivalent residual dose (radioactivity)

ERDA Electrical and Radio Development Association (Australia); Energy Research and Development Administration (US)

ERDAF Energy Research and Development in Agriculture and Food (US)

ERDE Engineering Research and Development Establishment; Explosives Research and Development Establishment

ERDF European Regional Development Fund

ERDIC Energy Research, Development and Information Centre

ERDL Engineering Research and Development Laboratory

ERDS emergency response data system

ERE *Ethniki Rizospastiki Enosis* (Greek: National Radical Union)

erec. erection

ERFA European Radio Frequency Agency

ERG electrical resistance gauge

ERGOM European Research Group on Management

ergon. ergonomics

ERI *Edwardus Rex et Imperator* (Latin: Edward King and Emperor)

ERIC Educational Resources Information Centre (US); energy rate input controller

ERIS Emergency Response Information System; Exo-atmospheric Re-entry

Vehicle Interceptor Subsystem (astronautics)
Erit. Eritrea
Erl. *Erläuterung* (German; explanatory note)
ERL Energy Research Laboratory
erm. ermine
ERM Exchange Rate Mechanism (finance)
Ernie electronic random number indicator equipment (premium bonds)
ERO European Regional Organization of the International Confederation of Free Trade Unions
Eropa Eastern Regional Organization for Public Administration
Eros earth resources observation satellite; experimental reflection orbital shot (astronautics)
erp effective radiated power
ERP European Recovery Programme
ERR energy release rate
erron. erroneous(ly)
ERS earnings-related supplement; earth resources satellite; emergency radio service; emergency response system; engine repair section; Ergonomics Research Society; Experimental Research Society (US)
ERT *Elliniki Radiophonia Tileorasis* (Greek: Hellenic National Radio and Television Institute); excess retention tax
ERTA Economic Recovery and Tax Act (US)
ERTS Earth Resources Technology Satellite; European Rapid Train System
ERU English Rugby Union
ERV English Revised Version (Bible)
erw. *erweitert* (German: enlarged or extended)
ERW enhanced radiation weapon
es eldest son; electrical sounding; electric starting
es. *esempio* (Italian: example)
Es einsteinium (element)
ES Dundee (UK vehicle registration); Econometric Society; Education Specialist; elastic scattering (physics); electronic structure (chemistry); electron synchotron (physics); electrostatic; El Salvador (international vehicle registration); energy spectrum; engine-sized (paper); Entomological Society; Estonia (international civil aircraft marking); exploratory shaft (mining)
ESA Ecological Society of America; Educational Supply Association; Entomological Society of America;

environmentally sensitive area; European Space Agency; Euthanasia Society of America
ESANZ Economic Society of Australia and New Zealand
ESAR electronically steerable array radar
ESB electrical stimulation of the brain; Electricity Supply Board (US); electric storage battery; Empire State Building; English Speaking Board; environmental specimen bank
ESBA English Schools' Badminton Association
ESBBA English Schools' Basket Ball Association
ESBTC European Space Battery Test Centre (US)
esc. *escompte* (French: discount); escutcheon
Esc. escape key (computing); escudo (Portuguese monetary unit)
ESC Economic and Social Council (UN); electronic stills camera; Energy Security Corporation (US); English Stage Company; English Steel Corporation; Entomological Society of Canada; European Space Conference; extended core storage (computing)
ESCA English Schools' Cricket Association; English Schools' Cycling Association
ESCAP Economic and Social Commission for Asia and the Pacific (UN)
eschat. eschatology
ESCO Educational, Scientific and Cultural Organization (UN)
ESCOM Electricity Supply Commission of South Africa
ESCU European Space Operations Centre
Esd. Esdras (Bible)
ESD echo-sounding device; Environmental Sciences Division (US); Euratom Safeguards Directorate
ESDAC European Space Data Centre
ESE east-southeast; engineers stores establishment
ESEF Electrotyping and Stereotyping Employers' Federation
ESES environmentally sound energy system
ESF European Science Foundation
ESG Education Support Grant; English standard gauge (engineering)
ESH Environmental Safety and Health; equivalent standard hours; European Society of Haematology

ESI Electricity Supply Industry; environment sensitivity index
ESITB Electricity Supply Industry Training Board
Esk. Eskimo
esl expected significant level
ESL English as a second language
ESLAB European Space Research Laboratory
ESMA Electrical Sign Manufacturers' Association
esn(tl). essential
ESN educationally subnormal
ESNZ Entomological Society of New Zealand
ESO Energy Services Operator; European Southern Observatory
ESOC European Space Operations Centre
ESOL English for speakers of other languages
ESOMAR European Society for Opinion Surveys and Market Research
ESOP employee share-ownership plan
esp. especially; *espressivo* (Italian: expressively; music)
Esp. *Espagne* (French: Spain); *España* (Spanish: Spain); Esperanto
ESP English for special purposes; English for specific purposes; extrasensory perception
espg. espionage
espr(ess). *espressivo* (Italian: expressively; music)
ESPRIT European strategic programme for research and development in information technology
Esq. Esquire
ESQA English Slate Quarries Association
esq° *esquerdo* (Portuguese: left)
ESRC Economic and Social Research Council; Electricity Supply Research Council
ESRO European Space Research Organization
ESRS European Society for Rural Sociology
ess. essence; *essentia* (Latin: essence; pharmacology); essential
Ess. Essex
ESS energy storage system
ESSA English Schools' Swimming Association; Environmental Science Services Administration (US)
ESSO Standard Oil Company
est. established; estate (law); estimate; estimated; estimation; estimator; estuary
Est. established; Estonia; Estonian

EST earliest start time; Eastern Standard Time; electric-shock treatment; electroshock therapy
estab. establish; established; establishment
ESTEC European Space Research and Technology Centre
estg estimating
Esth. Esther (Bible)
ESTI European Space Technology Institute
estn estimation
esu electrostatic unit
ESU English-Speaking Union
ESV earth satellite vehicle (astronautics); emergency shutdown valve (engineering)
et educational therapy; electric telegraph; engineering time; English text; English translation; entertainment tax; exchange telegraph
Et ethyl
ET Eastern Time; Egypt (international vehicle registration); embryo transfer (medicine); emerging technology (NATO); Employment Training; ephemeris time; equation of time (physics); Ethiopian Airlines (airline flight code); extraterrestrial; Sheffield (UK vehicle registration)
Eta *Euzkadi ta Askatasuna* (Basque: Nation and Liberty; Basque separatist organization)
ETA Entertainment Trades' Alliance; estimated time of arrival; European Teachers' Association
Étab. *Établissement* (French: business establishment)
ETAC Education and Training Advisory Council
et al. *et alibi* (Latin: and elsewhere); *et alii* (Latin: and others)
ETB English Tourist Board
etc *et cetera* (Latin: and the other things, and so forth)
ETC Eastern Telegraph Company; European Translation Centre
ETCTA Electrical Trades Commercial Travellers' Association
ETD estimated time of departure; extension trunk dialling (telecommunications)
ETE estimated time en route; evacuation-time estimate; Experimental Tunnelling Establishment
ETF electronic transfer of funds (banking)
eth. ether; ethical; ethics

Eth. Ethiopia; Ethiopian; Ethiopic
ETH *Eidgenössische Technische Hochschule*
(German: Federal Institute of
Technology); Ethiopia (international
vehicle registration)
ethnog. ethnography
ethnol. ethnological; ethnology
eti elapsed time indicator
ETI estimated time of interception;
extraterrestrial intelligence
ETJC Engineering Trades Joint Council
etkm every test known to man
ETMA English Timber Merchants'
Association; European Television
Magazine Association
eto estimated time off
ETO European Theatre of Operations
(World War II); European Transport
Organization
ETOP Environmental Threat and
Opportunity Profile (US)
etp estimated turnaround point;
estimated turning point
Etr. Etruscan
ETR engineering test reactor; estimated
time of return; experimental test reactor
(nuclear engineering); experimental
thermonuclear reactor (nuclear
engineering)
ETS Educational Testing Service (US);
estimated time of sailing; expiration of
time of service
ETSA Electricity Trust of South Australia
et seq *et sequens* (Latin: and the
following)
etsp entitled to severance pay
et sqq. *et sequentes / sequentia* (Latin: and
the following)
ETSU Energy Technology Support Unit
ETTA English Table Tennis Association
ETTU European Table Tennis Union
ETU Electricians Trade Union;
experimental test unit
ETUC European Trade Union
Confederation
ETUI European Trade Union Institute
et ux. *et uxor* (Latin: and wife)
ETV educational television; engine test
vehicle
ety. etymological; etymologist; etymology
Eu europium (element)
EU Bristol (UK vehicle registration);
Ecuatoriana (airline flight code,
Ecuador); *Estados Unidos* (Spanish:
United States); *États-Unis* (French:
United States); European Union;
Evangelical Union; experimental unit

EUA *Estados Unidos da América*
(Portuguese: United States of America);
Estados Unidos de América (Spanish:
United States of America); *États-Unis
d'Amérique* (French: United States of
America); European unit of account
(finance); examination under
anaesthesia (medicine)
Euc. Euclid (Greek mathematician)
EUCOM European Command (US;
military)
EUDISED European Documentation and
Information Service for Education
EUFA European Union Football
Association
EUFTT European Union of Film and
Television Technicians
eugen. eugenics
EUL Everyman's University Library
EUM *Estados Unidos Mexicanos* (Spanish:
Mexico)
EUMETSAT European Meteorological
Satellite System
EUP English Universities Press
Eur. Europe; European
Euratom European Atomic Energy
Commission
Eureca European retrievable carrier
(astronautics)
Eur Ing European Engineer
Eurip. Euripides
Euro$ Eurodollar
EURO European Regional Office (FAO)
EUROCAE European Organization for
Civil Aviation Electronics
EUROCEAN European Oceanographic
Association
EUROCHEMIC European Company for
the Chemical Processing of Irradiated
Fuels
EUROCOM European Coal Merchants'
Union
EUROFINAS Association of European
Finance Houses
EuroJazz European Community Youth
Jazz Orchestra
EUROM European Federation for Optics
and Precision Mechanics
EURONET European data-transmission
network
EUROP European Railway Wagon Pool
EUROSPACE European Industrial Space
Study Group
EUROTOX European Standing
Committee for the Protection of
Populations against the Risks of Chronic
Toxicity

Eus. Eusebius of Caesarea (ecclesiastical historian)
EUS Eastern United States
EUV extreme ultra-violet (physics)
EUW European Union of Women
ev efficient vulcanization
ev. *evangelisch* (German: Protestant)
eV *eingetragener Verein* (German: registered society); electronvolt (physics)
EV Chelmsford (UK vehicle registration); electric vehicle; English Version (Bible); entry vehicle (astronautics)
EVA Electric Vehicle Association; Engineer Vice-Admiral; ethene and vinyl acetate (plastic); extra vehicular activity (astronautics)
evac. evacuate; evacuated; evacuation
eval. evaluate; evaluated; evaluation
evan(g). evangelical; evangelist
evap. evaporate; evaporated; evaporation; evaporator
evce evidence
EVCS extravehicular communications system (astronautics)
ev(n)g evening
evol. evolution; evolutionary; evolutionist
EVR electronics video broadcasting system
EVT Educational and Vocational Training
EVW European Voluntary Workers
evy every
ew each way (betting)
EW early warning; Eastwest Airlines (airline flight code, Australia); electronic warfare; enlisted woman (US); Estonia (international vehicle registration); Peterborough (UK vehicle registration)
EWA Education Writers' Association
EWF Electrical Wholesalers' Federation
EWICS European Workshop for Industrial Computer Systems
EWL evaporative water loss
EWO Educational Welfare Officer; essential work order; European Women's Orchestra
EWP emergency war plan
EWR early-warning radar
EWRC European Weed Research Association
EWS emergency water supply; emergency welfare service
EWSF European Work Study Federation
ex. examination; examine; examined; examiner; example; excellent; except; excepted; exception; excess; exchange; exclude; excluding; exclusive; excursion;

excursus; execute; executed; executive; executor; exempt; exercise; export; express; extension; extra; extract
Ex. Exeter; Exeter College (Oxford); Exodus (Bible)
EX A/S Norving (airline flight code, Norway); Exeter (UK postcode); Norwich (UK vehicle registration)
exag. exaggerate; exaggeration
exam. examination; examine; examiner
examd examined
examn examination
ex aq. *ex aqua* (Latin: from water; medicine)
ex b. ex bonus (without bonus; finance)
exc. excellent; except; excepted; exception; exchange; excommunication; *excudit* (Latin: he/she engraved it); excursion
Exc. Excellency
ex cap. ex capitalization (without capitalization; finance)
exch. exchange
Exch. Exchequer
excl. exclamation; exclamatory; exclude; excluding; exclusive
exclam. exclamation; exclamatory
ex cp. ex coupon (without the interest on the coupon; finance)
exd examined
ex div. ex dividend (without dividend; finance)
exec. execute; execution; executive; executor
execx executrix
exempl. *exemplaire* (French: copy of printed work)
exes expenses
Exet. Exeter College (Oxford)
ex. g(r). *exempli gratia* (Latin: for example)
exh. exhaust; exhibition
exhib. exhibit; exhibition; exhibitioner; exhibitor
exhibn exhibition
Ex.-Im. Export-Import Bank (US)
ex int. ex interest (without interest; banking)
ex lib. *ex libris* (Latin: from the books or from the library of)
ex n. ex new (shares; stock exchange)
Exod. Exodus (Bible)
ex off. *ex officio* (Latin: by right of office)
Exon: *Exoniensis* (Latin: Bishop of Exeter)
exor executor
exp exponential (mathematics)
exp. expand; expansion; expedition;

expense; experience; experiment; experimental; expiration; expire; expired; export; exportation; exported; exporter; express; expression; expurgated

ex p. *ex parte* (Latin: on behalf of one party only)

EXP Exchange of Persons Office (UNESCO); expected (meteorology)

expdn expedition

exper. experimental

expl. explain; explanation; explanatory; explosion; explosive

exploit. exploitation

expn. exposition

EXPO exposition

exp. o. experimental order

expr. express

ex-Pres. ex-President

expt experiment

exptl experimental

exptr exporter

expurg. expurgate; expurgated

exr executor

exrx executrix

exs expenses

ext. extend; extension; extent; exterior; external; externally; extinct; extra; extract; extraction; *extractum* (Latin: extract; medicine); extreme

EXTD extend (meteorology)

EXTEL Exchange and Telegraph Company (news agency, UK)

EXTEND Exercise Training for the Elderly and/or Disabled

ext. liq. *extractum liquidum* (Latin: liquid extract)

extn extension

extr. extraordinary

extrad. extradition

exx examples; executrix

EY Bangor (UK vehicle registration)

EYC European Youth Campaign

EYR East Yorkshire Regiment

Ez. Ezra (Bible)

EZ Belfast (UK vehicle registration)

Ezek. Ezekiel (Bible)

Ezr. Ezra (Bible)

F

f face value (numismatics); femto-; f-number (photography); fail; farad (electricity); fast; fine; firm; fog; founded; franc

f focal length (physics); *forte* (Italian: loud; music); frequency (physics); fugacity (chemistry); function (mathematics)

f. facing; fair; farthing; father; fathom; feet; female; feminine (grammar); filly (horse racing); fine (metallurgy); flat; fluid; folio; following (page); foot; for; forecastle; form (botany); formula; foul (sport); founded; franc; freehold; from; furlong; furlough; guilder (Dutch monetary unit)

F Fahrenheit; fail; false (mathematics); farad; fast; Faversham (UK fishing port registration); Fellow; fighter (US); filial generation (genetics); fine (pencils); fluorine (element); f-number (photography); Fokker (aircraft); franc; France (international civil aircraft marking; international vehicle registration); Friday; spectral type (astronomy); thick fog (meteorology)

F Faraday constant (physics); force (physics)

F. family; Father; fathom; February; Federation; Fellow; female; feminine (grammar); *ferrovia* (Italian: railway); *fiat* (Latin: let it be made; medicine); fiction; filly (horse racing); finance; fine (metallurgy); fleet; folio; foolscap; foul (sport); *Frauen* (German: women); *freddo* (Italian: cold); French; *Frère* (French: Brother); Friday; *frio* (Portuguese/Spanish: cold)

Fa *factura* (Spanish: invoice)

fa fire alarm; first aid; first attack; free alongside (commerce); free aperture (optics); freight agent; friendly aircraft; fuel-air (ratio)

FA factor analysis (statistics); Factory Act; Faculty of Actuaries; family allowance; fanny adams; farm adviser; fatty acid (chemistry); field activities; field ambulance; field artillery; filtered air; Finance Act; financial adviser; fine art; fly ash; fuel ash; folic acid (biochemistry); Football Association; freight agent; fuck all; fuel assembly (nuclear engineering); Stoke-on-Trent (UK vehicle registration)

faa free of all averages (insurance)

FAA Federal Aviation Administration (US); Fellow of the Australian Academy (of Science); Film Artists' Association; Fleet Air Arm

FAAAS Fellow of the American Academy of Arts and Sciences; Fellow of the American Association for the Advancement of Science

FAAC Food Additives and Contaminants Committee

FAAO Fellow of the American Academy of Optometry

FAAP Fellow of the American Academy of Pediatrics

FAARM Fellow of the American Academy of Reproductive Medicine

FAAV Fellow of the Central Association of Agricultural Valuers

fab first aid box

f à b *franco à bord* (French: free on board; commerce)

fab. fabric; fabricate; fabrication (commerce); fabulous

FAB Flour Advisory Bureau; French-American-British; fuel-air bomb

fabbr. *fabbrica* (Italian: factory)

FABMDS field army ballistic missile defense system (US)

fabr. fabricate; fabrication

Fab. Soc. Fabian Society

fabx. fire alarm box

fac fast as can (be); *franc d'avarie commune* (French: free of general average; insurance)

fac. façade; facial; facility; facsimile; factor; factory; faculty

Fac. Faculty

FAC Federation of Agricultural Cooperatives; forwards air controller (military)

FACA Fellow of the American College of Anaesthetists; Fellow of the American College of Anaesthesiologists

FACC Fellow of the American College of Cardiology; Ford Aerospace and Communication Corporation (US)

FACCA Fellow of the Association of Certified and Chartered Accountants

FACCP Fellow of the American College of Chest Physicians

FACD Fellow of the American College of Dentistry

FACE Fellow of the Australian College of Education; field artillery computer

equipments; Financial Advertising Code of Ethics (US)

FACEM Federation of the Associations of Colliery Equipment Manufacturers

FACerS Fellow of the American Ceramic Society

facet. facetious

FACG Fellow of the American College of Gastroenterology

facil. facility

FACMTA Federal Advisory Council on Medical Training

FACOG Fellow of the American College of Obstetricians and Gynaecologists

FACOM Fellow of the Australian College of Occupational Medicine

FACP Fellow of the American College of Physicians

FACR Fellow of the American College of Radiology

FACRM Fellow of the Australian College of Reproductive Medicine

facs. facsimile

Facs Fellow of the American College of Surgeons

facsim. facsimile

fact(a). *factura* (Spanish: invoice)

FACT Federation Against Copyright Theft; fully automatic compiler-translator

fad free air delivered

FADO Fellow of the Association of Dispensing Opticians

FAE fuel-air explosive (military)

Faer. Faeroe Islands

FAeSI Fellow of the Aeronautical Society of India

FAGO Fellowship in Australia in Obstetrics and Gynaecology

FAGS Federation of Astronomical and Geophysical Services; Fellow of the American Geographical Society

Fah(r). Fahrenheit

FAHA Fellow of the Australian Academy of the Humanities

FAI *Fédération aéronautique internationale* (French: International Aeronautical Federation); Football Association of Ireland; fresh-air inlet

FAIA Fellow of the American Institute of Architects; Fellow of the Association of International Accountants; Fellow of the Australian Institute of Advertising

FAIAA Fellow of the American Institute of Aeronautics and Astronautics

FAIAS Fellow of the Australian Institute of Agricultural Science

FAIB Fellow of the Australian Institute of Builders
FAIBiol Fellow of the Australian Institute of Biology
FAIC Fellow of the American Institute of Chemists
FAIE Fellow of the Australian Institute of Energy
FAIEx Fellow of the Australian Institute of Export
FAIFST Fellow of the Australian Institute of Food Science and Technology
FAII Fellow of the Australian Insurance Institute
FAIM Fellow of the Australian Institute of Management
FAIP Fellow of the Australian Institute of Physics
Fak. *Faktura* (German: invoice)
FAK freights all kinds (shipping)
Falk. I(s). Falkland Islands
FALN *Fuerzas Armadas de Liberación Nacional* (Spanish: Armed Forces of National Liberation; Puerto Rico)
FALPA Fellow of the Incorporated Society of Auctioneers and Landed Property Agents
fam. familiar; family
FAM Free and Accepted Masons
FAMA Fellow of the American Medical Association; Fellow of the Australian Medical Association; Foundation for Mutual Assistance in Africa
FAMEME Fellow of the Association of Mining Electrical and Mechanical Engineers
FAMI Fellow of the Australian Marketing Institute
FAmNucSoc Fellow of the American Nuclear Society
FAMS Fellow of the Ancient Monuments Society; Fellow of the Indian Academy of Medical Sciences
f&a fore and aft
F&AP fire and allied perils (insurance)
F&C full and change (tides)
f&d fill and drain; freight and demurrage
f&f fixtures and fittings
F&Gs folded and gathered pages (bookbinding)
F&M foot and mouth disease
f&t fire and theft (insurance)
Fany First Aid Nursing Yeomanry
fao finish all over; for the attention of
FAO Fleet Accountant Officer; Food and Agriculture Organization (UN)

FAP Family Assistance Program (US); first aid post; *Força Aérea Portuguesa* (Portuguese: Portuguese Air Force); *franc d'avarie particulière* (French: free of particular average)
FAPA Fellow of the American Psychiatric Association
FAPHA Fellow of the American Public Health Association
FAPS Fellow of the American Phytopathological Society
faq fair average quality (commerce); free alongside quay (commerce); frequently asked questions (computing)
faqs fair average quality of season
far. farriery; farthing
Far. Faraday
FAR false alarm rate; Federal Aviation Regulations; free of claim for accident reported (insurance)
FArborA Fellow of the Arboricultural Association
FARE Federation of Alcoholic Rehabilitation Establishments
FARELF Far East Land Forces
fas firsts and seconds; free alongside ship (commerce)
FAS Faculty of Architects and Surveyors; Federation of American Scientists; Fellow of the Anthropological Society; Fellow of the Antiquarian Society; fetal/foetal alcohol syndrome (medicine); free alongside ship (commerce)
FASA Fellow of the Australian Society of Accountants
FASB Financial Accounting Standards Board (US)
fasc. *fasciculus* (Latin: bundle; anatomy, printing)
FASc Fellow of the Indian Academy of Sciences
FASCE Fellow of the American Society of Civil Engineers
FASE Fellow of the Antiquarian Society, Edinburgh
FASEB Federation of American Societies for Experimental Biology
FASI Fellow of the Architects' and Surveyors' Institute
FASS Federation of the Associations of Specialists and Subcontractors
FASSA Fellow of the Academy of Social Sciences in Australia
FAST factor analysis system; fast automatic shuttle transfer; first atomic ship transport; forecasting and

assessment in science and technology (EC)
fastnr fastener
fath. fathom
FATIS Food and Agriculture Technical Information Service (OEEC)
FAU Friends' Ambulance Unit
FAusIMM Fellow of the Australasian Institute of Mining and Metallurgy
fav. favour; favourite
FAVO Fleet Aviation Officer
FAWA Federation of Asian Women's Associations
fax facsimile transmission; fuel-air explosion
fb flat bar; fog bell; freight bill, fullback (sport); full board
FB Bristol (UK vehicle registration); Fenian Brotherhood; fire brigade; fisheries board; fishery board; flat bottom (railways); flying boat; foreign body (medicine); Forth Bridge; Free Baptist
F-B full-bore (rifles)
FBA Farm Buildings Association; Federal Bar Association (US); Federation of British Artists; Federation of British Astrologers; Fellow of the British Academy; fluorescent brightening agent (detergents); Freshwater Biological Association
FBAA Fellow of the British Association of Accountants and Auditors
f'ball football
fbc fallen building clause (insurance)
FBCM Federation of British Carpet Manufacturers
FBCO Fellow of the British College of Ophthalmic Opticians; Fellow of the British College of Ophthalmic Optometrists
FBCP Fellow of the British College of Physiotherapists
FBCS Fellow of the British Computer Society
fbcw fallen building clause waiver (insurance)
fbd freeboard
FBEA Fellow of the British Esperanto Association
FBEC(S) Fellow of the Business Education Council (Scotland)
FBFM Federation of British Film Makers
FBH fire brigade hydrant
FBHI Fellow of the British Horological Institute

FBHS Fellow of the British Horse Society
FBHTM Federation of British Hand Tool Manufacturers
FBI Federal Bureau of Investigation (US)
FBIBA Fellow of the British Insurance Brokers' Association
FBID Fellow of the British Institute of Interior Design
FBIM Fellow of the British Institute of Management
FBINZ Fellow of the Bankers' Institute of New Zealand
FBIPP Fellow of the British Institute of Professional Photography
FBIS Fellow of the British Interplanetary Society
FBL flight-by-light (aircraft)
FBM fleet ballistic missile
FBMA Food and Beverage Managers' Association
fbo for the benefit of
FBOA Fellow of the British Optical Association
FBOU Fellow of the British Ornithologists' Union
FBP final boiling point (chemistry)
FBPS Fellow of the British Phrenological Society
FBPsS Fellow of the British Psychological Society
fbr. fibre
FBR fast breeder reactor (nuclear engineering)
FBRAM Federation of British Rubber and Allied Manufacturers
fbro. *febrero* (Spanish: February)
FBS Fellow of the Botanical Society; forward-based system (military)
FBSC Fellow of the British Society of Commerce
FBSE Fellow of the Botanical Society, Edinburgh
FBSM Fellow of the Birmingham School of Music
FBSS failed back-surgery syndrome (medicine)
FBT *Fédération des bourses du travail* (French: Federation of Labour Exchanges; trade union); fringe benefit tax
FBu Burundi franc (monetary unit of Burundi)
FBU Fire Brigades Union
FBW fly-by-wire (aeronautics)
fby future budget year
fc fielder's choice (baseball); filing cabinet; *fin courant* (French: at the end of

this month); follow copy (printing); for cash; fuel cell

FC Federal Cabinet (Australia); fellow craft (Freemasonry); fencing club; *ferrocarril* (Spanish: railway); *fidei commissum* (Latin: bequeathed in trust); *fieri curavit* (Latin: the donor directed this to be done); fifth column; Fighter Command; fire cock; fire control; Fishmongers' Company; football club; Forestry Commission; Free Church; fuel cell; funnel cloud (meteorology); Oxford (UK vehicle registration)

FCA Farm Credit Administration (US); Federation of Canadian Artists; Fellow of the Institute of Chartered Accountants

FCAATSI Federal Council for the Advancement of Aborigines and Torres Strait Islanders (Australia)

FCA(Aust) Fellow of the Institute of Chartered Accountants in Australia

FCAI Fellow of the New Zealand Institute of Cost Accountants

FCAnaes Fellow of the College of Anaesthetists

fcap foolscap

FCAR free of claim for accident reported (insurance)

FCASI Fellow of the Canadian Aeronautics and Space Institute

FCAST forecast (meteorology)

FCB file control block (computing)

FCBA Federal Communications Bar Association; Fellow of the Canadian Bankers' Association

FCBSI Fellow of the Chartered Building Societies Institute

FCC Federal Communications Commission; Federal Council of Churches; first-class certificate; fluid catalytic cracking (chemical engineering)

FCCA Fellow of the Chartered Association of Certified Accountants

FCCEA Fellow of the Commonwealth Council for Educational Administration

FCCEd Fellow of the College of Craft Education

FCCS Fellow of the Corporation of Secretaries

FCCSET Federal Coordinating Council on Science, Engineering and Technology (US)

FCCT Fellow of the Canadian College of Teachers

FCD First Chief Directorate (KGB)

FCDA Federal Civil Defence Administration (US)

FCEC Federation of Civil Engineering Contractors

FCFC Free Church Federal Council

FCFI Fellow of the Clothing and Footwear Institute

fcg facing

FCGB Forestry Committee of Great Britain

FCGI Fellow of the City and Guilds of London Institute

FChS Fellow of the Society of Chiropodists

FCI *Fédération cynologique internationale* (French: International Federation of Kennel Clubs); Fellow of the Institute of Commerce

FCIA Fellow of the Canadian Institute of Actuaries; Fellow of the Corporation of Insurance Agents; Foreign Credit Insurance Association

FCIArb Fellow of the Chartered Institute of Arbitrators

FCIB Fellow of the Chartered Institute of Bankers; Fellow of the Corporation of Insurance Brokers

FCIBSE Fellow of the Chartered Institution of Building Services Engineers

FCIC Federal Crop Insurance Corporation (US); Fellow of the Chemical Institute of Canada

FCII Fellow of the Chartered Insurance Institute

FCILA Fellow of the Chartered Institute of Loss Adjusters

FCIM Fellow of the Chartered Institute of Marketing

FCIOB Fellow of the Chartered Institute of Building

FCIPA Fellow of the Chartered Institute of Patent Agents

FCIS Fellow of the Chartered Institute of Secretaries and Administrators

FCISA Fellow of the Chartered Institute of Secretaries and Administrators (Australia)

FCIT Fellow of the Chartered Institute of Transport; Four Countries International Tournament (basketball)

FCIV Fellow of the Commonwealth Institute of Valuers

FCMA Fellow of the Institute of Cost and Management Accountants

FCMS Fellow of the College of Medicine and Surgery

FCMSA Fellow of the College of
Medicine of South Africa
FCNA Fellow of the College of Nursing,
Australia
fco *franco* (French: free of charge)
f. co. fair copy (printing)
FCO Farmers' Central Organization;
fire-control officer; Foreign and
Commonwealth Office
FCOG(SA) Fellow of the South African
College of Obstetrics and Gynaecologists
FCollP Fellow of the College of
Preceptors
FCOphth Fellow of the College of
Ophthalmologists
FCOT Fellow of the College of
Occupational Therapists
fcp foolscap
FCP Fellow of the College of Clinical
Pharmacology; Fellow of the College of
Preceptors
FCPA Fellow of the Canadian
Psychological Association
FCPO Fleet Chief Petty Officer
FCPS Fellow of the College of Physicians
and Surgeons
FCP(SoAf) Fellow of the College of
Physicians, South Africa
FCPSO(SoAf) Fellow of the College of
Physicians and Surgeons and
Obstetricians, South Africa
fcs francs; warranted free of capture,
seizure, arrest, detainment and the
consequences thereof (insurance)
FCS Federation of Conservative
Students; Fellow of the Chemical Society
FCSD Fellow of the Chartered Society of
Designers
FCSP Fellow of the Chartered Society of
Physiotherapy
fcsrcc warranted free of capture, seizure,
arrest, detainment and the consequences
thereof and damage caused by riots and
civil commotions (insurance)
FCSSA Fellow of the College of
Surgeons, South Africa
FCST Federal Council of Surgeons, South
Africa
FCT Federal Capital Territory (Australia);
Fellow of the Association of Corporate
Treasurers
FCTB Fellow of the College of Teachers
of the Blind
FCTU Federation of Associations of
Catholic Trade Unionists
fcty factory
FCU fighter control unit

fd field; fiord; flight deck; focal distance;
ford; forward; found; founded; free
delivery; free discharge; free dispatch;
fund
FD Dudley (UK vehicle registration); *Fidei
Defensor* (Latin: Defender of the Faith);
finite difference (computing); fire
department; fleet duties; Fleetwood (UK
fishing port registration); free-delivered;
free delivery; Free Democrat
FDA First Division Association (trade
union); Food and Drug Administration
(US)
FD&C Food, Drug and Color Regulations
(US)
FDC Fire Detection Center (US); first day
cover (philately); *fleur de coin* (French:
mint condition; numismatics)
FDDI fibre distributed data interface
(computing)
FDF Food and Drink Federation
fdg funding
FDHO Factory Department, Home Office
FDI *Fédération dentaire internationale*
(French: International Dental
Federation)
FDIC Federal Deposit Insurance
Corporation (US); Food and Drink
Industries Council
FDIF *Fédération démocratique internationale
des femmes* (French: Women's
International Democratic Federation)
FDM finite-difference method
(computing); frequency-division
multiplexing (telecommunications)
FDO Fleet Dental Officer; for declaration
(purposes) only (taxation)
FDP *Freie Demokratische Partei* (German:
Free Democratic Party)
fdr founder
FDR Franklin Delano Roosevelt (US
President)
fdry foundry
FDS Fellow in Dental Surgery; flight-
director system (aeronautics)
FDSRCPSGlas Fellow in Dental Surgery
of the Royal College of Physicians and
Surgeons of Glasgow
FDSRCS Fellow in Dental Surgery of the
Royal College of Surgeons of England
FDSRCSE Fellow in Dental Surgery of
the Royal College of Surgeons of
Edinburgh
fe first edition; for example
Fe iron (element)
FE Far East; Folkestone (UK fishing port
registration); foreign editor; further

education; Lincoln (UK vehicle registration)

FEA Federal Energy Administration (US); Federal Executive Association (US); *Fédération internationale pour l'éducation artistique* (French: International Federation for Art Education)

FEAF Far East Air Force

FEANI *Fédération européenne d'associations nationales d'ingenieurs* (French: European Federation of National Associations of Engineers)

feb(b). *febbraio* (Italian: February)

Feb February

FEB Fair Employment Board (US); functional electronic block

fec *fecit* (Latin: made this)

FEC Federal Election Commission (US); First Edition Club; *Fondation européenne de la culture* (French: European Cultural Foundation); Foreign Exchange Certificate (China)

FECB Foreign Exchange Control Board

FECI Fellow of the Institute of Employment Consultants

Fed. Federal(ist); Federal Reserve Bank (US); Federated; Federation

FED Federal Reserve System

FEDC Federation of Engineering Design Consultants

FEER fundamental equilibrium exchange rate (banking)

FEF Far East Fleet

FEI *Fédération équestre internationale* (French: International Equestrian Federation); Financial Executive Institute (US)

FEIDCT Fellow of the Educational Institute of Design Craft and Technology

FEIS Fellow of the Educational Institute of Scotland

FEL free-electron laser

FELF Far East Land Forces

Fell. Fellow

FeLV feline leukaemia virus (microbiology)

fém *force électromotrice* (French: electromotive force, emf)

fem. female; feminine

FEM field-emission microscope (physics); field-emission microscopy (physics)

FEMA Federal Emergency Management Agency (US)

fenc. fencing

FEng Fellow of the Fellowship of Engineering

FENSA Film Entertainments National Service Association

FEO Fleet Engineer Officer

FEOGA *Fonds européen d'orientation et de garantie agriculturel* (French: European Agricultural Guidance and Guarantee Fund; EC)

FEPA Fair Employment Practices Act (US)

FEPC Fair Employment Practices Committee (US)

FEPEM Federation of European Petroleum Equipment Manufacturers

Fer. Fermanagh

FERA Federal Emergency Relief Administration

FERC Federal Energy Regulatory Commission

FERDU Further Education Review and Development Unit

Ferm. Fermanagh

ferr. *ferrovia* (Italian: railway)

ferv. *fervens* (Latin: boiling; pharmacology)

FES Federation of Engineering Societies; Fellow of the Entomological Society; Fellow of the Ethnological Society; foil, épée and sabre (fencing); F E Smith, Earl of Birkenhead (UK statesman and lawyer)

Fest. Festival

FET federal estate tax (US); federal excise tax (US); field-effect transistor; fossil-energy technology

FEU Further Education Unit

feud. feudal; feudalism

fev. *fevereiro* (Portuguese: February)

fév. *février* (French: February)

FEV forced expiratory volume (medicine)

FEX fleet exercise (US Navy)

ff *fecerunt* (Latin: made this); fixed focus; folios; following; forms; thick fog (nautical)

ff *fortissimo* (Italian: very loudly; music)

FF Bangor (UK vehicle registration); *Felicissimi Fratres* (Latin: Most Fortunate Brothers); Fellows; *Fianna Fáil* (Irish: warriors of Ireland; Irish political party); field force (military); Ford Foundation (US); frontier force (military); Tower Air (airline flight code; USA)

ffa free foreign agency; free from alongside (commerce)

FFA Fellow of the Faculty of Actuaries (Scotland); Fellow of the Institute of Financial Accountants; free fatty acid (biochemistry); Future Farmers of America

FFARACS Fellow of the Faculty of Anaesthetists of the Royal Australasian College of Surgeons

FFARCS Fellow of the Faculty of Anaesthetists of the Royal College Surgeons of England

FFARCSI Fellow of the Faculty of Anaesthetists of the Royal College of Surgeons of Ireland

FFAS Fellow of the Faculty of Architects and Surveyors

FFA(SA) Fellow of the Faculty of Anaesthetics (South Africa)

FFB Fellow of the Faculty of Building

FFC Foreign Funds Control

FFCM Fellow of the Faculty of Community Medicine

FFCMI Fellow of the Faculty of Community Medicine of Ireland

FFD Fellow of the Faculty of Dental Surgeons

FFDRCSI Fellow of the Faculty of Dentistry of the Royal College of Surgeons in Ireland

fff *fortississimo* (Italian: as loudly as possible; music)

FFF Free French Forces

FFHC Freedom from Hunger Campaign

FFHom Fellow of the Faculty of Homoeopathy

FFI Fellow of the Faculty of Insurance; Finance for Industry; free from infection; French Forces of the Interior

FFJ Franciscan Familiar of Saint Joseph

FFL *Forces françaises libres* (French: Free French Forces)

ffly faithfully

FFOM Fellow of the Faculty of Occupational Medicine

FFOMI Fellow of the Faculty of Occupational Medicine of Ireland

FFPath, RCPI Fellow of the Faculty of Pathologists of the Royal College of Physicians of Ireland

FFPHM Fellow of the Faculty of Public Health Medicine

FFPS Fauna and Flora Preservation Society; Fellow of the Faculty of Physicians and Surgeons

FFr French franc

FFRR full-frequency range recording

FFS *Front des Forces Socialistes* (French: Front of Socialist Forces; Algeria)

ffss full-frequency stereophonic sound

FFV First Families of Virginia (US)

FFWM free-floating wave meter

ffy faithfully

FFY Fife and Forfar Yeomanry

fg field goal (sport); fine grain; fog; fully good (commerce)

FG Afriana Afgan Airlines (airline flight code, Afghanistan); Brighton (UK vehicle registration); Federal Government; *Fine Gael* (Irish: tribe of the Gaels; Irish political party); fire guard; flue gas (engineering); fog (meteorology); foot guards; *frais généraux* (French: overheads); full gilt

fga foreign of general average (insurance); free of general average (insurance)

FGA Fellow of the Gemmonological Association

FGCM Fellow of the Guild of Church Musicians; field general court martial

FGDS *Fédération de la gauche démocrate et socialiste* (French: Federation of the Democratic and Socialist Left)

fgf fully good, fair (commerce)

FGI *Fédération graphique internationale* (French: International Graphical Federation); Fellow of the Institute of Certified Grocers

Fgn Foreign

FGO Fleet Gunnery Officer

FGS Fellow of the Geological Society

FGSM Fellow of the Guildhall School of Music and Drama

fgt freight

FGT federal gift tax (US)

FGTB *Fédération générale du travail de Belgique* (French: Belgian General Federation of Labour)

fh *fiat haustus* (Latin: make a draught; medicine); fog horn; fore hatch; forward hatch

FH Falmouth (UK fishing port registration); family history (medicine); fetal/foetal heart (medicine); field hospital; fire hydrant; flyhalf (rugby); Gloucester (UK vehicle registration)

F/H freehold

FHA Farmers' Home Administration (US); Federal Housing Administration (US); Finance Houses Association

FHAS Fellow of the Highland and Agricultural Society of Scotland

fhb family hold back

FHCIMA Fellow of the Hotel Catering and Institutional Management Association

FHH fetal/foetal heart heard (medicine)

FHI *Fédération haltérophile internationale* (French: International Weightlifting Federation)
FHLB Federal Home Loan Bank (US)
FHLBA Federal Home Loan Bank Administration (US)
FHLBB Federal Home Loan Bank Board (US)
fhld freehold
FHLMC Federal Home Loan Mortgage Corporation (US)
FHNH fetal/foetal heart not heard (medicine)
fhp friction horsepower
FHR Federal House of Representatives (Australia); fetal/foetal heart rate (medicine)
FHS Fellow of the Heraldry Society
FHSA Family Health Services Authority
FHSM Fellow of the Institute of Health Service Management
FHWA Federal Highway Administration (US)
fi for instance; free in (commerce)
FI Faeroe Islands; Falkland Islands; Fiji Islands; fire insurance; flow injection (engineering); Icelandair (airline flight code); Tipperary (Irish vehicle registration)
FIA Federal Insurance Administration; *Fédération internationale de l'automobile* (French: International Automobile Federation); Fellow of the Institute of Actuaries; full interest admitted (commerce)
FIAA *Fédération internationale athlétique d'amateur* (French: International Amateur Athletic Association); Fellow of the Institute of Actuaries of Australia
FIAA&S Fellow of the Incorporated Association of Architects and Surveyors
FIAAS Fellow of the Institute of Australian Agricultural Science
FIAB *Fédération internationale des associations de bibliothécaires* (French: International Federation of Library Associations and Institutions); Fellow of the International Association of Book-keepers
FIAF *Fédération internationale des archives du film* (French: International Federation of Film Archives)
FIAgrE Fellow of the Institution of Agricultural Engineers
FIAI *Fédération internationale des associations d'instituteurs* (French: International Federation of Teachers'

Associations); Fellow of the Institute of Industrial and Commercial Accountants
FIAJ *Fédération internationale des auberges de la jeunesse* (French: International Youth Hostel Federation)
FIAL Fellow of the International Institute of Art and Letters
FIAM Fellow of the Institute of Administrative Management; Fellow of the International Academy of Management
FIAP *Fédération internationale de l'art photographique* (French: International Federation of Photographic Art); Fellow of the Institution of Analysts and Programmers
FIAPF *Fédération internationale des associations de producteurs de films* (French: International Federation of Film Producers' Associations)
FIArbA Fellow of the Institute of Arbitrators of Australia
FIAS Fellow of the Institute of the Aerospace Sciences (US); Fellow Surveyor of the Incorporated Association of Architects and Surveyors
FIASc Fellow of the Indian Academy of Sciences
Fiat *Fabbrica Italiana Automobili Torino* (Italian: Italian Motor Works in Turin)
fib free into barge; free into bond; free into bunker
fib. fibula (medicine)
FIBA *Fédération internationale de basketball amateur* (French: International Amateur Basketball Federation); Fellow of the Institute of Business Administration (Australia)
FIBD Fellow of the Institute of British Decorators
FIBiol Fellow of the Institute of Biology
FIBOR Frankfurt Inter-Bank Offered Rate
FIBOT Fair Isle Bird Observatory Trust
FIBP Fellow of the Institute of British Photographers
FIBScot Fellow of the Institute of Bankers in Scotland
FIBST Fellow of the Institute of British Surgical Technicians
FIBT *Fédération internationale de bobsleigh et de tobogganning* (French: International Bobsleighing and Tobogganing Federation)
fic. fiction(al); fictitious
FIC Fellow of Imperial College, London; Fellow of the Institute of Chemistry; frequency interference control

FICA ## FICA # FICA

FIFF Fellow of the Institute of Freight Forwarders
FIFireE Fellow of the Institution of Fire Engineers
FIFO first in, first out (computing; accounting)
FIFSP *Fédération internationale des fonctionnaires supérieurs de police* (French: International Federation of Senior Police Officers)
FIFST Fellow of the Institute of Food Science and Technology
fig. figurative(ly); figure
FIG *Fédération internationale de gymnastique* (French: International Gymnastic Federation)
FIGasE Fellow of the Institution of Gas Engineers
FIGC *Federazione Italiana Gioco Calcio* (Italian: Italian Football Association)
FIGCM Fellow of the Incorporated Guild of Church Musicians
FIGED *Fédération internationale des grandes entreprises de distribution* (French: International Federation of Distributors)
FIGO *Fédération internationale de gynécologie et d'obstetrique* (French: International Federation of Gynaecology and Obstetrics)
FIGRS Fellow of the Irish Genealogical Research Society
FIH *Fédération internationale de hockey* (French: International Hockey Federation); *Fédération internationale des hôpitaux* (French: International Hospital Federation); Fellow of the Institute of Housing; Fellow of the Institute of Hygiene
FIHE Fellow of the Institution of Health Education
FIHort Fellow of the Institute of Horticulture
FIHospE Fellow of the Institute of Hospital Engineering
FIHsg Fellow of the Institute of Housing
FIHT Fellow of the Institution of Highways and Transportation
FIIA Fellow of the Institute of Internal Auditors
FIIC Fellow of the International Institute for Conservation of Historic and Artistic Works
FIIM Fellow of the Institution of Industrial Managers
FIInfSc Fellow of the Institute of Information Scientists
FIInst Fellow of the Imperial Institute

FIITech Fellow of the Institute of Industrial Technicians
FIJ *Fédération internationale de judo* (French: International Judo Federation); *Fédération internationale des journalistes* (French: International Federation of Journalists)
fil. filament; fillet; filter; filtrate
FIL *Fédération internationale de laiterie* (French: International Dairy Federation); Fellow of the Institute of Linguists
FILA *Fédération internationale de lutte amateur* (French: International Amateur Wrestling Federation)
FILDM Fellow of the Institute of Logistics and Distribution Management
FILE Fellow of the Institute of Legal Executives
FILO first in, last out
FILT *Fédération internationale de lawn tennis* (French: International Lawn Tennis Federation)
FIM *Fédération internationale des musiciens* (French: International Federation of Musicians); *Fédération internationale motocycliste* (French: International Motorcycle Federation); Fellow of the Institute of Metals; field-ion microscope; field-ion microscopy
FIMA Fellow of the Institute of Mathematics and its Applications
FIMarE Fellow of the Institute of Marine Engineers
FIMBRA Financial Intermediaries, Managers and Brokers Regulatory Association
FIMC Fellow of the Institute of Management Consultants
FIMechE Fellow of the Institution of Mechanical Engineers
FIMGTechE Fellow of the Institution of Mechanical and General Technician Engineers
FIMH Fellow of the Institute of Military History
FIMI Fellow of the Institute of the Motor Industry
FIMinE Fellow of the Institution of Mining Engineers
FIMIT Fellow of the Institute of Musical Instrument Technology
FIMLS Fellow of the Institute of Medical Laboratory Sciences
FIMM Fellow of the Institution of Mining and Metallurgy
FIMP *Fédération internationale de médecine*

physique (French: International Federation of Physical Medicine)
FIMS *Fédération internationale de médecine sportive* (French: International Federation of Sporting Medicine); Fellow of the Institute of Mathematical Statistics; field-ion mass spectrometer; field-ion mass spectrometry
FIMT Fellow of the Institute of the Motor Trade
fin. *ad finem* (Latin: at or near the end); final; finance; financial; financier; *finis* (Latin: the end); finish
Fin. Finland; Finnish
FIN Finland (international vehicle registration)
fina following items not available
FINA *Fédération internationale de natation amateur* (French: International Amateur Swimming Federation)
Findus Fruit Industries Ltd
Fin. Sec. Financial Secretary
FInstAM Fellow of the Institute of Administrative Management
FInstArb Fellow of the Institute of Arbitrators
FInstB Fellow of the Institution of Buyers
FInstCh Fellow of the Institute of Chiropodists
FInstD Fellow of the Institute of Directors
FInstE Fellow of the Institute of Energy
FInstFF Fellow of the Institute of Freight Forwarders
FInstLEx Fellow of the Institute of Legal Executives
FInstMC Fellow of the Institute of Measurement and Control
FInstO Fellow of the Institute of Ophthalmology
FInstP Fellow of the Institute of Physics
FInstPet Fellow of the Institute of Petroleum
FInstPI Fellow of the Institute of Patentees and Inventors
FInstPS Fellow of the Institute of Purchasing and Supply
FInstRE Fellow of the Institute of Radio Engineers
FInstSMM Fellow of the Institute of Sales and Marketing Management
FINucE Fellow of the Institution of Nuclear Engineers
fio for information only; free in and out (commerce)
FIOA Fellow of the Institute of Acoustics
FIOP Fellow of the Institute of Plumbing; Fellow of the Institute of Printing

FIP *Fédération internationale de philatélie* (French: International Philatelic Federation); *Fédération internationale pharmaceutique* (French: International Pharmaceutical Federation)
FIPA *Fédération internationale des producteurs agricoles* (French: International Federation of Agricultural Producers); Fellow of the Institute of Practitioners in Advertising
FIPENZ Fellow of the Institution of Professional Engineers, New Zealand
FIPG Fellow of the Institute of Professional Goldsmiths
FIPM Fellow of the Institute of Personnel Management
FIPR Fellow of the Institute of Public Relations
FIProdE Fellow of the Institution of Production Engineers
FIQ *Fédération internationale de quilleurs* (French: International Bowling Federation); Fellow of the Institute of Quarrying
FIQA Fellow of the Institute of Quality Assurance
FIQS Fellow of the Institute of Quantity Surveyors
fir flight information region; floating-in rate; fuel-indicator reading
fir. firkin
FIR far-infrared radiation
FIRA *Fédération internationale de rugby amateur* (French: International Amateur Rugby Federation); Furniture Industry Research Association
FIREE(Aust) Fellow of the Institute of Radio and Electronics Engineers (Australia)
FIRS *Fédération internationale de patinage à roulettes* (French: International Roller Skating Federation)
FIRSE Fellow of the Institute of Railway Signalling Engineers
FIRTE Fellow of the Institute of Road Transport Engineers
FIS family income supplement; farm improvement scheme; *Fédération internationale de sauvetage* (French: International Life Saving Federation); *Fédération internationale de ski* (French: International Ski Federation); Fellow of the Institute of Statisticians; flight information service; free into store; *Front Islamique du Salut* (French: Islamic Salvation Front; Algeria)
FISA *Fédération internationale des sociétés*

d'aviron (French: International Rowing Federation); *Fédération internationale de sport automobiles* (French: International Motoring Federation); Fellow of the Incorporated Secretaries Association

FISE *Fédération internationale syndicale de l'enseignement* (French: World Federation of Teachers' Unions); Fellow of the Institution of Sales Engineers; Fellow of the Institution of Sanitary Engineers; *Fonds international de secours à l'enfance* (French: United Nations Children's Fund)

fish. fishery; fishes; fishing

FISITA *Fédération internationale des sociétés d'ingénieus des techniques de l'automobile* (French: International Federation of Automobile Engineers' and Technicians' Associations)

FIST Fellow of the Institute of Science Technology

FISTC Fellow of the Institute of Scientific and Technical Communicators

FIStructE Fellow of the Institution of Structural Engineers

FISU *Fédération internationale du sport universitaire* (French: International University Sports Federation)

FISVA Fellow of the Incorporated Society of Valuers and Auctioneers

FISW Fellow of the Institute of Social Work

fit free in truck (commerce); free of income tax

FIT Federal Income Tax (US); *Fédération internationale des traducteurs* (French: International Federation of Translators)

FITA *Fédération internationale de tir à l'arc* (French: International Archery Federation)

FITCE *Fédération internationale des ingénieurs des télécommunications de la communauté européenne* (French: Federation of Telecommunications Engineers in the European Community)

FITD Fellow of the Institute of Training and Development

FITE Fellow of the Institution of Electrical and Electronics Technician Engineers

FITT *Fédération internationale de tennis de table* (French: International Table Tennis Federation)

fitw federal income tax withholding (US)

FIVB *Fédération internationale de volley-ball* (French: International Volleyball Federation)

fiw free in wagon (commerce); free into wagon (commerce)

FIWC Fiji Industrial Workers' Congress

FIWEM Fellow of the Institution of Water and Environmental Management

FIWO Fellow of the Institute of Social Workers

FIWSc Fellow of the Institute of Wood Science

fix. fixture

Fj. Fjord

FJ Air Pacific (airline flight code, Fiji); Exeter (UK vehicle registration)

FJA Future Journalists of America

Fjd Fjord

FJI Fellow of the Institute of Journalists; Fiji (international vehicle registration)

fk flat keel; fork

FK Dudley (UK vehicle registration); Falkirk (UK postcode); *Fundamental Katalog* (German: Fundamental Catalogue; astronomy)

FKC Fellow of King's College, London

FKCHMS Fellow of King's College Hospital Medical School

Fkr Faroese krone (monetary unit)

fl. *fleuve* (French: river); floor; *flores* (Latin: flowers; powdered drugs); florin; *floruit* (Latin: flourished); fluid; flute (music); guilder

f. l. *falsa lectio* (Latin: false reading)

Fl. Flanders; Flemish

FL Flag Lieutenant; Flight Lieutenant; Florida (zip code); Football League; Liechtenstein (international vehicle registration); Peterborough (UK vehicle registration)

Fla Florida

FLA Fellow of the Library Association; *fiat lege artis* (Latin: let it be done by rules of the art); Film Laboratory Association

flag. flageolot (music)

FLAI Fellow of the Library Association of Ireland

Flak *Fliegerabwehrkanone* (German: anti-aircaft gun or shellbursts)

FLCM Fellow of the London College of Music

FLCO Fellow of the London College of Osteopathy

fld field; filed

fldg folding

fl. dr. fluid dram

Flem. Flemish

flex. flexible

flg flagging; flooring; flying; following

FLHS Fellow of the London Historical Society
FLI Fellow of the Landscape Institute
FLIA Fellow of the Life Insurance Association
Flint. Flintshire
FLIP floating instrument platform (US Navy)
FLIR forward-looking infrared (military)
Flli *Fratelli* (Italian: Brothers)
FLN *Front de Libe[ac]ration Nationale* (French: National Liberation Front of Algeria)
FLOOD fleet observation of oceanographic data (US)
flops floating-point operations per second (computing)
flor. *floruit* (Latin: flourished)
Flor. Florence; Florentine; Florida
fl oz fluid ounce
flp fault location panel (aeronautics)
fl. pl. *flore pleno* (Latin: with double flowers)
FLQ *Front de Liberation du Québec* (French; Quebec Liberation Front; Canada)
flr florin
FLRA Federal Labor Relations Authority (US)
flrg flooring
fl. rt. flow rate
FLS Fellow of the Linnean Society
FLSA Fair Labor Standards Act (US)
flst flautist
Flt flight
F/Lt flight lieutenant
Flt Cmdr flight commander
fltg floating
Flt Lt flight lieutenant
Flt Off. flight officer
Flt Sgt flight sergeant
flu influenza
fluc. fluctuant; fluctuate; fluctuated; fluctuation
FLUC fluctuating (meteorology)
fluor. fluorescent; fluoridation; fluoride; fluorspar
fly. flyweight (boxing)
fm face measurement; facial measurement; farm; farmer; fathom; *femmes mariées* (French: married women); *fiat mistura* (Latin: let a mixture be made; medicine); fine measure; fine measurement; frequency modulation (radio); from
Fm facing matter (advertising); fermium (element)
FM Chester (UK vehicle registration); facilities management (computing); field magnet (electrical engineering); Field Marshal; figure of merit (aeronautics); Flight Mechanic; foreign mission; *Fraternitas Medicorum* (Latin: Fraternity of Physicians); *fraternité mondiale* (French: world brotherhood); freemason; frequency modulation (radio); Friars Minor
FMA Farm Management Association; Fellow of the Museums Association; Food Machinery Association
fman foreman
FMANU *Fédération mondiale des associations pour les Nations Unies* (French: World Federation of United Nations Associations)
FMANZ Fellow of the Medical Association of New Zealand
FMAO Farm Machinery Advisory Officer
FMAS Foreign Marriage Advisory Service
FMB Farmers' Marketing Board (Malawi); Federal Maritime Board (US); Federation of Master Builders
FMC Federal Maritime Commission (US); Fellow of the Medical Council; Forces Motoring Club; Ford Motor Company
FMCE Federation of Manufacturers of Construction Equipment
FMCG fast-moving consumer goods
FMCP Federation of Manufacturers of Contractors' Plant
FMCS Federal Mediation and Conciliation Service (US)
FMCW frequency modulated continuous wave
fmd formed
FMD foot and mouth disease
FMES Fellow of the Minerals Engineering Society
FMF fetal/foetal movements felt (medicine); Fiji Military Forces; Fleet Marine Force; Food Manufacturers' Federation
FMFPAC Fleet Marine Forces, Pacific (US)
FMG Federal Military Government (Nigeria); franc (monetary unit of Madagascar)
FMI Fellow of the Motor Industry; *Filii Mariae Immaculatae* (Latin: Sons of Mary Immaculate)
FMIG Food Manufacturers' Industrial Group
Fmk markka (Finnish monetary unit); Finnmark
fml formal

FMLN Farabundo Marti National Liberation Front (El Salvador)
fmn formation
FMO Fleet Medical Officer; Flight Medical Officer
FMPA *Fédération mondiale pour la protection des animaux* (French: World Federation for the Protection of Animals)
fmr(ly) former; formerly
FMRS Foreign Member of the Royal Society
FMS Federated Malay States; *Fédération mondiale des sourds* (French: World Federation of the Deaf); Fellow of the Institute of Management Studies; Fellow of the Medical Society; flexible manufacturing system (computing); flight-management system (aeronautics)
FMSA Fellow of the Mineralogical Society of America
FMTS field maintenance test station
FMVSS Federal Motor Vehicle Safety Standards (US)
fn footnote
FN Maidstone (UK vehicle registration)
fna for necessary action
FNA Fellow of the Indian National Science Academy; French North Africa
FNAEA Fellow of the National Association of Estate Agents
FNAL Fermi National Accelerator Laboratory
FNB Federal Narcotics Bureau
FNCB First National City Bank (US)
FNCO Fleet Naval Constructor Officer
fnd found; foundered
fndd founded
fndr founder
fndry foundry
fne fine
FNECInst Fellow of the North East Coast Institution of Engineers and Shipbuilders
FNI *Fédération naturiste internationale* (French: International Naturist Federation); Fellow of the Nautical Institute
FNIF Florence Nightingale International Foundation
FNILP Fellow of the National Institute of Licensing Practitioners
FNL Friends of the National Libraries
FNLA *Frente Nacional de Libertação de Angola* (Portuguese: National Front for the Liberation of Angola)

FNMA Federal National Mortgage Association
FNO fleet navigation officer
FNU *Fond des Nations Unies pour les réfugiés* (French: United Nations Refugee Fund); *Forces des Nations Unies* (French: United Nations Forces)
FNWC Fleet Numerical Weather Center (US)
FNZEI Fellow of the New Zealand Educational Institute
FNZIA Fellow of the New Zealand Institute of Architects
FNZIAS Fellow of the New Zealand Institute of Agricultural Science
FNZIC Fellow of the New Zealand Institute of Chemistry
FNZIE Fellow of the New Zealand Institution of Engineers
FNZIM Fellow of the New Zealand Institute of Management
FNZPsS Fellow of the New Zealand Psychological Society
fo fast operating; *firmato* (Italian: signed); free overside (commerce); fuel oil
fo. folio
f/o for orders (commerce); full out
FO federal official; Field Officer (military); firm offer (commerce); first officer; flying officer (air force); Foreign Office; formal offer (commerce); forward observer (military); full organ (music); Gloucester (UK vehicle registration); Western New South Wales Airlines (airline flight code, Australia)
FOB free on board (commerce)
FOBFO Federation of British Fire Organizations
FOBS fractional orbital bombardment system (military)
FOBTSU forward observer target survey unit
foc free of charge
FoC Father of the Chapel (trade unions)
FOC free of charge (commerce); free of claims
FOCL fibre-optic communications line
FOCOL Federation of Coin-Operated Launderettes
fo'c's'le forecastle (nautical)
FOCT flag officer carrier training
FOD free of damage
FODA Fellow of the Overseas Doctors' Association
FOE Fraternal Order of Eagles (US); Friends of the Earth
FOFA follow-on forces attack

FOFATUSA Federation of Free African Trade Unions of South Africa

F of F Firth of Forth

FOH front of house (theatre)

FOI freedom of information (US)

FOIA Freedom of Information Act (US)

FOIC flag officer in charge

fok fill or kill (stock exchange)

fol. folio; follow; followed; following

FOL Federation of Labour (New Zealand)

folg. following

foll. followed; following

FOM figure of merit (statistics)

FOMC Federal Open Market Committee (US)

FONA flag officer, naval aviation

FONAC flag officer, naval air command

FOOTSIE Financial Times Stock Exchange 100-Share Index

FOP forward observation post

foq free on quay (commerce)

for. foreign; foreigner; forensic; forest; forester; forestry; *forte* (Italian: loud; music)

For. forint (Hungarian monetary unit)

FOR Fellowship of Operational Research; flying objects research; free on rail

FORATOM *Forum atomique européen* (French: European Atomic Forum)

Ford Forum for the Restoration of Democracy (Kenya)

Forest Freedom Organization for the Right to Enjoy Smoking Tobacco

formn foreman; formation

form. wt formula weight (chemistry)

for. rts foreign rights

for's'l foresail (nautical)

fort full out rye terms (commerce)

fort. fortification; fortified; fortify

Fortran formula translation (computing)

Forts. *Fortsetzung* (German: continuation)

forz. *forzando* (Italian: with force; music)

fos free of stamp (finance); free on ship (commerce); free on steamer (commerce); free on station (commerce)

FOS Fisheries Organization Society

Fosdic film optical sensing device (computing)

fot free of tax (commerce); free on truck (commerce)

Found. foundation; foundry

4WD four-wheel drive

FOV field of view

fow first open water (commerce); free on wagon (commerce)

FOX Futures and Options Exchange (commerce)

fp *fiat pilula* (Latin: let a pill be made; medicine); fine paper; fine point (cricket); fireplace; fixed price; flameproof; flashpoint (chemistry); foolscap; footpath; foot pound; forward pass; freezing point; fresh paragraph; full point; fully paid

fp *forte piano* (Italian: loud then soft; music); freezing point

Fp. frontispiece

FP Federal Parliament; field punishment; filter paper; fire policy (insurance); fission product (nuclear engineering); floating policy (insurance); focal plane (optics); former pupil; fowl pest; Free Presbyterian; freezing point; fresh paragraph; fully paid; functional programming (computing); Leicester (UK vehicle registration)

FPA Family Planning Association; Film Production Association of Great Britain; Fire Protection Association; floating-point accelerator (computing); Foreign Press Association; free of particular average (insurance)

fpb fast patrol boat

fpbg fast patrol boat with guided missiles

fpc for private circulation

FPC Family Practitioner Committee; Federal Power Commission (US); Federation of Painting Contractors; fish protein concentrate; Flowers Publicity Council

FPEA Fellow of the Physical Education Association

FPF *Federaçao Portuguesa de Futebol* (Portuguese: Portuguese Football Federation)

FPHA Federal Public Housing Authority (US)

FPhS Fellow of the Philosophical Society of England

FPhyS Fellow of the Physical Society

FPI Federal Prison Industries

FPIA Fellow of the Plastics Institute of Australia

FPLA field-programmable logic array (electronics; computing)

fpm feet per minute

FPMI Fellow of the Pensions Management Institute

FPMR Federal Property Management Regulation (US)

FPO Field Post Office; fire prevention officer; fleet post office (US Navy)

FPRC Flying Personnel Research Committee

FPRI Fellow of the Plastics and Rubber Institute

fps feet per second; foot-pound-second (physics); frames per second (photography)

FPS Fellow of the Pharmaceutical Society; Fellow of the Philharmonic Society; Fellow of the Philological Society; Fellow of the Philosophical Society; Fellow of the Physical Society; Fluid Power Society (US)

fpsps feet per second per second

FPT fixed price tenders (commerce); forepeak tank (nautical)

fq fiscal quarter (finance)

FQS Federal Quarantine Service (US)

fr *folio recto* (Latin: right-hand page)

fr. fragment; frame; franc; free; frequent; from; front; fruit(ing)

fr. Froude number (physics)

Fr Father (religion); francium (element); *Frater* (Latin: Brother; Roman Catholic Church)

Fr. France; *Fratelli* (Italian: Brothers); *Frau* (German: Mrs); French; Friar; Friday

FR Faroe Islands (international vehicle registration); Federal Republic; Federal Reserve; fighter reconnaissance; fluorine rubber (chemistry); *Forum Romanum* (Latin: Roman Forum); Fraserburgh (UK fishing port registration); freight release; frequency rate; fusion reactor (nuclear engineering); Preston (UK vehicle registration); Ryanair (airline flight code, Ireland)

F/R folio reference

fra flame retardant additive

Fra *Frate* (Italian: Brother; Roman Catholic Church)

FRA forward rate agreement (finance)

FRACDS Fellow of the Royal Australian College of Dental Surgeons

FRACGP Fellow of the Royal Australian College of General Practitioners

FRACI Fellow of the Royal Australian Chemical Institute

FRACMA Fellow of the Royal Australian College of Medical Administrators

FRACO Fellow of the Royal Australian College of Ophthalmologists

FRACOG Fellow of the Royal Australian College of Obstetrics and Gynae-cologists

FRACP Fellow of the Royal Australian College of Radiologists

FRAD Fellow of the Royal Academy of Dancing

FRAeS Fellow of the Royal Aeronautical Society

FRAgSs Fellow of the Royal Agricultural Societies

FRAHS Fellow of the Royal Australian Historical Society

FRAI Fellow of the Royal Anthropo-logical Institute

FRAIA Fellow of the Royal Australian Institute of Architects

FRAIC Fellow of the Royal Architectural Institute of Canada

FRAIPA Fellow of the Royal Australian Institute of Public Administration

FRAM Fellow of the Royal Academy of Music

FRAME Fund for the Replacement of Animals in Medical Experiments

Franc. Franciscan

fr&cc free of riot and civil commotions (insurance)

Frank. Frankish

FRANZCP Fellow of the Royal Australian and New Zealand College of Psychiatrists

FRAP *Frente de Acción Popular* (Spanish: Popular Action Front; Chile)

FRAPI Fellow of the Royal Australian Planning Institute

FRAS Fellow of the Royal Asiatic Society; Fellow of the Royal Astronomical Society

FRASE Fellow of the Royal Agricultural Society of England

FRATE formulae for routes and technical equipment (railways)

fraud. fraudulent

FRB Federal Reserve Bank (US); Federal Reserve Board; Fisheries Research Board of Canada; *Frente de la Revolución Boliviana* (Spanish: Bolivian Revolutionary Front)

FRBS Fellow of the Royal Botanic Society; Fellow of the Royal Society of British Sculptors

FRC Federal Radiation Council (US); Federal Radio Commission (US); Flight Research Center (NASA)

FRCA Fellow of the Royal College of Art

Fr-Can French-Canadian

FRCCO Fellow of the Royal Canadian College of Organists

FRCD floating-rate certificate of deposit (banking); Fellow of the Royal College of Dentists of Canada

FRCGP Fellow of the Royal College of General Practitioners

FRCM Fellow of the Royal College of Music
FRCN Fellow of the Royal College of Nursing
FRCO Fellow of the Royal College of Organists
FRCO(CHM) Fellow of the Royal College of Organists with Diploma in Choir Training
FRCOG Fellow of the Royal College of Obstetricians and Gynaecologists
FRCP Fellow of the Royal College of Physicians, London.
FRCPA Fellow of the Royal College of Pathologists of Australasia
FRCP&S(Canada) Fellow of the Royal College of Physicians and Surgeons of Canada
FRCPath Fellow of the Royal College of Pathologists
FRCP(C) Fellow of the Royal College of Physicians of Canada
FRCPE(d) Fellow of the Royal College of Physicians of Edinburgh
FRCPGlas Fellow of the Royal College of Physicians and Surgeons of Glasgow
FRCPI Fellow of the Royal College of Physicians of Ireland
FRCPsych Fellow of the Royal College of Psychiatrists
FRCR Fellow of the Royal College of Radiologists
FRCS Fellow of the Royal College of Surgeons
FRCSCan Fellow of the Royal College of Surgeons of Canada
FRCScl Fellow of the Royal College of Science, Ireland
FRCSE(d) Fellow of the Royal College of Surgeons of Edinburgh
FRCSGlas Fellow of the Royal College of Physicians and Surgeons of Glasgow
FRCSI Fellow of the Royal College of Surgeons of Ireland
FRCSoc Fellow of the Royal Commonwealth Society
FRCVS Fellow of the Royal College of Veterinary Surgeons
frd friend
FR Dist. Federal Reserve District
fre *fracture* (French: invoice)
Fre. *Freitag* (German: Friday); French
FREconS Fellow of the Royal Economic Society
FRED Fast Reactor Experiment, Dounreay; figure reading electronic device

Free. freeway (US)
FREGG Free Range Egg Association
FREI Fellow of the Real Estate Institute (Australia)
Frelimo *Frente de Libertação de Moçambique* (Portuguese: Liberation Front of Mozambique)
freq. frequency; frequent(ly); frequentative (grammar)
FRES Federation of Recruitment and Employment Services; Fellow of the Royal Entomological Society
FRESH foil research hydrofoil
Fr.G. French Guiana
FRG Federal Republic of Germany
FRGS Fellow of the Royal Geographical Society
FRGSA Fellow of the Royal Geographical Society of Australasia
frgt freight
FRHB Federation of Registered House Builders
FRHistS Fellow of the Royal Historical Society
Frhr *Freiherr* (German: Baron)
FRHS Fellow of the Royal Horticultural Society
Fri. Fribourg; Friday
FRI Fellow of the Royal Institution; Food Research Institute
FRIA Fellow of the Royal Irish Academy
FRIAI Fellow of the Royal Institute of Architects of Ireland
FRIAS Fellow of the Royal Incorporation of Architects in Scotland; Fellow of the Royal Institute for the Advancement of Science
FRIBA Fellow of the Royal Institute of British Architects
fric(t). friction; frictional
FRIC Fellow of the Royal Institute of Chemistry
FRICS Fellow of the Royal Institution of Chartered Surveyors
FRIH Fellow of the Royal Institute of Horticulture (New Zealand)
FRIIA Fellow of the Royal Institute of International Affairs
FRIN Fellow of the Royal Institute of Navigation
FRINA Fellow of the Royal Institution of Naval Architects
FRIPA Fellow of the Royal Institute of Public Administration
FRIPHH Fellow of the Royal Institute of Public Health and Hygiene
Fris. Friesland; Frisian

Frk. *Frøken* (Danish, Norwegian: Miss); *Fröken* (Swedish: Miss)

Frl. *Fräulein* (German: Miss)

FRL full repairing lease

frld foreland; freehold

frm from

FRMCM Fellow of the Royal Manchester College of Music

FRMCS Fellow of the Royal Medical and Chirurgical Society

FRMedSoc Fellow of the Royal Medical Society

FRMetS Fellow of the Royal Meteorological Society

FRMS Fellow of the Royal Microscopical Society

FRN floating-rate note (finance)

FRNCM Fellow of the Royal Northern College of Music

FRNS Fellow of the Royal Numismatic Society

FRNSA Fellow of the Royal Navy School of Architects

FRO Fellow of the Register of Osteopaths; Fire Research Organization; fire risk only (insurance)

frof fire risk on freight (insurance)

front(is). frontispiece

FRP fibre-reinforced plastic; fibreglass-reinforced plastic; fuel-reprocessing plant

frpf fireproof

FRPharmS Fellow of the Royal Pharmaceutical Society

FRPS Fellow of the Royal Photographic Society

FRPSL Fellow of the Royal Philatelic Society, London

FRQ frequent (meteorology)

Frs. Frisian

FRS Federal Reserve System (US); Fellow of the Royal Society; Festiniog Railway Society; fuel research station

FRSA Fellow of the Royal Society of Arts

FRSAI Fellow of the Royal Society of Antiquaries of Ireland

FRSAMD Fellow of the Royal Scottish Academy of Music and Drama

FRSC Fellow of the Royal Society of Canada; Fellow of the Royal Society of Chemistry

FRSCM Fellow of the Royal School of Church Music

FRSE Fellow of the Royal Society of Edinburgh

FRSGS Fellow of the Royal Scottish Geographical Society

FRSH Fellow of the Royal Society for the Promotion of Health

FRSL Fellow of the Royal Society of Literature

FRSM Fellow of the Royal Society of Medicine

FRSNA Fellow of the Royal School of Naval Architecture

FRSNZ Fellow of the Royal Society of New Zealand

FRSS Fellow of the Royal Statistical Society

FRSSA Fellow of the Royal Scottish Society of Arts; Fellow of the Royal Society of South Africa

FRSSI Fellow of the Royal Statistical Society of Ireland

FRSSS Fellow of the Royal Statistical Society of Scotland

FRST Fellow of the Royal Society of Teachers

FRSTM&H Fellow of the Royal Society of Tropical Medicine and Hygiene

frt freight

frt fwd freight forward

FRTPI Fellow of the Royal Town Planning Institute

frt ppd freight prepaid

FRTS Fellow of the Royal Television Society

Fru fructose (biochemistry)

frum *fratrum* (Latin: of the brothers)

frust. *frustillatum* (Latin: in small portions; medicine)

FRVA Fellow of the Rating and Valuation Association

FRVC Fellow of the Royal Veterinary College

FRVIA Fellow of the Royal Victorian Institute of Architects

frwk framework

fr(w)y freeway

FRZSScot Fellow of the Royal Zoological Society of Scotland

fs factor of safety; *faire suivre* (French: please forward); far side; film strip; fire station; flight service; flying saucer; flying status; low fog over sea (meteorology)

fs. facsimile

FS Edinburgh (UK vehicle registration); Fabian Society; Faraday Society; feasibility study; *Ferrovie Stato Italia* (Italian: Italian State Railways); field security; financial secretary; financial statement; Fleet Surgeon; Flight Sergeant; Foreign Service; Forest Service (US); Friendly Society

fsa fuel storage area

FSA Farm Security Agency (US); Federal Security Agency (US); Fellow of the Society of Antiquaries; Field Survey Association; Financial Services Act; finite-state automaton (computing); foreign service allowance; Friendly Societies Act

FSAA Fellow of the Society of Incorporated Accountants and Auditors

FSAE Fellow of the Society of Art Education; Fellow of the Society of Automotive Engineers

FSAI Fellow of the Society of Architectural Illustrators

FSAIEE Fellow of the South African Institute of Electrical Engineers

FSAM Fellow of the Society of Art Masters

FSAS(cot) Fellow of the Society of Antiquaries of Scotland

FSASM Fellow of the South Australian School of Mines

FSBI Fellow of the Savings Bank Institute

FSC Federal Supreme Court (US); Fellow of the Society of Chiropodists; Field Studies Council; *Fratres Scholarum Christianorum* (Latin: Brothers of the Christian schools or Christian Brothers); Friends Service Council

FSCA Fellow of the Society of Company and Commercial Accountants

FSD full-scale deflection

FSDC Fellow of the Society of Dyers and Colourists

FSE Fellow of the Society of Engineers; field support equipment

FSF Fellow of the Institute of Shipping and Forwarding Agents

FSG Fellow of the Society of Genealogists

FSgt Flight Sergeant

FSGT Fellow of the Society of Glass Technology

FSH follicle-stimulating hormone (biochemistry)

FSHM Fellow of the Society of Housing Managers

FSI *Fédération spirite internationale* (French: International Spiritualist Federation); Free Sons of Israel

FSK frequency shift keying (telecommunications)

FSL First Sea Lord

FSLAET Fellow of the Society of Licensed Aircraft Engineers and Technologists

FSLIC Federal Savings and Loan Insurance Corporation (US)

FSLN *Frente Sandinista de Liberación Nacional* (Spanish: Sandinista National Liberation Front; Nicaragua)

FSLTC Fellow of the Society of Leather Technologists and Chemists

FSM *Fédération syndicale mondiale* (French: World Federation of Trade Unions); flying-spot microscope (electronics); Free Speech Movement (US)

FSMC Freeman of the Spectacle-Makers' Company

FSME Fellow of the Society of Manufacturing Engineers

FSN federal stock number

FSNA Fellow of the Society of Naval Architects

FSO field security officer; Fleet Signals Officer; Foreign Service Officer

FSP field security police; foreign service pay

FSR Field Service Regulations; Fleet Street Patent Law Reports

FSRP Fellow of the Society for Radiological Protection

FSS Fellow of the Royal Statistical Society; *Front des forces socialistes* (French: Socialist Forces Front; Algeria)

FSSI Fellow of the Statistical Society of Ireland

FSSU Federated Superannuation Scheme for Universities

FSTD Fellow of the Society of Typographic Designers

FSU family service unit

FSUC Federal Statistics Unit Conference

FSVA Fellow of the Incorporated Society of Valuers and Auctioneers

ft feint; *fiat* (Latin: let there be made); foot; formal training; feet; fort; full terms

ft. fortification; fortify

Ft forint (Hungarian monetary unit); Fort

FT feet (meteorology); Financial Times; Fischer-Tropsch (chemistry); Newcastle upon Tyne (UK vehicle registration)

FTA Free Trade Agreement; Freight Transport Association; Future Teachers of America

FTA (Index) Financial Times Actuaries Share Index

FTAM file transfer, access and management (computing)

FTASI Financial Times Actuaries All-Share Index

FTAT Furniture, Timber and Allied Trades Union
FTB fleet torpedo bomber
ftbrg. footbridge
FTC Federal Trade Commission (US); flight test center (US); flying training command; Full Technological Certificate (City and Guilds Institute)
FTCD Fellow of Trinity College, Dublin
FTCL Fellow of Trinity College of Music, London
FTD foreign technology division
FTDA Fellow of the Theatrical Designers and Craftsmen's Association
fte full-time equivalent
FTESA Foundry Trades Equipment and Supplies Association
ftg fitting
FTG Fuji Texaco Gas
fth(m). fathom
FTI Fellow of the Textile Institute
FTII Fellow of the Institute of Taxation
FT (Index) Financial Times Ordinary Share Index
ft-lb foot-pound
Ft Lieut Flight Lieutenant
FTM flying training manual; fractional test meal (medicine)
ft mist. *fiat mistura* (Latin: let a mixture be made; medicine)
FTO Fleet Torpedo Officer
FT Ord Financial Times (Industrial) Ordinary Share Index
FTP Fellow of Thames Polytechnic; file-transfer protocol (computing)
FTPA Fellow of the Town and Country Planning Association
ft pulv. *fiat pulvis* (Latin: let a powder be made)
ft/s feet per second
FTS Fellow of the Australian Academy of Technological Sciences and Engineering; Fellow of the Tourism Society; flying training school
FTSC Fellow of the Tonic Sol-Fa College
FTSE 100 Financial Times Stock Exchange 100-Share Index
fttr fitter
FTU Federation of Trade Unions (Hong Kong)
FTW free-trade wharf (commerce)
FTZ free-trade zone
FU Air Littoral (airline flight code, France); Farmers' Union; *Freie Universität* (German: Free University, Berlin); Lincoln (UK vehicle registration)
FUACE *Fédération universelle des*

associations chrétiennes d'étudiants (French: World Student Christian Federation)
FUEN Federal Union of European Nationalities
FUMIST Fellow of the University of Manchester Institute of Science and Technology
fund. fundamental
fur. furlong; further
furn. furnace; furnish; furnished; furniture
fus. fuselage; fusilier
fut. future; futures (finance)
FUW Farmers' Union of Wales
fv fire vent; fishing vessel; flush valve; *folio verso* (Latin: left-hand page)
FV Preston (UK vehicle registration)
FVRDE Fighting Vehicle Research and Development Establishment
FW formula weight (chemistry); fresh water; Lincoln (UK vehicle registration)
FWA Factories and Workshops Act; Family Welfare Association; Federal Works Agency (US); Fellow of the World Academy of Arts and Sciences
FWAG Farming and Wildlife Advisory Group
fwb four wheel brake; four-wheel braking
FWB Free Will Baptists
FWCC Friends' World Committee for Consultation
fwd forward; four-wheel drive; free water damage; fresh water damage; front-wheel drive
fwdg forwarding
FWeldI Fellow of the Welding Institute
FWFM Federation of Wholesale Fish Merchants
fwh flexible working hours
FWI Federation of West Indies; French West Indies
FWL Foundation of World Literacy
FWO Federation of Wholesale Organizations; Fleet Wireless Officer
FWPCA Federal Water Pollution Control Administration (US)
FWS fighter weapons school; fleet work study
FWSG farm water supply grant
fwt fair wear and tear; featherweight (boxing)
FX Bournemouth (UK vehicle registration); foreign exchange; Francis Xavier (Spanish Jesuit); special effects (theatre, cinema)
fxd fixed; foxed

fxg fixing
fxle forecastle (nautical)
FY Blackpool (UK postcode); fiscal year; Fowey (UK fishing port registration); Liverpool (UK vehicle registration)
FYC Family and Youth Concern
fyi for your information
FYM farmyard manure
FYP Five-Year Plan (economics)
fz *forzando/forzato* (Italian: accentuate strongly; music)
FZ Belfast (UK vehicle registration); freezing (meteorology); Free Zone; French Zone
FZA Fellow of the Zoological Academy (US)
FZDZ freezing drizzle (meteorology)
FZFG freezing fog (meteorology)
FZGB Federation of Zoological Gardens of Great Britain and Ireland
FZRA freezing rain (meteorology)
FZS Fellow of the Zoological Society
F-Zug *Fernschnellzug* (German: long-distance express train)

G

g acceleration of free fall (physics); gale (meteorology); gallon; gaseous (chemistry); gluon (physics); grade (mathematics); gram; gravity
g degeneracy (physics)
g. garage; *gauche* (French: left); gauge; gelding; gender; general; genitive; geographical; gilt; goal(keeper); gold; government; grand; great; green; grey; *gros/grosse* (French: large); guardian; guide; guilder; guinea; gunnery
G Galway (Irish fishing port registration); gauss (magnetism); general exhibition (Australian and US cinema certificate); German(y); giga-; Glasgow (UK postcode); gourde (Haitian monetary unit); grand; guarani (Paraguayan monetary unit); storm (meteorology); UK (international civil aircraft marking)
G conductance (physics); gravitational constant (physics)
G. German(y); good; green; Guernsey; Gulf
G3 Group of Three (economics)
G5 Group of Five (finance)
G7 Group of Seven (economics)
G10 Group of Ten (finance)
G24 Group of Twenty-Four (economics)
G77 Group of Seventy-Seven (developing economies)
ga general average (insurance)
Ga gallium (element)
Ga. Gallic; Georgia
GA Gaelic Athletic (club); Gamblers' Anonymous; garrison artillery; Garuda Indonesia (airline flight code); General Accident; general agent; General American (linguistics); general anaesthetic; General Assembly (UN); general assignment; general average (insurance); Geographical Association; Geologists' Association; Georgia (zip code); Glasgow (UK vehicle registration); goal attack (sport); government actuary; graphic arts
G/A general average (insurance); ground-to-air
GAA Gaelic Athletic Association (Ireland)
Gab. Gabon
GAB general arrangements to borrow (finance)
GABA gamma-amino buyric acid (medicine)
Gabba Wollongabba (Queensland Cricket Club ground, Brisbane)
Gael. Gaelic
GAFTA Grain and Free Trade Association
GAI guaranteed annual income (US); Guild of Architectural Ironmongers
gal gallon
Gal. Galatians (Bible); Galicia; Galway
GALAXY General Automatic Luminosity (high-speed scanner, Royal Observatory, Edinburgh)
gall. gallery; gallon
GALT gut-associated lymphoid tissue (medicine)
galv. galvanic; galvanize(d); galvanometer
Gam. Gambia
GAM guided aircraft missile
G&AE general and administrative expenses (accounting)
G and O gas and oxygen (medicine)
G&S Gilbert and Sullivan
G&T gin and tonic

GAO General Accounting Office (US)
GAP general assembly programme; Great American Public
GAPAN Guild of Air Pilots and Air Navigators
GAPCE General Assembly of the Presbyterian Church of England
gar. garage; garrison
GAR Grand Army of the Republic (US Civil War); guided aircraft rocket
gard. garden
GARIOA government aid and relief in occupied areas
GARP Global Atmospheric Research Programme
GAS general adaptation syndrome
GASC German-American Securities Corporation
GASP Group Against Smokers' Pollution (US)
gastroent. gastroenterological; gastroenterology
GATCO Guild of Air Traffic Control Officers
GATT General Agreement on Tariffs and Trade
GAUFCC General Assembly of Unitarian and Free Christian Churches
GAV gross annual value (accounting)
GAW guaranteed annual wage
GAWF Greek Animal Welfare Fund
GAYE give as you earn
gaz. gazette; gazetted; gazetteer
Gb gilbert (magnetism)
GB gall bladder; Gas Board; Girls' Brigade; Glasgow (UK vehicle registration); government and binding; Great Britain; guide book; gunboat; UK (international vehicle registration)
GBA Alderney (international vehicle registration); Governing Bodies Association
GB and I Great Britain and Ireland
GBCW Governing Body of the Church in Wales
GBDO Guild of British Dispensing Opticians
GBE Dame or Knight Grand Cross of the Order of the British Empire
GBG Guernsey (international vehicle registration)
GBGSA Governing Bodies of Girls' Schools Association
GBH grievous bodily harm
GBJ Jersey (international vehicle registration)

GBM Isle of Man (international vehicle registration)
gbo goods in bad order
GBP Great British Public
GBRE General Board of Religious Education
GBS George Bernard Shaw (Irish playwright and critic)
GBSM Graduate of the Birmingham and Midland Institute School of Music
GBTA Guild of Business Travel Agents
GBZ Gibraltar (international vehicle registration)
GC galactic centre (astronomy); gas chromatography; Gas Council; George Cross; gliding club; Goldsmiths' College; golf club; good conduct; government chemist; Grand Chancellor; Grand Chaplain; Grand Chapter; Grand Conductor; Grand Cross; Lina Congo (airline flight code); southwest London (UK vehicle registration)
GCA Girls' Clubs of America; ground-controlled approach; Guatemala (international vehicle registration)
G Capt Group Captain
GCB Dame or Knight Grand Cross of the Order of the Bath
GCBS General Council of British Shipping
GCC Gas Consumers' Council; Girton College, Cambridge; Gonville and Caius College, Cambridge; Gulf Cooperation Council
GCD general and complete disarmament; greatest common divisor (mathematics)
GCE General Certificate of Education; General College Entrance (US)
GCF greatest common factor (mathematics)
GCH Knight of the Grand Cross of the Hanoverian Order; Guild Certificate of Hairdressing
GCHQ Government Communications Headquarters
GCI ground-controlled interception (aeronautics)
GCIE Knight Grand Commander of the Order of the Indian Empire
GCIU Graphic Communications International Union (US)
GCL Guild of Cleaners and Launderers
GCLJ Knight Grand Cross of the Order of St Lazarus of Jerusalem
GCLH Grand Cross of the Legion of Honour
GCM general circulation model

(meteorology); general court martial;
Good Conduct Medal; greatest common
measure (statistics); greatest common
multiple (mathematics)

GCMG Dame or Knight Grand Cross of
the Order of St Michael and St George

GCMS gas-chromatography mass
spectroscopy

GCO Gun Control Officer (Navy)

GCON Grand Cross of the Order of the
Niger

GCR ground-controlled radar

GCRO General Council and Register of
Osteopaths

GCSE General Certificate of Secondary
Education

GCSG Knight Grand Cross of the Order
of St Gregory the Great

GCSI Knight Grand Commander of the
Order of the Star of India

GCSJ Knight Grand Cross of Justice of
the Order of St John of Jerusalem

GCStJ Bailiff or Dame Grand Cross of
the Most Venerable Order of the
Hospital of St John of Jerusalem

GCVO Dame or Knight Grand Cross of
the Royal Victorian Order

gd general duties; good; grand-daughter;
gravimetric density; ground

Gd gadolinium (element)

GD gestational day (obstetrics); Glasgow
(UK vehicle registration); goal defence
(netball); Graduate in Divinity; Grand
Duchess; Grand Duchy; Grand Duke;
Gunnery Division

GDBA Guide Dogs for the Blind
Association

GDC General Dental Council; General
Dynamics Corporation

GDI gross domestic income

Gdk Gdansk

gdn garden; guardian

Gdns Gardens

GDP gross domestic product

GDR German Democratic Republic

gds goods

Gds Guards

Gdsm. Guardsman

ge gilt edge (books)

Ge germanium (element)

GE garrison engineer; general election;
General Electric (US); Glasgow (UK
vehicle registration); Goole (UK fishing
port registration); gross energy;
Guernsey Airlines (airline flight code,
Channel Islands, UK)

GEA Garage Equipment Association

geb. *geboren* (German: born); *gebunden*
(German: bound)

GEBCO general bathymetric chart of the
oceans

Gebr. *Gebrüder* (German: brothers)

GEC General Electric Company (UK)

GED general educational development

gegr. *gegründet* (German: founded)

gel. gelatin

GEM genetically engineered micro-
organism; ground effect machine;
guidance evaluation missile; Guild of
Experienced Motorists

GEMS Global Environmental Monitoring
System (UN)

gen. gender; genealogy; general;
generally; generator; generic; genetic;
genetics; genital; genitive; genuine;
genus (biology)

Gen. General; Genesis (Bible); Geneva;
Genoa

gen. av. general average (insurance)

gend. *gendarme* (French: policeman)

geneal. genealogy

genit. genitive

Genl General

genn. *gennaio* (Italian: January)

gent. gentleman

Gents gentlemen (toilets)

GEO geostationary earth orbit;
geosynchronous earth orbit

geod. geodesy; geodetic

geog. geographer; geographic(al);
geography

geol. geologic; geological; geologist;
geology

geom. geometric; geometrical; geometry

geon gyro-erected optical navigation

geophys. geophysics

geopol. geopolitics

GEOREF International Geographic
Reference System

ger. gerund; gerundive

Ger. German(y)

GER gross energy requirement

Gerbil Great Education Reform Bill (UK)

Ges. *Gesellschaft* (German: company or
society)

GESP generalized extrasensory
perception

gest. *gestorben* (German: deceased)

Gestapo *Geheime Staats-Polizei* (German:
secret state police; Third Reich)

GETT Grants Equal To Tax (US)

GeV gigaelectronvolt (physics)

gez. *gezeichnet* (German: signed)

GF General Foods Ltd; glass fibre;

government form; gradient freezing; Guggenheim Foundation; Guinean franc; Gulf Air (airline flight code, Bahrain); southwest London (UK vehicle registration)

gfa good fair average (commerce); good freight agent (commerce)

GFCM General Fisheries Council for the Mediterranean (FAO)

GFD geophysical fluid dynamics

GFG Good Food Guide

GFH George Frederick Handel

GFOFs geared futures and options and funds (stock exchange)

GFR German Federal Republic

GFS Girls' Friendly Society

GFTU General Federation of Trade Unions (US)

GFWC General Federation of Women's Clubs

gg gas generator

GG gamma globulin (medicine); Girl Guides; Glasgow (UK vehicle registration); governor general; great gross; Grenadier Guards

GGA Girl Guides Association

GGC generalized genetic code

ggd great granddaughter

gge garage

ggr great gross (144 dozen)

ggs great grandson

GGSM Graduate of the Guildhall School of Music and Drama

GH general hospital; Ghana (international vehicle registration); Ghana Airways (airline flight code); Grangemouth (UK fishing port registration); Green Howards (military); Greenwich Hospital; growth hormone (biochemistry); southwest London (UK vehicle registration)

GHCIMA Graduate of the Hotel Catering and Institutional Management Association

ghe ground handling equipment

GHI Good Housekeeping Institute

GHMS Graduate of Homeopathic Medicine and Surgery

GHOST global horizontal sounding technique

GHQ General Headquarters (military)

GHRH growth-hormone-releasing hormone

GHS Girls' High School

GHz gigahertz

gi galvanized iron; gill (measuring unit)

Gi gilbert (magnetism)

GI Air Guinée (airline flight code, Guinea); galvanized iron; gastrointestinal; generic issue; Royal Glasgow Institute of the Fine Arts; general issue (US); government issue (US); Government of India; growth inhibitor (biochemistry); Tipperary (Irish vehicle registration)

GIA Garuda Indonesian Airways

Gib. Gibraltar

GIB Gulf International Bank

GIC *Guilde internationale des coopératrices* (French: International Cooperative Women's Guild)

GIE Graduate of the Institute of Engineers and Technicians

GIEE Graduate of the Institution of Electrical Engineers

GIFT gamete intrafallopian transfer (medicine)

GIGO garbage in, garbage out (computing)

GIMechE Graduate of the Institution of Mechanical Engineers

GINO graphical input output (computing)

GInstAEA Graduate of the Institute of Automotive Engineer Assessors

GInstT Graduate of the Institute of Transport

GINucE Graduate of the Institution of Nuclear Engineers

gio. *giovedi* (Italian: Thursday)

giov. *giovedi* (Italian: Thursday)

GIP glazed imitation parchment (paper)

GIS geological information system (computing); geographical information system (computing)

GISS Goddard Institute for Space Studies

giu. *giugno* (Italian: June)

GIUK Greenland, Iceland, United Kingdom

GJ southwest London (UK vehicle registration)

GJD Grand Junior Deacon (Freemasonry)

Gk Greek

GK goalkeeper; Greenock (UK fishing port registration); southwest London (UK vehicle registration)

GKA Garter King of Arms

GKC G(ilbert) K(eith) Chesterton

GKN Guest, Keen and Nettlefolds (engineering company)

GKS graphics kernel system (computing)

gl. gill; glass; gloss

g/l grams per litre

Gl. *Gloria* (Latin: glory)

GL Germanischer Lloyd (German shipping classification); Gloucester (UK postcode); gothic letter (printing); government laboratory; Grand Lodge (Freemasonry); Grand Luxe (cars); Gronlandsfly (airline flight code, Greenland); ground level; gun licence; Truro (UK vehicle registration)

4GL fourth-generation language (computing)

glab. glabrous (botany)

GLAB Greater London Arts Board

glam greying, leisured, affluent, married

Glam. Glamorgan(shire)

Glas. Glasgow

GLASS Gay, Lesbian Assembly for Student Support (US)

glau. glaucous (botany)

GLB Girls' Life Brigade

GLC gas-liquid chromatography (chemistry); Greater London Council; ground-level concentration (radioactivity); Guild of Lettering Craftsmen

GLCM Graduate of the London College of Music; ground-launched cruise missile

gld. guilder (Dutch currency unit)

GLDP Greater London Development Plan

GLM graduated length method (skiing)

GLOBECOM Global Communications System (US Air Force)

GLOMEX Global Oceanographic and Meteorological Experiment

GLORIA Geological Long Range Asdic

Glos. Gloucester(shire)

gloss. glossary

GLS Grand Lodge of Scotland (Freemasonry)

glt gilt (books)

GLT greetings letter telegram

gm gram

g m gram metre

gm² grams per square metre (paper)

GM Geiger-Müller; general manager; general merchandise; general mortgage; General Motors Corporation; Geological Museum; geometric mean; George Medal; gold medal(list); Grand Marshall; Grand Master (Freemasonry); grant-maintained (education); guided missile; Reading (UK vehicle registration)

GMAG Genetic Manipulation Advisory Group

G-man government man (FBI agent)

gmb good merchantable brand

GMB General, Municipal, Boilermakers (trade union); Grand Master of the Order of the Bath; Grand Master Bowman (archery)

GMBE Grand Master of the Order of the British Empire

GmbH *Gesellschaft mit beschränkter Haftung* (German: private limited company)

Gmc Germanic

GMC general management committee; General Medical Council; giant molecular cloud (astronomy); Guild of Memorial Craftsmen

GMF Glass Manufacturers' Federation

GMIE Grand Master of the Order of the British Empire

GMKP Grand Master of the Knights of St Patrick

GMMG Grand Master of the Order of St Michael and St George

GMO genetically modified organism

GMP Glass, Molders, Pottery, Plastics and Allied Workers International Union (US); Grand Master of the Order of St Patrick; gross material product; Gurkha Military Police

gmq good merchantable quality

GMR ground-mapping radar

GMS grant-maintained status (education)

GMSC General Medical Services Committee

GMSI Grand Master of the Order of the Star of India

GMST Greenwich Mean Sidereal Time

GMT Greenwich Mean Time; Greenwich Meridian Time

GMTV Good Morning Television (UK television)

GMV golden mosaic virus (microbiology)

GMW gram-molecular weight

GMWU General and Municipal Workers' Union

gn grandnephew; grandniece

gn. guinea

GN Air Gabon (airline flight code); Graduate Nurse (US); Granton (UK fishing port registration); southwest London (UK vehicle registration)

GNA *Agence Guinéenne de Press* (news agency, Guinea); Ghana News Agency; Guyana News Agency

GNAS Grand National Archery Society

GNC General Nursing Council

gnd ground

GND ground (meteorology)

GNMA Government National Mortgage Association (US)

GNP gross national product

Gnr gunner (military)
GNR *Guarda Nacional Republicana* (Portuguese: National Republican Guard)
GnRH gonadotrophin-releasing hormone (biochemistry)
gns guineas
GNTC Girls' Nautical Training Corps
GNVQ General National Vocational Qualification
GO gas operated; General Office(r); general order (military); great organ (music); Group Officer; southwest London (UK vehicle registration)
gob good ordinary brand
GOC General Officer Commanding; General Optical Council; Greek Orthodox Church
GOC-in-C General Officer Commanding-in-Chief
GOCO government-owned, contractor-operated
GOE General Ordination Examination
GOES Geostationary Operational Environmental Satellite (US)
GOM Grand Old Man
GOP Girls' Own Paper; Grand Old Party (US Republican Party)
Gopa Government Oil and Pipeline Agency
Gosplan *Gosudarstvennaya Planovaya* (Russian: State Planning Commission)
Gosud. *Gosudarstvo* (Russian: state)
Goth. Gothic
gou. gourde (Haitian monetary unit)
Gov. government; governor
Gov-Gen governor-general
govt government
gox gaseous oxygen (chemistry)
gp galley proofs (printing); geometrical progression (mathematics); great primer (printing); group
GP Gallup Poll; gas-permeable (contact lenses); general paralysis; general pause (music); general practitioner; general purpose; *Gloria Patri* (Latin: glory be to the Father); graduated pension; Graduate in Pharmacy; Grand Prix; southwest London (UK vehicle registration)
GPA General Practitioners' Association; grade point average (US; education)
GPALS Global Protection Against Limited Strikes
GPC general purposes committee
Gp Capt group captain
Gp Comdr group commander

gpd gallons per day
GPDST Girls' Public Day School Trust
gph gallons per hour
G Ph Graduate in Pharmacy
GPHI Guild of Public Health Inspectors
GPI general paralysis of the insane
GPIB general-purpose interface bus (computing)
GPKT Grand Priory of the Knights of the Temple
gpm gallons per minute
GPM graduated payments mortgage (US); Grand Past Master (Freemasonry)
GPMU Graphical, Paper and Media Union
GPO General Post Office; Government Printing Office (US)
GPR *genio populi Romani* (Latin: to the genius of the Roman people); ground-penetrating radar
gps gallons per second
GPS Global Positioning System (US); Graduated Pension Scheme; Great Public Schools (Australia)
GPSS General Purpose System Simulator
GPT Guild of Professional Toastmasters
GPU General Postal Union; General Public Utilities Corporation; *Gosudarstvennoye Politicheskoye Upravlenie* (Russian: State Political Administration)
GQ general quarters (military)
GQG *Grand Quartier Général* (French: General Headquarters)
gr. grade; grain (unit); gram; grammar; grand; great; greater; grey; gross; ground; group
Gr Gunner
Gr. Grecian; Greece; Greek
GR Aurigny Air Services (airline flight code, Channel Islands, UK); gamma ray; general reconnaissance; general relativity (physics); general reserve; *Georgius Rex* (Latin: King George); Gloucester (UK fishing port registration); grand recorder; Greece (international vehicle registration); ground rent; *Gulielmus Rex* (Latin: King William); Gurkha Rifles; Newcastle upon Tyne (UK vehicle registration)
GRA Game Research Association; Greyhound Racing Association
grad. gradient; grading; gradual; graduate(d)
GradIAE Graduate of the Institution of Automobile Engineers

GradIM Graduate of the Institute of Metals

GradInstBE Graduate Member of the Institution of British Engineers

GradInstP Graduate of the Institute of Physics

GradInstR Graduate of the Institute of Refrigeration

GradIPM Graduate of the Institute of Personnel Management

GradPRI Graduate of the Plastics and Rubber Institute

GradSE Graduate of the Society of Engineers

gram. grammar; grammarian; grammatical

GRAS generally regarded as safe (US)

GRBI Gardeners' Royal Benevolent Institution

Gr. Br. Great Britain

GRBS Gardeners' Royal Benevolent Society

GRC General Research Corporation

Gr. Capt. group captain

GRCM Graduate of the Royal College of Music

GRDF Gulf Rapid Deployment Force

GRE Graduate Record Examination (US); grant-related expenditure; Guardian Royal Exchange Assurance

gr. f. grey filly (horse racing)

GRI *Georgius Rex Imperator* (Latin: George, King and Emperor); guaranteed retirement income (New Zealand)

Gr-L Graeco-Latin

grm gram

grn green

GRN goods received note

gro. gross

GRO Gamma Ray Observatory; General Register Office; Greenwich Royal Observatory

GROBDM General Register Office for Births, Deaths and Marriages

gro. t. gross tons

grp group

GRP glass-reinforced plastic; glassfibre-reinforced plastic

grs grains; gross

GRS Great Red Spot (astronomy)

GRSC Graduate of the Royal Society of Chemistry

GRSE Guild of Radio Service Engineers

GRSM Graduate of the Royal Schools of Music

gr. t. gross ton

GRT gross registered tonnage

GRU *Glavnoye Razvedyvatelnoye Upravleniye* (Russian: Central Intelligence Office)

gr. wt gross weight

gry gross redemption yield (finance)

gs grandson; groundspeed (aeronautics); guineas

Gs gauss (magnetism)

GS General Schedule (US civil service); General Secretary; general service; General Staff (military); geographical survey; geological survey; Geological Society; goal shooter (netball); gold standard; grammar school; Luton (UK vehicle registration)

GSA General Services Administration (US); Girls Scouts of America; Girls' Schools Association; Glasgow School of Art

GS&W Great Southern and Western Railway (Ireland)

GSB Government Savings Bank

GSC General Service Corps; General Staff Corps

GSD general supply depot

GSE ground service equipment; ground support equipment

GSEE *Geniki Synomospondia Ergaton Hellados* (Greek: Greek General Confederation of Labour)

GSL Geological Society of London; group scout leader; guaranteed student loan (US)

gsm good sound merchantable quality; gram per square metre (paper)

GSM Garrison Sergeant-Major; general sales manager; General Service Medal; Member of the Guildhall School of Music and Drama

GSO General Staff Officer

GSP Good Service Pension; gross social product (economics)

G-spot Grafenberg spot (erogenous zone)

GSR galvanic skin reflex; galvanic skin response

GSS geostationery satellite; global surveillance system; Government Statistical Service

GST goods and services tax (Canada, New Zealand); Greenwich Sidereal Time; gust (meteorology)

g st garter stitch (knitting)

GSW gunshot wound

gt gas tight; gilt (books); great; gross tonnage; *gutta* (Latin: a drop; medicine)

GT gas turbine; gauge theory (physics); GB Airways (airline flight code,

Gibraltar); Good Templar; Grand Tiler (Freemasonry); *Gran Turismo* (Italian: grand touring; cars); greetings telegram; southwest London (UK vehicle registration)

Gt. Br(it). Great Britain

GTC General Teaching Council (Scotland); Girls' Training Corps; good till cancelled (commerce); good till countermanded (commerce); government training centre

GTCL Graduate of the Trinity College of Music, London.

gtd guaranteed

gte gilt top edge (books)

gtee guarantee

GTI *Gran Turismo Injection* (Italian: grand touring injection; cars)

gtm good this month

GTO *Gran Turismo Omologata* (Italian: certified for grand touring; cars)

gtr greater

GTR Grand Theory of Relativity

GTS gas turbine ship; General Theological Seminary (US)

gtt. *guttae* (Latin: drops; medicine); *guttatim* (Latin; drop by drop; medicine)

GTT glucose tolerance test (medicine)

gtw good this week

gu. guinea

Gu. Guinea

GU gastric ulcer; genito-urinary; Guam (zip code); Guernsey (UK fishing port registration); Guildford (UK postcode); southeast London (UK vehicle registration)

guar. guarantee(d)

Guat. Guatemala

gui. guitar

GUI Golfing Union of Ireland; graphic user interface (computing)

GUIDO Guidance Officer (astronautics)

guil. guilder (Dutch monetary unit)

Guin. Guinea

Gulag *Glavnoye Upravleniye Lagerei* (Russian: Soviet prison and labour camp system)

GUM genito-urinary medicine; *Gosudarstvenni Universalni Magazin* (Russian: Universal State Store)

gun. gunnery

GUR glucose utilization rate (medicine)

GUS Great Universal Stores (UK)

GUT grand unified theory (physics)

guttat. *guttatim* (Latin: drop by drop; medicine)

guv *gerecht und vollkommen* (German: correct and complete); governor

GUY Guyana (international vehicle registration)

gv gravimetric volume; gross valuation

GV *Grande Vitesse* (French: High Speed Train); Ipswich (UK vehicle registration)

GVH graft-versus-host (medicine)

GVHD graft-versus-host disease (medicine)

gvt government

GVW gross vehicle weight

GW George Washington (US president); gigowatt; Glasgow (UK fishing port registration); guided weapons; southeast London (UK vehicle registration)

GWP Government White Paper; gross world product

GWR Great Western Railway

GWS Glashow-Weinberg-Salam (physics)

GX southeast London (UK vehicle registration)

Gy gray (physics)

GY Grimsby (UK fishing port registration); Guyana Airways (airline flight code); southeast London (UK vehicle registration)

gym gymnasium; gymnastics

gyn. gynaecological; gynaecology

GZ Belfast (UK vehicle registration); ground zero

H

h hail (meteorology); hecto-

h height; Planck constant (physics); small increment (mathematics)

h. harbour; hard; hardness; heat; height; high; hip; hit (sport); horizontal; horn (music); horse;

hot; hour; house; hundred; husband

H halfpage (advertising); henry (physics); heroin; Hull (UK fishing port registration); Hungary (international vehicle registration); hydrogen (element)

H dose equivalent (medicine, physics);

Hamiltonian (physics); light exposure (photography, physics); magnetic field strength (physics)

H. halfpage (advertising); harbour; hard(ness) (pencils); hearts (cards); herbaceous; Holy; horn (music); hospital; hour; hydrant

H4 Solomon Islands (international aircraft marking)

ha hectare; heir apparent; high angle (gunnery); *hoc anno* (Latin: in this year)

Ha hahnium

Ha. Haiti(an); Hawaii(an)

HA Dudley (UK vehicle registration); hardy annual (horticulture); Harrow (UK postcode); Hautes-Alpes (French department); Hawaiian Airlines (airline flight code, USA); health authority; heavy artillery; high altitude; Highways Act; histamine (biochemistry); Historical Association; hockey asso-ciation; hour angle (astronomy); Hungary (international civil aircraft marking); Hydraulic Association of Great Britain

HAA heavy anti-aircraft; hepatitis-associated antigen (immunology)

HAAC Harper Adams Agricultural College (US)

HA&M Hymns Ancient and Modern

hab. habitat; habitation

Hab. Habakkuk (Bible)

HAB high-altitude bombing

hab. corp. *habeas corpus* (Latin: have the body; law)

habt. *habeat* (Latin: let him have)

HAC high-alumina cement; Honourable Artillery Company

had hereinafter described

haem. haemoglobin; haemorrhage

HAF Hellenic Air Force

Hag. Haggai (Bible)

hagiol. hagiology

HAI hospital-acquired infection

Hak. Soc. Hakluyt Society

hal. halogen

Hal. Orch. Hallé Orchestra

Ham. Hamburg

Han. Hanover(ian)

h&c hot and cold (water)

H&E Health and Efficiency (journal); heredity and environment

h&t hardened and tempered

H&W Harland and Wolff (Belfast shipyard)

Hants. Hampshire

HAP hazardous air pollutant

h. app. heir apparent

har. harbour

HARCVS Honorary Associate of the Royal College of Veterinary Surgeons

harm. harmonic; harmony

HARM high-speed anti-radiation missile

harp. harpsichord

HART Halt All Racist Tours (New Zealand)

Harv. Harvard University

HAS Headmasters' Association of Scotland; Health Advisory Service; Helicopter Air Service; Hospital Advisory Service

HASAWA Health and Safety at Work Act

HAT housing action trust; housing association trust

haust. *haustus* (Latin: draught; medicine)

HAV hepatitis A virus

HAWT horizontal-axis wind turbine

haz. hazard; hazardous

hb halfback (sports); handbook; hardback (books); homing beacon; human being

Hb haemoglobin (biochemistry)

HB Cardiff (UK vehicle registration); hard black (pencils); hardy perennial (horticulture); Herri Batasuna (Basque separatist party); House of Bishops; Switzerland and Liechtenstein (international civil aircraft marking)

HB&K Humboldt, Bonpland and Kunth (botany)

HBC high breaking capacity (electrical engineering); Historic Buildings Council; Hudson's Bay Company

HBCU Historically Black Colleges and Universities (US)

HBD had been drinking; has been drinking

Hbf *Hauptbahnhof* (German: central station)

hbk hardback (book)

HBLV human B-lymphotropic virus (medicine)

HBM Her or His Britannic Majesty/'s

H-bomb hydrogen bomb

HBP high blood pressure

hbr harbour

HBS Harvard Business School

Hbt Hobart (Australia)

HBV hepatitis B virus

hby hereby

hc habitual criminal; hand control; heating cabinet; high capacity; *honoris causa* (Latin: for the sake of honour); hot and cold (water)

h/c held covered (insurance)

HC Brighton (UK vehicle registration);

Ecuador (international civil aircraft marking); Hague Convention; Headmasters' Conference; Headteachers' Conference; health certificate; Heralds' College; High Church; High Commission(er); High Court; higher certificate; highly commended; Highway Code; hockey club; Holy Communion; home counties; *hors concours* (French: not for competition); House of Clergy; House of Commons; house of correction; housing centre; housing corporation

H/C held covered (insurance)

HCA Hospital Caterers' Association

HCAAS Homeless Children's Aid and Adoption Society

hcap handicap

HCB House of Commons Bill

HCBA Hotel and Catering Benevolent Association

hcc hydraulic cement concrete

hcd high current density

hce human-caused error

hcf highest common factor (mathematics); hundred cubic feet

HCF high-calorific fuel; high carbohydrate and fibre; highest common factor (mathematics); Honorary Chaplain to the Forces

HCFC hydrochlorofluorocarbon

hCG human chorionic gonadotrophin (biochemistry)

HCH Herbert Clark Hoover (US president); hexachlorocyclohexane (insecticide)

HCI Hotel and Catering Institute; human-computer interaction; human-computer interface

HCIL Hague Conference on International Law

HCIMA Hotel Catering and Institutional Management Association

HCJ High Court of Justice; Holy Child Jesus

hcl high cost of living

HCM High Court Master; Her or His Catholic Majesty

HCO Harvard College Observatory; Higher Clerical Officer

hcp handicap

HCP House of Commons paper

HCPT Historic Churches Preservation Trust

hcptr helicopter

HCR High Chief Ranger; highway contract route (US)

hcs high-carbon steel

HCS Home Civil Service

HCSA Hospital Consultants' and Specialists' Assocation

HCVC Historic Commercial Vehicle Club

hcw hot and cold water

hd hand; head; heavy duty; high density; *hora decubitus* (Latin: at bedtime; medicine)

HD herniated disc (medicine); high density; high dose (physics); Highland Division; Hodgkin's disease; home defence; honourable discharge; Hoover Dam; Huddersfield (UK postcode, vehicle registration); hydrogen-deuterium (chemistry)

H-D Hurter-Driffield (photography)

H/D Havre-Dunkirk (shipping)

HDA Hawkesbury Diploma in Agriculture (Australia); high-duty alloy

hdatz high-density air-traffic zone

hdbk handbook; hardback (book)

HDC high-dose chemotherapy (medicine); holder in due course (law)

HDCR Higher Diploma of the College of Radiographers

HDD head-down display (aeronautics, computing); heavy-duty diesel; Higher Dental Diploma

hdg heading

HDipEd Higher Diploma in Education

hdkf handkerchief

hdl. handle

HDL high-density lipo-protein (biochemistry, medicine)

HDLC high-level data link control (computing)

hdle hurdle (horse racing)

hdlg handling

HDM high-duty metal

hdn harden

HDP heavy-duty petrol; high-density polyethene (chemistry); high-density polyethylene (chemistry)

HDPE heavy-duty petrol

hdqrs headquarters

HDR high dose rate (physics); hot dry rock

HDTV high-definition television

HDV heavy-duty vehicle

hdw. hardware (computing)

hdwd hardwood; headword

he heat engine; *hic est* (Latin: here lies); hub end

He helium (element)

He. Hebrew

HE Her or His Excellency; high-energy; higher education; high explosive; His

Eminence; home establishment; horizontal equivalent; hydraulic engineer; Sheffield (UK vehicle registration)

HEA Health Education Authority; Horticultural Education Association

HEAO High Energy Astronomy Observatory; High Energy Astrophysical Observatory

Heb. Hebraic; Hebrew; Hebrews (Bible)

Hebr. Hebrew; Hebrides

HEC *hautes études commerciales* (French: higher commercial studies); Health Education Council; Higher Education Corporation

HECTOR Heated Experimental Carbon Thermal Oscillator Reactor

HEDCOM headquarters command (US Air Force)

HEF high-energy fuel

HEH Her or His Exalted Highness

hei high-explosive incendiary

HEIC Honourable East India Company

HEICS Honourable East India Company's Service

heir app. heir apparent

heir pres. heir presumptive

hel. helicopter

HEL high-energy laser

Hellen. Hellenic; Hellenism; Hellenistic

helo. heliport

HELP helicopter electronic landing path; Help Establish Lasting Peace

hem. haemoglobin; haemorrhage

HEMM heavy earth-moving machinery

HEO Higher Executive Officer; highly elliptic-inclined orbit

HEOS high-elliptic-inclined-orbit satellite

HEP human error probability (statistics); hydroelectric power

HEPC hydroelectric power commission (US)

HEPCAT helicopter pilot control and training

her. heraldic; heraldry; *heres* (Latin: heir)

Her. Hercules; Herefordshire

hera high-explosive rocket-assisted

HERALD Highly Enriched Reactor, Aldermaston, Berks

herb. herbaceous; herbalist; herbarium

hered. heredity

Herod. Herodotus (Greek historian)

herp(etol). herpetologist; herpetology

Hert. Hertford College (Oxford)

Herts. Hertfordshire

HERU Higher Education Research Unit

HET heavy-equipment transporter

HEU highly enriched uranium

HEW Department of Health, Education and Welfare (US)

hex hexadecimal (computing)

hex. hexachord; hexagonal

hexa. hexamethylene tetramine (rubber)

hf half; hold fire; horse and foot (military)

Hf hafnium (element)

HF hard firm (pencils); high frequency (radio); Holy Father; home fleet; home forces; Liverpool (UK vehicle registration)

Hfa Haifa (Israel)

HFARA Honorary Foreign Associate of the Royal Academy

hf bd half binding (books); half-bound (books)

HFC high-frequency current (electricity); hydrofluorocarbon (chemistry)

HFDF high frequency direction-finder

HFO heavy fuel oil; high frequency oscillation

HFR high flux reactor (nuclear engineering)

HFRA Honorary Foreign Member of the Royal Academy

hg hectogram

Hg mercury (element)

HG Harrogate (UK postcode); Haute-Garonnes (French department); High German; high grade; Her or His Grace; Holy Ghost; Home Guard; Horse Guards; Preston (UK vehicle registration)

HGCA Home Grown Cereals Authority

hgd hogshead

HGDH Her or His Grand Ducal Highness

HGH human growth hormone

HGMM Hereditary Grand Master Mason

h. g. pt hard gloss paint

hgr hangar; hanger

hgt height

HGTAC Home Grown Timber Advisory Committee

HGV heavy goods vehicle

HGW heat-generating waste; H(erbert) G(eorge) Wells

hg(w)y highway

hh hands (measuring of horses)

HH Carlisle (UK vehicle registration); double hard (pencils); Haiti (international civil aircraft marking); Harwich (UK fishing port registration); heavy hydrogen (chemistry, physics); Her or His Highness; Her or His Honour; Hesketh Hubbard Art Society; His Holiness

HHA half-hardy annual (horticulture); Historic Houses Association; *Hurriyet Haber Ajasi* (news agency, Turkey)
HHB half-hardy biennial (horticulture)
hhd hogshead
HHD Doctor of Humanities (US); hypertensive heart disease
HHDWS heavy handy deadweight scrap
HHFA Housing and Home Finance Agency (US)
HHH treble hard (pencils)
HHI Highland Home Industries
H-Hour Hour Hour
HHP half-hardy perennial (horticulture)
HHS Department of Health and Human Services (US)
HHV human herpesvirus
Hi. Hindi
HI Dominican Republic (civil aircraft marking); Hawaii (zip code); Hawaiian Islands; hearing impaired; height of instrument (surveying); *hic iacet* (Latin: here lies); high intensity; Tipperary (Irish vehicle registration)
HIA Housing Improvement Association
hi. ac. high accuracy
HIAS Hebrew Immigrant Aid Society (US)
Hib. Hibernia(n)
hicat high-altitude clear air turbulence
Hi. Com. High Command; High Commission(er)
HIDB Highlands and Islands Development Board
hier. hieroglyphics
hi-fi high fidelity
hifor high-level forecast
HIH Her or His Imperial Highness
HIL hazardous immiscible liquid (chemistry)
HILAC heavy-ion linear accelerator (nuclear physics)
HILAT high-latitude
HIM Her or His Imperial Majesty
Hind. Hindi; Hindu; Hindustan; Hindustani
HIP health-insurance plan (US)
HIPAR high-power acquisition radar
hipot high potential
Hipp. Hippocrates (Greek physician)
HIPS high-impact polystyrene
hirel high reliability
hi-res high resolution (physics)
HIS *his iacet sepultus/sepulta* (Latin: here lies)
hist. histologist; histology; historian; historic(al); history

histn historian
histol. histologist; histology
Hitt. Hittite
HIUS Hispanic Institute of the United States
HIV human immuno-deficiency virus
HIV–P human immuno-deficiency virus–positive
HJ Chelmsford (UK vehicle registration); *hic jacet* (Latin: here lies); high jump; *Hitler Jugend* (German: Hitler Youth)
HJS *hic jacet sepultus/sepulta* (Latin: here lies buried)
HK Chelmsford (UK vehicle registration); Colombia (international civil aircraft marking); Hong Kong; Hong Kong (international vehicle registration); housekeeper allowance (taxation); House of Keys (Manx Parliament)
hkf handkerchief
HJK Hashemite Kingdom of Jordan (international vehicle registration)
hl hectolitre; *hoc loco* (Latin: in this place)
Hl *Heilige* (German: Saint)
HL hard labour; Hartlepool (UK fishing port registration); Haute-Loire (French department); honours list; House of Laity; House of Lords; Sheffield (UK vehicle registration); South Korea (international civil aircraft marking)
HLA human lymphocyte antigen
HLBB Home Loan Bank Board (US)
HLD Doctor of Humane Letters
HLE high-level exposure (physics)
HLI Highland Light Infantry
HLL high-level language (computing)
HLNW high-level nuclear waste
hlpr helicopter
HLPR Howard League for Penal Reform
HLS Harvard Law School
HLW high-level waste (radioactivity)
HLWN highest low water of neap (tides)
hm hallmark; headmaster; headmistress; hectometre; *hoc mense* (Latin: in this month)
HM Air Seychelles (airline flight code); central London (UK vehicle registration); harbour master; harmonic mean (music); Haute-Marne (French department); hazardous waste (chemistry); headmaster; headmistress; heavy metal; Her or His Majesty/'s; home mission
HMA Head Masters' Association; high-memory area (computing)
HMAC Her or His Majesty's Aircraft Carrier

HMAS Her or His Majesty's Australian Ship

HMBDV Her or His Majesty's Boom Defence Vessel

HMC Head Masters' Conference; Her or His Majesty's Customs; Historical Manuscripts Commission; Horticultural Marketing Council; Hospital Management Committee; Household Mortgage Corporation

HMCA Hospital and Medical Care Association

HMCIC Her or His Majesty's Chief Inspector of Constabulary

HMCIF Her or His Majesty's Chief Inspector of Factories

HMCN Her or His Majesty's Canadian Navy

HMCS Her or His Majesty's Canadian Ship

HMCSC Her or His Majesty's Civil Service Commissioners

hmd humid

HMD Her or His Majesty's Destroyer

HMF heavy-metal fluoride; Her or His Majesty's Forces

HMFI Her or His Majesty's Factory Inspectorate

HMG heavy machine-gun; Her or His Majesty's Government

HMHS Her or His Majesty's Hospital Ship

HMI Her or His Majesty's Inspector(ate) (schools); human-machine interface (computing)

HMIED Honorary Member of the Institute of Engineering Designers

HMIP Her or His Majesty's Inspectorate of Pollution

HMIS Her or His Majesty's Inspector of Schools

HMIT Her or His Majesty's Inspector of Taxes

HML Her or His Majesty's Lieutenant

HMLR Her or His Majesty's Land Registry

HMML Her or His Majesty's Motor Launch

HMMS Her or His Majesty's Mine Sweeper

HMNZS Her or His Majesty's New Zealand Ship

HMO health maintenance organization (US)

HMOCS Her or His Majesty's Overseas Civil Service

hmp handmade paper

HMP Her or His Majesty's Prison; *hoc*

monumentum posuit (Latin: he/she erected this monument)

HMRT Her or His Majesty's Rescue Tug

hms hours, minutes, seconds

HMS heavy media separation (mining); Her or His Majesty's Service; Her or His Majesty's Service Ship

HMSO Her or His Majesty's Stationery Office

hmstd homestead

HMT Her or His Majesty's Trawler; Her or His Majesty's Treasury; Her or His Majesty's Tug

HMV His Master's Voice (record company)

HMWA Hairdressing Manufacturers' and Wholesalers' Association

hn *hac nocte* (Latin: tonight); horn (music)

HN Middlesbrough (UK vehicle registration)

HNC Higher National Certificate

HND Higher National Diploma

hndbk handbook

HNL helium-neon laser (physics)

Hnrs Honours

ho hold over

ho. house

Ho holmium (element)

HO Bournemouth (UK vehicle registration); habitual offender (law); head office; Home Office; Hydrographic Office

hoc held on charge

HoC House of Commons

HOC heavy organic chemical

HoD head of department

H of C House of Commons

H of K House of Keys

H of L House of Lords

H of R House of Representatives (US)

hol. holiday

HoL House of Lords

HOL Holocene (geology)

HOLC Home Owners' Loan Corporation (US)

Holl. Holland

Holland hope our love lasts and never dies; hope our love lives and never dies

Holmes Home Office Large Major Enquiry System (computer)

Hom. Homer (Greek poet)

homeo. homeopath; homeopathic; homeopathy

hon. honorary; honour; honourable

Hon. honorary; honorary member; honourable

Hond. Honduras

Hono. Honolulu

hons. Honours

Hon. Sec. honorary secretary

HOOD hierarchical object-orientated design

Hook. Sir William Hooker (botany)

Hook. fl Hooker fils (botany)

Hopeful hard-up old person expecting full useful life

hor. horizon; horizontal; horology

Hor. Horace (Roman poet)

hor. decub. *hora decubitus* (Latin: at bedtime; medicine)

HoReCa International Union of National Associations of Hotel, Restaurant and Café Keepers

horol. horological; horologist; horology

hort. horticultural; horticulturalist; horticulture

HORU Home Office Research Unit

Hos. Hosea (Bible)

hosp. hospital

Hotol horizontal take-off and landing aircraft (astronautics)

HOV high-occupancy vehicle

how. howitzer

hp half pay; heir presumptive; high power (electricity); hire purchase; horizontally polarized; horse power

HP America West Airlines (airline flight code); Coventry (UK vehicle registration); Handley Page (aircraft); hardy perennial (horticulture); Hautes-Pyrénées (French department); Hemel Hempstead (UK postcode); Hewlett-Packard (US electronics company); high performance; high power (electricity); high pressure; high priest; Himachal Pradesh (India); hire purchase; hot-pressed (paper); house physician; Houses of Parliament; hybrid perpetual (horticulture); Panama (international civil aircraft marking)

HPA Hospital Physicists' Association

HPC history of present complaint (medicine)

hpch. harpsichord

hpd harpsichord

HPS high-pressure steam; high-protein supplement

HPT high-pressure turbine

HPTA Hire Purchase Trade Association

HPV human papilloma virus

hq headquarters; *hoc quaere* (Latin: look for this)

HQ headquarters

HQBA headquarters base area

HQMC Headquarters, Marine Corps (US)

hr hail and rain (meteorology); home run (baseball); hour

Hr *Herr* (German: Mr/Sir); hussar

HR heart rate (medicine); Hereford (UK postcode); home rule; home run (baseball); Honduras (international civil aircraft marking); House of Representatives (US); human relations; Swindon (UK vehicle registration)

H-R Hertzsprung-Russell (astronomy)

HRA Health Resources Administration (US)

HRC Holy Roman Church

HRCA Honorary Royal Cambrian Academician

HRCT high-resolution computed tomography (medicine); high-resolution computerized tomography (medicine)

HRE Holy Roman Emperor; Holy Roman Empire

HREM high-resolution electron microscope

HRGI Honorary Member of the Royal Glasgow Institute of the Fine Arts

HRH Her or His Royal Highness

HRHA Honorary Member of the Royal Hibernian Academy

HRI Honorary Member of the Royal Institute of Painters in Water Colours

HRIP *hic requiescit in pace* (Latin: here rests in peace)

HRMS high-resolution mass spectrometry

Hrn *Herren* (German: Gentlemen/Sirs)

HROI Honorary Member of the Royal Institute of Oil Painters

HRP human remains pouch (military)

HRR higher reduced rate (taxation)

hrs hours

HRSA Honorary Member of the Royal Scottish Academy

hrsg *herausgegeben* (German: edited or published)

HRSW Honorary Member of the Royal Scottish Water Colour Society

HRT hormone replacement therapy (medicine)

hs hail and snow (meteorology); highest score; *hoc sensu* (Latin: in this sense); *hora somni* (Latin: at bedtime; medicine)

Hs *Handschrift* (German: manuscript)

HS Glasgow (UK vehicle registration); Haute-Saône (French department); Hawker Siddeley (aircraft); *hic sepultus/sepulta* (Latin: here is buried); high school; Home Secretary; hospital ship; house surgeon; sesterce (Roman coin); Thailand (international civil aircraft marking)

HSA Health Systems Agency (US)

HSAB hard and soft acids and bases (chemistry)

HSC Health and Safety Commission; Higher School Certificate

H Sch high school

HSD heat-storage device; high-speed diesel

HSDU hospital sterilization and disinfection unit

hse house

HSE Health and Safety Executive; *hic sepultus/sepulta est* (Latin: here lies buried)

hsekpr housekeeper

hsg housing

HSH Her or His Serene Highness

HSI human-system interaction (computing); human-system interface (computing)

HSL Huguenot Society of London

HSLA high-strength, low-alloy (steel)

HSM Her or His Serene Majesty

HSO Hamburg Symphony Orchestra

Hss *Handschriften* (German: manuscripts)

HSS Fellow of the Historical Society; high-speed steel

HSSU hospital sterile supply unit

HST Harry S Truman (US president); Hawaii Standard Time; highest spring tide; high-speed train; Hubble Space Telescope; hypersonic transport

HSV herpes simplex virus

HSWA Hazardous and Solid Waste Act (US); Hazardous and Solid Waste Amendments (US)

ht half time (sport); half-tone; heat; heavy tank; height; *hoc tempore* (Latin: at this time); *hoc titulo* (Latin: in or under this title)

HT Bristol (UK vehicle registration); half time (sport); Hawaii Time; heat treatment; high temperature; high tension (electricity); high tide; high treason; hybrid tea (rose)

h/t half-tone

HTA Horticultural Traders' Association; Household Textile Association

htb high-tension battery

htd heated

Hte *Haute* (French: High)

HTGR high-temperature gas-cooled reactor (nuclear engineering)

HTLV human T-cell lymphotropic virus

HTM heat-transfer medium

HTOL horizontal take-off and landing (astronautics)

htr heater

HTR high temperature reactor (nuclear engineering)

H Trin. Holy Trinity

hts half-time survey; high-tensile steel

Hts Heights

HTS high-temperature superconductor

HTT heavy tactical transport

HTTR high-temperature test reactor (nuclear engineering)

HTV Harlech Television

ht wkt hit wicket (cricket)

HU Bristol (UK vehicle registration); Harvard University; Hull (UK postcode)

HUAC House Un-American Activities Committee (US)

HUD head-up display (aeronautics, computing); Housing and Urban Development (US)

Hugo Human Genome Organization

HUJ Hebrew University of Jerusalem

HUKFORLANT hunter-killer forces, Atlantic (US Navy)

HUKS hunter-killer submarine (US Navy)

hum. human; humane; humanities; humanity; humble; humorous

Hum. humanities

HUMINT human intelligence (military)

HUMRRO Human Resources Research Office

HUMV human light vehicle (military)

hund. hundred

Hung. Hungarian; Hungary

Hunts. Huntingdonshire

HUP Harvard University Press

hur. hurricane

HURCN hurricane (meteorology)

Husat Human Science and Advanced Research Institute

husb. husband(ry)

hv high vacuum; high velocity

HV health visitor; high velocity; high voltage; *hoc verbum* (Latin: this word); central London (UK vehicle registration); Transavia Airlines (airline flight code, Netherlands); the Vatican (international civil aircraft marking)

HVA Health Visitors' Association

HVAC heating, ventilation, air conditioning; high-voltage alternating current

HVAR high-velocity aircraft rocket

HVCA Heating and Ventilating Contractors' Association

HVCert Health Visitor's Certificate
HVDC high-voltage direct current
HVEM high-voltage electron microscope
HVO *Hrvatsko vijece odbrane* (Croatian Defence Council)
HVP hydrolized vegetable protein
HVT half-value thickness (physics); health visitor teacher
hvy heavy
hw hit wicket (cricket)
h/w herewith; hot water; husband and wife
HW Bristol (UK vehicle registration); hazardous waste; high water; hot water
HWL Henry Wadsworth Longfellow (US poet); high-water line
HWLB high water, London Bridge
HWM high-water mark
HWONT high water, ordinary neap tides
HWOST high water, ordinary spring tides
HWR heavy-water reactor (nuclear physics)

HWS hot water system; hurricane warning system
HWW hot-and-warm worked (engineering)
hwy highway
HX Halifax (UK postcode); central London (UK vehicle registration)
hy heavy; highway
HY Bristol (UK vehicle registration)
hyb. hybrid
hyd. hydrate; hydraulic; hydrographic
hydrog. hydrographic
hydt hydrant
hyg. hygiene
hyp. hypodermic; hypotenuse (mathematics); hypothesis; hypothetical
hypo sodium thiosulphate
hypoth. hypothesis; hypothetical
Hz hertz (unit of frequency)
HZ dust haze (meteorology); Saudi Arabia (international civil aircraft marking); Tyrone (UK vehicle registration)
hzy hazy (meteorology)

I

i imaginary number (mathematics); one (Roman numerals)
i instantaneous current (physics); unit coordinate vector (mathematics)
i. *id* (Latin: that); incisor (tooth); indicate; interest (banking); intransitive (grammar); island
I electric current (physics); inti (Peruvian monetary unit); iodine (element); Italy (international civil aircraft marking; international vehicle registration); luminous intensity (physics); moment of inertia (mechanics); one (Roman numerals)
I. Idaho; *Iesus* (Latin: Jesus); *Imperator* (Latin: Emperor); *Imperatrix* (Latin: Empress); imperial; *Imperium* (Latin: Empire); inch (advertising); incumbent; independence; independent; India; Indian; *infidelis* (Latin: infidel or unbeliever); inspector; institute; instructor; intelligence; interceptor; international; interpreter; Ireland; Irish; island; isle; issue; Italian; Italy
ia immediately available; *in absentia*

(Latin: while absent); indicated altitude (aeronautics); initial appearance
iA *im Auftrage* (German: by order of)
Ia Indiana; Iowa
IA Antrim (UK vehicle registration); Incorporated Accountant; Indian Army; infected area; information anxiety; initial allowance (taxation); Institute of Actuaries; Inter-American; Iowa (zip code); Iraqi Airways (airline flight code)
I/A Isle of Anglesey
IAA Institute of Industrial Administration; International Academy of Astronautics; International Actuarial Association; International Advertising Association
IAAA Irish Amateur Athletic Association; Irish Association of Advertising Agencies
IAAE Institution of Automotive and Aeronautical Engineers (US)
IAAF International Amateur Athletic Federation
IAAP International Association of Applied Psychology

IAAS Incorporated Association of Architects and Surveyors
IAB Industrial Advisory Board; Industrial Arbitration Board; Inter-American Bank
IABA International Association of Aircraft Brokers and Agents
IABO International Association of Biological Oceanography
iac integration, assembly and checkout
IAC Industrial Advisory Council (US); Institute of Amateur Cinematographers
IACA Independent Air Carriers' Association
IACB International Advisory Committee on Bibliography (UNESCO)
IACCP Inter-American Council of Commerce and Production
IACOMS International Advisory Committee on Marine Societies (FAO)
IACP International Association for Child Psychiatry and Allied Professions; International Association of Chiefs of Police; International Association of Computer Programmers (US)
IACS International Annealed Copper Standard
IADB Inter-American Defense Board; Inter-American Development Bank
IADR International Association for Dental Research
IAE Institute of Atomic Energy (US); Institute of Automobile Engineers; Institute of Automotive Engineers
IAEA International Atomic Energy Agency
IAEC Israel Atomic Energy Commission
IAECOSOC Inter-American Economic and Social Council
IAEE International Association of Energy Economists
iaf interview after flight (aviation)
IAF Indian Air Force; Indian Auxiliary Force; International Astronautical Federation
IAFD International Association on Food Distribution
IAG International Association of Geodesy; International Association of Geology; International Association of Gerontology
IAGB&I Ileostomy Association of Great Britain and Ireland
IAgrE Institution of Agricultural Engineers
IAH International Association of Hydrogeologists; International Association of Hydrology

IAHA Inter-American Hotel Association
IAHM Incorporated Association of Headmasters
IAHP International Association of Horticultural Producers
IAHR International Association for Hydraulic Research; International Association for the History of Religions
IAI International African Institute
IAL Imperial Airways Limited; Imperial Arts League; Irish Academy of Letters
IALA International African Law Association; International Association of Lighthouse Authorities
IALL International Association of Law Libraries
IALS International Association of Legal Science
IAM Institute of Administrative Management; Institute of Advanced Motorists; Institute of Aviation Medicine; International Association of Machinists and Aerospace Workers (US); International Association of Meteorology; International Association of Microbiologists
IAMA Incorporated Advertising Managers' Association
IAMAP International Association of Meteorology and Atmospheric Physics
IAMC Indian Army Medical Corps
IAML International Association of Music Libraries
IAMS International Association of Microbiological Societies; International Association of Microbiological Studies
IANC International Airline Navigators' Council
IANE Institute of Advanced Nursing Education
IANEC Inter-American Nuclear Energy Commission
IAO in and out of cloud (meteorology); Incorporated Association of Organists
IAOC Indian Army Ordnance Corps
IAOS Irish Agricultural Organization Society
IAP International Academy of Pathology
IAPA Inter-American Press Association
IAPB International Association for the Prevention of Blindness
IAPG International Association of Physical Geography
IAPH International Association of Ports and Harbours
IAPO International Association of Physical Oceanography

IAPS Incorporated Association of Preparatory Schools

IAPSO International Association for the Physical Sciences of the Oceans

IAPT International Association for Plant Taxonomy

IARA Inter-Allied Reparations Agency

I. Arb. Institute of Arbitrators

IARC Indian Agricultural Research Council; International Agency for Research on Cancer

IARD International Association for Rural Development

IARF International Association for Religious Freedom

IARI Indian Agricultural Research Institute

IARO Indian Army Reserve of Officers

IARU International Amateur Radio Union

IAS immediate access store (computing); Indian Administrative Service; indicated air speed (aeronautics); Institute for Advanced Studies (US); Institute of the Aerospace Sciences; instrument approach system (aeronautics)

IASA International Air Safety Association

IASC Indian Army Service Corps

IASH International Association of Scientific Hydrography

IASI Inter-American Statistical Institute

iasor ice and snow on runway

IASS International Association for Scandinavian Studies; International Association of Soil Science

iat inside air temperature

IAT International Atomic Time

IATA International Air Transport Association; International Amateur Theatre Association

IATUL International Association of Technological University Libraries

IAU International Association of Universities; International Astronomical Union

IAUPL International Association of University Professors and Lecturers

IAV International Association of Vulcanology

IAVG International Association for Vocational Guidance

iaw in accordance with

IAW International Alliance of Women

IAWPRC International Association on Water Pollution Research and Control

ib. *ibidem* (Latin: in the same place)

IB Armagh (UK vehicle registration); Iberia (airline flight code, Spain); in

bond; incendiary bomb; industrial business; information bureau; instruction book; intelligence branch; International Bank for Reconstruction and Development; invoice book

IBA Independent Bankers' Association; Independent Broadcasting Authority; Industrial Bankers' Association; industrial buildings allowance (taxation); International Bar Association; International Bowling Association; Investment Bankers' Association

IBAA Investment Bankers' Association of America

IBAE Institution of British Agricultural Engineers

IBB Institute of British Bakers; International Bowling Board; Invest in Britain Bureau

IBBISB/BF&H International Brotherhood of Boilermakers, Iron Shipbuilders, Blacksmiths, Forgers and Helpers (US)

IBBR interbank bid rate (finance)

IBC International Broadcasting Corporation

IBD Incorporated Institute of British Decorators and Interior Designers

IBE Institute of British Engineers; International Bureau of Education (UNESCO)

IBEL interest-bearing eligible liability (finance)

IBEW International Brotherhood of Electrical Workers (US)

IBF Institute of British Foundrymen; International Badminton Federation; International Boxing Federation; international banking facility

IBG Incorporated Brewers Guild; Institute of British Geographers

IBI invoice book inwards (book-keeping)

ibid *ibidem* (Latin: in the same place)

IBID international bibliographical description

IBiol Institute of Biology

IBK Institute of Book-Keepers

IBM intercontinental ballistic missile; International Business Machines (computer manufacturer)

IBMBR interbank market bid rate (finance)

IBO invoice book outwards (book-keeping)

ibp initial boiling point

IBP Institute of British Photographers; International Biological Programme

IBPAT International Brotherhood of Painters and Allied Trades (US)
IBRD International Bank for Reconstruction and Development (World Bank)
IBRO International Bank Research Organization; International Brain Research Organization
IBS Institute of Bankers in Scotland; irritable bowel syndrome
IBST Institute of British Surgical Technicians
IBT International Brotherhood of Teamsters, Chauffeurs, Warehousemen and Helpers of America
IBTE Institution of British Telecommunications Engineers
i. bu. imperial bushel
IBWM International Bureau of Weights and Measures
ic index correction; instrument correction; integrated circuit; internal combustion; internal communication
i/c in charge; in command
IC Carlow (Irish vehicle registration); identity card; *Iesus Christus* (Latin: Jesus Christ); Imperial College of Science and Technology (London); Index Catalogue (astronomy); Indian Airlines (airline flight code); industrial court; information centre; *Inforpress Centroamericana* (news agency, Guatemala); integrated circuit (electronics); Intelligence Corps; internal combustion; ionization chamber (physics)
I-C Indo-China
ICA ignition control additive; Industrial Caterers' Association; Institute of Chartered Accountants; Institute of Company Accountants; Institute of Contemporary Arts; International Cartographic Association; International Chefs' Association; International Coffee Agreement; International Colour Authority; International Commercial Arbitration; International Commission on Acoustics; international commodity agreement; International Cooperation Administration; International Cooperative Alliance; International Council on Archives; International Court of Arbitration; International Cyclist Association; invalid care allowance
ICAA Invalid Children's Aid Association

ICAE International Commission on Agricultural Engineering
ICAEW Institute of Chartered Accountants in England and Wales
ICAI Institute of Chartered Accountants in Ireland; International Commission for Agricultural Industries
ICAM Institute of Corn and Agricultural Merchants
ICAN International Commission for Air Navigation
IC&CY Inns of Court and City Yeomanry
ICAO International Civil Aviation Organization
ICAP Institute of Certified Ambulance Personnel; International Congress of Applied Psychology
ICAR Indian Council of Agricultural Research
ICAS Institute of Chartered Accountants of Scotland; International Council of Aeronautical Sciences; International Council of Aerospace Sciences
ICB Institute of Comparative Biology
ICBA International Community of Booksellers' Associations
ICBD International Council of Ballroom Dancing
ICBHI Industrial Craft (Member) of the British Horological Institute
ICBM intercontinental ballistic missile
ICBN International Code of Botanical Nomenclature
ICBP International Council for Bird Preservation; International Council for Bird Protection
ICC Indian Claims Commission (US); intercounty championship; International Chamber of Commerce; International Children's Centre; International Congregational Council; International Convention Centre (Birmingham); International Correspondence Colleges; International Cricket Conference
ICCA International Cocoa Agreement
ICCB Intergovernmental Consultation and Coordination Board
ICCC International Conference of Catholic Charities
ICCE International Council of Commerce Employers
ICCF International Correspondence Chess Federation
ICCH International Commodities Clearing House
ICCPR International Covenant on Civil and Political Rights (UN)

ICCROM International Centre for Conservation at Rome
ICCS International Centre of Criminological Studies
ICD Institute of Cooperative Directors; International Classification of Diseases (WHO)
ICDO International Civil Defence Organization
ICDP International Confederation for Disarmament and Peace
Ice. Iceland; Icelandic
ICE ice, compress, elevation (treatment of bruised limbs); Institute of Chartered Engineers; Institute of Chemical Engineers; Institution of Civil Engineers; internal combustion engine; International Cultural Exchange
ICED International Council for Educational Development
ICEF International Council for Educational Films; International Federation of Chemical, Energy and General Workers' Unions
ICEI Institution of Civil Engineers of Ireland
Icel. Iceland; Icelandic
ICeram Institute of Ceramics
ICES International Council for the Exploration of the Sea
ICETT Industrial Council for Educational and Training Technology
ICF International Canoe Federation
ICFTU International Confederation of Free Trade Unions
icg icing
ICGS interactive computer-graphics system; International Catholic Girls' Society
ich. ichthyology
ICHCA International Cargo Handling Coordination Association
IChemE Institution of Chemical Engineers
ICHEO Inter-University Council for Higher Education Overseas
ICHPER International Council for Health, Physical Education and Recreation
ichth(yol). ichthyology
ICI Imperial Chemical Industries; International Commission on Illumination; Investment Casting Institute (US)
ICIA International Credit Insurance Association
ICIANZ Imperial Chemical Industries, Australia and New Zealand

ICID International Commission on Irrigation and Drainage
ICIDH International Classification of Impairments, Disabilities and Handicaps (WHO)
ICJ International Commission of Jurists; International Court of Justice
ICJW International Council of Jewish Women
ICL International Computers Limited; International Confederation of Labour
ICLA International Committee on Laboratory Animals
IcInd Iceland
ICM Institute for Complementary Medicine; Institute of Credit Management; Intergovernmental Committee for Migrations (UN); International Confederation of Midwives; Irish Church Missions
ICMMP International Committee of Military Medicine and Pharmacy
ICMS International Centre for Mathematical Sciences (Edinburgh)
ICN *in Christi nomine* (Latin: in Christ's name); Infection Control Nurse; International Council of Nurses
ICNA Infection Control Nurses' Association
ICNB International Code of Nomenclature of Bacteria
ICNP International Code of Nomenclature of Cultivated Plants
ICNV International Code of Nomenclature of Viruses
ICO Institute of Careers Officers; International Coffee Organization; Islamic Conference Organization
ICOM International Council of Museums
ICOMOS International Council of Monuments and Sites
icon. iconographical; iconography
ICON indexed currency option note
ICOR Intergovernmental Conference on Oceanic Research (UNESCO)
ICorrST Institution of Corrosion Science and Technology
ICPA International Commission for the Prevention of Alcoholism; International Cooperative Petroleum Association
ICPHS International Council for Philosophy and Humanistic Studies
ICPO International Criminal Police Organization (Interpol)
ICPU International Catholic Press Union
ICR intelligent character recognition (computing)

ICRC International Committee of the Red Cross

ICRF Imperial Cancer Research Fund

ICRP International Commission on Radiological Protection

ICRU International Commission on Radiation Units (and Measurements)

ICS Imperial College of Science and Technology (London); Indian Civil Service; instalment credit selling; Institute of Chartered Shipbrokers; International Chamber of Shipping; international consultancy service; International Correspondence School; investors' compensation scheme (finance)

ICSA Institute of Chartered Secretaries and Administrators

ICSB International Small Business Congress

ICSID International Council of Societies of Industrial Design

ICSLS International Convention for Safety of Life at Sea

ICSPE International Council of Sport and Physical Education

ICST Imperial College of Science and Technology (London)

ICSU International Council of Scientific Unions (UNESCO)

ICTA International Council of Travel Agents

ICTP International Centre for Theoretical Physics

ICTU Irish Congress of Trade Unions

ICTV International Committee on Taxonomy of Viruses

ICU intensive care unit (medicine); international code use (signals)

ICVA International Council of Voluntary Agencies

icw in connection with; interrupted continuous wave (telecommunications)

ICW Institute of Clerks of Works of Great Britain; International Congress of Women

ICWA Indian Council of World Affairs; Institute of Cost and Works Accountants

ICWG International Cooperative Women's Guild

ICWU International Chemical Workers Union (US)

ICYF International Catholic Youth Federation

ICZN International Code of Zoological Nomenclature

id. *idem* (Latin: the same)

Id. Idaho

ID Cavan (Irish vehicle registration); Idaho (zip code); identification; infectious disease(s); information department; inside diameter; Institute of Directors; Intelligence Department; Iraqi dinar (monetary unit)

IDA Industrial Diamond Association; International Development Association; Irish Dental Association; Islamic Democratic Association

IDB illicit diamond buyer; illicit diamond buying; Industrial Development Bank; Inter-American Development Bank; Internal Drainage Board

IDC industrial development certificate

ID card identification card

IDD insulin-dependent diabetes; international direct dialling (telecommunications)

IDDD international direct distance dialling (telecommunications)

iden(t). identification; identify; identity

IDF International Dairy Federation; International Democratic Fellowship; International Dental Federation; International Diabetes Federation

IDIB Industrial Diamond Information Bureau

IDL international date line; international driver's licence

IDLH immediately dangerous of life and health

IDMS integrated data-management system (computing)

IDN *in Dei nomine* (Latin: in God's name); integrated data network (computing)

IDP Institute of Data Processing; integrated data processing (computing); International Driving Permit; interplanetary dust particles (astronomy)

IDPM Institute of Data Processing Management

IDRC International Development Research Centre

IDS Income Data Services; Industry Department for Scotland; Institute of Development Studies

IDSM Indian Distinguished Service Medal

IDT industrial design technology

IDV International Distillers and Vintners

ie *id est* (Latin: that is); inside edge

IE Clare (Irish vehicle registration); index error; Indian Empire; Indoeuropean (languages); ion exchange (chemistry);

Irvine (UK fishing port registration);
Solomon Airlines (airline flight code)
IEA Institute of Economic Affairs;
Institution of Engineers, Australia;
International Economic Association;
International Energy Agency;
International Ergonomics Association
IEC industrial energy conservation;
integrated environmental control;
International Electrotechnical
Commission
IED improvised explosive device;
Information Engineering Directorate;
Institution of Engineering Designers
IEDD improvised explosive device
disposal
IEE Institute of Energy Economics (US);
Institution of Electrical Engineers
IEEE Institute of Electrical and
Electronics Engineers (US)
IEEIE Institution of Electrical and
Electronics Incorporated Engineers
IEF Indian Expeditionary Force
IEHO Institution of Environmental Health
Officers
IEI Industrial Engineering Institute;
Institution of Engineers of Ireland
IEME Inspectorate of Electrical and
Mechanical Engineers
IEng Incorporated Engineer
IER Institute of Environmental Research
IERE Institution of Electronic and Radio
Engineers
IES Indian Educational Service;
Institution of Engineers and
Shipbuilders in Scotland
IET interest equalization tax
IEW intelligence and electronic warfare
IExpE Institute of Explosives Engineers
if information feedback; *ipse fecit* (Latin:
he did it himself)
IF Cork (Irish vehicle registration);
inertial fusion (nuclear engineering);
infield (baseball); inside forward (sport);
Institute of Fuel; interferon (medicine);
intermediate frequency (electronics)
IFA Incorporated Faculty of Arts;
independent financial adviser;
instrumented fuel assembly;
International Federation of Actors;
International Fertility Association;
International Fiscal Association; Irish
Football Association
IFAC International Federation of
Automatic Control
IFAD International Fund for Agricultural
Development (UN)

IFALPA International Federation of Air
Line Pilots' Associations
IFAP International Federation of
Agricultural Producers
IFATCA International Federation of Air
Traffic Controllers' Associations
IFAW International Fund for Animal
Welfare
IFB invitation for bid (finance)
IFBPW International Federation of
Business and Professional Women
IFC International Finance Corporation;
International Fisheries Commission
IFCATI International Federation of
Cotton and Allied Textile Industries
IFCC International Federation of
Camping and Caravanning;
International Federation of Children's
Communities
IFCCPTE International Federation of
Commercial, Clerical, Professional and
Technical Employees
IFCO International Fisheries Cooperative
Organization
IFCTU International Federation of
Christian Trade Unions
IFE Institute for Energy Technology;
Institute of Fire Engineers; intelligent
front end (computing)
iff if and only if (logic, mathematics)
IFF Identification, Friend or Foe (radar);
Institute of Freight Forwarders
IFFA International Federation of Film
Archives
IFFPA International Federation of Film
Producers' Associations
IFFS International Federation of Film
Societies
IFFTU International Federation of Free
Teachers' Unions
IFGA International Federation of Grocers'
Associations
IFGO International Federation of
Gynaecology and Obstetrics
IFHE International Federation of Home
Economics
IFHP International Federation for
Housing and Planning
IFIP International Federation for
Information Processing
IFJ International Federation of Journalists
IFL International Friendship League
IFLA International Federation of
Landscape Architects; International
Federation of Library Associations
IFM International Falcon Movement
IFMC International Folk Music Council

IFMSA International Federation of Medical Students' Associations
IFOR International Fellowship of Reconciliation
IFORS International Federation of Operational Research Societies
IFP Inkatha Freedom Party (South Africa)
IFPA Industrial Film Producers' Association
IFPAAW International Federation of Plantation, Agricultural and Allied Workers
IFPCS International Federation of Unions of Employees in Public and Civil Services
IFPI International Federation of the Phonographic Industry
IFPM International Federation of Physical Medicine
IFPW International Federation of Petroleum (and Chemical) Workers
IFR instrument flying regulations (aeronautics); instrument flying rules (aeronautics); integral fast reactor (nuclear engineering)
IFRB International Frequency Registration Board
IFS Indian Forest Service; International Federation of Surveyors; Irish Free State
IFSPO International Federation of Senior Police Officers
IFST Institute of Food Science and Technology
IFSW International Federation of Social Workers
IFTA International Federation of Teachers' Associations; International Federation of Travel Agencies
IFTC International Film and Television Council
IFTU International Federation of Trade Unions
IFUW International Federation of University Women
IFWEA International Federation of Workers' Educational Associations
IFWL International Federation of Women Lawyers
ig. ignition
IG Ilford (UK postcode); imperial gallon; Indo-Germanic (languages); industrial group; inertial guidance; inner guard; Inspector General; Instructor in Gunnery; Irish Guards
IGA International Geographical Association; International Golf Association

IGasE Institution of Gas Engineers
IGCM Incorporated Guild of Church Musicians
IGD illicit gold dealer
IGF Inspector-General of Fortifications; International Gymnastic Federation
IGFA International Game Fish Association
IGFET insulated-gate field-effect transistor (electronics)
IGH Incorporated Guild of Hairdressers
IGM International Grandmaster (chess)
ign. ignite(s); ignition; *ignotus* (Latin: unknown)
IGO intergovernmental organization
IGPP Institute of Geophysics and Planetary Physics
IGRS Irish Genealogical Research Society
IGS Imperial General Staff; independent grammar school
IGU International Gas Union; International Geographical Union
IGWF International Garment Workers' Federation
IGY International Geophysical Year (1957-58)
IH Donegal (Irish vehicle registration); *Iacet hic* (Latin: here lies); industrial hygiene; Ipswich (UK fishing port registration)
IHA International Hotel Association
IHAB International Horticultural Advisory Service
IHB International Hydrographic Bureau
IHC intellectually handicapped child (New Zealand); Intercontinental Hotels Corporation
IHCA International Hebrew Christian Alliance
IHEU International Humanist and Ethical Union
IHF Industrial Hygiene Foundation; International Hockey Federation; International Hospitals Federation
IHM *Iesus Mundi Salvator* (Latin: Saviour of the World)
IHospE Institute of Hospital Engineering
ihp indicated horsepower
IHR Institute of Historical Research
IHRB International Hockey Rules Board
IHS *Iesus Hominum Salvatori* (Latin: Jesus Saviour of Mankind); *in hoc signo* (Latin: in this sign); Jesus (Greek)
IHSM Institute of Health Services Management
IHT Institution of Highways and Transportation

IHU Irish Hockey Union
II image intensifier (electronics); two (Roman numerals)
IIA International Institute of Agriculture
IIAC Industrial Injuries Advisory Council
IIAL International Institute of Arts and Letters
IIAS International Institute of Administrative Sciences
IIB *Institut international des brevets* (French: International Patent Institute)
IIBD&ID Incorporated Institute of British Decorators and Interior Designers
iid independent identically distributed (statistics)
IID insulin-independent diabetes
IIE Institute for International Education; International Institute of Embryology
IIEP International Institute of Educational Planning
IIHF International Ice Hockey Federation
III International Institute of Interpreters; Investors in Industry; three (Roman numerals)
IIM Institution of Industrial Managers
IInfSc Institute of Information Scientists
IIP *Institut international de la presse* (French: International Press Institute); International Ice Patrol; International Institute of Philosophy
IIR isobutylene-isoprene rubber (chemistry)
IIRS Institute for Industrial Research and Standards (Ireland)
IIS Institute of Information Scientists; International Institute of Sociology
IISO Institution of Industrial Safety Officers
IISS International Institute of Strategic Studies
IIT Indian Institute of Technology
iJ *im Jahre* (German: in the year)
IJ Down (UK vehicle registration)
IK Dublin (Irish vehicle registration)
IKBS intelligent knowledge-based system (computing)
Ikr. Icelandic króna (monetary unit)
il inside leg
IL Fermanagh (UK vehicle registration); Illinois (zip code); Ilyushin (aircraft); inside left (sport); Institute of Linguists; instrument landing (aeronautics); Israel (international vehicle registration)
I/L import licence
ILA induction linear accelerator (physics); Institute of Landscape Architects; instrument landing approach

(aeronautics); International Law Association; International Longshoremen's Association
ILAA International Legal Aid Association
ILAB International League of Antiquarian Booksellers
ILC International Law Commission (UN)
ILE Institution of Locomotive Engineers
ILEA Inner London Education Authority
ILEC Inner London Education Committee
ILF International Landworkers' Federation
ILGA Institute of Local Government Administration
ILGWU International Ladies' Garment Workers' Union (US)
ill. illustrate(d); illustration; illustrator; *illustrissimus* (Latin: most distinguished)
Ill. Illinois
illegit. illegitimate
illit. illiterate
illum. illuminate(d); illumination
illus(t). illustrate(d); illustration; illustrator
ILN Illustrated London News
ilo in lieu of
ILO industrial liaison officer; International Labour Organization (UN)
ILocoE Institution of Locomotive Engineers
ILP Independent Labour Party
ILR Independent Law Reports; independent local radio
ILRM International League for the Rights of Man
ILS Incorporated Law Society; instrument landing system (aeronautics)
ilt in lieu thereof
ILTF International Lawn Tennis Federation
ILU Institute of London Underwriters
ILW intermediate-level waste (nuclear engineering)
Im. Imperial
IM Galway (Irish vehicle registration); Indian Marines; Institute of Metals; interceptor missile; International Master (chess); intramuscular (medicine)
IMA Indian Military Academy; Institute of Mathematics and its Applications; International Music Association; Irish Medical Association
imag. imaginary; imagination; imagine
IM&AWU International Molders' and Allied Workers' Union (US)
IMarE Institute of Marine Engineers

IMARSAT International Maritime Satellite Organization

IMAS International Marine and Shipping Conference

IMB Institute of Marine Biology

IMC image motion compensation (photography); Institute of Management Consultants; Institute of Measurement and Control; instrument meteorological conditions (aeronautics); International Maritime Committee; International Missionary Council; International Music Council

IMCO Intergovernmental Maritime Consultative Organization (UN)

IMEA Incorporated Municipal Electrical Association

IMechE Institution of Mechanical Engineers

IMet Institute of Metals

I. Meth. Independent Methodist

IMF International Monetary Fund; International Motorcycle Federation; interplanetary magnetic field (astrophysics)

IMGTechE Institution of Mechanical and General Technician Engineers

IMinE Institution of Mining Engineers

IMINT image intelligence (military)

imit. imitate; imitation; imitative

IMM Institution of Mining and Metallurgy; International Mercantile Marine; International Monetary Market

immed. immediate

IMMTS Indian Mercantile Marine Training Ship

immun. immunity; immunization; immunology

IMO International Maritime Organization; International Meteorological Organization; International Miners' Organization

imp. imperative; imperfect; imperial; impersonal; implement; import(ed); important; importer; impression; imprimatur; *imprimé* (French: printer); imprint

Imp. *Imperator* (Latin: Emperor); *Imperatrix* (Latin: Empress); Imperial

IMP interface message processor (computing); International Match Point (bridge); interplanetary measurement probe

IMPA International Master Printers' Association

IMPACT implementation, planning and control technique

impce importance

imper. imperative

imperf. imperfect; imperforate (philately)

impers. impersonal

impf(t). imperfect

imposs. impossible

IMPR improving (meteorology)

impreg. impregnate; impregnated

improp. improper; improperly

impt important

imptr importer

impv. imperative

IMR individual medical report; infant mortality rate; Institute of Medical Research

IMRA Industrial Marketing Research Association

IMRAN international marine radio aids to navigation

IMRO Investment Management Regulatory Organization

IMS Indian Medical Service; industrial methylated spirit; Information Management System (computing); Institute of Management Services; International Musicological Society

IMSM Institute of Marketing and Sales Management

IMT immediate; immediately; International Military Tribunal

IMU International Mathematical Union

IMunE Institution of Municipal Engineers

IMVS Institute of Medical and Veterinary Science (Australia)

IMW Institute of Masters of Wine

in. inch/es

In indium (element)

In. India; Indian; Instructor (military)

IN Indiana (zip code); Indian Navy; Kerry (Irish vehicle registration)

INA Indian National Army; Institution of Naval Architects; International Newsreel Association; Iraqi News Agency

INAO *Institut national des appellations d'origine des vins et eaux-de-vie* (French wine producing authority)

inaug. inaugurate(d); inauguration

inbd inboard

Inbucon International Business Consultants

inc. include; included; including; inclusive; income; incomplete; incorporate; incorporated; increase; incumbent

Inc. Incorporated

INC in cloud (meteorology); Indian

National Congress; *in nomine Christi*
(Latin: in the name of Christ);
International Numismatic Commission
INCA International Newspaper Colour
Association
incalz. *incalzando* (Italian: increasing
speed and tone; music)
INCB International Narcotics Control
Board (UN)
incho. inchoate (law)
incid. incidental
incl. incline; include; included; includes;
including; inclusive
incog. *incognito* (Latin: unknown or
unrecognized)
incor(p). incorporated; incorporation
incorr. incorrect
INCPEN Industry Committee for
Packaging and the Environment
incr. increase; increased; increasing;
increment
INCR increase (meteorology)
incun. incunabula
in d. *in dies* (Latin: daily)
ind. independence; independent; index;
indicate; indication; indicative; indigo;
indirect; indirectly; industrial; industry
Ind. Independent (politics); India; Indian;
Indiana; Indies
IND India (international vehicle
registration); *in nomine Dei* (Latin: in
God's name); investigational new drug
(US pharmacology); investigative new
drug (US pharmacology)
indecl. indeclinable (grammar)
indef. indefinite
indic. indicating; indicative; indicator
Ind. Imp. *Indiae Imperator* (Latin: Emperor
of India)
indiv(id). individual
Ind. Meth. Independent Methodist
Indo-Eur. Indo-European
Indo-Ger. Indo-German(ic)
indre. indenture
induc. induction
indust. industrial; industrious;
industry
ined. *ineditus* (Latin: unpublished)
INER Institute of Nuclear Energy
Research
INET Institute of Nuclear Energy
Technology
in ex. *in extenso* (Latin: in full)
inf infinum (mathematics)
inf. infantry; inferior; infinitive; influence;
information; *infra* (Latin: below); *infusum*
(Latin: infusion; medicine)

INF intermediate-range nuclear forces;
International Naturist Federation
infin. infinitive
infirm. infirmary
infl. inflammable; inflated; inflect;
inflorescence (botany); influence;
influenced
infm information
info. information
infra dig. *infra dignitatem* (Latin:
undignified)
Ing. *Ingenieur* (German: engineer)
Ingl. *Inghilterra* (Italian: England)
INGO international non-governmental
organization
Inh. *Inhaber* (German: proprietor); *Inhalt*
(German: contents)
inhab. inhabitant
INI *in nomine Iesu* (Latin: in the name of
Jesus)
init. initial(ly); *initio* (Latin: in the
beginning)
inj. injection; injury
INJ *in nomine Jesu* (Latin: in the name of
Jesus)
INLA International Nuclear Law
Association; Irish National Liberation
Army
in lim. *in limine* (Latin: at the outset)
in loc. *in loco* (Latin: in place of)
in loc. cit. *in loco citato* (Latin: in the place
cited)
Inmarsat International Maritime Satellite
Organization
in mem. *in memoriam* (Latin: to the
memory of)
inn. innings (cricket)
INO inspectorate of naval ordnance
inorg. inorganic
INP Institute of Nuclear Physics
in pr. *in principio* (Latin: in the
beginning)
in pro. in proportion
inq. inquiry; inquisition
INR independent national radio; Index of
Nursing Research
INRI *Iesu Nazarenus Rex Iudaeorum* (Latin:
Jesus of Nazareth, King of the Jews)
in s. in situ
ins. inches; inscribe; inscription;
inspector; insular; insulate; insulated;
insulation; insurance
INS Indian Naval Ship; inertial
navigation system; International News
Service; Inverness (UK fishing port
registration)
INSA Indian National Science Academy

INSAG International Nuclear Safety
Advisory Group
insce insurance
inscr. inscribe; inscription
INSEA International Society for
Education through Art
INSEAD *Institut européen d'administration
des affaires* (French: European Institute of
Administrative Affairs)
insep. inseparable
INSET in-service training (education)
insol. insoluble
insolv. insolvent
insp. inspect; inspected; inspection;
inspector
Insp. Gen. inspector general
inst. instance; *instant* (Latin: current
month); instantaneous; institute;
institution; instruct; instruction;
instructor; instrument; instrumental
Inst. Institute
INST *in nomine Sanctae Trinitatis* (Latin: in
the name of the Holy Trinity)
INSTAB Information Service on Toxicity
and Biodegradibility (water pollution)
InstAct Institute of Actuaries
InstBE Institution of British Engineers
InstCE Institution of Civil Engineers
InstD Institute of Directors
InstE Institute of Energy
InstEE Institution of Electrical
Engineers
instl. installation
InstMet Institute of Metals
InstMM Institution of Mining and
Metallurgy
Instn Institution
InstP Institute of Physics
InstPet Institute of Petroleum
InstPl Institute of Patentees and
Inventors
instr. instruction; instructor; instrument;
instrumental
InstR Institute of Refrigeration
InstSMM Institute of Sales and Marketing
Management
InstT Institute of Transport
int. intelligence (military); intercept;
interest; interim; interior; interjection;
intermediate; internal; international;
interpret; interpretation; interpreter;
interval; intransitive; introit (music)
int. al. *inter alia* (Latin: among other
things)
INTAL Institute for Latin American
Integration (Buenos Aires)
int. comb. internal combustion

Intelsat International Telecommunications Satellite Consortium
intens. intensifier; intensify; intensive
inter. intermediate; interrogation mark
INTER intermittent (meteorology)
interj. interjection
internat. international
interp. interpreter
Interpol International Criminal Police
Commission
interrog. interrogate; interrogation;
interrogative
intl international
INTO Irish National (Primary) Teachers'
Organization
intr(ans). intransitive
in trans. in transit
intro(d). introduce; introduction;
introductory
INTSF intensify (meteorology)
INTST intensity (meteorology)
INTUC Indian National Trade Union
Congress
INucE Institution of Nuclear Engineers
inv. *invenit* (Latin: he/she designed this);
invent; invented; invention; inventor;
inversion; invert; investment; invoice
Inv. Inverness; Investment
inv. et del. *invenit et delineavit* (Latin:
he/she designed and drew this)
invt(y). inventory
Io. Iowa
IO India Office; inspecting officer;
integrated optics; intelligence officer;
Kildare (Irish vehicle registration)
I/O input-output (computing); inspecting
order
IOB Institute of Bankers; Institute of
Biology; Institute of Book-keepers;
Institute of Brewing; Institute of
Building
IOC Intergovernmental Oceanographic
Commission; International Olympic
Committee
IOCU International Organization of
Consumers' Unions
IoD Institute of Directors
IODE Imperial Order of Daughters of the
Empire (Canada)
IOE International Organization of
Employers
IoF Institute of Fuel
IOF International Order of Foresters;
International Oceanographic Foun-
dation; International Orienteering
Federation
I of E Institute of Export

I of M Isle of Man
IOGT International Order of Good Templars
IoJ Institute of Journalists
IOJ International Organization of Journalists
IOM Indian Order of Merit; Institute of Metals; Isle of Man
IOME Institute of Marine Engineering
IOMTR International Office for Motor Trades and Repairs
Ion. Ionic
IOO Inspecting Ordnance Officer
IOOF Independent Order of Oddfellows
IOP input/output processor (computing); Institute of Painters in Oil Colours; Institute of Petroleum; Institute of Physics; Institute of Plumbing; Institute of Printing
IOPAB International Organization for Pure and Applied Biophysics
IoS The Independent on Sunday (newspaper)
IOS integrated office system (computing)
IOSCO International Organization of Securities Commissions
IOSM Independent Order of the Sons of Malta
IoT Institute of Transport
IOU Industrial Operations Unit; I owe you
IOW inspector of works; Institute of Welding; Isle of Wight
ip identification point; incentive pay; indexed and paged; initial phase; input primary (electrical engineering)
IP Airlines of Tasmania (airline flight code, Australia); image processing (electronics); Imperial Preference; India Paper; innings pitched (baseball); in-patient (medicine); input primary (electrical engineering); instalment plan; Institute of Petroleum; Institute of Plumbing; Ipswich (UK postcode); Kilkenny (Irish vehicle registration)
IPA India Pale Ale; Insolvency Practitioners' Association; Institute of Park Administration; Institute of Practitioners in Advertising; International Phonetic Alphabet; International Phonetic Association; International Poetry Archives (Manchester); International Phonetic Academy; International Phonetic Association; International Publishers' Association; isopropanol (chemistry)
IPAA International Petroleum Asso-

ciation of America; International Prisoners' Aid Association
IPARS International Programmed Airline Reservation System
ipbm interplanetary ballistic missile
IPC International Petroleum Company (Peru); International Polar Commission; International Publishing Corporation; Iraq Petroleum Company
IPCA International Pest Control Association
IPCC Intergovernmental Panel on Climatic Change (UN)
IPCS Institution of Professional Civil Servants; intelligent process-control system (computing)
IPD individual package delivery
IPE Institution of Plant Engineers; Institution of Production Engineers; International Petroleum Exchange
IPF Irish Printing Federation
IPFA (Chartered) Institute of Public Finance and Accountancy
IPFC Indo-Pacific Fisheries Council (FAO)
IPG Independent Publishers' Guild; Industrial Painters' Group
iph impressions per hour
IPH industrial process heat; industrial process heating
IPHE Institution of Public Health Engineers
ipi *in partibus infidelium* (Latin: in the regions of unbelievers)
IPI Institute of Patentees and Inventors; Institute of Professional Investigators; International Press Institute
IPL information processing language (computing); initial program load (computing)
IPlantE Institution of Plant Engineers
IPLO Irish People's Liberation Organization
IPM immediate past master (Freemasonry); inches per minute; inches per month; Institute of Personnel Management
IPO input-process-output (computing); Israel Philharmonic Orchestra; initial public offering (US stock exchange)
IPP Institute for Plasma Physics
IPPA Independent Programme Producers' Association
IPPF International Planned Parenthood Federation
IPPR Institute for Public Policy Research

IPPS Institute of Physics and the Physical Society

IPPV intermittent positive-pressure ventilation (medicine)

IPR Institute of Public Relations

IPRA International Public Relations Association

IPRE Incorporated Practitioners in Radio and Electronics

IProdE Institution of Production Engineers

ips inches per second; instructions per second (computing)

Ips. Ipswich

IPS inches per second; Indian Police Service; Indian Political Service; Institute of Purchasing and Supply; Inter Press Service (news agency, Italy); International Confederation for Plastic Surgery; interpretative programming system (computing)

IPSA International Political Science Association

IPSE integrated project support environment (computing)

IPT Institute of Petroleum Technologists; interpersonal therapy

IPTO independent power take-off (astronautics)

IPTPA International Professional Tennis Players' Association

IPTS International Practical Temperature Scale (physics)

IPU Inter-Parliamentary Union

ipy inches per year

iq *idem quod* (Latin: the same as)

IQ Institute of Quarrying; intelligence quotient; international quota

IQA Institute of Quality Assurance

IQS Institute of Quantity Surveyors

ir inside radius

iR *im Ruhestand* (German: retired or emeritus)

Ir iridium (element)

Ir. Ireland; Irish

IR ice on runway (meteorology); incidence rate; index register; informal report; information retrieval; infrared; Inland Revenue; inside right (sport); inspector's report; Institute of Refrigeration; instrument reading; international registration; Iran (international vehicle registration); Iran Air (airline flight code); Iranian rial (monetary unit); isoprene rubber (chemistry); Offaly (Irish vehicle registration)

IRA individual retirement account (US); Institute of Registered Architects; Irish Republican Army

IRAD Institute for Research on Animal Diseases

iran inspect and repair as necessary

Iran. Iranian

IRAS Infrared Astronomical Satellite

IRB industrial revenue bond; Irish Republican Brotherhood

IRBM intermediate-range ballistic missile

IRC Industrial Reorganization Corporation; Infantry Reserve Corps; International Red Cross; international reply coupon; International Research Council

IRCert Industrial Relations Certificate

IRD International Research and Development Company

IRDA Industrial Research and Development Authority

Ire. Ireland

IRE Institute of Radio Engineers (US)

Irel. Ireland

IREE(Aust) Institution of Radio and Electronics Engineers (Australia)

IRF International Road Federation; International Rowing Federation

IRFB International Rugby Football Board

IRFU Irish Rugby Football Union

irid. iridescent

IRL Ireland (international vehicle registration)

IRNA Islamic Republic News Agency (Iran)

IRO industrial relations officer; Inland Revenue Office; International Relief Organization; International Refugee Organization

iron. ironic; ironical

IRPA International Radiation Protection Association

IRQ interrupt request (computing); Iraq (international vehicle registration)

irr. irredeemable (finance); irregular

IRR infrared radiation; Institute of Race Relations; internal rate of return (finance)

irreg. irregular; irregularly

IRRI International Rice Research Institute

IRRV Institute of Revenues, Rating and Valuation

IRS information retrieval system (computing); Internal Revenue Service (US)

IRTE Institute of Road Transport Engineers

IRU industrial rehabilitation unit; International Relief Union; International Road Transport Union

IRWC International Registry of World Citizens

is. island; isle

Is. Isaiah (Bible); Islam; Islamic; island/s; isle/s; Israel; Israeli

IS Iceland (international vehicle registration); Industrial Society; information science; information service; information system; input secondary (electrical engineering); International Society of Sculptors, Painters and Gravers; Irish Society; Mayo (Irish vehicle registration)

Isa. Isaiah (Bible)

ISA Independent Schools Association; International Sociological Association; International Standard Atmosphere (aeronautics)

ISAB Institute for the Study of Animal Behaviour

ISAC Industrial Safety Advisory Council

ISAM indexed sequential access method (computing)

ISAS Institute of Space and Astronautical Science (Japan)

ISBA Incorporated Society of British Advertisers

ISBN International Standard Book Number

ISC Imperial Service College; Imperial Staff College; Indian Staff Corps; International Seismological Centre; International Student Conference; International Sugar Council; International Supreme Council (Freemasonry)

ISCE International Society of Christian Endeavour

ISCh Incorporated Society of Chiropodists

ISCM International Society for Contemporary Music

ISCO Independent Schools Careers Organization; International Standard Classification of Occupations

ISD international standard depth; international subscriber dialling

ISDN Integrated Services Digital Network (telecommunications)

ISE Indian Service of Engineers; Institution of Structural Engineers; International Stock Exchange of the UK and the Republic of Ireland Limited

ISF International Shipping Federation; International Spiritualist Federation

ISGE International Society of Gastroenterology

ISH International Society of Haematology

ISHS International Society for Horticultural Science

ISI Indian Standards Institution; International Statistical Institute; Iron and Steel Institute

ISIS Independent Schools Information Service; International Shipping Information Services

ISJC Independent Schools Joint Council

ISK króna (Icelandic monetary unit)

isl. island; isle

ISM *Iesus Salvator Mundi* (Latin: Jesus, Saviour of the World); Imperial Service Medal; Incorporated Society of Musicians

ISME International Society for Musical Education

ISMRC Inter-Services Metallurgical Research Council

ISO Imperial Service Order; International Standards Organization; International Sugar Organization

isol. isolate; isolated; isolation

ISOL isolated (meteorology)

ISP Institute of Sales Promotion; International Study Programme

ISPA International Society for the Protection of Animals; International Sporting Press Association

ISPEMA Industrial Safety (Personal Equipment) Manufacturers' Association

ISQ *in statu quo* (Latin: in the same state or unchanged)

ISR information storage and retrieval; Institute of Social Research; International Society for Radiology

ISRB Inter-Services Research Bureau

ISRD International Society for Rehabilitation of the Disabled

ISRO International Securities Regulatory Organization

iss. issue

ISS Institute of Space Sciences; Institute for Space Studies; Institute for Strategic Studies; International Social Service

ISSA International Social Security Association

ISSN International Standard Serial Number

ISSS International Society of Soil Science

IST Indian Standard Time; information

sciences technology; Institute of Science Technology

ISTC Institute of Scientific and Technical Communicators; Iron and Steel Trades' Confederation

ISTD Imperial Society of Teachers of Dancing

ISTEA Iron and Steel Trades Employers' Association

isth. isthmus

IStructE Institution of Structural Engineers

ISU International Seamen's Union; International Shooting Union; International Skating Union

ISV independent software manufacturer; International Scientific Vocabulary

ISVA Incorporated Society of Valuers and Auctioneers

ISWG Imperial Standard Wire Gauge (engineering)

it inspection tag; internal thread; in transit

it. italic

It. Italian; Italy

IT ignition temperature; income tax; Indian Territory (US); industrial tribunal; infantry training; information technology; Inner Temple (law); International Table (physics); Leitrim (Irish vehicle registration)

ita Initial Teaching Alphabet

ITA Independent Television Authority; industrial and technical assistance; Industrial Transport Association; Institute of Air Transport; Institute of Travel Agents

ITAI Institution of Technical Authors and Illustrators

ital. italic/s

Ital. Italy; Italian

Italy I trust and love you

IT&T International Telephone and Telegraph Corporation

ITB Industry Training Board; International Time Bureau; Irish Tourist Board

itc installation time and cost

ITC Imperial Tobacco Company; Independent Television Commission; Industrial Training Council; International Tin Council; International Trade Centre; intertropical confluence (meteorology); investment tax credit (US)

ITCA Independent Television Contractors' Association

ITCZ intertropical convergence zone (meteorology)

ITDA indirect target damage assessment (military)

ITE Institute of Terrestrial Ecology

ITEME Institution of Technician Engineers in Mechanical Engineering

ITER international thermonuclear engineering reactor; international tokamak engineering reactor

ITF International Tennis Federation; International Trade Federations; International Transport Workers' Federation

ITGWF International Textile and Garment Workers' Federation

itin. itinerary

Itl. Italian

ITMA Institute of Trade Mark Agents; It's That Man Again! (BBC radio comedy series)

ITN Independent Television News

ITO International Trade Organization

ITS Industrial Training Service; Intermarket Trading System (US); International Trade Secretariat

ITT insulin tolerance test (medicine); International Telephone and Telegraph Corporation

ITTF International Table Tennis Federation

ITU intensive therapy unit (medicine); International Telecommunication Union (UN); International Temperance Union; International Typographical Union

ITV Independent Television; instructional television (US)

ITVA International Television Association

ITWF International Transport Workers' Federation

iu international unit (pharmacology)

IU immunizing unit; international unit (pharmacology); Izquierda Unida (Spanish: United Left); Limerick (Irish vehicle registration)

IUA International Union Against Alcoholism; International Union of Architects

IUAA International Union of Advertisers' Associations

IUAES International Union of Anthropological and Ethnological Sciences

IUAI International Union of Aviation Insurers

IUAO International Union for Applied Ornithology

IUAPPA International Union of Air Pollution Prevention Associations

IUB International Union of Biochemistry; International Universities Bureau

IUBS International Union of Biological Sciences

IUCD intra-uterine contraceptive device

IUCN International Union for the Conservation of Nature and Natural Resources

IUCr International Union of Crystallography

IUCW International Union for Child Welfare

IUD intra-uterine death (medicine); intra-uterine device (contraceptive)

IUE International Ultra-violet Explorer (astronomy); International Union of Electronic, Electrical, Salaried, Machine and Furniture Workers (US)

IUF International Union of Food and Allied Workers' Associations

IUFO International Union of Family Organizations

IUFRO International Union of Forest Research Organizations

IUGG International Union of Geodesy and Geophysics

IUGR intra-uterine growth retardation (medicine)

IUGS International Union of Geological Sciences

IUHPS International Union of the History and Philosophy of Science

IULA International Union of Local Authorities

IUMF *institut d'universitaires de formation des maîtres* (French: advanced teacher-education institute)

IUMI International Union of Marine Insurance

IUMSWA Industrial Union of Marine and Shipbuilding Workers of America

IUNS International Union of Nutritional Science

IUOE International Union of Operating Engineers (US)

IUPAB International Union of Pure and Applied Biophysics

IUPAC International Union of Pure and Applied Chemistry

IUPAP International Union of Pure and Applied Physics

IUPS International Union of Physiological Sciences

IUS inertial upper stage (astronautics); International Union of Students

IUSP International Union of Scientific Psychology

IUSY International Union of Socialist Youth

IUTAM International Union of Theoretical and Applied Mechanics

iv increased value; initial velocity; intravenous; intravenously; invoice value

iV *in Vertretung* (German: by proxy)

IV Air Gambia (airline flight code); four (Roman numerals); intravenous(ly); Inverness (UK postcode); invoice value

IVA individual voluntary arrangement (bankruptcy); invalidity allowance

IVB invalidity benefit

IVBF International Volleyball Federation

IVF in vitro fertilization (medicine)

IVR International Vehicle Registration

IVS International Voluntary Service

IVT intravehicular transfer (astronautics)

IVU International Vegetarian Union

iw indirect waste; inside width

IW Inspector of Works; Isle of Wight; Londonderry (UK vehicle registration)

IWA Inland Waterways Association; Institute of World Affairs

IWC International Whaling Commission; International Wheat Council

IWD Inland Waterways and Docks

IWEM Institution of Water and Environmental Management

IWG imperial wire gauge

IWGC Imperial War Graves Commission

IWM Imperial War Museum

IWO Institute of Welfare Officers

IWPC Institute of Water Pollution Control

IWS International Wool Secretariat

IWTA Inland Water Transport Association

IWW Industrial Workers of the World; International Workers of the World

IX *Iesus Christus* (Latin: Jesus Christ); Longford (Irish vehicle registration)

IY Imperial Yeomanry; Louth (Irish vehicle registration); Yemenia Yemen Airways (airline flight code, Yemen Arab Republic)

IYHF International Youth Hostels Federation

IYRU International Yacht Racing Union

iyswim if you see what I mean

IZ Mayo (Irish vehicle registration)

j current density (physics)

j. *jour* (French: day); *juris* (Latin: of law); *jus* (Latin: law)

J advance ratio (engineering); Durham (UK vehicle registration); jack (cards); Jacobean determinant (mathematics); Japan (international vehicle registration); Jersey (UK fishing port registration); joule; Jurassic (geology)

J angular momentum (physics); current density (physics)

J. Jacobean; *Jahr* (German: year); January; Jesus; jet; Jew(ish); Journal; Judaic; Judaism; Judge; July; June; Justice

J. *judex* (Latin: judge)

J2 Djibouti (international civil aircraft marking)

J3 Grenada (international civil aircraft marking)

J5 Guinea Bissau (international civil aircraft marking)

J6 St Lucia (international civil aircraft marking)

J7 Dominica (international civil aircraft marking)

J8 St Vincent (international civil aircraft marking)

Ja. January

JA Jamaica (international vehicle registration); Japan (international civil aircraft marking); joint account (banking); Judge Advocate; Justice of Appeal; Manchester (UK vehicle registration)

JAA Japan Aeronautic Association; Jewish Athletic Association

Jaat joint air attack team (military)

Jac. Jacobean

JAC Joint Apprenticeship Committee (US); Junior Association of Commerce (US)

Jacq. J. F./N. J. Jacquin (botany)

JACT Joint Association of Classical Teachers

JAD Julian Astronomical Day

JADB Joint Air Defense Board (US)

JAEC Japan Atomic Energy Commission; Joint Atomic Energy Committee (US Congress)

JAF Judge Advocate of the Fleet

JAFC Japan Atomic Fuel Corporation

Jafo just another fucking observer (military)

Jag Jaguar (cars)

JAG Judge Advocate General

JAIEG Joint Atomic Information Exchange Group

JAL Japan Airlines; jet approach and landing chart

Jam. Jamaica; James (Bible)

JAMA Journal of the American Medical Association

JAMPRESS (news agency, Jamaica)

jan. janitor

Jan January

JANA Jamahiriya News Agency (Libya)

J&K Jammu and Kashmir (India)

j&wo jettisoning and washing overboard (insurance)

JANET Joint Academic Network (computing)

janv. *janvier* (French: January)

jap. japanned

Jap. Japan; Japanese

JAP Jewish American Princess

jar. jargon

JARE Japanese Antarctic Research Expedition

Jas. James (Bible)

JAS Jamaica Agricultural Society; Junior Astronomical Society

jastop jet-assisted stop (aeronautics)

JATCC Joint Aviation Telecommunications Coordination Committee

JATCRU joint air traffic control radar unit

JATO jet-assisted take-off (aeronautics)

JATS joint air transportation service

jaund. jaundice

jav. javelin (athletics)

Jav. Java; Javanese

jb jet bomb; joint board; junction box

Jb. *Jahrbuch* (German: yearbook)

JB *Juris Baccalaureus* (Latin: Bachelor of Laws); junior beadle; Reading (UK vehicle registration)

JBAA Journal of the British Archaeological Association

JBC Jamaica Broadcasting Association; Japan Broadcasting Association

JBCNS Joint Board of Clinical Nursing Studies

Jber. *Jahresbericht* (German: annual report)

JBES Jodrell Bank Experimental Station

JBL Journal of Business Law
JBS John Birch Society (US)
jc joint compound
JC Bangor (UK vehicle registration);
Jesus Christ; Jockey Club; Julius Caesar;
Junior Chamber (of Commerce) (US);
junior college (US); *juris-consultus* (Latin:
jurisconsult; law); Justice Clerk;
justiciary case; juvenile court
JC Jewish Chronicle
J-C *Jésus-Christ* (French: Jesus Christ)
JCAC Joint Civil Affairs Committee (US)
JCAR Joint Commission on Applied
Radioactivity
JCB *Juris Canonici Baccalaureus* (Latin:
Bachelor of Canon Law); *Juris Civilis
Baccalaureus* (Latin: Bachelor of Civil
Law); Joseph Cyril Bamford (manu-
facturer of excavating machines)
JCC Jesus College, Cambridge; Joint
Consultative Committee; Junior
Chamber of Commerce
JCD *Juris Canonici Doctor* (Latin: Doctor
of Canon Law); *Juris Civilis Doctor*
(Latin: Doctor of Civil Law)
JCI Junior Chamber International
JCL job-control language (computing);
Juris Canonici Licentiatus (Latin:
Licentiate in Canon Law); *Juris Civilis
Licentiatus* (Latin: Licentiate in Civil
Law)
JCNAAF Joint Canadian Navy-Army-Air
Force
JC of C Junior Chamber of Commerce
JCP Japan Communist Party
JCR junior common room
JCS Joint Chiefs of Staff; Joint Common-
wealth Societies; Journal of the Chemical
Society
jct. junction
JCWI Joint Council for the Welfare of
Immigrants
jd joined
JD Diploma in Journalism; Jordan dinar
(monetary unit); Julian date (astrono-
my); junior deacon; junior dean; *Jurum
Doctor* (Latin: Doctor of Laws or Juris-
prudence); jury duty; Justice Depart-
ment (US); juvenile delinquent; central
London (UK vehicle registration)
JDA Japan Defence Agency
JDB Japan Development Bank
JDipMA Joint Diploma in Management
Accounting Services
JDL Jewish Defense League (US)
jds job data sheet
JE Manx Airlines (airline flight code, Isle

of Man, UK); Peterborough (UK vehicle
registration)
jea joint export agent
JEA Jesuit Educational Association; Joint
Engineering Association
JEC Joint Economic Committee (US
Congress)
JECI *Jeunesses étudiante catholique
internationale* (French: International
Young Catholic Students)
J. Ed. Journal of Education
Jeep general purpose (GP; vehicle)
Jer. Jeremiah (Bible); Jersey; Jerusalem
JERC Joint Electronic Research
Committee
JERI Japan Economic Research
Institute
jerob. jeroboam
Jes. Jesus
JESA Japanese Engineering Standards
Association
JESSI Joint European Submicron Silicon
Initiative
jet. jetsam; jettison
JET Joint European Torus (nuclear
engineering); Joint European Transport
JETCO Jamaican Export Trading
Company; Japan Export Trading
Company
JETP Journal of Experimental and
Theoretical Physics
JETRO Japan External Trade
Organization
jett. jettison
jeu. *jeudi* (French: Thursday)
Jew. Jewish
jf fog at a distance (meteorology)
JF Leicester (UK vehicle registration)
J/F journal folio (book-keeping)
JFET junction field-effect transistor
(electronics)
JFK John Fitzgerald Kennedy (US
President); John Fitzgerald Kennedy
Airport (New York)
JFM *Jeunesses fédéralistes mondiales*
(French: Young World Federalists)
JFTC Joint Fur Trade Committee
JFU Jersey Farmers' Union
jg junior grade
JG Maidstone (UK vehicle registration);
Swedair (airline flight code, Sweden)
JGTC Junior Girls' Training Corps
JGW Junior Grand Warden
(Freemasonry)
Jh. *Jahrehundert* (German: century)
JH Jubilee head (head of Queen Victoria;
numismatics); juvenile hormone

(biochemistry); Reading (UK vehicle
registration)
jha job hazard analysis
JHDA Junior Hospital Doctors'
Association
JHMO junior hospital medical officer
JHS *Jesus Hominum Salvator* (Latin: Jesus
Saviour of Men); junior high school
JHU Johns Hopkins University (US)
JHVH Jehovah
JI Journalists' Institute; Tyrone (UK
vehicle registration)
JIB joint intelligence bureau
jic just in case
JIC joint industrial council; joint
intelligence center (US); joint intelligence
committee (US)
JICRAR Joint Industry Committee for
Radio Audience Research
Jictar Joint Industry Committee for
Television Advertising Research
JIE Junior Institution of Engineers
JIJI *Jiji Tsushin-Sha* (news agency, Japan)
JIM Japan Institute of Metals
JINS juvenile in need of supervision (US)
JINucE Junior Member of the Institution
of Nuclear Engineers
JIOA joint intelligence objectives agency
JIS Jamaica Information Service; Japan
Industrial Standard; Jewish Information
Society; joint intelligence staff
JIT just-in-time (manufacturing)
JJ Judges; Justices; Maidstone (UK
vehicle registration)
JK Brighton (UK vehicle registration)
jkt jacket; job knowledge test
Jl journal
Jl. July
JL Japan Airlines (airline flight code);
Lincoln (UK vehicle registration)
JLA Jewish Librarians' Association
JLB Jewish Lads' Brigade
JLC Jewish Labor Committee (US)
JLP Jamaica Labour Party
JM Air Jamaica (airline flight code);
Reading (UK vehicle registration)
JMA Japanese Meteorological Agency
JMB James Matthew Barrie (Scottish
playwright and novelist); Joint
Matriculation Board
JMBA Journal of the Marine Biological
Association
JMCS Junior Mountaineering Club of
Scotland
JMJ Jesus, Mary and Joseph (Roman
Catholic Church)
JMSAC Joint Meteorological Satel-

lite Advisory Committee
jn join; junction; junior
JN Chelmsford (UK vehicle registration)
JNA Jordan News Agency
jnc. junction
JNC joint negotiating committee
jnd just noticeable difference
JNEC Jamaican National Export
Corporation
JNF Jewish National Fund
jnl journal
jnlst journalist
jnr junior
JNR Japanese National Railways
jns just noticeable shift
jnt joint
JNTO Japan National Tourist
Organization
jnt stk joint stock
JO job order; *Journal Official* (French:
Official Gazette); junior officer; Oxford
(UK vehicle registration)
Jo. Bapt. John the Baptist
joc. jocose; jocular
JOC *Jeunesse ouvrière chrétienne* (French:
Young Christian Workers); joint
operations center (US)
jod joint occupancy date
J. of E. Journal of Education
JOG junior offshore group (yachting)
Johan. Johannesburg
join. joinery
Jon. Jonah (Bible)
Josh. Joshua (Bible)
JOT joint observer team
jour. journal(ist); journey; journeyman
JOVIAL Jules' own version of
international algorithmic language
(devised by Jules Schwarz; computing)
jp precipitation within sight of station
(meteorology)
JP Adria Airways (airline flight code,
Yugoslavia); jet propelled; jet pro-
pulsion; Justice of the Peace; Liverpool
(UK vehicle registration)
JPA Jamaica Press Association
JPC joint planning council; joint
production council; Judge of the Prize
Court
JPCAC Joint Production, Consultative
and Advisory Committee
JPL Jet Propulsion Laboratory (US);
Journal of Planning Law
Jpn Japan
JPRS Joint Publications Research Service
(US)
JPS jet-propulsion system; Jewish

Publications Society (US); Joint Parliamentary Secretary; joint planning staff; Junior Philatelic Society

JPTO jet-propelled take-off (astronautics)

JQ Trans Jamaica Airlines (airline flight code)

jr *jour* (French: day)

Jr Junior

Jr. journal; juror

JR *Jacobus Rex* (Latin: King James); joint resolution; Judges' Rules; Jurist Reports; Newcastle upon Tyne (UK vehicle registration)

JRAI Journal of the Royal Anthropological Institute

JRC Junior Red Cross

JS Chosonminhang Korean Airways (airline flight code, DPR of Korea); Inverness (UK vehicle registration); Japan Society (US); judgment summons (law); judicial separation (law)

JSAWC Joint Services Amphibious Warfare Centre

JSB joint-stock bank

JSC Johnson Space Center (Texas)

JSD Doctor of Juristic Science

JSDC Joint Service Defence College

Jsey Jersey

JSLS Joint Services Liaison Staff

JSP Jackson structured programming (computing); Japan Socialist Party

JSPS Japan Society for the Promotion of Science

JSS joint services standard

JSSC Joint Services Staff College; joint shop stewards' committee

J-stars joint surveillance and targeting acquisition radar system

jt joint; joint tenancy (law)

JT Bournemouth (UK vehicle registration)

JTA Jewish Telegraphic Agency (news agency, Israel)

JTC Junior Training Corps

Jt Ed. Joint Editor

JTIDS Joint Tactical Information Distribution System

jtly jointly

JTO jump take-off (aircraft)

JTS job training standards

JTST jet stream (meteorology)

JTUAC Joint Trade Union Advisory Committee

ju joint use

Ju Junkers (German aircraft)

Ju. June

JU *JAT-Jugoslovenski Aerotransport* (airline flight code, Yugoslavia); Leicester (UK vehicle registration)

jud. judgment; judicial; judo

Jud. Judah (Bible); Judaism; Judea; Judge; Judges (Bible); Judith (Bible)

JUD *Juris Utriusque Doctor* (Latin: Doctor of Canon and Civil Law)

judgt judgment

juev. *jueves* (Spanish: Thursday)

JUGFET junction-gate field-effect transistor (electronics)

juil. *juillet* (French: July)

jul. *julho* (Portuguese: July); *julio* (Spanish: July)

Jul. July

Jun. June; junior

junc. junction

jun. part. junior partner

Junr Junior

JurD *Juris Doctor* (Latin: Doctor of Law)

jurisd. jurisdiction

jurisp. jurisprudence

jus(t). justice

JUSMAG Joint United States Military Advisory Group

juss. jussive (grammar)

Juss. Jussieu (botany)

Just. Justinian

juv. juvenile

Juv. Juvenal (Roman poet)

JUWTFA Joint Unconventional Warfare Task Force, Atlantic

jux. juxtaposition

Jv. Java; Javanese

JV joint venture (commerce); junior varsity (US); Lincoln (UK vehicle registration)

JW Birmingham (UK vehicle registration); Jehovah's Witness/es; junior warden

JWB Jewish Welfare Board; joint wages board

JWEF Joinery and Woodwork Employers' Federation

jwlr jeweller

jwo jettisoning and washing overboard (insurance)

JWS Joint Warfare Staff

JWV Jewish War Veterans

JX Huddersfield (UK vehicle registration); Jesus Christ

Jy July; jury

JY Exeter (UK vehicle registration); Jersey European Airways (airline flight code, Channel Islands, UK); Jordan (international civil aircraft marking)

JZ Down (UK vehicle registration)

K

k constant (mathematics); curvature (mathematics); kilo-; knit
k thermal conductivity (physics)
k. cumulus (meteorology); karat (US); keel; killed; king; knight; knot; kopeck (Russian monetary unit); kosher; krona (Swedish monetary unit); krone (Danish and Norwegian monetary unit)
K Kampuchea (international vehicle registration); capacity; Cretaceous (geology); kelvin; kilo- (computing); kina (monetary unit of Papua New Guinea); king (chess); kip (Laotian monetary unit); Kirkpatrick (catalogue of Domenico Scarlatti's works); Kirkwall (UK fishing port registration); Köchel number (in catalogue of Mozart works); kwacha (Zambian monetary unit); kyat (Burmese monetary unit); Liverpool (UK vehicle registration); potassium (element); solar constant (astronomy); strikeout (baseball); one thousand
K equilibrium constant (chemistry); kinetic energy (physics)
K. *Kald* (Norwegian: cold); *Kall* (Swedish; cold); *Kalt* (German: cold); King('s); King's College (Cambridge); *koel* (Dutch: cold); *Kold* (Danish: cold); *Krinda* (Danish: women); *Krinne* (Norwegian: women); *Krinnor* (Swedish: women)
K9 canine (military)
KA Dragonair (airline flight code, Hong Kong); Kilmarnock (UK postcode); King of Arms; Knight of St Andrew (Russia); Liverpool (UK vehicle registration)
KADU Kenya African Democratic Union
KAK *Kungl Automobil Klubben* (Swedish: Royal Automobile Club)
Kal. *Kalendae* (Latin: calends, the first day of the month)
Kan(s). Kansas
k&b kitchen and bathroom
KANTAFU Kenya African National Traders' and Farmers' Union
KANU Kenyan African National Union
KANUPP Karachi Nuclear Power Plant (Pakistan)
kao. kaolin
KAO Kuiper Airborne Observatory
Kap. *Kapital* (German: capital; finance); *Kapitel* (German: chapter)
Kar. Karachi
KAR King's African Rifles

Karel. Karelia(n)
Kash. Kashmir
KASSR Karelian Autonomous Soviet Socialist Republic
kb kilobar (physics); knit into back of stitch (knitting)
KB kilobyte (computing); King's Bench; king's bishop (chess); Knight Bachelor; Knight of the Bath; knowledge base (computing); *Koninkrijk België* (Flemish: Kingdom of Belgium); Liverpool (UK vehicle registration)
KBASSR Kabardino-Balkar Autonomous Soviet Socialist Republic
KBC King's Bench Court
kbd keyboard
KBD King's Bench Division
KBE Knight Commander of the Black Eagle (Russia); Knight Commander of the Order of the British Empire
KBES knowledge-based expert system (computing)
Kbhvn *København* (Danish: Copenhagen)
Kbl Kabul (Afghanistan)
KBP king's bishop's pawn (chess)
KBS Knight of the Blessed Sacrament; knowledge-based system (computing)
KBW King's Bench Walk (Temple, London)
kbyte kilobyte (computing)
kc kilocycle (physics)
KC Kansas City; Kennel Club; King's College; King's Counsel; King's Cross (London); Knight Commander; Knight of the Crescent (Turkey); Knights of Columbus (Roman Catholic Church); Liverpool (UK vehicle registration)
KCA Keesing's Contemporary Archives
kcal kilocalorie
KCB Knight Commander of the Order of the Bath
KCC King's College, Cambridge; (Knight) Commander of the Order of the Crown (Belgium and the Congo Free State)
K-cell killer cell (immunology)
KCH King's College Hospital (London); Knight Commander of the Hanoverian Order
KCHS Knight Commander of the Order of the Holy Sepulchre
KCIE Knight Commander of the Order of the Indian Empire
KCL King's College, London

KCLJ Knight Commander of the Order of St Lazarus of Jerusalem
KCMG Knight Commander of the Order of St Michael and St George
KCNA Korean Central News Agency
kcs kilocycles per second
Kcs koruna (Czech and Slovak monetary unit)
KCSA Knight Commander of the Military Order of the Collar of St Agatha of Paterna
KCSG Knight Commander of the Order of St Gregory the Great
KCSI Knight Commander of the Order of the Star of India
KCSJ Knight Commander of the Order of St John of Jerusalem (Knights Hospitaller)
KCSS Knight Commander of the Order of St Silvester
KCVO Knight Commander of the Royal Victorian Order
kd killed
KD kiln dried; knock down (auction sales); knocked down (commerce); *Kongeriget Danmark* (Danish: Kingdom of Denmark); Kuwaiti dinar (monetary unit); Liverpool (UK vehicle registration)
KDC knocked-down condition (commerce)
KDF *Kraft durch Freude* (German: Strength Through Joy; Nazi holiday organization)
KDG King's Dragoon Guards
kdlcl knocked down in less than carloads
KDM *Kongelige Danske Marine* (Danish: Royal Danish Navy)
KE kinetic energy; Korean Air (airline flight code, Republic of Korea); Maidstone (UK vehicle registration)
KEAS knots equivalent airspeed (aeronautics)
Keb Keble College (Oxford)
Kef. Keflavik (Iceland)
KEH King Edward's Horse
Ken. Kensington; Kentucky; Kenya
Kent. Kentucky
KEO King Edward's Own
keV kiloelectronvolt (physics)
KEY keep extending yourself
KF Liverpool (UK vehicle registration)
KFA Kenya Farmers' Association
KFAED Kuwait Fund for Arab Economic Development
KFL Kenya Federation of Labour
kfm *kaufmännisch* (German: commercial)
Kfm. *Kaufman* (German: merchant)

Kfz. *Kraftfahrzeug* (German: motor vehicle)
kg keg; kilogram
KG Cardiff (UK vehicle registration); Knight of the Order of the Garter; *Kommanditgesellschaft* (German: limited partnership)
KGB *Komitet Gosudarstvennoi Bezopasnosti* (Russian: Committee of State Security, USSR)
KGC Knight of the Golden Circle (US anti-federal organization); Knight of the Grand Cross
kg cal. kilogram calorie
KGCB Knight Grand Cross of the Bath
KGCSG Knight Grand Cross of the Order of St Gregory the Great
kgf kilogram-force (physics)
Kgf. *Kriegsgefangener* (German: prisoner-of-war)
Kgl. *Königlich* (German: Royal)
Kgn Kingston (Jamaica)
Kgs Kings (Bible)
KGS known geological structure
KGV Knight of Gustavus Vasa (Sweden)
kH kilohertz
KH Hull (UK vehicle registration); kennel huntsman; King's Hussars; Knight of the Hanoverian Order; Kyrnair (airline flight code, Corsica)
KHC Honorary Chaplain to the King
KHDS Honorary Dental Surgeon to the King
KHM King's Harbour Master
KHNS Honorary Nursing Sister to the King
KHP Honorary Physician to the King
KHS Honorary Surgeon to the King; Knight of the Order of the Holy Sepulchre
kHz kilohertz
ki. kitchen
KI Waterford (Irish vehicle registration)
KIA killed in action
KIAS knots indicated airspeed (aeronautics)
kid. kidney
K-i-H Kaiser-i-Hind (Emperor of India; medal)
kil(d). kilderskin (brewing cask)
Kild. Kildare
Kilk. Kilkenny
Kinc. Kincardine (Scotland)
kind. kindergarten
kingd. kingdom
Kinr. Kinross (Scotland)
KIO Kuwait Investment Office

Kirk. Kirkcudbright (Scotland)
KISS keep it simple, stupid (US); Kurs Information Service System (German stock exchange)
kit. kitchen
kJ kilojoule
KJ knee jerk (medicine); Knight of St Joachim; Maidstone (UK vehicle registration)
KJV King James Version (Bible)
KK Kabushiki Kaisha (Japanese: joint stock company); Maidstone (UK vehicle registration)
KKK Ku Klux Klan
KKt king's knight (chess)
KKtP king's knight's pawn
kl kilolitre
KL KLM (Royal Dutch Airlines; airline flight code, Netherlands); Kuala Lumpur; Maidstone (UK vehicle registration)
klax. klaxon
KLH Knight of the Legion of Honour (France)
KLJ Knight of the Order of St Lazarus of Jerusalem
KLM *Koninklijke Luchtvaart Maatschappij* (Dutch: Royal Dutch Airlines)
KLSE Kuala Lumpur Stock Exchange
km kilometre
KM Air Malta (airline flight code); King's Medal; Knight of Malta; Maidstone (UK vehicle registration)
KMO Kobe Marine Observatory (Japan)
kmph kilometres per hour
KMT Kuomintang (Chinese Nationalist Party)
KMUL Karl Marx Universitäy Leipzig
kmw. kilomegawatt
kmwhr kilomegawatt hour
kn knot (nautical); krona (Swedish monetary unit); krone (Danish and Norwegian monetary unit)
KN king's knight; King's Norton (Birmingham mint mark; numismatics); kip (Laotian monetary unit); *Kongeriket Norge* (Norwegian: Kingdom of Norway); Maidstone (UK vehicle registration)
KNA Kenya News Agency; *Kongelig Norsk Automobil-klubb* (Norwegian: Royal Norwegian Automobile Club)
KNM *Kongelige Norske Marine* (Norwegian: Royal Norwegian Navy)
KNP king's knight's pawn (chess); Kruger National Park (South Africa)

KNPC Kuwait National Petroleum Company
Knt Knight
ko keep off; keep out; kick off (football); knock out
KO knock out; Maidstone (UK vehicle registration)
KOC Kuwait Oil Company
KOD kick-off drift (navigation)
K of C Knights of Columbus (Roman Catholic Church)
K of K Kitchener of Khartoum
K of P Knights of Pythias (US)
KOM Knight of the Order of Malta
Komintern *Kommunistícheskii Internatsionál* (Russian: Communist International)
Komp. *Kompanie* (German: company)
Komsomol *Kommunisticheski Soyuz Molodezki* (Russian: Communist Union of Youth)
kop. kopeck (Russian monetary unit)
Kor. Koran; Korea(n)
KORR King's Own Royal Regiment
KOSB King's Own Scottish Borderers
KOYLI King's Own Yorkshire Light Infantry •
kp key personnel
KP Flitestar (airline flight code, South Africa); King's Parade; king's pawn; kitchen police (US military); Knight of the Order of St Patrick; Maidstone (UK vehicle registration)
kpc kiloparsec
KPD *Kommunistische Partei Deutschlands* (German: German Communist Party)
KPDR Korean People's Democratic Party
KPFSM King's Police and Fire Service Medal
kph kilometres per hour
KPL *Khao San Pathet Lao* (news agency, Kampuchea)
KPM King's Police Medal
Kpmtr *Kapellmeister* (German: conductor; music)
KPNLF Khmer People's National Liberation Front
KPNO Kitt Peak National Observatory (US)
KPP Keeper of the Privy Purse
kpr keeper
KPU Kenya People's Union
KQ Kenya Airways (airline flight code); line squall (meteorology)
kr. krona (Swedish monetary unit); króna (Icelandic monetary unit); krone (Danish and Norwegian monetary unit)

Kr krypton (element)
KR King's Regiment; King's Regulations; king's rook; Maidstone (UK vehicle registration)
KRC Knight of the Red Cross
KRE Knight of the Order of the Red Eagle
KRL knowledge representation language (computing)
KRP king's rook's pawn (chess)
KRR King's Royal Rifles
KRRC King's Royal Rifle Corps
krt cathode ray tube
ks storm of drifting snow (meteorology)
KS Edinburgh (UK vehicle registration); Kansas (zip code); Kaposi's sarcoma (medicine); King's Scholar; King's School; Kipling Society; Kitchener Scholar; *Konungariket Sverige* (Swedish; Kingdom of Sweden)
KSC Kennedy Space Center (US); King's School, Canterbury; Knight of St Columba
ksf key success factor
KSG Knight of the Order of St Gregory the Great
KSh Kenya shilling (monetary unit)
KSI Knight of the Order of the Star of India
KSJ Knight of the Order of St John of Jerusalem
ksl kidney, spleen, liver
KSLI King's Shropshire Light Infantry
KSM Korean Service Medal; *Kungliga Svenska Marinen* (Swedish: Royal Swedish Navy)
KSS Knight of the Order of St Silvester
KSSR Kazakh Soviet Socialist Republic
KSSU KLM, SAS, Swissair and UTA (airline organization)
KStJ Knight of the Order of St John of Jerusalem
KSU Kansas State University
kt karat (US); kilotonne; knot (nautical)
Kt Knight
KT Kingston-upon-Thames (UK

postcode); Knight of the Thistle; Knight Templar; knot (meteorology); Maidstone (UK vehicle registration)
Kt Bach. Knight Bachelor
Kto *Konto* (German: account; banking)
KU Kuwait Airways (airline flight code); Sheffield (UK vehicle registration)
KUNA Kuwait News Agency
kutd keep up to date
Kuw. Kuwait
kV kilovolt
KV Coventry (UK vehicle registration); *Köchel Verzeichnis* (German: Köchel catalogue, of Mozart works); Transkei Airways (airline flight code, South Africa)
kVA kilovolt-ampère
kVAr kilovar (electrical engineering)
kVp kilovolt peak
kW kilowatt
KW Kirkwall, Orkney (UK postcode); Sheffield (UK vehicle registration)
kWh kilowatt hour
KWIC key word in context
KWOC key word out of context
KWT Kuwait (international vehicle registration)
KX Cayman Airways (airline flight code); Luton (UK vehicle registration)
ky. kyat (Burmese monetary unit)
Ky Kentucky
KY Kentucky (zip code); Kirkcaldy (UK fishing port registration; postcode); Kol Israel (Israeli broadcasting service); Sheffield (UK vehicle registration)
kybd keyboard
KYODO *Kyodo Tsushini* (news agency, Japan)
Kyr. *Kyrie eleison* (Greek: Lord, have mercy)
kz duststorm or sandstorm (meteorology)
KZ Antrim (UK vehicle registration); killing zone (military); *Konzentration-slager* (German: concentration camp)

L

l lightning (meteorology); liquid (chemistry); lira (Italian monetary unit); litre
l length; orbital angular momentum quantum number (physics)
l. elbow; lake; lambda; land; large; late;

lateral; latitude; law; leaf; league; leasehold; left; legitimate; length; *libra* (Latin: pound sterling); light; line; link; literate; little; loch; long; lost; lough; low
L fifty (Roman numerals); inductor (physics); lambert (physics); language;

learner (driver); lempira (Honduran monetary unit); Liberal; *Libra* (Latin: pound sterling); lift (aeronautics); linear; litre; live (electricity); Liverpool (UK postcode); Luxembourg (international vehicle registration); orbital angular momentum quantum number (physics); stage left (theatre)

L angular momentum (physics); Avogadro constant (chemistry); Lagrangian function (physics); latent heat; length; longitude; luminance (physics); luminosity (astronomy); radiance (physics); self-inductance (electrical engineering); sound intensity (physics)

L. Labour; Lady; Lake; Lancers; large; Latin; law; League; left; lethal; *liber* (Latin: book); Liberal; *libra* (Latin: pound sterling); Licentiate; Lieutenant; line; link; Linnaeus (botany); lira (Italian monetary unit); Loch; *locus* (Latin: place); Lodge; London; Lord; lost (sport); Lough; low

la landing account; leading article; *lege artis* (Latin: as directed; medicine); lighter than air

la. last

La lanthanum (element)

La. Lancastrian; Lane; Louisiana

LA Lancaster (UK postcode); LAN (airline flight code, Chile); large aperture (photography); Latin America; Latin American; law agent; leave allowance; left atrial (medicine); left atrium (medicine); legal adviser; Legislative Assembly; letter of authority; Library Association; Licensing Act; licensing authority; Lieutenant-at-Arms; linear accelerator (physics); Literate in Arts; Liverpool Academy; Llanelly (UK fishing port registration); Lloyd's agent; local agent; local anaesthetic; local association; local authority; long acting; Los Angeles; Louisiana (zip code); low altitude; northwest London (UK vehicle registration)

LAA League of Advertising Agencies (US); Library Association of Australia; Libyan Arab Airlines; Lieutenant-at-Arms; Life Assurance Advertisers (US); light anti-aircraft

LAADS Los Angeles Air Defense Sector (US)

LAAOH Ladies' Auxiliary, Ancient Order of Hibernians

LAAR liquid-air accumulator rocket

lab. label; laboratory; labour; labourer

Lab. Laborite (US); Labour; Labrador

LAB linear alkyl benzene (chemistry); load aboard barge; low-altitude bombing

LABA Laboratory Animal Breeders' Association (US)

lac. lacquer; lactation

LAC Laboratory Animals Centre; leading aircraftman; Licentiate of the Apothecaries' Company; London Athletic Club; long-run average cost (finance)

LACES London Airport cargo electronic processing scheme; Los Angeles Council of Engineering Societies (US)

LACONIQ laboratory computer on-line inquiry (computing)

LACSA *Lineas Aéreas Costarricenses* (Spanish: Costa Rican Airlines)

LACSAB Local Authorities' Conditions of Service Advisory Board

LACW leading aircraftwoman

lad. ladder

LAD language acquisition device (linguistics); light aid detachment

ladar laser detection and ranging

Ladp Ladyship

L. Adv. Lord Advocate

LAE linear algebraic equation (mathematics)

laev. *laevus* (Latin: left)

LaF Louisiana French

LAF *L'Académie Française* (French: French Academy)

LAFC Latin-American Forestry Commission

LAFTA Latin American Free Trade Association

lag. lagoon

Lah. Lahore

LAH Licentiate of the Apothecaries' Hall (Dublin)

LAHS low altitude, high speed

LAI leaf area index (botany); Library Association of Ireland; *Logos Agencia de Informacion* (news agency, Spain)

LAIA Latin American Integration Association

LAL *Laboratoire de l'accélérateur linéaire* (French: Linear Accelerator Laboratory)

lali lonely aged low income

lam. laminate; laminated

Lam. Lamarck (botany); Lamentations (Bible)

LAM *Liberalium Artium Magister* (Latin

Master of the Liberal Arts); London Academy of Music

LAMA Locomotive and Allied Manufacturers' Association of Great Britain

Lamb. Lambeth

LAMC Livestock Auctioneers' Market Committee of England and Wales

LAMCO Liberian-American-Swedish Mineral Corporation

LAMDA London Academy of Music and Dramatic Art

LAMIDA Lancashire and Merseyside Industrial Development Association

Lamp. Lampeter (Wales)

LAMP low-altitude manned penetration; Lunar Analysis and Mapping Program (US)

LAMS launch acoustic measuring system

LAMSAC Local Authorities' Management Services and Computer Committee

LAN inland (meteorology); *Linea Aérea Nacional* (Spanish: National Airlines); local apparent noon; local-area network (computing)

LANBY large automatic navigation buoy

Lanc. Lancaster; Lancers

Lancs. Lancashire

L&D loans and discounts; loss and damage

L&ID London and India Docks

L&NRR Louisville and Nashville Railroad (US)

L&NWR London and North-Western Railway

L&SWR London and South-Western Railway

L&YR Lancashire and Yorkshire Railway

Lan. Fus. Lancashire Fusiliers

lang. language

Lang. Languedoc

LANICA *Lineas Aéreas de Nicaragua* (Spanish: Nicaraguan National Airlines)

LANL Los Alamos National Laboratory (US)

LANRAC Land Army Reunion Association Committee

LanR(PWV) Lancashire Regiment (Prince of Wales' Volunteers)

LANSA *Lineas Aéreas Nacionales* (Spanish: National Airlines; Peru)

Lantirn low-altitude navigation and targeting infrared system (military)

LAO Laos (international vehicle registration); Licentiate in the Art of Obstetrics

LAOAR Latin American Office of Aerospace Research (US Air Force)

Lap. Lapland; Lappish

LAP Laboratory of Aviation Psychology (US); *Lineas Aéreas Paraguayas* (Spanish: Paraguayan Air Lines)

LAPD Los Angeles Police Department

LAPES low-altitude parachute extraction system

LAPO Los Angeles Philharmonic Orchestra

LAPT London Association for the Protection of Trade

LAR leaf area ratio (botany); Libya (international vehicle registration); life assurance relief (taxation); limit address register (computing)

LARA light armed reconnaissance aircraft

larg. *largamente* (Italian: broadly; music); *largeur* (French: width); *largo* (Italian: very slowly; music)

LARO Latin American Regional Office (FAO)

LARSP language assessment, remediation and screening procedure

laryngol. laryngologist; laryngology

LAS Land Agents' Society; large astronomical satellite; League of Arab States; Legal Aid Society; London Archaeological Service; Lord Advocate of Scotland; low-altitude satellite; lower airspace

Laser light amplification by stimulated emission of radiation

LASER London and South Eastern Library Region

LASH lighter aboard ship (commerce)

LASL Los Alamos Scientific Laboratory (US)

LASMO London and Scottish Marine Oil

LASP low-altitude space platform

LASS lighter-than-air submarine simulator

lat. lateral; latitude; *latus* (Latin: wide)

Lat. Latin; Latvia; Latvian

LAT local apparent time; Los Angeles Times

LATCC London air traffic control centre

LATCRS London air traffic control radar station

lat. ht latent heat

Latv. Latvia

Latvn Latvian

lau. laundry

LAUK Library Association of the United Kingdom

laun. launched

LAUTRO Life Assurance and Unit Trust Regulatory Organization

lav. lavatory

LAV light armoured vehicle; *Lineas Aéreas Venezolanas* (Spanish: Venezuelan Airlines); lymphadenopathy-associated virus (HIV)

law. lawyer

LAW League of American Writers; light anti-tank weapon

LAWRS limited airport weather reporting system

LAWS low-altitude wind shear (meteorology)

lax. laxative

LAX Los Angeles international airport

lb landing barge; left back (sport); leg bye (cricket); letter box; *libra* (Latin: pound; weight); link belt

Lb *Lectori benevolo* (Latin: to the kind reader)

LB *Litterarum Baccalaureus* (Latin: Bachelor of Letters); Liberia (international vehicle registration); light bomber; Lloyd Aereo Boliviano (airline flight code); local board; northwest London (UK vehicle registration)

LBA late booking agent (ticket tout)

LB&SCR London, Brighton and South Coast Railway

lb. ap. pound, apothecaries'

lb. av. pound, avoirdupois

LBB leak before break (engineering)

Lbc. Lübeck

LBC Land Bank Commission; London Broadcasting Company

LBCH London Bankers' Clearing House

LBCM Licentiate of the Bandsmen's College of Music; London Board of Congregational Ministers

LBD League of British Dramatists

L/Bdr Lance-Bombardier

lbf pound-force (physics)

lb-ft pound-foot

LBH length, breadth, height

LBJ Lyndon Baines Johnson (US President)

LBO leveraged buy-out (commerce)

LBP length between perpendiculars

lbr labour; lumber

Lbs *Lectori benevolo salutem* (Latin: to the kind reader, greeting)

LBS Libyan Broadcasting Service; lifeboat station; London Business School

LBSM Licentiate of Birmingham and Midland Institute School of Music

LBV landing barge vehicle; late bottled vintage (port wine)

lbt pound troy

lbw leg before wicket (cricket)

LBW live body weight

lc label clause; law courts; lead covered; leading cases; legal currency; letter card; letter of credit; little change (meteorology); *loco citato* (Latin: in the place cited); low-calorie; low-carbon; lower case (printing)

LC Cross of Leo; landing craft; Langerhans cells (medicine); Leander Club; left centre (theatre); Legislative Council; letter of credit; level crossing; Library of Congress (US); Lieutenant-Commander; liquid chromatography (chemistry); livestock commissioner; Loganair (airline flight code, UK); Lord Chamberlain; Lord Chancellor; Lower Canada; northwest London (UK vehicle registration)

L/C letter of credit

LCA Library Club of America; Licensed Company Auditor; low-cost automation

LCAD London Certificate in Art and Design

LCAP loosely coupled array of processors (computing)

lcb longitudinal centre of buoyancy

LCB left centre back (theatre); Liquor Control Board (US); London Convention Bureau; Lord Chief Baron

LCC leadless chip carrier (computing); life-cycle cost (accounting, computing); life-cycle costing (accounting, computing); load-carrying capability (engineering); London Chamber of Commerce; London County Council

LCCC Library of Congress Catalog Card (US)

LCD liquid-crystal display (electronics); Lord Chamberlain's Department; Lord Chancellor's Department; lower court decisions; lowest common denominator (mathematics)

LCDT London Contemporary Dance Theatre

lce lance

LCE Licentiate in Civil Engineering; London Commodity Exchange

lcf longitudinal centre of flotation; lowest common factor (mathematics)

lcg longitudinal centre of gravity

LCGB Locomotive Club of Great Britain

LCh *Licentiatus Chirurgiae* (Latin: Licentiate in Surgery); Lord Chancellor

LCIGB Locomotive and Carriage Institution of Great Britain and Ireland

LCJ Lord Chief Justice

lcl lower control limit

LCL less-than-carload lot (commerce); less-than-container load (commerce); Licentiate in Canon Law

LCLS Livestock Commission Levy Scheme

LCM landing craft mechanized; least common denominator (mathematics); lowest common multiple (mathematics); life-cycle management (computing); London College of Music

Lcn Lincoln

LCN load classification number (aeronautics); local civil noon

LCO landing craft officer; launch control officer

L-Col. Lieutenant-Colonel

L-Corp. Lance-Corporal

LCP last complete programme; least-cost planning; Licentiate of the College of Preceptors; liquid-crystal polymer (chemistry); London College of Printing; low-cost production

LCP&SA Licentiate of the College of Physicians and Surgeons of America

LCP&SO Licentiate of the College of Physicians and Surgeons of Ontario

L/Cpl Lance-Corporal

LCPS Licentiate of the College of Physicians and Surgeons

l/cr *lettre de crédit* (French: letter of credit)

LCS London Cooperative Society

LCSP London and Counties Society of Physiologists

LCST Licentiate of the College of Speech Therapists

LCT landing craft tank; local civil time

lcty locality

LCU large close-up (photography)

LCV Licentiate of the College of Violinists

ld land; lead (printing); legal dose; light difference; line of departure; line of duty; load

Ld Limited (company); Lord

LD *Litterarum Doctor* (Latin: Doctor of Letters or Literature); Lady Day; *Laus Deo* (Latin: praise be to God); learning-disabled; *lepide dictum* (Latin: wittily said); lethal dose; Liberal and Democratic; Libyan dinar (monetary unit); Licentiate in Divinity; Light Dragoons; *Litera Dominicalis* (Latin: Dominical letter); Llandrindod Wells (UK postcode); London Docks; low

density; Low Dutch; northwest London (UK vehicle registration)

L/D letter of deposit

Lda *Sociedade de responsabilidade limitada* (Portuguese: limited company)

LDA Lead Development Association

ldb light distribution box

ldc long-distance call; lower dead centre

LDC least developed country; less-developed country; local distribution company

LDDC London Docklands' Development Corporation

LDEG *laus Deo et gloria* (Latin: praise and glory be to God)

LDentSc Licentiate in Dental Science

Lderry Londonderry

ldg landing; leading; loading; lodging

Ldg Leading (in air force and navy ranks)

Ldge Lodge

L. d'H Légion d'Honneur (France)

LDiv Licentiate in Divinity

ldk lower deck

ldmk landmark

Ldn London

LDN less-developed nation

LDOS Lord's Day Observance Society

Ldp Ladyship; Lordship

LDP Liberal-Democratic Party (Japan); London daily price (finance); long-distance path

LDPE low-density polyethylene (packaging material)

ldr leader; ledger; lodger

LDR low dose rate

ldry laundry

lds loads

LDS Latter-day Saints; *laus Deo semper* (Latin: praise be to God for ever); Licentiate in Dental Surgery

LDSc Licentiate in Dental Science

LDT licensed deposit taker (finance)

LDV Local Defence Volunteers (World War II)

LDX long-distance xerography

LDY Leicestershire and Derbyshire Yeomanry

le leading edge; left eye; library edition; light equipment; limited edition; low explosive

Le leone (monetary unit of Sierra Leone)

Le. Lebanese; Lebanon

LE Egyptian pound (monetary unit); Labour Exchange; Leicester (UK postcode); Link Airways (airline flight code, South Africa); London Electricity;

low energy; northwest London (UK vehicle registration)
lea. league; leather; leave
LEA Local Education Authority
LEAJ Law Enforcement and Administration of Justice (US)
LEAP Life Education for the Autistic Person; lift-off elevation and azimuth programmer; Loan and Educational Aid Programme
Leb. Lebanese; Lebanon
LEB London Electricity Board
LEC Local Enterprise Company
lect. *lectio* (Latin: lesson); lecture; lecturer
lectr lecturer
led. ledger
LED light-emitting diode (electronics)
LEDC Lighting Equipment Development Council
LEFM linear elastic fracture mechanics
leg. legal; legate; legation; *legato* (Italian: bound or smoothly; music); legion; legislation; legislative; legislature; legitimate
legg. *leggero* (Italian: light or rapid; music)
legis. legislation; legislative; legislature
legit. legitimate
Leics. Leicester; Leicestershire
Leip. Leipzig
Leit. Leitrim
LEL Laureate in English Literature
LEM lunar excursion module (astronautics)
LEMA Lifting Equipment Manufacturers' Association
LEO low Earth orbit (astronautics); Lyons Electronic Office (computer)
LEP Large Electron-Positron (CERN collider)
LEPMA Lithographic Engravers' and Plate Makers' Association
LEPORE long-term and expanded program of oceanic research and exploration (US)
LEPRA Leprosy Relief Association
LEPT long-endurance patrolling torpedo
les. lesbian
LES launch escape system; Liverpool Engineering Society
LèsL *Licencié ès lettres* (French: Bachelor of Arts)
LèsS *Licencié ès sciences* (French: Bachelor of Science)
LESS least-cost estimating and scheduling
let. letter

LET linear energy transfer (physics)
LETS Local Employment and Trade System
LEU low-enriched uranium (physics)
lev lunar excursion vehicle
Lev. Levant; Leviticus (Bible)
lex. lexicon
LEX land exercise
lexicog. lexicographer; lexicographic; lexicography
LEY Liberal European Youth
lf leaf; ledger folio; life float; light face (printing)
LF Lancashire Fusiliers; *Linjeflyg* (airline flight code, Sweden); low frequency (radio); northwest London (UK vehicle registration)
lfa local freight agent
LFA less-favoured area
LFAS Licentiate of the Faculty of Architects and Surveyors
LFB London Fire Brigade
LFBC London Federation of Boys' Clubs
lfc low-frequency current
LFC Lutheran Free Church
LFCDA London Fire and Civil Defence Authority
LFD least fatal dose; low-fat diet
LFE laboratory for electronics
Lfg *Lieferung* (German: delivery)
LFO low-frequency oscillator
LFRD lot fraction reliability deviation
lft leaflet
LFTU landing force training unit
lg common logarithm; long
lg. lagoon; large
LG Chester (UK vehicle registration); Lady Companion of the Order of the Garter; landing ground; Lewis gun; Lieutenant-General; Life Guards; David Lloyd George (UK prime minister); London Gazette; Low German; Luxair (airline flight code, Luxembourg)
LGAR Ladies of the Grand Army of the Republic (US)
LGB Local Government Board
LGC lunar (module) guidance computer
lge large; league
LGEB Local Government Examination Board
L-Gen Lieutenant-General
LGer Low German
LGIO Local Government Information Office
LGk Late Greek
LGM little green men; Lloyd's Gold Medal

LGPRA Local Government Public Relations Association
LGr Late Greek
LGR leasehold ground rent; local government reports
LGSM Licentiate of the Guildhall School of Music
LGTB Local Government Training Board
lgth length
lg tn long ton
LGU Ladies' Golf Union
lh left half (sport); left hand; left-handed
LH left half (sport); left hand; left-handed; Leith (UK fishing port registration); licensing hours; Licentiate in Hygiene; Light Horse (military); Lufthansa (airline flight code, Germany); luteinizing hormone (biochemistry); northwest London (UK vehicle registration)
LHA landing helicopter assault; local health authority; local hour angle; Lord High Admiral; lower hour angle
lhb left halfback (sport)
LHC Large Hadron Collider (CERN); Lord High Chancellor
LHCIMA Licentiate of the Hotel Catering and Institutional Management Association
lhd left-hand drive
LHD *Literarum Humaniorum Doctor* (Latin: Doctor of Humanities or Literature)
LHDC lateral homing depth charge
LHeb Late Hebrew
LHMC London Hospital Medical College
LHO livestock husbandry officer
lhr lumen-hour (physics)
LHRC Light and Health Research Council
LHRH luteinizing-hormone-releasing hormone (biochemistry)
LHS left hand side
LHSM Licentiate of the Institute of Health Services Management
LHT Lord High Treasurer
LHWN lowest high water neap (tides)
li letter of introduction; longitudinal interval
li. link; lira (Italian monetary unit)
Li lithium (element)
LI Leeward Islands; Liberal International; Licentiate in Instruction (US); Light Infantry; Lincoln's Inn; Littlehampton (UK fishing port registration); Long Island (New York); Westmeath (Irish vehicle registration)
LIA Laser Industry Association (US); Lead Industries Association (US);

Leather Industries of America; Lebanese International Airways
LIAB Licentiate of the International Association of Book-Keepers
LIAT London International Arbitration Trust
lib. *liber* (Latin: book); liberation; liberty; librarian; library; libretto
Lib. Liberal; Liberia; Libra
LIB *Legum Baccalaureus* (Latin: Bachelor of Laws)
LIBA Lloyd's Insurance Brokers' Association
lib. cat. library catalogue
Lib. Cong. Library of Congress (US)
Lib Dem Liberal Democrat
LIBER *Ligue des bibliothèques européennes de recherche* (French: League of European Research Libraries)
LIBID London Inter-Bank Bid Rate (finance)
LIBOR London Inter-Bank Offered Rate (finance)
libst librettist
lic. licence; licensed
Lic Licentiate
Lic. *Licenciado* (Spanish: Bachelor)
LIC Lands Improvement Company; linear integrated circuit (electronics)
LicAc Licentiate of Acupuncture
LICeram Licentiate of the Institute of Ceramics
LicMed Licentiate in Medicine
LicTheol Licentiate in Theology
LICW Licentiate of the Institute of Clerks of Works
LID *Legum Doctor* (Latin: Doctor of Laws)
lidar light detection and ranging
LIDC Lead Industries Development Council
Lieut. lieutenant
Lieut-Cdr lieutenant-commander
Lieut-Col. lieutenant-colonel
Lieut-Com. lieutenant-commander
Lieut-Gen. lieutenant-general
Lieut-Gov. lieutenant-governor
LIFFE London International Financial Futures and Options Exchange
LIFireE Licentiate of the Institution of Fire Engineers
LIFO last in first out
Lig. Liguria; Limoges
LIHG *Ligne internationale de hockey sur glace* (French: International Ice Hockey Federation)
LILO last in last out
lim. limit; limited

Lim. Limerick
LIM Licentiate of the Institute of Metals
LIMEAN London Inter-Bank Mean Rate
limo limousine
lin. line; lineal; linear; liniment
linac linear accelerator (physics)
Linc. Lincoln College (Oxford)
Lincs. Lincolnshire
lin. ft linear foot
ling. linguistics
Linn. (Carolus) Linnaeus (Swedish botanist)
lino linoleum
LInstP Licentiate of the Institute of Physics
LIOB Licentiate of the Institute of Building
LIP life insurance policy
LIPM Lister Institute of Preventive Medicine
LIPS logical inferences per second (computing)
liq. liquid; liquor
LIRA Linen Industry Research Association
Lis. Lisbon
LISA Library and Information Science Abstracts
LISM Licentiate of the Incorporated Society of Musicians
LISP list processing (computing)
lit. literal; literally; literary; literature; litre; litter; little
Lit lira (Italian monetary unit)
LitB *Litterarum Baccalaureus* (Latin: Bachelor of Letters or Literature)
lit. crit. literary criticism
LitD *Litterarum Doctor* (Latin: Doctor of Letters or Literature)
lith. lithograph; lithography
Lith. Lithuania; Lithuanian
litho(g). lithograph; lithographic; lithography
lithol. lithology
Lit. Hum. *Literae Humaniores* (Latin: faculty of classics and philosophy; Oxford)
LitM *Litterarum Magister* (Latin: Master of Letters or Literature)
Lit. Sup. Times Literary Supplement
LittB *Litterarum Baccalaureus* (Latin: Bachelor of Letters or Literature)
LittD *Litterarum Doctor* (Latin: Doctor of Letters or Literature)
LittM *Litterarum Magister* (Latin: Master of Letters or Literature)
liturg. liturgical; liturgy

LIUNA Laborers' International Union of North America
liv. *livraison* (French: delivery; commerce)
Liv. Liverpool; Livy (Roman historian)
liv. st. *livre sterling* (French: pound sterling)
lj life jacket
LJ Bournemouth (UK vehicle registration); Library Journal; long jump (athletics); Lord Justice; Sierra National Airlines (airline flight code; Sierra Leone)
LJC London Juvenile Courts
LJJ Lords Justices
LK Lerwick (UK fishing port registration); northwest London (UK vehicle registration)
lkd locked
lkg locking
lkg(e) leakage (commerce)
lkr locker
ll live load; *loco laudato* (Latin: in the place quoted); lower left; lower limit
ll. leaves; *leges* (Latin: laws); lines
LL Bell-Air (airline flight code, New Zealand); Late Latin; Law Latin; Law List; Lebanese pound (monetary unit); lending library; Lend Lease; limited liability; Liverpool (UK fishing port registration); Llandudno (UK postcode); London Library; Lord-Lieutenant; lower limb (medicine); Low Latin; northwest London (UK vehicle registration)
LL. laws; lines; Lords
L/L *Lutlang* (Norwegian: limited company)
LLA Lady Literate in Arts
LL. AA. II. *Leurs Altesses Impériales* (French: Their Imperial Highnesses)
LL. AA. RR. *Leurs Altesses Royales* (French: Their Royal Highnesses)
LLB *Legum Baccalaureus* (Latin: Bachelor of Laws)
llc lower left centre
LLCM Licentiate of London College of Music
LLCO Licentiate of the London College of Osteopathy
LLD *Legum Doctor* (Latin: Doctor of Laws)
Llds Lloyd's (insurance)
LLE low-level exposure (radioactivity)
LL. EE. *Leurs Éminences* (French: Their Eminencies); *Leurs Excellences* (French: Their Excellencies)
LLett Licentiate of Letters
LLGDS land-locked and geographically disadvantaged

lli latitude and longitude indicator

LLI Lord Lieutenant of Ireland

LLL Licentiate in Laws; loose leaf ledger; low-level logic (computing)

LLLW liquid low-level waste (radioactivity)

LLM *Legum Magister* (Latin: Master of Laws)

LLMCom Master of Laws in Commercial Law

LL. MM. *Leurs Majestés* (French: Their Majesties)

LLN League for Less Noise

LLNW low-level nuclear waste

LLRW low-level radioactive waste

LLS lunar logistics system (astronautics)

LLSV lunar logistics system vehicle (astronautics)

LLU lending library unit

LLV lunar logistics vehicle (astronautics)

LLW low-level waste (radioactivity)

lm land mine; light metal; *locus monumenti* (Latin: place of the monument); lumen (physics)

l. M. *laufenden Monats* (German: of the current month)

Lm Maltese lira (monetary unit)

LM ALM (Antillean Airlines, airline flight code, Netherlands Antilles); Legion of Merit; Licentiate in Medicine; Licentiate in Midwifery; Licentiate in Music; light metal; liquid metal; load management (engineering); London Museum; long metre (music); Lord Marquis (Scotland); Lord Mayor; lunar module (astronautics); northwest London (UK vehicle registration)

LMA Linoleum Manufacturers' Association; low moisture avidity

LMBC Lady Margaret Boat Club (St John's College, Cambridge); Liverpool Marine Biological Committee

LMC liquid-metal coolant (nuclear engineering); Lloyd's Machinery Certificate; Local Medical Committee

LMCC Licentiate of the Medical Council of Canada

lmd leafmould

LMD local medical doctor; long metre double (music)

LME London Metal Exchange

LMed Licentiate in Medicine

LMG light machine gun

LMH Lady Margaret Hall (Oxford)

LMI Logistics Management Institute (US)

LMO lens-modulated oscillator; light machine oil

LMP last menstrual period (medicine); lunar module pilot

LMR London Midland Region (British Rail)

LMRCP Licentiate in Midwifery of the Royal College of Physicians

LMRSH Licentiate Member of the Royal Society for the Promotion of Health

LMRTPI Legal Member of the Royal Town Planning Institute

LMS laser mass spectrometry; Licentiate in Medicine and Surgery; local management of schools; London Mathematical Society; London Medical Schools; London, Midland and Scottish Railway; London Missionary Society; loss of memory syndrome (medicine)

LMSSA Licentiate in Medicine and Surgery, Society of Apothecaries

LMT length, mass, time (physics); local mean time (astronomy)

LMus Licentiate in Music

LMVD Licensed Motor Vehicle Dealer (New Zealand)

LMW low molecular weight (biochemistry)

LMX London Market Excess of Loss (Lloyd's)

ln natural logarithm

Ln. Lane

LN Jamahiriya Libyan Arab Airlines (airline flight code); King's Lynn (UK fishing port registration); Lincoln (UK postcode); liquid nitrogen; lymph node (medicine); northwest London (UK vehicle registration); Norway (international civil aircraft marking)

LNat Liberal National

LNC League of Nations Covenant

LNER London and North Eastern Railway

LNG liquefied natural gas

Lnrk Lanarkshire

LNS land navigation system

LNT liquid-nitrogen temperature

LNU League of Nations Union

LNWR London and North-Western Railway

lo lubricating oil

l/o *leur ordre* (French: their order)

Lo. loam; local; Lord; low

LO *Landsorganisationen i Sverige* (Swedish: General Federation of Swedish Trade Unions); launch operator; liaison officer; London (UK fishing port registration); London office; LOT-Polish Airlines

(airline flight code); northwest London (UK vehicle registration)
loa length over all
LOA leave of absence; light observation aircraft
LOB left on base (baseball); line of balance; Location of Offices Bureau
LOBAL long-base-line buoy
LOBAR long-base-line radar
loc letter of credit; lines of communication
loc. local; location; locative (grammar)
LOC launch operations centre; Library of Congress (US); locally (meteorology)
LOCA loss-of-coolant accident (nuclear engineering)
loc. cit. *loco citato* (Latin: in the place cited)
loc. laud. *loco laudato* (Latin: in the place cited with approval)
locn location
loco. locomotion; locomotive
loc. primo cit. *loco primo citato* (Latin: in the place first cited)
LOD limit of detection
LOF loss of flow; loss of fluid; loss of function
L of C Library of Congress (US); lines of communication
L of N League of Nations
LOFT low-frequency radio telescope
log. logarithm; logic; logical; logistic
LOH light observation helicopter
LOI lunar orbit insertion
LOLA library on-line acquisition; lunar orbit landing approach
LOM Loyal Order of Moose (US)
LOMA Life Office Management Association (US)
Lomb. Lombard; Lombardy
lon. longitude
Lon(d). London; Londonderry
Londin: *Londiniensis* (Latin: (Bishop) of London)
long. Longitude
Long. Longford
longl longitudinal
Lonrho London Rhodesian (finance)
LOOM Loyal Order of Moose (US)
lop line of position (navigation)
LOPAR low-power acquisition radar
loq. *loquitur* (Latin: he/she speaks)
LOR light output ratio; lunar orbit rendezvous
LORAC long-range accuracy
LORAD long-range detection
LORAN long-range navigation

LORAPH long-range passive homing system
LORCS League of Red Cross and Red Crescent Societies
LORV low observable re-entry vehicle
LOS Latin Old Style; Law of the Seas; line of sight; loss of signal
LOSS large-object salvage system
lot. lotion
Lot *Polskie Linie Lotnicze* (Polish: Polish Air Lines)
LOT large orbital telescope
LOTC London over the Counter market (finance)
Lou. Louisiana
LOX liquid oxygen
loy. loyal; loyalty
LOYA League of Young Adventurers
lp last paid; latent period; launch platform; limp; long primer (type size); low pressure
Lp Ladyship; Lordship
LP Labour Party; large paper (books); large post (paper size); last post; legal procurator; Liberal Party; Libertarian Party; life policy; Limited Partnership; linear programming (computing); liquid petroleum; liquid propellant; northwest London (UK vehicle registration); long playing (gramophone records); Lord Provost; low pressure; lumbar puncture (medicine)
L/P letterpress; life policy
LPA Leather Producers' Association for England; Local Productivity Association
lpc low pressure chamber
LPC Lord President of the Council
LPE London Press Exchange
LPEA Licentiate of the Physical Education Association
LPed Licentiate in Pedagogy
LPG liquefied petroleum gas
LPh Licentiate in Philosophy
lpi lines per inch
lpm lines per millimetre; lines per minute
LPN Licensed Practical Nurse
LPNA Lithographers' and Printers' National Association (US)
LPO local post office; local purchasing officer; London Philharmonic Orchestra
L'pool Liverpool
LPRP Laotian People's Revolutionary Party
LPS London Philharmonic Society; Lord Privy Seal
LPSO Lloyd's Policy Signing Office
LPU low pay unit

lpw lumens per watt (optics)
Lpz. Leipzig
lq *lege quaeso* (Latin: please read)
LQ letter quality (computing)
lqdr liquidator
LQR Law Quarterly Review
LQT Liverpool quay terms (commerce)
lr landing report; log run; long range; long run; lower
lR *laufen de Rechnung* (German: current account)
Lr Lancer; lawrencium (element); ledger; lira (Italian monetary unit)
LR LACSA (airline flight code, Costa Rica); Lancaster (UK fishing port registration); Land Registry; Law Report; left-right; left-to-right; liquor ratio (dyeing); liquor-to-goods ratio (dyeing); Lloyd's Register; Lowland Regiment; Loyal Regiment; northwest London (UK vehicle registration)
LRA Local Radio Association
LRAC Law Reports, Appeal Cases; long-run average cost (finance)
LRAD Licentiate of the Royal Academy of Dancing
LRAM Licentiate of the Royal Academy of Music
LRB London Residuary Body; London Rifle Brigade
LRC Labour Representation Committee; Leander Rowing Club; London Rowing Club
LRCA London Retail Credit Association
LRCh Law Reports, Chancery Division
LRCM Licentiate of the Royal College of Music
LRCP Licentiate of the Royal College of Physicians
LRCPE(d) Licentiate of the Royal College of Physicians of Edinburgh
LRCPI Licentiate of the Royal College of Physicians of Ireland
LRCPSGlas Licentiate of the Royal College of Physicians and Surgeons of Glasgow
LRCS League of Red Cross Societies; Licentiate of the Royal College of Surgeons of England
LRCSE Licentiate of the Royal College of Surgeons of Edinburgh
LRCSI Licentiate of the Royal College of Surgeons in Ireland
LRCVS Licentiate of the Royal College of Veterinary Surgeons
LREC Local Research Ethics Committee (medicine)

LRHL Law Reports, House of Lords
LRIBA Licentiate of the Royal Institute of British Architects
LRKB Law Reports, King's Bench
LRP Law Reports, Probate Division; long-range planning
LRPS Licentiate of the Royal Photographic Society
LRQB Law Reports, Queen's Bench
LRR lower reduced rate (taxation)
Lrs Lancers
LRS Land Registry Stamp; Lloyd's Register of Shipping
LRSC Licentiate of the Royal Society of Chemistry
LRSM Licentiate of the Royal Schools of Music
LRT light rail transit; London Regional Transport; long-range transport
LRTF long-range theatre nuclear forces
LRTI lower respiratory tract infection (medicine)
LRU least recently used; line replaceable unit
LRV light rail vehicle; lunar roving vehicle
LRWES long-range weapons experimental station
ls landing ship; left side; letter signed; litres per second; local sunset; *locus sigilli* (Latin: the place of the seal); long sight; low speed; lump sum
LS Edinburgh (UK vehicle registration); Law Society; Leading Seaman; Leeds (UK postcode); legal seal; Lesotho (international vehicle registration); letter service; Licensed Surveyor; Licentiate in Surgery; liminal sensitivity (psychology); Linnean Society; *locus sigilli* (Latin: place of the seal); London Scottish; London Sinfonietta; long shot (cinema); loudspeaker; Syrian pound (monetary unit)
LSA Land Settlement Association; leading supply assistant; Licence in Agricultural Sciences; Licentiate of the Society of Apothecaries
LSAA Linen Supply Association of America
LS&GCM Long Service and Good Conduct Medal
LSB least significant bit (computing); London School Board
lsc *loco supra citato* (Latin: in the place before cited)
LSC Licentiate in Sciences; London Salvage Corps; Lower School Certificate

LScAct Licentiate in Actuarial Science
LSCF least squares curve fitting (statistics)
LSCS lower segment Caesarean section (obstetrics)
Lsd *Librae, solidi, denarii* (Latin: pounds, shillings and pence)
LSd Sudanese pound (monetary unit)
LSD League of Safe Drivers; least significant digit (computing); Lightermen, Stevedores and Dockers; lysergic acid diethylamide (hallucinogenic drug)
lsd li. leased line
lse limited signed edition
LSE London School of Economics and Political Science; London Stock Exchange
L-Sgt lance-sergeant
LSHTM London School of Hygiene and Tropical Medicine
LSI Labour and Socialist International; large-scale integration (electronics); large-scale integrated (electronics)
LSJ London School of Journalism
LSJM *laus sit Jesu et Mariae* (Latin: praise be to Jesus and Mary)
LSL landing ship logistic; low-speed logic
lsm *litera scripta manet* (Latin: the written word remains)
LSM laser scanning microscope; least-squares method (mathematics, physics); linear synchronous motor (electrical engineering)
LSO London Symphony Orchestra
LSQ line squall (meteorology)
LSS large-scale structure; large-scale system; Licentiate in Sacred Scripture; Lifesaving Service; life-saving station; life-support system
LSSc Licentiate in Sanitary Science
lst local standard time
LST landing ship (for) tanks; landing ship (for) transport; Licentiate in Sacred Theology; local sidereal time (astronomy); local standard time
LSU Louisiana State University
LSZ limited speed zone (New Zealand)
lt landed terms; landing team; large tug; light; local time; *locum tenens* (Latin: holding temporary position); long ton; loop test
Lt Lieutenant; Light (military)
LT Leading Telegraphist; letter telegram; Licentiate in Teaching; Licentiate in Theology; Lithuania (international vehicle registration); London Transport; Lowestoft (UK fishing port registration); low temperature; low tension (electrical engineering); LTU (*Lufttransport-Unternehmen GmbH*, airline flight code, Germany); northwest London (UK vehicle registration); Turkish lira (monetary unit)
LTA Lawn Tennis Association; lighter than air; London Teachers' Association
LTAA Lawn Tennis Association of Australia
LT&SR London, Tilbury and Southend Railway
ltb low-tension battery
LTB London Tourist Board; London Transport Board
LTBT Limited Test Ban Treaty
LTC Lawn Tennis Club
Lt-Cdr lieutenant-commander
LTCL Licentiate of Trinity College of Music, London
Lt-Col. lieutenant-colonel
Lt-Com. lieutenant-commander
Ltd limited (company)
LTDP long-term defence programme
LTE London Transport Executive
LTF Lithographic Technical Foundation
ltg lettering; lighting
ltge lighterage (commerce)
Lt-Gen. lieutenant-general
Lt-Gov. lieutenant-governor
LTh(eol). Licentiate in Theology
LTH light training helicopter
LTI Licentiate of the Textile Institute
LTIB Lead Technical Information Bureau
Lt Inf. Light Infantry
LTL less-than-truckload-lot (US commerce)
LTM Licentiate in Tropical Medicine; London Terminal Market
ltn. lightning
ltng. arr. lightning arrester
LTO leading torpedo operator
LTOM London Traded Options Market
LTOS Law Times, Old Series
ltr letter; lighter; litre
LTRA Lands Tribunal Rating Appeals
LtRN Lieutenant, Royal Navy
LTRS Low Temperature Research Station
LTSC Licentiate of Tonic Sol-Fa College
LTTE Liberation Tigers of Tamil Eelam (Sri Lanka)
lu(g). *luglio* (Italian: July)
l/u laid up; lying up (shipping)
Lu lutetium (element)
Lu. Lucerne
LU Liberal Unionist; northwest London

(UK vehicle registration); loudness unit; Luton (UK postcode); Theron Airways (airline flight code, South Africa)

LUA Liverpool Underwriters' Association

lub(r). lubricant; lubricate; lubrication

LUC London Underwriters Centre

LUCOM lunar communication system

lug. luggage; lugger

LUG light utility glider; local users group (computing)

LUHF lowest useful high frequency (electronics)

LULOP London Union List of Periodicals

lum. lumbago; lumber; luminous

LUM lunar excursion vehicle

LUMAS lunar mapping system

lun. *lundi* (French: Monday); *lunedi* (Italian: Monday); *lunes* (Spanish: Monday)

LUNCO Lloyd's Underwriters Non-Marine Claims Office

LUOTC London University Officers' Training Corps

LUS Land Utilization Survey

LUSCS lower uterine segment Caesarean section (obstetrics)

LUSI lunar surface inspection

lusing. *lusingando* (Italian: coaxing or caressing; music)

LUT launch umbilical tower (astronautics); look-up table (computing)

Luth. Lutheran

lux. luxurious

Lux. Luxembourg

LuxF Luxembourg franc (monetary unit)

lv low voltage

lv. leave; *livre* (French: book)

Lv lev (Bulgarian monetary unit)

LV Argentina (international civil aircraft marking); Latvia (international vehicle registration); licensed victualler; light and variable (meteorology); Liverpool (UK vehicle registration); luncheon voucher

LVA Licensed Victuallers' Association

LVI *laus Verbo Incarnato* (Latin: praise to the Incarnate Word); low viscosity index

LVLO local vehicle licensing office

LVN licensed vocational nurse (US)

LVO Lieutenant of the Royal Victorian Order

lvs leaves

LVS Licentiate in Veterinary Science

LVT landing vehicle, tracked

lw long wave (radio frequency); lumens per watt

LW left wing (sport); light weight; long wave (radio frequency); low water; northwest London (UK vehicle registration)

LWA London Welsh Association

lwb long wheelbase

LWEST low water equinoctial spring tide

LWF Lutheran World Federation

LWL length at waterline (shipping); load waterline (shipping)

LWM low water mark

LWONT low water, ordinary neap tide

LWOST low water, ordinary spring tide

LWR light-water reactor (nuclear engineering)

LWRA London Waste Regulation Authority

LWT London Weekend Television

LWV League of Women Voters (US)

lx lux (physics)

LX Crossair (airline flight code, Switzerland); Luxembourg (international civil aircraft marking); northwest London (UK vehicle registration)

Lxmbrg Luxembourg

LXX Septuagint (Bible)

ly light year

Ly. Lyon (France)

LY El Al Israel Airlines (airline flight code); Lithuania (international civil aircraft marking); Londonderry (UK fishing port registration); northwest London (UK vehicle registration)

lyr. lyric; lyrical; lyrics

LYR layer; layered (meteorology)

LZ Armagh (UK vehicle registration); Bulgaria (international civil aircraft marking)

lzy lazy

M

m metre; milli- (one-thousandth); million
m apparent magnitude (astronomy); magnetic moment (physics); mass (chemistry); meta- (chemistry); molality (chemistry)
m. maiden over (cricket); male; *manipulus* (Latin: handful); mare; mark (monetary unit); married; masculine; master; mate; measure; medical; medicine; medium; memorandum; meridian; *meridies* (Latin: noon); meridional; midday; middle; mile; mill (monetary unit); *mille* (French: 1,000); minim (measure); minor; minute; *misce* (Latin: mix; medicine); mist (meteorology); mixture; moderate; *mois* (French: month); molar (tooth); month; moon; morning; *mort/morte* (French: dead); *morto* (Italian: dead); mountain
M em (printing); loti (monetary unit of Lesotho); Mach (aeronautics); magnetization (physics); Malta (international vehicle registration); Manchester (UK postcode); mature audience (Australian cinema certification); medium (size); mega- (one million); mesomeric effect (chemistry); Messier Catalogue (astronomy); metal (chemistry); Milford (UK fishing port registration); million; minim (measure); Monday; Motorway; mud (cartography); mutual inductance (electrical engineering); sea mile (navigation); 1,000 (Roman numerals)
M absolute magnitude (astronomy); mass; moment (of a force)
M. *Magister* (Latin: Master); magistrate; majesty; Manitoba; March; mark (German monetary unit); marquess; marquis; martyr; master; May; medal; medieval; member; Methodist; metronome (music); metropolitan; *mezza/mezzo* (Italian: half); Middle; militia; minesweeper; Monday; *Monsieur* (French: Mr or Sir); *monte* (Italian: mount); mother; mountain
M1 money in circulation
M3 total money supply
ma manufacturing assembly; map analysis; menstrual age
m/a my account (book-keeping)
mA milliampere (electricity)
Ma Mach number (aeronautics)
Ma. *Mater* (Latin: Mother)

MA Chester (UK vehicle registration); Magistrates' Association; Malev (airline flight code, Hungary); Manpower Administration (US); Maritime Administration (US); Massachusetts (zip code); Master of Arts; Mathematical Association; medieval archaeology; mental age (psychology); Middle Ages; Military Academy; military assistant; military attaché; *Missionarius Apostolicus* (Latin: Apostolic missionary); mobility allowance; Morocco (international vehicle registration); Mountaineering Association
MAA Manufacturers' Agents Association of Great Britain; master-at-arms; Mathematical Association of America; Member of the Architectural Association; Motor Agents' Association; Mutual Aid Association (US); Mutual Assurance Association (US)
MAAF Mediterranean Allied Air Forces
ma'am madam
MA&F Ministry of Agriculture and Fishing
MAAS Member of the American Academy of Arts and Sciences
MAAT Member of the Association of Accounting Technicians
mabp mean arterial blood pressure
MABS marine air base squadron (US)
mac mackintosh (raincoat)
Mac. Macao; Maccabees
MAc Master of Accountancy
MAC maximum allowable concentration; multiplexed analogue component (television); Municipal Assistance Corporation
MACA Mental After Care Association
MACC military aid to the civilian community
MACE Member of the Association of Conference Executives; Member of the Australian College of Education
Maced. Macedonia; Macedonian
mach. machine; machinery; machinist
MACM Member of the Association of Computing Machines
macroecon. macroeconomics
MACS Member of the American Chemical Society
Mad. Madeira
MAD magnetic anomaly detection;

maintenance, assembly and disassembly; major affective disorder (psychiatry); mean absolute deviation; mutual assured destruction

Madag. Madagascar

MADD Mothers Against Drunk Driving (US)

MADO Member of the Association of Dispensing Opticians

Madr. Madras; Madrid

mae mean absolute error

MaE Master in Engineering

MAE Master of Aeronautical Engineering; Master of Art Education; Master of Arts in Education

MA(Econ) Master of Arts in Economics

MA(Ed) Master of Arts in Education

MAEE Marine Aircraft Experimental Establishment

maesto. *maestoso* (Italian: majestic; music)

MAFA Manchester Academy of Fine Arts

MAFF Ministry of Agriculture, Fisheries and Food

mag. magazine; *maggio* (Italian: May); magnesium; magnet; magnetic; magnetism; magneto; magnitude; magnum

Mag. Magyar

MAg Master of Agriculture

Magd Magdalen College (Oxford); Magdalene College (Cambridge)

MAgEc Master of Agricultural Economics

magg. *maggio* (Italian: May); *maggiore* (Italian: major; music)

maglev magnetic levitation

MAgr Master of Agriculture

MAgrSc Master of Agricultural Science

mah(og). mahogany

MAI *Magister in Arte Ingeniaria* (Latin: Master of Engineering); mean annual increment (forestry); Member of the Anthropological Institute

MAIAA Member of the American Institute of Aeronautics and Astronautics

MAIB Marine Accident Investigation Branch

MAICE Member of the American Institute of Consulting Engineers

MAIChE Member of the American Institute of Chemical Engineers

maint. maintenance

MAISE Member of the Association of Iron and Steel Engineers

maj. major; majority

Maj. major (military)

Maj.-Gen. major-general

Mal. Malachi (Bible); Malay; Malayan; Malaysia; Malaysian; Malta; *Maréchal* (French: marshal)

MAL Malaysia (international vehicle registration)

MALD Master of Arts in Law and Diplomacy

mall. malleable

MAM multiple allocation memory (computing)

MAMBO Mediterranean Association for Marine Biology and Oceanography

MAMEME Member of the Association of Mining Electrical and Mechanical Engineers

man. management; manager; manual; manually; manufacture; manufacturer

Man. Manchester; Manila; Manitoba

MAnaes Master of Anaesthesiology

Manch. Manchester; Manchuria

mand. mandamus (High Court order); mandolin (music)

m&b mild and bitter (beer)

M&B May & Baker (pharmaceutical company); Mills & Boon (publishing company)

M&E music and effects

Man. Dir. managing director

m&r maintenance and repairs

m&s maintenance and supply

M&S Marks & Spencer (department stores)

Man. Ed. managing editor

manf. manufacturer

MANF May, August, November, February (finance)

mang. B manganese bronze

Manit. Manitoba

man. op. manually operated

man. pr. *mane primo* (Latin: early in the morning; medicine)

Mans. mansion; mansions

Mansf. Mansfield College (Oxford)

manuf(ac). manufacture; manufactured; manufacturer; manufacturing

Manweb Merseyside and North Wales Electricity Board

MAO Master of Obstetric Art; monoamine oxidase

MAOI monoamine oxidase inhibitor (antidepressant)

MAOT Member of the Association of Occupational Therapists

MAOU Member of the American Ornithologists' Union

MAP major air pollutant; Manufacturing Automation Protocol (computing);

maximum average price; mean arterial blood pressure; medical aid post; Ministry of Aircraft Production; modified American plan (US)
MAppSc Master of Applied Science
MAPsS Member of the Australian Psychological Society
mar. marimba (music); marine; maritime; marriage; married; *martedì* (Italian: Tuesday); *marzo* (Italian: March)
Mar. March
MAR marginal age relief (taxation); Master of Arts in Religion; memory address register (computing)
MARAC Member of the Australasian Register of Agricultural Consultants
marc. *marcato* (Italian: marked; music)
MARC machine-readable cataloguing (bibliography)
March. Marchioness
MArch Master of Architecture
marg. margarine; margin; marginal
mar. insce marine insurance
marit. maritime
mar. lic. marriage licence
MARMAP Marine Resources Monitoring Assessment and Prediction (US)
Marq. marquess; marquis
MARS meteorological automatic reporting station; meteorological automatic reporting system
mart market
mart. martyr
MARV manoeuvrable re-entry vehicle (military)
mas. masculine
MAS Master of Applied Science; Military Agency for Standardization
MASAE Member of the American Society of Agricultural Engineers
masc. masculine
MASc Master of Applied Science
MASC Member of the Australian Society of Calligraphers
MASCE Member of the American Society of Civil Engineers
mascon mass concentration (astronomy)
maser microwave amplification by stimulated emission of radiation
MASH mobile army surgical hospital (US)
MASME Member of the American Society of Mechanical Engineers
Mass. Massachusetts
MA(SS) Master of Arts in Social Science
mat. maternity; matinée; matins; matrix; matte; mature; maturity (finance)

MAT marine, aviation and transport (insurance); Master of Arts in Teaching
MATA multiple answering teaching aid
math. mathematical; mathematically; mathematician; mathematics (Canada, US)
MATh Master of Arts in Theology
maths mathematics
MATIF *marché à terme des instruments financiers* (French: financial futures market)
matr. matrimonial; *matrimonium* (Latin: marriage)
matric. matriculate; matriculation (examination)
MATS Military Air Transport Service (US Air Force)
MATSA Managerial Administrative Technical Staff Association
Matt. Matthew (Bible)
MATTS multiple airborne target trajectory system (military)
MATV master antenna television
Maur. Mauritius
Mau Re Mauritanian rupee (monetary unit)
MAusIMM Member of the Australian Institute of Mining and Metallurgy
MAW marine air wing (US); medium assault weapon
max. maxim; maximum
mb magnetic bearing; main battery; medium bomber; millibar (meteorology); *misce bene* (Latin: mix well); motor barge; motorboat
MB Chester (UK vehicle registration); maritime board; mark of the Beast; marketing board; maternity benefit; Medal of Bravery (Canada); medical board; *Medicinae Baccalaureus* (Latin: Bachelor of Medicine); megabit (electronics); megabyte (computing); methyl bromide (fire retardant); metropolitan borough; millibar (meteorology); motor barge; motorboat; municipal borough; *Musicae Baccalaureus* (Latin: Bachelor of Music)
Mba Mombasa
MBA Master of Business Administration
MBAC Member of the British Association of Chemists
MBAcA Member of the British Acupuncture Association
mbar millibar (meteorology)
MBASW Member of the British Association of Social Workers
mbc maximum breathing capacity

MBC metropolitan borough council; municipal borough council

MBCO Member of the British College of Ophthalmic Opticians/Optometrists

MBCPE Member of the British College of Physical Education

MBCS Member of the British Computer Society

MBdgSc Master of Building Science

MBE Member of the Order of the British Empire

MBF Musicians Benevolent Fund

MBFR mutual and balanced force reduction (military)

mbH *mitbeschränkter Haftung* (German: with limited liability)

MBHI Member of the British Horological Institute

MBIFD Member of the British Institute of Funeral Directors

MBIM Member of the British Institute of Management

MBK missing, believed killed (military)

MBKSTS Member of the British Kinematograph, Sound and Television Society

MBM Master of Business Management

MBNOA Member of the British Naturopathic and Osteopathic Association

MBO management buyout (finance); management by objectives

MBOU Member of the British Ornithologists' Union

MBP mean blood pressure

MBPICS Member of the British Production and Inventory Control Society

MBPsS Member of the British Psychological Society

mbr member

MBR microwave background radiation (astronomy)

MBS Manchester Business School

MBSc Master of Business Science

MBT main battle tank (military); mean body temperature (medicine)

MBuild Master of Building

Mbyte megabyte (computing)

mc megacycle; *mois courant* (French: current month); motorcycle

m/c machine; motorcycle

MC machinery certificate; *Magister Chirurgiae* (Latin: Master of Surgery); Magistrates' Court; magnetic course (navigation); marginal cost; Marine Corps (US); Maritime Commission (US); marriage certificate; Master of Ceremonies; medical certificate; medical college; Medical Corps (US); *Medium Coeli* (Latin: mid-heaven; astronomy); Member of Congress (US); Member of Council; mess committee; Methodist Church; military college; Military Cross; Missionaries of Charity; molecular cloud (astronomy); Monaco (international vehicle registration); Monday Club (politics); Monte Carlo; Morse code; motor contact; northeast London (UK vehicle registration)

M/C Manchester; marginal credit (finance)

MCA Management Consultants' Association; Manufacturing Chemists Association; Master of Commerce and Administration; Matrimonial Causes Act; monetary compensatory amount; multi-channel analyser (electronics); multiple channel analyser (electronics); multi-criteria analysis; multiple classification analysis

MCAB Marine Corps air base (US)

MCAM Member of the CAM Foundation

MC&G mapping, charting and geodesy

MCB Marine Corps Base (US); Master in Clinical Biochemistry; memory control block; miniature circuit breaker; multiple-cratering bomblets (military)

MCBSI Member of the Chartered Building Societies Institute

MCC Manchester Computer Centre; Marylebone Cricket Club; Maxwell Communications Corporation; Melbourne Cricket Club; member of the county council; metropolitan county council; mid-course correction (navigation)

MCCA Minor Counties Cricket Association

MCCC Middlesex County Cricket Club

MCCD RCS Member in Clinical Community Dentistry of the Royal College of Surgeons

MCD Master of Civic Design; Movement for Christian Democracy

MCDS management control data system

MCE Master of Civil Engineering

MCFP Member of the College of Family Physicians (Canada)

MCG Melbourne Cricket Ground

MCGA multi-colour graphics array (computing)

MCGB Master Chef of Great Britain

McGU McGill University (Canada)

Mch. Manchester

MCh(ir) *Magister Chirurgiae* (Latin: Master of or in Surgery)

MChD *Magister Chirurgiae Dentalis* (Latin: Master of Dental Surgery)

MChE Master of Chemical Engineering

MChemA Master in Chemical Analysis

MChOrth *Magister Chirurgiae Orthopaedicae* (Latin: Master of Orthopaedic Surgery)

MChS Member of the Society of Chiropodists

mcht merchant

mchy machinery

mci malleable cast iron

MCIBSE Member of the Chartered Institution of Building Services Engineers

MCIM Member of the Chartered Institute of Marketing

MCIOB Member of the Chartered Institute of Building

M. CIRP *Membre. Collège internationale pour recherche et production* (French: Member of the International Institution for Production Engineering Research)

MCIS Member of the Chartered Institute of Secretaries; Member of the Institute of Chartered Secretaries and Administrators

MCIT Member of the Chartered Institute of Transport

MCL Master of or in Civil Law; maximum contaminant levels; maximum contamination levels

MClinPsychol Master of Clinical Psychology

MCISc Master of Clinical Science

MCM Monte Carlo method (mathematics); multi-stage conventional munitions

MCMES Member of the Civil and Mechanical Engineers' Society

Mco Morocco

mcol. musicological; musicologist; musicology

MCollH Member of the College of Handicrafts

mcolst musicologist

MCom Master of Commerce

MCommH Master of Community Health

MConsE Member of the Association of Consulting Engineers

MCOphth Member of the College of Ophthalmologists

MCP male chauvinist pig; Master of City Planning (US); Member of Colonial Parliament; Member of the College of Preceptors

MCPP Member of the College of Pharmacy Practice

MCPS Mechanical Copyright Protection Society; Member of the College of Physicians and Surgeons

MCR mass communications research; middle common room; mobile control room

MCS Madras Civil Service; Malayan Civil Service; Master of Commercial Science; Military College of Science; monitoring and control system

MCSEE Member of the Canadian Society of Electrical Engineers

MCSP Member of the Chartered Society of Physiotherapy

MCST Member of the College of Speech Therapists

MCT mainstream corporation tax; Member of the Association of Corporate Treasurers

MCU main control unit; medium close-up (photography)

MCW modulated continuous wave (telecommunications)

Md Maryland; mendelevium (element)

M/d months after date (commerce)

MD Air Madagascar (airline flight code); *main droite* (French: right hand); malicious damage; managing director; *mano destra* (Italian: right hand); map distance; market day; Maryland (zip code); medical department; *Medicinae Doctor* (Latin: Doctor of Medicine); memorandum of deposit (banking); mentally deficient; mess deck; Middle Dutch; military district; mini-disc; molecular dynamics; Monroe Doctrine; musical director; northeast London (UK vehicle registration)

MDA methylenedioxyamphetamine (hallucinogenic drug); minimum detectable activity; minimum detectable amount; monochrome display adaptor (computing); multiple disciminant analysis (finance); Muscular Dystrophy Association

MDAM multi-dimensional access memory (computing)

MDAP Mutual Defense Assistance Program (US)

M-day mobilization day (US)

MdB *Mitglied des Bundestag* (German: Member of the Bundestag)

MDB *Movimento Democrático Brasileiro*

(Spanish: Brazilian Democratic Movement)

MDC metropolitan district council; minimum detectable concentration; modification and design control; more developed country

MDD minimal detectable dose

Mddx Middlesex

MDentSc Master in Dental Science

MDes Master of Design

MDG medical director-general

MDHB Mersey Docks and Harbour Board

m. dict. *more dicto* (Latin: in the manner directed; medicine)

MDip Master of Diplomacy

mdise merchandise

MDiv Master of Divinity

mdl model

MDL minimum detectable level (radioactivity)

Mdlle *Mademoiselle* (French: Miss)

Mdm Madam

MDMA methylenedioxy-methamphetamine (hallucino-genic drug; Ecstacy)

Mdme *Madame* (French: Mrs)

mdn median

mdnt midnight

MDP Mongolian Democratic Party

MDQ minimum detectable quantity

MDR memory data register (computing); minimum daily requirement

Mds *Mesdames* (French: Ladies)

MDS main dressing station; Master of Dental Surgery

MDSc Master of Dental Science

mdse merchandise

MDT mean downtime (computing); Mountain Daylight Time (US)

MDu Middle Dutch

MDU Medical Defence Union

MDV Doctor of Veterinary Medicine

MDW military defence works

Mdx Middlesex

me maximum effort; mobility equipment

Me Maine (US); *Maître* (French: Master; law); Messerschmitt (German aircraft); methyl (chemistry)

ME Maine (zip code); managing editor; marine engineer; marine engineering; marriage encounter (US); Master of Education; Master of Engineering; mechanical engineer; mechanical engineering; Medical Examiner (US); Medway (UK postcode); metabolizable energy (medicine); Methodist Episcopal; Middle East; Middle Eastern; Middle

East Airlines (airline flight code, Lebanon); Middle English; military engineer; milled edge; mining engineer; mining engineering; Montrose (UK fishing port registration); Most Excellent; mottled edges (books); myalgic encephalomyelitis; northeast London (UK vehicle registration)

MEA Member of the European Assembly; Middle East Airlines

MEAF Middle East Air Force

meas. measurable; measure; measurement

MEB Midlands Electricity Board

MEBA/NMU Marine Engineer Beneficial Association/National Maritime Union (US)

MEc Master of Economics

MEC marginal efficiency of capital (finance); Master of Engineering Chemistry; Member of Executive Council; Methodist Episcopal Church; Middle East Command

MECAS Middle East Centre for Arab Studies

mech. mechanic; mechanics; mechanical; mechanically; mechanism; mechanize; mechanized

MechE Mechanical Engineer

ME(Chem) Master of Chemical Engineering

MECI Member of the Institute of Employment Consultants

MECO main engine cut off (astronautics)

MEcon Master of Economics

med. medal; medallist; median; medical; medicine; medieval; medium

Med. Mediterranean

MEd Master of Education

MED maximum equivalent dose; minimum effective dose; Municipal Electricity Department (New Zealand)

Med. Gr. Medieval Greek

medic medical practitioner; medical student

Medico Medical International Corporation (US); Medical Corporation Organization (US)

Medit. Mediterranean

med. jur. medical jurisprudence

MEDLARS Medical Literature Analysis and Retrieval System (US)

Med. Lat. Medieval Latin

MedRC Medical Reserve Corps

MedScD Doctor of Medical Science

med. tech. medical technician; medical technology

MEE Master of Electrical Engineering
ME(Elec) Master of Electrical Engineering
MEF Mediterranean Expeditionary Force; Middle East Force
meg megabyte (computing)
meg. megacycle; megaton; megawatt; megohm
mega- one million
MEIC Member of the Engineering Institute of Canada
Mej. *Mejuffrouw* (Dutch: Miss)
MEK methyl ethyl ketone (solvent)
Melan. Melanesia; Melanesian
Melb. Melbourne
MELF Middle East Land Forces
mem. member; *memento* (Latin: remember); memoir; memoirs; memorandum; memorial
ME(Mech) Master of Mechanical Engineering
memo. memorandum
MENA Middle East News Agency
Mencap Royal Society for Mentally Handicapped Children and Adults
MEng Master of Engineering
mensur. mensuration
mentd mentioned
MEO marine engineering officer
MEP *Mahajana Eskath Peramuna* (Sinhalese: People's United Front; Sri Lanka); Master of Engineering Physics; mean effective pressure; Member of the European Parliament
MEPA Master of Engineering and Public Administration
mer. mercantile; merchandise; *mercoledì* (Italian: Wednesday); *mercredi* (French: Wednesday); mercury; meridian; meridional
Mer. Merionethshire
merc. mercantile; *mercoledì* (Italian: Wednesday); mercury
Merc. Mercedes
MERLIN medium energy reactor, light water industrial neutron source; multi-element radio-linked interferometer network (astronomy)
Mert. Merton College (Oxford)
MèsA *Maître ès arts* (French: Master of Arts)
MESc Master of Engineering Science
Messrs *Messieurs* (French: gentlemen)
met. metallurgical; metallurgist; metallurgy; metaphor; metaphysical; metaphysics; meteorological; meteorology; metronome; metropolitan

Met. Metropolitan Opera House (New York); Metropolitan Police
metal(l). metallurgical; metallurgy
metaph. metaphor; metaphorical; metaphysical; metaphysically; metaphysics
METAR meteorological airfield report
met. bor. metropolitan borough
MetE Metallurgical Engineer
meteor(ol). meteorological; meteorology
Meth. Methodist
meths methylated spirits
M-et-L Maine-et-Loire (French department)
M-et-M Meurthe-et-Moselle (French department)
m. et n. *mane et nocte* (Latin: morning and night; medicine)
MetR Metropolitan Railway (London)
Metro *Chemin de fer métropolitan* (French: metropolitan railway; Paris underground railway system)
metrol. metrological; metrology
metrop(ol). metropolis; metropolitan
metsat meteorological satellite
Mev. *Mevrouw* (Dutch: Miss)
MeV megaelectronvolt
MEW measure of economic welfare (finance); microwave early warning (system) (military)
Mex. Mexican; Mexico
MEX Mexico (international vehicle registration)
MEXE Military Engineering Experimental Establishment
Mex. Sp. Mexican Spanish
mez. *mezzo/mezza* (Italian: half or medium; music)
Mez mezzo-soprano
MEZ *Mitteleuropäische Zeit* (German: Central European Time)
mezzo. mezzotint
mf *mezzo forte* (Italian: moderately loudly; music); motherfucker
mF millifarad
MF machine finish (paper); machine finished (paper); magnetic field; Master of Forestry; medium frequency (telecommunications); melamine-formaldehyde; Middle French; mill finish; motherfucker; multi-frequency; northeast London (UK vehicle registration)
M/F male or female
MFA Master of Fine Arts
MFAMus Master of Fine Arts in Music
MFARCS Member of the Faculty of

Anaesthetists of the Royal College of
Surgeons
MFB Metropolitan Fire Brigade
MFC Mastership in Food Control; motor-
fuel consumption
MFCM Member of the Faculty of
Community Medicine
mfd manufactured
MFD minimum fatal dose
mfg manufacturing
MFH Master of Foxhounds; mobile field
hospital
MFHom Member of the Faculty of
Homeopathy
MFlem Middle Flemish
MFLOPS million floating-point
operations per second (computing)
MFM modified frequency modulation
(computing)
MFN most favoured nation (commerce)
MFOM Member of the Faculty of
Occupational Medicine
MFP mean free path (physics)
MFPA Mouth and Foot Painting
Artists
mfr. manufacture; manufacturer
MFr Middle French
mfre manufacture
MFS Master of Food Science; Master of
Foreign Study
mfst manifest
mft moto freight tariff
m. ft. *mistura fiat* (Latin: let a mixture be
made; medicine)
MFV motor fleet vessel
mg milligram; mixed grain; morning
Mg magnesium (element)
MG machine-glazed (paper); machine
gun; *main gauche* (French: left hand);
Major-General; make good (building);
Morris Garages (sports cars); motor
generator; northeast London (UK
vehicle registration)
MGA Major-General in charge of
Administration; Mushroom Growers'
Association
mgawd make good all works disturbed
MGB metropolitan green belt;
Ministerstvo Gosudarstvennoi Bezopasnosti
(Russian: Ministry of State Security;
Soviet secret police); motor gunboat
MGC Machine Gun Corps; Marriage
Guidance Council; Marriage Guidance
Councillor
mg. cu. m. milligrammes per cubic
metre
MGD million gallons a day

MGDS RCS Member in General Dental
Surgery of the Royal College of
Surgeons
mge message
MGGS Major-General, General Staff
MGI Member of the Institute of
Certificated Grocers
MGk Medieval Greek; Modern Greek
M. Glam Mid Glamorgan
MGM Metro-Goldwyn-Mayer (US cinema
studios); mobile guided missile
MGN Mirror Group Newspapers
Mgn Dir. Managing Director
MGO Master General of the Ordnance;
Master of Gynaecology and
Obstetrics
MGP manufactured-gas plant
mgr manager
Mgr Manager; *Monseigneur* (French: my
lord); Monsignor (Roman Catholic
Church)
MGr Medieval Greek
MGR modular gas-cooled reactor (nuclear
engineering)
Mgrs Managers; *Monseigneurs* (French:
my lords); Monsignors (Roman Catholic
Church)
mgs metre-gram-second
mgt management
mH millihenry (physics)
MH magnetic heading (navigation); main
hatch (nautical); Malaysian Airlines
(airline flight code); marital history;
Master of Horse; Master of Horticulture;
Master of Hounds; Master of Hygiene;
Medal of Honor (US); mental health;
Middlesbrough (UK fishing port
registration); military hospital; Ministry
of Health; northeast London (UK vehicle
registration)
MHA Master in Hospital Administration
(US); Member of the House of Assembly
(Australia, Canada); Mental Health
Administration (US); Methodist Homes
for the Aged
MHCIMA Member of the Hotel Catering
and Institutional Management
Association
MHD magnetohydrodynamics (physics)
MHE Master of Home Economics
MHeb Middle Hebrew
MHF massive hydraulic fracture; massive
hydraulic fracturing; medium high
frequency
MHG Middle High German
MHK Member of the House of Keys (Isle
of Man)

MHLG Ministry of Housing and Local Government
M. Hon. Most Honourable
MHortSc Master of Horticultural Science
MHR Member of the House of Representatives (Australia, US)
MHRA Modern Humanities Research Association
MHRF Mental Health Research Fund
MHS medical history sheet; Member of the Historical Society; message-handling system (computing)
MHTGR modular high-temperature gas-cooled reactor (nuclear engineering)
MHum Master of Humanities
MHW mean high water
MHWNT mean high water neap tide
MHWST mean high water spring tide
MHy Master of Hygiene
MHz megahertz
mi. mile; mill (monetary unit; Canada, US); minute
Mi. Minor; Mississippi
MI malleable iron; Marshall Islands (international civil aircraft marking); Michigan (zip code); Military Intelligence; Ministry of Information; moment of inertia; mounted infantry; myocardial infarction (medicine); Wexford (Irish vehicle registration)
MI5 Military Intelligence, section five (UK counter-intelligence organization)
MI6 Military Intelligence, section six (UK intelligence and espionage organization)
MIA Master of International Affairs; missing in action
MIAA&S Member of the Incorporated Association of Architects and Surveyors
MIAeE Member of the Institute of Aeronautical Engineers
MIAgrE Member of the Institution of Agricultural Engineers
MIAM Member of the Institute of Administrative Management
MIAP Member of the Institution of Analysts and Programmers
MIAS Member of the Institute of Accounting Staff
MIBE Member of the Institution of British Engineers
MIBF Member of the Institute of British Foundrymen
MIBiol Member of the Institute of Biology
MIBK methyl isobutyl ketone (solvent)
MIBritE Member of the Institution of British Engineers

MIB(Scot) Member of the Institute of Bankers in Scotland
Mic. Micah (Bible)
MICE Member of the Institution of Civil Engineers
MICEI Member of the Institution of Civil Engineers of Ireland
MICFor Member of the Institute of Chartered Foresters
Mich. Michaelmas; Michigan
MIChemE Member of the Institution of Chemical Engineers
MICorrST Member of the Institution of Corrosion Science and Technology
MICR magnetic ink character recognition (computing)
micro(s). microscope; microscopist; microscopy
micro- one-millionth part
Micro. Micronesia
microbiol. microbiology
MICS Member of the Institute of Chartered Shipbrokers
MICV mechanized infantry combat vehicle (military)
mid. middle; midnight
Mid. Midlands; Midshipman
MIDAS measurement information and data analysis (computing); missile defence alarm system
Midd(l)x Middlesex
MIDELEC Midlands Electricity Board
MIDI musical instrument digital interface
Midl. Midlands; Midlothian
Mid. Lat. Middle Latin
MIDPM Member of the Institute of Data Processing Management
midw. midwest; midwestern
MIE(Aust) Member of the Institution of Engineers, Australia
MIED Member of the Institution of Engineering Designers
MIEE Member of the Institution of Electrical Engineers
MIEEE Member of the Institute of Electrical and Electronics Engineers
MIEI Member of the Institution of Engineering Inspection
MIE(Ind) Member of the Institution of Engineers, India
MIES Member of the Institution of Engineers and Shipbuilders, Scotland
MIEx Member of the Institute of Export
MIExpE Member of the Institute of Explosives Engineers
MIF milk in first (tea-making)

MIFA Member of the Institute of Field Archaeologists
MIFF Member of the Institute of Freight Forwarders
MIFG shallow fog (meteorology)
MIFireE Member of the Institute of Fire Engineers
MiG Mikoyan and Gurevich (Russian fighter aircraft)
MIG metal-inert gas
MIGasE Member of the Institution of Gas Engineers
MIGeol Member of the Institution of Geologists
MIH Master of Industrial Health; Member of the Institute of Housing
MIHort Member of the Institute of Horticulture
MIHT Member of the Institution of Highways and Transportation
MIIE Member of the Institution of Industrial Engineers
MIIM Member of the Institute of Industrial Managers
MIInfSc Member of the Institute of Information Sciences
mike microphone
mil. mileage; military; militia
Mil. Milan
MIL Member of the Institute of Linguists; one million (US)
Mil. Att. military attaché
MILGA Member of the Institute of Local Government Administrators
milit. military
mill. million; *millionen* (German: million)
milli- one-thousandth part
MILocoE Member of the Institution of Locomotive Engineers
Milw. Milwaukee
MIM Member of the Institute of Metals
MIMarE Member of the Institute of Marine Engineers
MIMC Member of the Institute of Management Consultants
MIMD multiple instruction, multiple data (computing)
MIMechE Member of the Institution of Mechanical Engineers
MIMGTechE Member of the Institution of Mechanical and General Technician Engineers
MIMI Member of the Institute of the Motor Industry
MIMinE Member of the Institution of Mining Engineers

MIMM Member of the Institution of Mining and Metallurgy
MIMS Monthly Index of Medical Specialties
MIMT Member of the Institute of the Motor Trade
MIMunE Member of the Institution of Municipal Engineers
min. mineralogical; mineralogy; minim (measure); minimum; mining; ministerial; minor; minute
Min. Minister; Ministry
MIND National Association for Mental Health
mineral. mineralogical; mineralogy
Minn. Minnesota
Min. Plen. Minister Plenipotentiary
Min. Res. Minister Resident; Minister Residentiary
MINS minor in need of supervision
MInstAM Member of the Institute of Administrative Management
MInstBE Member of the Institution of British Engineers
MInstD Member of the Institute of Directors
MInstE Member of the Institute of Energy
MInstEnvSci Member of the Institute of Environmental Sciences
MInstMC Member of the Institute of Measurement and Control
MInstME Member of the Institution of Mining Engineers
MInstMM Member of the Institution of Mining and Metallurgy
MInstP Member of the Institute of Physics
MInstPet Member of the Institute of Petroleum
MInstPI Member of the Institute of Patentees and Inventors
MInstPkg Member of the Institute of Packaging
MInstPS Member of the Institute of Purchasing and Supply
MInstR Member of the Institute of Refrigeration
MInstRA Member of the Institute of Registered Architects
MInstT Member of the Institute of Transport
MInstTM Member of the Institute of Travel Managers in Industry and Commerce
MInstWM Member of the Institute of Wastes Management

MINucE Member of the Institution of Nuclear Engineers

min. wt minimum weight

Mio Miocene (geology)

MIOB Member of the Institute of Building

MIOSH Member of the Institution of Occupational Safety and Health

mip mean indicated pressure

MIP marine insurance policy; maximum investment plan; Member of the Institute of Plumbing; monthly investment plan

MIPA Member of the Institute of Practitioners in Advertising

MIPM Member of the Institute of Personnel Management

MIPR Member of the Institute of Public Relations

MIProdE Member of the Institution of Production Engineers

MIPS million instructions per second (computing)

MIQ Member of the Institute of Quarrying

MIr Middle Irish

MIRA Member of the Institute of Registered Architects; Motor Industry's Research Association

MIRAS mortgage interest relief at source

MIRD medical internal radiation dose

MIRED micro reciprocal degrees

MIREE(Aust) Member of the Institution of Radio and Electronics Engineers (Australia)

MIRT Member of the Institute of Reprographic Technicians

MIRTE Member of the Institute of Road Transport Engineers

MIRV multiple independently targetted re-entry vehicle (military)

Mis Mississippian (geology)

MIS management information system; manufacturing information system; marketing information system; Member of the Institute of Statisticians; meteorological information system; Mining Institute of Scotland

misc. miscellaneous; miscellany

MISD multiple instruction, single data (computing)

MIS(India) Member of the Institution of Surveyors (India)

miss. miscarriage

Miss. Mission; Missionary; Mississippi

mist. *mistura* (Latin: mixture; medicine)

mistrans. mistranslation

MIStructE Member of the Institution of Structural Engineers

Mit. *Mittwoch* (German: Wednesday)

MIT Massachusetts Institute of Technology

MITA Member of the Industrial Transport Association

MITD Member of the Institute of Training and Development

MITE Member of the Institution of Electrical and Electronics Technician Engineers

MITI Ministry of International Trade and Industry (Japan)

MITL magnetically insulated transmission line

MITT Member of the Institute of Travel and Tourism

Mitts minutes of telecommunications traffic

MIWEM Member of the Institution of Water and Environmental Management

mixt. mixture

MJ Luton (UK vehicle registration); megajoule; Ministry of Justice

MJA Medical Journalists' Association

MJD management job description

MJI Member of the Institute of Journalists

MJQ Modern Jazz Quartet

MJS Member of the Japan Society

MJSD March, June, September, December (finance)

MJur *Magister Juris* (Latin: Master of Law)

mk mark (German monetary unit); markka (Finnish monetary unit)

Mk mark (category or model)

MK Air Mauritius (airline flight code); Malawi kwacha (monetary unit); Milton Keynes (UK postcode); northeast London (UK vehicle registration)

mkd marked

MKO Mauna Kea Observatory (Hawaii)

mks marks (monetary units); metre-kilogram-second

mksA metre-kilogram-second-ampere

mkt market

ml machine language; mail; mean level; millilitre; mine-layer

ML Licentiate in Midwifery; Master of Law; Master of Laws; Master of Letters; maximum likelihood (statistics); *Medicinae Licentiatus* (Latin: Licentiate in Medicine); Medieval Latin; Methil (UK fishing port registration); Motherwell (UK postcode); motor launch; muzzle-loading (firearms); northeast London (UK vehicle registration)

MLA Master in Landscape Architecture;

Master of Landscape Architecture;
Master of the Liberal Arts; Medical
Library Association; Member of the
Legislative Assembly; Modern Language
Association (US)
MLArch Master in Landscape
Architecture; Master of Landscape
Architecture
MLC Meat and Livestock Commission;
Member of the Legislative Council
(Australia, India)
MLCOM Member of the London College
of Osteopathic Medicine
mld mould; moulded
MLD Master of Landscape Design;
minimal lethal dose
mldg moulding
mle maximum loss expectancy
MLF *Mouvement de libération des femmes*
(French: Women's Liberation
Movement); multilateral (nuclear) force
(military)
MLG Middle Low German
MLib(Sc) Master of Library Science
MLitt *Magister Litterarum* (Latin: Master of
Letters)
Mlle *Mademoiselle* (French: Miss)
MLO military liaison officer
MLR minimum lending rate; Modern
Language Review; multiple linear
regression (statistics)
MLRS multiple-launch rocket system
MLS Master of Library Science; medium
long shot (cinema); microwave landing
system (aeronautics); mixed language
system; multi-language system
MLSO medical laboratory scientific
officer
MLW mean low water
MLWN(T) mean low water neap (tide)
MLWS(T) mean low water spring (tide)
mm made merchantable; millimetre;
mutatis mutandis (Latin: with the
necessary changes)
m'm madam
MM Maelzel's metronome (music);
maintenance manual; Majesties;
malignant melanoma (medicine);
Martyrs; Master Mason (Freemasonry);
Master Mechanic; Master of Music;
Medal of Merit; mercantile marine;
Messieurs (French: gentlemen); Military
Medal; music master; northeast London
(UK vehicle registration)
MMA Metropolitan Museum of Art;
Music Masters' Association
MMath Master of Mathematics

MMB Milk Marketing Board
MMC Monopolies and Mergers
Commission
MMD Movement for Multi-party
Democracy (Zambia)
MMDA money market deposit account
(US)
MMDS multi-point microwave
distribution system (radio)
Mme *Madame* (French: Mrs)
MME Master of Mechanical Engineering;
Master of Mining Engineering; Master of
Music Education
MMechE Master of Mechanical
Engineering
MMed Master of Medicine
MMedSci Master of Medical Science
Mmes *Mesdames* (French: Ladies)
MMet Master of Metallurgy
MMetE Master of Metallurgical
Engineering
mmf magnetomotive force (physics)
MMG medium machine gun (military)
MMGI Member of the Mining, Geological
and Metallurgical Institute of India
mmHg millimetre of mercury
MMI man-machine interaction; man-
machine interface; Municipal Mutual
Insurance
MMin Master of Ministry
MMM Member of the Order of Military
Merit (Canada)
MMO medium machine oil
mmp mixture melting point (chemistry)
MMP Military Mounted Police
MMQ minimum manufacturing
quantity
MMR mass miniature radiography
(medicine); measles, mumps, rubella
MMRBM mobile medium-range ballistic
missile (military)
MMS Marine Meteorological Services;
Member of the Institute of Management
Services; Methodist Missionary Society;
Moravian Missionary Society; multi-
mission modular spacecraft
MMSA Master of Midwifery of the
Society of Apothecaries
MMSc Master of Medical Science
MMT methylcyclopentadienyl manganese
tricarbonyl (petrol additive)
MMU memory management unit
(computing); million monetary units
(finance)
MMus Master of Music
MMusEd Master of Musical Education
mn *maison* (French: house); million;

mutato nomine (Latin: with the name changed)

mn. midnight

Mn manganese (element); Modern

MN Commercial Airways (airline flight code, South Africa); magnetic north; Maldon (UK fishing port registration); Master of Nursing; Merchant Navy; Minnesota (zip code)

MNA Master of Nursing Administration; Member of the National Assembly (Quebec)

MNAD Multi-National Airmobile Division (NATO)

MNAEA Member of the National Association of Estate Agents

MNAS Member of the National Academy of Sciences (US)

MNC multi-national company

MND Ministry of National Defence

MnE Modern English

MNE multi-national enterprise

MNECInst Member of the North East Coast Institution of Engineers and Shipbuilders

mng managing

MnGk Modern Greek

mngmt management

mngr manager

MnGr Modern Greek

MNI Member of the Nautical Institute

MNIMH Member of the National Institute of Medical Herbalists

Mnl. Manila

mnm minimum

Mnr *Mjnheer* (Dutch: Mr or Sir)

MNR marine nature reserve; mean neap rise (tides); Mozambique National Resistance

MNT mean neap tide

MNurs Master of Nursing

mo mail order; modus operandi; money order

m-o months old

mo. moment; month; mouth

Mo molybdenum (element)

Mo. Missouri; Monday

MO mail order; manually operated; mass observation; Master of Obstetrics; Master of Oratory; medical officer; medical orderly; meteorological office; military operations; Missouri (zip code); modus operandi; money order; monthly order; motor-operated; municipal officer; Reading (UK vehicle registration)

MoA Ministry of Aviation

MOA memorandum of agreement

MO&G Master of Obstetrics and Gynaecology

mob. mobile; mobilization; mobilize

mobizn. mobilization

MOBS multiple-orbit bombardment system

MoC mother of the chapel (trade unions)

MOC management and operating contractor

mod. moderate; *moderato* (Italian: moderate tempo; music); modern; modification; modified; modulus (mathematics)

MoD Ministry of Defence

MOD mail order department; Ministry of Overseas Development

mod. cons. modern conveniences

mod. dict. *modo dicto* (Latin: as prescribed; medicine)

modem modulator demodulator (computing)

modif. modification

mod. praes. *modo praescripto* (Latin: in the manner directed; medicine)

Mods Honour Moderations (Oxford University examination)

modto *moderato* (Italian: moderate tempo; music)

MODU mobile offshore drilling unit

MOEH medical officer for environmental health

M of A Ministry of Agriculture, Fisheries and Food

M of W Ministry of Works

MoH Ministry of Housing and Local Government

MOH Master of Otter Hounds; Medal of Honor; medical officer of health

MOHLG Ministry of Housing and Local Government

Moho Mohorovicic Discontinuity (geology)

MOI military operations and intelligence; Ministry of Information; Ministry of the Interior

mol mole (chemistry)

mol. molecular; molecule

MOL manned orbital laboratory (astronautics); Ministry of Labour

Mold(v). Moldavia; Moldavian

mol. wt molecular weight

mom middle of month

MOM milk of magnesia

MOMA Museum of Modern Art (New York)

MOMI Museum of the Moving Image (London)

mon. monastery; monastic; monetary; monitor; monsoon

Mon. Monaco; Monaghan; Monday; Monmouthshire; *Montag* (German: Monday); Montana

MONEP *Marché des options négotiables de Paris* (French: Paris traded option market)

Mong(ol). Mongolia; Mongolian

Monm. Monmouthshire

monog. monograph

Mons. *Monsieur* (French: Mr)

Mont. Montana; Montgomeryshire

Montgom. Montgomeryshire

Montr. Montreal

mop mother-of-pearl

MOPA master oscillator power amplifier (electronics)

moped motorized pedal cycle

MOPH Military Order of the Purple Heart (US)

MOPS mail order protection scheme

mor. *morendo* (Italian: dying away; music); morocco (bookbinding)

Mor. Moroccan; Morocco

MOR middle of the road

MORC Medical Officer Reserve Corps

mor. dict. *more dicto* (Latin: in the manner directed; medicine)

MORI Market and Opinion Research International

morn. morning

morph. morphological; morphology

mor. sol. *more solito* (Latin: in the usual manner; medicine)

mort. mortal; mortality; mortar; mortgage; mortuary

mos. months

Mos. Moscow; Moselle

MOS magneto-optical system; metal-oxide-silicon (electronics); metal-oxide semiconductor (electronics); Ministry of Supply

mot. motor; motorized

MoT Ministry of Transport

MOTNE meteorological operational telecommunications network

MOUSE minimum orbital unmanned satellite of the earth

mov. *movimento* (Italian: movement; music)

MOV motor-operated valve (engineering)

movt movement

MOW Ministry of Works (New Zealand)

Moz. Mozambique

mp meeting point; melting point; *mezzo piano* (Italian: moderately softly; music); mile post (cartography); months after payment; mooring post

MP Madhya Pradesh (India); medium pressure; Member of Parliament; Mercator's projection (cartography); Methodist Protestant; Metropolitan Police; mile post (cartography); Military Police; Military Policeman; *mille passum* (Latin: 1,000 paces); Minister Plenipotentiary; miscellaneous papers; miscellaneous publications; Mounted Police; Mounted Policeman; northeast London (UK vehicle registration)

M/P memorandum of partnership

MPA Master of Professional Accounting; Master of Public Administration; Master Printers Association; Music Publishers' Association

MPAA Motion Picture Association of America

MPAGB Modern Pentathlon Association of Great Britain

MPB Missing Persons Bureau (US)

MPBW Ministry of Public Building and Works

MPC mathematics, physics, chemistry; maximum permissible concentration; megaparsec; Metropolitan Police College; Metropolitan Police Commissioner

MPD maximum permissible dose

MPE Master of Physical Education; maximum permissible exposure (radioactivity)

MPEA Member of the Physical Education Association

MPer Middle Persian

mpg miles per gallon

mph miles per hour

MPh Master of Philosophy

MPH Master of Public Health

MPhil Master of Philosophy

mpi mean point of impact

MPI Max Planck Institute

MPIA Master of Public and International Affairs

MPL maximum permissible level

MPLA *Movimento Popular de Libertação de Angola* (Portuguese: Popular Movement for the Liberation of Angola)

mpm metres per minute

MPO management and personnel office; Metropolitan Police Office; military post

office; mobile printing office; mobile publishing office
mpp most probable position
MPP Member of the Provincial Parliament (Ontario)
MPR *Majelis Permusyawaratan Rakyat* (Bahasa Indonesia: People's Consultative Assembly; Indonesia); Mongolian People's Republic
MPRISA Member of the Public Relations Institute of South Africa
MPRP Mongolian People's Revolutionary Party
mps metres per second
MPs Master of Psychology
MPS manufacturer's part specification; marginal propensity to save; Medical Protection Society; Member of the Philological Society; Member of the Physical Society; metres per second
MPsSc Master of Psychological Science
MPsych Master of Psychology
MPsyMed Master of Psychological Medicine
m. pt melting point
MPTA Municipal Passenger Transport Association
MPTP methylphenyltetrahydropyridine
MPU microprocessor unit (computing)
Mpy *Maatschappij* (Dutch: company)
mq. mosque
MQ metol-quinol (photographic developing fluid)
Mqe Martinique
mr memorandum receipt
Mr Master; Mister
MR Air Mauritanie (airline flight code, Mauritius); magnetic resonance; Manchester (UK fishing port registration); map reference; Master of the Rolls; match rifle; mate's receipt (commerce); mental retardation; metabolic rate; Middlesex Regiment; Minister Residentiary; motivation research; motivational research; motorways regulations; municipal reform; Swindon (UK vehicle registration)
MRA Maritime Royal Artillery; Moral Rearmament
MRAC Member of the Royal Agricultural College
MRACP Member of the Royal Australasian College of Physicians
MRACS Member of the Royal Australasian College of Surgeons

MRadA Member of the Radionic Association
MRAeS Member of the Royal Aeronautical Society
MRAF Marshal of the Royal Air Force
MRAIC Member of the Royal Architectural Institute of Canada
MRAS Member of the Royal Academy of Science; Member of the Royal Asiatic Society; Member of the Royal Astronomical Society
MRB Mersey River Board
MRBM medium-range ballistic missile
MRBS Member of the Royal Botanic Society
MRC Medical Registration Council; Medical Research Council; Medical Reserve Corps; Model Railway Club
MRCA multi-role combat aircraft
MRCGP Member of the Royal College of General Practitioners
MRC-LMB Medical Research Council Laboratory of Molecular Biology
MRCO Member of the Royal College of Organists
MRCOG Member of the Royal College of Obstetricians and Gynaecologists
MRCP Member of the Royal College of Physicians
MRCPA Member of the Royal College of Pathologists of Australia
MRCPath Member of the Royal College of Pathologists
MRCPE Member of the Royal College of Physicians of Edinburgh
MRCPGlas Member of the Royal College of Physicians and Surgeons of Glasgow
MRCPI Member of the Royal College of Physicians of Ireland
MRCPsych Member of the Royal College of Psychiatrists
MRCS Member of the Royal College of Surgeons
MRCSE Member of the Royal College of Surgeons of Edinburgh
MRCSI Member of the Royal College of Surgeons of Ireland
MRCVS Member of the Royal College of Veterinary Surgeons
MRD machine-readable dictionary
MRe Mauritanian rupee (monetary unit)
MRE Master of Religious Education; meal, ready to eat (military); Microbiological Research Establishment; Mining Research Establishment
MRG Minority Rights Group

MRGS Member of the Royal Geographical Society
MRH Member of the Royal Household
MRHS Member of the Royal Horticultural Society
MRI magnetic resonance imaging (medicine); Member of the Royal Institution
MRIA Member of the Royal Irish Academy
MRIAI Member of the Royal Institute of the Architects of Ireland
MRIC Member of the Royal Institute of Chemistry
MRIN Member of the Royal Institute of Navigation
MRINA Member of the Royal Institute of Naval Architects
MRIPHH Member of the Royal Institute of Public Health and Hygiene
mrkr marker
MRM mechanically removed meat (food processing)
MRMetS Member of the Royal Meteorological Society
mRNA messenger ribonucleic acid
mrng morning
MRO Member of the Register of Osteopaths
MRP manufacturer's recommended price; Master in Regional Planning; Master of Regional Planning
MRPharmS Member of the Royal Pharmaceutical Society
Mrs Mistress (married title)
MRS Market Research Society
MRSC Member of the Royal Society of Chemistry
MRSH Member of the Royal Society for the Promotion of Health
MRSL Member of the Royal Society of Literature
MRSM Member of the Royal Society of Medicine; Member of the Royal Society of Musicians of Great Britain
MRSPE Member of the Royal Society of Painter-Etchers and Engravers
MRSPP Member of the Royal Society of Portrait Painters
MRST Member of the Royal Society of Teachers
MRT mass rapid transport
MRTPI Member of the Royal Town Planning Institute
MRU manpower research unit; mobile repair unit

MRUSI Member of the Royal United Service Institution
MRV multiple re-entry vehicle (military)
MRVA Member of the Rating and Valuation Association
ms mail steamer; manuscript; margin of safety; maximum stress; mild steel; millisecond
m/s metres per second; months after sight (finance)
Ms Miss or Mrs
MS Edinburgh (UK vehicle registration); Egyptair (airline flight code); mail steamer; main sequence (astronomy); *mano sinistra* (Italian: left hand); manuscript; mass spectrometer; mass spectrometry; Master of Science (US); Master of Surgery; Mauritius (international vehicle registration); media studies; medical staff; medium shot (photography); *memoriae sacrum* (Latin: sacred to the memory of); mess sergeant; milestone (cartography); minesweeper; Ministry of Supply; Mississippi (zip code); motor ship (US); multiple sclerosis; municipal surveyor
MSA Malaysia-Singapore Airways; Master of Science and Arts; Master of Science in Agriculture; Media Studies Association; Member of the Society of Apothecaries; Merchant Shipping Act; Metropolitan Statistical Area (US); Mineralogical Society of America; Motor Schools' Association of Great Britain; Mutual Security Agency (US)
MSAE Master of Science in Aeronautical Engineering (US); Member of the Society of Automotive Engineers (US)
MSAgr Master of Science in Agriculture
MSAICE Member of the South African Institution of Civil Engineers
MSAInstMM Member of the South African Institute of Mining and Metallurgy
MS&R Merchant Shipbuilding and Repairs
MSArch Master of Science in Architecture
MSAutE Member of the Society of Automobile Engineers
MSB Maritime Safety Board; Metropolitan Society for the Blind; most significant bit (computing)
MSBA Master of Science in Business Administration
MSBus Master of Science in Business
msc moved, seconded and carried

msc. miscellaneous
MSc Master of Science
MSC Manchester Ship Canal; Manpower Services Commission; medical staff corps; Metropolitan Special Constabulary
MScA Master of Science in Agriculture
MScApp Master of Applied Science
MSc(Arch) Master of Science in Architecture
MScD Doctor of Medical Science (US); Master of Dental Science
MSCE Master of Science in Civil Engineering
MSc(Econ) Master of Science in Economics
MSc(Ed) Master of Science in Education
MSChE Master of Science in Chemical Engineering
MSc(Hort) Master of Science in Horticulture
MSCI Index Morgan Stanley Capital International World Index (finance)
MScMed Master of Medical Science
MSc(Nutr) Master of Science in Nutrition
MSCP Master of Science in Community Planning
MSD Doctor of Medical Science; Master of Science in Dentistry; Master Surgeon Dentist; most significant digit (computing)
MSDent Master of Science in Dentistry
MS-DOS Microsoft Disk Operating System (trademark; computing)
MSE Master of Science in Education; Master of Science in Engineering; Member of the Society of Engineers
MSEd Master of Science in Education
MSEE Master of Science in Electrical Engineering
MSEM Master of Science in Engineering Mechanics; Master of Science in Engineering of Mines
MSF Manufacturing, Science and Finance Union; Master of Science in Forestry; *Médecins sans frontières* (French: Doctors Without Frontiers; charity); mine-sweeping flotilla
msg. message
MSG monosodium glutamate (flavour enhancer)
msgr messenger
Msgr *Monseigneur* (French: my lord); Monsignor (Roman Catholic Church)
MSgt Master Sergeant (US military)
MSH Master of Staghounds; melanocyte-stimulating hormone

MSHE(c) Master of Science in Home Economics
Mshl Marshal
MSHyg Master of Science in Hygiene
MSI *Movimento Sociale Italiano* (Italian: Italian Social Movement)
MSIAD Member of the Society of Industrial Artists and Designers
MSIE Master of Science in Industrial Engineering
m'sieur *monsieur* (French: Mr or Sir)
MSINZ Member of the Surveyors' Institute of New Zealand
MSJ Master of Science in Journalism
MSL Master of Science in Linguistics; mean sea level
MSLS Master of Science in Library Science
MSM Master of Sacred Music; Master of Science in Music; Meritorious Service Medal
MSME Master of Science in Mechanical Engineering
MSMed Master of Medical Science
MSMetE Master of Science in Metallurgical Engineering
MSMus Master of Science in Music
MSN Master of Science in Nursing
MSO Member of the Society of Osteopaths
MSocIS *Membre de la société des ingénieurs et scientifiques de France* (French: Member of the Society of Engineers and Scientists of France)
MSocSc Master of Social Science/s
MSPE Master of Science in Physical Education
MSPH Master of Science in Public Health
MSPhar(m) Master of Science in Pharmacy
MSPHE Master of Science in Public Health Engineering
MSQ managing service quality
MSR main supply route; mean spring rise (tides); Member of the Society of Radiographers; missile-site radar (military)
MSS manuscripts; Master of Social Science; Master of Social Service; Member of the Royal Statistical Society
MSSE Master of Science in Sanitary Engineering (US)
mst measurement
MST Master of Sacred Theology; Master of Science in Teaching; mean spring tide; mean survival time; Mountain Standard Time (US)

MStat Master of Statistics
MSTD Member of the Society of Typographic Designers
Mstr Master
MSTS Military Sea Transportation Service (US Navy)
MSUL Medical Schools of the University of London
MSurv Master of Surveying
MSurvSc Master of Surveying Science
MSw Middle Swedish
MSW Master in Social Work; Master of Social Work; Master of Social Welfare; medical social worker; municipal solid waste
MSY maximum sustainable yield
mt metric ton; missile test; mount; mountain; Mountain Time (US)
mt. megaton
Mt metical (Mozambican monetary unit); mount; mountain
MT magnetic tape; mail transfer; malignant tumour; mandated territory; Maryport (UK fishing port registration); mass transport; mean time; mechanical transport; megaton; Middle Temple (law); Montana (zip code); motor tanker; motor transport; Mountain Time (US); northeast London (UK vehicle registration)
M/T empty; mail transfer
MTA minimum terms agreement; Music Teachers' Association; Music Trades' Association
MTAI Member of the Institute of Travel Agents
MTB motor torpedo boat
MTBF mean time between failures (computing)
MTC Mechanized Transport Corps; Music Teacher's Certificate
MTCA Ministry of Transport and Civil Aviation
mtd mounted
MTD maximum tolerated dose; mean temperature difference; Midwife Teacher's Diploma
MTech Master of Technology
MTEFL Master in the Teaching of English as a Foreign Language
MTFS medium-term financial strategy
mtg meeting; mortgage; mounting
mtge mortgage
mtgee mortgagee
mtgor mortgagor
mth month
MTh Master of Theology

MTI *Magyar Tavariti Iroda* (news agency, Hungary); moving-target indication (radar); moving-target indicator (radar)
mtl material
mtl. *monatlich* (German: monthly)
MTL mean tide level
MTM methods-time measurement
mtn motion; mountain
MTN multilateral trade negotiations
MTNA Music Teachers' National Association
MTO made to order; mechanical transport officer
MTP Master of Town Planning
mtr meter
MTR mean time to restore (US Air Force); minimum time rate
Mt Rev. Most Reverend
Mts Mountains; Mounts
MTS Master of Theological Studies; Merchant Taylors' School; motor transport service; multi-channel television sound (US)
MTTR mean time to repair; mean time to restore
MTU magnetic tape unit (computing); missile training unit (US Air Force)
MTV motor torpedo vessel; music television (US)
m/u make-up
MU maintenance unit; Manchester United Football Club; marginal utility; monetary unit; Mothers' Union; Musicians' Union; northeast London (UK vehicle registration)
MUC Missionary Union of the Clergy
MUF multiple usable frequency (telecommunications)
MUFTI minimum use of force tactical intervention (military)
mun(ic). municipal; municipality
MUniv Master of the University
mus. museum; music; musical; musician
musa multiple unit steerable aerial; multiple unit steerable antenna
MusB *Musicae Baccalaureus* (Latin: Bachelor of Music)
MusD *Musicae Doctor* (Latin: Doctor of Music)
MusM *Musicae Magister* (Latin: Master of Music)
musn musician
mut. mutilate; mutual
MUX multiplexer
mv market value; mean variation; *mezza voce* (Italian: half voice or softly; music); motor vessel

mV millivolt
MV Ansett WA (airline flight code, Australia); market value; megavolt; merchant vessel; motor vessel; muzzle velocity (firearms); southeast London (UK vehicle registration)
MVB Bachelor of Veterinary Medicine
MVD Doctor of Veterinary Medicine; *Ministerstvo Vnutrennikh Del* (Russian: Ministry for Internal Affairs)
MVEE Military Vehicles and Engineering Establishment
MVetMed Master of Veterinary Medicine
MVetSc Master of Veterinary Science
MVL motor-vehicle licence
MVO male voice over; Member of the Royal Victorian Order
MVP Most Valued Player (baseball award)
MVS(c) Master of Veterinary Science
mvt movement
mW milliwatt
MW Malawi (international vehicle registration); Master of Wine; medium wave (radio frequency); megawatt; Middle Welsh; mixed waste (nuclear engineering); molecular weight; Most Worshipful; Most Worthy; Swindon (UK vehicle registration)
M/W midwife
MWA Mystery Writers of America
MWC municipal-waste combustion

MWeldI Member of the Welding Institute
MWF Medical Women's Federation
mwg music wire gauge
MWGM Most Worshipful Grand Master (Freemasonry); Most Worthy Grand Master (Freemasonry)
MWh megawatt hour
MWI municipal-waste incineration; municipal-waste incinerator
MWIA Medical Women's International Association
MWO Meteorological Watch Office
MWP mechanical wood pulp
MWPA Married Women's Property Act
Mx maxwell (magnetism); Middlesex
MX Mexicana (airline flight code); missile, experimental; southeast London (UK vehicle registration)
mxd mixed
mxm maximum
my million years
my. myopia
MY motor yacht; southeast London (UK vehicle registration)
myc. mycological; mycology
MYOB mind your own business
MYRA multi-year rescheduling agreement (finance)
myst. mysteries; mystery
myth(ol). mythological; mythology
Mz Mesozoic (geology)
MZ Belfast (UK vehicle registration)

N

n en (printing); nano-; neutron; north; northern; revolutions per second
n indefinite number (mathematics); number density (chemistry, physics); principal quantum number (physics); refractive index (optics)
'n' and
n. nail; name; nasal; *natus* (Latin: born); nautical; naval; neap; near; negative; nephew; nerve; net (commerce); neuter; neutral; new; night; nominative; noon; norm; normal; north; northern; *nostro* (Latin: our); note; *notre* (French: our); noun; *nous* (French: us/we); number
N en (printing); knight (chess); naira (Nigerian monetary unit); near; neutral (electrical engineering); Newry (UK fishing port registration); newton

(physics); ngultrum (monetary unit of Bhutan); nitrogen (element); north; northern; north London (UK postcode); Norway (international vehicle registration); nuclear; nucleon (physics); USA (international civil aircraft marking)
N neutron number (physics)
N. national; nationalist; navigation; navy; new; Norse; north; northern; November; nullity (law); nurse; nursing
n/a not applicable; not available
Na Nebraska; sodium (element)
NA Manchester (UK vehicle registration); Narcotics Anonymous (US); National Academician (US); National Academy; National Airlines; National Archives; National Army; National Assembly;

Nautical Almanac; naval architect; naval attaché; naval auxiliary; Netherlands Antilles (international vehicle registration); neutral axis (engineering); new account (banking); *Nomina Anatomica* (Latin: Anatomical Names); noradrenaline (biochemistry); North America; North American; *Notias Argentinas* (news agency, Argentina); numerical aperture (optics); nursing auxiliary

N/A new account (banking); no account (banking); no advice (banking); non-acceptance (banking, commerce); not available

naa not always afloat (shipping)

NAA National Aeronautic Association (US); National Association of Accountants (US); National Automobile Association (US); Nursing Auxiliaries' Association

NAAA National Alliance of Athletic Associations

NAABC not always afloat but safe aground (shipping)

NAACP National Association for the Advancement of Colored People (US)

NAAFA National Association to Aid Fat Americans

NAAFI Navy, Army and Air Force Institutes

NAAQS National Ambient Air Quality Standard (US)

NAAS National Agricultural Advisory Service

NAB National Advisory Body for Public Sector Higher Education; National Alliance of Businessmen; National Assistance Board; National Association of Broadcasters (US); National Australia Bank; naval air base; naval amphibious base; New American Bible; News Agency of Burma

NABC National Association of Boys' Clubs

NABS National Advertising Benevolent Society

NAC National Advisory Council; National Agriculture Centre; National Airways Corporation (US); National Anglers' Council; National Archives Council; National Association for the Childless

NACA National Advisory Committee for Aeronautics

NACAB National Association of Citizens Advice Bureaux

NACCAM National Coordinating Committee for Aviation Meteorology

NACCB National Accreditation Council for Certification Bodies

NACEIC National Advisory Council on Education for Industry and Commerce

NACF National Art Collections Fund

NaCl sodium chloride (salt)

NACM National Association of Colliery Managers

NACNE National Advisory Committee on Nutrition Education

NACODS National Association of Colliery Overmen, Deputies and Shotfirers

NACOSS National Approved Council for Security Systems

NACRO National Association for the Care and Resettlement of Offenders

NACTST National Advisory Council on the Training and Supply of Teachers

nad no appreciable difference

nad. nadir

NAD National Academy of Design (US); naval aircraft department; naval air division; no abnormality detected (medicine); not on active duty

NADC naval aide-de-camp

NADEC National Association of Development Education Centres

NADFAS National Association of Decorative and Fine Arts Societies

NADGE NATO Air Defence Ground Environment

NADOP North American Defense Operational Plan

NADW North Atlantic deep water

NADWARN Natural Disaster Warning System (US)

NAE National Academy of Engineering (US); naval aircraft establishment

NAEA National Association of Estate Agents

NAEP National Assessment of Educational Progress (US)

NAEW NATO Airborne Early Warning

Naewoe Naewoe Press (news agency, South Korea)

NA f. Netherlands Antillean guilder (monetary unit)

NAFD National Association of Funeral Directors

NAFO National Association of Fire Officers; Northwest Atlantic Fisheries Organization

N. Afr. North Africa

NAFTA New Zealand and Australia Free

Trade Agreement; North American Free Trade Agreement; North Atlantic Free Trade Area

nag net annual gain

Nag. Nagasaki (Japan)

NAG National Association of Goldsmiths

NAGC National Association for Gifted Children

NAGS National Allotments and Gardens Society

Nah. Nahum (Bible)

NAHA National Association of Health Authorities

Nahal *No'ar Halutzi Lohem* (Hebrew: Pioneer and Military Youth; Israel)

NAHAT National Association of Health Authorities and Trusts

NAHB National Association of Home Builders (US)

NAHT National Association of Head Teachers

NAI non-accidental injury

NAIR national arrangements for incidents involving radioactivity (US)

NAIRU non-accelerating inflation rate of unemployment

NAITA National Association of Independent Travel Agents

NAK negative acknowledgement (telecommunications)

NAL National Aerospace Laboratory (US)

NALC National Association of Letter Carriers

NALGO National and Local Government Officers' Association

N. Am. North America; North American

NAM National Association of Manufacturers (US)

NAMAS National Measurement and Accreditation Service

NAMH National Association for Mental Health

NAMMA NATO MRCA Management Agency

NAMS national air-monitoring sites (US)

NAN News Agency of Nigeria

NANC non-adrenergic non-cholinergic

NAND not AND (computing, electronics)

N&Q Notes and Queries

NAO National Audit Office

Nap. Naples; Napoleon; Napoleonic

NAP National Association for the Paralysed

NAPA National Association of Performing Artists (US)

NAPE National Association for Port Employees

NAPF National Association of Pension Funds

naph. naphtha (chemistry)

NAPO National Association of Probation Officers; National Association of Property Owners

NAPT National Association for the Prevention of Tuberculosis

nar. narrow

NAR net assimilation rate (botany)

narc. narcotic/s

NARM natural and accelerator-produced radioactive material

NAS National Academy of Sciences (US); National Adoption Society; National Association of Schoolmasters; naval air station; Noise Abatement Society; nursing auxiliary service

NASA National Aeronautics and Space Administration (US)

NASD National Amalgamated Stevedores and Dockers; National Association of Securities Dealers

NASDA National Space Development Agency (Japan)

NASDAQ National Association of Securities Dealers Automated Quotations system (US)

Nash. Nashville (US)

NASL North American Soccer League

Nass. Nassau (Bahamas)

NASS naval air signals school

NAS/UWT National Association of Schoolmasters/Union of Women Teachers

NASW National Association of Social Workers (US)

nat normal allowed time

nat. national; nationalist; native; natural; naturalize; naturalized; naturist; *natus* (Latin: born)

Nat. Natal

N. At. North Atlantic

NAT National Arbitration Tribunal

NATCS National Air Traffic Control Service

NATE National Association for the Teaching of English

NATFHE National Association of Teachers in Further and Higher Education

Nat. Hist. natural history

Nativ. Nativity

natl national

NATLAS National Testing Laboratory Accreditation Scheme

NATO North Atlantic Treaty Organization

nat. phil. natural philosophy

NATS National Air Traffic Services (US); Naval Air Transport Service (US)

nat. sc(i). natural science/s

NatScD Doctor of Natural Science

Natsopa National Society of Operative Printers and Assistants; National Society of Operative Printers, Graphical and Media Personnel

N. Att. Naval Attaché

NATTKE National Association of Theatrical, Television and Kine Employees

NATTS National Association of Trade and Technical Schools

natur. naturalist

NatWest National Westminster Bank

naut. nautical

nav. naval; navigable; navigation; navigator

NAV net asset value (finance)

Navaids navigation aids

NAVAIR Naval Air Systems Command (US)

Nav. E. Naval Engineer

navig. navigable; navigation; navigator

NAVS National Anti-Vivisection Society

NAVSAT navigational satellite

NAWB National Association of Workshops for the Blind

NAWC National Association of Women's Clubs

NAWO National Alliance of Women's Organizations

NAYC National Association of Youth Clubs; Youth Clubs UK

NAYT National Association of Youth Theatres

naz. *nazionale* (Italian: national)

Nazi *Nationalsozialisten* (German: National Socialist)

nb no ball (cricket); *nota bene* (Latin: note well)

Nb nimbus (meteorology); niobium (element)

NB Manchester (UK vehicle registration); narrow-bone; naval base; Nebraska; needle biopsy (medicine); New Brunswick (Canada); North Britain; *nota bene* (Latin: note well)

NBA National Basketball Association (US); National Book Award (US); National Boxing Association (US); National Building Agency; Net Book Agreement; North British Academy

NBC National Basketball Committee (US); National Book Council; National Boys' Club; National Broadcasting Company (US); National Bus Company; nuclear, biological and chemical (warfare or weapons)

NBCD natural binary-coded decimal (computing)

NBD negative binomial distribution (statistics)

NbE north by east

NBER National Bureau of Economic Research (US)

nbg no bloody good

NBI National Benevolent Institution

NBK National Bank of Kuwait

nbl not bloody likely

NBL National Book League

NBP normal boiling point (chemistry)

NBPI National Board for Prices and Incomes

NBR National Buildings Record; nitrile-butadiene rubber

nbre *noviembre* (Spanish: November)

NBRI National Building Research Institute

NBS National Bureau of Standards (US)

NBTS National Blood Transfusion Service

NBV net book value (accounting)

NbW north by west

nc no charge

NC Manchester (UK vehicle registration); national certificate; national congress; national council; national curriculum; Nature Conservancy; New Caledonia; New Church; nickel-cadmium (electric cells); nitrocellulose; nitrogen compound (chemistry); no change; not changing (meteorology); no charge; normally closed; North Carolina (zip code); Northern Command; numerical control; numerically controlled; Nurse Corps (US)

N/C new charter; nitrocellulose; no charge

NCA National Certificate of Agriculture; National Childminding Association; National Cricket Association; no copies available

NCAA National Collegiate Athletic Association; Northern Counties Athletic Association

NCACC National Civil Aviation Consultative Committee

NCAR National Center for Atmospheric Research (US)

NCARB National Council of Architectural Registration Boards (US)

NCB National Children's Bureau; National Coal Board; no claim bonus (insurance)

NCBA National Cattle Breeders' Association

NCBAE no claim bonus as earned (insurance)

NCBW nuclear, chemical and biological warfare

NCC National Climatic Center (US); National Computing Centre; National Consumer Council; National Council of Churches (US); National Curriculum Council; Nature Conservancy Council

NCCI National Committee for Commonwealth Immigrants

NCCJ National Conference of Christians and Jews

NCCL National Council for Civil Liberties (Liberty)

NCCS national command and control system; National Council for Civic Responsibility

NCCVD National Council for Combating Venereal Diseases

ncd no can do

NCD naval construction department

NCDAD National Council for Diplomas in Art and Design

NCDL National Canine Defence League

NCERT National Council for Educational Research and Training

NCET National Council for Educational Technology

NCFT National College of Food Technology

NCH National Children's Home; National Clearing House

n. Chr. *nach Christus* (German: after Christ)

nci no common interest

NCI National Cancer Institute (US); New Community Instrument (finance)

NCIC National Cancer Institute of Canada; National Crime Information Center (US)

NCL National Central Library; National Chemical Laboratory; National Church League

NCLC National Council of Labour Colleges

NCN National Council of Nurses

NCNA New China News Agency

NCNC National Convention of Nigeria and the Cameroons; National Convention of Nigerian Citizens

NCO non-commissioned officer

ncp normal circular pitch (engineering)

NCP National Car Parks Ltd; National Country Party (Australia); national cycling proficiency

NCPL National Centre for Programmed Learning

NCPS non-contributory pension scheme

NCPT National Congress of Parents and Teachers (US)

NCR National Cash Register Company Ltd; no carbon required (paper)

NCRE Naval Construction Research Establishment

NCRL National Chemical Research Laboratory

NCRP National Council on Radiation Protection and Measurement (US)

NCS National Communications System (US)

NCSC National Companies and Securities Commission (Australia); National Computer Security Center (US)

NCSE National Council for Special Education

NCSS National Council of Social Service

NCT National Chamber of Trade; National Childbirth Trust

NCTA National Community Television Association (US)

NCTE National Council of Teachers of English (US)

NCU National Communications Union; National Cyclists' Union

ncup no commission until paid

NCV no commercial value

NCVCCO National Council of Voluntary Child Care Organizations

NCVO National Council for Voluntary Organizations

NCVQ National Council for Vocational Qualifications

NCW National Council of Women

nd next day; no date; not dated; no decision; no deed; not deeded; no delay; no demand; non-delivery; not drawn (banking); nothing doing

Nd neodymium (element)

ND Manchester (UK vehicle registration); national debt; National Diploma; Naturopathic Diploma; neutral density (photography); no date; non-delivery; North Dakota (zip code)

N-D *Notre-Dame* (French: Our Lady)

NDA National Diploma in Agriculture; National Dairymens' Association; non-destructive analysis (engineering); non-destructive assay (engineering)
NDAC National Defense Advisory Committee (US)
N. Dak. North Dakota
NDB non-directional beacon (aeronautics)
NDC National Dairy Council; National Defence College; NATO Defence College
NDCS National Deaf Children's Society
NDD National Diploma in Dairying; National Diploma in Design
NDE near-death experience; non-destructive evaluation (engineering); non-destructive examination (engineering)
NDF National Diploma in Forestry
NDH National Diploma in Horticulture
NDIC National Defence Industries Council
Ndl. The Netherlands
NDN National District Nurse Certificate
ndp normal diametric pitch (engineering)
NDP National Democratic Party; net domestic product; New Democratic Party (Canada)
NDPS National Data Processing Service
NDRC National Defence Research Committee
NDSB Narcotic Drugs Supervisory Body (UN)
NDT non-destructive testing (engineering); non-distributive trade (commerce)
NDTA National Defense Transportation Association (US)
NDU Nursing Development Unit
ne northeast; northeastern; not essential; not exceeding
n/e new edition; no effects (banking)
Ne neon (element)
Ne. Nepal(ese); Netherlands
NE Manchester (UK vehicle registration); national emergency; National Executive; Naval Engineer; Nebraska (zip code); Newcastle (UK fishing port registration; postcode); new edition; New England; news editor; no effects (banking); northeast; northeastern; nuclear energy; nuclear explosion; nuclear explosive
N/E new edition; no effects (banking); not entered (accounting)
NEA National Education Association (US); National Endowment for the Arts (US); North East Airlines
NEAC New English Art Club

NEACP National Emergency Airborne Command Post (US)
NEAF Near East Air Force
NEAFC North-East Atlantic Fisheries Commission
Neapol. Neapolitan
NEARELF Near East Land Forces
Neb(r). Nebraska
NEB National Electricity Board; National Energy Board (US); National Enterprise Board; New English Bible
NEBSS National Examinations Board for Supervisory Studies
nec not elsewhere classified
NEC National Economic Council (US); National Electric Code (US); National Electronics Council; National Equestrian Centre; National Executive Committee; National Exhibition Centre (Birmingham); National Extension College (Cambridge); Nippon Electrical Company (Japan)
NECCTA National Educational Closed Circuit Television Association
NECInst North East Coast Institution of Engineers and Shipbuilders
necr. necrosis
necrol. necrology
necy necessary; necessity
NED no evidence of disease (medicine)
NEDC National Economic Development Council; North East Development Council
NEDO National Economic Development Office
NEEB North Eastern Electricity Board
NEF noise exposure forecast
neg. negation; negative; negatively; negligence; negotiate
Neg. Negro
Neh. Nehemiah (Bible)
NEH National Endowment for the Humanities
nei *non est inventus* (Latin: he/she/it has not been found); not elsewhere indicated
NEI Netherlands East Indies
NEL National Electronics Laboratory (US); National Engineering Laboratory
nem con. *nemine contradicente* (Latin: no one contradicting)
ne/nd new edition, no date given
N. Eng. New England; northern England
neol. neologism
nep new edition pending
Nep. Nepal; Nepales; Neptune (planet)
NEP New Economic Policy

NEPA National Environmental Policy Act (US)
NEPP National Energy Policy Plan (US)
NEQ non-equivalence (electronics)
NERA National Emergency Relief Administration (US)
NERC Natural Environment Research Council
nes not elsewhere specified
NESB non-English speaking background
NESC National Electric Safety Code (US)
NESTOR neutron source thermal reactor
net not earlier than
NET National Educational Television (US)
Neth. Netherlands
Neth. Ant. Netherlands Antilles
n. et m. *nocte et mane* (Latin: night and morning; medicine)
neur(ol). neurological; neurology
neuro. neurotic
neut. neuter; neutral; neutralize; neutralized; neutralizer
Nev. Nevada
NEW net economic welfare (US)
Newf. Newfoundland
New M. New Mexico
new par. new paragraph
news. newsagency; newsagent
New Test. New Testament (Bible)
nf near face (engineering); no fool; noun feminine
N/f no funds
NF Manchester (UK vehicle registration); National Formulary (US pharmacology); National Front; New Forest; Newfoundland; New French; no funds (banking); noise factor (telecommunications); noise figure (telecommunications); Norman French (language); *nouveau franc* (French: new franc)
nfa no further action
NFA National Farmers' Association; National Federation of Anglers; National Food Administration (US)
NFAL National Foundation of Arts and Letters
NFB National Film Board (Canada)
NFBPM National Federation of Builders' and Plumbers' Merchants
NFBTE National Federation of Building Trades Employers
nfc not favourably considered
NFC National Football Conference (US); National Freight Consortium

NFCO National Federation of Community Organizations
Nfd Newfoundland
NFD Newfoundland; no fixed date
NFDM non-fat dry milk
NFER National Foundation for Educational Research
NFFC National Film Finance Corporation
NFFE National Federation of Federal Employees (US)
NFFPT National Federation of Fruit and Potato Trades
NFHA National Federation of Housing Associations
NFI National Federation of Ironmongers
NFL National Football League (US, Canada)
Nfld Newfoundland
nfm nearest full moon; next full moon
NFMPS National Federation of Master Printers in Scotland
NFMS National Federation of Music Societies
NFO National Freight Organization
NFPW National Federation of Professional Workers
nfr no further requirements
NFRN National Federation of Retail Newsagents
NFS National Fire Service; National Flying Services; National Forest Service; network file service (computing); not for sale
NFSE National Federation of the Self-Employed (and Small Businesses)
NFT National Film Theatre
NFU National Farmers' Union
NFUW National Farmers' Union of Wales
NFWI National Federation of Womens' Institutes
NFYFC National Federation of Young Farmers' Clubs
ng narrow gauge (railways); no good; not given
Ng Neogene (geology)
Ng. Norwegian
NG Lauda Air (airline flight code, Austria); narrow gauge (railways); National Gallery; National Government; National Guard (US); National Guardsman (US); New Grenada; new growth (medicine); New Guinea; nitroglycerine; Noble Grand (Freemasonry); Noble Guard (Freemasonry); no go; no good; North German; Norwich (UK vehicle

registration); not good; Nottingham (UK postcode)

NGA National Glider Association; National Graphical Association

NGC National Grid Company; New General Catalogue (astronomy)

NGF nerve growth factor

NGk New Greek

NGL natural-gas liquid

NGmc North Germanic

NGNP nominal gross national product

NGO non-gazetted officer (India); non-governmental organization

NGr New Greek

NGRC National Greyhound Racing Club

NGRS Narrow Gauge Railway Society

NGS National Geographic Society; nuclear generating station

ngt *négociant* (French: merchant)

NGT National Guild of Telephonists

NGTE National Gas Turbine Establishment

NGU non-gonococcal urethritis (medicine)

NGV natural-gas vehicle

NH All Nippon Airways (airline flight code); National Hunt; naval hospital; New Hampshire (zip code); Northampton (UK vehicle registration); northern hemisphere; Northumberland Hussars

NHA National Horse Association of Great Britain; National Housing Agency (US)

NHBC National House-Building Council

NHBRC National House-Builders' Registration Certificate

NHC National Hunt Committee

NHD Doctor of Natural History

N. Heb. New Hebrew; New Hebrides

NHF National Hairdressers' Federation

NHG New High German

NHI National Health Insurance

NHK *Nippon Hoso Kyokai* (Japanese: Japan Broadcasting Corporation)

NHL National Hockey League (US)

NHLBI National Heart, Lung and Blood Institute (US)

NHMF National Heritage Memorial Fund

NHMRCA National Health and Medical Research Council of Australia

NHO Navy Hydrographic Office

nhp nominal horsepower

NHR National Housewives Register; National Hunt Rules

NHS National Health Service

NHSTA National Health Service Training Authority

NHTPC National Housing and Town Planning Council

Ni nickel (element)

NI National Insurance; Native Infantry; Naval Instructor; Naval Intelligence; new impression; News International; Northern Ireland; North Island (New Zealand); Wicklow (Irish vehicle registration)

NIA National Intelligence Authority (US); Newspaper Institute of America

NIAAA Northern Ireland Amateur Athletic Association

NIAB National Institute of Agricultural Botany

NIACRO Northern Ireland Association for the Care and Resettlement of Offenders

NIAE National Institute of Agricultural Engineering

NIAID National Institute of Allergy and Infectious Diseases

Nibmar no independence before majority African rule

NIBSC National Institute for Biological Standards Control

nic not in contract

Nic. Nicaragua; Nicaraguan

NIC National Incomes Commission; National Insurance contribution; newly industrialized country; Nicaragua (international vehicle registration)

Nica(r). Nicaragua; Nicaraguan

NiCad nickel-cadmium (battery)

NICAM near-instantaneous companded audio multiplex (electronics)

NiCd nickel-cadmium (battery)

NICEC National Institute for Careers Education and Counselling

NICEIC National Inspection Council for Electrical Installation Contracting

NICF Northern Ireland Cycling Federation

NICG Nationalized Industries Chairmen's Group

NICRA Northern Ireland Civil Rights Association

NICS Northern Ireland Civil Service

NICU neonatal intensive care unit (medicine)

NID National Institute for the Deaf; National Institute of Design (India); Naval Intelligence Division; Northern Ireland District

NIDC Northern Ireland Development Council

NIDD non-insulin-dependent diabetes

NIES Northern Ireland Electricity Service

NIESR National Institute of Economic and Social Research

NIF note issuance facility (finance)

NIFES National Industrial Fuel Efficiency Service

Nig. Nigeria; Nigerian

NIH National Institutes of Health (US); North Irish Horse

NIHCA Northern Ireland Hotels and Caterers Association

NIHE National Institute for Higher Education (Ireland)

NII Nuclear Installations Inspectorate

NIIP National Institute of Industrial Psychology

NILP Northern Ireland Labour Party

nimby not in my backyard

NIMH National Institute of Medical Herbalists; National Institute of Mental Health

n. imp. new impression

NIMR National Institute for Medical Research

NIN national information network

NINO no inspector, no operator (system)

NIO National Institute of Oceanography

NIOSH National Institute for Occupational Safety and Health (US)

nip. nipple (engineering)

Nip. Nippon; Nipponese

ni. pri. *nisi prius* (Latin: unless previously)

N. Ir. Northern Ireland

NIRA National Industrial Recovery Act (US)

NIRC National Industrial Relations Court

N. Ire. Northern Ireland

NIREX Nuclear Industry Radioactive Waste Executive

NIRS National Institute of Radiological Sciences (US)

nis not in stock

NIS new Israeli shekel (monetary unit)

NISA National Independent Supermarkets' Association

NISC National Industrial Safety Committee

NIST National Institute of Standards and Technology (US)

NISTRO Northern Ireland Science and Technology Regional Organization

NISW National Institute for Social Workers

NIT national intelligence test; negative income tax

NIV New International Version (Bible)

NIWAAA Northern Ireland Women's Amateur Athletic Association

nJ *nächsten Jahres* (German: next year)

NJ Brighton (UK vehicle registration); Namakwaland Lugiens (airline flight code, South Africa); New Jersey (zip code); nose job

NJA National Jewellers' Association

NJAC National Joint Advisory Council

NJC National Joint Council

NJCC National Joint Consultative Committee

NJNC National Joint Negotiating Committee

NK Luton (UK vehicle registration); not known

NKGB *Narodny Komissariat Gosudarstvennoi Bezopasnosti* (Russian: People's Commissariat of State Security)

NKr Norwegian krone (monetary unit)

NKVD *Narodnyi Komissariat Vnutrennikh Del* (Russian: People's Commissariat of Internal Affairs)

NKz new kwanza (Angolan monetary unit)

nl new line (printing); *non licet* (Latin: it is not permitted); *non liquet* (Latin: it is not clear)

Nl National

NL National Labour; National League (US baseball); National Liberal; Navy League; Navy List; Netherlands (international vehicle registration); Newcastle upon Tyne (UK vehicle registration); New Latin; no liability (Australian companies); northern latitude

NLB National Library for the Blind

NLC National Liberal Club; National Library of Canada

NLCB National Lottery Charities Board

NLCS North London Collegiate School

NLD National League for Democracy (Burma)

nlf nearest landing field

NLF National Labour Federation; National Liberal Federaton; National Liberation Front; National Loans Fund

NLI National Library of Ireland

NLLST National Lending Library for Science and Technology

NLM Natonal Library of Medicine

NLMC National Labour Management Council

NLN National League for Nursing

NLO naval liaison officer

NLP natural language processing

(computing); Natural Law Party (UK);
neighborhood loan program (US)
NLQ near letter quality (computing)
NLRB National Labor Relations Board
(US)
NLS National Library of Scotland
nlt not later than; not less than
NLW National Library of Wales
nly northerly
NLYL National League of Young Liberals
nm nanometre; nautical mile; new moon;
nocte et mane (Latin: night and morning;
medicine); non-metallic; noun masculine
nm. nutmeg
nM *nächsten Monats* (German: next
month)
Nm. *Nachmittag* (German: afternoon);
next matter (advertising)
N/m newton per metre; no mark/s
(commerce)
NM Luton (UK vehicle registration);
Mount Cook Airline (airline flight code,
New Zealand); national marketing;
nautical mile (meteorology); New
Mexico (zip code); nuclear medicine
NMA National Management Association;
National Medical Association
NMB National Maritime Board
nmc no more credit
NMC National Marketing Council;
National Meteorological Center (US)
N. Mex. New Mexico
NMFS National Marine Fisheries Service
(US)
NMGC National Marriage Guidance
Council
NMHA National Mental Health
Association
NMHF National Mental Health
Foundation (US)
NMP net material product (economics)
NMR nuclear magnetic resonance
NMRI nuclear magnetic resonance
imaging (medicine)
NMS National Market System (US)
NMSQT National Merit Scholarship
Qualifying Test (US)
NMSS National Multiple Sclerosis Society
(US)
nmt not more than
NMTF National Market Traders'
Federation
NMU National Maritime Union
NMW national minimum wage
nn. names; notes; nouns
NN Air Martinique (airline flight code);
Newhaven (UK fishing port

registration); no name; Northampton
(UK postcode); Nottingham (UK vehicle
registration)
N/N not to be noted
NNE north-northeast
NNEB National Nursery Examination
Board
NNF Northern Nurses' Federation
NNHT Nuffield Nursing Homes Trust
NNI noise and number index; noise
nuisance index
NNMA Nigerian National Merit Award
NNOM Nigerian National Order of Merit
NNP net national product (economics)
NNR National Nature Reserve
NNSA National Nuclear Safety
Administration (US)
NNT nuclear non-proliferation treaty
NNW north-northwest
no natural order; normally open; not out
(cricket)
no. north; northern; number; *numéro*
(French: number)
No nobelium (element)
No. north; northern; Norway;
Norwegian; number
NO Aus-Air (airline flight code,
Australia); Chelmsford (UK vehicle
registration); naval officer; naval
operations; navigation officer; New
Orleans; Nuffield Observatory; nursing
officer
N/O no orders (banking)
No. 10 Number 10 Downing Street
(London) (residence of prime minister)
NOA National Opera Association;
National Orchestral Association; not
otherwise authorized
NOAA National Oceanic and
Atmospheric Administration (US)
NOAO National Optical Astronomy
Observatories (US)
nob. *nobis* (Latin: for or on our part);
noble
NOB naval operating base
noc notation of content; not otherwise
classified
NOC National Olympic Committee; not
otherwise classified
NOCD not our class, dear
No. Co. northern counties
noct. *nocte* (Latin: at night; medicine)
NOD Naval Ordnance Department; night
observation device
NODA National Operatic and Dramatic
Association
NODC non-OPEC developing country

noe notice of exception; not otherwise enumerated

NOERC North of England Regional Consortium

nohp not otherwise herein provided

noibn not otherwise indexed by name

NOIC naval officer in charge

NOISE National Organization to Insure a Sound-controlled Environment (US)

nok next of kin

NOL Naval Ordnance Laboratory (US)

nol. con. *nolo contendere* (Latin: I do not wish to contend)

nol. pros. *nolle prosequi* (Latin: do not prosecute; law)

nom. nomenclature; nominal; nominated; nomination; nominative

nom. cap. nominal capital (finance)

nomen. nomenclature

nomin. nominative

nomm. nomination

nom. nov. *nomen novum* (Latin: new name)

NOMSS National Operational Meteorological Satellite System (US)

noncom. non-commissioned

Noncon. Nonconformist

non cul. *non culpabilis* (Latin: not guilty)

non-cum non-cumulative (finance)

non obs(t). *non obstante* (Latin: notwithstanding)

non pros. *non prosequitur* (Latin: he does not prosecute; law)

non rep(etat). *non repetatur* (Latin: do not repeat; medicine)

non res. non-resident

non seq. *non sequitur* (Latin: it does not follow)

nonst(an)d. non-standard

non-U not upper-class

nop not otherwise provided (for)

NOP National Opinion Poll; not our publication

nor. normal; north; northern

Nor. Norman; Normandy; north; northern; Norway; Norwegian; Norwich

NOR not OR (computing)

NORAD North American Air Defense Command

Norf. Norfolk

norm. normal; normalized

Norm. Norman; Normandy

NORM not operationally ready maintenance

NORML National Organization for the Reform of Marijuana Laws (US)

NORS not operationally ready supplies; not operationally ready supply

north. northern

Northants. Northamptonshire

Northd Northumberland

North(u)mb. Northumberland

Norvic: *Norvicensis* (Latin: (Bishop) of Norwich)

Norw. Norway; Norwegian

NORWEB North Western Electricity Board

NORWICH knickers off ready when I come home

nos not otherwise specified

nos. numbers; *numéros* (French: numbers)

Nos. numbers

NOS *Nederlandse Omroep Stichting* (Dutch: Netherlands Broadcasting Corporation)

NOSC Naval Ordnance Systems Command (US Navy)

NOSIG no significant change (meteorology)

not. notice

Not. Notary

NOTAR no-tail rotor (aircraft)

NOTB National Ophthalmic Treatment Board

Notimex *Noticias Mexicanas* (news agency, Mexico)

Nottm Nottingham

Notts. Nottinghamshire

notwg notwithstanding

nouv. *nouvelle* (French: new)

nov. novel(ist); *novembre* (French, Italian: November); novice; novitiate

Nov. November

Novosti *Agentstvo Pechati Novosti* (news agency, Russia)

NoW News of the World (newspaper)

NOW National Organization for Women (US); negotiable order of withdrawal (US banking); New Opportunities for Women

NOX nitrogen oxide

noy not out yet

noz. nozzle

np neap (tides); near point; net personality (law); net proceeds; new paragraph; new pattern; new pence; nickel-plated; *nisi prius* (Latin: unless previously); non-participating; no place of publication given (bibliography); no printer; no publisher; normal pitch; not paginated; nursing procedure

n/p net proceeds

Np napalm; neap (tides); neper

(telecommunications); neptunium (element)

NP national park; National Party; National Power; Nationalist Party; neuropsychiatric; neuropsychiatry; Newport (UK postcode); New Providence (Bahamas); nitro proof (firearms); Nobel Prize; non-polar (chemistry); notary public; noun phrase; nurse practitioner (US); Worcester (UK vehicle registration)

NPA National Park Authority; National Pigeon Association; New People's Army (Phillipines); Newspaper Publishers' Association

NPACI National Production Advisory Council on Industry

NPBA National Pig Breeders' Association

NPC National People's Congress (China); National Petroleum Council (US); National Ports Council; National Press Club (US); Northern People's Congress (Nigeria)

NPD *Nationaldemokratische Partei Deutschlands* (German: National Democratic Party); new product development; north polar distance (navigation)

npf not provided for

NPF National Progressive Front (Syria); Newspaper Press Fund

NPFA National Playing Fields Association

NPG National Portrait Gallery; Nuclear Planning Group (NATO)

NPh nuclear physics

NPK nitrogen, phosphorus and potassium (fertilizers)

n. pl. noun plural

npn n-type p-type n-type semiconductor (electronics)

NPN non-protein nitrogen

npna no protest for non-acceptance (commerce)

np/nd not published, no date given

npo *ne per oris* (Latin: not by mouth)

NPO New Philharmonia Orchestra

np or d no place or date

npp no passed proof

NPP nuclear power plant

NPR National Public Radio (US); noise power ratio

NPRA National Petroleum Refiners Association

nps nominal pipe size; no prior service

NPS National Portrait Society; *Norsk Presse Service* (news agency, Norway);

nuclear power source; nuclear power station

npt normal pressure and temperature

NPT non-proliferation treaty

npu *ne plus ultra* (Latin: nothing beyond or extreme point)

NPU National Pharmaceutical Union; National Postal Union; not passed urine (medicine)

NPV net present value (finance); no par value (shares)

NPW nuclear-powered warship

nqa net quick assets (finance)

NQOC not quite our class

nr near; net register; no risk (insurance); number

Nr *Nummer* (German: number)

NR Leicester (UK vehicle registration); National Register; natural rubber; naval rating; Navy Regulations; no risk (insurance); Norontair Canada (airline flight code); North Riding (Yorkshire); Norwich (UK postcode)

nra never refuse anything

NRA National Reclamation Association; National Recovery Administration (US); National Rehabilitation Association (US); National Recreation Area; National Rifle Association; National Rivers Authority; nuclear-reaction analysis

NRAA National Rifle Association of America

NRAO National Radio Astronomy Observatory (US)

NRC National Redemption Council (Ghana); National Research Council; Nuclear Regulatory Commission (US)

NRCA National Retail Credit Association

NRCC National Research Council of Canada

NRD National Register of Designers; National Registered Designer

NRDC National Research Development Corporation; Natural Resources Defense Council (US)

NRDS neonatal respiratory distress syndrome (medicine)

NREM non-rapid eye movement

NRF National Relief Fund

NRFL Northern Rugby Football League

NRI National Resources Institute

NRK *Norsk Rikskringkasting* (Norwegian: Norwegian Broadcasting Company)

NRL National Reference Library; Naval Research Library (US)

NRM National Resistance Movement (Uganda)

NRMA National Roads and Motorists Association (Australia)
nrml normal
NROR normal rate of return (finance)
NROTC Naval Reserve Officer Training Corps
NRP nuclear reprocessing plant
NRPB National Radiological Protection Board
NRR net reproduction rate
NRs Nepalese rupee (monetary unit)
NRS National Readership Survey; National Rose Society
NRT net registered tonnage
NRTA National Retired Teachers Association
NRV net realizable value (finance); non-return valve
Nrw. Norwegian
NRZ non-return to zero (computing)
ns nanosecond; Naval Staff (Graduate of the Royal Naval Staff College, Greenwich); near side; new series; nickel steel; not satisfactory; not specified; not sufficient (banking)
n/s non-smoker; not sufficient (banking)
Ns nimbostratus (meteorology)
NS Glasgow (UK vehicle registration); *Nachschrift* (German: postscript); National Service; National Society; natural science; naval service; New Ross (Irish fishing port registration); new series; Newspaper Society; New Style (calendar); NFD (airline flight code, Germany); nimbostratus (meteorology); non-smoker; not significant; Nova Scotia; nuclear science; nuclear ship; Numismatic Society
N-S *Notre-Seigneur* (French: Our Lord)
NSA National Security Agency (US); National Shipping Authority (US); National Skating Association; National Standards Association (US); National Student Association (US); New Society of Artists; non-sterling area; Nursery School Association
NSACS National Society for the Abolition of Cruel Sports
NSAE National Society of Art Education
NSAFA National Service Armed Forces Act
NSAID non-steroidal anti-inflammatory drug (medicine)
NSB National Savings Bank; National Science Board (US)
NSBA National Sheep Breeders' Association

NSC National Safety Council; National Savings Committee; National Security Council (US); National Sporting Club; National Steel Corporation
NSCA National Society for Clean Air
NSCR National Society for Cancer Relief
NSD naval supply depot
NSDAP *Nationalsozialistische Deutsche Arbeiterpartei* (German: National Socialist German Workers' Party; Nazis)
NSERC Natural Sciences and Engineering Research Council (US)
nsf not sufficient funds (banking)
NSF National Science Foundation
NSFGB National Ski Federation of Great Britain
NSG non-statutory guidelines (National Curriculum)
NSGT non-self-governing territory/ies
NSHEB North of Scotland Hydroelectric Board
NSI National Security Information (US)
n. sing. noun singular
NSL National Sporting League
NSM non-stipendiary minister
NSO naval staff officer
n. sp. new species
NSPCC National Society for the Prevention of Cruelty to Children
NSPE National Society of Professional Engineers (US)
nspf not specially provided for
NSRA National Small-bore Rifle Association
NSS national sample survey; New Shakespeare Society; normal saline solution (medicine)
NSSA National School Sailing Association
NSSU National Sunday School Union
nst non-slip thread
NST Newfoundland Standard Time
NSTP Nuffield Science Teaching Project
NSU non-specific urethritis (medicine)
NSW New South Wales
NSY New Scotland Yard
nt net terms; net tonnage; normal temperature
NT National Teacher (Ireland); National Theatre; National Trust; neap tide; Newport (UK fishing port registration); New Testament (Bible); New Translation; Northern Territory (Australia); no-trump (bridge); not titled; Nurse Teacher; Shrewsbury (UK vehicle registration)

NTA National Technical Association (US); net tangible assets
NTB non-tariff barrier (economics); *Norsk Telegrambyra* (news agency, Norway)
NTC negative temperature coefficient (physics)
NTD not top drawer
NTDA National Trade Development Association
NTEU National Treasury Employees Union (US)
ntfy notify
NTG North Thames Gas
NTGB North Thames Gas Board
NTGk New Testament Greek
Nth north
Nthb. Northumberland
nthn northern
NTIA National Telecommunications and Information Administration (US)
ntl no time lost
NTL non-threshold logic (electronics)
NTM non-tariff measure (economics)
nto not taken out
NTO naval transport officer
ntp no title page
NTP normal temperature and pressure (physics)
NTS National Trust for Scotland; Nevada Test Site; not to scale
NTSB National Transportation Safety Board (US)
NTSC National Television System Committee (US)
NTV Nippon Television
NTVLRO National Television Licence Records Office
nt wt net weight
nu name unknown; number unobtainable
Nu ngultrum (monetary unit of Bhutan)
NU National Union; *Nations Unies* (French: United Nations); natural uranium; Northern Union; Nottingham (UK vehicle registration); number unobtainable; Southwest Airlines (airline flight code, Japan)
NUAAW National Union of Agricultural and Allied Workers
NUBE National Union of Bank Employees
nuc(l). nuclear
NUCPS National Union of Civil and Public Servants
NUCUA National Union of Conservative and Unionists Associations
nud. nudism; nudist
NUDETS nuclear detection system

NUGMW National Union of General and Municipal Workers (UK)
NUI National University of Ireland
NUIW National Union of Insurance Workers
NUJ National Union of Journalists
NUJMB Northern Universities Joint Matriculation Board
NUL National Urban League (US)
num. number; numeral; numerical; numerologist; numerology
Num. Numbers (Bible)
NUM National Union of Mineworkers; New Ulster Movement
NUMAST National Union of Marine, Aviation and Shipping Transport Officers
numis(m). numismatics
NUOS naval underwater ordnance station
NUPE National Union of Public Employees
NUR National Union of Railwaymen
NUS National Union of Seamen; National Union of Students
NUT National Union of Teachers
N-u-T Newcastle-upon-Tyne
NUTG National Union of Townswomen's Guilds
NUTN National Union of Trained Nurses
nutr. nutrition
NUU New University of Ulster
NV *Naamloze Vennootschap* (Dutch: public limited company); needle valve; Nevada (zip code); New Version (Bible); non-vintage; non-voting (shares); Norske Veritas (shipping classification); Northampton (UK vehicle registration); Northwest Territorial Airways (airline flight code, Canada)
N/V non-vintage; no value (banking)
NVB National Volunteer Brigade
NVC non-verbal communication
NVG night-vision goggles (military)
NVGA National Vocational Guidance Association (US)
NVM Nativity of the Virgin Mary; non-volatile matter (chemistry)
NVQ National Vocational Qualification
NVRS National Vegetable Research Station
nw nanowatt; net weight; no wind
NW Leeds (UK vehicle registration); North Wales; northwest; northwestern; Northwest Airlines (airline flight code, US); northwest London (UK postcode)
NWC National War College (US)

NWEB North Western Electricity Board
Nwfld Newfoundland
NWFP North-West Frontier Province
(Pakistan)
nwg national wire gauge
NWGA National Wool Growers'
Association
NWI Netherlands West Indies
NWIDA North West Industrial
Development Association
nwl natural wavelength
NWP North-Western Province (India)
NWS National Weather Service (US);
normal water surface
n. wt net weight
nwt non-watertight
NWT Northwest Territories (Canada)
NWTV North West Television
NX Dudley (UK vehicle registration);
Nationair Canada (airline flight code)
NY Cardiff (UK vehicle registration); New
Year; New York (zip code)
NYA National Youth Administration (US)
NYC New York City
NYCSCE New York Coffee, Sugar and
Cocoa Exchange
NYD not yet diagnosed (medicine)
nyl. nylon
NYME New York Mercantile Exchange
NYMT National Youth Music Theatre
NYO National Youth Orchestra
NYOS National Youth Orchestra of
Scotland

NYP not yet published
NYPD New York Police Department
NYR not yet returned
NYS New York State
NYSE New York Stock Exchange
NYT National Youth Theatre; New York
Times
NYU New York University
NZ Air New Zealand (airline flight code);
Londonderry (UK vehicle registration);
neutral(ity) zone; New Zealand; New
Zealand (international vehicle
registration)
NZBC New Zealand Broadcasting
Corporation
NZDSIR New Zealand Department of
Scientific and Industrial Research
N. Zeal. New Zealand
NZEF New Zealand Employers'
Federation; New Zealand Expeditionary
Force
NZEFIP New Zealand Expeditionary
Force in the Pacific (World War II)
NZEI New Zealand Educational Institute
NZFL New Zealand Federation of Labor
NZIA New Zealand Institute of
Architects
NZLR New Zealand Law Reports
NZMA New Zealand Medical Association
NZPA New Zealand Press Association
NZRFU New Zealand Rugby Football
Union
NZRN New Zealand Registered Nurse

O

o overcast (meteorology)
o' of
o. occasional; octavio (printing); off; old;
only; *optimus* (Latin: best); order; organ;
out (baseball); over; overseer; owner
O blood type; opium; order (computing;
mathematics); Ordovician (geology);
oxygen (element); *octarius* (Latin: pint;
pharmacology)
O. observe; observer; occiput (obstetrics);
occupation; ocean; octavo; October;
oculus (Latin: eye); Oddfellows; *oeste*
(Spanish, Portuguese: west); office;
officer; Ohio; old; operation; orange;
order; ordinary; Orient; *Osten* (German:
east); *ottava* (Italian: octave); *ouest*
(French: west); over (cricket); *ovest*
(Italian: west); owner

o/a on account (of); on or about
OA Birmingham (UK vehicle
registration); objective analysis; office
address; office automation; Officers'
Association; *Officier d'Académie* (French:
Officer of the Academy; education); old
account (banking); oleic acid
(chemistry); Olympic Airways (airline
flight code, Greece); operational
analysis; osteoarthritis; overall
OAA *Organisation pour l'alimentation et
l'agriculture* (French: Food and
Agriculture Organization; FAO);
Outdoor Advertising Association of
Great Britain
OACI *Organisation de l'aviation civile
internationale* (French: International Civil
Aviation Organization)

oad overall depth
OAG Official Airline Guide (US)
oah overall height
o. alt. hor. *omnibus alternis horis* (Latin: every other hour)
OAM Medal of the Order of Australia
OAMDG *omnia ad majorem Dei gloriam* (Latin: all to the greater glory of God)
OANA Organization of Asian News Agencies
O&A October and April (invoices)
O&C Oxford and Cambridge (examinations board)
O&E Operations and Engineering (US)
O&M Ogilvie and Mather (advertising agency); organization and method
O&O Oriental and Occidental Steamship Company; owned and operated
oao off and on
OAO one and only; Orbiting Astronomical Observatory
OAP old age pension(er)
OAPC Office of Alien Property Custodian (US)
OAPEC Organization of Arab Petroleum Exporting Countries
OAr Old Arabic
OAR Order of Augustinian Recollects (Roman Catholic Church)
OAS offensive air support; on active service; *Organisation de l'Armée Secrète* (French: Secret Army Organization; Algeria); Organization of American States
OASIS optimal aircraft sequencing using intelligent systems
OAT outside air temperature
OATC Oceanic Air Traffic Control
OATUU Organization of African Trade Union Unity
OAU Organization of African Unity
ob ordinary building (timber)
ob. *obiit* (Latin: he/she died); *obiter* (Latin: incidentally); obligation; oboe; observation; obsolete; obstetric/s
o/b on or before
Ob. Obadiah (Bible)
OB Birmingham (UK vehicle registration); Oban (UK fishing port registration); observed bearing; obstetric/s; obstetrician (US); off-Broadway (theatre); official board; Old Bailey; old bonded (whisky); old boy; Order of Barbados; order of battle; Order of the Bath; ordinary business (life assurance); ordnance board; outside

broadcast; Peru (international civil aircraft marking)
OBA optical bleaching agent (detergents)
Obad. Obadiah (Bible)
OBAFGKMRNS oh be a fine girl, kiss me right now, Susan (mnemonic for Draper classification of stars by temperature and brightness)
obb(l). *obbligato* (Italian: obligatory; music)
ÖBB *Österreichische Bundesbahnen* (German: Federal Railways of Austria)
OBC old boys' club
ob. dk observation deck
obdt obedient
OBE Officer of the Order of the British Empire; out-of-body experience
OBEV Oxford Book of English Verse
ob-gyn(e) obstetrics-gynaecology
OBI Order of British India
obit. obituary
obj. object; objection; objective
objn objection
obl. obligation; oblige; oblique; oblong
OBLI Oxford and Buckinghamshire Light Infantry
OBM Ordnance benchmark (surveying)
OBO ore-bulk-oil (ship)
Obogs on-board oxygen-generating system (military)
ob. ph. oblique photograph(y)
obre *octobre* (French: October)
obs. obscure; observation; observatory; observe; observed; observer; obsolete; obstetric/s; obstetrician
Obs. Observatory; Observer (newspaper)
obsc. obscure
OBSC obscure; obscured (meteorology)
obscd obscured
obsol. obsolescent; obsolete
obsp *obiit sine prole* (Latin: died without issue)
obst. oboist
obstet. obstetric/s; obstetrician
obstn obstruction
obt obedient
obtd obtained
OBU offshore banking unit
obv. obverse
OBV ocean boarding vessel
oc office copy; official classification; on centre (architecture); only child; open charter (shipping); open cover; *opere citato* (Latin: in the work cited); over-the-counter
o'c o'clock
o/c officer commanding; overcharge

Oc. Ocean
OC Birmingham (UK vehicle registration); Observer Corps; Office of Censorship (US); officer commanding; operating characteristics (electrical engineering); operations centre; oral contraceptive; Order in Council; Order of Canada; orienteering club; original cover (philately); Oslo Convention; overseas command; overseas country
oca ocarina (music)
OCA Old Comrades Association
OCAM(M) *Organisation commune africaine et malgache/africaine, malgache et mauritienne* (French: African and Malagasy/African, Malagasy and Mauritian Common Organization)
O. Carm. Order of the Brothers of the Blessed Virgin Mary of Mount Carmel (Carmelites)
O. Cart. Order of Carthusians
OCAS Organization of Central American States
OCatal. Old Catalan
OCAW Oil, Chemical and Atomic Workers International Union
Oc. B/L ocean bill of lading (shipping)
occ. occasion(al); occasionally; occident(al); occupation; occurrence
occas. occasional; occasionally
occn occasion
OCD obsessive compulsive disorder (medicine); Office of Civil Defense (US); on-line communications driver (computing); *Ordo/Ordinis Carmelitarum Discalceatorum* (Latin: Order of Discalced Carmelites)
OCDE *Organisation de coopération et de développement economiques* (French: Organization for Economic Cooperation and Development/OECD)
OCDM Office of Civil Defense Mobilization (US)
OCDS Overseas College of Defence Studies (Canada)
O/Cdt officer-cadet
oceanog. oceanography
OCelt Old Celtic
OCF Officiating Chaplain to the Forces
och. ochre
OCNL occasional; occasionally (meteorology)
OCorn Old Cornish
OCR optical character reader; optical recognition; *Ordo/Ordinis Cisterciensium Reformatorum* (Latin: Order of Reformed Cistercians; Trappists)

OCS Officer Candidate School (US); Old Church Slavonic; outer continental shelf
OCSO Order of the Reformed Cistercians of the Strict Observance (Trappists)
ocst. overcast (meteorology)
oct. octave (music); octavo (printing)
Oct. October
OCTU officer cadet training unit
OCTV open-circuit television
OCU Operational Conversion Unit
OCUC Oxford and Cambridge University Club
ocul. *oculis* (Latin: to the eyes)
OCV open-circuit voltage
od *oculus dexter* (Latin: right eye; medicine); olive drab (military); optical density; outer diameter; outside diameter
od. *oder* (German: or)
OD Doctor of Ophthalmology; Doctor of Optometry; Doctor of Osteopathy; Exeter (UK vehicle registration); Lebanon (international civil aircraft marking); *oculus dexter* (Latin: right eye; medicine); officer of the day; Old Dutch; olive drab (military); operations division; Order of Distinction (Jamaica); ordinary seaman; Ordnance datum; ordnance department; organization development; other denominations; outer diameter; outside diameter; overdose
O/D on deck; on demand; overdraft; overdrawn
ODA open document architecture (computing); Operating Department Assistant (medicine); Overseas Development Administration
ODan Old Danish
ODAS Ocean Data Station
ODC Order of Discalced Carmelites
ODCh Chaplain for Other Denominations
ODE ordinary differential equation (mathematics)
ODECA *Organizacion de estados centroamericanos* (Spanish: Organization of Central American States)
ODESSA Ocean Data Environmental Sciences Services Acquisition; *Organisation der SS-Angehörigen* (German: Organization of SS members)
ODETTE Organization for Data Exchange Through Tele-Transmission in Europe
ODI Overseas Development Institute
ODM Ministry of Overseas Development
ODO outdoor officer (customs)
ODP official development planning;

overall development planning; open-door policy

ODs other denominations

ODV *eau de vie* (French: water of life; cognac)

oe omissions excepted; open end

Oe oersted (unit of magnetic force)

OE Austria (international civil aircraft marking); Birmingham (UK vehicle registration); Office of Education (US); Old English; Old Etonian; omissions excepted; on examination (medicine); Order of Excellence (Guyana); original error; outboard engine

OEA Overseas Education Association; oxygen-enriched air

OEC oxygen-enriched combustion

OECD Organization for Economic Cooperation and Development

OECS Organization of Eastern Caribbean States

OED Oxford English Dictionary

OEDIPUS Oxford English Dictionary Interpretation, Proofing and Updating System

OEEC Organization for European Economic Cooperation

OEF Organization of Employers' Federations and Employers in Developing Countries

OEL occupational exposure limit (radiation)

OEM original equipment manufacturer (computing)

OEO Office of Economic Opportunity (US)

OEP Office of Economic Preparedness (US)

OER Officers' Emergency Reserve; Organization for European Research

o'er over

OES ocean energy system; Office of Economic Stabilization (US); Order of the Eastern Star; Organization of European States

OET Office of Education and Training

of optional form; outside face

OF Birmingham (UK vehicle registration); Oddfellows; oil-filled; oil-fired; old-face (type); Old French; operating forces; operational forces; Order of the Founder (Salvation Army); oxidizing flame

OFEMA *Office français d'exportation de matériel aéronautique* (French: Office for the Export of Aeronautical Material)

off. offer; offered; office; officer; official; officinal

offcl official

Offer Office of Electricity Regulation

offg offering; officiating

offic. official; officially

offr officer

Ofgas Office of Gas Supply

OFlem Old Flemish

OFM Order of Friars Minor (Franciscans)

OFMCap. Order of Friars Minor Capuchin (Franciscans)

OFMConv. Order of Friars Minor Conventual (Franciscans)

OFr Old French

OFR Order of the Federal Republic of Nigeria

OFris Old Frisian

OFS Orange Free State

Ofsted Office for Standards in Education

OFT Office of Fair Trading

Oftel Office of Telecommunications

Ofwat Office of Water Services

og original gum (philately); own goal (sport)

OG Air Guadeloupe (airline flight code); Birmingham (UK vehicle registration); Officer of the Guard; ogee (architecture); Olympic Games; original gangster (US); original gravity (brewing); original gum (philately); outside guard

OGael Old Gaelic

ÖGB *Österreichischer Gewerkschaftsbund* (German: Austrian Federation of Trade Unions)

OGL open general licence (commerce)

OGM ordinary general meeting

OGO orbiting geophysical observatory

Ogpu *Otdelenie Gosudarstvenni Politcheskoi Upravi* (Russian: United State Political Administration; Soviet secret police)

OGS Oratory of the Good Shepherd

oh observation helicopter; office hours; *omni hora* (Latin: hourly); on head; open hearth; overhead

OH Birmingham (UK vehicle registration); Finland (international civil aircraft marking); Ohio (zip code); old head (of Queen Victoria; numismatics)

OHBMS On Her or His Britannic Majesty's Service

ohc overhead cam(shaft)

OHD organic heart disease

OHDETS over-horizon detection system

OHG *Offene Handelsgesellschaft* (German: partnership); Old High German

OHMS On Her or His Majesty's Service

OHN occupational health nurse

OHNC occupational health nursing certificate
OHP overhead projector
OHS occupational health service; open hearth steel (metallurgy)
ohv overhead valve
OI Belfast (UK vehicle registration); office instruction; Old Irish; operating instructions
OIC officer in charge; *Organisation internationale du commerce* (French: International Trade Organization); Organization of Islamic Conference
OIcel Old Icelandic
OIG *organisation intergouvernementale* (French: intergovernmental organization)
OIPC *Organisation internationale de police criminelle* (French: International Criminal Police Organization; Interpol)
OIr Old Irish
OIS organizer industrial safety
OIt Old Italian
OIT *Organisation international du travail* (French: International Labour Organization)
oj open joint; open joist
OJ Birmingham (UK vehicle registration); orange juice (US); Order of Jamaica
OJAJ October, January, April, July (finance)
OJCS Office of the Joint Chiefs of Staff
OJR old Jamaica rum
OJT on the job training
OK all correct; Birmingham (UK vehicle registration); *oculus laevus* (Latin: left eye); Czech Republic and Slovakia (international civil aircraft marking); Oklahoma (zip code); orl korrect
oka otherwise known as
OKH *Oberkommando der Heeres* (German: Army High Command; World War II)
Okla Oklahoma
Okt. *Oktober* (German: October)
ol. *oleum* (Latin: oil; medicine); olive
Ol. Olympiad; Olympic
OL Birmingham (UK vehicle registration); *oculus laevus* (Latin: left eye); Oldham (UK postcode); Old Latin; on-line (computing); operating licence; Order of Leopold; Ordnance Lieutenant; outside left (sport); overflow level; overhead line
OLC Oak Leaf Cluster (military)
Old Test. Old Testament (Bible)
O-level ordinary level (examinations)
OLG Old Low German
Oli. Oligocene (geology)

OLQ officer-like qualities
OLRT on-line real time (computing)
om old measurement; *omni mane* (Latin: every morning; medicine)
Om. Oman
OM Air Mongol-MIAT (airline flight code, Mongolian PR); Birmingham (UK vehicle registration); old man; *Optimus Maximus* (Latin: greatest and best); Order of Merit; ordnance map
OMB Office of Management and Budget (US)
OMC operation and maintenance costs
OMCap Order of Friars Minor of St Francis Capuccinorum
OMCS Office of the Minister for the Civil Service
OMI Oblate/s of Mary Immaculate
OMM Officer of the Order of Military Merit (Canada)
omn. hor. *omni hora* (Latin: every hour; medicine)
omn. noct. *omni nocte* (Latin: every night; medicine)
OMO one-man operation; one-man operator
oms output per man shift
OMS orbital manoeuvring system (astronautics); *Organisation mondiale de la santé* (French: World Health Organization)
on *omni nocte* (Latin: every night; medicine)
ON Air Nauru (airline flight code, Australia); Birmingham (UK vehicle registration); octane number; Old Norse; Ontario; Order of the Nation (Jamaica); orthopaedic nurse
on appro. on approval
ONC Ordinary National Certificate; Orthopaedic Nursing Certificate
OND Ophthalmic Nursing Diploma; Ordinary National Diploma
ONERA *Office national d'études et de recherches aerospatiales* (French: National Office of Aerospace Study and Research)
ONF Old Norman French; Old Northern French
ONG *organisation non-gouvernementale* (French: non-governmental organization)
ONGC Oil and Natural Gas Commission (US)
ONI Office of Naval Intelligence
ono or near(est) offer
onomat. onomatopoeia; onomatopoeic
ONorth Old Northumbrian

ONorw Old Norwegian
ONR Office of Naval Research (US)
ont ordinary neap tide
Ont. Ontario (Canada)
ONZ Order of New Zealand
o/o on order; order of
O/o offers over
OO Belgium (international civil aircraft marking); Chelmsford (UK vehicle registration); observation officer; once-over; operation order; orderly officer; Skywest Airlines (airline flight code, Australia)
OOBE out-of-body experience
OOD object-oriented design (computing); officer of the day; officer of the deck
OOG officer of the guard
OOL object-oriented language (computing)
OON Officer of the Order of the Niger
ooo of obscure origin
o/o/o out of order
OOP object-oriented programming (computing)
OOT out of town
OOW officer of the watch
op old pattern; open pattern; opposite prompt side (theatre); out of print; overproof (alcohol)
op. opaque; opera; *opera* (Latin: works); operation(al); operator; opinion; opposite; optical; *optimus* (Latin: excellent); *opus* (Latin: work)
Op. Opus (music)
OP Birmingham (UK vehicle registration); observation post (military); old people; Old Persian; old prices; open policy (insurance); opposite prompt side (theatre); *Ordo/Ordinis Praedictatorum* (Latin: Order of Preachers; Dominicans); osmotic pressure; other people('s); out of print; outpatient; overproof (alcohol)
OPA Office of Price Administration (US); Orbis Press Agency (news agency, Czech Republic)
op-amp operational amplifier (electronics)
op art optical art
OPAS Occupational Pensions Advisory Service
OPB Occupational Pensions Board
OPC ordinary Portland cement; outpatients' clinic; Overseas Press Club of America
op. cit. *opere citato* (Latin: in the work cited)

OPCON operational control
OPCS Office of Population Censuses and Surveys
OPD outpatients' department
OPDAR optical detection and ranging
OPEC Organization of Petroleum Exporting Countries
Op-Ed opposite editorial (newspaper layout)
OPEIU Office and Professional Employees International Union (US)
OPEP *Organisation des pays exportateurs de pétrole* (French: Organization of Petroleum Exporting Countries; OPEC)
OPers Old Persian
OPEX operational, executive and administrative personnel (UN)
opg opening
OPg Old Portuguese
OPG orthopantomogram (dentistry)
ophthal. ophthalmic; ophthalmologist; ophthalmology
ophthalmol. ophthalmologist; ophthalmology
opl operational
OPM Office of Personnel Management; operations per minute; other people's money (US); output per man
OPMA Overseas Press and Media Association
opn operation; opinion; option; *ora pro nobis* (Latin: pray for us)
OPO one-person operation; one-person operator
OPol Old Polish
opp. opportunity; opposed; opposite; opposition; opuses
OPP oriented polypropene (plastic packaging); out of print at present
oppy opportunity
OPQ occupational personality questionnaire
opr. operate; operator
OPr Old Provençal
OP riots Old Price riots (theatre)
OPruss Old Prussian
ops operations
OP's other people's
opt. optative (grammar); optical; optician; optics; optimal; optimum; option(al)
OptD Doctor of Optometry
OQ Officer of the National Order of Quebec
or operationally risky; operational requirement; operations requirement; operations room; out of range; overhaul and repair; owner's risk (insurance)

or. orange; oratorio; orient(al); orientalist; original; other
Or Oriel College (Oxford)
OR Air Comores (airline flight code, Comoros); official receiver; official referee; Old Roman; operating room; operational research; operations research; orderly room; Oregon (zip code); other ranks (military); outside right (sport); owner's risk (insurance); Portsmouth (UK vehicle registration)
ÖR Österraichischer Rundfunk (Austrian broadcasting service)
Oracle optional reception of announcements by coded line electronics (teletext service)
orat. oration; orator; oratorical; oratorically; oratorio; oratory
orb owner's risk of breakage (insurance)
ORB oceanographic research buoy; omnidirectional radio beacon
ORBIS orbiting radio beacon ionospheric satellite
ORBIT on-line retrieval of bibliographical information
ORC Officers' Reserve Corps (US); Overseas Research Council
ORCA Ocean Resources Conservation Association
orch. orchestra(l); orchestrated by; orchestration
orchd orchestrated by
ord owner's risk of damage (insurance)
ord. ordain; ordained; order; ordinal; ordinance; ordinary; ordnance
ordn. ordnance
Ore. Oregon
ORE occupational radiation exposure
Oreg. Oregon
ORESCO Overseas Research Council
orf owner's risk of fire (insurance)
org. organ; organic; organism; organist; organization; organize; organized
ORGALIME *Organisme de liaison des industries métalliques européennes* (French: Liaison Group for the European Metal Industries)
organ. organic; organization
orgst organist
orient. oriental(ist)
orig. origami; origin; original; orginally; originate; originated
ORIT *Organización regional inter-americana de trabajadores* (Spanish: Inter-American Regional Organization of Workers)
Ork(n). Orkney Islands

orl owner's own risk of leakage (insurance)
ORL otorhinolaryngology (medicine)
orn. ornament(al); ornithology
ornith(ol). ornithological; ornithology
ORNL Oak Ridge National Laboratory (US)
OROM optical read-only memory (computing)
orph. orphan(age)
orr owner's risk rates (insurance)
ors others
ORS Old Red Sandstone (geology); Operational Research Society
orse otherwise
ORSL Order of the Republic of Sierra Leone
ORT Organization for Rehabilitation by Training (US)
orth. orthography; orthopaedic/s
Orth. Orthodox
ORuss Old Russian
ORV off-road vehicle
os ocean station; *oculus sinister* (Latin: left eye); oil switch; old series; only son; on station; outside (measurement)
o/s on sale; out of service; out of stock; outsize; outstanding (banking)
Os osmium (element)
OS Austrian Airlines (airline flight code); Glasgow (UK vehicle registration); *oculus sinister* (Latin: left eye); Old Saxon; Old School; old series; Old Side; Old Style (calendar); operating system (computing); Ordinary Seaman; Ordnance Survey; out of stock; outsize
OSA Office of the Secretary of the Army (US); Official Secrets Act; old style antique (typography); Order of the Hermit Friars of St Augustine (Augustinians); Overseas Sterling Area
OSAF Office of the Secretary of the Air Force (US)
OS&W oak, sunk and weathered (building)
OSax Old Saxon
OSB Order of St Benedict (Benedictines)
osc overseas staff college (military)
osc. oscillator
OSC Order of St Clare (Poor Clares)
OScan(d) Old Scandinavian
OSCAR Orbital Satellites Carrying Amateur Radio; Organization for Sickle Cell Anaemia Research
OSD Office of the Secretary of Defense (US); Order of St Dominic (Dominicans)
OSE operational support equipment

o'seas overseas
OSerb Old Serbian
OSF Order of St Francis (Franciscans)
OSFC Order of Friars Minor of St Francis Capuchin
o/sg outstanding
OSHA Occupational Safety and Health Administration (US)
OSI Office of Scientific Integrity (US); on-site inspection; open systems interconnection (computing)
O/Sig Ordinary Signalman
Osl. Oslo
OSl(av) Old Slavonic
OSL Old Style Latin
OSM Order of the Servants of Mary (Servites)
OSN Office of the Secretary of the Navy (US)
OSNC Orient Steam Navigation Company
OSO orbiting solar observatory
osp *obiit sine prole* (Latin: died without issue)
OSp Old Spanish
OSR Office of Science and Research
OSRB Overseas Service Resettlement Bureau
OSRD Office of Scientific Research and Development (US)
OSRO Office for Special Relief Operations (FAO)
OSS Office of Space Sciences (US); Office of Strategic Services (US)
O. SS. S *Ordo/Ordinis Sanctissimae Trinitatis Salvatoris* (Latin: Order of the Most Holy Saviour; Bridgettines)
O. SS. T *Ordo/Ordinis Sanctissimae Trinitatis Redemptionis Captivorum* (Latin: Order of the Most Holy Trinity for the Redemption of Captives; Trinitarians)
ost ordinary spring tide
OST Office of Science and Technology (US)
osteo. osteopath; osteopathic; osteopathy
OSTI Office of Scientific and Technical Information (US); Organization for Social and Technological Innovation (US)
OStJ Officer of the Order of St John of Jerusalem
OSU Order of St Ursula (Ursulines)
OSUK Ophthalmological Society of the United Kingdom
OSV ocean station vessel
OSw Old Swedish
OT occupational therapist; occupational

therapy; off time; Old Testament (Bible); Old Teutonic; operating theatre (medicine); Overland Telegraph (Australia); overseas trade; overtime; Portsmouth (UK vehicle registration)
OTA Office of Technology Assessment (US)
OTAN *Organisation du traité de l'Atlantique nord* (French: North Atlantic Treaty Organization; NATO)
OTASE *Organisation du traité de défense collective pour l'Asie du sud-est* (French: South-East Asia Treaty Organization; SEATO)
OTB off-track betting (US)
otbd outboard
OTC officer in tactical command (US); officers' training corps; officers' transit camp; one-stop inclusive tour charter; Organization for Trade Cooperation; over-the-counter
OTE on-target earnings
OTEC ocean thermal-energy conversion
OTeut Old Teutonic
OTF off the film (photography)
OTH over the horizon (telecommunications)
otol. otological; otology
OTS Office of Technical Services; officers' training school; opportunities to see (advertising)
ott. *ottava* (Italian: octave; music); *ottobre* (Italian: October)
Ott. Ottawa
OTT over the top
OTT-FNB Oy Suomen Tietoimisto (news agency, Finland)
OTU operational training unit
OTurk Old Turkish
OU Bristol (UK vehicle registration); official use; Open University; Oxford University
OUAC Oxford University Appointments Committee; Oxford University Athletic Club
OUAFC Oxford University Association Football Club
OUBC Oxford University Boat Club
OUCC Oxford University Cricket Club
OUDS Oxford University Dramatic Society
OUP Official Unionist Party (Northern Ireland); Oxford University Press
OURC Oxford University Rifle Club
OURFC Oxford University Rugby Football Club

OURT Order of the United Republic of Tanzania

out. outlet

outbd outboard

ov. ovary; over; overture

Ov. Ovid (Roman poet)

OV Birmingham (UK vehicle registration)

ovbd overboard

ovc other valuable consideration (law)

ovc. overcast (meteorology)

ovfl. overflow

OVH overhead projector

ovhd overhead

ovld overload

ovno or very near offer

ÖVP *Österreichische Volkspartei* (German: People's Party; Austria)

ovpd overpaid

Ovra *Opera di vigilanza e di repressione dell'anti-fascismo* (Italian secret police)

ovrd. override

ow old woman; one way; out of wedlock

OW Office of Works; Old Welsh; Portsmouth (UK vehicle registration)

O/W oil in water

OWC Ordnance Weapons Command

OWF optimum working frequency

OWI Office of War Information (US); operating while intoxicated (motor vehicle; US)

OWLS Oxford Word and Language Service

OWRS Office of Water Regulations and Standards (US)

OWS ocean weather service; ocean weather ship; ocean weather station

Ox. Oxford

OX Birmingham (UK vehicle registration); Oxford (UK postcode)

Oxbridge Oxford and Cambridge (universities)

Oxf. Oxford(shire)

Oxfam Oxford Committee for Famine Relief

Oxon. *Oxonia* (Latin: Oxfordshire); *Oxoniensis* (Latin: of Oxford)

OY Denmark (international civil aircraft marking); northwest London (UK vehicle registration)

oys. oysters

oz ounce

OZ Belfast (UK vehicle registration)

oz ap apothecaries' ounce

oz av(dp) avoirdupois ounce

oz T troy ounce

P

p page; paragraph; pass; passed; pence; penny; pint; population; present; proton; shower (meteorology)

p electric dipole moment (physics); momentum (physics); *piano* (Italian: softly; music); pressure (physics)

p. page; pamphlet; paragraph; part; participle; particle; *partim* (Latin: in part); pass; passed; past; peak; pectoral; *per* (Latin: by or for); perch; percussion; person; peseta (monetary unit); peso (monetary unit); piastre (monetary unit); *pied* (French: foot); pint; pipe; *pius* (Latin: holy); plaster; polar; pole; *pondere* (Latin: by weight); population; port; *post* (Latin: after); *pouce* (French: inch); *pour* (French: for or per); power; *primus* (Latin: first); *pro* (Latin: for); professional; purl (knitting)

P 400 (Roman numerals); North Korea (international civil aircraft marking); park; parking; pass; passed; pawn (chess); pedestrian; pedestrian crossing;

Permian (geology); pharmacy; phosphate; phosphorus (element); polynomial (computing); port; Portsmouth (UK fishing port registration); Portugal (international vehicle registration); positive; postage; Post Office; power; pressure; proprietary; Protestant; public; pula (monetary unit of Botswana)

P parity (physics)

P. *Papa* (Italian: Pope); parson; Pastor; *pater* (Latin: father); pedal (music); *Père* (French: Father); perennial (horticulture); period; personnel; pitch; *populus* (Latin: people); positive; post; postage; posterior (medicine); Presbyterian; President; Priest; Prince; probate; probation; pro-consul; Progressive; prompt side (theatre); Protestant; public; pupil

P2 Papua New Guinea (international civil aircraft marking)

P4 Aruba (international aircraft marking)

P45 DSS unemployment benefit form
pa participial adjective; per annum;
permanent address; personal
appearance; press agent
pa. past
p/a personal account
pA *per Adresse* (German: care of)
Pa pascal (physics); protactinium
(element)
Pa. Pennsylvania
PA Guildford (UK vehicle registration);
Paisley (UK postcode); Pakistan Army;
Panama (international vehicle
registration); Pan American World
Airways (airline flight code); particular
average (insurance); Patients'
Association; Pennsylvania (zip code);
performance assessment; pernicious
anaemia; personal accident (insurance);
personal account; personal allowance
(taxation); personal appearance;
personal assistant; pitch angle
(engineering); political agent; Port
Adjutant (military); power amplifier;
power of attorney; Prefect Apostolic
(Roman Catholic Church); press agent;
Press Association; press attaché; private
account; product analysis; prosecuting
attorney; public accountant; public
address; publicity agent; Publishers'
Association; purchasing agent
P/A power of attorney; private
account
PAA Pan American Airways; peracetic
acid (chemistry); polyacrylic acid
(chemistry)
PAADC Principal Air Aide-de-camp
PABLA problem analysis by logical
approach
PABX private automatic branch exchange
(telecommunications)
pac passed advanced class (Military
College of Science)
Pac. Pacific
PAC Pacific Air Command (US); Pan-
African Congress; Pan-American
Congress; political action committee;
powdered activated carbon (chemistry);
Public Accounts Committee; Public
Assistance Committee; put-and-call
(stock exchange option)
PACAF Pacific Air Forces (US Air Force)
PACE performance and cost evaluation;
Police and Criminal Evidence Act;
precision analogue computing
equipment
Pacif. Pacific

PACOM Pacific Command (US)
PACS Pacific area communications
system
PACT Producers' Alliance for Cinema
and Television
pad. padding; paddock; padlock
PaD Pennsylvania Dutch
PAD packet assembler/disassembler
(computing); passive air defence;
payable after death
PADAR passive detection and ranging
(military)
PADLOC passive detection and location
of counter-measures (military)
p. Adr. *per Adresse* (German: care of)
p. ae. *partes equales* (Latin: equal parts;
medicine)
paf *puissance au frein* (French: brake
horsepower)
PAF peripheral address field
(computing)
PaG Pennsylvania German
PAg Professional Agronomist
PAGB Proprietary Association of Great
Britain
PAHO Pan American Health
Organization
paint. painter; painting
PAIS Public Affairs Information Service
(US)
Pak. Pakistan; Pakistani
PAK Pakistan (international vehicle
registration)
Pak Re Pakistan rupee (monetary unit)
pal. palace; palaeography; palaeontology
Pal. Palace; Palaeocene (geology);
Palestine; Palestinian
PAL Parcel Air Lift (US); peripheral
availability list (computing); phase
alternation line (television); Philippine
Airlines
palaeob(ot). palaeobotanical; palaeo-
botany
palaeog. palaeographical; palaeography
palaeontol. palaeontology
PALS permissive action link systems
(computing)
pam(ph). pamphlet
PAM pulse-amplitude modulation
(telecommunications)
PAMA Pan-American Medical
Association; Press Advertisement
Managers' Association
pan. panchromatic (photography);
panorama; panoramic; pantomime;
pantry
Pan. Panama; Panamanian

PAN *Partido Acción Nacional* (Spanish: National Action Party; Mexico)
PANA Pan-African News Agency
PANAFTEL Pan-African Telecommunications Network
PanAm Pan American World Airways
Pan. Can. Panama Canal
P&E plant and equipment
P&G Proctor & Gamble (pharmaceutical manufacturing company)
P&L profit and loss
P&O Peninsular and Oriental Steam Navigation Company
p&p post and packing
P&RT physical and recreational training
PANS procedures for air navigation services
panto pantomime
PAO Prince Albert's Own (regiment); public affairs officer
Pap. Papua; Papuan
PAP People's Action Party (Singapore); *Polska Agencja Prasowa* (news agency, Poland)
Pap-NG Papua-New Guinea
PAPS periodic armaments planning system
par planed all round (carpentry)
par. paragraph; parallax; parallel; paraphrase; parenthesis; parish; parochial
Par. Paraguay; Paraguayan
PAR perimeter acquisition radar; phased-array radar; precision approach radar; programme analysis review; pulse acquisition radar
para. paragraph
parab. parabola
par. aff. *pars affecta* (Latin: (to the) part affected; medicine)
paras paratroopers
parch. parchment
Par. Ch. parish church
paren. parenthesis
parens. parentheses
Parl. parliament; parliamentarian; parliamentary
parl. agt parliamentary agent
parl. proc. parliamentary procedure
Parly Sec. parliamentary secretary
PARM programme analysis for resource management
part. partial; participate; participial; participle; particle; particular; partition; partner; partnership
part. aeq. *partes aequales* (Latin: in equal parts; medicine)

pas power-assisted steering
pas. passive (grammar)
PAS public-address system
Pasok Panhellenic Socialist Movement
pass. passage; passenger; *passim* (Latin: here and there throughout); passive (grammar)
Pass. Passover
PASSIM Presidential Advisory Staff on Scientific Management
pat. patent; patented; pattern
PAT point after touchdown (American football); preauthorized automatic transfer (banking); Professional Association of Teachers
Pata. Patagonia; Patagonian
PATA Pacific Area Travel Association
patd patented
path(ol). pathological; pathology
Pat. Off. Patent Office
pat. pend. patent pending
PAU Pan American Union; programmes analysis unit
pav. pavilion
PAW powered all the way
PAWA Pan American World Airways
PAWC Pan-African Workers' Congress
PAWR Public Authority for Water Resources (US)
PAX private automatic telephone exchange
PAYE pay as you earn (taxation); pay as you enter
paymr paymaster
payt payment
PAYV pay as you view
pb passed ball (baseball)
Pb lead (element)
PB Air Burundi (airline flight code); Guildford (UK vehicle registration); pass book; permanent base; personal best (athletics); Pharmacopoeia Britannica; phenobarbitone (pharmacology); *Philosphiae Baccalaureus* (Latin: Bachelor of Philosophy); plastic-bonded; Plymouth Brethren; pocket book; power brakes; Prayer Book; premium bond; Primitive Baptists; Publications Board (US); purl into back of stitch (knitting)
PBA poor bloody assistant; Professional Bowlers Association (US); Public Buildings Administration (US)
PBAB please bring a bottle
PBC powerboat club
PBI poor bloody infantry; protein-bound iodine (medicine)

pbk paperback (books)
PBM permanent benchmark (surveying)
PBR payment by results
PBS Public Broadcasting Service
pbt profit before tax (finance)
PBT pay-back time (accounting)
PBX private branch telephone exchange
pc parsec (astronomy); per cent; personal computer; petty cash; postcard; *post cibum* (Latin: after meals; medicine)
pc. percentage; pica (printing); piece; price
PC Fiji Air (airline flight code); Guildford (UK vehicle registration); Panama Canal; paper chromatography (chemistry); Parish Council(lor); Parliamentary Commissioner; parsec; *Partie Communiste* (French: Communist Party); Past Commander; Paymaster Captain; Peace Commissioner (Ireland); Peace Corps (US); perpetual curate; personal computer; pioneer corps (military); pitch circle (machinery); Plaid Cymru (political party); Police Constable; political correctness; politically correct; polo club; polycarbonate (chemistry); polypropene carbonate (plastic); polypropylene carbonate (plastic); Poor Clares (religious order); Portland cement; port of call; post commander; preparatory commission; Press Council; pre-stressed concrete; Prince Consort; printed circuit (electronics); Prison Commission; Privy Council; Privy Councillor; process control; professional corporation (US); Progressive Conservative (Canada); public convenience; pulverized coal
P/C petty cash; price/s current
PCA Parliamentary Commissioner for Administration; Permanent Court of Arbitration
PCB petty cash book; polychlorinated piphenyl (pollutant); printed-circuit board (electronics); private car benefits (insurance)
pcc precipitated calcium carbonate (chemistry)
PCC parochial church council; *Partido Comunista de Cuba* (Spanish: Communist Party of Cuba); political consultative committee; Press Complaints Commission; Privy Council cases
PCE *Partido Comunista de España* (Spanish: Communist Party of Spain); Postgraduate Certificate of Education
pcf pounds per cubic foot

PCF *Parti Communiste Français* (French: French Communist Party); pistol, centre fire (firearms)
PCFC Polytechnics and Colleges Funding Council
P. Ch. parish church
pci pounds per cubic inch
PCI *Partito Comunista Italiano* (Italian: Italian Communist Party)
pcl parcel
PCL printer control language (computing)
pcm per calendar month
PCM pulse-code modulation (telecommunications)
PCMI photochromic microimage
PCMO principal colonial medical officer
PCN *Partido de Conciliación Nacional* (Spanish: National Conciliation Party; El Salvador); personal communications network (computing)
PCOB Permanent Central Opium Board (UN)
PCP Past Chief Patriarch; phenylcyclo-hexylpiperidine (hallucinogenic drug); polychloroprene (rubber)
PCR Pedestrian Crossings Regulations
PCRS Poor Clergy Relief Society
pcs pieces; prices
PCS Principal Clerk of Session (Scotland)
PCSP Permanent Commission for the South Pacific
pct per cent
PCTFE polychlorotrifluoroeth(yl)ene (plastic)
PCU power control unit; power conversion unit; pressurization control unit
PCV passenger-controlled vehicle; Peace Corps Volunteers (US); pressure containment vessel
PCZ Panama Canal Zone
PCZST Panama Canal Zone Standard Time
pd paid; passed; *per diem* (Latin: daily); pitch diameter (engineering); poop deck; postage due; postdated; potential difference (physics); preliminary design
p/d postdated
Pd palladium (element)
PD Guildford (UK vehicle registration); *per diem* (Latin: daily); Peterhead (UK fishing port registration); *Pharmaciae Doctor* (Latin: Doctor of Pharmacy); *Philosophiae Doctor* (Latin: Doctor of Philosophy); polar distance; Police

Department (US); port dues; *posdata* (Spanish: postscript); postal district; preventive detainee; preventive detention; production department; Progressive Democrat (Ireland); property damage (insurance); Public Defender (US); public domain (computing)
P/D price/dividend
PDA *pour dire adieu* (French: to say goodbye); predicted drift angle (navigation)
PdB *Pedagogiae Baccalaureus* (Latin: Bachelor of Pedagogy; US)
PDC *Partido Demócrata Cristiano* (Spanish: Christian Democratic Party; El Salvador); personnel dispatch centre; personnel dispersal centre
PdD *Pedagogiae Doctor* (Latin: Doctor of Pedagogy; US)
PDE Projectile Development Establishment
P-de-C Pas-de-Calais (French department)
P-de-D Puy-de-Dôme (French department)
PDFLP Popular Democratic Front for the Liberation of Palestine
PDG Paymaster Director-General; *président directeur général* (French: chairman and managing director)
PDGF platelet-derived growth factor (biochemistry; medicine)
pdi predelivery inspection
PDL poverty datum line
PdM *Pedagogiae Magister* (Latin: Master of Pedagogy; US)
PDM pulse-duration modulation (telecommunications)
pdn production
PDN public data network
PDP program development plan (NASA); programmed data processing
pdq pretty damn quick
pdr pounder
PDR People's Democratic Republic; precision depth recorder; price-dividend ratio
PDS Parkinson's Disease Society; Party of Democratic Socialism (German political party); programming documentation standards (computing)
PDSA People's Dispensary for Sick Animals
PDSR Principal Director of Scientific Research
PDT Pacific Daylight Time

pe personal estate (law); printer's error
Pe *Padre* (Spanish: Father; Roman Catholic Church)
PE Guildford (UK vehicle registration); personal effects (insurance); Peru (international vehicle registration); Peterborough (UK postcode); Petroleum Engineer (US); physical education; plastic explosive; pocket edition; Poole (UK fishing port registration); polyeth(yl)ene; Port Elizabeth (South Africa); potential energy (physics); Presiding Elder; printer's error; probable error; procurement executive; Professional Engineer (US); Protestant Episcopal
P/E port of embarkation; price-earnings ratio
PEA Physical Education Association of Great Britain and Northern Ireland
PEC photoelectric cell; Protestant Episcopal Church
ped. pedal; pedestal; pedestrian
PedD *Pedagogiae Doctor* (Latin: Doctor of Pedagogy)
pediat. pediatrics
PEDir Director of Physical Education
Peeb. Peebles
PEEP pilot's electronic eye-level presentation
PEI Prince Edward Island (Canada)
p. ej. *por ejemplo* (Spanish: for example)
Pek. Peking
PEL permissible exposure level; permissible exposure limit
Pemb. Pembroke College (Oxford, Cambridge)
Pembs. Pembrokeshire
pen. penal; penetration; peninsula(r)
Pen Pennsylvanian (geology)
Pen. Peninsula; Penitentiary
PEN International Association of Poets, Playwrights, Editors, Essayists and Novelists
PEng Member of the Society of Professional Engineers; Registered Professional Engineer (Canada)
Penn. Pennsylvania
penol. penology
pent. pentagon
Pent. Pentateuch; Pentecost
PEP personal equity plan; political and economic planning
PEPP Professional Engineers in Private Practice (US)
per *per procurationem* (Latin: on behalf of)
per. percentile; period; person

Per. Persian

PER price-earnings ratio; Professional and Executive Recruitment; Professional Employment Register

PERA Production Engineering Research of Great Britain

per an(n). *per annum* (Latin: yearly)

P/E ratio price-earnings ratio

perc. percussion

per con *per contra* (Latin: on the other side; book-keeping)

perd. *perdendosi* (Italian: dying away; music)

perf. perfect; perfection; perforate; perforated; perforation; performance; performed (by); performer

perh. perhaps

peri(g). perigee

perjy perjury

perk(s) perquisite/s

PERK perchloroeth(yl)ene (solvent)

perm permanent wave (hair-dressing)

perm. permanent; permission; permutation

PERME Propellants, Explosives and Rocket Motor Establishment

perp. perpendicular; perpetual

per pro. *per procurationem* (Latin: by proxy)

pers. person; personal; personally; perspective

Pers. Persia; Persian

pert. pertaining

PERT performance evaluation and review technique (computing, management); programme evaluation and review technique (computing, management); project evaluation and review technique (computing, management)

Peru(v). Peruvian

PESC Public Expenditure Survey Committee

Pesh. Peshawar (Pakistan)

pet. petroleum; petrological; petrologist; petrology

Pet. Peter (Bible); Peterhouse (Cambridge); Petronius (Roman satirist)

petn petition

PETP polyeth(yl)ene terephthalate (polyester)

petr. petrification; petrify; petrology

Petra Jordan News Agency

Petriburg: *Petriburgensis* (Latin: (Bishop) of Peterborough)

petro. petrochemical

petrog. petrography

petrol. petrology

PETS posting and enquiry terminal system (computing)

p. ex. *par exemple* (French: for example)

pf pfennig (German monetary unit); *piano e forte* (Italian: soft then loud; music); *pianoforte* (Italian: piano); *più forte* (Italian: louder); pneumatic float; pro forma (invoice)

pf. perfect; preferred (stock; finance); proof

PF Guildford (UK vehicle registration); panchromatic film; Patriotic Front; phenol-formaldehyde; plain face (building); power factor; Procurator-Fiscal; public funding; pulverized fuel

PFA Professional Footballers' Association

PFB preformed beams (building)

PFBR prototype fast breeder reactor (nuclear engineering)

pfc passed flying college

Pfc Private first-class (US Army)

pfce performance

pfd preferred (finance)

Pfd *Pfund* (German: pound)

PFD position fixing device

pfd sp. preferred spelling

PFF pathfinder force

pfg pfennig (German monetary unit)

PFLP Popular Front for the Liberation of Palestine

PFM pulse-frequency modulation (telecommunications)

PFR prototype fast reactor (nuclear engineering)

PFRT preliminary flight rating test

PFSA *pour faire ses adieux* (French: to say goodbye)

pft acct piano(forte) accompaniment

PFV *pour faire visite* (French: to make a call)

pfx prefix

pg pay group; paying guest; *persona grata* (Latin: acceptable person); proof gallon (alcohol); proving ground

pg. page

Pg Palaeogene (geology)

Pg. Portugal; Portuguese

PG Guildford (UK vehicle registration); parental guidance (cinema certification); Past Grand (Freemasonry); paying guest; postgraduate; Preacher General; pregnant; *prisonnier de guerre* (French: prisoner of war); Procurator-General

PGA Professional Golfers' Association ·

pgc per gyrocompass (navigation)

PGCE Postgraduate Certificate of Education
PG Cert Postgraduate Certificate
PGD Past Grand Deacon (Freemasonry)
PG Dip Postgraduate Diploma
PgDn page down (keyboard)
PGM Past Grand Master
pgn pigeon
PGR population growth rate; psychogalvanic response (psychology)
pgt per gross ton
PgUp page up (keyboard)
ph precipitation hardening (engineering)
ph. phase; philosopher; philosophy
pH acidity/alkalinity scale (chemistry)
Ph Phanerozoic (geology)
PH Guildford (UK vehicle registration); Netherlands (international civil aircraft marking); Perth (UK postcode); petroleum hydrocarbon; Plymouth (UK fishing port registration); Polynesian Airlines (airline flight code); previous history (medicine); public health; public house; Purple Heart (US military award)
PHA Public Health Act; Public Housing Administration (US); public housing authority
PHAB Physically Handicapped and Able-Bodied (charity)
phal. phalanx
phar(m). pharmacist; pharmacopoeia; pharmacy
Phar(m)B *Pharmaciae Baccalaureus* (Latin: Bachelor of Pharmacy)
Phar(m)D *Pharamciae Doctor* (Latin: Doctor of Pharmacy)
pharm. pharmaceutical; pharmacist; pharmacology; pharmacopoeia; pharmacy
Phar(m)M *Pharmaciae Magister* (Latin: Master of Pharmacy)
pharmacol. pharmacology
pharm. chem. pharmaceutical chemistry
PhB *Philosophiae Baccalaureus* (Latin: Bachelor of Philosophy)
ph. brz. phosphor bronze
PHC Pharmaceutical Chemist; primary health care
PhD *Philosophiae Doctor* (Latin: Doctor of Philosophy)
PHD Doctor of Public Health
PhDEd Doctor of Philosophy in Education
PHE Public Health Engineer
PhG Graduate in Pharmacy (US)
PHI permanent health insurance; Public Health Inspector

PHIBLANT Amphibious Forces, Atlantic (US Navy)
PHIBPAC Amphibious Forces, Pacific (US Navy)
phil. philological; philology; philosopher; philosophical; philosophy
Phil. Philadelphia; Philharmonic; Philippians (Bible); Philippines; philology
Phila. Philadelphia
Philem. Philemon (Bible)
Phil. I(s). Philippine Islands
philol. philological; philology
philos. philosopher; philosophical; philosophy
Phil. Soc. Philharmonic Society
Phil. Trans. Philosophical Transactions of the Royal Society of London
PhL Licentiate in Philosophy; Licentiate of Philosophy
PHLS Public Health Laboratory Service
PhM *Philosophiae Magister* (Latin: Master of Philosophy)
PhmB Bachelor of Pharmacy
PHN Public Health Nurse
Phoen. Phoenician; Phoenix
phon. phonetic; phonetically; phonetics; phonology
phot(og). photograph; photographer; photographic; photography
photom. photometrical; photometry
php pounds per horsepower; pump horsepower
phr. phrase; phraseology
phren(ol). phrenological; phrenology
PHS Public Health Service (US)
phys. physical; physically; physician; physicist; physics; physiological; physiology
phys. ed. physical education
physiog. physiography
physiol. physiological; physiologist; physiology
phys. sc. physical science
pi professional indemnity (insurance)
PI Cork (Irish vehicle registration); Pasteur Institute; per inquiry; personal injury; petrol injected; Philippine Islands; photographic interpretation; photographic interpreter; pimp (US); principal investigator (US); private investigator; programmed instruction (computing)
PIA Pakistan International Airlines Corporation; peripheral interface adaptor (computing)

piang. *piangendo* (Italian: plaintive; music)
pianiss. *pianissimo* (Italian: very soft; music)
PIAT projector infantry anti-tank (weapon)
PIB Petroleum Information Bureau
PIBOR Paris Inter-Bank Offered Rate (finance)
pic. piccolo (music); pictorial; picture
PIC product of incomplete combustion; programmable interrupt controller (computing)
PID personal identification device
PIDS primary immune deficiency syndrome (medicine)
PIE Paedophile Information Exchange; Proto-Indo-European (language)
pigmt pigment
pigmtn pigmentation
PIH pregnancy-induced hypertension
PIK payment in kind
pil. *pilula* (Latin: pill; medicine)
PIL payment in lieu
PILL programmed instruction language learning (computing)
PILOT programmed inquiry, learning or teaching (computing)
PIM personal information manager (computing); pulse interval modulation (telecommunications)
PIMS profit impact of market strategy
PIN personal identification number
P-in-C Priest-in-Charge
Pind. Pindar (Greek poet)
PINS person in need of supervision (US)
pinx(it) *pinxit* (Latin: he/she painted it)
PIO parallel input/output (computing); photographic interpretation officer; public information office (US military); public information officer (US military)
PIPO parallel in, parallel out (computing)
Pippy person inheriting parent's property
PIRA Paper Industries Research Association
PISO parallel in, serial out (computing)
PITCOM Parliamentary Information Technology Committee
pix pictures (movies)
pixel picture element (computing)
pizz. *pizzicato* (Italian: pinched or plucked; music)
pj physical jerks; pyjamas
PJ Guildford (UK vehicle registration); Netherlands Antilles (international civil aircraft marking); petajoule (physics); Presiding Judge; Probate Judge; pyjamas

pk pack; package; park; peak; peck
PK Guildford (UK vehicle registration); Indonesia and West Irian (international civil aircraft marking); Pakistan International Airlines (airline flight code); personal knowledge; psychokinesis
pkg packing; parking
pkg. package
PKP *Polskie Koleje Panstwowe* (Polish: Polish State Railways)
pkt packet; pocket
PKU phenylketonuria (medicine)
pkwy parkway (US)
pl. place; plain; plate; platoon; plural; pole
Pl. Place; Plate; Platz
PL Aeroperu (airline flight code, Peru); Guildford (UK vehicle registration); partial loss (insurance); passenger liability (insurance); patrol leader (scouting); Paymaster Lieutenant; Peel (UK fishing port registration); Plimsoll line (shipping); Plymouth (UK postcode); Poet Laureate; Poland (international vehicle registration); position line; Primrose League; product liability (law); product licence; programmed learning; programming language (computing); public law; public library
pla passengers' luggage in advance
Pla. Plaza
PLA People's Liberation Army (China); Port of London Authority
plan. planet; planetarium
plas. plaster; plastic
plat. plateau; platform; platinum; platonic; platoon
PLATO programmed logic for automated learning operation (computing)
Plaut. Plautus (Roman playwright)
plc public limited company
PLC Poor Law Commissioners; product life cycle; public limited company
plcy policy
pld payload
PLD potentially lethal damage; programmable logic device (computing)
Ple Pleistocene (geology)
pleb. plebeian
Plen. plenipotentiary
plf(f) plaintiff
PLG private/light goods (vehicle)
plgl. plateglass
Pli Pliocene (geology)

PLI *Partito Liberale Italiano* (Italian: Italian Liberal Party)
PLM Paris-Lyons-Mediterranean (Railway); pulse-length modulation (telecommunications)
plmb. plumber; plumbing
plng planning
PLO Palestine Liberation Organization
PLP Parliamentary Labour Party
PLR public lending right
Pls plates (books)
Pl Sgt platoon sergeant
PLSS personal life-support system (astronautics); portable life-support system (astronautics)
plstc plastic
plstr plasterer
plt pilot
pltc. political
pltf plaintiff
plu. plural
PLU people like us
plup(f). pluperfect
plur. plural; plurality
Pluto pipe line under the ocean (World War II)
Ply. Plymouth
plywd plywood
pm permanent magnet; post master; *post meridiem* (Latin: after noon); post mortem; premium; premolar (tooth)
Pm promethium (element)
PM Guildford (UK vehicle registration); parachute mine; particular metre (music); peculiar metre (music); Past Master; Paymaster; phase modulation (telecommunications); *piae memoriae* (Latin: of pious memory); Pipe Major; Police Magistrate; *polícia militare* (Italian: military police); Pope and Martyr; Postmaster; *post meridiem* (Latin: after noon); post mortem; preventive maintenance; predictive maintenance; prime minister; product manager; provost marshal (military)
PMA Pakistan Medical Association; papillary, marginal, attached (dentistry); paramethoxyamphetamine (hallucinogenic drug); personal military assistant; phenylmercuric acetate (chemistry); Purchasing Management Association (US)
PMAF Pharmaceutical Manufacturers' Association Foundation (US)
PM&ATA Paint Manufacturers' and Allied Trades Association

PM&R physical medicine and rehabilitation
PMB Potato Marketing Board
PMBX private manual branch exchange (telecommunications)
PMC Personnel Management Centre; plaster-moulded cornice (building)
PMD Program for Management Development (US)
PME protective multiple earthing (electronics)
PMF probable maximum flood
PMG Pall Mall Gazette; Paymaster General; Postmaster General; Provost Marshal General (military)
pmh past medical history; per man-hour
pmk postmark
PML prime minister's list; probable maximum loss (insurance)
PMM pulse-mode multiplex (telecommunications)
PMMA polymethylmethacrylate (synthetic resin)
PMO principal medical officer
PM of F Presidential Medal of Freedom
pmr paymaster
PMRAFNS Princess Mary's Royal Air Force Nursing Service
PMS Pantone Matching System (colour printing); premenstrual syndrome; processor-memory-switch (computing); project management system
pmt payment
PMT photomechanical transfer (photography); premenstrual tension; project management team
PMV predicted mean vote
PMX private manual exchange (telecommunications)
pn percussion note; percussive note; please note; promissory note (commerce)
PN Brighton (UK vehicle registration); Pakistan Navy; postnatal; Preston (UK fishing port registration); promissory note
P/N part number; promissory note (commerce)
Pna Panama
PNA Pakistan National Airlines; paranitroaniline (dye); Philippines News Agency; Psychiatric Nurses Association
PNB Philippine National Bank
PNC Palestinian National Council; People's National Congress (Guyana)
PND postnatal depression
PNdB perceived noise decibel/s

pndg pending
pneu(m). pneumatic
PNEU Parents' National Educational Union
png *persona non grata* (Latin: unacceptable person)
PNG Papua New Guinea; Papua New Guinea (international vehicle registration)
pnl panel
PNLM Palestine National Liberation Movement
PNO principal nursing officer
PNO People's National Party (Jamaica)
pnr pioneer; prior notice required
Pnt. Pentagon (US)
PNTO principal naval transport officer
pntr painter
PNV *Partido Nacional Vesco* (Spanish: Basque National Party)
pnxt *pinxit* (Latin: he/she painted it)
PNYA Port of New York Authority
Pnz. Penzance
po part of; *per os* (Latin: by mouth; medicine); postal order; power oscillator; previous order; putout (baseball)
Po polonium (element)
PO parcels office; parole officer; *par ordre* (French: by order); Passport Office; Patent Office; personnel officer; petty officer; Philharmonic Orchestra; pilot officer; Portsmouth (UK vehicle registration; postcode); postal order; Post Office; power-operated; Province of Ontario; public office; public officer; Pyrénées-Orientales (French department)
POA Prison Officers' Association
POAC Post Office Advisory Council
POB Post Office box
POC port of call; product of combustion (chemistry)
POD pay on death; pay on delivery; Pocket Oxford Dictionary; port of debarkation; Post Office Department (US)
POE port of embarkation; port of entry
POED Post Office Engineering Department
poet. poetic(al); poetry
POETS day piss off early tomorrow's Saturday
POEU Post Office Engineers Union
P of W Prince of Wales
poi. poison; poisonous

pol. polar; polarize; police; political; politician; politics
Pol. Poland; Polish
POL Patent Office Library; petroleum, oil and lubricants; problem-oriented language (computing)
pol. ad. political adviser
pol. econ. political economy
pol. ind. pollen index
Polis Parliamentary On-Line Information Service
polit. political; politics
poll. pollution
pol. sci. political science
Poly. Polynesia; Polynesian; Polytechnic; polyvinyl
POM prescription-only medication; prescription-only medicine
Ponsi person of no strategical importance (military)
pont. br. pontoon bridge
Ponti person of no tactical importance (military)
POO Post Office order
pop point of purchase; popular
pop. popular; popularly; population
POP plaster of Paris; point of purchase; Post Office preferred; proof of purchase
POPA Property Owners Protection Association
por payable on receipt; pay on receipt; pay on return; port of refuge
por. porosity; porous; portion; portrait
PORIS Post Office Radio Interference Station
porn. pornography
port. portable; portrait; portraiture
Port. Portugal; Portuguese
pos point of sale
pos. position; positive
POS point of sale; Port of Spain (Trinidad)
POSH port out, starboard home (preferred choice of cabins on luxury liners)
posn position
pos. pro. possessive pronoun
poss. possession; possessive (grammar); possible; possibly
POSSLQ person of opposite sex sharing living quarters
post. posthumous
POST Parliamentary Office of Science and Technology; point-of-sales terminal
posth(um). posthumous; posthumously
pot. potash; potassium; potential; potentiometer

poul. poultry
POUNC Post Office Users' National Council
POV point of view (cinema); privately owned vehicle
POW please oblige with; Prince of Wales; prisoner of war
powd. powder
pp pages; parcel post; past participle; per person; *per procurationem* (Latin: by proxy); *pianissimo* (Italian: very quietly; music); play or pay; post-paid; *post prandium* (Latin: after a meal; medicine); prepaid; present position; privately printed
pp. pages
PP Brazil (international civil aircraft marking); Luton (UK vehicle registration); Pacific plate (geology); parcel post; parish priest; parliamentary papers; *Partido Popular* (Spanish: Popular Party; Spain); *Pastor Pastorum* (Latin: Shepherd of the Shepherds); Past President; *Pater Patriae* (Latin: Father of his Country); *Patres* (Latin: Fathers); petrol point; polyprop(yl)ene (chemistry); prepositional phase
ppa polyphosphoric acid (chemistry)
PPA Pakistan Press Association; *Parti Populaire Algérian* (French: Popular Party of Algeria); Periodical Publishers' Association; Pools Proprietors' Association; Pre-School Playgroup Association
ppb parts per billion
PPB paper, printing and binding; party political broadcast; planning-programming-budgeting; private posting box
PPBAS planning-programming-budgeting-accounting system
PPBS planning-programming-budgeting system
PPC *Patres Conscripti* (Latin: Conscript Fathers; Roman Senate); *pour prendre congé* (French: to take leave); Professional Purposes Committee; progressive patient care; Public Power Corporation (US)
PPCLI Princess Patricia's Canadian Light Infantry
PPCS Primary Producers' Cooperation Society (New Zealand)
ppd post-paid; prepaid
PPE personal protective equipment; philosophy, politics and economics
PPF personal property floater (insurance)

PPFA Planned Parenthood Federation of America
pph. pamphlet
PPH paid personal holidays (US); post-partum haemorrhage (medicine)
ppi parcel post insured
PPI Pakistan Press International; plan position indicator; policy proof of interest (insurance); producer price index
PPITB Printing and Publishing Industry Training Board
PPK *Polizei Pistole Kriminal* (German: police criminal pistol; firearm)
PPL private pilot's licence
pple participle
ppm pages per minute; parts per million; pulse per minute
PPM pulse-position modulation (telecommunications)
PPMA Produce Packaging and Marketing Association
ppp *pianissimo* (Italian: as quietly as possible; music)
PPP Pakistan's People's Party; People's Progressive Party; personal pension plan; private patients plan; psychology, philosophy and physiology; purchasing power parity (economics)
PPPPL private pilot's licence
PPPS post post post-scriptum
ppr paper; present participle; proper
PPR printed paper rate (postage)
PPRA Past President of the Royal Academy
p. pro. *per procurationem* (Latin: by proxy)
PPS Parliamentary Private Secretary; post post-scriptum; Principal Private Secretary
ppt. precipitate (chemistry)
pptd precipitated (chemistry)
pptg precipitating (chemistry)
pptn precipitation (chemistry)
ppty property
PPU Peace Pledge Union; Primary Producers' Union
pq preceding question; previous question
PQ parliamentary question; *Parti Québecois* (French: Quebec Party; Canada); personality quotient; Province of Quebec
pr painter; pair; paper; parcel repair; per; *per rectum* (Latin: by the rectum; medicine); power
pr. prayer; preferred (stock); present; pressure; price; print; printed; printer;

printing; pronoun; proof; proper; prove; provincial

Pr praseodymium (element)

Pr. *Praca* (Portuguese: Square); Priest; Prince; Protestant; Provençal

PR Bournemouth (UK vehicle registration); parliamentary report; partial remission (medicine); partial response; *Parti Républicain* (French: Republican Party; France); pattern recognition (computing); payroll; percentile rank; performance ratio; personal representative (law); Philippine Airlines (airline flight code); photographic reconnaissance; Pipe Rolls; plotting and radar; *Populus Romanus* (Latin: the Roman people); postal regulations; preliminary report; Pre-Raphaelite; press release; press representative; Preston (UK postcode); prize ring (boxing); production rate; profit rate; progress report; project report; proportional representation; public relations; Puerto Rican; Puerto Rico; purchase request

PRA President of the Royal Academy; Public Roads Administration (US)

prag. pragmatic; pragmatism

pram perambulator

PRB People's Republic of Bulgaria; Pre-Raphaelite Brotherhood (artists)

PRBS President of the Royal Society of British Sculptors

PRC People's Republic of China; Postal Rate Commission (US); *post Romam conditam* (Latin: after the foundation of Rome); Price Regulation Committee (US)

PRCA President of the Royal Cambrian Academy; Public Relations Consultants' Association

prchst parachutist

prcht parachute

PRCP President of the Royal College of Physicians

prcs process

PRCS President of the Royal College of Surgeons

prcst precast

PRE Petroleum Refining Engineer; President of the Royal Society of Painter-Etchers and Engravers

Preb. prebend; prebendary

prec. preceding; precision

Prec. Precentor

pred. predicate; predicative

pref. preface; prefatory; prefect;

preferable; preferably; preference; preferred; prefix

Pref. Prefect

prefab prefabricated

prehist. prehistoric(al); prehistory

prej. prejudice

Prela *Prensa Latina* (news agency, Cuba)

prelim. preliminary

prem. premium

premed premedical

PrEng Professional Engineer

prep. preparation; preparatory; preposition

prepd prepared

prepg preparing

prepn preparation

pres. present; presentation; presidency; presidential; presumed; presumptive

Pres. Presbyterian; President

press. pressure

presv. preservation; preserve

pret. preterite (grammar)

prev. previous; previously

prf proof

PRF Petroleum Research Fund; pulse recurrence frequency (electronics); pulse repetition frequency (electronics)

prfnl professional

prfr proofreader

PRHA President of the Royal Hibernian Academy

pri. primate; primer; priority; private

PRI *Partido Revolucionario Institucional* (Spanish: Institutional Revolutionary Party; Mexico); *Partito Repubblicano Italiano* (Italian: Italian Republican Party); Plastics and Rubber Institute; President of the Royal Institute of Painters in Water Colours

PRIA President of the Royal Irish Academy

PRIAS President of the Royal Incorporation of Architects in Scotland

PRIBA President of the Royal Institute of British Architects

PRII Public Relations Institute of Ireland

prim. primary; primate; primer; primitive

primip. primipara (mother who has given birth to one child)

prin. principal; principle

Prin. Principal; Principality

print. printing

prism. prismatic

PRISM program reliability information system for management (US)

priv. private; privative

prm premium

PRM personal radiation monitor
prn *pro re nata* (Latin: as the situation demands; medicine)
pro. procedure; proceed; procure; profession(al); prostitute
Pro. Provost
Pr. O press officer
PRO Public Record Office; public relations officer
pro-am professional-amateur (sport)
prob. probability; probable; probably; probate; problem
prob. off. probation officer
proc. procedure; proceedings; process
Proc. proceedings; proctor
Proc. Roy. Soc. Proceedings of the Royal Society
prod. produce; produced; producer; product; production
prof. profession; professional
Prof. professor
Prof. Eng. Professional Engineer (US)
prog. prognosis; program (computing); programme; progress; progressive
Prog. Progressive
PROI President of the Royal Institute of Oil Painters
proj. project; projectile; projection; projector
prol. prologue
prom. promenade; promontory; promote(r); promotion
PROM programmable read-only memory (computing)
pron. pronomial; pronoun; pronounce; pronounceable; pronounced; pronouncement; pronouncing; pronunciation
pron. a. pronomial adjective
pro. note promissory note (finance)
pronunc. pronunciation
prop. propeller; proper; properly; property; proposition; proprietary; proprietor
PROP Preservation of the Rights of Prisoners
propl proportional
propn proportion
propr proprietor
props properties (theatre)
PRORM Pay and Records Office, Royal Marines
pros. prosodical; prosody; prospectus rate (advertising)
PROS preventive maintenance, repair and operational services
Pros. Atty Prosecuting Attorney

prost. prostate (medicine); prostitution
Prot. Protectorate; Protestant
pro tem. *pro tempore* (Latin: for the time being)
prov. proverb; proverbial; proverbially; province; provincial; provisional
Prov. Provençal; Provence; Proverbs (Bible); Province; Provost
Prov. GM Provincial Grand Master (Freemasonry)
Provo Provisional (member of the Irish Republican Army)
prox *proximo* (Latin: in or of next month)
prox. acc. *proxime accessit* (Latin: he/she came nearest)
prox luc. *proxima luce* (Latin: the day before)
pr. p. present participle
PRP petrol refilling point; profit-related pay; performance-related pay
pr. pr. *praeter propter* (Latin: about or nearly)
PRR pulse repetition rate (electronics)
prs pairs
PRs Pakistan rupee (monetary unit)
PRS Performing Right Society Limited; President of the Royal Society
PRSA President of the Royal Scottish Academy; Public Relations Society of America
prsd pressed
PRSE President of the Royal Society of Edinburgh
PRSH President of the Royal Society of the Promotion of Health
Pr. ST Prairie Standard Time (US)
PRSW President of the Royal Scottish Water Colour Society
PRT personal rapid transit (US); petroleum revenue tax
prtg printing
Pru Prudential Assurance Company Limited
PRU photographic reconnaissance unit
PRUAA President of the Royal Ulster Academy of Arts
Prus. Prussia; Prussian
prv *pour rendre visite* (French: to return a call)
PRV pressure-reducing valve
PRWA President of the Royal West of England Academy
PRWS President of the Royal Society of Painters in Water Colours
ps particle size; passed school of instruction (military); *post scriptum* (Latin: postscript); pull switch

ps. pieces; pseudonym
Ps positronium (chemistry); Psalm
Ps. Psalms (Bible)
PS Aberdeen (UK vehicle registration); paddle steamer; Parliamentary Secretary; *Partido Socialista* (Portuguese: Socialist Party); *Parti Socialiste* (French: Socialist Party); passenger steamer; Pastel Society; penal servitude; Permanent Secretary; Philological Society; phrase structure (linguistics); Police Sergeant; *post scriptum* (Latin: postscript); power steering; press secretary; *Presse Services* (news agency, France); private secretary; Privy Seal; prompt side (theatre); Provost Sergeant; public school
psa passed staff college (RAF)
Psa. Psalms (Bible)
PSA Passenger Shipping Association; Petty Sessions Area; phase-shift analysis (physics); Photographic Society of America; pleasant Sunday afternoon; Political Studies Association of the United Kingdom; President of the Society of Antiquaries; Prices Surveillance Authority (Australia); Property Services Agency
PSAB Public Schools Appointments Bureau
PSAC President's Science Advisory Committee (US)
p's and q's please's and thank-you's (manners)
PSAT Preliminary Scholastic Aptitude Test (US)
PSB pistol, small-bore; Postal Savings Bureau (Japan); Premium Savings Bond
PSBA Public School Bursars' Association
PSBR public sector borrowing requirement
psc passed staff college (military)
PSC *Parti Social Chrétien* (French: Francophone Christian Social Party; Belgium); Professional Services Committee; Public Service Commission (US)
PSCD patrol service central depot
PSD *Partido Social Democrata* (Portuguese: Social Democratic Party); pay supply depot; Petty Sessional Division (law)
PSDI *Partito Socialista Democratico* (Italian: Italian Democratic Socialist Party)
PSDR public sector debt requirement
PSE Pacific Stock Exchange; programming support environment

(computing); project support environment (computing)
pseud. pseudonym
psf pounds per square foot
PSHFA Public Servants Housing Finance Association
psi pounds per square inch
PSI *Partito Socialista Italiano* (Italian: Italian Socialist Party); Pharmaceutical Society of Ireland; Policy Studies Institute
psia pounds per square inch, absolute
PSIAD President of the Society of Industrial Artists and Designers
psid pounds per square inch, differential
psig pounds per square inch, gauge
PSIS Permanent Secretaries Committee on the Intelligence Services
PSIUP *Partito Socialista Italiano di Unità Proletaria* (Italian: Italian Socialist Party of Proletarian Unity)
PSK phase shift keying (telecommunications)
PSL Paymaster Sublieutenant; private-sector liquidity (economics); public-sector loan
PSL/PSA problem statement language/problem statement analyser (computing)
psm passed school of music (Royal Military School of Music)
PSM product sales manager
PSMA President of the Society of Marine Artists
PSNC Pacific Steam Navigation Company
PSO personal staff officer; principal scientific officer
PSOE *Partido Socialista Obrero Español* (Spanish: Spanish Workers Socialist Party)
PSP *Pacifistich Socialistische Partij* (Dutch: Pacifist Socialist Party; Netherlands); phenolsulphonphthalein (medicine)
PSRO Professional Standards Review Organization (US)
Pss Psalms
PSS physiological saline solution (medicine); postscripts; Printing and Stationery Service; professional services section
PSSC Personal Social Services Council
psso pass slipped stitch over (knitting)
PST Pacific Standard Time (Canada, US)
pstl postal
PSU *Partito Socialista Unitario* (Italian: Unitary Socialist Party); police support

unit; power supply unit (computing);
process support unit
p. surg. plastic surgery
PSV public service vehicle
PSW psychiatric social worker
psych. psychic(al); psychological;
psychologist; psychology
psychoanal. psychoanalysis
psychol. psychological; psychologist;
psychology
pt part; part time; past tense; patient;
payment; pint; point; point of turn(ing);
port; primary target; *pro tempore* (Latin:
for the time being)
pt. preterite (grammar)
Pt platinum (element); point; port
PT Brazil (international civil aircraft
marking); Newcastle upon Tyne (UK
vehicle registration); Pacific Time (US);
patrol torpedo (US); *perte totale* (French:
total loss); perturbation theory (physics);
phase transition (physics); physical
therapy; physical training;
physiotherapist; Port Talbot (UK
fishing port registration); postal
telegraph; post town; preferential
treatment; previously treated
(medicine); Public Trustee; pupil
teacher; purchase tax
Pta peseta (Spanish monetary unit);
Pretoria
PTA Parent-Teacher Association;
Passenger Transport Authority; post-
traumatic amnesia (medicine);
preferential trade area; Printing Trades
Alliance
ptbl. portable
PT boat patrol torpedo boat (US)
PTBT partial test-ban treaty
PTC personnel transfer capsule (diving);
photographic type composition; primary
training centre
ptd painted; printed
Pte Plate; Private; private limited
company
PTE Passenger Transport Executive; post-
test examination
pt ex(ch). part exchange
PTFCE polytrifluoroeth(yl)ene
(chemistry)
PTFE polytetrafluorethylene (chemistry)
ptg painting; printing
Ptg Pleistogene (geology)
Ptg. Portugal; Portuguese
PTH public teaching hospital (US)
PTI physical training instructor; Press
Trust of India

PTM pulse-time modulation
(telecommunications)
ptn partition; portion
PTN pay through the nose; public
telephone network; public
transportation network
ptnr partner
PTO Patent and Trademark Office (US);
please turn over; power take-off
(astronautics); public telecommunications operator; Public Trustee Office
ptp past participle
ptpg participating
pt/pt point to point (horse racing)
ptr printer
pts parts; payments; pints; points; ports
Pts. Portsmouth
PTS Philatelic Traders' Society; printing
technical school
ptsc passed technical staff college
(military)
PTSD post-traumatic stress disorder
(medicine)
pts/hr parts per hour
Ptsmth Portsmouth
PTT Postal, Telegraph and Telephone
Administration
pt-tm. part-time
PTV public television
ptw per 1,000 words
pty party
Pty Proprietary
pu paid up
Pu plutonium (element)
PU Chelmsford (UK vehicle registration);
passed urine (medicine); pick-up; Pluna
(*Primerias Lineas Uruguayas de Navegación
Aerea*, airline flight code, Uruguay);
polyurethane; processing unit
(computing); public utility
pub. public; publican; publication; public
house; published; publisher; publishing
Pub. publishers' announcement
(advertising)
pubd published
pub. doc. public document
publ. public; publican; publication;
publicity; published; publisher;
publishing
pubn publication
pubr publisher
pub. wks public works
PUC papers under consideration; pick-up
car; Public Utilities Commission (US)
pud. pudding
PUD pick up and deliver(y); planned unit
development (US)

pug. pugilist
PUHCA Public Utility Holding Company Act (US)
pulv. *pulvis* (Latin: powder; medicine)
pums permanently unfit for military service
pun. punish(ment)
punc. punctuation
Punj. Punjab
PUO pyrexia (fever) of unknown origin
PUP People's United Party; Princeton University Press (US)
pur. purchase; purchased; purchaser; purification; purify; purple; pursuit
purch. purchaser
purp. purple
PURV powered underwater research vehicle
pus permanently unfit for service
PUS Parliamentary Undersecretary; Permanent Undersecretary
PUWP Polish United Workers' Party
pv *per vaginam* (Latin: by the vagina; medicine)
PV Ipswich (UK vehicle registration); patrol vessel; *petite vitesse* (French: goods or slow train); pole vault; positive vetting; power-voltage; pressure vessel; pressure-volume
PVA polyvinyl acetate (synthetic resin); polyvinyl alcohol (chemistry)
PVB polyvinyl butyral (chemistry)
pvc pigment volume concentration (paint)
PVC polyvinyl choloride (synthetic resin)
PVCH polyvinylcyclohexane (chemistry)
PVD peripheral vascular disease (medicine)
PVDA *Partij van de Arbeid* (Dutch: Labour Party; Netherlands)
PVDC polyvinylidenechloride (chemistry)
PVF polyvinyl fluoride (synthetic resin)
PVG polyvinylene glycol (chemistry)
PVO principal veterinary officer
PVP polyvinyl pyrrolidone (synthetic resin)
PVR premature voluntary retirement
PVS persistent vegetative state (medicine); post-Vietnam syndrome;

post-viral syndrome (myalgic encephalomyelitis)
pvt(e) private
Pvt. Private (military)
PVT polyvinyltoluene; pressure, volume, temperature
PVTCA polyvinyltrichloroacetate (chemistry)
pw per week
PW Norwich (UK vehicle registration); Padstow (UK fishing port registration); policewoman; power windows; prisoner of war; public works; pulse width (electronics)
PWA person with Aids (medicine); Public Works Administration (US)
PWC postwar credits
pwd powered
PWD Public Works Department
PWE Political Welfare Executive
PWLB Public Works Loan Board
PWM pulse-width modulation (telecommunications)
PWO Prince of Wales's Own
pwp price when perfect
pwr power
PWR pressurized-water reactor (nuclear engineering)
pwr supply power supply
pwt pennyweight
px Pedro Ximénez (grape)
PX Ai Niugini (airline flight code, Papua New Guinea); physical examination; please exchange; Portsmouth (UK vehicle registration); Post Exchange (US); private exchange (telecommunications)
pxt *pinxit* (Latin: he/she painted it)
py pyridine (chemistry)
PY Middlesbrough (UK vehicle registration); Paraguay (international vehicle registration); Surinam Airways (airline flight code)
PYO pick your own
pyro(tech). pyrotechnics
Pz Palaeozoic (geology)
PZ Belfast (UK vehicle registration); LAP (*Lineas Aereas Paraguayas*, airline flight code, Paraquay); Penzance (UK fishing port registration); Surinam (international civil aircraft marking)
PZS President of the Zoological Society

Q

q quark (physics)
q electric charge (physics); specific humidity (meteorology); squall (meteorology)
q. *quaere* (Latin: inquire); *quaque* (Latin: every); quart; quarter; quarterly; quarto; *quasi* (Latin: almost); queen; quench; query; question; quick; quintal (100kg); quire
Q coulomb (unit of electricity); quality (electronics); quartermaster; Quaternary; Queen (chess); Queensland; query; quetzal (Guatemalan monetary unit)
Q quality factor (electrical engineering); quantity of electricity (physics); quantity of heat (physics); quantity of light (physics)
Q. quantity; quarterly; Quartermaster; quarter-page (advertising); quarto (manuscripts); Quebec; Queen/'s; Queensland; question; Sir Arthur Quiller-Couch (UK writer)
Q. *quadrans* (Latin: farthing)
qa quick assembly
QA qualification approval; quality assurance; quarters allowance
QAB Queen Anne's Bounty (Church of England fund)
QADS quality-assurance data system
QAIMNS Queen Alexandra's Imperial Military Nursing Service
Q&A question and answer
Qantas Queensland and Northern Territory Aerial Service (Australian airline)
QARANC Queen Alexandra's Royal Army Nursing Corps
QARNNS Queen Alexandra's Royal Naval Nursing Service
QAS quaternary ammonium sulphanilamide (chemistry)
QB quarterback (American football); Queen's Bench (law); queen's bishop (chess)
Qbc Quebec
QBD Queen's Bench Division
qbi quite bloody impossible
QBP queen's bishop's pawn
QC Air Zaire (airline flight code); quality control; Quartermaster Corps; Queen's College; Queen's Consort; Queen's Counsel; quit claim (law)
QCD quantum chromodynamics

QCE quality-control engineering
QCH Queen Charlotte's Hospital
QC Is Queen Charlotte Islands (Canada)
QCR quality-control reliability
QCT quality-control technology
QCVSA Queen's Commendation for Valuable Service in the Air
qd *quaque die* (Latin: every day; medicine); *quasi dicat* (Latin: as if one should say); *quasi dictum* (Latin: as if said)
QDRI qualitative development requirement information (US)
qds *quater in die sumendus* (Latin: to be taken four times a day; medicine)
qe *quod est* (Latin: which is)
QE quantum efficiency (physics); quantum electronics
QE2 Queen Elizabeth II (cruise ship)
QED quantum electrodynamics; *quod erat demonstrandum* (Latin: which was to be proved)
QEF *quod erat faciendum* (Latin: which was to be done)
QEH Queen Elizabeth Hall (London)
QEI *quod erat inveniendum* (Latin: which was to be discovered or found out)
QEO Queen Elizabeth's Own
QER Quarterly Economic Review
QF Qantas Airways (airline flight code, Australia); quality factor (electronics); quick-firing
QFSM Queen's Fire Service Medal for Distinguished Service
QFT quantum field theory (physics)
QG Quartermaster-General; *quartiere generale* (Italian: headquarters); *quartier-général* (French: headquarters)
QGM Queen's Gallantry Medal
qh *quaque hora* (Latin: every hour)
QHC Queen's Honorary Chaplain
QHDS Queen's Honorary Dental Surgeon
QHM Queen's Harbour Master
QHNS Queen's Honorary Nursing Sister
QHP Queen's Honorary Physician
QHS Queen's Honorary Surgeon
qid *quater in die* (Latin: four times a day; medicine)
QIP *quiescat in pace* (Latin: may he/she rest in peace)
QISAM queued indexed sequential access method (computing)
qk quick

QKt queen's knight (chess)
QKtP queen's knight's pawn (chess)
ql *quantum libet* (Latin: as much as you please; medicine); quarrel; quintal (100 kg)
QL Lesotho Airways (airline flight code); Queen's Lancers; query language (computing)
Qld Queensland
qlty quality
qly quarterly
qm *quaque mane* (Latin: every morning; medicine); *quomodo* (Latin: by what means)
QM Air Malawi (airline flight code); quantum mechanics (physics); Quartermaster; Queen's Messenger
QMAAC Queen Mary's Army Auxiliary Corps
QMC Quartermaster Corps; Queen Mary College (London)
Q. Mess. Queen's Messenger
QMG Quartermaster-General
QMGF Quartermaster-General to the Forces
Qmr Quartermaster
QMR qualitative material requirement
QMS Quartermaster-Sergeant
qn *quaque nocte* (Latin: every night; medicine); question; quotation
Qn Queen
QN queen's knight (chess)
QNI Queen's Nursing Institute
QNP queen's knight's pawn (chess)
QNS quantity not sufficient
qnt quintet
qnty quantity
QO qualified in ordnance (Navy); qualified officer
QOCH Queen's Own Cameron Highlanders
QOOH Queen's Own Oxfordshire Hussars
Q(ops) Quartering (operations)
QOR qualitative operational requirement
qp *quantum placet* (Latin: as much as seems good; medicine)
QP qualification pay; queen's pawn (chess); query processing (computing)
QPC Qatar Petroleum Company
QPFC Queen's Park Football Club (Scotland)
q. pl. *quantum placet* (Latin: as much as seems good; medicine)
QPM Queen's Police Medal
QPR Queen's Park Rangers (football club)

qq. quartos; questions
qq. hor. *quaque hora* (Latin: every hour; medicine)
qq. v. *quae vide* (Latin: which see)
qr quarter; quarterly; quire (paper)
QR Quarterly Review; queen's rook (chess); quick response (marketing); riyal (monetary unit)
QRA quick reaction alert (military aircraft)
QRIH Queen's Royal Irish Hussars
QRP queen's rook's pawn (chess)
QRR Queen's Royal Rifles
qrs quarters
QRV Qualified Valuer, Real Estate Institute of New South Wales
qs *quantum sufficit* (Latin: as much as will suffice); quarter section (land)
QS quadraphonic-stereophonic (audio equipment); quantity surveyor; quarantine station; quarter sessions; Queen's Scholar; quick sweep (building)
QSE qualified scientist and engineer
QSM Queen's Service Medal (New Zealand)
QSO quasi-stellar object (quasar; astronomy); Queen's Service Order (New Zealand)
QSS quasi-stellar source (astronomy)
QSTOL quiet short take-off and landing (aeronautics)
QSTS quadruple screw turbine ship
qt quart; quartet; quiet
qt. quantity
qtly quarterly
qto quarto
QTOL quiet take-off and landing (aeronautics)
qtr quarter
qty quantity
qu. quart; quarter; quarterly; queen; query; question
QU Uganda Airlines (airline flight code)
quad. quadrangle; quadrant; quadrilateral; quadruple(t); quadruplicate
qual. qualification; qualitative; quality
qualgo quasi-autonomous local government organization
qualn qualification
quango quasi-autonomous non-governmental organization; quasi-autonomous national government organization
quant. quantitative; quantity
quant. suff. *quantum sufficit* (Latin: as much as will suffice; medicine)

quar(t). quarter; quarterly
quasar quasi-stellar object (astronomy)
quat. *quattuor* (Latin: four; medicine)
QUB Queen's University, Belfast
Que. Quebec
ques. question
questn. questionnaire
quins quintuplets
Quins Harlequins (rugby football club)
quint. quintuplicate
QUIP query interactive processor
(computing)
quor. quorum
quot. quotation; quote

quotid. *quotidie* (Latin: daily; medicine)
qv *quantum vis* (Latin: as much as you
wish; medicine); *quod vide* (Latin: which
see)
QV Lao Aviation (airline flight code,
Laos)
QVR Queen Victoria Rifles
Qwerty standard typewriter keyboard
(from key arrangement)
QWL quality of work(ing) life
QX Horizon Air (airline flight code, US)
qy quay; query
qz quartz
QZ Zambia Airways (airline flight code)

R

r ribonucleoside (biochemistry)
r internal resistance (electricity); polar
coordinate (mathematics); position
vector (mathematics); radius; radius
vector; rate of increase (ecology)
r. radius; railroad (US); railway; rain;
range; rare; ratio; received; recipe; *recto*
(Latin: on the right hand page); red;
replacing; reply; reserve; residence;
resides; response; retired; right; rises;
road; rod; rouble (Russian monetary
unit); rubber (cards); ruled; run
(baseball, cricket); rupee
R eight (medieval Roman numerals);
radical (chemistry); radius; Ramsgate
(UK fishing port registration); rand
(South African monetary unit); ratio
(mathematics); Réaumur (temperature
scale); resistance (electrical engineering);
restricted (Australian, US cinema
certification); return (tickets); reverse
(gear); roentgen (physics); rook (chess)
R. rabbi; Radical (politics); radiology;
radius; railroad (US); railway; *Rapido*
(Italian: express train); *Recht* (German:
law); *recipe* (Latin: take; medicine);
recommendation; rector; red; redactor;
Regiment; *Regina* (Latin: Queen);
registered; registered at the US Patent
Office; Regius; regular (clothing size);
relative (navigation); reliability; report;
Republic; Republican; reserve; response;
Respublica (Latin: Republic); reward; *Rex*
(Latin: King); Rifles (military); right;
River; road; Roman; Romania;
Romanian; Rome; rosary; rouble; route;
Royal; *Rue* (French: street); run (nautical)

R molar gas constant (chemistry)
ra. radio
Ra radium (element)
RA Argentina (international vehicle
registration); Nottingham (UK vehicle
registration); rain (meteorology);
Ramblers' Association; Rear-Admiral;
reduction of area; Referees' Association;
Regular Army (US); *República Argentina*
(Spanish: Argentine Republic);
Resettlement Administration (US);
rheumatoid arthritis (medicine); Road
Association; Royal Academician; Royal
Academy; Royal Artillery; Royal Nepal
Airlines (airline flight code); Russia
(international civil aircraft marking)
R/A refer to acceptor (finance); return to
author
RAA Rabbinical Alliance of America;
Regional Arts Association; Royal
Academy of Arts; Royal Artillery
Association; Royal Australian Artillery
RAAF Royal Australian Air Force; Royal
Auxiliary Air Force
RAAFNS Royal Australian Air Force
Nursing Service
RAAMC Royal Australian Army Medical
Corps
RAANC Royal Australian Army Nursing
Corps
Rab. Rabat (Morocco)
Rabb. Rabbinate; Rabbinic(al)
RABDF Royal Association of British
Dairy Farmers
RABI Royal Agricultural Benevolent
Institution
RAC Railway Association of Canada;

Regional Advisory Committee (TUC);
Regional Advisory Council; Royal Aero
Club; Royal Agricultural College
(Cirencester); Royal Armoured Corps;
Royal Automobile Club
RACA Royal Automobile Club of
Australia
RACE rapid automatic checkout
equipment; Research and Development
in Advanced Communication
Technologies for Europe
RACGP Royal Australian College of
General Practitioners
RAChD Royal Army Chaplains'
Department
RACI Royal Australian Chemical Institute
RACO Royal Australian College of
Ophthalmologists
RACOG Royal Australian College of
Obstetricians and Gynaecologists
RACON radar beacon
RACP Royal Australasian College of
Physicians
RACS Royal Arsenal Cooperative
Society; Royal Australasian College of
Surgeons
rad radiation absorbed dose; rapid
automatic drill
rad. radar; radian; radiator; radical; radio;
radiologist; radiology; radiotherapist;
radiotherapy; radius
Rad. Radical (politics); Radnorshire
(Wales)
RAD Royal Academy of Dancing; Royal
Albert Docks
RADA Royal Academy of Dramatic Art
radar radio detection and ranging
RADAR Royal Association for Disability
and Rehabilitation
RADAS random access discrete address
system
RADC Royal Army Dental Corps
RADCM radar counter-measures
raddol. *raddolcendo* (Italian: becoming
calmer; music)
RADIUS Religious Drama Society of
Great Britain
RAdm. Rear-Admiral
radmon radiological monitor(ing)
radn radiation
RADRON radar squadron (US Air Force)
rae radio astronomy explorer
RAE Royal Aerospace Establishment;
Royal Australian Engineers
RAEC Royal Army Educational Corps
RAeroC Royal Aero Club of the United
Kingdom

RAeS Royal Aeronautical Society
RAF *Rote Armee Faktion* (German: Red
Army Faction); Royal Aircraft Factory;
Royal Air Force
RAFA Royal Air Forces Association;
Royal Australian Field Artillery
RAFBF Royal Air Force Benevolent Fund
RAFES Royal Air Force Educational
Service
RAFG Royal Air Force Germany
RAFMS Royal Air Force Medical Services
RAFR Royal Air Force Regiment
RAFRO Royal Air Force Reserve of
Officers
RAFSAA Royal Air Force Small Arms
Association
RAFSC Royal Air Force Staff College
RAFTC Royal Air Force Transport
Command
RAFVR Royal Air Force Volunteer
Reserve
rag river assault group
RAGA Royal Australian Garrison
Artillery
RAH Royal Albert Hall (London)
RAHS Royal Australian Historical Society
RAI *Radiotelevisione Italiana* (Italian:
Italian Broadcasting Corporation); Royal
Anthropological Institute
RAIA Royal Australian Institute of
Architects
RAIC Royal Architectural Institute of
Canada
Raj. Rajasthan (India)
RAK random act of kindness (US)
rall. *rallentando* (Italian: becoming slow;
music)
RALS remote augmented lift system
(aeronautics)
ram relative atomic mass
RAM radar absorbing material
(aeronautics); random-access memory
(computing); reverse annuity mortgage;
rocket-assisted motor; Royal Academy
of Music; Royal Air Maroc (Moroccan
airline); Royal Arch Masons
(Freemasonry)
RAMAC Radio Marine Associated
Companies; random-access memory
accounting (computing)
ramb. rambler (rose)
RAMC Royal Army Medical Corps
RAN request for authority to negotiate;
Royal Australian Navy
RANC Royal Australian Naval College
RANCOM random communication
satellite

R&A Royal and Ancient Golf Club of St Andrews
R&B rhythm and blues
R&CC riot and civil commotions
R&D research and development
R&E research and engineering
R&I *Regina et Imperatrix* (Latin: Queen and Empress); *Rex et Imperator* (Latin: King and Emperor)
r&m reports and memoranda
R&M reliability and marketing
R&R rescue and resuscitation; rest and recreation; rock and roll
R&T research and technology
R&VA Rating and Valuing Association
RANN Research Applied to National Needs (US)
RANR Royal Australian Naval Reserve
RANVR Royal Australian Naval Volunteer Reserve
RAOB Royal Antediluvian Order of Buffaloes
RAOC Royal Army Ordnance Corps
RAOU Royal Australian Ornithologists' Union
rap. rapid
RAP ready-assembled price; Regimental Aid Post; remedial action plan; remedial action programme
RAPC Royal Army Pay Corps
RAPID Register for the Ascertainment and Prevention of Inherited Diseases
RAPRA Rubber and Plastics Research Association of Great Britain
RAR Royal Australian Regiment
RARDE Royal Armament Research and Development Establishment
RARE *Réseaux associés pour la recherche européenne* (French: Associate Networks for European Research; computing)
RARO Regular Army Reserve of Officers
RAS rectified air speed (aeronautics); Royal Agricultural Society; Royal Asiatic Society; Royal Astronomical Society
RASE Royal Agricultural Society of England
raser radio-frequency amplification by stimulated emission of radiation
RASH rain shower (meteorology)
RASN rain and snow (meteorology)
rat. rateable; rating; ration
RAT rocket-assisted torpedo
RATAN radar and television aid to navigation
RATO rocket-assisted take-off
RATP *Régie autonome des transports parisiens* (French: Paris transport authority)
RAuxAF Royal Auxiliary Air Force
RAVC Royal Army Veterinary Corps
rb right back (sport); rubber band
Rb rubidium (element)
RB Botswana (international vehicle registration); Nottingham (UK vehicle registration); radiation belt (astronomy); radiation burn; reconnaissance bomber; representative body; *República Boliviana* (Spanish: Republic of Bolivia); review body; Rifle Brigade; Ritzaus Bureau (news agency, Denmark); Royal Ballet; Syrian Arab Airlines (airline flight code)
RBA Royal Society of British Artists
RBAF Royal Belgian Air Force
RBC red blood cell (medicine); red blood count (medicine); Royal British Colonial Society of Artists
RBE relative biological effectiveness (radiation)
RBerks Royal Berkshire Regiment
RBG Royal Botanical Gardens
rbi require better information; runs batted in (baseball)
RBI resource-based industry; right back inside (skating); runs batted in (baseball)
RBK&C Royal Borough of Kensington and Chelsea
rbl. rouble (Russian monetary unit)
RBL Royal British Legion
RBn radio beacon
RBN Registry of Business Names
RBNA Royal British Nurses' Association
RBO right back outside (skating)
RBS Royal Society of British Sculptors
RBSA Royal Birmingham Society of Artists
rbt roundabout
RBT random breath testing
RBY Royal Bucks Yeomanry
rc radio code; radio coding; reinforced concrete; release clause; reverse course; right centre; rotary combustion; rubber-cushioned
RC Nottingham (UK vehicle registration); racing club (cycling); red cell (blood); Red Cross; Reformed Church; reinforced concrete; reproductive capacity; Republican Convention (US); research centre; Reserve Corps; resin-coated (photography); resistor-capacitor; rifle club; right of centre (theatre); road club (cycling); Roman Catholic; rough cutting (building); Royal College; Royal Commission; Taiwan (international vehicle registration)

R/C recredited
RCA Central African Republic
(international vehicle registration);
Rabbinical Council of America;
Racecourse Association; Radio
Corporation of America; Royal
Cambrian Academy; Royal Canadian
Academy of Arts; Royal College of Art;
Royal Company of Archers; Rural
Crafts' Association
RCAC Royal Canadian Armoured Corps
RCAF Royal Canadian Air Force
RCamA Royal Cambrian Academy
RCAMC Royal Canadian Army Medical
Corps
RCASC Royal Canadian Army Service
Corps
RCB Congo (international vehicle
registration); right centre back (theatre)
RCC recovery control centre; rescue
coordination centre; Roman Catholic
Chaplain; Roman Catholic Church;
Rural Community Council
RCCh Roman Catholic Church
rcd received
RCD Regional Cooperation for
Development (Asia); residual current
device (electricity)
RCDC Royal Canadian Dental Corps
RCDS Royal College of Defence Studies
RCE rotary combustion engine
(engineering)
rcf relative centrifugal force
RCFCA Royal Canadian Flying Clubs'
Association
RCGA Royal Canadian Golf Association
RCGP Royal College of General
Practitioners
RCGS Royal Canadian Geographical
Society
RCH Chile (international vehicle regis-
tration); railway clearing house
RCHA Royal Canadian Horse Artillery
RCHM Royal Commission on Historical
Monuments
rci radar coverage indicator
RCI Royal Canadian Institute
RCJ Royal Courts of Justice
RCL Royal Canadian Legion; ruling case
law
RCM radar counter-measures; radio
counter-measures; regimental court
martial; Royal College of Midwives;
Royal College of Music
RCMP Royal Canadian Mounted Police
RCN Royal Canadian Navy; Royal
College of Nursing

RCNC Royal Corps of Naval
Constructors
RCNR Royal Canadian Naval Reserve
RCNT Registered Clinical Nurse Teacher
RCNVR Royal Canadian Naval Volunteer
Reserve
RCO Royal College of Organists
RCOG Royal College of Obstetricians and
Gynaecologists
RCP Royal College of Physicians
RCPath Royal College of Pathologists
RCPE(d) Royal College of Physicians,
Edinburgh
RCPI Royal College of Physicians of
Ireland
RCPSG Royal College of Physicians and
Surgeons of Glasgow
RCPsych Royal College of Psychiatry
rcpt receipt
RCR Royal College of Radiologists
RCS reaction control system
(astronautics); reactor coolant system
(nuclear engineering); reactor cooling
system (nuclear engineering); remote
control system; Royal Choral Society;
Royal College of Science; Royal College
of Surgeons of England; Royal
Commonwealth Society; Royal Corps of
Signals; Royal Counties Show
RCSB Royal Commonwealth Society for
the Blind
RCSE(d) Royal College of Surgeons of
Edinburgh
RCSI Royal College of Surgeons in
Ireland
RCSS random communication satellite
system
RCST Royal College of Science and
Technology
rct receipt; recruit
RCT regimental combat team; registered
clinical teacher; remote control
transmitter; Royal Corps of Transport
RCU remote control unit; road-
construction unit; rocket counter-
measure unit
rcvr receiver
RCVS Royal College of Veterinary
Surgeons
rd relative density; rendered; *rive droite*
(French: right bank); road; rod; round;
running days (shipping); rutherford
(physics)
Rd radium; Road
RD radiation dose; Reading (UK vehicle
registration); *récemment dégorgé* (French:
recently disgorged; wines); refer to

drawer (banking); registered dietician (US); *República Dominicana* (Spanish: Dominican Republic); research department; Royal Dragoons; Royal Naval and Royal Marine Forces Reserve Decoration; Rural Dean; Rural Delivery (New Zealand)

R/D refer to drawer (banking)

RDA *Rassemblement Démocratique Africain* (French: African Democratic Rally); recommended daily allowance; recommended dietary allowance; Retail Distributors' Association; Royal Defence Academy; Royal Docks Association

RD&D research, development and demonstration

RD&E research, development and engineering

RDAT rotary-head digital audio tape

RDB Research and Development Board (military); Royal Danish Ballet; Rural Development Board

RDC Royal Defence Corps; running-down clause (insurance); Rural District Council

RDCA Rural District Councils' Association

rdd required delivery date

RDD random digital dialing (marketing)

RDE Research and Development Establishment

RDF radio direction finder; radio direction finding; Rapid Deployment Force (military); Royal Dublin Fusiliers

RDI Royal Designer for Industry (Royal Society of Arts)

rDNA ribosomal DNA

RDPL Laos (international civil aircraft marking)

rdr radar

rds. roadstead (shipping)

RDS radio data system; respiratory distress syndrome (medicine); Royal Drawing Society; Royal Dublin Society

RDT&E research, development, testing and engineering

RDV rendezvous

RDX Research Department Explosive

rdy ready

RDy Royal Dockyard

RDZ radiation danger zone

re right end (American football)

re. regarding to; with reference to

Re Reynolds number (physics); rhenium (element); rupee (Indian monetary unit)

RE rare earth (chemistry); real estate (US); Reformed Episcopal; religious

education; renewable energy; revised edition; Right Excellent; right eye (medicine); Royal Engineers; Royal Exchange; Royal Society of Painter-Etchers and Engravers; Stoke-on-Trent (UK vehicle registration)

REA Radar and Electronics Association; request for engineer's authorization; Rural Electrification Administration (US)

reac. reactor

REAC Regional Education Advisory Committee (TUC)

REACH Retired Executives' Action Clearing House

react research education and aid for children with potentially terminal illness

Rear-Adm. Rear-Admiral

reasm. reassemble

REB regional examining body

rec. receipt; receive; *recens* (Latin: fresh; medicine); recent; reception; recipe; record; recorded; recorder; recording; recreation

REC Railway Executive Committee; regional electricity company

recap. recapitulate; recapitulation

recce reconnaissance; reconnoitre

recd received

recep. reception

recip. reciprocal; reciprocity

recirc. recirculate

recit. recitation; recitative (music)

reclam. reclamation

recm. recommend

RECMF Radio and Electronic Component Manufacturers' Federation

recog. recognition; recognize

recom. recommend

recon. reconciliation; recondition; reconnaissance; reconnoitre; reconsign(ment); reconstruct(ion)

recond. recondition

REconS Royal Economic Society

reconst. reconstruct; reconstruction

recpt receipt

recr. receiver

recryst. recrystallized (chemistry)

rec. sec. recording secretary

rect. receipt; rectangle; rectangular; *rectificatus* (Latin: rectified; medicine); rectify

Rect. rector; rectory

recv(ee) recreational vehicle (US)

red. redeemable (finance); reduce; reduced; reduction

redisc. rediscount

redox. reduction-oxidation (chemistry)
Red R Register of Engineers for Disaster relief
redupl. reduplicate; reduplication; reduplicative
ref. refer; referred; referee; reference; refined; reform; reformed; reformation; reformer; refrigerated ship; refund; refunding; refuse
refash. refashioned
Ref. Ch. Reformed Church
refd referred; refund
refl. reflect; relection; reflective; reflex; reflexive
Reform. Reformatory
Ref. Pres. Reformed Presbyterian
refrig. refrigerate; refrigeration; refrigerator
Ref. Sp. Reformed Spelling
reg. regent; regiment; region; register; registered; registrar; registration; registry; regular; regularly; regulation; regulator
Reg. Regent; Regent's Park College (Oxford); *Regina* (Latin: Queen)
REGAL range and elevation guidance for approach and landing (aeronautics)
regd registered
Reg-Gen. Registrar-General
Reg. Prof. Regius Professor
regr. registrar
Regt Regent; Regiment
regtl regimental
Reg. TM registered trademark
REHAB Rehabilitation Evaluation of Hall and Baker (medicine; psychiatry)
reinf. reinforce
reinfmt reinforcement
reit. reiteration (printing)
REIT real-estate investment trust (US)
rej. reject
rel. relate; relating; relation; relative; relatively; release; released; relic; *relié* (French: bound); religion; religious; *reliquiae* (Latin: relics)
REL recommended exposure limit (radiation)
rel. pron. relative pronoun
rem roentgen equivalent man (unit of radioactivity)
rem. remark/s; remit(tance)
REM rapid eye movement (physiology)
REME Royal Electrical and Mechanical Engineers
remitt. remittance
Ren. Renaissance
Renf. Renfrewshire (Scotland)

Renfe *Red Nacional de Ferrocarriles Españoles* (Spanish state railways)
REngDes Registered Engineering Designer
renv. renovate; renovation
REO regional education officer
rep. repair; repaired; repeat; *repetatur* (Latin: let it be repeated; medicine); repertory (theatre); report; reported; reporter; represent; representing; representative; reprint
Rep. Representative (US); Republic; Republican
REP recovery and evacuation program (US)
REPC Regional Economic Planning Council
repl. replace; replaced; replacement; replicate
repo. repossess
repr. represent; representative; represented; representing; reprint; reprinted
repro. reproduced; reproduction
rept receipt; report
repub. republished
Repub. Republic; Republican
req. request; require; required; requisition
reqd required
reqn requisition
reqs requires
RER renewable energy resource/s
RERO Royal Engineers Reserve of Officers
res. rescue; research; researcher; reservation; reserve; reserved; reservoir; reside/s; residence; resident; resigned; resolution
RES renewable energy source; renewable energy system; Royal Entomological Society of London
resgnd resigned
resig. resignation
resp. respective; respectively; respiration; respondent; responsibility
res. phys. resident physician
res. sec. resident secretary
rest(r). restaurant; restoration; restrict; restriction
Rest. Restoration
ret. retain; retire; retired; return; returned
retd. retained; retired; returned
R. et I. *Regina et Imperatrix* (Latin: Queen and Empress); *Rex et Imperator* (Latin: King and Emperor)
retnr retainer

RETRA Radio, Electrical and Television Retailers' Association
RETRO retrofire officer (astronautics)
rev. revenue; reverse; reversed; review; reviewed; revise; revised; revision; revolution; revolve; revolver; revolving
Rev. Revelation (Bible); Reverend; Review
REV re-entry vehicle (astronautics)
rev. a/c revenue account
Revd Reverend
rev. ed. revised edition
Rev. Stat. Revised Statutes
Rev. Ver. Revised Version (Bible)
rew. reward; rewind
Reykjvk Reykjavik (Iceland)
rf radio frequency; range finder; rapid fire; reception fair (telecommunications); reef; relative flow; rheumatic fever; right field(er) (baseball); rough finish (paper)
rf. *rinforzando* (Italian: reinforcing; music)
Rf rufiyaa (monetary unit of the Maldives); rutherfordium (chemistry)
RF radio frequency; reconnaissance fighter; regular forces (military); representative fraction (cartography); *République française* (French: French Republic); research foundation; Reserve Force (military); Rockefeller Foundation; Royal Fusiliers; rugby football; Rwanda franc (monetary unit); Stoke-on-Trent (UK vehicle registration)
RFA Royal Field Artillery; Royal Fleet Auxiliary
RFAC Royal Fine Art Commission
rfb right fullback (sport)
RFC Reconstruction Finance Corporation; Royal Flying Corps; Rugby Football Club
RFD radio-frequency device; reporting for duty; rural free delivery (US postal service)
RFDS Royal Flying Doctor Service (Australia)
RFE Radio Free Europe
RFH Royal Festival Hall (London)
RFI radio-frequency interference; request for information; right forward inside (skating)
RFL Rugby Football League
Rfn Rifleman
RFN Registered Fever Nurse
RFO right forward outside (skating)
rfp retired on full pay
RFPC radio-frequency pulse compression (electronics)
RFQ request for quotation (commerce)

RFR Royal Fleet Reserve
rfrd referred
RFS Registry of Friendly Societies; Royal Forestry Society
RFSU Rugby Football Schools' Union
RFU Rugby Football Union
rfz. *rinforzando* (Italian: reinforcing; music)
rg right guard (American football); *rive gauche* (French: left bank)
RG Newcastle upon Tyne (UK vehicle registration); Reading (UK postcode); reserve guard; Varig (airline flight code, Brazil)
Rga Riga (Latvia)
RGA remote geological analysis; residual-gas analyser; Royal Garrison Artillery; Royal Guernsey Artillery
RGB red, green and blue (colour television)
rgd registered; reigned
rge range
R-Genl Registrar-General
RGG Royal Grenadier Guards
RGH Royal Gloucestershire Hussars
RGI Royal Glasgow Institute of the Fine Arts
RGJ Royal Green Jackets
rgn region
Rgn Rangoon
RGN Registered General Nurse
RGNP real gross national product (economics)
RGO Royal Greenwich Observatory
RGS Royal Geographical Society
RGSA Royal Geographical Society of Australasia
Rgt Regiment
RGT relativistic gravitational theory
rgtl regimental
rh right alf; right hand; right-handed
Rh rhesus factor (medicine); rhodium (element)
RH Haiti (international vehicle registration); Hull (UK vehicle registration); Redhill (UK postcode); relative humidity (meteorology); remote handled; remote handling; right hand; right-handed; Rochester (UK fishing port registration); Royal Highlanders (Black Watch); Royal Highness; Royal Hospital
RHA Regional Health Authority; Road Haulage Association; Royal Hibernian Academy; Royal Horse Artillery
RHAF Royal Hellenic Air Force (Greece)
RHamps Royal Hampshire Regiment

rhap. rhapsody
RHAS Royal Highland and Agricultural Society of Scotland
RHB Regional Hospital Board; right halfback (sport)
rhbdr rhombohedron
RHBNC Royal Holloway and Bedford New College (London)
rhd right hand drive
rheo. rheostat
rheol. rheological; rheology
rhet. rhetoric(al)
RHF Royal Highland Fusiliers
RHG Royal Horse Guards
RHHI Royal Hospital and Home for Incurables (Putney)
RHistS Royal Historical Society
RHM Rank Hovis McDougall
RHMS Royal Hibernian Military School
rhom(b). rhombic; rhomboid; rhombus
rhp rated horsepower
RHQ regimental headquarters
RHR Royal Highland Regiment (Black Watch)
rhs right-hand side; round-headed screw
RHS Royal Highland Show; Royal Historical Society; Royal Horticultural Society; Royal Humane Society
RHSI Royal Horticultural Society of Ireland
RHV Registered Health Visitor
ri reflective insulation; rubber insulated; rubber insulation
RI Dublin (Irish vehicle registration); Indonesia (international vehicle registration); radio interference; radioisotope; Railway Inspectorate; refractive index; Regimental Institute; *Regina et Imperatrix* (Latin: Queen and Empress); *Registro Italiano Navale* (Italian shipping classification); reinsurance; religious instruction; report of investigation; *Rex et Imperator* (Latin: King and Emperor); Rhode Island (zip code); Rockwell International Corporation; Rotary International; Royal Institute of Painters in Water Colours; Royal Institution
RIA Royal Irish Academy
RIAA Recording Industry Association of America
RIAC Royal Irish Automobile Club
RIAF Royal Indian Air Force
RIAI Royal Institute of the Architects of Ireland
RIAM Royal Irish Academy of Music

RIAS Royal Incorporation of Architects in Scotland
RIASC Royal Indian Army Service Corps
RIB Racing Information Bureau; rigid-hull inflatable boat; Rural Industries Bureau
RIBA Royal Institute of British Architects
RIBI Rotary International in Great Britain and Ireland
RIC Radio Industry Council; Royal Irish Constabulary
RICA Research Institute for Consumer Affairs
RICE rest, ice, compression, elevation (treatment of sports injuries)
RICO Racketeer Influenced and Corrupt Organizations Act (US)
RICS Royal Institution of Chartered Surveyors
RIE recognized investment exchange (commerce); Royal Indian Engineering College
RIF reduction in force (military); Royal Inniskilling Fusiliers
Rif. Brig. Rifle Brigade
RIIA Royal Institute of International Affairs
RIM Mauritania (international vehicle registration); Royal Indian Marines
RIN reference indicator number (aeronautics); Royal Indian Navy
RINA Royal Institution of Naval Architects
rinf. *rinforzando* (Italian: reinforcing; music)
RINVR Royal Indian Naval Volunteer Reserve
RIO reporting in and out
RIOP Royal Institute of Oil Painters
rip. *ripieno* (Italian: all instrumentalists; music)
RIP *requiescat in pace* (Latin: may he/she rest in peace)
RIPA Royal Institute of Public Administration
RIPH&H Royal Institute of Public Health and Hygiene
RIrF Royal Irish Fusiliers
RIS Research Information Service
RISC reduced-instruction-set computer
rit. *ritardando* (Italian: holding back; music); *ritenuto* (Italian: held back; music)
RIT Rorschach inkblot test (psychiatry)
RITA reusable interplanetary transport approach vehicle
riten. *ritenuto* (Italian: held back; music)

riv. river
RJ Manchester (UK vehicle registration); ramjet; road junction (military); Royal Jordanian Airlines (airline flight code)
RJA Royal Jersey Artillery
RJE remote job entry (computing)
RJLI Royal Jersey Light Infantry
RJM Royal Jersey Militia
RK Air Afrique (airline flight code, Côte d'Ivoire); northwest London (UK vehicle registration); religious knowledge
RKKA *Rabochekrest'yanshi Krasny* (Russian: Red Army of Workers and Peasants)
RKO Radio-Keith-Orpheum (US cinema/broadcasting company)
rky rocky
Rl rouble; Royal
RL Aeronica (airline flight code, Nicaragua); Lebanon (international vehicle registration); reference library; research laboratory; rocket launcher; Rugby League; Truro (UK vehicle registration)
RLD retail liquor dealer (US)
RLF Royal Literary Fund
R Lincolns Royal Lincolnshire Regiment
RLL run length limited (computing)
RLO railway liaison officer; returned letter office
RLPAS Royal London Prisoners' Aid Society
RLPO Royal Liverpool Philharmonic Orchestra
RLPS Royal Liverpool Philharmonic Society
Rls rial (Iranian monetary unit)
RLS Robert Louis Stevenson (Scottish novelist and poet)
RLSS Royal Life Saving Society
rlwy railway
rly railway; relay
rm ream (paper); room
RM Carlisle (UK vehicle registration); Madagascar (international vehicle registration); radiation monitoring; radio monitoring; Registered Midwife; Reichsmark (former German monetary unit); remote monitoring; Resident Magistrate; riding master; Romford (UK postcode); Royal Mail; Royal Marines
RMA Royal Marine Artillery; Royal Marines Association; Royal Military Academy; Royal Musical Association
RMB renminbi (Chinese monetary unit)
RMC regional meteorological centre; Royal Military College

RMCC Royal Military College of Canada
RMCM Royal Manchester College of Music
RMCS Royal Military College of Science
rmd ready money down
RMedSoc Royal Medical Society, Edinburgh
RMetS Royal Meteorological Society
RMFVR Royal Marine Forces Volunteer Reserves
RMH Royal Marsden Hospital (London)
RMI Resource Management Initiative (NHS)
RMIT Royal Melbourne Institute of Technology
RMLI Royal Marine Light Infantry
rmm relative molecular mass (chemistry)
RMM Mali (international vehicle registration)
RMN Registered Mental Nurse
RMO regimental medical officer; regional medical officer; resident medical officer; Royal Marine Office
RMP Royal Marine Police; Royal Military Police
RMPA Royal Medico-Psychological Association
RMRA Royal Marines Rifle Association
rms rooms; root mean square (mathematics)
RMS radiation-monitoring system; Railway Mail Service (US); remote monitoring system; root mean square (mathematics); Royal Mail Service; Royal Mail Ship; Royal Mail Steamer; Royal Microscopical Society; Royal Society of Miniature Painters
RMSchMus Royal Marines School of Music
RMSM Royal Military School of Music
RMT National Union of Rail, Maritime and Transport Workers
rn reception nil (telecommunications)
Rn radon (element); region
RN Niger (international vehicle registration); Preston (UK vehicle registration); Registered Nurse (US); Royal Naval; Royal Navy; Runcorn (UK fishing port registration)
RNA ribonucleic acid; Royal Naval Association
RNAS Royal Naval Air Service; Royal Naval Air Station
RNAW Royal Naval Aircraft Workshop
RNAY Royal Naval Aircraft Yard
R 'n' B rhythm and blues
RNB Royal Naval Barracks

RNBT Royal Naval Benevolent Trust
RNC Republican National Committee (US); Royal Naval College
RNCM Royal Northern College of Music
rnd round
RND Royal Naval Division
RNEC Royal Naval Engineering College
Rnf. Renfrewshire (Scotland)
RNF Royal Northumberland Fusiliers
RNIB Royal National Institute for the Blind
RNID Royal National Institute for the Deaf
RNLAF Royal Netherlands Air Force
RNLI Royal National Lifeboat Institution
RNLO Royal Naval Liaison Officer
RNMDSF Royal National Mission to Deep Sea Fishermen
RNMH Registered Nurse for the Mentally Handicapped
RNMS Royal Naval Medical School
RNoN Royal Norwegian Navy
RNPFN Royal National Pension Fund for Nurses
R 'n' R rock and roll
RNR Royal Naval Reserve
RNRA Royal Naval Rifle Association
rns runs
RNS Royal Numismatic Society
RNSA Royal Naval Sailing Association
RNSC Royal Naval Staff College
RNSR Royal Naval Special Reserve
RNSS Royal Naval Scientific Service
RNT Registered Nurse Teacher; Registered Nurse Tutor; Royal National Theatre
RNTE Royal Naval Training Establishment
RNTNEH Royal National Throat, Nose and Ear Hospital
RNTU Royal Naval Training Unit
RNVR Royal Naval Volunteer Reserve
RNVSR Royal Naval Volunteer Supplementary Reserve
RNWMP Royal Northwest Mounted Police
rnwy runway
RNXS Royal Naval Auxiliary Service
RNZAC Royal New Zealand Armoured Corps
RNZAF Royal New Zealand Air Force
RNZIR Royal New Zealand Infantry Regiment
RNZN Royal New Zealand Navy
RNZNVR Royal New Zealand Naval Volunteer Reserve
ro rowed over (rowing); run out (cricket)

ro. *recto* (Latin: on the right-hand page); roan
Ro *recto* (Latin: on the right-hand page)
RO Luton (UK vehicle registration); radar observer; radar operator; radio operator; Radio Orchestra; receiving office; receiving officer; receiving order; record/s office; recruiting officer; regimental order; registered office; relieving officer; reserved occupation; returning officer; rial Omani (monetary unit of Oman); Romania (international vehicle registration); Rothesay (UK fishing port registration); Royal Observatory; Tarom (airline flight code; Romania)
ROA record of achievement (education); Reserve Officers' Association; return on assets (finance)
ROAM return on assets managed (finance)
ROAR right of admission reserved
ROB remaining on board
ROC return on capital (finance); Royal Observer Corps
ROCE return on capital employed (finance)
ROE return on equity (finance); Royal Observatory, Edinburgh
ROF Royal Ordnance Factory
Roffen: *Roffensis* (Latin: (Bishop) of Rochester)
R of O Reserve of Officers
ROG receipt of goods
ROI region of interest; return on investment (finance); Royal Institute of Oil Painters
ROK South Korea (international vehicle registration)
Rolls Rolls-Royce
rom. roman (type)
Rom. Roman; Romance (language); Romanic (languages); Romania; Romanian; Romans (Bible)
ROM read-only memory (computing)
Rom. Cath. Roman Catholic
Rom-Press Romanian News Agency
RON remain overnight
RONA return on net assets (finance)
rop run of paper (publishing)
RORC Royal Ocean Racing Club
ro-ro roll on-roll off (ferries)
Ros. Roscommon
ROSE Research Open Systems in Europe (computing)
ROSLA raising of school-leaving age

RoSPA Royal Society for the Prevention of Accidents
rot. rotary; rotating; rotation; rotor
Rot. Rotterdam
ROT remedial occupational therapy; rule of thumb
ROTC Reserve Officers' Training Corps (US)
ROU Uruguay (international vehicle registration)
rout. routine
ROV remotely operated vehicle
ROW right of way
Rox. Roxburghshire (Scotland)
Roy. Royal(ty)
rp reception poor (telecommunications); regimental policeman; reply paid
Rp rupiah (Indonesian monetary unit)
RP Northampton (UK vehicle registration); Philippines (international vehicle registration); radiation protection; reaction product (chemistry); Received Pronunciation; recommended practice; recommended price; recovery phase; redundancy payment; Reformed Presbyterian; regimental police; regimental policeman; registered plumber; Regius Professor; reinforced plastic; reply paid; reprint(ing); *República Portuguesa* (Portuguese: Republic of Portugal); repurchase agreement (US); research paper; return of premium (insurance); *Révérend Père* (French: Reverend Father); rocket projectile; Royal Society of Portrait Painters; rules of procedure
RPA radiation protection adviser; record of personal achievement (education); Registered Plumbers' Association
RPB recognized professional body (finance)
RPC rapid Portland cement; Republican Party Conference (US); request the pleasure of your company; Royal Pioneer Corps
RPD *Rerum Politicarum Doctor* (Latin: Doctor of Political Science); regional port director
RPE radio production executive; Reformed Protestant Episcopal
RPF Rwanda Patriotic Front
rpg rounds per gun
RPG report program generator (computing); rocket-propelled grenade (military); role-playing game
rph revolutions per hour
RPhilS Royal Philharmonic Society

RPI retail price index
rplca replica
rpm revolutions per minute
RPM reliability performance measure; resale price maintenance; revolutions per minute
RPMS Royal Postgraduate Medical School
RPN Registered Psychiatric Nurse
RP/ND reprinting, no date
RPO railway post office; regional personnel officer; Royal Philharmonic Orchestra
RPQ request for price quotation
RPR *Rassemblement pour la République* (French: Rally for the Republic)
rprt report
rps revolutions per second
RPS radiological protection service; rapid processing system; Royal Philharmonic Society; Royal Photographic Society
RPSGB Royal Pharmaceutical Society of Great Britain
rpt repeat; report; reprint
RPV remotely piloted vehicle (military)
RQ regraded quality (tyres); remoulded quality (tyres); request for quotation (commerce); respiratory quotient (medicine)
RQL reference quality level
RQMS regimental quartermaster sergeant
rqmt requirement
rqr. require; requirement
rr continuous rain (meteorology); ready reckoner
rr. rare
RR Nottingham (UK vehicle registration); radiation resistance; railroad (US); Remington Rand (US company); research report; return rate; Right Reverend; road race (cycling); Rolls-Royce; Royal Air Force (airline flight code, UK); rural route (US)
RRA Rapid Reaction Force (military); Royal Regiment of Artillery
RRB Race Relations Board
RRC Road Racing Club; Royal Red Cross
RRE Royal Radar Establishment
RRF Royal Regiment of Fusiliers
RRL Registered Record Librarian; Road Research Laboratory
RRM renegotiable-rate mortgage (US)
rRNA ribosomal RNA
RRP recommended retail price
RR. PP. *Révérends Pères* (French: Reverend Fathers)
RRR return receipt requested (US)

RRS Royal Research Ship
RRT rail rapid transit
rs rain and snow/sleet (meteorology); right side
Rs rupees
RS Aberdeen (UK vehicle registration); Received Standard (English); reconnaissance squadron; reconnaissance strike; recording secretary; recruiting service; Reformed Spelling; remote sensing; research station; respiratory system; Revised Statutes (law); Royal Scots (military); Royal Society
R/S rejection slip
RSA Republic of South Africa; Returned Services Association (New Zealand); Road Safety Act; Royal Scottish Academician; Royal Scottish Academy; Royal Society for the Encouragement of Arts, Manufactures and Commerce; Royal Society of Arts; Royal Society of Australia
RSAA Royal Society for Asian Affairs
RSAD Royal Surgical Aid Society
RSAF Royal Small Arms Factory
RSAI Royal Society of Antiquaries of Ireland
RSAMD Royal Scottish Academy of Music and Drama
RSAS Royal Surgical Aid Society
rsb range safety beacon
RSC Royal Shakespeare Company; Royal Society of Canada; Royal Society of Chemistry; Rules of the Supreme Court
RSCDS Royal Scottish Country Dance Society
rsch research
RSCJ *Religiosae Sacratissimi Cordis Jesus* (Latin: Nuns of the Most Sacred Heart of Jesus or Sacred Heart Society)
RSCM Royal School of Church Music
RSCN Registered Sick Children's Nurse
RSD recovery, salvage and disposal; Royal Society of Dublin
RSE Received Standard English; Royal Society of Edinburgh
RSF rough sunk face (building); Royal Scots Fusiliers
RSFS Royal Scottish Forestry Society
RSFSR Russian Soviet Federative Socialist Republic
RSG rate-support grant; recirculating steam generator; regional seat of government (civil defence); Royal Scots Greys (military)
RSGB Radio Society of Great Britain

RSGS Royal Scottish Geographical Society
RSH Royal Society for the Promotion of Health
RSHA *Reichssicherheitshauptamt* (German: Reich Security Central Office; Nazi secret police)
RSI regional staff inspector; repetitive strain injury; Royal Sanitary Institute
RSJ rolled steel joist (building)
RSL Returned Services League (Australia); Royal Society of Literature
RSLA raising of school-leaving age
RSM regimental sergeant major; regional sales manager; Royal School of Mines; Royal Society of Medicine; Royal Society of Musicians; San Marino (international vehicle registration)
RSMA Royal Society of Marine Artists
RSME Royal School of Military Engineering
rsn reason
RSNA Radiological Society of North America
RSNC Royal Society for Nature Conservation
RSNZ Royal Society of New Zealand
RSO radiological safety officer; Radio Symphony Orchestra; railway sorting office; railway suboffice; range safety officer (military); recruiting staff officer; resident surgical officer; Royal Scottish Orchestra; rural suboffice
RSocMed Royal Society of Medicine
rsp rain stops play; rain stopped play
RSPB Royal Society for the Protection of Birds
RSPCA Royal Society for the Prevention of Cruelty to Animals
RSPP Royal Society of Portrait Painters
rsq. rescue
RSRE Royal Signals and Radar Establishment
RSS *Regiae Societatis Socius* (Latin: Fellow of the Royal Society); Royal Statistical Society
RSSA Royal Scottish Society of Arts
RSSPCC Royal Scottish Society for the Prevention of Cruelty to Children
RSTM&H Royal Society of Tropical Medicine and Hygiene
rstr. restricted
RSU road safety unit
RSUA Royal Society of Ulster Architects
RSV Revised Standard Version (Bible)
RSVP *répondez, s'il vous plaît* (French: please reply)

rsvr reservoir
RSW Royal Scottish Society of Painters in Water Colours
RSWC right side up with care
RSwN Royal Swedish Navy
rt right; right tackle (American football)
RT Ipswich (UK vehicle registration); radiation therapy; radio telegraph; radio telegraphy; radio telephone; radio telephony; reaction time; reading test; received text; return ticket; room temperature; round table; round trip
R/T radio telegraph; radio telegraphy
RTA reciprocal trade agreement; road traffic accident; Road Traffic Act
RTB return to base (military)
RTBA rate to be agreed
RTBF *Radio-Télévision Belge de la Communauté Française* (French broadcasting company)
rtc. ratchet
RTC Road Transport Corporation (India); Round Table Conference
rtd retired; returned
rtd ht retired hurt (cricket)
RTDS real time data system (computing)
rte route
RTE *Radio Telefis Éireann* (Gaelic: Irish Radio and Television); real-time execution (computing)
RTECS Registry of Toxic Effects of Chemical Substances
RTF *Radiodiffusion-Télévision Française* (French television company)
rtg rating
RTG radio-isotope thermo-electric generator; relativistic theory of gravitation (physics)
Rt Hon. Right Honourable
RTI Round Table International
RTITB Road Transport Industry Training Board
RTK right to know
RTL real-time language (computing); resistor-transistor logic (electronics)
RTM registered trademark
rtn retain; return
rtng returning
RTO railroad transportation officer (US); railway transport officer
RTOL reduced take-off and landing (aeronautics)
RTP rated thermal power (engineering); room temperature and pressure (physics)
RTPI Royal Town Planning Institute

RTR Royal Tank Regiment
RTRA Road Traffic Regulation Act
Rt Rev. Right Reverend
RTS Religious Tract Society; reserve tug service; Royal Television Society; Royal Toxophilite Society
RTSA Retail Trading Standards Association
RTT(Y) radioteletype
RTTC Road Time Trials Council (cycling)
RTU return to unit (military); returned to unit (military)
Rt W Right Worshipful
RTW ready to wear
rty rarity
RTYC Royal Thames Yacht Club
RTZ Rio Tinto Zinc Corporation Limited
Ru ruthenium (element)
Ru. Russia; Russian
RU Bournemouth (UK vehicle registration); Burundi (international vehicle registration); Readers' Union; registered user; reprocessed uranium; Rugby Union
RUA Royal Ulster Academy of Painting, Sculpture and Architecture
RUAS Royal Ulster Agricultural Society
rub. rubber
RUC Royal Ulster Constabulary
RUCR Royal Ulster Constabulary Reserve
rud. rudder
RUF revolving underwriting facility (banking)
RUG restricted users group (computing)
RUI Royal University of Ireland
RUKBA Royal United Kingdom Beneficent Association
rumpie rural upwardly mobile professional
RUPP road used as public path
RUR Royal Ulster Regiment
RURAL Society for the Responsible Use of Resources in Agriculture and on the Land
Rus. Russia; Russian
RUS Russia (international vehicle registration)
RUSI Royal United Services Institute for Defence Studies
RUSM Royal United Service Museum
Russ. Russia; Russian
Rut(d). Rutland
rv random variable (statistics); rendezvous
RV Portsmouth (UK vehicle registration); rateable value; recreational vehicle (US); re-entry vehicle (astronautics); rendezvous; research vessel; Revised

Version (Bible); Rifle Volunteers
RVC Rifle Volunteer Corps; Royal
Veterinary College
RVCI Royal Veterinary College of Ireland
RVLR Road Vehicles Lighting
Regulations
RVM Royal Victorian Medal
RVO Royal Victorian Order
RVR runway visual range
RVSVP *répondez vite, s'il vous plait*
(French: please reply quickly)
RVU research vessel unit
Rw. Rwanda
RW Coventry (UK vehicle registration);
rainwater; right of way; Right
Worshipful; Right Worthy; Royal
Warrant; runway
RWA Race Walking Association; Royal
West of England Academy; Rwanda
(international vehicle registration)
RWAFF Royal West African Frontier
Force
R War. R Royal Warwickshire Regiment
RWAS Royal Welsh Agricultural
Society
rwd rear-wheel drive
RWD radioactive-waste disposal
RWEA Royal West of England Academy
RWF Radio Wholesalers' Federation;
Royal Welch Fusiliers
RwFr Rwanda franc (monetary unit)
RWGM Right Worshipful Grand Master
(Freemasonry)

RWGR Right Worthy Grand
Representative (Freemasonry)
RWGS Right Worthy Grand Secretary
(Freemasonry)
RWGT Right Worthy Grand Templar
(Freemasonry); Right Worthy Grand
Treasurer (Freemasonry)
RWGW Right Worthy Grand Warden
(Freemasonry)
R Wilts Yeo. Royal Wiltshire
Yeomanry
RWK Queen's Own Royal West Kent
Regiment
RWM radioactive waste management
RWP rainwater pipe
RWS Royal Society of Painters in Water
Colours
rwy railway
RX Reading (UK vehicle registration);
Rye (UK fishing port registration)
ry railway
RY Air Rwanda (airline flight code);
Leicester (UK vehicle registration);
Ramsey (UK fishing port registration)
RYA Royal Yachting Association
RYC in reply to your cable
RYS Royal Yacht Squadron
rz return to zero
RZ Antrim (UK vehicle registration)
RZSI Royal Zoological Society of
Ireland
RZSS(cot) Royal Zoological Society of
Scotland

S

s second; solid (chemistry)
s. school; sea; seaman; section; see; semi-;
series; sermon; set; shilling; *siècle*
(French: century); *siehe* (German: see);
sign; signed; *sine* (Latin: without); single;
singular (grammar); *sinister* (Latin: left);
sinistra (Italian: left); sire; sister; slow;
small; snow; socialist; society; *solidus*
(Latin: shilling); solo; son; soprano;
south; southern; spherical; steamer;
steel; stem; stock; stratus (cloud);
substantive (grammar); succeeded; suit;
sun; sunny; summer; surplus
s/ *sur* (French: on)
S saint; Schilling (Austrian monetary
unit); *Señor* (Spanish: Mr); Sheffield
(UK postcode); siemens (electrical
engineering); *Signor* (Italian: Mr);

Signora (Italian: Mrs); Silurian
(geology); silver; Skibbereen (Irish
fishing port registration); slow; small;
solar mass (astronomy); south; southern;
sucre (Ecuadorian monetary unit);
sulfur/sulphur (element); summer;
summer loading (shipping); Sunday;
Sweden (international vehicle
registration)
S. Sabbath; sable (heraldry); sacral
(anatomy); saint; *San* (Italian: saint);
Sankt (German: saint); *Santo/Santa*
(Italian: saint); *Sao* (Portuguese: saint);
satisfactory; Saturday; Saxon; School;
Scotland; Scottish; Sea; secondary;
secret; secretary; section; *segno* (Italian:
sign; music); *Seite* (German: page);
Senate; *Señor* (Spanish: Mr); sentence;

September; *sepultus* (Latin: buried); series; ship; signaller; signature; *Signor* (Italian: Mr); *Signora* (Italian: Mrs); Socialist; Society; *Socius* (Latin: Fellow); solar; soprano; south; southern; spades (cards); staff; statute (law); submarine; summer; sun; Sunday; Sweden

S2 Bangladesh (international civil aircraft marking)

S7 Seychelles (international civil aircraft marking)

S9 Sao Tomé (international civil aircraft marking)

sa safe arrival; *secundum artem* (Latin: by skill; medicine); see also; semiannual (horticulture); sex appeal; *siehe auch* (German: see also); *sine anno* (Latin: without date); soluble in alkali (chemistry); special agent; storage area; subject to approval; subsistence allowance

sa. sable (heraldry)

Sa. Saturday

SA Aberdeen (UK vehicle registration); Salvation Army; sandstorm (meteorology); Saudi Arabia; Saudi Arabian; seaman apprentice; Secretary of the Army (US); semiannual (horticulture); sex appeal; small arms; *sociedad anónima* (Spanish: public limited company); *sociedade anónima* (Portuguese: public limited company); *société anonyme* (French: public limited company; Belgium, France, Luxembourg, Switzerland); Society of Antiquaries; Society of Arts; Society of Authors; Soil Association; *Son Altesse* (French: Her or His Highness); South Africa; South African; South African Airways (airline flight code); South America; South American; South Australia; South Australian; *Sturm Abteilung* (German: storm troopers; Nazi organization); subject to approval; surface area; surface-to-air (missile); Swansea (UK fishing port registration; postcode)

S/A subject to acceptance; survivorship agreement (banking; US)

SAA small arms ammunition; South African Airways; Speech Association of America; Standards Association of Australia; surface-active agent (chemistry)

SAAA Scottish Amateur Athletic Association

Saab *Svensk Aeroplan Aktiebolag* (Swedish aircraft and car manufacturer)

SAAF South African Air Force

SAAFA Special Arab Assistance Fund for Africa

SAAU South African Agricultural Union

sab. *sábado* (Portuguese: Saturday) *sabato* (Italian: Saturday)

Sab. Sabbath

SAB Science Advisory Board; Scientific Advisory Board; Society of American Bacteriologists; soprano, alto, bass; South Atlantic Bight

SABA Scottish Amateur Boxing Association

Sabat. Sabbatical

SABC Scottish Association of Boys' Clubs; South African Broadcasting Corporation

Sabena *Société anonyme belge d'exploitation de la navigation aérienne* (Belgian World Airlines)

SABMIS seaborne antiballistic missile intercept system

sabo. sabotage

SABRA South African Bureau of Racial Affairs

SABS South African Bureau of Standards

SAC Scientific Advisory Committee; Scottish Automobile Club; Senior Aircraftman; short-run average cost (finance); small-arms club; South Atlantic coast; State Athletic Commission (US); Strategic Air Command (US)

SACEUR Supreme Allied Commander Europe

SACL South African Confederation of Labour

SACLANT Supreme Allied Commander Atlantic

SACO *Sveriges Akademikers Centralorganisation* (Swedish: Swedish Confederation of Professional Associations)

SACP South African Communist Party

Sacr. Sacramento (US); sacrist

SACSEA Supreme Allied Command, SE Asia

SACSIR South African Council for Scientific and Industrial Research

SACW Senior Aircraftwoman

SAD seasonal affective disorder (psychiatry)

SADCC Southern Africa Development Coordinating Committee; Southern Africa Development Coordinating Conference

SADF South African Defence Force

SADG *Société des architectes diplômés* (French: Society of Government-Certified Architects)
SADIE scanning analogue to digital input equipment
SADT structured analysis and design technique (computing)
SAE self-addressed envelope; Society of Automotive Engineers (US); stamped addressed envelope
SAEF stock exchange automatic execution facility
SAF Secretary of the Air Force (US); Society of American Foresters; Strategic Air Force (US)
safe stamped addressed foolscap envelope
S. Afr. South Africa; South African
S. Afr. D. South African Dutch
SAFU Scottish Amateur Fencing Union
SAG Screen Actors' Guild (US)
SAGA Society of American Graphic Artists
SAGB Spiritualist Association of Great Britain
SAGE semiautomatic ground environment (military)
SAH Supreme Allied Headquarters
Sai. Saigon
SAID sexual allegations in divorce
SAIF South African Industrial Federation
SAIMR South African Institute of Medical Research
SAIRR South African Institute of Race Relations
sal. salary
SAL South Arabian League; surface airlifted mail
Salop Shropshire
SALP South African Labour Party
SALR saturated adiabatic lapse rate (medicine)
SALT Strategic Arms Limitation Talks; Strategic Arms Limitation Treaty
salv. salvage
Salv. Salvador
sam. *samedi* (French: Saturday)
Sam. Samaria; Samaritan; Samoa; *Samstag* (German: Saturday); Samuel (Bible)
S. Am. South America
SAM surface-to-air missile
Samar. Samaritan
SAMC South African Medical Corps
S. Amer. South America; South American
SAMH Scottish Association for Mental Health

san. sanitary; sanatorium
sanat. sanatorium
SANCAD Scottish Association for National Certificates and Diplomas
sand. sandwich
s&d song and dance
S&F stock and fixtures (insurance)
S&FA shipping and forwarding agents
S&H shipping and handling
S&L savings and loan association (US)
S&M sadism and masochism; sausages and mash; stock and machinery (insurance)
s&s sex and shopping (popular fiction)
SANDS Stillbirth and Neonatal Death Society
s&sc sized and supercalendered (paper)
S&T Salmon and Trout Association; supply and transport
Sane Schizophrenia - A National Emergency
SANE Committee for a Sane Nuclear Policy (US)
sanit. sanitary; sanitation
SANR subject to approval, no risk
sans sans serif (printing)
Sans(k). Sanskrit
SANZ Standards Association of New Zealand
SAO Scottish Association of Opticians
SAOS Scottish Agricultural Organization Society
sap soon as possible
SAP South African Police
SAPA South African Press Association; South African Publishers' Association
sapfu surpassing all previous foul-ups; surpassing all previous fuck-ups
sapl sailed as per list (shipping)
Sar. Sarawak; Sardinia; Sardinian
SAR search and rescue; *Son Altesse Royale* (French: Her or His Royal Highness); Sons of the American Revolution; South African Republic
SARAH search and rescue homing (radar); surgery assistant robot acting on the head (brain surgery)
SARBE search and rescue beacon equipment
Sarl. *société à responsabilité limitée* (French: private limited company; Belgium, France, Luxembourg, Switzerland)
SARSAT search and rescue satellite-aided tracking
Sarum: *Sarumensis* (Latin: (Bishop) of Salisbury)

Sas. *società in accomandita* (Italian: limited partnership)
SAS Scandinavian Airline System; *Societatis Antiquariorum Socius* (Latin: Fellow of the Society of Antiquaries); *Son Altesse Sérénissime* (French: Her or His Most Serene Highness); Special Air Service (military)
SASc Small Arms School Corps
SASE self-addressed stamped envelope
Sask. Saskatchewan
SASO Senior Air Staff Officer; South African Students' Organization
SASR Special Air Service Regiment
sat. satellite; saturate; saturated
Sat. Saturday; Saturn
S. At. South Atlantic
SAT scholastic aptitude test (US); Senior Member of the Association of Accounting Technicians; ship's apparent time; South Australian Time; standard assessment task (education)
SATB soprano, alto, tenor, bass
SATCO signal automatic air traffic control system
SATEX semiautomatic telegraph exchange
satn saturation
SATRO Science and Technology Regional Organization
S. Aus(tral). South Australia; South Australian
sav sale at valuation; stock at valuation
SAVS Scottish Anti-Vivisection Society
SAW space at will (advertising); submerged arc welding; surface acoustic wave (telecommunications)
SAWS synoptic automatic weather station
sax. saxophone
Sax. Saxon; Saxony
SAYE save as you earn
sb single-breasted (clothing); small bore (rifle); smooth bore; stolen base (baseball)
sb. substantive (grammar)
Sb antimony (element)
SB Air Caledonie International (airline flight code, New Caledonia); Glasgow (UK vehicle registration); sales book; Sam Browne (military webbing); savings bank; *Scientiae Baccalaureus* (Latin: Bachelor of Science); selection board; Serving Brother; short bill (commerce); sick bay; Signal Boatswain; signal book; simultaneous broadcast; small business (commerce); sodium borate (chemistry);

South Britain; Special Branch (police); Statute Book; stillborn (medicine); stretcher bearer; sub-branch
SBA School of Business Administration; sick-bay attendant; sick-berth attendant; Small Business Administration (US); standard beam approach (aeronautics)
SBAA Sovereign Base Areas Administration
SBAC Society of British Aerospace Companies
SBB *Schweizerische Bundesbahnen* (German: Swiss Federal Railways)
SBBNF Ship and Boat Builders' National Federation
SBC School Broadcasting Council; single-board computer; small bayonet cap (electrical engineering)
SbE south by east
SBE Southern British English (dialect)
SBGI Society of British Gas Industries
SBH Scottish Board of Health
SBIC small business investment company (US)
SBM single buoy mooring
SBNO Senior British Naval Officer
s'board starboard
SBOT Sacred Books of the Old Testament
SBP systolic blood pressure (medicine)
SBR styrene-butadiene rubber
sbre *septiembre* (Spanish: September)
SBS sick-building syndrome; Special Boat Service (military)
SBStJ Serving Brother of the Order of St John of Jerusalem
SBT segregated ballast tanks (shipping)
SBU strategic business unit
SBV seabed vehicle
SbW south by west
sc salvage charges; self-contained; single column (printing); small capitals (printing); staff college; steel casting; supercalendered (paper)
sc. scale; scene; science; scientific; screw; scruple (unit of weight); *sculpsit* (Latin: he/she carved or engraved it); sculptor
s/c self-contained; *son compte* (French: his account)
Sc scandium (element); stratocumulus (meteorology)
Sc. Scandinavia; Scandinavian; science; Scotch; Scotland; Scots; Scottish; sculptor
SC Cruzeiro (airline flight code, Brazil); Edinburgh (UK vehicle registration); safe custody; sailing club; Salvage Corps; same case (law); Sanitary Corps (US); School Certificate (Australia; New

Zealand); Schools Council; Scilly (UK fishing port registration); Security Council (UN); self-contained; *Senatus Consultum* (Latin: decree of the Senate); senior counsel; service certificate; Sessions Cases (law); shooting club; short course; Signal Corps; single column (printing); skating club; skiing club; small craft; social club; solar cell; South Carolina (zip code); Southern Command (military); special case; special constable; special constabulary; sports club; staff captain; staff college; staff corps; standing committee/ conference; Star of Courage (Canada); statutory committee; stratocumulus (meteorology); stress corrosion (engineering); Suffolk and Cambridge-shire (Regiment); Supreme Court; surface contamination; swimming club

SCA sickle-cell anaemia

SCAAA Southern Counties Amateur Athletic Association

SCAHT Scottish Churches Architectural Heritage Trust

Scan(d). Scandinavia; Scandinavian

SCAO Senior Civil Affairs Officer

SCAP Supreme Command Allied Powers; Supreme Commander Allied Powers

SCAPA Society for Checking the Abuses of Public Advertising

scaps small capitals (printing)

SCAR Scientific Committee on Antarctic Research; Special Committee on Antarctic Research

SCARA selective compliance assembly robot arm

Scarab submerged craft assisting repair and burial

ScB *Scientiae Baccalaureus* (Latin: Bachelor of Science)

SCB Solicitors Complaints Bureau; Speedway Control Board

ScBC Bachelor of Science in Chemistry

ScBE Bachelor of Science in Engineering

SCBU special care baby unit

scc single column centimetre (printing)

SCC Sea Cadet Corps; Society of Church Craftsmen

SCCA Sports Car Club of America

SCCAPE Scottish Council for Commercial, Administrative and Professional Education

SCCL Scottish Council for Civil Liberties

scd scheduled

ScD *Scientiae Doctor* (Latin: Doctor of Science)

SCD sickle-cell disease

SCDA Scottish Community Drama Association

SCDC Schools Curriculum Development Committee

ScDHyg Doctor of Science in Hygiene

ScDMed Doctor of Science in Medicine

sce. scenario

SCE schedule compliance evaluation; Scottish Certificate of Education

scf standard cubic feet

SCF Save the Children Fund; Senior Chaplain to the Forces

scfh standard cubic feet per hour

scfm standard cubic feet per minute

scg scoring

Sc. Gael. Scottish Gaelic

SCGB Ski Club of Great Britain

sch. schedule; scholar; scholarship; scholastic; *scholium* (Latin: note); school; schooner

Sch. schedule (taxation); Schilling (Austrian monetary unit); School

sched. schedule

schem. schematic

scherz. *scherzando* (Italian: playful or humorous; music)

SchMusB Bachelor of School Music

schol. scholar; scholarship; scholastic; *scholium* (Latin: note)

schr schooner

sci single column inch (advertising)

sci. science; scientific

SCI Scottish Central Institutions; Society of the Chemical Industry

SCID severe combined immuno-deficiency disease (medicine)

sci. fa. *scire facias* (Latin: that you cause to know)

sci-fi science fiction

SCIT Special Commissioners of Income Tax

SCK Servants of Christ the King

SCL Scottish Central Library; Student in Civil Law; Student of Civil Law

SCLC Southern Christian Leadership Conference (US)

SCLI Somerset and Cornwall Light Infantry

ScM *Scientiae Magister* (Latin: Master of Science)

SCM State Certified Midwife; Student Christian Movement; summary court-martial

SCMA Society of Cinema Managers of

Great Britain and Ireland (Amalgamated)

SCMES Society of Consulting Marine Engineers and Ship Surveyors

ScMHyg Master of Science in Hygiene

SCNE Select Committee on National Expenditure

SCNO Senior Canadian Naval Officer

SCOBEC Scottish Business Education Council

SCOFF Society for the Conquest of Flight Fear

S. Con. Res. Senate concurrent resolution (US)

SCONUL Standing Conference of National and University Libraries

SCOR Scientific Committee on Oceanic Research; Standing Committee on Refugees

Scot. Scotch; Scotland; Scotsman; Scottish

ScotBIC Scottish Business in the Community

SCOTEC Scottish Technical Education Council

SCOTUS Supreme Court of the United States

SCOTVEC Scottish Vocation Education Council

SCOUT shared currency option under tender (commerce)

SCP Social Credit Party (Canada)

SCPC single channel per carrier (telecommunications)

SCPR Scottish Council of Physical Recreation

SCPS Society of Civil and Public Servants

scr. scrip (finance); script; scruple (unit of weight)

SCR selective catalytic reaction (chemical engineering); selective catalytic reactor (chemical engineering); senior common room; silicon-controlled rectifier (electronics)

SCRE Scottish Council for Research in Education

SCREAM Society for the Control and Registration of Estate Agents and Mortgage Brokers

Script. Scriptural; Scripture/s

SCS Soil Conservation Service; space communications system

SCSA Soil Conservation Society of America

SCSI small computer systems interface

SCSS Scottish Council of Social Service

SCTR Standing Conference on Telecommunications Research

SCU Scottish Cricket Union; Scottish Cycling Union; Scottish Cyclists' Union

SCUA Suez Canal Users' Association

scuba self-contained underwater breathing apparatus

sculp(t). *sculpsit* (Latin: he/she carved it); sculptor; sculptress; sculptural; sculpture

SCV *Stato della Città del Vaticano* (Italian: Vatican City State)

SCWS Scottish Cooperative Wholesale Society

SCY Truro (Isles of Scilly, UK vehicle registration)

SCYA Scottish Christian Youth Assembly

sd safe deposit; said; sailed; same date; *sans date* (French: no date); semi-detached; several dates; sewed (books); short delivery (commerce); *siehe dies* (German: see this); signed; *sine die* (Latin: without a day or date); sound; standard deviation (statistics)

SD Diploma in Statistics; Glasgow (UK vehicle registration); *salutem dicit* (Latin: he/she sends greeting); *Scientiae Doctor* (Latin: Doctor of Science); sea-damaged; Secretary of Defense (US); semi-detached; *Senatus Decreto* (Latin: by decree of the Senate); send direct; senile dementia; senior deacon; sequence date; service dress (military); short delivery (commerce); *Sicherheitsdienst* (German: Security Service; Nazi organization); sight draft (finance); Signal Department; Signal Division; South Dakota (zip code); special delivery; special duty; staff duties; stage door; standard deviation (statistics); State Department (US); submarine detector; Sudan Airways (airline flight code); Sunderland (UK fishing port registration); supply depot; Swaziland (international vehicle registration)

S/D school district (US); sight draft (finance)

SDA *Schweizerische Depeschenagentur* (news agency, Switzerland); Scottish Development Agency; Scottish Dinghy Association; Scottish Diploma in Agriculture; Seventh Day Adventist; Social Democratic Alliance

S. Dak. South Dakota

SD&T staff duties and training

SDAT senile dementia of the Alzheimer type (medicine)

S-DAT stationary digital audio tape
SDC Society of Dyers and Colourists; submersible decompression chamber
SDD Scottish Development Department; subscriber direct dialling (telephony)
SDECE *Service de documentation étrangère et de contre-espionage* (French counterintelligence agency)
SDF Social Democratic Federation
SDG *Soli Deo Gloria* (Latin: Glory to God Alone)
SDHE spacecraft data-handling equipment
SDI selective dissemination of information; Strategic Defense Initiative (US)
SDIO Strategic Defense Initiative Office (US)
sdl. saddle
SDL special duties list
SDLP Social Democratic and Labour Party (Northern Ireland)
SDMJ September, December, March, June (finance)
SDO senior dental officer; senior duty officer; station duty officer; subdivisional officer
S. Doc. Senate document (US)
SDP Social Democratic Party; social, domestic and pleasure (insurance)
SDR special dispatch rider; special drawing rights (finance)
SDS scientific data system; Sisters of the Divine Saviour; *Sozialistischer Deutscher Studentenbund* (German: Federation of German Socialist Students); strategic defense system (US); Students for a Democratic Society (US)
SDT Society of Dairy Technology
SDU Social Democratic Union
se single end; single ended; single engine; single entry (book-keeping); special equipment; standard error (statistics); straight edge
Se selenium (element)
SE Aberdeen (UK vehicle registration); Salcombe (UK fishing port registration); sanitary engineering; Society of Engineers; software engineering (computing); *Son Eminence* (French: His Eminence); *Son Excellence* (French: Her or His Excellence); southeast; southeastern; southeast London (UK postcode); Staff Engineer; Standard English; Stirling engine; stock exchange; stopped end (building); Sweden (international civil aircraft marking)

SEA South-East Asia
SEAAC South-East Asia Air Command
SEAC School Examination and Assessment Council; South-East Asia Command; Standard Eastern Automatic Computer
SEAL sea-air-land (US Navy)
SEALF South-East Asia Land Forces
SEAN State Enrolled Assistant Nurse
SE&CR South Eastern and Chatham Railway
SEAQ stock exchange automated quotations
SEATO South-East Asia Treaty Organization
SEATS Stock Exchange Alternative Trading Service
SEB Southern Electricity Board
sec secant (mathematics)
sec. second; secondary; seconded; secretary; section; sector; *secundum* (Latin: according to); security
SEC Securities and Exchange Commission (US)
SECAM *séquence electronique couleur avec mémoire* (French: electronic colour sequence with memory; television)
SECC Scottish Exhibition and Conference Centre
Sec. Gen. Secretary General
sech hyperbolic secant (mathematics)
sec. leg. *secundum legem* (Latin: according to law)
Sec. Leg. Secretary of the Legation
sec. nat. *secundum naturam* (Latin: according to rule)
sect. section
secy secretary
sed. sedative; sediment
SED Scottish Education Department; shipper's export declaration
SEDAR submerged electrode detection and ranging (navigation)
sedt sediment
sedtn sedimentation
SEE Senior Electrical Engineer; Society of Environment Engineers
SEEA *Société européenne d'énergie atomique* (French: European Atomic Energy Society)
SEEB Southeastern Electricity Board
Seeboard Southeastern Electricity Board
SEF Shipbuilding Employers' Federation
seg. segment; segregate; *segue* (Italian: follows; music)
SEG socio-economic grade
SEH St Edmund Hall (Oxford)

SEIF *Secretaria de Estado da Informação e Turismo* (Portuguese: State Information and Tourist Board)

SEIS submarine escape immersion suit

seismol. seismological; seismology

SEIU Service Employees International Union (US)

sel. select; selected; selection; *selig* (German: deceased)

Sel(w) Selwyn College (Cambridge)

Selk. Selkirk

SELNEC South-East Lancashire, North-East Cheshire

sem. semester; semicolon; seminary

Sem. Seminary; Semitic

SEM scanning electron microscope; scanning electron microscopy

semi semi-detached house

semp. *sempre* (Italian: always; music)

sen. senior; *senza* (Italian: without; music)

Sen. Senate; Senator; Seneca (Roman writer); senior

SEN special educational needs; State Enrolled Nurse

S en C *société en commandite* (French: limited partnership)

S en NC *société en nom collectif* (French: partnership)

Sen. M. senior master

Sen. Mist. senior mistress

Senr senior

sent. sentence

SEO senior executive officer; senior experimental officer; Society of Education Officers

seoo *sauf erreur ou omission* (French: errors or omissions excepted)

sep. sepal; separable; separate; separated; separation

Sep. September; Septuagint

SEP simplified employee pension (US)

SEPM Society of Economic Palaeontologists and Mineralogists

sepn separation

SEPON Stock Exchange Pool Nominees Limited

sept. *septem* (Latin: seven); *septembre* (French: September); *septiembre* (Spanish: September)

Sept. September; Septuagint

seq. sequel; sequence; *sequens* (Latin: the following); *sequente* (Latin: and in what follows); *sequitur* (Latin: it follows)

seq. luce *sequenti luce* (Latin: the following day; medicine)

seqq. *sequentia* (Latin: the following);

sequentibus (Latin: in the following places)

ser. serial; series; sermon; servant; service

SERA Socialist Environment and Resources Association

Serb. Serbia; Serbian

SERC Science and Engineering Research Council

Serg(t). sergeant

Serj(t). serjeant

SERL Services Electronics Research Laboratory

SERLANT Service Forces, Atlantic (US Navy)

SERPAC Service Forces, Pacific (US Navy)

Serps state earnings-related pension scheme

SERT Society of Electronic and Radio Technicians

serv. servant; service

SES Singapore Stock Exchange; socio-economic status (US)

SESCO secure submarine communications

SESDAQ Stock Exchange of Singapore Dealing and Automated Quotation System

SESI Stock Exchange of Singapore Index

SESO senior equipment staff officer

sess. session

set. *setembro* (Portuguese: September); settlement

SET Securities Exchange of Thailand; selective employment tax

SETI search for extraterrestrial intelligence

S-et-L Saône-et-Loire (French department)

S-et-M Seine-et-Marne (French department)

S-et-O Seine-et-Oise (French department)

sett. *settembre* (Italian: September)

sev. sever; several

SEV severe (meteorology)

sevl. several

sew. sewage; sewer(age)

SEW safety-equipment worker

sex. sextet; sexual

Sexag. Sexagesima

sext. sextant

sf sacrifice fly (baseball); *sans frais* (French: no expenses); science fiction; *sforzando* (Italian: strongly accentuated; music); signal frequency; sinking fund (finance); *sub finem* (Latin: towards the end)

Sf Surinam guilder (monetary unit)
SF Edinburgh (UK vehicle registration); Finland (international vehicle registration); San Francisco; science fiction; senior fellow; Sherwood Foresters (military); shipping federation; signal frequency (telecommunications); sinking fund (finance); Sinn Fein; Society of Friends; special facilities; special forces; standard frequency (electrical engineering)
SFA Scottish Football Association; sweet Fanny Adams; sweet fuck all
SFBMS Small Farm Business Management Scheme
Sfc Sergeant first class (US)
SFC specific fuel consumption; surface (meteorology)
sfgd safeguard
SFI *Société financière internationale* (French: International Finance Corporation)
SFInstE Senior Fellow, Institute of Energy
SFL Scottish Football League; sequenced flashing lights (aeronautics)
sfm surface feet per minute
SFO senior flag officer; Serious Fraud Office; Superannuation Funds Office
SFOF spaceflight operations facility (NASA)
sfp *sforzato-piano* (Italian: strong accent, then soft; music)
SFr Swiss franc
SFR sinking fund rate of return (finance)
SFT supercritical fluid technology
SFTCD Senior Fellow, Trinity College Dublin
SFU signals flying unit; suitable for upgrade
sfz *sforzando* (Italian: strongly accentuated; music)
sg specific gravity; steel girder
sg. singular (grammar)
Sg. surgeon
SG Edinburgh (UK vehicle registration); *Sa Grâce* (French: Her or His Grace); *Sa Grandeur* (French: Her or His Highness); Scots Guards; Seaman Gunner; Secretary General; senior grade (US education); Seyfert galaxy (astronomy); ship and goods; singular (grammar); Society of Genealogists; Solicitor General; spin-glass (crystal); Stevenage (UK postcode); Surgeon General
SGA small for gestational age (medicine); Society of Graphic Art
SGB *Schweizerischer Gewerkschaftsbund*

(German: Swiss Federation of Trade Unions)
SGBI Schoolmistresses' and Governesses' Benevolent Institution
SgC Surgeon Captain
SgCr Surgeon Commander
sgd signed
SGD Senior Grand Deacon (Freemasonry)
sgdg *sans garantie du gouvernement* (French: without government guarantee; patents)
SGF Scottish Grocers' Federation
SGHWR steam-generating heavy-water reactor
sgl. single
S. Glam. South Glamorgan
SgLCr surgeon lieutenant-commander
SGM Sea Gallantry Medal
SGO squadron gunnery officer
SGP Singapore (international vehicle registration)
SgRA surgeon rear-admiral
Sgt sergeant
SGT Society of Glass Technology
Sgt Maj. sergeant major
SGU Scottish Gliding Union; Scottish Golf Union
SgVA surgeon vice-admiral
SGW Senior Grand Warden (Freemasonry)
sh hyperbolic sine (mathematics); sacrifice hit (baseball); second-hand; slant height; slope height
sh. shall; share; sheep; sheet; shilling; shower
Sh. Shakespeare; Shipwright
SH Edinburgh (UK vehicle registration); Sahsa (*Servicio Aero de Honduras*, airline flight code); Scarborough (UK fishing port registration); Schleswig-Holstein; school house; scrum-half (rugby); showers (meteorology); small head (numismatics); southern hemisphere
SHA Scottish Hockey Association; Secondary Heads Association; sidereal hour angle (astronomy, navigation); Special Health Authority
SHAC Shelter Housing Aid Centre
SHAEF Supreme Headquarters Allied Expeditionary Force
Shak(es). William Shakespeare (English playwright and poet)
SH&MA Scottish Horse and Motormen's Association
SHAPE Supreme Headquarters Allied Powers, Europe (NATO)

SHC specific heat capacity
SHCJ Society of the Holy Child Jesus
shd should
S/HE Sundays and holidays excepted (shipping)
Shef(f). Sheffield
Shet(l). Shetland Islands
SHEX Sundays and holidays excepted (shipping)
Sh. F. shareholders' funds
SHF super-high frequency
SHHD Scottish Home and Health Department
shipt shipment
SHM simple harmonic motion (physics); Society of Housing Managers
SHMO senior hospital medical officer
sho shutout (baseball)
SHO senior house officer
shoran short-range navigation
shp shaft horsepower
SHP single-flowered hardy perennial (rose); single-flowered hybrid perpetual (rose)
shpg shipping
shpt shipment
SHQ station headquarters; supreme headquarters
shr. share
shrap. shrapnel
Shrops. Shropshire
SHS Shire Horse Society; *Societatis Historicae Socius* (Latin: Fellow of the Historical Society)
sht sheet (books)
SHT single-flowered hybrid tea (rose)
shtg. shortage
shv *sub hac voce / hoc verbo* (Latin: under this word)
SHW safety, health and welfare
si sum insured
Si silicon (element)
SI Dublin (Irish vehicle registration); Sandwich Islands (Hawaii); seriously ill; Shetland Isles; Smithsonian Institution; Society of Illustrators (US); South Island (New Zealand); staff inspector; Star of India; Staten Island (New York); statutory instrument; *Système International (d'Unités)* (French: International System of Units)
SIA Society of Investment Analysts; Spinal Injuries Association
SIAC Securities Industry Automation Corporation (US)
SIAD Society of Industrial Artists and Designers

SIAM Society of Industrial and Applied Mathematics (US)
Sib. Siberia; Siberian
SIB Savings and Investment Bank; Securities and Investments Board; self-injurious behaviour (medicine); Shipbuilding Industry Board; Special Investigation Branch (police)
SIBOR Singapore Inter-Bank Offered Rate
sic. *siccus* (Latin: dry; pharmacology)
Sic. Sicilian; Sicily
SIC Scientific Information Center (US); Standard Industrial Classification
SICOT *Société internationale de chirurgie orthopédique et de traumatologie* (French: International Society of Orthopaedic Surgery and Traumatology)
SID Society for International Development; *Spiritus in Deo* (Latin: her or his spirit is with God); sudden ionospheric disturbance (radio)
SIDA Swedish International Development Authority; *Syndrome Immuno-Déficitaire Acquis* (French: acquired immune deficiency syndrome)
SIDS sudden infant death syndrome (medicine)
SIEC Scottish Industrial Estates Corporation
SIESO Society of Industrial and Emergency Service Officers
SIF selective identification feature; stress-intensity factor (engineering)
SIFS special instructors flying school
sig. signal; signature; *signetur* (Latin: let it be written or labelled); signification; signifies
Sig. *signa* (Latin: write; medicine); signature; *Signor* (Italian: Mr); *Signore* (Italian: Sir)
SIG signature of engraver present (numismatics); special-interest group
SIGAC Scottish Industrial Groups Advisory Council
sig. fig. significant figures (mathematics)
sigill. *sigillum* (Latin: seal)
SIGINT signals intelligence
SIGMA Science in General Management
Sigmn Signalman (Navy)
sign. signature
sig. n. pro. *signa nomine proprio* (Latin: label with the proper name; medicine)
Sig. O. signal officer
SIL *Société internationale de la lèpre* (French: International Leprosy Association)
Sil. Silesia; Silesian

sim. similar; similarly; simile
SIM self-inflicted mutilation; *Société internationale de musicologie* (French: International Musicological Society); survey information on microfilm
SIMA Scientific Instrument Manufacturers' Association of Great Britain; Steel Industry Management Association
SIMC *Société internationale pour la musique contemporaine* (French: International Society for Contemporary Music)
Simca *Société industrielle de mécanique et carrosserie automobiles* (French car manufacturing company)
SIMD single instruction, multiple data (computing)
SIME Security Intelligence Middle East
SIMG *Societas Internationalis Medicinae Generalis* (Latin: International Society of General Medicine)
SIMM single in-line memory module (computing, electronics)
SIMPL Scientific, Industrial and Medical Photographic Laboratories
sin sine (mathematics)
sin. sinecure; *sinistra* (Italian: left)
SinDrs Doctor of Chinese
sing. singular (grammar); *singulorum* (Latin: of each; medicine)
Sing. Singapore
sinh hyperbolic sine (mathematics)
Sinh. Sinhalese
SINS ship's inertial navigation system
SIO senior intelligence officer; serial input/output (computing)
SIOP single integrated operation plan (US military)
SIP supplemental income plan (US); *Svensk-Internationella Pressbyran* (news agency, Sweden)
SIPC Securities Investor Protection Corporation (US)
SIPO serial in, parallel out (computing)
SIPRC Society of Independent Public Relations Consultants
SIPRI Stockholm International Peace Research Institute
SIR small income relief (taxation)
SIRA Scientific Instrument Research Association
sis. sister
SIS Secret Intelligence Service (MI6); Security Intelligence Service (New Zealand)

SISD single instruction, single data (computing)
SISO serial in, serial out (electronics); single input, single output (electronics)
SISS submarine integrated sonar system
SISTER Special Institutions for Scientific and Technological Education and Research
sit stopping in transit; storing in transit
sit. sitting-room; situation
SIT Society of Industrial Technology; Society of Instrument Technology; spontaneous ignition temperature (engineering)
SITA *Société internationale de télécommunications aéronautiques* (French: International Society of Aeronautical Telecommunications); Students' International Travel Association
SITC standard international trade classification
sitcom situation comedy (television)
SITPRO Simpler Trade Procedures Board
sitt. sitting-room
sit(s). vac. situations vacant
SIUNA Seafarers International Union of North America
SI unit *Système international unit* (French: International System of Units)
SIW self-inflicted wound
sj sub judice (law)
SJ Glasgow (UK vehicle registration); Society of Jesus (Jesuits); Southern Air (airline flight code, New Zealand); supersonic jet
SJA St John Ambulance
SJAA St John Ambulance Association
SJAB St John Ambulance Brigade
SJC standing joint committee; Supreme Judicial Court (US)
SJD *Scientiae Juridicae Doctor* (Latin: Doctor of Juridical or Juristic Science)
S. J. Res. Senate joint resolution (US)
sk sack; sick
sk. sketch
SK Inverness (UK vehicle registration); Saskatchewan; Scandinavian Airline System (airline flight code, Sweden); Sealed Knot (historical re-enactment society); Stockport (UK postcode)
skamp station keeping and mobile platform (unmanned sea vessel)
SKC Scottish Kennel Club
S Ken. South Kensington (London)
SKF *Svenska Kullagerfabriken* (Swedish steel-making organization)
Skm Stockholm

skpo slip one, knit one, pass slipped stitch over (knitting)

Skr Sanskrit; Skipper

SKr Swedish krona (monetary unit)

Skt Sanskrit

sl salvage loss (insurance); *secundum legem* (Latin: according to rule); seditious libel; *sine loco* (Latin: without place; bibliography); support line

sl. sleet; slightly; slip

Sl. Slovak; Slovakian

SL Dundee (UK vehicle registration); salvage loss (insurance); scout leader; sea level; second lieutenant; security list; serjeant-at-law; short lengths (building); Slough (UK postcode); Slovenia (international civil aircraft marking); solicitor-at-law; source language; southern league; south latitude; squadron leader

SLA Scottish Library Association; special landscape area; Special Libraries Association (US); Symbionese Liberation Army

SLADE Society of Lithographic Artists, Designers, Engravers and Process Workers

SLAET Society of Licensed Aircraft Engineers and Technologists

SLAM standoff land-attack missile

slan *sine loco, anno, vel nomine* (Latin: without place, year, name; bibliography)

SLAR side-looking airborne radar (military)

SLAS Society for Latin American Studies

S. Lat. south latitude

Slav. Slavic; Slavonian; Slavonic

SLBM submarine-launched ballistic missile

SLC Scottish Leaving Certificate; Statute Law Committee; Surgeon Lieutenant-Commander

SLCM sea-launched cruise missile; ship-launched cruise missile; submarine-launched cruise missile

sld sailed; sealed; sold; solid

SLD self-locking device; Social and Liberal Democrats

SLDP Social and Liberal Democratic Party

S. Ldr Squadron Leader

SLE systemic lupus erythematosus

Slena Sierre Leone News Agency

s. l. et a. *sine loco et anno* (Latin: without place and year; bibliography)

S level scholarship level (education); special level (education)

slf straight line frequency (telecommunications)

SLF Scottish Landowners' Federation

SLFP Sri Lanka Freedom Party

SLIC Savings and Loan Insurance Corporation (US)

SLIM South London Industrial Mission

Slipar short light pulse alerting receiver (military aircraft)

SLLA Scottish Ladies Lacrosse Association

SLLW solid low-level waste (radioactivity)

SLM ship-launched missile

SLMA Student Loan Marketing Association (US)

SLMC Scottish Ladies' Mountaineering Club

slnd *sine loco nec data* (Latin: without indication of date or place; bibliography)

SLO senior liaison officer

slp *sine legitime prole* (Latin: without lawful issue); slip

SLP Scottish Labour Party; Socialist Labor Party (US)

SLR satellite laser ranging; self-loading rifle; single lens reflex (photography)

SL Rs Sri Lanka rupee (monetary unit)

SLSC surf life-saving club

SLTA Scottish Licensed Trade Association

Slud salivate, lachrymate, urinate, defecate (military)

SLV space launch vehicle; standard launch vehicle

SLW solid low-level waste (radioactivity)

sly slowly; southerly

sm. small

s/m sadomasochism; sadomasochist

Sm samarium (element)

SM Aberdeen Airways (airline flight code, UK); Glasgow (UK vehicle registration); sadomasochism; sadomasochist; sales manager; *Sa Majesté* (French: Her or His Majesty); *sanctae memoriae* (Latin: of holy memory); *Scientiae Magister* (Latin: Master of Science); *Seine Majestät* (German: Her or His Majesty); senior magistrate; Sergeant Major; service mark (US registered proprietary name); service module (astronautics); shipment memorandum; Shoreham (UK fishing port registration); short metre (music); silver medal; silver medallist; Sisters of Mercy; Society of Miniaturists; Sons of Malta; Staff Major; stage manager

(theatre); standard model (astronomy); state militia (US); station master; stipendiary magistrate; strategic missile; *Sua Maestà* (Italian: Her or His Majesty); Submarine Duties; *Su Magestad* (Spanish: Her or His Majesty); Surgeon Major; Sutton (UK postcode)
SMA Surplus Marketing Administration (US)
SMAC Standing Medical Advisory Committee
SMATV satellite master antenna television
SMAW shielded metal-arc welding
SMB Bachelor of Sacred Music; *Sa Majesté Britannique* (French: Her or His Britannic Majesty)
SMBA Scottish Marine Biological Association
SMBG self-monitoring of blood glucose (medicine)
SMC *Sa Majesté Catholique* (French: Her or His Catholic Majesty); Scottish Mountaineering Club
sm. caps small capitals (printing)
SMC(Disp) Dispensing Certificate of the Worshipful Company of Spectacle Makers
SMD Doctor of Sacred Music; short metre double (music); submarine mine depot
SME *Sancta Mater Ecclesia* (Latin: Holy Mother Church); Surinam (international vehicle registration)
SMERSH *Smert Shpionam* (Russian: death to spies; KGB organization)
SMetO senior meteorological officer
SMG submachine gun
SMHD Higher Diploma in Ophthalmic Optics of the Worshipful Company of Spectacle Makers
SMHI Swedish Meteorological and Hydrological Institute
SMHO Sovereign Military Hospitaller Order (Malta)
SMI *Sa Majesté Impériale* (French: Her or His Imperial Majesty)
SMIA Sheet Metal Industries Association
SMIEEE Senior Member of the Institute of Electrical and Electronics Engineers (US)
SMIRE Senior Member of the Institute of Radio Engineers (US)
Smith. Inst. Smithsonian Institution (Washington)
SMJ Sisters of Mary and Joseph
smk. smoke

sml. simulate; simulation; simulator; small
SML Science Museum Library
SMLE short magazine Lee-Enfield (rifle)
SMM Master of Sacred Music; *Sancta Mater Maria* (Latin: Holy Mother Mary)
SMMB Scottish Milk Marketing Board
SMMT Society of Motor Manufacturers and Traders Limited
SMO senior medical officer; Sovereign Military Order
smorz. *smorzando* (Italian: gradually slower and softer; music)
smp *sine mascula prole* (Latin: without male issue)
SMP statutory maternity pay
SMPS Society of Master Printers of Scotland
SMPTE Society of Motion Picture and Television Engineers (US)
SMR *Sa Majesté Royale* (French: Her or His Royal Majesty); standard Malaysian rubber; standard metabolic rate (medicine)
SMRE Safety in Mines Research Establishment
SMRTB Ship and Marine Requirements Technology Board
SMS secondary modern school
SMSO senior maintenance staff officer
SMT ship's mean time
SMTA Scottish Motor Trade Association
SMTF Scottish Milk Trade Federation
SMTO senior mechanical transport officer
SMW standard metal window
SMWIA Sheet Metal Workers' International Association (US)
sn *secundum naturam* (Latin: according to nature); serial number; series number; service number; *sine nomine* (Latin: without name); *sub nomine* (Latin: under a specified name)
sn. snow
s/n signal to noise ratio
Sn tin (element)
SN Dundee (UK vehicle registration); Sabena Belgian World Airlines (airline flight code); Secretary of the Navy (US); Senegal (international vehicle registration); Sergeant Navigator; shipping note; snow (meteorology); supernova (astronomy); Swindon (UK postcode)
S/N shipping note; signal-to-noise (electronics)
snafu situation normal, all fouled up; situation normal, all fucked up

SNAME Society of Naval Architects and Marine Engineers (US)
SNAP Shelter Neighbourhood Action Project; systems for nuclear auxiliary power
SNB sellers no buyers (stock exchange)
SNCB *Société nationale des chemins de fer belges* (French: Belgian National Railways)
SNCC Student Non-Violent Coordinating Committee
SNCF *Société nationale des chemins de fer français* (French: French National Railways)
Snd sound
SND Sisters of Notre Dame
SNF spent nuclear fuel; strategic nuclear forces (US)
SNFA Standing Naval Force, Atlantic
SNFU Scottish National Farmers' Union
Sng. Singapore
SNG substitute natural gas; synthetic natural gas
SNH Scottish National Heritage
SNIF short-term note issuance facility (finance)
SNIG sustainable non-inflationary growth
SNL standard nomenclature list
SNLR services no longer required
SNLV strategic nuclear launch vehicle
SNM Society of Nuclear Medicine (US); Somali National Movement
SNO senior naval officer; senior navigation officer; senior nursing officer
SNOBOL string-oriented symbolic language (computing)
SNP Scottish National Party
SNPA Scottish Newspaper Proprietors' Association
Snr senior
Sñr *Señor* (Spanish: Mr)
SNR signal-to-noise ratio (electronics); Society for Nautical Research
Snra *Senhora* (Portuguese: Mrs)
Sñra *Señora* (Spanish: Mrs)
Sñrta *Señorita* (Spanish: Miss)
SNSC Scottish National Ski Council
SNTPC Scottish National Town Planning Council
SNTS Society for New Testament Studies
so seller's option; shipping order; *siehe oben* (German: see above); strike out; substance of
so. sonata; south; southern
So. south; southern
SO Aberdeen (UK vehicle registration);

scientific officer; Scottish Office; section officer; seller's option; senior officer; shale oil; signal officer; Sligo (Irish fishing port registration); sorting office; Southampton (UK postcode); special order; staff officer; standing order; stationery office; statistical office; suboffice; supply officer; symphony orchestra
S/O section officer; shipowner
SOA state of the art
SOAD Staff Officer, Air Defence
SOAP subjective, objective, analysis, plan (medicine)
SOAS School of Oriental and African Studies (University of London)
SOB Senate office building; silly old bastard; silly old blighter; silly old bugger; son of a bitch; state office building
soc. social; socialist; society; sociology
Soc. Socialist; *società* (Italian: company or partnership); Society; Socrates (Greek philosopher)
SOC Scottish Ornithologists' Club; slightly off colour
SocCE(France) *Sociétés des ingénieurs civils de France* (French: Society of Civil Engineers of France)
Soc. Dem. Social Democrat
sociol. sociological; sociologist; sociology
SOCist Cistercians of Common Observance
SOCO scene-of-crime officer (police)
SOCONY Standard Oil Corporation of New York
SOCS Society of County Secretaries
soc. sci. social science; social scientist
socy society
sod. sodium
SODAC Society of Dyers and Colourists
SODEPAX Committee on Society, Development and Peace
SODOMEI Japanese Federation of Trade Unions
SODS ship's operatic and dramatic society (Royal Navy)
SOE Special Operations Executive; state-owned enterprise
SOED Shorter Oxford English Dictionary
SOES Small Order Execution System (finance; US)
SOF soluble organic fraction (chemistry); sound on a film (cinema)
SOFAA Society of Fine Art Auctioneers
sofar sound fixing and ranging

SOFCS self-organizing flight-control system
SOFFEX Swiss Options and Financial Futures Exchange
Sofia-Pres Sofia Press Agency (news agency, Bulgaria)
S. of S. Secretary of State; Song of Songs (Bible)
S. of Sol. Song of Solomon (Bible)
S. of T. Sons of Temperance
S. of TT School of Technical Training
SOGAT Society of Graphical and Allied Trades
SOHIO Standard Oil Company of Ohio
Sohyo *Nihon Rodo Kumiai So Hygikai* (Japanese: General Council of Japanese Trade Unions)
SO(I) staff officer (intelligence)
SO-in-C signal officer-in-chief
sol shipowner's liability (insurance)
sol. solicitor; soluble; solution
Sol. Solicitor; Song of Solomon (Bible)
SOL shit out of luck (US); strictly out of luck
SOLACE Society of Local Authority Chief Executives
Sol. Gen. Solicitor General
soln solution
solr solicitor
solv. solvent
soly solubility
Som. Somerset; Somerville College (Oxford)
SOM Society of Occupational Medicine
SOMA Society of Mental Awareness
SOME Senior Ordnance Mechanical Engineer
Som. Sh. Somali shilling (monetary unit)
sonar sound navigation and ranging
SO(O) staff officer (operations)
sop. soprano
SOP sleeping-out pass; standard operating procedure
Sopac-News South Pacific News Service (news agency, New Zealand)
soph. sophomore
Soph. Sophocles (Greek playwright and poet)
SoR sale or return
SORD submerged-object recovery device
sos *si opus sit* (Latin: if necessary; medicine)
SOS save our souls (distress signal); Secretary of State; senior officers' school; services of supply
SOSc Society of Ordained Scientists
SoSh Somali shilling (monetary unit)

sost. *sostenuto* (Italian: sustained)
SOTS Society for Old Testament Study
Sou. south; southern; Southampton
sov shut-off valve
sov. sovereign
SOV subject-object-verb (linguistics)
Sov. Soviet
Sov. Un. Soviet Union
sowc senior officers' war course
Soweto Southwestern Townships (South Africa)
sp self-propelled; *senza pedale* (Italian: without pedal; music); *sine prole* (Latin: without issue); single phase (electrical engineering); special position (advertising); *sposa* (Italian: wife); starting point; starting price; stop payment (banking)
sp. space; special; specie; species; specific; specimen; speed; spelling; spirit; sport
Sp. Spain; Spaniard; Spanish; Spring
SP Dundee (UK vehicle registration); Poland (international civil aircraft marking); *Saint-Père* (French: Holy Father); Salisbury (UK postcode); *Sanctissimus Pater* (Latin: Most Holy Father); Self-Propelled (gun); service pistol; service police (military); shore patrol; Sisters of Providence; Socialist Party; soil pipe; spark plug; Staff Paymaster; starting price (betting); stirrup pump; stop payment; stop press; stretcher party; submarine patrol; *Summus Pontifex* (Latin: Supreme Pontiff); supply point; supra protest (finance)
SpA *società per azioni* (Italian: public limited company)
SPA Saudi Press Agency; Society for Personnel Administration (US)
SPAA Scottish Passenger Agents' Association
SPAB Society for the Protection of Ancient Buildings
Spam spiced ham (tradename)
Sp. Am. Spanish American
Span. Spaniard; Spanish
SPANA Society for the Protection of Animals in North Africa
SPANDAR space and range radar (NASA)
Sp. Ar. Spanish Arabic
SPAR superprecision-approach radar
SPAS *Societatis Philosophicae Americanae Socius* (Latin: Fellow of the American Philosophical Society)

SPATC South Pacific Air Transport Council

SPC Society for the Prevention of Crime

SPCA Society for the Prevention of Cruelty to Animals (US)

SPCK Society for Promoting Christian Knowledge

spd subject to permission to deal (finance)

SPD Salisbury Plain District; south polar distance (astronomy); *Sozialdemokratische Partei Deutschlands* (German: Social Democratic Party of Germany)

SPDA single-premium deferred annuity

SPE Society for Pure English; Society of Petroleum Engineers; solid-phase epitaxy (electronics)

spec. special; specific; specifically; specification; specimen; spectrum; speculation

SPEC Society for Pollution and Environmental Control; South Pacific Bureau for Economic Cooperation

special. specialized

specif. specifically; specification

specs specifications; spectacles

Spectre Special Executive for Counter-Intelligence, Revenge and Extortion (fictional crime organization in the James Bond stories of Ian Fleming)

Sp. Ed. Specialist in Education (US)

SPF South Pacific Forum; sun protection factor

spg self-propelled gun

SPG Society for the Propagation of the Gospel; Special Patrol Group

SPGA Scottish Professional Golfers' Association

SPGB Socialist Party of Great Britain

sp. gr. specific gravity

sp. ht specific heat

SPI selected period investment (finance); Society of the Plastics Industry (US)

SPIRE spatial inertial reference equipment (navigation)

spirit. *spiritoso* (Italian: with spirit; music); spiritualism; spiritualistic

SPIW special-purposes individual weapon

spl *sine prole legitima* (Latin: without legitimate issue)

SPLA Sudan People's Liberation Army

spm *sine prole mascula* (Latin: without male issue)

SPMO senior principal medical officer

SPMU Society of Professional Musicians in Ulster

SPN stop press news

SPNC Society for the Promotion of Nature Conservation

SPNM Society for the Promotion of New Music

SPNR Society for the Promotion of Nature Reserves

SPO senior press officer

SPÖ *Sozialistische Partei Österreichs* (German: Austrian Socialist Party)

SPOD Sexual Problems of the Disabled (Royal Association for Disability and Rehabilitation)

SPOE Society of Post Office Engineers

sport. sporting

SPOT satellite positioning and tracking

spp. species (plural)

SPQR *Senatus Populusque Romanus* (Latin: The Senate and People of Rome); small profits, quick return

spr. spring; sprinkle

Spr Sapper (military)

SPR Society for Psychical Research; strategic petroleum reserve

SPRC Society for the Prevention and Relief of Cancer

SPREd Society of Picture Researchers and Editors

SPRINT solid-propellant rocket-intercept missile (military)

sprl *société de personnes à responsabilité limitée* (French: private limited company)

SPRL Society for the Promotion of Religion and Learning

sps *sine prole supersite* (Latin: without surviving issue)

SPS Scottish Painters' Society; Super Proton Synchrotron (CERN); syndiotactic polystyrene (plastic)

SPSL Society for the Protection of Science and Learning

SPSO senior principal scientific officer

SPSP St Peter and St Paul

sp. surf. specific surface (chemistry)

spt seaport; support

sptg sporting

SPTL Society of Public Teachers of Law

SPUC Society for the Protection of the Unborn Child

SPURV self-propelled underwater research vessel

SPVD Society for the Prevention of Venereal Disease

sq staff qualified (military)

sq. sequence; *sequens* (Latin: the following); squadron; square

Sq. Squadron; Square

SQ sick quarters; Singapore Airlines (airline flight code); squall (meteorology); stereophonic-quadrophonic (audio equipment); survival quotient
SQA software quality assurance (computing)
sq cm square centimetre/s
sqd. squad
sqdn squadron
Sqdn Ldr squadron leader
sq. ft square foot/feet
sq. in. square inch/es
sq. km square kilometre/s
SQL standard query language (computing); structured query language (computing)
sq. m square metre/s
sq. mi. square mile/s
sq. mm square millimetre/s
SQMS staff quartermaster sergeant
sqn squadron
Sqn Ldr squadron leader
SqnQMS squadron quartermaster sergeant
SqnSM squadron sergeant major
SqO squadron officer
sqq. *sequentia* (Latin: the following)
squid superconducting quantum interference device (electronics)
sq. yd square yard/s
sr self-raising; senior; shipping receipt; short rate
Sr *Senhor* (Portuguese: Mr or Sir); senior; *Señor* (Spanish: Mr or Sir); Sir; sister; strontium (element)
SR Dundee (UK vehicle registration); Saudi riyal (Saudi Arabian monetary unit); Senate resolution (US); service rifle; Seychelles rupee (monetary unit); Socialist Revolutionary Party (USSR); Society of Radiographers; sodium ricinoleate (in toothpaste); Sons of the Revolution (US); Southern Railway; Southern Region (railways); special relativity (physics); Special Reserve (military); standard rate (taxation); stimulus-response (psychology); Stranraer (UK fishing port registration); Sunderland (UK postcode); Sveriges Radio (Swedish broadcasting corporation); Swissair (airline flight code, Switzerland); synchrotron radiation (physics); synthetic rubber
S/R sale or return
Sra *Senhora* (Portuguese: Mrs); *Señora* (Spanish: Mrs)

SRA Squash Rackets Association
SRAC short-run average cost (finance)
SRAM short-range attack missile; static random access memory (computing)
SR&CC strikes, riot and civil commotion
SRB solid rocket booster
SRBM short-range ballistic missile
SRBP synthetic resin-bonded paper
SRC sample return container; Science Research Council; *sociedad regular colectiva* (Spanish: partnership); solvent-refined coal; standard reference compound; Students' Representative Council; Swiss Red Cross
SRCh State Registered Chiropodist
SRCN State Registered Children's Nurse
SRD service rum diluted
SRDE Signals Research and Development Establishment
SRE *Sancta Romana Ecclesia* (Latin: Holy Roman Church)
S. Rept Senate report (US)
S. Res. Senate resolution (US)
SRG standard reformed gas; Strategic Research Group
SRHE Society for Research into Higher Education
SRI *Sacrum Romanum Imperium* (Latin: Holy Roman Empire)
SRIS Science Reference Information Service
Srl. *società a responsabilità limitata* (Italian: private limited company)
SRls Saudi riyal (Saudi Arabian monetary unit)
SRM short-range missile; speed of relative movement
SRN Saunders Roe (hovercraft manufacturers); State Registered Nurse
SRNA Shipbuilders and Repairers National Association
SRO self-regulatory organization (finance); single room occupancy; sold right out; standing room only; Statutory Rules and Orders; Supplementary Reserve of Officers
SRP State Registered Physiotherapist; suggested retail price; supply refuelling point
SRS *Societatis Regiae Sodalis* (Latin: Fellow of the Royal Society)
SRSA Scientific Research Society of America
Srta *Senhorita* (Portuguese: Miss); *Señorita* (Spanish: Miss)
SRU Scottish Rugby Union
SRY Sherwood Rangers Yeomanry

SS screw steamer; *sensu stricto* (Latin: in the strict sense); *senza sordini* (Italian: without mutes; music); simplified spelling; stainless steel; steamship; *supra scriptum* (Latin: written above)

ss. sections; *semis* (Latin: half; medicine); shortstop (baseball); subsection

s/s same size

SS Aberdeen (UK vehicle registration); *Sacra Scriptura* (Latin: Holy Scripture); saints; *Santa Sede* (Italian: Holy See); *Sa Sainteté* (French: His Holiness); *Schutzstaffel* (German: Protection Squad; Nazi military organization); secondary school; Secretary of State; secret service; security service; short sleeves; Sidney Sussex College (Cambridge); social security; sodium sulphate (chemistry); Southend-on-Sea (UK postcode); Staff Surgeon; stainless steel; standard size; steamship; St Ives (UK fishing port registration); *Strada Statale* (Italian: National Highway); Straits Settlements; Sunday school; surface to surface (missile)

SS. saints; *sanctissimus* (Latin: most holy)

S/S same size (illustrations); silk screen (printing); steamship

SSA Scottish Schoolmasters' Association; Social Security Administration (US); Society of Scottish Artists; standard spending assessment

SSAC Scottish Sub-Aqua Club; Social Security Advisory Committee

SSAE stamped self-addressed envelope

SSAFA Soldiers', Sailors' and Airmen's Families Association

SSAP Statement of Standard Accounting Practice

SSB *Sacrae Scripturae Baccalaureus* (Latin: Bachelor of Sacred Scripture); Social Security Board (US)

SSBN strategic submarine, ballistic nuclear (US Navy)

SSC Scottish Ski Club; Sculptors' Society of Canada; Secondary School Certificate (India); Short Service Commission; small-saver certificate (US); *Societas Sanctae Crucis* (Latin: Society of the Holy Cross); Solicitor before the Supreme Court (Scotland); Species Survival Commission; Superconducting Super Collider (physics)

SScD Doctor of Social Science

SSD *Sacrae Scripturae Doctor* (Latin: Doctor of Sacred Scripture); Social Services Department

SS. D *Sanctissimus Dominus* (Latin: Most Holy Lord)

SSE Society of St Edmund; south-southeast

SSEB South of Scotland Electricity Board

SSEC Secondary School Examinations Council

SSEES School of Slavonic and East European Studies (University of London)

SSF single-seater fighter (aircraft); Society of St Francis

SSFA Scottish Schools' Football Association; Scottish Steel Founders' Association

S/Sgt Staff Sergeant

SSHA Scottish Special Housing Association

SSI Scottish Symphony Orchestra; site of scientific interest; small-scale integration (electronics); Social Services Inspectorate; Society of Scribes and Illuminators; supplemental security income (US)

SSJE Society of St John the Evangelist

SSL *Sacrae Scripturae Licentiatus* (Latin: Licentiate in Sacred Scripture)

SSM Society of the Sacred Mission; Staff Sergeant Major; surface-to-surface missile

SSMA Stainless Steel Manufacturers' Association

SSN severely subnormal; standard serial number

SSO senior scientific officer; senior supply officer; staff signal officer; station staff officer

ssp. subspecies

SSP statutory sick pay

SSPCA Scottish Society for the Prevention of Cruelty to Animals

sspp. subspecies (plural)

SS. PP. *Sancti Patres* (Latin: Holy Fathers)

SSQ station sick quarters (military)

SSR Soviet Socialist Republic

SSRA Scottish Squash Rackets Association

SSRC Social Science Research Council

SSRI Social Science Research Institute (US)

SSS Secretary of State for Scotland; Selective Service System (US military); sick sinus syndrome (medicine); single-screw ship; South Shields (UK fishing port registration); standard scratch score (golf)

SSSI site of special scientific interest

SSSR *Soyuz Sovietskikh Sotsialisticheskikh Respublik* (Russian: Union of Soviet Socialist Republics)

SSStJ Serving Sister, Order of St John of Jerusalem

SST Society of Surveying Technicians; supersonic transport

SSTA Scottish Secondary Teachers' Association

SSU Sunday School Union

SSW Secretary of State for War; south-southwest; special security wing (prisons)

SSWA Scottish Society of Women Artists

st select time; short ton; static thrust; steam trawler

st. stanza; state; statement; statute; stem; stet (printing); stitch (knitting); stone (weight); strait; street; stumped (cricket)

St saint; stratus (meteorology); Street

St. Statute; Strait; Street

ST Inverness (UK vehicle registration); septic tank; shipping ticket; speech therapist; spring tide; Standard Time; Stockton (UK fishing port registration); Stoke-on-Trent (UK postcode); stratus (meteorology); Sudan (international civil aircraft marking); Summer Time; Sunday Times; surface trench (building); surtax

sta. station; stationary

Sta *Santa* (Italian, Portuguese, Spanish: female saint)

STA Sail Training Association; Science and Technology Agency (US); Scottish Typographical Association; Society of Typographic Arts; Swimming Teachers' Association

stab. stabilization; stabilized; stabilizer; stable

stacc. staccato (music)

Staffs. Staffordshire

STAGS Sterling Transferable Accruing Government Securities

STANAG Standard NATO Agreement

stand. standard; standardized

St And. St Andrews (Scotland)

START Strategic Arms Reduction Talks

stat. statics; *statim* (Latin: immediately; medicine); stationary; statistic(al); statistics; statuary; statue; statute

STATE simplified tactical approach and terminal equipment (military)

Stat. Hall Stationers' Hall (London)

stats statistics

STAUK Seed Trade Association of the United Kingdom

STB *Sacrae Theologiae Baccalaureus* (Latin: Bachelor of Sacred Theology)

stbd starboard

stbt steamboat

STC Samuel Taylor Coleridge (English poet); satellite test centre; Senior Training Corps; short-title catalogue; Standard Telephones and Cables Limited; state total cost; State Trading Corporation (India)

std standard; started

Std. *Stunde* (German: hour)

STD *Sacrae Theologiae Doctor* (Latin: Doctor of Sacred Theology); sexually transmitted disease; Society of Typographic Designers; subscriber trunk dialling

Ste *Sainte* (French: female saint)

Sté *société* (French: company)

STE Society of Telecom Executives

STEL short-term exposure level (radiation); short-term exposure limit (radiation)

STEM scanning transmission electron microscope; scanning transmission electron microscopy

sten. stenographer; stenography

Sten gun Shepherd & Turpin, Enfield gun (sub-machine gun; World War II)

steno(g). stenographer; stenography

STEP special temporary employment programme

ster(eo). stereophonic; stereotype; sterling

St. Ex. Stock Exchange

stg sterling

StGB *Strafgesetzbuch* (German: Penal Code)

stge storage

STGWU Scottish Transport and General Workers' Union

Sth South

STh Scholar in Theology

sthn southern

STI Straits Times Index (Singapore Stock Exchange)

STINGS stellar inertial guidance system (aeronautics)

stip. stipend; stipendiary; stipulation

stir surplus to immediate requirements

Stir. Stirlingshire

stk stock

STL *Sacrae Theologiae Lector* (Latin: Professor or Reader of Sacred Theology); *Sacrae Theologiae Licentiatus* (Latin: Licentiate in Sacred Theology); Standard Telecommunications Laboratories;

studio-to-transmitter link (telecommunications)

stlg sterling

STLO Scientific Technical Liaison Office(r)

STM *Sacrae Theologiae Magister* (Latin: Master of Sacred Theology); scanning tunnelling microscope; scanning tunnelling microscopy; short-term memory

STMS short-term monetary support (EMS)

stmt statement

stn stain; station

St° *Santo* (Portuguese: saint)

STO sea transport officer; senior technical officer; standing order

STOL short take-off and landing (aircraft)

STOLVCD short take-off and landing, vertical climb and descent (aircraft)

S'ton Southampton

STOP Students Tired of Pollution

STOPP Society of Teachers Opposed to Physical Punishment

S to S ship to shore; station to station

stp standard temperature and pressure

STP *Sacrae Theologiae Professor* (Latin: Professor of Sacred Theology); scientifically treated petroleum (oil substitute); sewage treatment plant; standard temperature and pressure

STPMA Scottish Theatrical Proprietors' and Managers' Association

str seater; steamer; surplus to requirements

str. straight; strait; street; strength; string; stringer (journalism); stringed (music); strings (music); stroke (rowing); strong; structural; structure

Str. Strait; Street

STRAC strategic air command (US); strategic army corps

Strad. Stradivarius (make of violins)

STRAD signal transmitting, receiving and distribution

stratig. stratigraphy

strd stranded

strep. streptococcus

STRICOM Strike Command (US)

string. *stringendo* (Italian: intensifying; music)

STRIVE Society for the Preservation of Rural Industries and Village Enterprises

STROBE satellite tracking of balloons and emergencies

Sts saints

STS Scottish Text Society; space transportation system (astronautics)

STSO senior technical staff officer

st. st. stocking stitch (knitting)

STTA Scottish Table Tennis Association

STUC Scottish Trades Union Congress

stud. student

Stuka *Sturzkampfflugzeug* (German: dive bomber; World War II)

STV Scottish Television Limited; single transferable vote; standard test vehicle; subscription television

stvdr. stevedore

stwy stairway

su set up; *siehe unten* (German: see below)

Su. Sudan(ese); Sunday

SU Aeroflot (airline flight code, Russia); Egypt (international civil aircraft marking); Glasgow (UK vehicle registration); Scripture Union; Southampton (UK fishing port registration); Soviet Union; strontium unit (physics)

SUA State Universities Association (US)

sub. subaltern; sub-editor; *subito* (Italian: immediately or suddenly); subject; subjunctive; submarine; subordinated; subscription; subsidiary; subsidy; subsistence; substantive; substitute; suburb; suburban; subvention; subway

SUB supplemental unemployment benefits (US)

subd. subdivision

sub-ed. sub-editor

subj. subject; subjective; subjectively; subjunctive

SUBLANT Submarine Forces, Atlantic (US Navy)

Sub L(ieu)t Sub-Lieutenant

subord. cl. subordinate clause

SUBPAC Submarine Forces, Pacific (US Navy)

SUBROC submarine rocket

subs. subsidiary; subsistence

subsc. subscription

subsec. subsection

subs(e)q. subsequent; subsequently

subsp. subspecies

subst. substantive; substantively; substitute

substand. substandard

suc. succeed; success; successor, suction

succ. succeed; success; successor

suf. suffix

suff. sufficient; suffix

Suff. Suffolk; Suffragan

Suffr. Suffragan

sug. suggest; suggestion
SUIT Scottish and Universal Investment Trust
suiv. *suivant* (French: following)
Sult. Sultan; Sultana
sum. *sumat/sumendum* (Latin: let her/him take or let it be taken; medicine); summary; summer
SUM surface-to-underwater missile
sums. summons
Sun(d). Sunday
SUNFED Special United Nations Fund for Economic Development
SUNS sonic underwater navigation system
SUNY State University of New York
sup. superficial; superfine; superior; superlative; supine (grammar); supplement(ary); supply; *supra* (Latin: above); supreme
sup. ben. supplementary benefit
Sup. Ct Superior Court; Supreme Court
Supdt Superintendent
super. superficial; superfine; superior; supernumerary
superhet. supersonic heterodyne (telecommunications)
superl. superlative
supp(l). supplement(ary)
Supp. Res. Supplementary Reserve (of officers)
supr supervisor
supr. superior; supreme
Supt Superintendent
supvr supervisor
sur. surface; surplus
Sur. Surrey
surg. surgeon; surgery; surgical
Surg. C(om)dr Surgeon Commander
Surg. Gen. Surgeon General
Surg. Lt-Cdr Surgeon Lieutenant-Commander
Surg. Maj. Surgeon Major
surr. surrender; surrogate
Surr. Surrey
surro. surrogate
surv. survey(ing); surveyor; survive; surviving
SURV standard underwater research vessel
Surv. Gen. surveyor general
Sus. Sussex; Susanna (Apocrypha)
SUS Scottish Union of Students; Students' Union Society
susp. suspend; suspension
Suss. Sussex
SUSY supersymmetry (physics)

SUT Society for Underwater Technology
Suth. Sutherland
sv sailing vessel; save (baseball); side valve; *sub verbo/voce* (Latin: under the word or heading); surrender value (insurance)
s/v surrender value (insurance)
Sv sievert (physics)
SV safety valve; *Sancta Virgo* (Latin: Holy Virgin); *Sanctitas Vestra* (Latin: Your Holiness); Saudi-Saudi Arabian Airlines (airline flight code)
svc. service
SVC superior vena cava (medicine)
svce service
SVD swine vesicular disease
svg saving
svgs savings
S-VHS super-VHS
SVO Scottish Variety Orchestra; subject-verb-object (linguistics); superintending veterinary officer
svp *s'il vous plait* (French: if you please)
SVP saturated vapour pressure
SVQ Scottish vocational qualification
svr *spiritus vini rectificatus* (Latin: rectified spirit of wine; medicine)
SVS still-camera video system
SVTP sound velocity, temperature, pressure
svv *sit venia verbo* (Latin: forgive the expression)
s. vv. *sub verbis* (Latin: under the words or headings)
svy survey
sw salt water; sea water; short wave (radio)
sw. switch
s/w sea water; seaworthy
Sw. Sweden; Swedish; Swiss
SW Air Namibia (airline flight code); Glasgow (UK vehicle registration); senior warden; shipper's weight; shock wave; short wave (radio); small woman (clothing size); South Wales; southwest; southwestern; southwest London (UK postcode); standard weight
S/W software (computing)
SWA Namibia (international vehicle registration)
Swab. Swabia; Swabian
SWACS space warning and control system
Swalk sealed with a loving kiss
SWANU South West Africa National Union

SWANUF South West Africa National United Front

SWAPO South-West Africa People's Organization

S/WARE software (computing)

SWAT Special Weapons and Tactics (police unit)

swb short wheelbase

SWB South Wales Borderers (military)

swbd switchboard

SWCI software configuration item (computing)

swd sewed (bookbinding)

SWE Society of Women Engineers

Sweb South Wales Electricity Board; Southwest Electricity Board

Swed. Sweden; Swedish

SWET Society of West End Theatre

SwF Swiss franc (monetary unit)

SWF single white female

SWG standard wire gauge

SWH solar water heating

SWIE South Wales Institute of Engineers

SWIFT Society for Worldwide Interbank Financial Transmission

SWIMS Study of Women in Men's Society (US)

Swing Sterling warrant into gilt-edged stock (finance)

Swit(z). Switzerland

SWL safe working load

SWLA Society of Wildlife Artists

SWMF South Wales Miners' Federation

SWO station warrant officer

SWOA Scottish Woodland Owners' Association

SWOPS single well oil-production system

SWOT strengths, weaknesses, opportunities, threats (marketing)

SWP safe working pressure; Socialist Workers' Party

SWPA South-West Pacific Area

SWR standing-wave ratio (telecommunications)

SWRB Sadler's Wells Royal Ballet

SWS static water supply

Swtz. Switzerland

SWWJ Society of Women Writers and Journalists

Sx Sussex

SX Edinburgh (UK vehicle registration); Greece (international civil aircraft marking); Sundays excepted (shipping)

SXT sextant

Sy. Seychelles; supply; Surrey; Syria

SY Seychelles (international vehicle registration); Shrewsbury (UK postcode); steam yacht; Stornoway (UK fishing port registration)

SYB The Statesman's Yearbook

Syd. Sydney (Australia)

S. Yd Scotland Yard

SYHA Scottish Youth Hostels Association

syl(l). syllable; syllabus

sym. symbol(ic); symmetrical; symmetry; symphonic; symphony; symptom

symp. symposium

symph. symphony

syn. synchronize; synonym(ous); synonymy; synthetic

sync. synchronization

Syncom synchronous communications satellite

synd. syndicate; syndicated

synon. synonymous

synop. synopsis

synth. synthesizer (music); synthetic

Sy. PO supply petty officer

syr. syrup

Syr. Syria; Syriac; Syrian

SYR Syria (international vehicle registration)

syst. system; systematic

sz. size

SZ Down (UK vehicle registration)

T

t hour angle (astronomy); thickness; tonne

t Celsius temperature

t. table; tabulated; tackle (sport); taken; tare (commerce); teaspoon(ful); teeth; tempo (music); *tempore* (Latin: in the time of); tenor; tense (grammar); terminal; territorial; territory; thunder;

time; *tome* (French: volume); ton; tonne; *tonneau* (French: ton); town(ship); transit; transitive (grammar); troy; tun; turn

T telephone; temperature (meteorology); tera-; tesla (physics); Thailand (international vehicle registration); trainer (aircraft); Tralee (Irish fishing port registration); tropical loading (shipping); true

T kinetic energy (physics); period (physics); thermodynamic temperature; torque

T. tablespoon; tablespoonful; *tace* (Italian: be silent; music); tanker; target; tea (rose); teacher; telegraph; telegraphic; telephone; tempo (music); temporary; tenor (music); Territorial; Territory; Testament; thermometer; third of a page (advertising); Thursday; time; torpedo; transaction; translation; transport; transportation; transverse (obstetrics); Treasury; Trinity; true; Tuesday; Turkish; twist (knitting)

T2 Tuvalu (international civil aircraft marking)

T3 Kiribati (international civil aircraft marking)

T7 San Marino (international civil aircraft marking)

ta target area; time and attendance; travel allowance; true altitude

ta. tableau; tablet

Ta tantalum (element)

TA Exeter (UK vehicle registration); table of allowances (taxation); Taunton (UK postcode); teaching assistant (US); telegraphic address; temporary admission; Territorial Army; thermal analysis (physics); tithe annuity; training adviser; transit authority (US); travel allowance

T/A technical assistant; temporary assistant

TAA Territorial Army Association; test of academic aptitude; Trans-Australia Airlines; Transportation Association of America

TA&VRA Territorial Auxiliary and Volunteer Reserve Association

tab. table; tablet; tabulate; tabulation; tabulator

TAB tabulator (keyboard); Technical Assistance Board (UN); Total Abstinence Brotherhood; Totalizator Administration Board (Australia, New Zealand); Totalizator Agency Board (Australia, New Zealand); typhoid, paratyphoid A, paratyphoid B (vaccine)

TABA Timber Agents' and Brokers' Association of the United Kingdom

Tac. Tacitus (Roman historian)

TAC Tactical Air Command (US Air Force); Technical Assistance Committee (UN); Television Advisory Committee;

The Athletics Congress; Tobacco Advisory Committee; Trades Advisory Council

TACAN tactical air navigation

tach. tachometer

TACL Training for Action-Centred Leadership

TACMAR tactical multi-function array radar

TACS tactical air-control system

TACV tracked air-cushion vehicle

Tads target acquisition and designation sight (military)

TAF Tactical Air Force

TAFE technical and further education

tafu things are fouled up; things are fucked up

tafubar things are fouled/fucked up beyond all recognition (computing)

Tag. Tagalog (language)

TAG The Adjutant-General (US)

T/Agt transfer agent (US)

Tai. Taiwan

TAI *temps atomique international* (French: International Atomic Time)

tal. *talis* (Latin: such)

Tal. Talmud Torah (Judaism)

TAL traffic and accident loss (insurance)

TALISMAN Transfer Accounting Lodgement for Investors and Stock Management (stock exchange)

tal. qual. *talis qualis* (Latin: average quality)

Tam. Tamil (language)

TAM tactical air missile; Television Audience Measurement

Tamba Twins and Multiple Births Association

tan tangent (mathematics)

T&A tits and ass; tonsillectomy and adenoidectomy (medicine); tonsils and adenoids (medicine)

T&AFA Territorial and Auxiliary Forces Association

T&AVR Territorial and Army Volunteer Reserve

t&b top and bottom

T&CPA Town and Country Planning Association

T&E test and evaluation; tired and emotional (drunk); travel and entertainment; trial and error

t&g tongue and groove (timber)

T&G Transport and General Workers' Union

t&o taken and offered (betting)

t&p theft and pilferage (insurance)

t&s toilet and shower
T&S transport and supply
T&SG Television and Screenwriters' Guild
T&T Trinidad and Tobago
Tang. Tanganyika; Tangier
tanh hyperbolic tangent (mathematics)
TANJUG *Novinska Agencija Tanjug* (news agency, Yugoslavia)
TANS terminal-area navigation system; Territorial Army Nursing Service
TANU Tanganyika African National Union
TAO Technical Assistance Operations (UN)
TAOC Tactical Air Operations Center (US)
TAP Technical Assistance Program (US); *Transportes Aéreos Portugueses* (Portuguese: Portuguese Airlines); *Tunis Afrique Presse* (news agency, Tunisia)
Tapline Trans-Arabian Pipeline Company (Saudi Arabia)
TAPPI Technical Association of the Pulp and Paper Industry (US)
TAPS Trans-Alaska Pipeline System
tar. tariff; tarpaulin
TAR terrain-avoidance radar; Territorial Army Regulations; thrust-augmented rocket
TARA Technical Assistant, Royal Artillery; Territorial Army Rifle Association
TARAN test and replace as necessary
TARDIS time and relative dimensions in space
tarfu things are really fouled up (computing); things are really fucked up (computing)
TARO Territorial Army Reserve of Officers
TARS Technical Assistance Recruitment Service (UN)
Tas. Tasmania; Tasmanian
TAS torpedo antisubmarine; true air speed (aeronautics)
TASI time-assignment speech interpolation (telecommunications)
Tasm. Tasmania; Tasmanian
TASMO tactical air support of maritime operations
TASR terminal area surveillance radar
Tass *Telegrafnoye Agentsvo Sovetskovo Soyuza* (Russian: Telegraph Agency of the Soviet Union)
TASS Transport Aircraft Servicing Specialist (RAF)

TAT tired all the time (medicine); transatlantic telephone cable
TATSA transportation aircraft test and support activity
Tatts Tattersall's (Australian lottery company)
TAUN Technical Assistance of the United Nations
TAURUS Transfer and Automated Registration of Uncertified Stock (stock exchange)
taut. tautology
t.-à-v. *tout-à-vous* (French: yours ever)
tav. tavern
TAVR Territorial and Army Volunteer Reserve
TAVRA Territorial Auxiliary and Volunteer Reserve Association
taw twice a week
TAWOC taking away without owner's consent (car theft)
taxn taxation
tb take back (printing); temporary buoy; total bases (baseball); trial balance (book-keeping); true bearing (navigation); tuberculosis
Tb terbium (element)
TB Liverpool (UK vehicle registration); torpedo boat; torpedo bomber; training battalion; training board; Treasury Bill; trial balance (book-keeping); tuberculosis
tba to be advised; to be agreed; to be announced
TBA tyres, batteries and accessories
tb&s top, bottom and sides
TBCEP tri-beta-chloroethyl phosphate (flame retardant)
tbcf to be called for
tbd to be decided; to be determined
TBD torpedo-boat destroyer
TBF Teachers Benevolent Fund
TBI total body irradiation (medicine)
T-bill Treasury bill
tbl through back of loop (knitting)
TBL through bill of lading (commerce)
TBM tactical ballistic missile; temporary benchmark; terabit memory (computing)
TBO time between overhauls; total blackout (theatre)
T-bond Treasury bond
tbs(p). tablespoon; tablespoonful
TBS talk between ships; tight building syndrome; training battle simulation
TBT tributyl tin (used in paint)
tc temperature control; terra cotta; till cancelled; time check; traveller's cheque;

true course (navigation); twin carburettors

Tc technetium (element)

TC Air Tanzania (airline flight code); Bristol (UK vehicle registration); Tank Corps; Tariff Commission (US); Tax Cases (law); technical college; temporary clerk; Temporary Constable; tennis club; touring club; town clerk; town council; town councillor; training centre; training college; training corps; Transport Command (military); traveller's cheque; *tre corde* (Italian: three strings or release soft pedal; music); Trinity College; Trinity Cross (Trinidad and Tobago Order); tropical cyclone (meteorology); Trusteeship Council (UN); tungsten carbide (chemistry); Turkey (international civil aircraft marking); twin carburettors

TCA trichloroacetic acid (herbicide); tricyclic antidepressant (drug)

TCB take care of business (US); Thames Conservancy Board

TCBM transcontinental ballistic missile

TCC time compression coding (telecommunications); Transport and Communications Commission (UN); Trinity College, Cambridge; Troop Carrier Command (US)

TCCB Test and County Cricket Board

TCD Trinity College, Dublin

TCDD tetrachlorodibenzodioxin (pollutant)

tcf trillion cubic feet

TCF Temporary Chaplain to the Forces; time-correction factor; Touring Club of France

TCFB Transcontinental Freight Bureau

tchg teaching

tchr teacher

TCI *Touring Club Italiano* (Italian: Italian Touring Club)

TCL trichloroeth(yl)ene (solvent); Trinity College (of Music), London

TCM Trinity College of Music (London)

TCMA Telephone Cable Makers' Association

TCO test control office; *Tjänstemännens Centralorganisation* (Swedish: Central Organization of Salaried Employees); Trinity College, Oxford

TCP trichlorophenylmethyliodialicyl (antiseptic)

TCPA Town and Country Planning Association

TCS target cost system; traffic control station (US)

tctl tactical

TCU towering cumulus (meteorology); Transportation, Communications, International Union

td tank destroyer; technical data; *ter in die* (Latin: three times a day; medicine); test data; time delay; tractor-drawn

td. touchdown

TD Galashiels (UK postcode); Manchester (UK vehicle registration); Tactical Division (military); tank destroyer; Teaching Diploma; *Teachta Dála* (Gaelic: Member of the Dáil); technical development; technical drawing; Territorial (Efficiency) Decoration; Tilbury Docks; torpedo depot; touchdown (sport); traffic director (US); Treasury Department (US); trust deed; Tunisian dinar (monetary unit)

TDB Total Disability Benefit

tdc top dead centre (engineering)

TDC Temporary Detective Constable; through-deck cruiser; top dead centre (engineering)

TDD telecommunications device for the deaf; Tubercular Diseases Diploma

TDDL time division data link (telecommunications)

TDG twist drill gauge

TDI toluene-2,4-diisocyanate (chemistry)

TDL tunable diode laser

TDM telemetric data monitor; time-division multiplexing (telecommunications)

TDMA time-division multiple access (telecommunications)

TDN total digestible nutrients

TDO tornado (meteorology)

TDP technical development plan

tdr *tous droits réservés* (French: all rights reserved)

TDR Treasury deposit receipt (finance)

TDRSS tracking and data-relay satellite system

tds *ter die sumendum* (Latin: to be taken three times a day; medicine)

TDS tabular data stream (computing)

te thermal efficiency; tinted edge (paper); trailing edge; trial and error; turbine engine; twin-engined

t/e time expired; twin-engined

Te tellurium (element)

TE Manchester (UK vehicle registration); telecommunications engineering; trace element; trade expenses; transverse electric (telecommunications)

TEA Terminal Education Age

TEAC Technical Educational Advisory Council

tec detective

TEC Training and Enterprise Council

tech(n). technical; technically; technician; technique; technology

Tech(CEI) Technician (Council of Engineering Institutions)

technol. technological; technologically; technology

TEE Telecommunications Engineering Establishment; Torpedo Experimental Establishment; Trans-Europe Express (railway)

TEF toxicity equivalence factor

TEFL Teaching English as a Foreign Language

teg top edges gilt (books)

Teh. Tehran

tel. telegram; telegraph; telegraphic; telephone

TEL tetraethyl lead (petrol additive); transporter-erector-launcher (astronautics)

telecom. telecommunication/s

teleg. telegram; telegraph; telegraphic; telegraphy

teleph. telephone; telephony

telex teleprinter exchange; teletype exchange

TELNET teletype network (computing)

tel. no. telephone number

TEM Territorial Efficiency Medal; transmission electron microscope; transmission electron microscopy

TEMA Telecommunications Engineering and Manufacturing Association

temp. temperance; temperate; temperature; tempo; temporal; temporary; *tempore* (Latin: in the time of)

Templar tactical expert mission-planner (military computing)

temp. prim. *tempo primo* (Italian: at the original pace; music)

tempy temporary

ten. tenant; tenement; tenor; *tenuto* (Italian: held or sustained; music)

tency tenancy

Tenn. Tennessee

TENS transcutaneous electrical nerve stimulation (medicine)

TeolD Doctor of Theology

TEPP tetraethyl pyrophosphate (pesticide)

ter. terrace; territorial; territory

Ter. Terence (Roman poet)

terat. teratology

TERCOM terrain contour mapping (aeronautics); terrain contour matching (aeronautics)

term. terminal; terminate; termination; terminology

terr. terrace; territorial; territory

tert. tertiary

TES Times Educational Supplement

Tesco T.E. Stockwell and Sir John Cohen (food shopping chain)

TESL teaching English as a second language

TESOL teaching of English to speakers of other languages

Tessa Tax Exempt Special Savings Account

test. testament; testator; testatrix; testimonial; testimony

TET Teacher of Electrotherapy

T.-et-G. Tarn-et-Garonne (French department)

TETOC technical education and training for overseas countries ·

tet. tox. tetanus toxin

TEU twenty-foot equivalent unit (shipping)

Teut. Teuton; Teutonic

TeV teraelectronvolt (physics)

TEWT tactical exercise without troops (military)

Tex. Texan; Texas

text. textile/s

text. rec. *textus receptus* (Latin: the received text)

tf tabulating form; tax-free; training film; *travaux forcés* (French: hard labour)

TF Iceland (international civil aircraft marking); Reading (UK vehicle registration); task force; Telford (UK postcode); Territorial Force; thin film (electronics); tropical freshwater (shipping)

TFA Tenant Farmers' Association; total fatty acids

TFAP Tropical Forest Action Plan

tfc traffic

TFECG Training and Further Education Consultative Group

tfr transfer

TFR Territorial Force Reserve

TFSC Turkish Federated State of Cyprus

TFU telecommunications flying unit

TFW tactical fighter wing (military)

TFX tactical fighter experimental (aircraft)
tg tail gear; tangent (mathematics); type genus (biology)
TG Cardiff (UK vehicle registration); Guatemala (international civil aircraft marking); Tate Gallery (London); temporary gentleman; Thai Airways International (airline flight code); thank God; Theater Guild (US); Togo (international vehicle registration); training group; transformational-generative grammar; transformational grammar; Translators' Guild (London)
TGA thermal gravimetric analysis (chemistry)
TGAT Task Group on Assessment and Testing (education)
tgb tongued, grooved and beaded (carpentry)
TGB Très Grande Bibliothèque (French national library)
TGEW Timber Growers England and Wales Ltd
TGI Target Group Index (marketing)
TGIF thank God it's Friday
TGM torpedo gunner's mate
T-group training group
tgt target
TGT turbine gas temperature (aeronautics)
TGV *train à grande vitesse* (French: high speed train)
TGWU Transport and General Workers' Union
th hyperbolic tangent (mathematics)
th. thermal
Th thorium (element)
Th. theatre; theology; Thursday
TH Swansea (UK vehicle registration); *Technische Hochschule* (German: technical college or university); Teignmouth (UK fishing port registration); Territory of Hawaii; toothed border (numismatics); town hall; Toynbee Hall; Transport House; Trinity Hall; Trinity House
Thai. Thailand
thanat. thanatology
ThB *Theologicae Baccalaureus* (Latin: Bachelor of Theology)
ThD *Theologicae Doctor* (Latin: Doctor of Theology)
THE Technical Help to Exporters (UK Standards Institute)
theat. theatre; theatrical
Theoc. Theocritus (Greek poet)
theol. theologian; theological; theology

Theoph. Theophrastus (Greek philosopher)
theor. theorem; theoretical; theory
theos. theosophical; theosophist; theosophy
therap(eut). therapeutic/s
therm. thermometer; thermometry
thermochem. thermochemistry
thermodyn. thermodynamics
thermom. thermometer; thermometry
thes. thesis
THES Times Higher Education Supplement
thesp. thespian
Thess. Thessalonians (Bible); Thessaly
THHM Trinity House high water mark
thi time handed in
THI temperature-humidity index
thk thick
ThL Theological Licentiate
ThM *Theologiae Magister* (Latin: Master of Theology)
thnks thanks
tho' though
thor. thorax
thoro. thoroughfare
thou. 1,000
thp thrust horsepower
thr. their; through; thrust
THR total hip replacement (medicine)
3i Investors in Industry
three Rs reading, writing and arithmetic
throt. throttle
thru through
ThSchol Scholar in Theology
Thuc. Thucydides (Greek historian)
Thur(s). Thursday
THWM Trinity (House) high water mark
THz terahertz (physics)
Ti titanium (element)
Ti. Tiberius (Roman emperor); Tibet
TI Costa Rica (international civil aircraft marking); Limerick (Irish vehicle registration); technical inspection; technical institute; temperature indication; temperature indicator; Texas Instruments Corporation (US); thermal imaging; toluene-insoluble (chemistry); Tourist Information Bureau
T/I target identification; target indicator
TIA Tax Institute of America
tib trimmed in bunkers
Tib. Tibet; Tibetan
TIB Tourist Information Bureau
TIBOR Tokyo Inter-Bank Offered Rate (finance)

TIC taken into consideration (law); tourist information centre
tid *ter in die* (Latin: three times a day; medicine)
TIE Theatre in Education
TIF telephone influence factor; telephone interference factor; *Transports Internationaux par Chemin de Fer* (French: International Rail Transport)
TIG tungsten inert gas (welding)
TIGR Treasury Investment Growth Receipts (bond)
TIH Their Imperial Highnesses
TILS Technical Information and Library Service
tim time is money
Tim. Timothy (Bible)
timp. timpani (music)
TIMS The Institute of Management Sciences
TIN taxpayer identification number (US)
TINA there is no alternative (Margaret Thatcher catchphrase)
tinct. tincture
TIO technical information officer
Tip. Tipperary
TIP terminal interface processor (computing)
TIR *Transport International Routier* (French: International Road Transport)
TIRC Tobacco Industry Research Committee
TIROS television and infrared observation satellite
tis. tissue
TIS technical information service
tit. title; titular
Tit. Titus (Bible)
TJ Cameroon (international civil aircraft marking); Liverpool (UK vehicle registration); talk jockey; terajoule (physics); triple jump (athletics)
tk tank; truck
Tk taka (Bangladeshi monetary unit)
TK Exeter (UK vehicle registration); Turkish Airlines (airline flight code)
TKO technical knockout (boxing)
tkr tanker
tks thanks
tkt ticket
tl test link; thunderstorm (meteorology); time length; title list; total load; total loss (insurance); trade list
Tl thallium (element)
TL Central African Republic (international civil aircraft marking); Lincoln (UK vehicle registration); target

language; Torpedo Lieutenant; total loss (insurance); trade-last (US); transmission line; Turkish lira (monetary unit)
T/L time loan (banking); total loss (insurance)
tlb temporary lighted buoy
TLC tender loving care; total lung capacity (medicine); Trades and Labour Council (Australia)
tld tooled
TLG Theatrical Ladies' Guild
tlo total loss only (insurance)
TLO technical liaison officer
tlr tailor; trailer
TLR Times Law Reports; twin-lens reflex (photography)
TLS Times Literary Supplement; typed letter, signed
tltr translator
TLU table look-up (computing)
TLV threshold-limit value (electronics)
TLWM Trinity (House) low-water mark
tm temperature meter; true mean (navigation)
Tm thulium (element)
TM LAM (*Linhas Aereas de Moçambique*, airline flight code, Mozambique); Luton (UK vehicle registration); tactical missile; technical manual; technical memorandum; test manual; Their Majesties; tone modulation (telecommunications); trademark; trained man; training manual; transcendental meditation; trench mortar; tropical medicine; Turing machine (computing)
TMA Theatrical Management Association; Trans-Mediterranean Airways (Lebanon)
TMB travelling medical board
tmbr timber
TMD theatre missile defence (military)
tme time
TMI Three Mile Island (US)
tmkpr timekeeper
TML tetramethyl lead (chemistry); three-mile limit (shipping)
TMMG Teacher of Massage and Medical Gymnastics
TMO telegraph money order; telegraphic money order
TMP thermomechanical pump
tmpry temporary
tmr timer
TMT turbine motor train
TMV tobacco mosaic virus; true mean value

tn technical note; telephone number; ton; tonne; town; train; transportation
TN Australian Airlines (airline flight code); Newcastle upon Tyne (UK vehicle registration); Tennessee (zip code); Tonbridge (UK postcode); Tongo (international civil aircraft marking); Troon (UK fishing port registration); true north; Tunisia (international vehicle registration)
TNC Theatres National Committee; total numerical control; transnational corporation
TNF theatre nuclear forces (military)
tng training; turning
TNG The Newspaper Guild (US)
TNIP Transkei National Independence Party (South Africa)
TNM tactical nuclear missile; tumour, node, metastasis (medicine)
T-note Treasury note (finance)
TNP *Théâtre National Populaire* (French theatre company)
TNPG The Nuclear Power Group
tnpk. turnpike
TNT trinitrotoluene (explosive)
TNW theatre nuclear weapon (military)
TNX trinitroxylene (chemistry)
to take-off; turnover
To. Togo
TO Nottingham (UK vehicle registration); table of organization (management); technical officer; telegraph office; telegraphic order; telephone office; telephone order; torpedo officer; trained operator; transport officer; Truro (UK fishing port registration); turn over (page)
T/O turnover
tob. tobacco; tobacconist
Tob. Tobit (Bible)
ToB Tour of Britain (cycling)
TOB temporary office building
Toc H Talbot House (Christian aid organization based at Talbot House; from telegraphic code for TH)
TOD time of delivery; trade and operations division
toe ton oil equivalent
TOE theory of everything (physics)
TOEFL test of English as a foreign language; testing of English as a foreign language
TOET test of elementary training
TOF time of flight (physics)
TOFC trailer on flat car (railways)
tog(r). together

Tok. Tokyo
TOL Tower of London
tom(at). tomato; *tomus* (Latin: volume)
TOM *territoire d'outre mer* (French: overseas territory); total organic matter (chemistry)
TOMCAT theatre of operations missile continuous-wave anti-tank weapon
TOMS Total Ozone Mapping Spectrometer
TON total organic nitrogen (chemistry)
tonn. tonnage
Tony Antoinette Perry Award (Broadway theatre)
TOO time of origin; to order only (commerce)
TOP technical office protocol (computing); temporarily out of print
TOPIC Teletext Output Price Information Computer (stock exchange)
topog. topographer; topographical; topography
topol. topological; topology
TOPS Training Opportunities Scheme
tor time of receipt; time of reception
Tor. Toronto
TOR Tertiary Order Regular of St Francis
torn. tornado
torp. torpedo
tos temporarily out of service; temporarily out of stock; terms of service
TOSD Tertiary Order of St Dominic
TOSF Tertiary Order of St Francis
Toshiba Tokyo Shibaura Denki KK (Japanese corporation)
tot time on target; time over target
tot. total
TOTC time-on-target computation (military)
tote totalizator
TOTP Top of the Pops (BBC television music programme)
Tou. Toulon (France)
tour. tourism; tourist
tourn. tournament
TOW tube-launched optically tracked wire-guided (antitank missile); tug-of-war
tox. toxic; toxicology
toxicol. toxicological; toxicologist; toxicology
tp target practice; taxpayer; teaching practice; test panel; title page; *timbre-poste* (French: postage stamp); toilet paper; to pay; *tout payé* (French: all expenses paid); township; troop; true position

TP Portsmouth (UK vehicle registration); TAP-Air Portugal (airline flight code); taxpayer; technical paper; technical publication; teleprinter; teleprocessing (computing); *tempo primo* (Italian: at the original tempo; music); *tempore Paschale* (Latin: at Easter); test panel; third party (insurance); town planner; town planning; transaction processing (computing); Transvaal Province; treaty port; trigonometric point (surveying); true position; turning point (surveying)

TPC The Peace Corps (US); Trade Practices Commission (Australia)

tpd tons per day

tph tons per hour

tpi teeth per inch (engineering); tracks per inch (computing); turns per inch (engineering)

TPI Tax and Price Index; terminal phase initiation (computing); threads per inch (engineering); tons per inch (shipping); totally and permanently incapacitated; transpolyisoprene (synthetic gutta percha); Tropical Products Institute

tpk turnpike

TPLF Tigrean People's Liberation Front

tpm tons per minute

TPM third-party maintenance

TPO travelling post office; tree preservation order

Tpr Trooper (military)

TPR temperature, pulse, respiration (medicine)

TPS toughened polystyrene

tpt trumpet; transport

tptr trumpeter

tq *tale quale* (Latin: as is)

TQ tel quel (exchange rate); Torquay (UK postcode); total quality (quality control)

TQM total quality management

tr. *tinctura* (Latin: tincture; medicine); trace; track; tragedy; train; trainee; transaction; transfer; transitive; translate; translated; translation; translator; transport; transportation; transpose (printing); transposition; treasurer; treble (music); trill (music); troop; truck; trumpet; trumpeter; trust; trustee

Tr terbium (chemistry); Triassic (geology)

TR Gabon (international civil aircraft marking); Portsmouth (UK vehicle registration); target rifle; tariff reform; Telephone Rentals plc; *tempore reginae/regis* (Latin: in the time of the queen or king); Territorial Reserve; test

run; Theodore Roosevelt (US President); tons registered; tracking radar; *Transbrasil S/A Linhas Aereas* (airline flight code, Brazil); transmit-receive (telecommunications); Truro (UK postcode); trust receipt; Turkey (international vehicle registration)

T/R transmitter-receiver

TRA Thoroughbred Racing Association (US)

trac. tracer; tractor

TRACALS traffic control and landing system (aeronautics)

TRACE task reporting and current evaluation; test equipment for rapid checkout evaluation (aeronautics)

trad. tradition(al); *traduttore* (Italian: translator); *traduzione* (Italian: translation)

TRADA Timber Research and Development Association

trag. tragedian; tragedy; tragic; tragical

TRAMPS temperature regulator and missile power supply

trannie transistor radio

trans. transaction; transfer; transferred; transit; transitive; transitory; translate; translated; translation; translator; transparent; transport; transportation; transpose (printing); transposition; transverse

Trans. Transvaal

transcr. transcribed; transcription

transf. transferred

transl. translate; translated; translation; translator

translit. transliterate; transliteration

transp. transport; transportation

trany transparency

trav. travel; traveller; travels

Trb. Tribune

trbn. trombone

TRC Thames Rowing Club; Tobacco Research Council

tr. co. trust company

tr. coll. training college

Trd Trinidad

TRDA Timber Research and Development Association

tre(as). treasurer; treasury

tree trustee

trem transport emergency (card; carried by vehicles transporting chemicals)

trem. *tremolando* (Italian: trembling; music); tremulant (organ music)

trf tariff

trf. transfer

TRF tuned radio frequency
trg touring; training
trg. triangle (music)
TRG Tory Reform Group
TRH Their Royal Highnesses
TRI Television Reporters International; Textile Research Institute (US)
trib. tribal; tributary; tribute
TRIC Television and Radio Industries Club
trid. *triduum* (Latin: three days; medicine)
trig. trigger; trigonometric; trigonometrical; trigonometry
TRIGA training, research and isotope-production reactors–General Atomic (engineering)
trigon. trigonometric; trigonometrical; trigonometry
trike trichloroeth(yl)ene (solvent); tricycle
trim. *trimestre* (Latin: quarter)
Trin. Trinidad; Trinity; Trinity College (Oxford); Trinity Hall (Cambridge)
Trip. Tripos (Cambridge University examination)
tripl. triplicate
triple A anti-aircraft artillery
trit. triturate
TRJ turboramjet (engine)
TRLFSW tactical range landing-force support weapon
trlr trawler
TRM trademark
trml terminal
trn technical research note
TRNC Turkish Republic of Northern Cyprus
trng touring; training
TRO temporary restraining order
trom(b). trombone
trombst trombonist
trop. tropic(al)
Trop. Can. Tropic of Cancer
Trop. Cap. Tropic of Capricorn
trop. med. tropical medicine
trp troop (military)
TRRL Transport and Road Research Laboratory
trs. transfer; transpose (printing); trustees
TRSB time reference scanning beam
trsd transferred; transposed
TRSR taxi and runway surveillance radar
TRSSGM tactical range surface-to-surface guided missile
trt turret
Truron: *Truronensis* (Latin: (Bishop) of Truro)
try truly

ts temperature switch; tensile strength; test summary; till sale; turbine ship; twin screw; type specification
TS Cleveland (UK postcode); Dundee (UK vehicle registration); *tasto solo* (Italian: one key alone; music); Television Society; Theosophical Society; tool steel; tough shit; Tourette's Syndrome (medicine); training ship; transition state (chemistry); Treasury Solicitor; tub-sized (paper); Tunisia (international civil aircraft marking); typescript
T/S trans-shipment
TSA The Securities Association Ltd; time-series analysis (statistics); total surface area; Training Services Agency
TSB Trustee Savings Bank
TSD Tertiary of St Dominic
TSDS two-speed destroyer sweeper
TSE Tokyo Stock Exchange; Toronto Stock Exchange
TSF two-seater fighter
tsfr transfer
T. Sgt technical sergeant
TSh Tanzanian shilling (monetary unit)
TSH Their Serene Highnesses; thyroid-stimulating hormone (biochemistry)
tsi tons per square inch
TSO trading standards officer
tsp. teaspoon; teaspoonful
TSR tactical strike reconnaissance; terminate and stay resident (computing); torpedo-spotter reconnaissance; Trans-Siberian Railway
TSRB Top Salaries Review Body
tss typescripts
TSS time-sharing system; toxic shock syndrome (medicine); turbine steamship; twin-screw steamer; twin-screw steamship
TSSA Transport Salaried Staffs' Association
tstr tester
tsu this side up
tsvp *tournez s'il vous plait* (French: please turn over)
TSW Television South West
TT Chad (international civil aircraft marking); Exeter (UK vehicle registration); Tarbert (UK fishing port registration); technical training; teetotal; teetotaller; telegraphic transfer (banking); Tertiary (geology); tetanus toxoid; *Tidningarnes Telegrambyra* (news agency, Sweden); time trial (cycling); torpedo tube; Tourist Trophy (motor-

cycling); transit time; Trinidad and Tobago (international vehicle registration); Trust Territories; tuberculin tested (dairying)

TTA Travel Trade Association

TTBT Threshold Test Ban Treaty

TTC teachers' training course; technical training centre; Technical Training Command (military)

TTF Timber Trade Federation

ttfn ta-ta for now (Tommy Handley catchphrase)

TTL through the lens (photography); to take leave; transistor-transistor logic (electronics)

Tto Toronto

TTS teletypesetter; teletypesetting

TTT team time trial (cycling); Tyne Tees Television Ltd

TTTC Technical Teachers Training College

TTY teletypewriter (US)

Tu. Tudor; Tuesday

TU Chelmsford (UK vehicle registration); Côte d'Ivoire (international civil aircraft marking); thermal unit; toxic unit; trade union; traffic unit (telecommunications); training unit; transmission unit (telecommunications); Tunis Air (airline flight code); Tupolev (Russian aircraft)

TUAC Trade Union Advisory Committee

tub. tubular (tyre)

tuberc. tuberculosis

TUC Trades Union Congress

TUCC Transport Users' Consultative Committee; Transport Users' Consultative Council

TUCGC Trades Union Congress General Council

Tue(s). Tuesday

TUG Telephone Users' Group

TULRA Trade Union and Labour Relations Act

TUM Trades Union Movement

tuppenny twopenny

turb. turbine; turboprop

TURB turbulence (meteorology)

turboprop turbine propelled

Turk. Turkey; Turkish

turp(s). turpentine

tv terminal velocity; test vehicle

TV Nottingham (UK vehicle registration); television; terminal velocity; test vehicle; transvestite

TVA *taxe à/sur la valeur ajoutée* (French:

value-added tax); Tennessee Valley Authority

TVEI Technical and Vocational Education Initiative

tvl travel

Tvl Transvaal

TVP textured vegetable protein

TVR television rating; temperature variation of resistance (physics)

TVRO television receive only (antenna)

tw tail wind

TW Chelmsford (UK vehicle registration); Trans World Airways (airline flight code, US); travelling wave (telecommunications); Twickenham (UK postcode)

T-W three-wheeler (motorcycle; US)

TWA Thames Water Authority; time-weighted average; Trans-World Airlines

TWh terawatt hour (electricity)

TWIMC to whom it may concern

TWN teleprinter weather network

TWO this week only

TWOC taking without owner's consent (car theft)

twp township

TWT transonic wind tunnel; travelling-wave tube (electronics)

TW3 That Was The Week That Was (BBC television series)

TWU Transport Workers' Union (US)

TWX teletypewriter exchange service (US)

twy twenty

tx tax; taxation

TX Cardiff (UK vehicle registration); Texas (zip code)

Ty territory; truly

TY Benin (international civil aircraft marking); Newcastle upon Tyne (UK vehicle registration)

TYC Thames Yacht Club

tyo two-year-old (horse racing)

typ. typical; typing; typist; typographic; typographical; typography

typh. typhoon

typo. typographer; typographic; typographical; typographical error; typography

typog. typographer; typographic; typographical; typography

typw. typewriter; typewriting; typewritten

Tyrol. Tyrolean; Tyrolese

TZ Belfast (UK vehicle registration); Mali (international civil aircraft marking)

U

u ugly threatening sky (meteorology); unified atomic mass unit (chemistry)
u. uncle; *und* (German: and); unit; unsatisfactory; *unter* (German: under); upper; utility
U Unionist; Universal (cinema certification; suitable for unaccompanied children); University; upper class; uranium (element); urinal; you
U. Union; Unionist; unit; United; University; unsatisfactory; upper; Utah
ua under age; *unter anderem* (German: among other things); *usque ad* (Latin: as far as)
U/a underwriting account (insurance)
UA Leeds (UK vehicle registration); Ulster Association; United Airlines (airline flight code, US); United Artists Corporation; University of Alabama
UAA United Arab Airlines
UAB Unemployment Assistance Board; Universities Appointments Board; University of Alabama in Birmingham
UABS Union of American Biological Societies
UAC Ulster Automobile Club
UADW Universal Alliance of Diamond Workers
UAE United Arab Emirates
UAI *Union des associations internationales* (French: Union of International Associations)
UAL United Airlines
UAM underwater-to-air missile
u&lc upper and lower case (printing)
u&o use and occupancy
UAOD United Ancient Order of Druids (Friendly Society)
UAOS Ulster Agricultural Organization Society
UAP United Australia Party
UAPT *Union africaine des postes et télécommunications* (French: African Postal and Telecommunications Union)
UAR United Arab Republic
UARS upper-atmosphere research satellite
UART universal asynchronous receiver/transmitter (electronics)
uas upper airspace
UAS University Air Squadron
UAU Universities Athletic Union
UAW United Automobile Workers (US)

uAwg *um Antwort wird gebeten* (German: an answer is requested)
UB Leeds (UK vehicle registration); Southall (UK postcode); United Brethren; Upper Bench (law)
UB40 unemployment benefit form 40
UBC University of British Columbia (Vancouver)
UBF Union of British Fascists
UBI Understanding British Industry
U-boat *Unterseeboot* (German: submarine)
UBR Uniform Business Rate (taxation); University Boat Race
UBS United Bible Societies
uc *una corda* (Italian: on one string or use soft pedal; music); upper case (printing)
u/c undercharge (commerce)
Uc Universal, particularly suitable for children (cinema certification)
UC central London (UK vehicle registration); Ladeco (airline flight code, Chile); *una corda* (Italian: on one string or use soft pedal; music); under construction; undercover; University College; upcast shaft (engineering); up centre (theatre); Upper Canada; urban council; *urbe condita* (Latin: the city being built); uterine contraction (obstetrics)
UCA United Chemists' Association
UCAE Universities' Council for Adult Education
UCAR Union of Central African Republics
UCATT Union of Construction, Allied Trades and Technicians
ucb unless caused by
UCBSA United Cricket Board of South Africa
UCC Union Carbide Corporation; Universal Copyright Convention; University Computing Company
UCCA Universities' Central Council on Admissions
UCCD United Christian Council for Democracy
UCD University College, Dublin; upper critical depth (oceanography)
UCET Universities Council for Education of Teachers
UCH University College Hospital (London)
UCHD usual childhood diseases
UCI *Union cycliste internationale* (French:

International Cyclists' Union);
University of California, Irvine

UCITS Undertakings for Collective Investment in Transferable Securities (finance)

UCJG *Alliance universelle des unions chrétiennes de jeunes gens* (French: World Alliance of Young Men's Christian Associations)

ucl upper cylinder lubricant (engineering)

UCL University College, London; upper control limit

UCLA University of California at Los Angeles

UCM University Christian Movement

UCMJ uniform code of military justice (US)

UCMSM University College and Middlesex School of Medicine

UCNS Universities' Council for Non-academic Staff

UCNW University College of North Wales

UCR Uniform Crime Report (US)

UCS Union of Concerned Scientists; University College School (London); Upper Clyde Shipbuilders

UCSB University of California, Santa Barbara

UCSD University of California, San Diego

UCSW University College of South Wales

UCTA United Commercial Travellers' Association of Great Britain and Ireland

UCV United Confederate Veterans (US)

UCW Union of Communication Workers; University College of Wales

UCWRE Underwater Countermeasures and Weapons Research Establishment

ud unfair dismissal; *ut dictum* (Latin: as directed; medicine)

UD Oxford (UK vehicle registration); United Dairies

U/D under deed (US)

UDA Ulster Defence Association

UDAG Urban Development Action Grant (US)

udc upper dead centre

UDC United Daughters of the Confederacy; universal decimal classification; Urban Development Corporation; Urban District Council

UDCA Urban District Councils' Association

UDE Underwater Development Establishment

UDEAC *Union douanière et économique de l'Afrique centrale* (French: Central African Customs and Economic Union)

UDEAO *Union douanière des états d'Afrique d'Ouest* (French: Customs Union of West African States)

udf *und die folgende* (German: and the following)

UDF Ulster Defence Force; Union Defence Force (South Africa); Union of Democratic Forces (Bulgaria); *Union pour la démocratie française* (French: French Democratic Union)

u. dgl. *und dergleichen* (German: and the like)

UDI unilateral declaration of independence

UDM Union of Democratic Mineworkers

UDP United Democratic Party

UDR Ulster Defence Regiment; *Union des démocrates pour la république* (French: Union of Democrats for the Republic)

UDSR *Union démocratique et socialiste de la résistance* (French: Democratic and Socialist Union of the Resistance)

ue unexpired

UE Dudley (UK vehicle registration); university entrance (examination) (New Zealand)

UEA Universal Esperanto Association; University of East Anglia

UED University Education Diploma

uef universal extra fine (screw)

UEF *Union européenne des fédéralistes* (French: European Union of Federalists); *Union européenne féminine* (French: European Union of Women)

UEFA Union of European Football Associations

UEI Union of Educational Institutions

UEIC United East India Company

UEL United Empire Loyalists

UEO *Union de l'Europe occidentale* (French: Western European Union); unit education officer; unit educational officer

UEP *Union européenne de paiements* (French: European Payments Union)

UEPS *union européenne de la presse sportive* (French: European Sports Press Union)

UER *Union européenne de radiodiffusion* (French: European Broadcasting Union); university entrance requirements; unsatisfactory equipment report

UETA universal engineer tractor, armoured (US)

UETRT universal engineer tractor, rubber-tyred (US)

UF Brighton (UK vehicle registration); United Free Church of Scotland; urea-formaldehyde; utilization factor (lighting)
UFA *Universum Film-Aktiengesellschaft* (German: Universal Film Company)
UFAW Universities Federation for Animal Welfare
UFC United Free Church; Universities' Funding Council
UFCW United Food and Commercial Workers International Union (US)
uff. *ufficiale* (Italian: official)
UFF Ulster Freedom Fighters
UFO unidentified flying object
ufp unemployed full pay
UFT unified field theory (physics); United Federation of Teachers (US)
UFTAA Universal Federation of Travel Agents' Association
UFTU Union of Free Trades Union (Romania)
UFU Ulster Farmers' Union
UFW United Farm Workers of America
u/g underground
Ug(an). Uganda; Ugandan
UG Leeds (UK vehicle registration)
UGC University Grants Committee
UGLE United Grand Lodge of England (Freemasonry)
UGT *Unión General de Trabajadores* (Spanish: General Union of Workers)
UGWA United Garment Workers of America
UH Cardiff (UK vehicle registration); upper half
UHA Union House of Assembly (South Africa)
UHB urban haute bourgeoisie
UHCC Upper House of the Convocation of Canterbury
UHCY Upper House of the Convocation of York
UHF ultra-high frequency
UHT ultra-heat-treated; ultra-high temperature
UHV ultra-high vacuum; ultra-high voltage
ui *ut infra* (Latin: as below)
u/i under instruction
UI Londonderry (UK vehicle registration); unemployment insurance (US); user interface (computing)
UIA Union of International Associations
UIAA *Union internationale des associations d'alpinisme* (French: International Union of Alpine Associations); *Union inter-*

nationale des associations d'annonceurs (French: International Union of Advertisers' Associations)
UIC *Union internationale des chemins de fer* (French: International Union of Railways)
UICC *Union internationale contre le cancer* (French: International Union against Cancer)
UICN *Union internationale pour la conservation de la nature et de ses resources* (French: International Union for Conservation of Nature and Natural Resources)
UICPA *Union internationale de chimie pure et appliquée* (French: International Union of Pure and Applied Chemistry)
UIE *Union internationale des étudiants* (French: International Union of Students)
UIEO Union of International Engineering Organizations
UIHPS *Union internationale d'histoire et de philosophie des sciences* (French: International Union of the History and Philosophy of Science)
UIJS *Union internationale de la jeunesse socialiste* (French: International Union of Socialist Youth)
UIL *Unione Italiana del Lavoro* (Italian: Italian Federation of Trade Unions); United Irish League
UIP *Union internationale de patinage* (French: International Skating Union); *Union internationale de physique pure et appliquée* (French: International Union of Pure and Applied Physics); *Union interparlementaire* (French: Inter-Parliamentary Union)
UIPC *Union internationale de la presse catholique* (French: International Catholic Press Union)
UIPM *Union internationale de pentathlon moderne* (French: International Modern Pentathlon Union)
UIS *Union internationale de secours* (French: International Relief Union)
UISB *Union internationale des sciences biologiques* (French: International Union of Biological Sciences)
UISM *Union internationale des syndicats des mineurs* (French: Miners' Trade Unions International)
UISPP *Union internationale des sciences préhistoriques et prohistoriques* (French: International Union of Prehistoric and Prohistoric Sciences)

UIT *Union internationale des télécom-munications* (French: International Telecommunications Union); unit investment trust

UITP *Union internationale des transports publics* (French: International Union of Public Transport)

UIU Upholsterers' International Union of North America

UJ Shrewsbury (UK vehicle registration); Union Jack; universal joint (engineering)

UJC Union Jack Club (London)

UJD *Utriusque Juris Doctor* (Latin: Doctor of Civil and Canon Law)

UK Air UK (airline flight code); Birmingham (UK vehicle registration); United Kingdom

UK(A) United Kingdom (Allcomers) (athletics)

UKA Ulster King of Arms; United Kingdom Alliance

UKAC United Kingdom Automation Council

UKADGE United Kingdom Air Defence Ground Environment

UKAEA United Kingdom Atomic Energy Authority

UKAPE United Kingdom Association of Professional Engineers

UKBG United Kingdom Bartenders' Guild

UKCC United Kingdom Central Council for Nursing, Midwifery and Health Visiting

UKCIS United Kingdom Chemical Information Service

UKCOSA United Kingdom Council for Overseas Students' Affairs

UKCSBS United Kingdom Civil Service Benefit Society

UKCTA United Kingdom Commercial Travellers' Association

UKDA United Kingdom Dairy Association

uke ukulele

UKFBPW United Kingdom Federation of Business and Professional Women

UKgal UK gallon

UKIAS United Kingdom Immigrants' Advisory Service

UKIRT United Kingdom Infrared Telescope

UKISC United Kingdom Industrial Space Committee

UKLF United Kingdom Land Forces

UKMF(L) United Kingdom Military Forces (Land)

UKMIS United Kingdom Mission

UK(N) United Kingdom (National) (athletics)

UKOOA United Kingdom Offshore Operators Association

UKOP United Kingdom Oil Pipelines

UKPA United Kingdom Pilots' Association

UKPIA United Kingdom Petroleum Industry Association Ltd

Ukr. Ukraine; Ukrainian

UKSATA United Kingdom South Africa Trade Association

UKSLS United Kingdom Services Liaison Staff

UKSMA United Kingdom Sugar Merchant Association Ltd

UKW *Ultrakurzwelle* (German: ultra-short wave)

ul upper left; upper limit

UL Air Lanka (airline flight code, Sri Lanka); central London (UK vehicle registration); Ullapool (UK fishing port registration); university library; up left (theatre); upper limb (medicine)

ULA uncommitted logic array (computing)

ULC up left centre (theatre)

ULCC ultra-large crude carrier (shipping); University of London Computer Centre

ULCI Union of Lancashire and Cheshire Institutes

ULF ultra-low frequency; upper limiting frequency

ULICS University of London Institute of Computer Science

ULM ultrasonic light modulator; universal logic module

ULMS underwater long-range missile system

ULP University of London Press

ULS unsecured loan stock (finance)

ULSEB University of London School Examinations Board

ult. ultimate; ultimately; *ultimo* (Latin: last month)

ULT United Lodge of Theosophists

ult. praes. *ultimum praescritum* (Latin: last prescribed)

ULV ultra-low volume

u/m undermentioned

um. unmarried

UM Air Zimbabwe (airline flight code); Leeds (UK vehicle registration); Mauritanian ougiya (monetary unit); University of Minnesota

UMA *Union du Maghreb Arabe* (French: Arab Maghreb Union)
UMB *Union mondiale de billard* (French: World Billiards Union)
umbl. umbilical
UMC University of Missouri, Columbia
UMCP University of Maryland, College Park
UMDS United Medical and Dental Schools
UMEJ *Union mondiale des étudiants juifs* (French: World Union of Jewish Students)
UMF Umbrella Makers' Federation
UMFC United Methodist Free Churches
UMIST University of Manchester Institute of Science and Technology
UMNO United Malays National Organization; United Malaysia National Organization
ump. umpire
UMT universal military training
UMTS universal military training service; universal military training system
UMW United Mine Workers (US)
un. unified; union; united; unsatisfactory
UN Eastern Australia Airlines (airline flight code); Exeter (UK vehicle registration); United Nations
UNA United Nations Association
UNAA United Nations Association of Australia
unab. unabridged
unacc(omp). unaccompanied
UNACC United Nations Administrative Committee and Coordination
UNACOM universal army communication system
unan. unanimous
UNARCO United Nations Narcotics Commission
unasgd unassigned
unatt. unattached
unattrib. unattributed
UNAUS United Nations Association of the United States
unauthd unauthorized
unb(d). unbound
UNB universal navigation beacon; University of New Brunswick
UNBRO United Nations Border Relief Operation
unc. uncertain; uncle
UNC uncirculated (numismatics); *Union Nationale Camerounaise* (French: Cameroon National Union/Cameroon People's Democratic Movement); United

Nations Command; University of North Carolina
UNCAST United Nations Conference on the Applications of Science and Technology
UNCC United Nations Cartographic Commission
UNCCP United Nations Conciliation Commission for Palestine
UNCDF United Nations Capital Development Fund
UNCED United Nations Conference on Environment and Development
UNCIO United Nations Conference on International Organization
uncir(c). uncirculated
UNCITRAL United Nations Commission on International Trade Law
unclas(s). unclassified
UNCLE United Network Command for Law Enforcement (fictitious security organization; US television series *The Man from UNCLE*)
UNCLOS United Nations Conference on the Law of the Sea
UNCOK United Nations Commission on Korea
uncond. unconditional
uncor. uncorrected
UNCSTD United Nations Conference on Science and Technology for Development
UNCTAD United Nations Conference on Trade and Development
UNCURK United Nations Commission for Unification and Rehabilitation of Korea
UND University of North Dakota
UNDC United Nations Disarmament Commission
undergrad. undergraduate
UNDP United Nations Development Programme
UNDRO United Nations Disaster Relief Organization
undsgd undersigned
undtkr undertaker
Une unnilennium (element)
UNE underground nuclear explosion
UNEC United Nations Education Conference
UNECA United Nations Economic Commission for Asia
UNEDA United Nations Economic Development Administration
UNEF United Nations Emergency Force

UNEP United Nations Environment
Programme
UNESCO United Nations Economic,
Scientific and Cultural Organization
UNETAS United Nations Emergency
Technical Aid Service
unexpl. unexplained; unexploded;
unexplored
UNFAO United Nations Food and
Agriculture Organization
UNFB United Nations Film Board
UNFC United Nations Food Conference
UNFICYP United Nations (Peacekeeping)
Force in Cyprus
UNFPA United Nations Fund for
Population Activities
ung. *unguentum* (Latin: ointment)
UNGA United Nations General Assembly
Unh unnilhexium (element)
UNHCR United Nations High
Commission for Refugees
UNHQ United Nations Headquarters
UNHRC United Nations Human Rights
Commissioner
Uni. University College (Oxford)
UNI *Ente Nazionale Italiano di Unificazione*
(Italian: Italian Standards Association);
United News of India
UNIA Universal Negro Improvement
Association (US)
UNIC United Nations Information Centre
UNICA *Union internationale du cinéma
d'amateurs* (French: International Union
of Amateur Cinema)
UNICE *Union des industries de la
communauté européenne* (French: Union of
Industries of the European Community)
UNICEF United Nations Children's Fund
UNICOM universal integrated
communication system
UNIDO United Nations Industrial
Development Organization
UNIDROIT *Institut international pour
l'unification du droit privé* (French:
International Institute for the Unification
of Private Law)
unif. uniform
UNIFIL United Nations Interim Force in
Lebanon
UNIMA *Union internationale des
marionnettes* (French: International
Union of Puppeteers)
UNIO United Nations Information
Organization
UNIP United National Independence
Party (Zambia)
UNIPEDE *Union internationale des*

*producteurs et distributeurs d'énergie
électrique* (French: International Union of
Producers and Distributors of Electrical
Energy)
unis. unison (music)
UNIS United Nations International
School
UNISCAT United Nations Expert
Committee on the Application of Science
and Technology
UNISIST Universal System for
Information in Science and Technology
Unit. Unitarian(ism)
Unita *União Nacional para a Independência
Total de Angola* (Portuguese: National
Union for the Total Independence of
Angola)
UNITAR United Nations Institute for
Training and Research
univ. universal; universally; university
Univ. Universalist; University; University
College (Oxford)
UNIVAC universal automatic computer
UNJSPB United Nations Joint Staff
Pension Board
unkn. unknown
UNKRA United Nations Korean
Reconstruction Agency
UNLC United Nations Liaison Committee
unm. unmarried
UNM University of New Mexico
UNMC United Nations Mediterranean
Commission
UNO United Nations Organization
unop. unopposed
unp. unpaged; unpaid
Unp unnilpentium (element)
UNP United National Party (Sri Lanka)
UNPA United Nations Postal
Administration
UNPC United Nations Palestine
Commission
UNPCC United Nations Conciliation
Commission for Palestine
unpd unpaged; unpaid
UNPROFOR United Nations Protection
Force in Yugoslavia
unpub(d). unpublished
Unq unnilquadium (element)
UNREF United Nations Refugee
Emergency Fund
UNRISD United Nations Research
Institute for Social Development
UNRPR United Nations Relief for
Palestine Refugees
UNRRA United Nations Relief and
Rehabilitation Administration

UNRWA United Nations Relief and Works Agency for Palestine Refugees in the Near East
Uns unnilseptium (element)
unsat. unsatisfactory; unsaturated
UNSC United Nations Security Council; United Nations Social Commission
UNSCC United Nations Standards Coordinating Committee
UNSCCUR United Nations Scientific Conference on the Conservation and Utilization of Resources
UNSCOB United Nations Special Committee on the Balkans
UNSCOP United Nations Special Committee on Palestine
UNSF United Nations Special Fund for Economic Development
UNSG United Nations Secretary-General
UNSR United Nations Space Registry
UNSW University of New South Wales
UNTAA United Nations Technical Assistance Administration
UNTAB United Nations Technical Assistance Board
UNTAC United Nations Transitional Authority for Cambodia
UNTAG United Nations Transition Assistance Group (Namibia)
UNTAM United Nations Technical Assistance Mission
UNTC United Nations Trusteeship Council
UNTT United Nations Trust Territory
UNWCC United Nations War Crimes Commission
uo *und ofters* (German: and often)
UO Exeter (UK vehicle registration)
uoc ultimate operating capability
UOD ultimate oxygen demand (water conservation)
U of A University of Alaska
U of NC University of North Carolina
U of S University of Saskatchewan
UOFS University of the Orange Free State (South Africa)
U of T University of Toronto
up. underproof (alcohol); unpaid; upper
UP Bahamasair (airline flight code, Bahamas); Newcastle upon Tyne (UK vehicle registration); Ulster Parliament; Union Pacific; United Party; United Presbyterian; United Press; University of Paris; University of Pennsylvania; University of Pittsburgh; unsaturated polyester; Upper Peninsula (US); Uttar Pradesh

UPA *Union postale arabe* (French: Arab Postal Union); United Productions of America (cinema company)
UPC Uganda People's Congress; *Union des Populations Camerounaises* (French: Union of the Populations of Cameroon); United Presbyterian Church; Universal Postal Convention; universal product code
upd unpaid
UPD united port district; Urban Planning Directorate
UPGC University and Polytechnic Grants Committee
UPGWA United Plant Guard Workers of America
uphd uphold (law)
uphol. upholsterer; upholstery
UPI United Press International
UPIGO *Union professionelle internationale des gynécologues et obstétriciens* (French: International Union of Professional Gynaecologists and Obstetricians)
UPIU United Paperworkers International Union (US)
UPNI Unionist Party of Northern Ireland
UPOA Ulster Public Officers' Association
UPOW Union of Post Office Workers
UPP United Peasant Party (Poland); United Press of Pakistan (news agency)
UPR unearned premiums reserve (insurance); Union Pacific Railroad
UPS uninterrupted power supply; United Parcel Service (US); United Publishers' Services
UPU Universal Postal Union (UN)
UPUP Ulster Popular Unionist Party
uPVC unplasticized polyvinyl chloride
UPW Union of Post Office Workers
UPWA United Packinghouse Workers of America
ur. urinary; urine
Ur. uranium; Urdu; Uruguay; Uruguayan
UR Luton (UK vehicle registration); Ukraine (international civil aircraft marking); unconditioned reflex; unconditioned response; uniform regulations; up right (theatre); urban renewal
URA Urban Renewal Administration (US)
Uran. Uranus
urb. urban
URBM ultimate-range ballistic missile
URC United Reform Church; up right centre (theatre)
Urd. Urdu
URF *Union des services routiers des chemins*

de fer européens (French: Union of European Railways Road Services)
urg. urgent
URI upper respiratory infection (medicine)
URL Unilever Research Laboratory
urol. urology
URSI *Union radio scientifique internationale* (French: International Scientific Radio Union)
URTI upper respiratory tract infection (medicine)
URTU United Road Transport Union
Uru. Uruguay
Urupabol Uruguay, Paraguay and Bolivia (international commission)
URW United Rubber, Cork, Linoleum and Plastic Workers of America
us *ubi supra* (Latin: where mentioned above); *ut supra* (Latin: as above)
u/s unserviceable; useless
US Glasgow (UK vehicle registration); *ufficio stampa* (Italian: press office); ultrasound scanning (medicine); Uncle Sam; unconditioned stimulus; Union of South Africa; United Service (US); United States (of America); unsaleable; US Air (airline flight code)
U/S unserviceable; useless
USA United States Army; United States of America; United States of America (international vehicle registration); United Synagogues of America
USA/ABF United States of America Amateur Boxing Federation
USAAC United States Army Air Corps
USAAF United States Army Air Force
USAC United States Air Corps; United States Auto Club
USAEC United States Atomic Energy Commission
USAF United States Air Force
USAFA United States Air Force Academy
USAFC United States Army Forces Command
USAFE United States Air Forces in Europe
USAFI United States Armed Forces Institute
USAFR United States Air Force Reserve
USAID United States Agency for International Development
USAMC United States Army Materiel Command
USAMedS United States Army Medical Service
USAR United States Army Reserve

USAREUR United States Army, Europe
USASA United States Army Security Agency
USASigC United States Army Signal Corps
USASMC United States Army Supply and Maintenance Command
USAT United States Army Transport
USATDC United States Army Training and Doctrine Command
USATEC United States Army Test and Evaluation Command
USAWC United States Army Weapons Command
USBC United States Bureau of the Census
USBM United States Bureau of Mines
USC Ulster Special Constabulary; United Services Club; United Somali Congress; United States Code; United States Congress; United States of Colombia; University of South Carolina; University of Southern California; up stage centre (theatre)
USCA United States Code Annotated
USCC United States Circuit Court
USCCA United States Circuit Court of Appeals
USCG United States Coast Guard
USCGA United States Coast Guard Academy
USCGC United States Coast Guard Cutter
USCGR United States Coast Guard Reserve
USCGS United States Coast and Geodetic Survey
USCL United Society for Christian Literature
USCRC United States Citizens Radio Council
USCSC United States Civil Service Commission
USCSupp. United States Code Supplement
USDA United States Department of Agriculture
USDAW Union of Shop, Distributive and Allied Workers
USDOE United States Department of Energy
USEA United States Energy Association
U/sec. Undersecretary
USECC United States Employees' Compensation Commission
USES United States Employment Service
usf. *und so fort* (German: and so on)

USF United States Forces
USFL United States Football League
USG United States Government; United States Standard Gauge (railways)
USGA United States Golf Association
USgal United States gallon
USGPO United States Government Printing Office
USGS United States Geological Survey
USh Uganda shilling (monetary unit)
USHA United States Housing Authority
USI United Schools International; United Service Institution; United States Industries
USIA United States Information Agency
USIS United States Information Service
USITC United States International Trade Commission
USL United States Legation; United States Lines
USLTA United States Lawn Tennis Association
USM ultrasonic machining; underwater-to-surface missile; United States Mail; United States Marines; United States Mint; unlisted securities market (stock exchange)
USMA United States Military Academy
USMC United States Marine Corps; United States Maritime Commission
USMH United States Marine Hospital
USMS United States Maritime Service
USN United States Navy
USNA United States National Army; United States Naval Academy
USNC United States National Committee
USNG United States National Guard
USNI United States Naval Institute
USNO United States Naval Observatory
USNR United States Naval Reserve
USNRC United States Nuclear Regulatory Commission
USNS United States Navy Ship
USO United Service Organization (US military entertainments organization)
US of A United States of America
USP unbleached sulphite pulp (paper manufacture); unique selling proposition (advertising); United States Patent; United States Pharmacopeia
USPat United States Patent
USPC Ulster Society for the Preservation of the Countryside
USPG United Society for the Propagation of the Gospel
USPHS United States Public Health Service

USPO United States Post Office
USPS United States Postal Service
USR United States Reserves; Universities' Statistical Record
USRA Universities Space Research Association (US)
USRC United States Reserve Corps
USS Undersecretary of State; *Union Syndicale Suisse* (French: Swiss Federation of Trade Unions); United States Senate; United States Service; United States Ship; United States Steamer; United States Steamship; Universities Superannuation Scheme
USSAF United States Strategic Air Force
USSB United States Shipping Board
USSC(t) United States Supreme Court
USSR Union of Soviet Socialist Republics
USSS United States Steamship
UST undersea technology
USTA United States Tennis Association; United States Trademark Association
USTC United States Tariff Commission
USTS United States Travel Service
usu. usual; usually
USV United States Volunteers
USVA United States Volleyball Association
USVB United States Veterans' Bureau
USVI United States Virgin Islands
usw. *und so weiter* (German: and so forth)
USW ultra-short wave; underwater sea warfare
USWA United Steelworkers of America
USWB United States Weather Bureau
USWI United States West Indies; urban solid-waste incinerator
ut universal trainer; untrained; urinary tract; user test
ut. utility
Ut. Utah
UT Leicester (UK vehicle registration); ultrasonic testing; ultrasonic transducer; Union Territory (India); unit trust; universal time (astronomy); University of Texas; urinary tract (medicine); UTA (*Union des Transports Aériens*, airline flight code, France); Utah (zip code)
U/T under trust
UTA Ulster Transport Authority; Union de Transports Aériens (French airline); Unit Trust Association
UTC *universel temps coordonné* (French: Coordinated Universal Time); University Training Corps
Utd United
UTDA Ulster Tourist Development Association

ut dict. *ut dictum* (Latin: as directed;
medicine)
ute utility (pick-up truck; Australia)
utend. *utendus* (Latin: to be used;
medicine)
U3A University of the Third Age
UTI urinary-tract infection (medicine)
ut inf. *ut infra* (Latin: as below)
UTK University of Tennessee,
Knoxville
UTS ultimate tensile strength
ut sup. *ut supra* (Latin: as above)
UTU United Transportation Union (US)
UTWA United Textile Workers of
America
uU *unter Umständen* (German:
circumstances permitting)
UU central London (UK vehicle
registration); Ulster Unionist
UUA Unitarian Universalist Association
(US)
UUM underwater-to-underwater missile
UUUC United Ulster Unionist Coalition;
United Ulster Unionist Council
UUUP United Ulster Unionist Party
uuV *unter üblichem Vorbehalt* (German:
errors and omissions excepted)
UV central London (UK vehicle
registration); ultraviolet
UVA ultraviolet radiation (between 320m
and 380m wavelength)

UVAS ultraviolet astronomical satellite
uvaser ultraviolet amplification by
stimulated emission of radiation
UVB ultraviolet radiation (between 280m
and 320m wavelength)
UVF Ulster Volunteer Force
UVL ultraviolet light
uw underwater; unladen weight
UW central London (UK vehicle
registration); University of Washington
U/W under will (law); underwriter
UWA University of Western Australia
UWC Ulster Workers' Council
UWCE Underwater Weapons and
Countermeasures Establishment
UWI University of the West Indies
UWIST University of Wales Institute of
Science and Technology
UWT Union of Women Teachers
UWUA Utility Workers Union of America
UWUSA United Workers' Union of South
Africa
ux. *uxor* (Latin: wife)
UX Shrewsbury (UK vehicle registration)
UXB unexploded bomb
UY Cameroon Airlines (airline flight
code); Universal Youth; Worcester (UK
vehicle registration)
Uz. Uzbek; Uzbekistan(i)
UZ Belfast (UK vehicle registration);
University of Zurich

V

v five (Roman numerals); variable
absorption (spectroscopy); *versus* (Latin:
against); very; victory; visibility;
volt(age); volume
v image distance (optics); specific volume
(chemistry); velocity
v. vacuum; vagrant; vale; valley; valve;
vein; *vel* (Latin: or); ventilator; ventral;
verb(al); verse; version; *verso* (Latin: on
the lefthand (page); books); *versus* (Latin:
against); vertical; very; via; vicar(age);
vice; *vide* (Latin: see); village; violin;
virus; viscosity; visibility; vision
(medicine); vocative (grammar); voice
(music); volcano; voltage; volume; *von*
(German: of); *votre* (French: your); vowel
V electric potential (electricity); five
(Roman numerals); potential energy
(physics); vanadium (element); Vatican

City (international vehicle registration);
Venerable; verb (grammar);
Vergeltungswaffe (German: reprisal
weapon (rocket missiles); World War II);
Victoria; victory; volt; Viscount(ess)
V volume (capacity)
V. Venerable; version; Very; vespers; *Via*
(Italian: Street); Vicar; Vice; Viscount;
Viscountess; *volti* (Italian: turn over;
music); voltmeter; Volunteer/s
V1 *Vergeltungswaffe 1* (German: reprisal
weapon 1 (rocket missile); World
War II); *violino primo* (Italian: first
violin)
V2 Antigua (international civil aircraft
marking); *Vergeltungswaffe 2* (German:
reprisal weapon 2 (rocket missile);
World War II); *violino secondo* (Italian:
second violin)

V3 Belize (international civil aircraft marking)
V5 Namibia (international civil aircraft marking)
V8 Brunei (international civil aircraft marking)
va value analysis; verb active; verbal adjective; viola (music)
Va Virginia (US)
VA Peterborough (UK vehicle registration); value-added; value analysis (commerce); Veterans' Administration (US); VIASA (*Venezolana Internacional de Aviación*, airline flight code, Venezuela); Vicar Apostolic; Vice-Admiral; Victoria and Albert Order; Virginia (zip code); Voice of America (radio); Volunteer Artillery; Volunteers of America; *Vostra Altezza* (Italian: Your Highness); *Votre Altesse* (French: Your Highness); *Vuestra Alteza* (Spanish: Your Highness)
V/A voucher attached
va&i verb active and intransitive
VAB vehicle assembly building (NASA)
VABF Variety Artists' Benevolent Fund
VABM vertical angle benchmark (surveying)
vac. vacancy; vacant; vacation; vacuum
VAC vector analogue computer
vacc. vaccination; vaccine
vac. dist. vacuum distilled; vacuum distillation
vac. pmp vacuum pump
VAD Voluntary Aid Detachment (Red Cross)
VADAS voice-activated domestic appliance system
V-Adm Vice-Admiral
VAF Variety Artists' Federation
vag. vagabond; vagina; vagrancy; vagrant
VAH Veterans' Administration Hospital (US)
val. valley; valuable; valuation; value; valued
valid. validate; validation
valn valuation
Valpo Valparaiso
vamp. vampire
van advantage (tennis)
VAN value-added network (computing)
van. vanguard; vanilla
Vanc. Vancouver (Canada)
V&A Victoria and Albert Museum (London)
V&M Virgin and Martyr

v&t vodka and tonic
V&V verification and validation (computing)
VAPI visual approach path indicator (aeronautics)
vapor. vaporization
vap. prf vapour proof
var. variable; variant; variation; variety; variometer; various
VAR value-added reseller (computing); visual aural range; volunteer air reserve; *Votre Altesse Royale* (French: Your Royal Highness)
varactor variable reactor (electronics)
Varig (Empresa da) Viacão Aérea Rio Grandense (Brazilian airline)
varistor variable resistor (electronics)
var. lect. *vario lectio* (Latin: a variant reading)
varn. varnish
varsity university
vas. vasectomy
VASARI Visual Art System for Archiving and Retrieval of Images (computing)
vasc. vascular
Vascar. visual average speed computer and recorder
VASI visual approach slope indicator (aeronautics)
VASP Viacão Aérea São Paulo (Brazilian airline)
Vat. Vatican
VAT value-added tax
VATE versatile automatic test equipment
Vat. Lib. Vatican Library
vaud. vaudeville
v. aux. auxiliary verb
VAV variable air volume
VAWT vertical-axis wind turbine
VAX virtual address extension (DEC computer range; trademark)
vb vehicle borne; verb(al); vertical bomb
VB Birmingham European Airways (airline flight code, UK); Maidstone (UK vehicle registration); verbal constituent (grammar); volunteer battalion
vbl verbal
V bomber aircraft category
vc valuation clause; vehicular communication; visual communication
vc. (violin)cello (music)
VC Coventry (UK vehicle registration); Vatican City; velo club (cycling); venture capital (finance); Veterinary Corps (US); vice-chairman; vice-chamberlain; vice-chancellor; vice-consul; Vickers Commercial (aircraft manufacturers);

Victoria Cross; Viet Cong; vinyl chloride
VCA vinyl carbonate (chemistry); Volunteer Civic Association (US)
VCAS Vice-Chief of the Air Staff
VCC Veteran Car Club of Great Britain; Vice-Chancellors Committee
VCCS voltage-controlled current source (electronics)
VCDS Vice-Chief of the Defence Staff
Vce Venice
VCE variable-cycle engine
VCG vertical centre of gravity; Vice-Consul-General
VCGS Vice-Chief of the General Staff
VCH Victoria County History; vinyl cyclohexene (chemistry)
vch. vehicle
c. Chr. *vor Christus* (German: before Christ)
VCI volatile corrosion inhibitor
vcl. (violin)cello (music); vehicle
vcm vacuum
VCM vinyl chloride monomer (plastic)
VCNS Vice-Chief of the Naval Staff
vcnty vicinity
VCO Viceroy's Commissioned Officer (India); voltage controlled oscillator; voluntary county organizer (Women's Institute)
VCPI virtual control program interface (computing)
Vcr Vancouver (Canada)
VCR video cassette recorder; visual control room (airfields)
vcs voices
V. Cz. Vera Cruz (Mexico)
vd vapour density; various dates; void
VD veneral disease; Victorian Decoration; Volunteer Decoration
V-Day Victory Day
Vdc volts direct current
VDC Volunteer Defence Corps
v. def. verb defective
v. dep. verb deponent
VDH valvular disease of the heart
VDI virtual device interface (computing)
v. diff. very difficult (mountaineering)
VDJ video disc jockey
VDM *Verbi Dei Minister* (Latin: Minister of the Word of God); Vienna Development Method (computer notation)
VDQS *vins délimités de qualité supérieure* (French: superior-quality wine)
VDR variable-diameter rotor; video-disc recording

VDRL venereal disease research laboratory
VDS variable-depth sonar
VDT video tape terminal; visual display terminal (computing)
VDU visual display unit
VDW van der Waals (chemistry)
ve. *veuve* (French: widow)
VE Avensa (airline flight code, Venezuela); Peterborough (UK vehicle registration); valve engineer(ing); vocational education; *Vostra Eccellenza* (Italian: Your Excellency); *Votre Éminence* (French: Your Eminence); *Vuestra Excelencia* (Spanish: Your Excellency)
VEB *Volkseigener Betrieb* (German: People's Concern; former East German nationalized company)
vec. vector
ved. *vedova* (Italian: widow)
VE Day Victory in Europe Day (8 May 1945)
veg. vegetable; vegetarian; vegetation
veh. vehicle; vehicular
vel. vellum; velocity; velvet
ven. *vendredi* (French: Friday); veneer; *venerdì* (Italian: Friday); venereal; venery; venison; venom(ous); ventral; ventricle
Ven. Venerable; Venetian; Venezuela; Venezuelan; Venice; Venus
Venet. Venetian
Venez. Venezuela; Venezuelan
vent. ventilate; ventilation; ventriloquist
ver. verification; verify; vermilion; verse; version
Ver. *Verein* (German: association or company)
VER vertical (meteorology)
VERA versatile reactor assembly; vision electronic recording apparatus
veränd. *verändert* (German: revised)
verb. *verbessert* (German: improved or revised)
verb. et lit. *verbatim et literatim* (Latin: word for word and letter for letter; law)
verb. sap. *verbum satis sapienti* (Latin: a word is enough to the wise)
verdt verdict
Verf. *Verfasser* (German: author)
Verl. *Verlag* (German: publisher)
verm. vermiculite; vermilion
vern. vernacular
vers versed sine; versine (mathematics)
vers. version

verso *reverso* (Latin: other side; left hand page in books)

vert. vertebra(l); vertical; vertigo

Very Rev(d). Very Reverend

ves. *vesica* (Latin: bladder; medicine); *vesicula* (Latin: blister; medicine); *vespere* (Latin: in the evening; medicine); vessel; vestry

vesp. *vespere* (Latin: in the evening; medicine)

VESPER Voluntary Enterprises and Services and Part-time Employment for the Retired

vet. veteran; veterinarian; veterinary surgeon

Vet. Admin. Veterans' Administration (US)

veter. veterinarian; veterinary surgeon

VetMB Bachelor of Veterinary Medicine

vet. sci. veterinary science

vet. surg. veterinary surgeon

vf very fair (meteorology); very fine (numismatics)

VF Norwich (UK vehicle registration); Vicar Forane (Roman Catholic Church); video frequency; voice-frequency (telecommunications)

VFA Victorian Football Association (Australia)

VFD verified free distribution; volunteer fire department (US)

VFL Victorian Football League (Australia)

VFM value for money (accounting)

VFO variable-frequency oscillator (electronics)

VFOAR Vandenberg Field Office of Aerospace Research (US Air Force)

VFR visual flight rules (aeronautics)

VFT very fast train (Australia)

VFU vertical format unit (computing)

VFW Veterans of Foreign Wars (US)

vfy verify

vg *verbigracia* (Spanish: for example); *verbi gratia* (Latin: for example); very good

Vg. Virgin (ecclesiastical)

VG Norwich (UK vehicle registration); *vaisseau de guerre* (French: warship); very good; Vicar General; Vice Grand (Freemasonry); *Votre Grâce* (French: Your Grace); *Votre Grandeur* (French: Your Highness)

VGA video graphics array (computing)

vgc very good condition

vgl. *vergleiche* (German: compare)

VGPI visual glide path indicator (aeronautics; World War II)

vh vertical height; very high

VH Air Burkina (airline flight code, Burkina Faso); Australia (international civil aircraft marking); Huddersfield (UK vehicle registration); *Votre Hautesse* (French: Your Highness)

vhb very heavy bombardment

VHC very highly commended

VHD video high density

VHE very high energy

VHF very high fidelity; very high frequency

VHO very high output

VHP Vishwa Hindu Parishad (India; radical Hindu group)

VHS video home system (trademark)

VHT very high temperature

VHV very high vacuum

vi verb intransitive; *vide infra* (Latin: see below)

VI Vancouver Island (Canada); vertical interval (cartography); Virgin Islands; viscosity index; volume indicator

VIA Visually Impaired Association

viad. viaduct

VIASA *Venezolana Internacional de Aviácion, SA* (Spanish: Venezuelan International Airways)

VIB vertical integration building

vib. vibraphone; vibrate; vibration

vic. vicar(age); vicinity; victory

Vic. Victoria (Australia)

VIC Victoria Institute of Colleges

Vic. Ap(os). Vicar Apostolic

Vice-Adm. Vice-Admiral

Vic. Gen. Vicar General

vid. *vide* (Latin: see); *vidua* (Latin: widow)

VID virtual image display (computing)

Vien. Vienna

VIF variable import fee

vig(n). vignette

vil. village

v. imp. verb impersonal

v. imper. verb imperative

vin. vinegar

VIN vehicle identification number (US)

vind. vindicate; vindication

vini. viniculture

VIO veterinary investigation officer

VIP vasoactive intestinal polypeptide (medicine); very important person

vir. *viridis* (Latin: green)

Vir(g). Virgil (Roman poet); Virgo

VIR *Victoria Imperatrix Regina* (Victoria, Empress and Queen)

Virg. Virginia

v. irr. verb irregular

vis. viscosity; visibility; visible; visual
Vis. Viscount(ess)
VIS Veterinary Investigation Service; visibility (meteorology)
visc. viscosity
Visc(t). Viscount(ess)
VISS VHS index search system
VISTA Volunteers in Service to America
vit. vitreous
VITA Volunteers for International Technical Assistance
viti. viticulture
vitr. *vitreum* (Latin: glass)
vit. stat. vital statistics
viv. *vivace* (Italian: lively; music)
vivi. vivisection
vix. *vixit* (Latin: he/she lived)
viz *videlicet* (Latin: namely)
vJ *vorigen Jahres* (German: of last year)
VJ Gloucester (UK vehicle registration); Vaucluse Junior (yacht; Australia); video jockey
VJ Day Victory over Japan Day (15 August 1945)
vk vertical keel
VK Air Tungaru (airline flight code, Republic of Kiribati); Newcastle upon Tyne (UK vehicle registration)
vl *varia lectio* (Latin: a variant reading)
vl. violin
VL Lincoln (UK vehicle registration); Vulgar Latin
vla viola
VLA Very Large Array (radio telescopes)
Vlad. Vladivostock
VLB vertical-lift bridge
VLBC very large bulk carrier (shipping)
VLBW very low birth weight (medicine)
VLCC very large crude carrier (shipping)
vle violone (music); double-bass viol (music)
VLF very low frequency
vln violin
VLR very long range (aircraft); Victoria Law Reports
VLSI very large scale integration (electronics)
vltg. voltage
vlv. valve; valvular
v. M. *vorigen Monats* (German: last month)
VM Manchester (UK vehicle registration); velocity modulation (physics); Victory Medal; Viet Minh; Virgin Mary; volatile matter (chemistry); *Votre Majesté* (French: Your Majesty)
V-Mail victory mail (US military)

VMC visual meteorological conditions (aeronautics)
VMCCA Veteran Motor Car Club of America
VMD *Veterinariae Medicinae Doctor* (Latin: Doctor of Veterinary Medicine)
VMH Victoria Medal of Honour (Royal Horticultural Society)
VMS virtual machine system (computing); Voluntary Medical Services Medal
vmt very many thanks
vn verb neuter; violin
VN Middlesbrough (UK vehicle registration); Vietnam; Vietnam (international civil aircraft marking, international vehicle registration); Vietnam Airlines (airline flight code); Vietnamese
Vna Vienna
V-neck v-cut neck (clothing)
VNM Victoria National Museum (Canada)
vo *verso* (Latin: left hand (page); books)
VO Nottingham (UK vehicle registration); Tyrolean Airways (airline flight code, Austria); valuation officer; verbal order; very old (brandy, port, etc); veterinary officer; (Royal) Victorian Order; voice-over (broadcasting)
VOA Voice of America (radio); Volunteers of America
voc. vocal(ist); vocation; vocative (grammar)
VOC Vehicle Observer Corps
vocab. vocabulary
VOCAL Voluntary Organizations Communication and Language
vocat. vocative (grammar)
voc-ed vocational education
voctl vocational
VOD velocity of detonation
VODAT voice-operated device for automatic transmission
vol. volatile; volcanic; volcano; volume; voluntary; volunteer
volc. volcanic; volcano
vols volumes
volum. volumetric (chemistry)
voly voluntary
VONA vehicle of the new age (computerized shuttle)
VOP very oldest procurable (brandy, port, etc)
VOR very-high-frequency omnirange radio range (navigation); very-high-frequency omnidirectional radio range (navigation)
vorm. *vormals* (German: formerly);

vormittags (German: in the morning)
Vors. *Vorsitzender* (German: chairman)
vou. voucher
vox pop *vox populi* (Latin: voice of the people)
voy. *voyez* (French: see)
vp vanishing point; vapour pressure; variable pitch; verb passive
VP Birmingham (UK vehicle registration); VASP (*Viacão Aèrea São Paulo*, airline flight code, Brazil); vent pipe (building); verb phrase (grammar); vice-president; vice-principal; victory points; *vita patris* (Latin: during the life of her/his father)
VPC *vente par correspondence* (French: mail order)
vpd vehicles per day
VP-F Falkland Islands (international civil aircraft marking)
v. ph. vertical photography
vph vehicles per hour
VPL visible panty line
VP-LA Anguilla (international civil aircraft marking)
VP-LMA Montserrat (international civil aircraft marking)
VP-LV Virgin Islands (international civil aircraft marking)
vpm vehicles per mile
Vpo Valparaiso
VPO Vienna Philharmonic Orchestra
VPP value payable post (India); Volunteer Political Party
V. Pres. Vice-President
VPRGS Vice-President of the Royal Geographical Society
VPRP Vice-President of the Royal Society of Portrait Painters
VPRS Vice-President of the Royal Society
vps vibrations per second
VPZS Vice-President of the Zoological Society
VQMG Vice-Quartermaster-General
VQ-T Turks and Caicos Islands (international civil aircraft marking)
vr variant reading; *vedi retro* (Italian: please turn over); verb reflexive
VR Manchester (UK vehicle registration); *Transportes Aereos de Cabo Verde* (airline flight code, Cape Verde Island) variant reading; velocity ratio (physics); Vicar Rural; *Victoria Regina* (Latin: Queen Victoria); virtual reality (computing); voltage regulator; Volunteer Reserve; vulcanized rubber
VRA Vocational Rehabilitation Administration (US)

VRAM video random access memory (computing)
VRB variable (meteorology)
VR-B Bermuda (international civil aircraft marking)
VRC Vehicle Research Corporation; Volunteer Rifle Corps
VR-C Cayman Islands (international civil aircraft marking)
VRD Royal Naval Volunteer Reserve Officers' Decoration
v. refl. verb reflexive
V. Rev. Very Reverend
vrg veering
VR-G Gibraltar (international civil aircraft marking)
VR-H Hong Kong (international civil aircraft marking)
Vri. *Vrijdag* (Dutch: Friday)
VRI *Victoria Regina et Imperatrix* (Latin: Victoria, Queen and Empress); visual rule instrument (aeronautics)
VRM variable rate mortgage (US)
VRO vehicle registration office
Vry Viceroy
vs variable speed; *vide supra* (Latin: see above); *volti subito* (Italian: turn over quickly; music)
vs. *versus* (Latin: against)
VS Luton (UK vehicle registration); Venerable Sage (Freemasonry); Veterinary Surgeon; *vieux style* (French: Old Style; calendar); Virgin Atlantic Airways (airline flight code, UK); *volti subito* (Italian: turn over quickly; music); *Vostra Santità* (Your Holiness); *Votre Sainteté* (French: Your Holiness)
VSAM virtual storage access method (computing)
VSB vestigial sideband (telecommunications)
vsby visibility
VSC Volunteer Staff Corps
VSCC very superior old (brandy, port, etc); Vintage Sports Car Club
VSD vendor's shipping document
VSEPR valence-shell electron pair repulsion
VSI vertical speed indicator (navigation)
V-sign victory sign
VSL venture scout leader
VSM vestigial sideband modulation (telecommunications)
vsn vision
VSO verb-subject-object (linguistics); very superior old (brandy, port, etc); Vienna State Opera; Voluntary Service Overseas

VSOP very special old pale; very superior old pale (brandy, port, etc)
VSP vertical speed (meteorology)
VSQ very special quality
VSR very short range; very special reserve (wine)
vst violinist
V-STOL vertical and short take-off and landing (aircraft)
VSW vitrified stoneware
VSWR voltage standing-wave ratio (telecommunications)
vt vacuum technology; variable transmission; verb transitive
Vt Vermont
VT India (international civil aircraft marking); Stoke-on-Trent (UK vehicle registration); variable time; vatu (monetary unit of Vanuatu); Vermont (zip code)
VTC Volunteer Training Corps; voting trust certificate
Vte *Vicomte* (French: Viscount)
Vtesse *Vicomtesse* (French: Viscountess)
vtg voting
VTL variable threshold logic (computing)
VTO vertical take-off (aircraft)
VTOHL vertical take-off, horizontal landing (aircraft)
VTOL vertical take-off and landing (aircraft)
VTOVL vertical take-off, vertical landing (aircraft)

VTR video tape recorder; video tape recording
VU Manchester (UK vehicle registration); volume unit (acoustics)
vul(g). vulgar; vulgarly
Vul(g). Vulgate (Bible)
vv *vice versa* (Latin: the other way around); *viva voce* (Latin: spoken aloud)
vv. verbs; verses; violins; voices (music); volumes
v/v volume in volume (chemistry)
VV Northampton (UK vehicle registration)
VVD *Volkspartij voor Vrijheid en Democratie* (Dutch: People's Party for Freedom and Democracy)
vve *veuve* (French: widow)
vv. ll. *variae lectiones* (Latin: variant readings)
VV. MM. *Vos Majestés* (French: Your Majesties)
VVO very very old (brandy, port, etc)
VW Chelmsford (UK vehicle registration); Very Worshipful; *Volkswagen* (German: people's car; German motor manufacturer)
VWH Vale of the White Horse
vx vertex
VX Aces (*Aerolineas Centrales de Colombia*, airline flight code, Colombia); Chelmsford (UK vehicle registration)
vy various years (bibliography); very
VY Leeds (UK vehicle registration)
VZ Tyrone (UK vehicle registration)

W

w dew (meteorology); waist; warm; water; watt (electricity); week; white; wide; wife; with; woman
w. waist; wall; war; warm; waste; water; weather; week; weight; west; western; wet; white; wicket (cricket); wide (cricket); width; wife; win; wind; wire; with; woman; won; wooden; word; work; wrong
W tungsten (element); Wales; water closet; Waterford (Irish fishing port registration); watt (electricity); west; western; west London (UK postcode); winter loading (shipping); women's (clothing); won (South Korean monetary unit)

W weight (physics); work (physics)
W. Wales; Warden; Wednesday; Welsh; Wesleyan; west; western; white; wide; widow; widowed; widower
wa with answers
WA Sheffield (UK vehicle registration); Warrington (UK postcode); Washington (zip code); Welfare Administration (US); West Africa; West African; Western Australia; Westminster Abbey; Whitehaven (UK fishing port registration); wing attack (netball); with average (insurance); withholding agent (US banking); Woodworkers of America (trade union)
WAA Women's Auxiliary Association

WAAA Women's Amateur Athletic Association
WAAAF Women's Auxiliary Australian Air Force
WAAC Women's Army Auxiliary Corps
WAAE World Association for Adult Education
WAAF Women's Auxiliary Air Force; Women's Auxiliary Australian Air Force
WAAS Women's Auxiliary Army Service; World Academy of Art and Science
WAC Women's Army Corps (US); World Aeronautical Chart
WACB World Association for Christian Broadcasting
WACC World Association for Christian Communications
WACCC Worldwide Air Cargo Commodity Classification
WACSM Women's Army Corps Service Medal
Wad(h). Wadham College (Oxford)
WADEX word and author index
WADF Western Air Defence (US)
WADS wide-area data service
wae when actually employed
WAF West African Forces; with all faults; Women in the Air Force
WAFC West African Fisheries Commission (FAO)
WAFFLE wide angle fixed field locating equipment
W. Afr. West Africa; West African
WAFS Women's Auxiliary Ferrying Squadron (US); Women's Auxiliary Fire Service
WAG Gambia (international vehicle registration); Writers' Action Group
WAGBI Wildfowl Association of Great Britain and Ireland
WAGGGS World Association of Girl Guides and Girl Scouts
WAIF World Adoption International Fund
WAIS Wechsler Adult Intelligence Scale (psychology)
Wal. Walloon
WAL Sierra Leone (international vehicle registration)
wam wife and mother
WAM work analysis and measurement; wrap around mortgage (US)
WAN Nigeria (international vehicle registration); wide-area network (computing)
Wand. Wanderers (football)
w&i weighing and inspection

W&L Washington and Lee University (US)
W&M William and Mary
w&s whisky and soda
w&t wear and tear (taxation)
WANS Women's Australian National Service
WAOS Welsh Agricultural Organization Society
WAP work assignment plan; work assignment procedure
WAPC Women's Auxiliary Police Corps
WAPOR World Association for Public Opinion Research
war. warrant
War. Warsaw; Warwickshire
WAR West Africa Regiment
WARC Western Air Rescue Center (US); World Administrative Radio Conference; World Alliance of Reformed Churches
Warks. Warwickshire
warn. warning
warr(ty). warranty
WASA Welsh Amateur Swimming Association
Wash. Washington
WASP white Anglo-Saxon Protestant; Women Airforce Service Pilots (US)
WAST Western Australia Standard Time
Wat. Waterford
WAT weight, altitude, temperature (aeronautics); word association test (psychology)
WATA World Association of Travel Agencies
WATS Wide Area Telephone Service (US)
W. Aus(t). Western Australia
WAVES Women Accepted for Volunteer Emergency Service (US Navy)
WAWF World Association of World Federalists
WAY World Assembly of Youth
WAYC Welsh Association of Youth Clubs
wb wage board; waste ballast; water ballast; waveband; waybill; westbound; wheel base; wool back (knitting)
Wb Weber (magnetism)
WB Sheffield (UK vehicle registration); warehouse book; Warner Brothers Pictures Incorporated; water board; waveband (telecommunications); waybill (commerce); weather bureau; Wechsler-Bellevue (intelligence test); weekly benefits (insurance); World Bank for Reconstruction and Development

WBA West Bromwich Albion (football club); World Boxing Association
WBAFC Weather Bureau Area Forecast Center (US)
WBAN Weather Bureau, Air Force and Navy (US)
WBC white blood cell (medicine); white blood count (medicine); World Boxing Council
WBF World Bridge Federation
WBGT wet-bulb globe temperature (meteorology); wet-bulb globe thermometer (meteorology)
wbi will be used
WbN west by north
wbs walking beam suspension (engineering); without benefit of salvage (insurance)
WbS west by south
WBS whole-body scan (medicine)
WBT wet-bulb temperature (meteorology)
wc walking club; watch committee; water closet; water cock; wheelchair; without charge
WC Chelmsford (UK vehicle registration); war cabinet; war council; water closet; Wesleyan Chapel; west central London (UK postcode); Western Command (military); working capital; workmen's compensation
W/C water closet; Wing Commander
WCA Wholesale Confectioners' Alliance; Wildlife and Countryside Act; Women's Christian Association
WCAT Welsh College of Advanced Technology
WCC War Crimes Commission; World Council of Churches
W/Cdr Wing Commander
WCEU World Christian Endeavour Union
WCF World Congress of Faiths
WCG Worldwide Church of God
WCL World Confederation of Labour
WCP World Climate Programme; World Council of Peace
WCRA Weather Control Research Association; Women's Cycle Racing Association
WCT World Championship Tennis
WCTU Women's Christian Temperance Union
WCWB World Council for the Welfare of the Blind
wd ward; warranted; weed; wood; word; would; wound

w/d warranted; well developed
WD (Windward Islands) Dominica (international vehicle registration); Dudley (UK vehicle registration); War Department; Watford (UK postcode); well developed; Wexford (Irish fishing port registration); wing defence (netball); Works Department
W/D withdrawal (banking); wind direction
WDA Welsh Development Agency; writing-down allowance (taxation)
WDC War Damage Commission; War Damage Corporation (US); Woman Detective Constable; Women's Diocesan Association; World Data Centre
wdf wood door and frame
wdg winding
Wdr Wardmaster (Navy)
WDS Woman Detective Sergeant
wd sc. wood screw
WDSPR widespread (meteorology)
wdth width
WDV written-down value (taxation)
w/e weekend; week ending
We. Wednesday
WE Sheffield (UK vehicle registration); War Establishment
wea. weapon; weather
WEA (Royal) West of England Academy; Workers' Educational Association
WE&FA Welsh Engineers' and Founders' Association
WEARCON weather observation and forecasting control system
WEC wave energy converter; wind energy converter; World Energy Conference
WECOM Weapons Command (US)
Wed. Wednesday
WEDA Wholesale Engineering Distributors' Association
Wednes. Wednesday
Weds. Wednesday
wef with effect from
WEFC West European Fisheries Conference
WEFT wings, engine, fuselage tail (aeronautics)
Wel. Welsh
weld. welding
Well. Wellington (New Zealand)
WEN Women's Environmental Network
Wes. Wesleyan
WES Women's Engineering Society; World Economic Survey
WES/PNEU Worldwide Education

Service of Parents' National Educational Union

west. western

Westm. Westmeath; Westminster; Westmorland

WET West European Time; Western European Time

WETUC Workers' Educational Trade Union Committee

WEU Western European Union

Wex(f). Wexford

wf wrong font (printing)

WF Sheffield (UK vehicle registration); Wakefield (UK postcode); Wells Fargo and Company (US); white female (US); wing forward (sport)

WFA White Fish Authority; Women's Football Association; World Friendship Association

w factor will factor (psychology)

WFB World Fellowship of Buddhists

WFC World Food Council

w. fd wool forward (knitting)

WFD World Federation of the Deaf

WFDY World Federation of Democratic Youth

WFEO World Federation of Engineering Organizations

WFF World Friendship Federation

WFGA Women's Farm and Garden Association

Wfl Worshipful

WFL Women's Freedom League

WFMH World Federation for Mental Health

WFMW World Federation of Methodist Women

WFN World Federation of Neurology

WFP World Food Programme (FAO)

WFPA World Federation for the Protection of Animals

WFSW World Federation of Scientific Workers

WFTU World Federation of Trade Unions

WFUNA World Federation of United Nations Associations

w. fwd wool forward (knitting)

wg weighing; wing

WG Grenada (international vehicle registration); Sheffield (UK vehicle registration); water gauge; weight guaranteed; Welsh Guards; West German; West Germanic (languages); West Germany; William Gilbert Grace (English cricketer); wire gauge; Working Group

WGA Writers' Guild of America

WGC Welwyn Garden City; Worthy Grand Chaplain (Freemasonry)

Wg/Cdr Wing Commander

Wg Comdr Wing Commander

W. Ger. West German; West Germanic (languages); West Germany

WGG Worthy Grand Guardian (Freemasonry); Worthy Grand Guide (Freemasonry)

WGI world geophysical interval

w. gl. wired glass

W. Glam. West Glamorgan

WGM Worthy Grand Master (Freemasonry)

WGmc West Germanic (languages)

WGPMS warehouse gross performance measurement system

WGS Worthy Grand Sentinel (Freemasonry)

WGU Welsh Golfing Union

wh. wharf; which; whispered; white

w/h withholding

W h watt hour (electricity)

WH Manchester (UK vehicle registration); water heater; Weymouth (UK fishing port registration); wheelers (cycling); White House (US); wing half (sport); withholding (banking)

WHA World Health Assembly (WHO); World Hockey Association

WHAM Winning Hearts And Minds (Vietnam War propaganda campaign)

W'hampton Wolverhampton

whb wash-hand basin

whd warhead

whf wharf

WhF Whitworth Fellow

whfg. wharfage

whfr wharfinger

Whi. Whitehall (London)

whis. whistle

whmstr weightmaster

WHO White House Office (US); World Health Organization

WHOA! Wild Horse Organized Assistance (US)

WHOI Woods Hole Oceanographic Institution (US)

whp water horse power

whr whether

WHRA World Health Research Centre

whs(e). warehouse

WhSh Whitworth Scholar

whsl(e). wholesale

whsmn warehouseman

whsng warehousing

whs. stk warehouse stock

WHTSO Welsh Health Technical Services Organization
why what have you?
wi when issued (finance)
WI Rottnest Airbus (airline flight code, Australia); Waterford (Irish vehicle registration); West Indian; West Indies; Windward Islands; Wisbech (UK fishing port); Wisconsin (zip code); Women's Institute; wrought iron
WIA wounded in action
WIBC Women's International Bowling Congress (US)
WICA Warsaw International Consumer Association
Wick. Wicklow
wid. widow(er)
WID West India Docks (London)
WIDF Women's International Democratic Federation
WIF West Indies Federation
Wig. Wigtown(shire)
Wigorn: *Wigorniensis* (Latin: (Bishop) of Worcester)
Wilco will comply
WILPF Women's International League for Peace and Freedom
Wilts. Wiltshire
WIN Work Incentive (US)
Winch. Winchester
W. Ind. West Indian; West Indies
Wind. I. Windward Islands
Wing Cdr Wing Commander
Wings warrants in negotiable government securities (finance)
Winn. Winnipeg
wint. winter
Winton: *Wintoniensis* (Latin: (Bishop) of Winchester)
WIP waste incineration plant; work in progress
WIPO World Intellectual Property Organization
WIRA Wool Industries Research Association
WIRDS weather information reporting and display system
Wis. Wisconsin
WISC. Wechsler Intelligence Scale for Children
Wisd. Wisden (cricket); Wisdom of Solomon (Bible)
WISP wide-range imaging spectrometer
wit. witness
WITA Women's International Tennis Association
withdrl withdrawal

witht without
Wits. Witwatersrand
WIZO Women's International Zionist Organization
WJ Labrador Airways (airline flight code, Canada); Sheffield (UK vehicle registration)
WJC World Jewish Congress
WJEC Welsh Joint Education Committee
wk warehouse keeper; weak; week; well-known; work; wreck
Wk Walk
WK Coventry (UK vehicle registration); Wick (UK fishing port registration)
wkds weekdays
wkg working
wkly weekly
WKN weaken(ing) (meteorology)
wkr worker; wrecker
wks weeks; works
wks. workshop
wkt wicket (cricket)
wl wool
w/l wavelength
WL Oxford (UK vehicle registration); St Lucia (international vehicle registration); *wagon-lit* (French: sleeping car); waiting list; water line; wavelength; West Lothian; Women's Liberation
WLA Women's Land Army
WLB War Labor Board (US)
wld would
Wld Ch. World Championship
wldr welder
WLF Women's Liberal Federation
wl fwd wool forward (knitting)
WLGS Women's Local Government Society
WHLB Women's League of Health and Beauty
WLI workload index
WLM Women's Liberation Movement
Wln Wellington (New Zealand)
W. long. west longitude
W. Loth. West Lothian
WLPSA Wild Life Preservation Society of Australia
WLR Weekly Law Reports
WLRI World Life Research Institute
WLS weighted least squares (statistics)
WLTBU Watermen, Lightermen, Tugmen and Bargemen's Union
WLU World Liberal Union
WLUS World Land Use Survey
wly westerly
wlz waltz
WM Liverpool (UK vehicle registration);

war memorial; wattmeter; white male (US); wire mesh; Worshipful Master (Freemasonry)

W/M weight or measurement (shipping)

WMA Working Mothers' Association; World Medical Association

WMAA Whitney Museum of American Art

WMC War Manpower Commission (US); Ways and Means Committee; working men's club; Working Men's College; World Meteorological Centre; World Methodist Council

WMCIU Working Men's Club and Institute Union Ltd

w. midl. West Midlands

wmk watermark

WMM World Movement of Mothers

WMO World Meteorological Organization

WMP with much pleasure

WMS Wesleyan Missionary Society; World Magnetic Survey

WMTC Women's Mechanized Transport Corps

WN Southwest Airlines (airline flight code, US); Swansea (UK vehicle registration); Wigan (UK postcode)

WNA winter North Atlantic (shipping)

wndp with no down payment

WNE Welsh National Eisteddfod

wnl within normal limits

WNLF Women's National Liberal Federation

WNO Welsh National Opera

WNP Welsh Nationalist Party

WNW west-northwest

wo walkover (sport); *wie oben* (German: as mentioned above); written order (commerce)

w/o without; written off (accounting)

WO Cardiff (UK vehicle registration); walkover (sport); War Office; warrant officer; welfare officer; wireless operator; Workington (UK fishing port registration); written order

woa without answers

WOA Wharf Owners' Association

WOAR Women Organized Against Rape

wob washed overboard

woc without compensation

WOCA world outside centrally planned economic areas

WOC(S) waiting on cement (to set) (building)

woe without equipment

Woe. *Woensdag* (Dutch: Wednesday)

WOF Warrant of Fitness (vehicles; New Zealand)

W/offr welfare officer

wog war office general stores; water, oil, or gas; with other goods; worker on government service

wol wharf-owner's liability

Wolfs. Wolfson College (Oxford)

WOM wireless operator mechanic

WOMAN World Organization for Mothers of All Nations

won wool on needle (knitting)

WOO warrant ordnance officer; World Oceanographic Organization

wop with other property; without personnel

wope without personnel or equipment

Wor. worshipful

WOR without our responsibility

Worc. Worcester College (Oxford)

WORC Washington Operations Research Council (US)

Worcs. Worcestershire

workh. workhouse

WORM write once read many (times) (computing)

WOSAC worldwide synchronization of atomic clocks

WOSB War Office Selection Board

WOSD weapons operational systems development

WOTCHA wonderful old thing, considering her/his age

WOW waiting on weather; Women Against the Ordination of Women

wp waste paper; waste pipe; weather permitting; wild pitch (baseball); will proceed; without prejudice (law); word processing; word processor; working party

Wp. Worship(ful)

WP weather permitting; Western Province (South Africa); West Point (US); White Paper (government); wire payment (US); without prejudice (law); Worcester (UK vehicle registration); word processing; word processor; working paper; working party; working pressure; Worthy Patriarch (Freemasonry); Worthy President (Freemasonry)

WPA Water Polo Association; Western Provident Association; with particular average (insurance); Work Progress Administration (US); Work Projects Administration (US); World Parliament Association; World Pool-Billiard

Association; World Presbyterian
Alliance
wpb wastepaper basket
WPB War Production Board (US)
WPBL Women's Professional Basketball
League (US)
WPBSA World Professional Billiards and
Snooker Association
WPC War Pensions Committee; Woman
Police Constable; wood-plastic
composite; wood-polymer composite;
World Petroleum Congress
WPCA Water Pollution Control
Administration (US)
WPCF Water Pollution Control
Federation (US)
wpe white porcelain enamel
WPFC West Pacific Fisheries
Commission
Wpfl worshipful
wpg waterproofing
WPGA Women's Professional Golfers'
Association
WPHC Western Pacific High
Commission
WPI wholesale price index; World Press
Institute
WPL warning-point level
wpm words per minute (shorthand,
typing)
WPMSF World Professional Marathon
Swimming Federation
wpn weapon
WPO *Wiener Philharmonisches Orchester*
(German: Vienna Philharmonic
Orchestra)
WPRL Water Pollution Research
Laboratory
wps with prior service
wr warehouse receipt; war risk
(insurance); water repellent
WR Royal Tongan Airlines (airline flight
code, Tonga); Leeds (UK vehicle
registration); ward room; warehouse
receipt; war reserve; Western Region
(railways); West Riding (Yorkshire);
Willelmus Rex (Latin: King William);
Worcester (UK postcode)
WRA War Relocation Authority (US);
Water Research Association
WRAAC Women's Royal Australian
Army Corps
WRAAF Women's Royal Australian
Air Force
WRAC Women's Royal Army
Corps
WRAF Women's Royal Air Force

WRANS Women's Royal Australian
Naval Service
WRAP weapons readiness analysis
program (US)
WRC Water Research Centre; Welding
Research Council (US)
WRE Weapons Research Establishment
w. ref. with reference (to)
w. reg. with regard (to)
WRI war risks insurance; Women's Rural
Institute
wrn wool round needle (knitting)
WRNR Women's Royal Naval Reserve
WRNS Women's Royal Naval Service
wrnt warrant
wro war risks only (insurance)
WRO Weed Research Organization
WRP Workers' Revolutionary Party
WRRA Women's Road Records
Association (cycling)
wrt with respect to; wrought (iron)
WRU Welsh Rugby Union; Wesleyan
Reform Union; who are you?
WRVS Women's Royal Voluntary
Service
WS Bristol (UK vehicle registration);
Walsall (UK postcode); water-soluble;
weapon system; Western Samoa
(international vehicle registration); West
Saxon; wind speed; Writer to the Signet
(Scottish law)
WSA War Shipping Administration
(US)
W. Sam. Western Samoa
WSC World Series Cricket
WSCF World Student Christian
Federation
WSI Writers and Scholars International
WSJ Wall Street Journal
WSM Women's Suffrage Movement
wsp water supply point
WSPU Women's Social and Political
Union
WSSA Welsh Secondary Schools
Association
WSTN World Service Television
News
WSTV World Service Television
WSU Wichita State University
WSW west-southwest
wt warrant; watertight; weight;
without
WT Leeds (UK vehicle registration);
Nigeria Airlines (airline flight code);
warrant telegraphist (Navy); war
transport; watertight; Westport (Irish
fishing port registration); wireless

telegraphy; wireless telephony;
withholding tax
W/T wireless telegraphy
WTA winner takes all; Women's Tennis
Association; World Transport Agency
WTAA World Trade Alliance Association
WTAU Women's Total Abstinence
Union
Wtb. *Wörterbuch* (German: dictionary)
WTC Wheat Trade Convention
wtd wanted; warranted; watered;
watertight door
Wtf. Waterford
WTG wind turbine generator
WTH whole-tree harvesting
wthr weather
WTIS World Trade Information
Service
WTMH watertight manhole
WTN Worldwide Television News
WTO Warsaw Treaty Organization;
World Tourism Organization
WTP willing(ness) to pay
wtr water; winter; writer
WTRC Wool Textile Research Council
WTS Women's Transport Service
WTT World Team Tennis
WTTA Wholesale Tobacco Trade
Association of Great Britain and
Northern Ireland
WTUC World Trade Union Conference
WU Leeds (UK vehicle registration);
Western Union
WUCT World Union of Catholic
Teachers
WUF World Underwater Federation
WUJS World Union of Jewish Students
WUPJ World Union for Progressive
Judaism
WUR World University Round Table
WUS World University Service
WUSL Women's United Service League
w/v water valve; weight to volume
(chemistry)
WV Brighton (UK vehicle registration);
St Vincent and the Grenadines
(international vehicle registration);
water valve; West Virginia (zip code);
Wolverhampton (UK postcode)
W. Va. West Virginia
WVA World Veterinary Association
wvd waived

WVD *Wereldverbond van Diamant
Bewerkers* (Dutch: Universal Alliance of
Diamond Workers)
WVF World Veterans' Federation
WVS Women's Voluntary Service
WVT water vapour transmission; water
vapour transfer
WVU West Virginia University
ww white wall (car tyres)
w/w weight for weight; weight in weight
(chemistry)
WW Leeds (UK vehicle registration);
wall-to-wall (estate agency); warehouse
warrant; warrant writer; Who's Who;
World War; worldwide
WW1 World War One
WW2 World War Two
WWDC World War Debt Commission
W. Wdr Warrant Wardmaster
WWDSHEX weather working days,
Sundays and holidays excluded
(shipping)
Wwe *Witwe* (German: widow)
WWF Worldwide Fund for Nature;
World Wildlife Fund
WWMCCS World Wide Military
Command and Control System
WWO wing warrant officer
WWSSN worldwide standard
seismograph network
WWSU World Water Ski Union
WWW Who Was Who; World Weather
Watch (WMO)
WWY Queen's Own Warwickshire and
Worcestershire Yeomanry
WX Ansett Express (airline flight code,
Australia); Leeds (UK vehicle
registration); weather (meteorology);
women's extra large (clothing)
wxy warning
Wy. Wycliffe; Wyoming
WY Oman Aviation Services (airline
flight code); Leeds (UK vehicle
registration); Wyoming (zip code)
Wyo. Wyoming
WYR West Yorkshire Regiment
wysiwyg what you see is what you get
(computing)
Wz. *Warenzeichen* (German: trademark)
WZ Belfast (UK vehicle registration);
Weltzeit (German: universal time)
WZO World Zionist Organization

X

x cross; ex (commerce, finance, etc); extra; hoar-frost (meteorology); multiplied by (mathematics)

X adults only (cinema classification); Christ; Cross; experiment(al); explosive; extension; extra; extraordinary; his/her mark (signature); kiss; location (cartography); sex chromosome; 10 (Roman numerals); X-ray

xa ex all (without benefits; finance)

XA Mexico (international civil aircraft marking)

xan. xanthene (chemistry); xanthic (chemistry)

xb ex bonus (without bonus shares; finance)

XB Mexico (international civil aircraft marking)

Xber December

xbre *décembre* (French: December)

xbt exhibit

XBT expendable bathythermograph

xc ex capitalization (without capitalization; finance); ex coupon (without coupon interest; finance)

XC cross-country; Mexico (international civil aircraft marking)

xcl excess current liabilities (insurance)

xcp ex coupon (without coupon; finance)

xcpt except

XCT X-ray computed tomography (medicine)

xd ex dividend (without dividend; finance)

x'd executed

xdiv ex dividend (without dividend; finance)

x'd out crossed out

Xdr crusader

XDR extended dynamic range (cassettes)

Xe xenon (element)

Xen. Xenophon (Greek historian)

Xer. Xerox copier; Xerox copy

xf extra fine

xfer transfer

xfmr transformer

xg crossing

x-height typesize (based on the letter x)

xhst exhaust

xhy extra heavy

xi ex interest (without interest; finance)

XI Belfast (UK vehicle registration); X-ray imaging (medicine)

xint excellent

XL extra large

xlwb extra-long wheelbase

XM experimental missile

Xmas Christmas

xmit transmit

XMS extended memory specification (computing)

xmsn transmission

xmtr transmitter

xn ex new (without right to new shares; finance)

Xn Christian

x/nt excellent

Xnty Christianity

XO executive officer

x out cross out

XP Christ; Christianity; express paid

xpl. explosive

xplt exploit

xpn expansion

xq cross-question

xr ex right (without rights; finance)

Xr examiner

XR X-ray

Xrds crossroads

XRE X-ray emission

x ref. cross reference

x. rts ex rights (without rights; finance)

xs expenses

Xt Christ

XT Burkina Faso (international civil aircraft marking)

xtal crystal

X-tgd cross-tongued (building)

Xth tenth

Xtian Christian

xtra extra

xtry extraordinary

Xty Christianity

XU Cambodia (international civil aircraft marking)

XUV extreme ultraviolet

xw ex warrants (without warrants; finance)

x/wb extra-long wheelbase

XX double-strength ale; heavy (meteorology); 20 (Roman numerals)

XXX triple-strength ale

XY Burma (international civil aircraft marking)

xyl. xylophone

XZ Armagh (UK vehicle registration)

Y

y dry air (meteorology)

y altitude; lateral axis (aeronautics)

y. yacht; yard; year; yellow; young(est)

Y sex chromosome; yen (Japanese monetary unit); YMCA; YMHA; Youghal (Irish fishing port registration); yttrium (element); yuan (Chinese monetary unit); YWCA; YWHA;

Y admittance (electricity); hypercharge (physics)

Y. Yeomanry; Yugoslavia

YA Afghanistan (international civil aircraft marking); Taunton (UK vehicle registration); York-Antwerp Rules (insurance); young adult

YABA Young American Bowling Alliance

YACC yet another compiler-compiler (computing)

YAG yttrium-aluminium garnet (artificial diamond)

YAL Young Australia League

Y&D yards and docks (US Navy)

Y&LR York and Lancaster Regiment

Y&R Young and Rubicam (advertising agency)

YAR York-Antwerp Rules (insurance)

Y-ARD Yarrow-Admiralty Research Department

YAS Yorkshire Agricultural Society

YASSR Yakut Autonomous Soviet Socialist Republic

Yavis young, attractive, verbal, intelligent and successful (US)

Yb ytterbium (element)

YB Taunton (UK vehicle registration); yearbook

YC Taunton (UK vehicle registration); yacht club; Yale College (US); Young Conservative; youth club

YCA Youth Camping Association

YC&UO Young Conservative and Unionist Organization

YCL Young Communist League (US)

YCNAC Young Conservative National Advisory Committee

YCS Young Catholic Students

yct yacht

ycw you can't win

YCW Young Christian Workers

yd yard

YD Taunton (UK vehicle registration); Yemeni dinar (monetary unit); Yugoslav dinar (monetary unit)

y'day yesterday

ydg yarding

yds yards

YE central London (UK vehicle registration); Your Excellency

YEA Yale Engineering Association (US)

yearb. yearbook

YEB Yorkshire Electricity Board

yel. yellow

Yel. NP Yellowstone National Park (US)

Yem. Yemen(i)

yeo. yeoman; yeomanry

YEO youth employment officer

YER yearly effective rate of interest (finance)

YES Youth Employment Service; Youth Enterprise Scheme

yesty yesterday

YF central London (UK vehicle registration)

YFC Young Farmers' Club

YFCU Young Farmers' Club of Ulster

YG Leeds (UK vehicle registration)

YH central London (UK vehicle registration); Yarmouth (UK fishing port registration); young head (of Queen Victoria; numismatics); youth hostel

YHA Youth Hostels Association

YHANI Youth Hostels Association of Northern Ireland

YHVH Jehovah or Yahweh

YHWH Jehovah or Yahweh

Yi(d). Yiddish; Yiddisher

YI Dublin (Irish vehicle registration); Iraq (international civil aircraft marking)

YIG yttrium-iron garnet

Yip(pie) Youth International Party member (US)

YJ Brighton (UK vehicle registration); Vanuatu (international civil aircraft marking)

YK Cyprus Turkish Airlines (airline flight code); central London (UK vehicle registration); Syria (international civil aircraft marking)

YL Latvia (international civil aircraft marking); central London (UK vehicle registration); yield limit

YLI Yorkshire Light Infantry

YM central London (UK vehicle registration); YMCA

YMBA Yacht and Motor Boat Association

YMCA Young Men's Christian Association
YMCath.A Young Men's Catholic Association (US)
YMCU Young Men's Christian Union
YMFS Young Men's Friendly Society
YMHA Young Men's Hebrew Association
YN Air Creebec (airline flight code, Canada); central London (UK vehicle registration); Nicaragua (international civil aircraft marking)
YNP Yellowstone National Park (US)
yo yarn over (knitting); year/s old
YO central London (UK vehicle registration); York (UK postcode)
yob backward boy; year of birth
YOC Young Ornithologists' Club (RSPB)
yod year of death
yom year of marriage
Yonhap United Press Agency (news agency, South Korea)
YOP Youth Opportunities Programme
Yorks Yorkshire
yp year's purchase (finance)
YP Aero Lloyd (airline flight code, Germany); central London (UK vehicle registration); yield point (mechanics); young person; young people; young prisoner
YPA Young Pioneers of America
YPFB Yacimientos Petrolíferos Fiscales Bolivianos (Bolivian state petroleum organization)
YPSCE Young People's Society of Christian Endeavour (US)
YPSL Young People's Socialist League (US)
YPTES Young People's Trust for Endangered Species
yr year; younger; your
YR central London (UK vehicle registration); Romania (international civil aircraft marking)
YRA Yacht Racing Association
yrbk yearbook
YRis Yemen riyal (monetary unit)
yrly yearly
yrs years; yours
yrs ty yours truly
Ys. Yugoslavia; Yugoslavian

YS El Salvador (international civil aircraft marking); Glasgow (UK vehicle registration); yield strength (mechanics); Young Socialists
YSA Young Socialist Alliance (US)
YSO young stellar object (astronomy)
yst youngest
yt yacht
YT central London (UK vehicle registration); Yukon Territory
ytb yarn to back (knitting)
YTD year to date (accounting)
ytf yarn to front (knitting)
YTKTK you're too young to know
YTS Youth Training Scheme
YU central London (UK vehicle registration); Dominair (airline flight code, Dominican Republic); Yale University (US); Yugoslavia (international civil aircraft marking)
Yugo. Yugoslavia
Yuk. Yukon
YUP Yale University Press
yuppie young upwardly-mobile professional; young urban professional
YV central London (UK vehicle registration); Venezuela (international civil aircraft marking; international vehicle registration)
YVF Young Volunteer Force
YVFF Young Volunteer Force Foundation
YW central London (UK vehicle registration); YWCA
YWCA Young Women's Christian Association
YWCTU Young Women's Christian Temperance Union
YWHA Young Women's Hebrew Association
YWS Young Wales Society; Young Workers' Scheme
YX central London (UK vehicle registration)
YY central London (UK vehicle registration)
YZ Londonderry (UK vehicle registration); *Transportes Aereos da Guiné-Bissau* (airline flight code, Guinea Bissau)

Z

z haze (meteorology)
z charge number (chemistry)
z. zenith; zero; zone
Z Dublin (Irish vehicle registration); zaïre (monetary unit of Zaïre); Zambia (international vehicle registration); Zimbabwe (international civil aircraft marking)
Z impedance (electricity); proton number (physics)
Z. *Zeit* (German: time); zero; Zion; *Zoll* (German: customs); zone; *zuid* (Dutch: south)
za. *zirca* (German: approximately)
ZA Albania (international civil aircraft marking); Dublin (Irish vehicle registration); South Africa (international vehicle registration); ZAS Airline (airline flight code, Egypt)
Zag. Zagreb
Zam. Zambia
Zan. Zanzibar
ZANU Zimbabwe African National Union
Zanz. Zanzibar
ZAP zero anti-aircraft potential (military)
ZAPU Zimbabwe African People's Union
z. B. *zum Beispiel* (German: for example)
ZB Cork (Irish vehicle registration); Monarch Airlines (airline flight code, UK); Zen Buddhist; zero beat
ZBB zero-base budgeting (US finance)
ZC Dublin (Irish vehicle registration); Royal Swazi National Airways (airline flight code, Swaziland); Zionist Congress
ZD Dublin (Irish vehicle registration); Virgin Air (airline flight code, Virgin Islands); Zener diode (electronics); zenith distance (astronomy); zero defect
Z-day zero day (military)
ZE Dublin (Irish vehicle registration); Lerwick (UK postcode)
ZEBRA zero energy breeder reactor assembly (nuclear engineering)
Zech. Zechariah (Bible)
Zeep zero energy experimental pile (nuclear engineering)
ZEG zero economic growth (economics)
Zeke Ezekiel (Bible)
zen. zenith
ZENITH zero energy nitrogen heated thermal reactor (nuclear engineering)

Zeph. Zephaniah (Bible)
Zepp. zeppelin
zero-g zero gravity
ZETA zero energy thermonuclear apparatus (nuclear engineering); zero energy thermonuclear assembly (nuclear engineering)
ZETR zero energy thermonuclear apparatus (nuclear engineering); zero energy thermonuclear assembly (nuclear engineering)
ZF Cork (Irish vehicle registration); zero frequency; zone of fire (military)
ZFGBI Zionist Federation of Great Britain and Ireland
ZG Dublin (Irish vehicle registration); Zoological Gardens
z. H. *zu Händen* (German: attention of, care of)
ZH Dublin (Irish vehicle registration); zero hour
ZI Dublin (Irish vehicle registration); zone of interior (military)
Ziana Zimbabwe Inter-Africa News Agency
ZIFT zygote intrafallopian transfer (medicine)
zip zone improvement plan (US)
ZJ Dublin (Irish vehicle registration)
ZK Cork (Irish vehicle registration); New Zealand (international civil aircraft marking)
zl freezing drizzle (meteorology)
Zl zloty (Polish monetary unit)
ZL Dublin (Irish vehicle registration); New Zealand (international civil aircraft marking)
ZM Galway (Irish vehicle registration)
Zn zinc (element)
ZN Meath (Irish vehicle registration)
ZO Dublin (Irish vehicle registration); Zionist Organization
ZOA Zionist Organization of America
zod. zodiac
zoogeog. zoogeography
zool. zoological, zoologist, zoology
ZP Donegal (Irish vehicle registration); Paraguay (international civil aircraft marking)
ZPG zero population growth
ZQ Ansett New Zealand (airline flight code)

Zr zirconium (element)
ZR freezing rain (meteorology); Wexford (Irish vehicle registration)
ZRE Zaïre (international vehicle registration)
Zs. *Zeitschrift* (German: periodical, journal)
ZS Dublin (Irish vehicle registration); South Africa (international civil aircraft marking); Zoological Society
ZSI Zoological Society of Ireland
ZST zone standard time
z. T. *zum Teil* (German: partly)
ZT Cork (Irish vehicle registration); South Africa (international civil aircraft registration); zone time
Ztg *Zeitung* (German: newspaper)
ZU Dublin (Irish vehicle registration); South Africa (international civil aircraft marking)
Zulu. Zululand
ZUM Zimbabwe Unity Movement
Zur. Zürich
ZV Dublin (Irish vehicle registration)
zw *zwischen* (German: between)
ZW Kildare (Irish vehicle registration); Zimbabwe (international vehicle registration)
ZX Air BC (airline flight code, Canada); Kerry (Irish vehicle registration)
ZY Louth (Irish vehicle registration)
zz zigzag
zZ *zur Zeit* (German: at present)
Zz *zingiber* (Latin: ginger; medicine)
ZZ vehicle temporarily imported from abroad (UK vehicle registration)

Appendices

ROMAN NUMERALS

I *or* i = 1   V *or* v = 5   X *or* x = 10   L *or* l = 50
C *or* c = 100   D *or* d = 500   M *or* m = 1000

1	= I	30		= XXX
2	= II	31		= XXXI
3	= III	32	etc.	= XXXII
4	= IV (also IIII)[1]	40		= XL (also XXXX)
5	= V	41		= XLI
6	= VI	42	etc.	= XLII
7	= VII	50		= L
8	= VIII	60		= LX
9	= IX	70		= LXX
10	= X	80		= LXXX
11	= XI	90		= XC (also LXXXX)
12	= XII	100		= C
13	= XIII	101		= CI
14	= XIV	102	etc.	= CII
15	= XV	150		= CL
16	= XVI	200		= CC
17	= XVII	300		= CCC
18	= XVIII	400		= CD (also CCCC)
19	= XIX	500		= D (also IↃ)[2]
20	= XX	600		= DC (also IↃC)
21	= XXI	700		= DCC (also IↃCC)
22	= XXII	800		= DCCC (also IↃCCC)
23	= XXIII	900		= CM
24	= XXIV	1000		= M
25	= XXV	2000		= MM
26	= XXVI	5000		= $\bar{V}$[3]
27	= XXVII	10,000		= $\bar{X}$
28	= XXVIII	100,000		= $\bar{C}$
29	= XXIX	1,000,000		= $\bar{M}$

[1] In modern use IV is preferred to IIII although IIII can still be seen on clock faces etc.

[2] In ancient and mediaeval times the symbol Ↄ, called the *apostrophus*, was used after I to express the number 500 and repeated after IↃ to express numbers ten times greater, as IↃↃ=5000, IↃↃↃ=50,000. Preceding such a number with the symbol C, repeated as many times as the symbol Ↄ appeared, multiplied the number by two, thus CCIↃↃ=10,000, CCCIↃↃↃ=100,000.

[3] In mediaeval times and later, a line over a symbol indicated a multiple of a thousand.

GREEK ALPHABET

A	α	alpha	a	Ξ	ξ	xi	x
B	β	beta	b	O	o	omicron	o
Γ	γ	gamma	g	Π	π	pi	p
Δ	δ	delta	d	P	ρ	rho	r
E	ε	epsilon	e	Σ	σ or ς	sigma	s
Z	ζ	zeta	z	T	τ	tau	t
H	η	eta	ē	Y	υ	upsilon	u
Θ	θ	theta	th	Φ	φ	phi	ph
I	ι	iota	i	X	χ	chi	ch/kh (pronounced *hh* as in *loch*)
K	κ	kappa	k				
Λ	λ	lambda	l	Ψ	ψ	psi	ps
M	μ	mu	m	Ω	ω	omega	ō
N	ν	nu	n				

RUSSIAN ALPHABET

А	а	a		Т	т	t
Б	б	b		У	у	u (pronounced oo as in *boot*)
В	в	v				
Г	г	g		Ф	ф	f
Д	д	d		X	х	kh (pronounced *hh* as in *loch*)
E	e	e/ye (as in *yet*)				
Ё	ё	ë/yo (as in *yawn*)		Ц	ц	ts
Ж	ж	zh		Ч	ч	ch
З	з	z		Ш	ш	sh
И	и	i (pronounced ee as in *sheep*)		Щ	щ	shch
				Ъ	ъ	indicates that the preceding consonant is not palatalized
Й	й	ǐ/y				
К	к	k				
Л	л	l		Ы	ы	i/ȳ
М	м	m		Ь	ь	indicates that the preceding consonant is palatalized
Н	н	n				
О	о	o		Э	э	e (as in *led*)
П	п	p		Ю	ю	yu (as in *universal*)
Р	р	r		Я	я	ya (as in *yard*)
С	с	s				

+	plus, the sign of addition: also of positive (*Elec. and Mag.*), and compression (*Eng.*)	∟	right angle
		ᐯ	equiangular
		△	triangle
−	minus, the sign of subtraction; also of negative (*Elec. and Mag.*), and tension (*Eng.*)	□	square
		▭	rectangle, or parallelogram
		⊙	circle
×	the sign of multiplication	◠	circumference
÷	the sign of division	◖	semicircle
:	is to ⎤	⌐ᴑ	quadrant
::	as ⎬ the signs of proportion	⌒	arc
:	is to ⎦	~	difference
∵	because	0	the cipher, zero
∴	therefore	°	degrees, 'minutes, "seconds,'''thirds
=	equals; the sign of equality	'	feet, "inches
≡	equivalent to, representing, varies	c	constant
α	as infinity	d	differential (in calculus)
√	square root	f	integration (in calculus)
∛	cube root	E	modulus of elasticity
∜	fourth root, etc.	F or f	functions
ⁿ√	nth root	g	gravity
∓	is unequal to	k	coefficient
>	is greater than	M	modulus
≯	is not greater than	n	any number
<	is less than	δ	variation
≮	is not less than	Δ	finite difference
‖	is parallel to	ε	base of hyperbolic logarithms
╫	is not parallel to	λ	latitude
⊥	is perpendicular to	π	ratio of circumference to diameter
±	equilateral		= 3·14159
∠	angle	R, r, ϱ	radius
∠ s	angles	Σ	sum of finite quantities

CHEMICAL ELEMENTS

Element	Symbol	Atomic number	Element	Symbol	Atomic number
actinium	Ac	89	neodymium	Nd	60
aluminium	Al	13	neon	Ne	10
americium	Am	95	neptunium	Np	93
antimony	Sb	51	nickel	Ni	28
argon	Ar	18	niobium	Nb	41
arsenic	As	33	nitrogen	N	7
astatine	At	85	nobelium	No	102
barium	Ba	56	osmium	Os	76
berkelium	Bk	97	oxygen	O	8
beryllium	Be	4	palladium	Pd	46
bismuth	Bi	83	phosphorus	P	15
boron	B	5	platinum	Pt	78
bromine	Br	35	plutonium	Pu	94
cadmium	Cd	48	polonium	Po	84
caesium	Cs	55	potassium	K	19
calcium	Ca	20	praseodymium	Pr	59
californium	Cf	98	promethium	Pm	61
carbon	C	6	protactinium	Pa	91
cerium	Ce	58	radium	Ra	88
chlorine	Cl	17	radon	Rn	86
chromium	Cr	24	rhenium	Re	75
cobalt	Co	27	rhodium	Rh	45
copper	Cu	29	rubidium	Rb	37
curium	Cm	96	ruthenium	Ru	44
dysprosium	Dy	66	samarium	Sm	62
einsteinium	Es	99	scandium	Sc	21
erbium	Er	68	selenium	Se	34
europium	Eu	63	silicon	Si	14
fermium	Fm	100	silver	Ag	47
fluorine	F	9	sodium	Na	11
francium	Fr	87	strontium	Sr	38
gadolinium	Gd	64	sulphur	S	16
gallium	Ga	31	tantalum	Ta	73
germanium	Ge	32	technetium	Tc	43
gold	Au	79	tellurium	Te	52
hafnium	Hf	72	terbium	Tb	65
helium	He	2	thallium	Tl	81
holmium	Ho	67	thorium	Th	90
hydrogen	H	1	thulium	Tm	69
indium	In	49	tin	Sn	50
iodine	I	53	titanium	Ti	22
iridium	Ir	77	tungsten	W	74
iron	Fe	26	unnilhexium	Unh	106
krypton	Kr	36	unnilpentium	Unp	105
lanthanum	La	57	unnilquadium	Unq	104
lawrencium	Lr	103	unnilseptium	Uns	107
lead	Pb	82	uranium	U	92
lithium	Li	3	vanadium	V	23
lutetium	Lu	71	xenon	Xe	54
magnesium	Mg	12	ytterbium	Yb	70
manganese	Mn	25	yttrium	Y	39
mendelevium	Md	101	zinc	Zn	30
mercury	Hg	80	zirconium	Zr	40
molybdenum	Mo	42			

CHEMISTRY

<> *or* ⚬	antimony	♄	lead
⚬̣ *or* o-o	arsenic	☿	mercury
♂̸	cobalt	☽	silver
♀	copper	♃	tin
☉	gold	4	zinc
♂	iron		

BOTANY

0	absent	☉	monocarpous
①	annual	§	naturalized plant
②	biennial	0	none
⌒	climbing plant	†	ornamental plant
△	evergreen	♃	perennial
♂	male	?	doubtful
♀	female	!	personally verified
☿	hermaphrodite	♀☿♂ *or* ♀♂̸♀ polygamous
×	hybrid	)	winding to left
∞	number indefinite	(	winding to right
8 *or* ♂−♀	monœcious	♄	woody-stem plant
♀♂ *or* ♂̸:♀	diœcious	‡	useful plant

339

ASTRONOMY

⊙	the sun	☍	opposition
●	new moon	△	trine
☽	first quarter of the moon	□	quadrature
○	full moon	☊	ascending node
☾	last quarter of the moon	☋	descending node
☿	Mercury	+	north
♀	Venus	−	south
⊕ *or* ♂ Earth		*a*	right ascension
♂	Mars	ß	celestial latitude
♃	Jupiter	δ	declination
♄	Saturn	*e*	eccentricity
♅	Uranus	*i*	inclination to the ecliptic
♆	Neptune	λ	longitude
○	planet	μ	mean daily motion
☄	comet	π	longitude of perihelion
①, ②, etc., *or* *1, *2, etc. asteroids,		*q*	perihelion distance of a comet
	in order of discovery	ø	latitude
✳	fixed star	°	degree of arc
☌	conjunction	′	minute(s) of arc
		″	second(s) of arc

ZODIAC

♈	Aries, the ram (Mar 21–Apr 21)	♎	Libra, the scales (Sep 24–Oct 23)
♉	Taurus, the bull (Apr 22–May 21)	♏	Scorpio, the scorpion (Oct 24–Nov 22)
♊	Gemini, the twins (May 22–June 22)	♐	Sagittarius, the archer (Nov 23–Dec 21)
♋	Cancer, the crab (June 23–Jul 23)	♑	Capricorn, the goat (Dec 22–Jan 20)
♌	Leo, the lion (Jul 24–Aug 23)	♒	Aquarius, the water-carrier (Jan 21–Feb 19)
♍	Virgo, the virgin (Aug 24–Sep 23)	♓	Pisces, the fishes (Feb 20–Mar 20)